SHAKESPEARE: THE CRITICAL HERITAGE
VOLUME 5 1765–1774

THE CRITICAL HERITAGE SERIES

GENERAL EDITOR: B. C. SOUTHAM, M.A., B. LITT. (OXON.)

Formerly Department of English, Westfield College, University of London

For a list of books in the series see the back end paper

SHAKESPEARE

THE CRITICAL HERITAGE

VOLUME 5 1765–1774

Edited by
BRIAN VICKERS

*Professor of English and Renaissance Literature,
ETH, Zürich*

.

ROUTLEDGE & KEGAN PAUL: LONDON, HENLEY AND BOSTON

First published in 1979
by Routledge & Kegan Paul Ltd
39 Store Street,
London WC1E 7DD,
Broadway House,
Newton Road,
Henley-on-Thames,
Oxon RG9 1EN and
9 Park Street,
Boston, Mass. 02108, USA

British Library Cataloguing in Publication Data

Shakespeare, the critical heritage.
Vol. 5: 1765–1774—(The critical heritage series).
1. Shakespeare, William—Criticism and interpretation—
Addresses, essays, lectures
I. Title II. Vickers, Brian
822.3'3   PR2975   79–40169
ISBN 0 7100 8788 8

Set in Monophoto Garamond
by Thomson Press (India) Limited, New Delhi
and printed in Great Britain by
Lowe & Brydone Printers Limited
Thetford, Norfolk

TO THE MEMORY OF

MY MOTHER

22 NOVEMBER 1914

TO

10 MAY 1977

General Editor's Preface

The reception given to a writer by his contemporaries and near-contemporaries is evidence of considerable value to the student of literature. On one side we learn a great deal about the state of criticism at large and in particular about the development of critical attitudes towards a single writer; at the same time, through private comments in letters, journals or marginalia, we gain an insight upon the tastes and literary thought of individual readers of the period. Evidence of this kind helps us to understand the writer's historical situation, the nature of his immediate reading-public, and his response to these pressures.

The separate volumes in the *Critical Heritage Series* present a record of this early criticism. Clearly, for many of the highly productive and lengthily reviewed nineteenth- and twentieth-century writers, there exists an enormous body of material; and in these cases the volume editors have made a selection of the most important views, significant for their intrinsic critical worth or for their representative quality—perhaps even registering incomprehension!

For earlier writers, notably pre-eighteenth century, the materials are much scarcer and the historical period has been extended, sometimes far beyond the writer's lifetime, in order to show the inception and growth of critical views which were initially slow to appear.

Shakespeare is, in every sense, a special case, and Professor Vickers is presenting the course of his reception and reputation extensively, over a span of three centuries, in a sequence of six volumes, each of which will document a specific period.

In each volume the documents are headed by an Introduction, discussing the material assembled and relating the early stages of the author's reception to what we have come to identify as the critical tradition. The volumes will make available much material which would otherwise be difficult of access and it is hoped that the modern reader will be thereby helped towards an informed understanding of the ways in which literature has been read and judged.

B. C. S.

Contents

CONTENTS

Preface

The aims of this series have been set out fully in the prefaces to previous volumes, and can be summed up briefly as being to present an integrated picture of Shakespeare's reception in England up to the beginning of the nineteenth century. The range of material included attempts to do justice to Shakespeare's special position: he is firmly established as England's greatest writer, yet the very text of his plays is uncertain, doubtful in thousands of places, subject to continual alteration by editors who only slowly begin to establish the basic principles of textual criticism, their work being criticized by readers and reviewers whose own knowledge ranges from the enlightened to the utterly uninformed. He is a giant of the past, yet unlike any other dramatist he is being performed every week of every theatrical season in a multitude of theatres throughout the British Isles. His plays are universally admired, yet found lacking on almost every important head. Critics complain about them, actors interpret them, producers alter them: what is not liked is either abandoned or transformed. We must remind ourselves from time to time that no other major writer, and very few minor ones, has ever suffered the whole-scale surgery, in the supposed interest of being kept alive, that Shakespeare underwent. As a writer of the past (a fairly recent past it might seem to us, but evidently a remote one to post-Restoration taste), his language, ideas, and use of dramatic conventions are only imperfectly understood, and a vast expenditure of energy is visible in this period in reconstructing the historical context as an aid to understanding, and appreciating, his work.

To do justice to this range of activity is the main problem confronting the editor of these volumes. It is made more difficult by other factors. One is the sheer amount of comment produced in this period, a deluge of books, essays, newspaper reviews, poems, letters, and much else. There were a number of times when I recalled, grimly, Johnson's comment that 'a man will turn over a library to make a book'. It had better be said that while I aim at completeness of coverage as far as printed books are concerned (completeness of discovering and reading, that is, not of reprinting), for the journals and newspapers I have been necessarily selective, due partly to the limits of my own knowledge and energy, due also to the rather poor state of information concerning the existence, and authorship, of essays and reviews in this field. It is to be hoped that a full-scale research project will soon be undertaken by co-operation between scholars and librarians in several centres, to produce a basic bibliography of eighteenth-century serials. At the moment, for instance, it is very difficult to find even complete files of the major newspapers of the period. Scholars working in England can journey between the Bodleian and the British Library, but to find a more complete file of the *St. James's Chronicle*, say, they must go to the Guildhall Library, if they are fortunate enough to discover (as I did only recently) that one exists there. The situation regarding other sources is far worse, and it seems to me a matter of urgency that an international committee be set up with the goal of assembling, through the medium of microfilm, a universally available complete file of all serials in this period. The English cultural heritage has been fragmented over the years, destroyed and dispersed, yet much of it can still be re-assembled, if the energy and organizing power exist.

Once the journals have been located there is the problem of authorship, since most of the essays and reviews in this period were published anonymously. Work has begun on the identification of authorship in such journals as the *Gentleman's Magazine*, the *Monthly Review*, and the *Critical Review*, and we are all indebted to such scholars as B. C. Nangle,[1] Claude E. Jones,[2] J. M. Kuist,[3] and Arthur Sherbo.[4] Yet information becomes available slowly, and whether one hears about it or not often depends on chance. Thus in Vol. 3 (published in 1975; text completed in 1972), I printed an interesting essay on Shakespeare and Otway from the *Gentleman's Magazine*, not knowing its author. In a book published in 1973 Bertram Davis[5] identified it as the work of Sir John Hawkins, on the evidence of Laetitia-Matilda Hawkins, *Anecdotes, Biographical Sketches and Memoirs* (London, 1823). Item No. 116 in Vol. 3, therefore, should now be ascribed to Hawkins.

Another authorship problem concerns a series of reviews, published between 1763 and 1770 in the *Critical Review*, which discuss all the major Shakespeare productions of the period: Heath, Johnson, Steevens, Kenrick, Mrs Montagu, and others. That these are by one hand is clear from the reviewer's frequent cross-references to earlier pieces by him in this magazine, a feature which is unique in my reading experience of eighteenth-century journals. Another unusual feature is their stress on the need to know regional English in order to understand Shakespeare's language. Since this is a frequent theme of George Steevens in his 1773 and 1778 editions of Shakespeare, and since the author of these reviews shows a detailed knowledge of Shakespeare's text and of recent Shakespeare criticism, I attributed the last item printed in Vol. 4, a review of Heath's *Revisal of Shakespeare's Text*, to Steevens. Hardly had that volume appeared (*nescit vox missa reverti*), while working on the 1778 edition by Steevens, I reached the notes to *As You Like It*, 1.2.21, on the word 'quintaine'. The reviewer of Dr Johnson's edition in the *Critical Review* (item No. 208 below) had given a good explanation of this word, which in the 1773 edition Steevens quoted and signed 'The Critical Review' (iii, p. 246). In 1778, however, the note is signed 'Mr. Guthrie' (iii, p. 281). It follows that it was Guthrie who reviewed Johnson in the *Critical*, a review which quotes Guthrie's own earlier *Essay on English Tragedy*, refers back to the review of Heath, and is itself referred to in a number of subsequent reviews.[6] Indeed, another note from the review of Johnson was referred to already in the 1773 edition (vii, p. 124; 1778: vii, p. 139) as being by 'the late Mr. Guthrie' (he died in March 1770). Hardly had I made the deduction that Guthrie is responsible for the whole series of reviews than a letter arrived from Professor Arthur Sherbo announcing that he had arrived at the same conclusion a few months earlier, another instance of simultaneous discovery, which may be galling for the investigators at the moment but at least leaves little doubt about the identification.

Readers may be referred to a forthcoming article by Professor Sherbo for a full discussion of the matter, but as regards Shakespeare criticism I can list the items which we jointly assign to Guthrie. They are the reviews of Heath's *Revisal* in March and April 1765 (xix, pp. 161–9, 250–5: No. 204 in Vol. 4); Kenrick's *Review* of Johnson in November (xx, pp. 332–6); Johnson's edition (No. 208 below); Tyrwhitt's *Observations* in December 1765 (xx, pp. 455–7); Steevens's twenty Quartos and Kenrick's *Defence* in January 1766 (xxi, pp. 26–33, 79); Barclay on Kenrick in April (xxi, pp. 301–7); the first edition of Farmer's *Essay* in January 1767, and the second in November (xxiii, pp. 47–53;

xxiv, pp. 400); Warner's glossary in March 1768, and Capell's edition in November of that year (xxv, pp. 214–16; xxvi, pp. 321–33); and Mrs Montagu's book in May 1769 (xxvii, pp. 350–5). I am in agreement with Professor Sherbo on all these items, and would add the following definite identifications: the review of the *Castrated Letter* in October 1763 (xvi, pp. 306–9), which is referred to in the Heath review as being by the same pen (see Vol. 4, p. 566, note); the 'Answers to Correspondents' in March 1766 concerning the Johnson reviews, which is evidently by the original reviewer (xxi, pp. 238–40); and the review of *Anecdotes of Polite Literature* in July 1764 (xvii, pp. 435–42), which echoes Guthrie's known views on Shakespeare in his 1747 *Essay on English Tragedy* (Vol. 3, pp. 198f., especially the claim that Shakespeare used Latin sources for *Macbeth* and *Hamlet*), and in which, as Professor Sherbo points out, the reviewer announces that he 'for some time past, has had a considerable share in our Review' (p. 439). Other reviews including Shakespeare criticism which may well have been written by Guthrie are: of *The Castle of Otranto*, second edition, in June 1765 (xix, p. 469); of Kenrick's *Falstaff's Wedding* in February and April 1766 (xxi, pp. 149, 319); of Colman's *Lear* in February 1768 (xxv, pp. 148–9).

The identification of anonymous reviews is always a hazardous task if it can only rely on internal evidence. In the case of Guthrie we have the external evidence of Steevens, many similarities with Guthrie's signed publications, and his own linking of the whole series of reviews. There is other evidence for Guthrie's career as a reviewer. Recently J. M. Kuist identified Guthrie as the author of a long essay on English literature from Chaucer to Milton which appeared in the *Gentleman's Magazine* in instalments in 1738–9;[7] C. E. Jones[8] noted the testimony of Percival Stockdale that Guthrie had worked for the *Critical Review* for several years before his death in 1770; and Arthur Sherbo has cited a number of contemporary references to Guthrie's association with this journal.[9] Two more pieces of evidence that I should like to draw attention to both concern James Boswell. In his journal for 25 March 1768 Boswell recorded going

to Percy Coffee-house, Rathbone Place, to meet Mr. Guthrie, the historian and Critical Reviewer, who had fought the battle of Douglas in the *Review*, and had praised my *Account of Corsica*. He was an old gentleman about sixty, had on a white coat and a crimson satin waistcoat with broad gold lace, and a bag-wig. We had port and madeira and a hearty supper. He had a great deal of the London author.

Boswell found it 'curious to sit with the very person whom in a little I should look upon as an awful reviewer,' but Guthrie was genial and generous, and Boswell exchanged praise and 'a genteel compliment' with him.[10] If viewed in the flush of success there, a powerful and respected literary figure, rather different is the estimate of Guthrie's career as a reviewer contained in a memorial of him written by his brother Hary at Boswell's request, now in the Boswell papers at Yale: 'He wrote much in the Critical Reviews, which its said gained him many enemies, by the freedoms he used in his criticisms'.[11] No doubt much more information about Guthrie, and about the eighteenth-century literary world, remains to be tapped, once we have the clues.

In compiling this volume I have been primarily indebted to the British Library, the Bodleian, and Cambridge University Library, to the staff of whose reading rooms and photographic services I extend especial thanks. The sentence from Guthrie's memorial is printed with permission of Yale University and the McGraw-Hill Book Company [William Heinemann, Ltd] and I am most grateful to Mrs Marion S. Pottle, Cataloguer of the Boswell Papers at Yale University, for checking the documents for me. For permission to print Garrick's *Hamlet* adaptation I thank the trustees of the Folger Library, its director, Professor O. B. Hardison, and its first editor, Professor George Winchester Stone, Jr. In the closing stages of preparing this volume I have been much helped by a generous grant from the Schweizerischer Nationalfonds zur Förderung der wissenschaftlichen Forschung. Arthur Sherbo has kept up an informative correspondence, and D. J. Fleeman answered an enquiry very fully. For checking material in English libraries I am again indebted to Ian Thomson, and for help with the typescript and proofs I thank Ilse Fannenböck, Barbara Häberli and Gabrielle Meyer.

B. W. V.

NOTES

1 Nangle (ed.), *The Monthly Review. First Series*, 1749–1789. *Indexes of Contributors and Articles* (Oxford, 1934).

2 Jones, 'Contributors to *The Critical Review* 1756–1785', *Modern Language Notes*, 61 (1946), pp. 433–41; 'Dramatic Criticism in the *Critical Review*, 1756–1785', *Modern Language Quarterly*, 20 (1959), pp. 18–26, 133–44.

3 Kuist, '*The Gentleman's Magazine* in the Folger Library: The History and Significance of the Nichols Family Collection', *Studies in Bibliography*, 29 (1976), pp. 307–22. The Folger owns a special file copy, containing 'identifications of hundreds of the magazine's anonymous contributors', which Professor Kuist is preparing for publication.

4 Sherbo (ed.), *New Essays by Arthur Murphy* (East Lansing, Mich., 1963); 'Samuel Johnson and the *Gentleman's Magazine*, 1750–1755', in *Johnsonian Studies*, ed. M. Wahba (Cairo, 1962), pp. 133–59; 'The Uses and Abuses of Internal Evidence', *Bulletin of the New York Public Library*, 63 (1959), pp. 5–22; and many other articles.

5 Davis, *A Proof of Eminence. The Life of Sir John Hawkins* (Blooming-ton, Ind., 1973), p. 33. Arthur Sherbo drew attention to this in his review of my Vol. 3 in *Renaissance Quarterly*, 29 (1976), p. 291.

6 At xix, p. 162 Guthrie refers to an earlier review at xvi, pp. 306ff.; at xx, p. 322 to xix, p. 165; at xx, p. 402 to xix, p. 167; at xx, p. 456 to xx, p. 322; at xxi, p. 26 to xx, p. 322; at xxi, p. 31 to 'our Review of Johnson's Shakespeare'; at xxi, p. 86 to xx, p. 403; at xxiii, p. 50 to xxi, p. 21; at xxiv, p. 400 to xxiii, p. 47; at xxv, p. 215 to xx, p. 409; at xxvi, p. 325 to xxi, p. 26 and xix, p. 161; at xxvi, p. 332 to xxiii, pp. 47 and 50; etc. At xxvii, p. 353, indeed, reviewing Mrs Montagu, Guthrie seems to grow tired of giving page-references to his own reviews, writing: 'As we have, upon too many occasions to be enumerated here, shewn...'.

7 Kuist, *op. cit.* in n. 3 above, p. 316.

8 Jones, 'Contributors', *op. cit.* in n. 2 above, pp. 436, 440–1.

9 Sherbo, forthcoming study.

10 *Boswell In Search of A Wife* 1766–1769, ed. F. Brady and F. A. Pottle (London, 1957), pp. 154–5; further references to Guthrie at pp. 163, 176. The editors also ascribe to Guthrie the running of *Old England: or the constitutional Journal*, which appeared (under the pseudonym of Jeffrey Broadbottom) between 1743 and 1753.

11 According to Marion S. Pottle, 'the Memorial consists of two and a half folio pages, dated Edinburgh, 8 July 1776'. I learned of its existence from *The Correspondence and Other Papers of James Boswell relating to the making of the 'Life of Johnson'*, ed. M. Waingrow (London, 1969), p. 234, n. 10.

Introduction

No author's works were ever investigated by so many, and such able commentators, in the same space of time as SHAKESPEARE's have been, within the last half century.

That judgment by Francis Gentleman, made in 1770,[1] represents a growing realization of the unique place held by Shakespeare in English scholarship and criticism. The 'last half century' had seen editions of Shakespeare by Pope, Theobald, Warburton, Hanmer, an anonymous editor in 1745,[2] Dr Johnson, and Edward Capell (No. 220), many of these being reissued or re-published in smaller formats. George Steevens was at work on an enlarged version of Johnson's edition, to be published in 1773 (Nos 212, 240), while Gentleman himself was to annotate Bell's acting edition of 1774. One editor (Charles Jennens) started a complete edition, issuing the plays separately, and other scholars who had proposed complete editions included William Kenrick, William Dodd, and Richard Warner. The amount of criticism that appeared can be gauged by a glance at the dates allotted to the volumes in this edition. The sense of having experienced a unique burst of literary concentration is found in the two main reviews[3] on the publication of the 1773 Johnson-Steevens edition. Writing in the *Critical Review*, an anonymous reviewer (perhaps Percival Stockdale) began: 'No writer, ancient or modern, has so much attracted admiration, and exercised the ingenuity of commentators, as the celebrated English poet whose productions now lie before us' (xxxvi, p. 345). The editor of the *Monthly Review*, Ralph Griffiths, was more expansive:

Among the accumulated proofs of the high esteem in which the writings of Shakespeare are held, in the present age, we may consider the multiplicity of editions which his plays have undergone in a few years as not the least. This multiplicity perhaps surpasses all other examples in the annals of literature: SUCH a tribute of praise, we believe, has never been paid to any other writer.—But the Immortal Bard (who, possibly,

1

by the way, never imagined that his works would have passed a second edition) richly deserves every honour that can be paid to the memory of so astonishing a genius; and to the EXALTED, and almost infinitely VARIOUS, merit of his productions. (xlix, p. 419)

The idolatry of Shakespeare, which began in the 1740s[4] and 1750s, grows to overwhelming proportions in this period, continuing well into the nineteenth century.[5] He is the supreme dramatist and poet: this is agreed by George Steevens (No. 211: England's 'NOBLEST POET'), T. W. (No. 216: greatest of tragedians), David Garrick (No. 222: 'the greatest dramatic poet in the world'), the anonymous orator at the 1769 Jubilee (No. 223), Francis Gentleman (No. 227: on the murder scene in *Macbeth*), John Armstrong (No. 230: 'perhaps excelled all other dramatic poets'), John Potter (No. 233: 'the first Dramatic Author in the World'), and Horace Walpole (No. 237: Shakespeare transcends 'such subaltern genius's as Euripides and Sophocles'). This estimate led increasingly to patriotic or nationalistic fervour. 'England may justly boast the honour of producing' Shakespeare, Garrick wrote in 1769 (No. 222), and in the previous year Edward Capell had begun the dedication[6] to his remarkable edition by describing Shakespeare's works as

a part of the kingdom's riches. They are her estate in fame, that fame which letters confer upon her; the worth and value of which or sinks or raises her in the opinion of foreign nations, and she takes her rank among them according to the esteem which these are held in. It is then an object of national concern that they should be sent into the world with all the advantage which they are in their own nature capable of receiving; and who performs the office rightly is in this a benefactor to his country, and somewhat entitl'd to her good will. The following great productions stand foremost in the list of these literary possessions; are talk'd of wherever the name of *Britain* is talk'd of, that is (thanks to some late counsels) wherever there are men.

The value of this national heritage has been diminished by textual corruptions, 'numerous and gross blemishes, spots in the sun's body, which prevent his glory breaking forth'; Capell's task has been to 'set this glorious Poet in his due state of brightness', so that the world can properly appreciate

these most exquisite portraits of nature, in which Man and his manners, together with all the subtle workings of the passions he is endu'd with,

2

are more largely and finely pencil'd out, and with higher colouring than can else be met with in the writings of any age or nation whatsoever . . .

Nature quitted Rome and Athens, J. R. proclaimed, and 'To Britain with Extasy flew' (No. 231); writing in prose, but no less enthusiastically, Thomas Hawkins saw Shakespeare as surpassing 'old Greece and Rome', becoming 'the Dramatic Poet of the English . . . the boast and wonder of our nation' (No. 241).

The patriotic adulation was intense but hardly articulate. That Shakespeare was a genius who scorned the Rules had been a recurrent *topos* in Shakespeare criticism since the end of the seventeenth century. In this period the concept of Shakespeare's genius emerges as an entity justifying separate discussion, as in William Duff's enthusiastic but vapid *Critical Observations On The Writings Of The Most Celebrated Original Geniuses In Poetry* (No. 226), namely Homer, Shakespeare, and Ossian(!),[7] Elizabeth Montagu's extremely successful *Essay on the Writings and Genius of Shakespeare* (No. 221, 1769: six editions by 1785), and Paul Hiffernan's odd *Dramatic Genius* (No. 228), in which bardolatry finds architectural and artistic expression. Similar adulation can be found in the poetry of the period, such as John Ogilvie's 'Ode to the Genius of Shakespeare',[8] and the anonymous 'The Rapture: On viewing the Tomb of Shakespeare at Stratford-upon-Avon'.[9] Enthusiasm is not always articulate, perhaps, but in this genre writers evaded discussion by attributing superhuman or magical powers to Shakespeare, especially in the creation of character. Capell described him as 'this *Proteus*, who could put on any shape that either serv'd his interest or suited his inclination' (No. 220). For Elizabeth Montagu 'Shakespeare seems to have had the art of the Dervise in the Arabian tales, who could throw his soul into the body of another man' (No. 221). To Edward Burnaby Greene, Shakespeare's pen was 'the magician's wand commanding the soul of his reader; an AMALTHEA's horn, decorated with all the flowers of luxuriant genius' (No. 229). Those three quotations come from works published in 1768, 1769, and 1770, symptomatic of the increasing assertiveness of adulation at that time.

Literary history and literary criticism express the same enthusiastic approval, tempered by some qualifications, largely along lines traditional since the formulation of English Neo-classicism by Dryden, Rymer, Dennis, and Gildon. If Shakespeare had faults they were those of his age: this idea, taken to extremes, resulted in an extraordinarily false picture of English sixteenth-century humanism, as I have remarked before.[10] To exalt his achievement that of the age had to be depressed, a new Dark Ages proclaimed. 'Shakespeare's plays were to be acted in a paltry tavern, to an unlettered audience just emerging from barbarity' (Mrs Montagu). In Hiffernan's Shakespeare Temple the 'great Poet' is represented crowned by 'a sun, rising in all his glory after having dissipated and expelled from our British Theatre the long incumbent clouds of Gothic ignorance and barbarism that are to be seen flying from the victorious lustre' (No. 228). If Shakespeare's audience enjoyed the clown-scene in *Othello*, Francis Gentleman remarked contemptuously, 'taste must have been in a very gothic state truly' (*The Dramatic Censor*, 1770, I, p. 139). These and other excuses are of wider significance than they may seem in isolation, since in the controversy over Shakespeare's learning—which in turn involves important evaluations of his artistic self-awareness—it was taken for granted that he lived in an uneducated, or even illiterate age, and therefore could have very little 'art'.

If 'Art or Nature' continues to function as a critical category, so do 'Rules or Genius', 'Beauties and Faults'. As against historians who have proposed clear-cut changes of taste in the eighteenth century, I want to stress the remarkable homogeneity of attitudes between Dryden and Johnson. Certainly that naive model of the History of Ideas in which 'movements' give way to each other *en bloc*, the one disappearing just as the other emerges, must be abandoned: whatever new elements there are in this period exist side by side with the old. Such a poetic pronouncement as the following could have been made at any time 'within the last half-century': Shakespeare will always 'crown the Triumphs' of the Elizabethan age.

> Above Controul, above each classic Rule,
> His Tutress Nature, and the World his School.
> On Pinions fancy-plum'd, to him was giv'n
> The Pow'r to scale INVENTION'S BRIGHTEST HEAV'N;
> Bid the charm'd Soul to raptur'd Heights aspire,
> And wake in ev'ry Breast congenial Fire.

George Keate's *Ferney* was in fact published in 1770, but similar utterances can be found to the end of this century and beyond.

The discussion of Shakespeare's beauties and faults began with Dryden, continuing uninterruptedly into this period, one of the most influential examples being Lord Kames's *Elements of Criticism* in 1762 (No. 193 in Vol. 4), which had 10 editions by the end of the century, and 28 by 1840. In his posthumously published *Origin of the English Drama* (1773) Thomas Hawkins saw the function of this collection of early plays not as being to present sixteenth-century drama for what it was but largely as a kind of excuse for Shakespeare, 'to illustrate the beauties and extenuate the faults of this great man' (No. 241). Much of the criticism so far reviewed belongs to the 'Beauties' school; the Fault-finders are less numerous, but in them the attitudes of Thomas Rymer are still flourishing. Francis Gentleman, whose whole work exists around these opposed categories, pursues Shakespeare remorselessly for his lacunae in plotting or motivation, for 'inconsistency', 'indecency', and 'inhumanity' (No. 227). John Potter, another man of the theatre, applies the normal Neoclassic categories of Characters, Sentiments, and Moral to *Othello*, emerging with Rymer-like criticisms of the 'very trifling circumstances' of Iago's resentment, or the trifles on which Othello's jealousy is founded (No. 233).

Another long-lived critical idea, deriving from the first adapters of Shakespeare in the 1670s and 1680s, Dryden and Tate, was expressed in the extreme metaphor for his beauties and faults, 'jewels amid rubbish'. In an anonymous 'History of Shakespeare' in the *London Magazine* for August 1769 (which, as Samuel Schoenbaum has shown,[11] became a model for later biographies) we have the following judicious estimate:

In this way of writing he was an absolute original, and of such a peculiar cast, as hath perpetually raised and confounded the emulation of his successors; a compound of such very singular blemishes, as well as beauties, that these latter have not more mocked the toil of every aspiring undertaker to emulate them, than the former, as flaws intimately united to diamonds, have baffled every attempt of the ablest artists to take them out, without spoiling the whole. (xxxviii, p. 404)

For Ralph Griffiths[12] the text of Shakespeare was perhaps irretrievably corrupt, 'But how wonderfully do the jewels emit their radiance thro' the rubbish in which they have been buried'.

It is not without significance that what we might call the harder, purer Neo-classic attitudes in this period are largely to be found in theatrical circles, with actors such as Gentleman, Potter, and (in some respects at least, notably his defence of the Unities),

Hiffernan. It is as if the theatre, immersed in its own activities and traditions, were a generation behind contemporary taste. The older concept of decorum, interpreted with disapproving rigidity, can be seen throughout Gentleman's work, bulking largely even in the small selection reprinted here (No. 227). Macbeth's 'blanket of the dark' is 'a low and improper idea', while the imagery of 'Vaulting ambition', he finds, 'leans towards the burlesque', and the whole speech is full of 'strained figures'. He is particularly upset at Lady Macbeth's 'Was the hope drunk' speech: 'surely we must blame a lady of high rank for descending to such a vulgar and nauseous allusion as the paleness and sickness of an inebriated state'. According to strict Neo-classic principles comedy has no place in tragedy, Hamlet's wit must then be offensive, and the Porter's scene in *Macbeth* is 'commendably omitted in presentation',[13] as is that of the murder of Lady Macduff on stage, which would be 'farcically horrid'. In *Othello* (*The Dramatic Censor*, I, pp. 133–40), Gentleman is constantly outraged by the language of Iago, 'egregiously offensive', 'trifling or abominable', 'indecent and improper', and as for Roderigo, 'we can by no means approve such a character ... in tragical composition; he is only to be laughed at, and that cannot be deemed a proper feeling for serious pieces'. Nor can Gentleman stomach Hamlet's stratagem to dispose of Rosencrantz and Guildenstern: we 'lament such low chicanery in a character of dignity'. As with Rymer on Arbaces and Iago,[14] we find the Neo-classic idea that superior characters should behave in a superior manner confronted with their actual evil behaviour in drama (not to mention life), a collision of theory and practice which is often resolved by stating that while such evil may happen (as in Lady Macbeth, say) it ought never to be represented. How dramatists could write tragedy, or even comedy, without showing human vice or destructiveness is a question that Neo-classicism never answered. For the older school of taste, represented by Gentleman, poetic justice is still desired, hence his unqualified approval of Tate's happy end for *Lear*.

II

In the theatre the situation remains much as have defined it in the preceding volumes. Shakespeare is still the bread-and-butter of the London theatres: in the period 1747 to 1776 approximately 20 per cent of performances at Drury Lane, and approximately 16 per cent at Covent Garden, were of Shakespeare. Of the most popular plays, as computed by G. W. Stone, Jr,[15] both houses performed *Romeo and Juliet* (the most popular play in the period, with a total of 141 performances at Drury Lane, 188 at Covent Garden), *Hamlet* (114 and 81 performances), *King Lear* (82 and 53), *Macbeth* (76 and 58). Of the 10 most popular tragedies at Drury Lane four were by Shakespeare; at Covent Garden those four, plus *Othello* (61 performances). Of the 15 leading comedies at Drury Lane three were Shakespeare's (*Much Ado*: 106; *Cymbeline*: 96; *The Tempest*: 78); of the top 15 comedies at Covent Garden only two were Shakespeare's (*The Merry Wives*: 85; *The Merchant of Venice*: 57), but of history plays *Richard III* was the most successful of all, with 100 performances at Drury Lane and 113 at Covent Garden. *Henry VIII* had 54 performances at Drury Lane, which also saw no less than 43 performances of Colman's *A Fairy Tale*, an inept mangling of *A Midsummer Night's Dream* (see Vol. 4, pp. 22f.).

Looking through these statistics one point stands out. The sure box-office success of Shakespeare needs to be contrasted with the paucity of new drama performed. The other six most popular tragedies at Drury Lane were Congreve's *The Mourning Bride*, which dates from 1697 (78 performances), Otway's *The Orphan* (1680: 76) and *Venice Preserved* (1682: 64), Rowe's *The Fair Penitent* (1703:72) and *Jane Shore* (1714:62), and Aaron Hill's version of Voltaire's *Zaire, Zara* (1736:62). At Covent Garden the non-Shakespearian tragedies were, again, *Jane Shore* (93 performances), Nat Lee's *Alexander the Great or the Rival Queens* (1677:74) and *Theodosius* (1680:48), Henry Jones's *The Earl of Essex* (1753:57), and Ambrose Phillips's adaptation of Racine's *Andromaque, The Distrest Mother* (1712:51). Of the 20 most popular tragedies in London in 1765, then, only one had been written within a dozen years, Jones's *Earl of Essex* (and there had been a version of that story by John Banks in 1681). In comedy we find several Restoration plays holding the stage, and even two by Ben Jonson, though earlier comedies were liable to rather drastic alterations in language and structure to fit a new moral propriety: Garrick's version of *The Country Wife* in 1766 bowed to decorum by omitting Horner, while the 1777 revival of *The*

Beggar's Opera at Covent Garden sent Macheath to the hulks for three years.[16] In comedy, and especially in farces and afterpieces, the managers were willing to risk contemporary dramatists. But in general theatrical taste was extremely conservative.

Of the most frequently performed Shakespeare plays a number had suffered alterations, greater or lesser: *King Lear* by Tate (No. 23 in Vol. 1), *Richard III* by Cibber (No. 38 in Vol. 2), *The Tempest* by Dryden and D'Avenant (No. 9 in Vol. 1), and three smaller-scale touchings-up by Garrick: *Romeo and Juliet* (No. 117 in Vol. 3), *Macbeth* (No. 100), and *Cymbeline* (see Vol. 4, pp. 19f.). Even *Henry VIII* owed much of its theatrical success to the vastly increased splendour of the coronation procession (No. 192 in Vol. 4). The opportunities of seeing an undoctored Shakespeare play on the London stage in this period were rather limited, and given the nature of theatrical taste that was perhaps just as well. The adaptations continued to succeed in the theatre, and to find explicit approval. John Potter recommends Garrick's *Romeo and Juliet*, since Shakespeare 'had neglected to heighten the Catastrophe to so great a degree of distress as it was capable of being carried' (No. 233). Elsewhere he praises adaptations on structural grounds, preferring, as did many of his contemporaries (see Vol. 4, pp. 16ff.), the adapters' attempts to satisfy the canons of unity. The reaction of the Neo-classic critic when confronted with Shakespeare has always been to change the poetic text to conform to the critical system. So we see Francis Gentleman's pen uncontrollably moving towards re-writing *Hamlet*, so that 'the innocent characters, Polonius and Ophelia, might have been saved', wishing that the precipitate flight of Malcolm and Donalbain in *Macbeth* 'was altered, as it easily might be, by giving a few speeches of spirit and dutiful affection to one or both the princes ...', and offering to re-write the opening of *King Lear* ('the whole affair might have been thrown into a much better light ...').

Three adaptations were performed in this period, arousing mixed responses. In 1768 George Colman produced a version of *King Lear* which cut more of Tate and included more of Shakespeare (No. 218): he did so in the face of almost unanimous praise of Tate. Colman's preface is a curious document, rejecting Tate for the right reasons, yet lacking the courage to take his convictions to their proper conclusion. He acutely notes that the love-interest added by Tate makes 'Cordelia's indifference to her father more probable' but makes her lose on the side of 'real virtue': alterations of design, that is, can produce damaging changes of motive. But although Colman expresses the universal eighteenth-century nausea at the blinding of Gloucester ('insignificant, cruel, offensive, shocking, ludicrous' were the words Francis Gentleman applied to it), he is unable to remove it since it is 'so closely interwoven with the fable'. This may show his respect for the integrity of the text, but on the other hand he will not restore the Fool, since if he did the play would so 'sink into burlesque' that it 'would not be endured on the modern stage'. Yet Colman wishes to preserve as much of the authentic text as possible, at times with ridiculous results, as when Lear's 'How dost, my boy? art cold' (p. 35) is addressed to no one on stage, certainly not Kent. Yet if he wanted to be true to Shakespeare why did he retain so much of Tate's turgid and bombastic verse?

Critical reaction to Colman's 'revival' varied according to the provenance of the critic. The literary reviewers, who could be expected to represent up-to-date or at least informed taste, welcomed it.[17] Benjamin Victor, playwright, treasurer of Drury Lane, and historian of the theatre, recorded that the 'Intent' of Colman's

Alteration was, to clear this celebrated Tragedy from the Love Scenes of *Edgar* and *Cordelia*, which were introduced into this Play by the Poet Laureat Mr. *Tate*.—This Love Business has been ever ridiculed by the Connoisseurs and Admirers of *Shakespeare*; and yet when the above Alteration was performed, the Play-going People, in general, seemed to lament the Loss of those Lovers in the Representation.[18]

Colman's adaptation failed, in fact, because it did not give the audience that mixture of pathos and sentiment which they were accustomed to in tragedy. As Cecil Price puts it,[19] 'the alterations robbed the play of its normal appeal to sensibility. Colman had gone too far, too fast. This was the kind of mistake Garrick seldom made'.

Sensibility was explicitly catered for by Richard Cumberland in his *Timon of Athens*, 1771 (No. 232). Apemantus' part was drastically reduced, and Timon was cured of misanthropy—thus almost all the satire, and a great deal of 'offensive' language could be omitted altogether. Cumberland made Timon a more aged figure, with a daughter Evanthe who is loved by Alcibiades. In addition to modish *tendresse* Cumberland followed Neo-classic principles by applying poetic justice against the two chief villains, Lucullus and Lucius. Each had buried his dishonestly acquired treasure, only for it to be discovered, in one case by Timon himself digging it up. Thus Cumberland reverses the whole plot-movement of the Timon fable, Timon is compensated for all his losses, and ceases to be in any sense a tragic figure. Yet his situation is still worked up by a pathetic sensibility until he finally dies, in what is surely a completely unnecessary death, if structural unity is at all a criterion. Although agreeing with the Neo-classical verdict that Shakespeare's play is 'extremely faulty in point of Regularity', John Potter had enough sense of the design of the whole to note that the satiric banquet in Act I is 'absolutely neces-sary to the Plan', and that Evanthe, although 'a good example of filial piety', is 'of but little service to the main Design of the Piece' (No. 233). The reviewers[20] were less critical than usual.

The most remarkable adaptation of the period, and the greatest sacrifice to contemporary taste, was Garrick's *Hamlet* (1772: No. 236), for accurate knowledge of which we are largely indebted to George Winchester Stone, Jr.[21] Garrick was in France and Italy from 1763 to 1765, and as Professor Stone says, 'there can be little doubt that one motivating factor in this alteration was the signi-ficance Garrick attached to French criticism' (*op. cit.* in note 21, p. 893). In 1761 Voltaire, in his *Appel à toutes les nations de l'Europe*,[22] had delivered his famous attack on *Hamlet*, enlarging on the earlier one in his preface to *Sémiramis*,[23] in both of which he had especially mocked the gravediggers' scene. Although it became a matter of national pride to refute Voltaire, his objections were symptomatic of the general European Neo-classic disapproval of comic scenes in tragedy, and similar expressions of outraged decorum can be found in English critics, such as George Stubbes in 1736 (Vol. 3, p. 61), or the author of the anonymous essay of 1752 (Vol. 4, p. 561). Even Thomas Wilkes, a theatre-historian more usually content to endorse majority taste, wrote in 1759[24] that the gravediggers' scene is a specimen 'that will always make us laugh, unless we remember the place in which we find it'.

Garrick left the play largely untouched up to Act IV, retaining some theatre-cuts but restoring others,[25] and used a better text than other acting-editions. Yet once arrived at Act V he set about his surgical task with great aesthetic self-righteousness. 'I had sworn I would not leave the stage', he wrote to Sir William Young on 10 January 1773, 'till I had rescued that noble play from all the rubbish of the 5th act. I have brought it forth without the grave Diggers, Ostrick, & the Fencing Match'.[26] 'I have destroyed ye Grave diggers, (those favourites of the people)', he wrote to a French friend a week earlier, '& almost all of ye 5th Act'; and to another friend in France, 'I have thrown away the gravediggers, & all ye fifth Act, . . . —this is a great revolution in our theatrical history'.[27] Garrick's vocabulary—'rubbish', 'destroyed', 'thrown away'—leaves us in no doubt of his reforming zeal, or, destructive intent. He was encouraged in the process by George Steevens (No. 235) who, as we will see, seems to have had a special animus towards *Hamlet*. Garrick certainly meant what he said by cutting 'almost all' of the fifth act: of the 1,002 lines remaining in Shakespeare's play from the point at which my excerpt begins below, Garrick deletes 898, leaving 104, and adds 37 lines of his own. This makes an amazing difference to the play, as every reader can see. Garrick cuts most of Act IV, scenes 5, 6, 7, and Act V, scenes 1, 2. Hamlet does not leave Denmark, Claudius and Laertes do not plot against Hamlet's life. Since the voyage to England is omitted, so are the deaths of Rosencrantz and Guildenstern. The gravediggers do not appear, nor does Osric. Since there is no plot against Hamlet there is no duel, poisoned rapier, and drink. The final catastrophe, then, can only derive from the quarrel between Hamlet and Laertes over Ophelia's madness (not her death or burial), which Claudius stops by setting his guards on Hamlet, who promptly stabs him. Gertrude runs offstage in a fit of madness, '*Hamlet runs upon Laertes's sword and falls*', but reconciles Horatio and Laertes before he dies. Fortinbras, needless to say, does not return.

Professor Stone notes that the adaptation 'held the stage for eight years and was played thirty-seven times', Garrick receiving 'during his four remaining years on the stage £3,426.14.10 for this alteration alone. Scarcely any other play brought in more box receipts' (pp. 893f.). Popularity, if not value, may be gauged by cash takings, but one wonders how many people came to see Garrick as Hamlet rather than his adaptation; and how many would have come if the original play had been performed. I have assembled all the contemporary reactions I could find, since this is a key issue for the taste of the period. George Steevens, in several reviews, puffs the adaptation vigorously, as was to be expected (No. 237b,c,d,e,g,h), but the reviews in the *Macaroni and Theatrical Magazine* (No. 237f), the *Westminster Magazine* (No. 237i), and the *London Chronicle*[28] were just as favourable.

It would seem as if the only dissenting voice in this period (there were to be many soon afterwards) was Horace Walpole's. Writing to William Mason on 9 January 1773 he commented tartly: 'Mr. Garrick has cut out the scene of the gravediggers in *Hamlet*. I hope he will be rewarded with a place in the French Academy'.[29] Indeed 'the French were pleased', for a correspondent of Garrick's in November 1774 had visited Voltaire, enjoying 'a most gracious reception. We talked of your alteration of *Hamlet*, which he very greatly approves, and exprest himself very highly in your praise' (Stone, *op. cit.* in note 21, p. 901). Two years later Voltaire, in his *Letter à l'Académie française*, in the course of yet another attack on *Hamlet*, recorded that the gravediggers had been cut with great success.[30] Yet in 1780 they were restored at Drury Lane, by public demand.

The modern reader is unlikely to become as indignant about Garrick's *Hamlet* as did some Victorian critics. We are less prone to bardolatry, perhaps; we have a more detached, or a more historical view; such 'desperate mutilations', to use James Boaden's words (*The Private Correspondence of David Garrick* (London, 1831), I, p. 454), have become commonplace in our time. Yet Horace Walpole's objections (No. 237j) still stand, and could be taken further. Now that the text is generally available it will be interesting to see how many readers feel, with Professor Stone, that the criticism of his *Hamlet* by such men as James Boaden, Thomas Davies, Isaac Reed, Benjamin Victor, John Genest, Percy Fitzgerald, T. A. Lounsbury, and F. A. Hedgcock—all authorities on the eighteenth-century theatre, several of them biographers of Garrick—was 'unjust to Garrick both as a dramatist and as an admirer of Shakespeare'.

III

This is not the first time that a discussion of Garrick has had to dwell on the extraordinary contradictions between his professed admiration for Shakespeare, and his actual theatrical practice. It is impossible to resolve these contradictions, and it is difficult

to reach a balanced estimate of Garrick because of the mixture
of panegyric and denigration which attended his whole career.
Although, as my previous discussions have shown (Vol. 3,
pp. 11ff.; Vol. 4, pp. 24ff.), Shakespeare was well established in
the London theatre before Garrick appeared, and many other
managers and actors devoted much of their working lives to the
presentation of Shakespeare, a myth was soon established according to which Garrick alone had credit for re-discovering him, or
for interpreting him properly. Many of the eulogies which linked
Garrick and Shakespeare were the grossest flattery.[31] In one of
the innumerable poems addressed to him, the actor Quin comes
back from the dead to recount meeting Ryan, another famous
actor of the past, who enquires after Garrick ('the monarch')
and the state of the theatre:

> I told him (and I told him true)
> The stage would dwindle but for you:
> That Rowe and Shakespeare's tragic strain, ⎫
> Jonson and Congreve's comic vein, ⎬
> Were ONLY heard at Drury-Lane. ⎭
> *Buffoonery* was gaining ground,
> And sense oblig'd to yield to sound.[32]

Not only saviour of the stage at large, Garrick was supposed to
have reclaimed Shakespeare single-handed, by a deliberate exertion
of will. An exceptionally full version of this naively unhistorical
account (which is still accepted by some modern admirers of
Garrick) is given by a correspondent in the *London Museum* for
1770 (p. 172):

Could Shakespeare arise to hear his own compositions melodized with
new emendations from his tongue, the bard would hardly believe his
own ears, or that his productions could be raised to such a summit of
praise. For had not Mr. Garrick's genius rescued many of the poet's
beauties from the rust of antiquity by his excellence of acting, they
might have lain like diamonds in the deep dust of libraries, unnoticed,
for the want of some skilful artist to polish them for the view of mankind. Garrick by Shakespeare rose; Shakespeare, by Garrick, has been
handed up to higher fame than ever any idea he could form to himself
could produce. The bard of Stratford is at once the greatest dramatic
prodigy the world hath brought forth; and our British actor the most
capital performer yet born, to elucidate and ornament the sublimest
language.

The idea that Garrick was the best commentator on Shakespeare was widely expressed. The anonymous *Life of Mr. James Quin, Comedian* (1766) was dedicated to David Garrick, 'he who is at once the real representative, and only just commentator of Shakespeare' (Sig. A_2^r). Richard Warner, dedicating his Shakespeare glossary to Garrick in 1768, took for granted 'the allow'd connexion of your name with that of our immortal Bard as the Guardian of his Fame', and cited the 'intimate acquaintance you have had with his writings, the very *minutiae* of which you have made your study' (No. 219).

If Garrick's name was closely linked with Shakespeare's before 1769, after that date it was indissolubly so. The Stratford Shakespeare Jubilee was one of the most remarkable manifestations of popular taste in the eighteenth century, and has attracted so much attention recently[33] that there is no need to add yet another detailed account here. It was not a serious cultural event—there was no theatre in Stratford, and no Shakespeare play was or could be performed. With a firework display, an oratorio, a public breakfast, a ball, an elaborate procession of 217 people, 170 of them dressed as Shakespeare characters, it was more like a popular pageant or annual festival. The climax of the proceedings was Garrick's declamation of his Jubilee *Ode* (No. 222), a poetical assemblage that has been mocked from that day to this.[34] Of slightly greater critical significance is the Jubilee oration (No. 223), itself a cento of received ideas, yet looking on to later stages in bardolatry, as with its praise of Shakespeare's language as representing the union 'of the prophet and the poet'. The celebrations themselves were marked by scenes of chaos, due to torrential rain, floods, inadequate transport and accommodation, overcrowding, extravagantly high prices, and a series of accidents, from benches collapsing to Garrick's tipsy barber inflicting a large cut while shaving him on the great day of the *Ode*. At times the accounts read like a disastrous farce, and indeed Garrick lost some £2,000 in the process; yet with his genius for knowing what would please he re-enacted the *Ode* and the pageant in the more reliable setting of his own theatre. His concoction of *The Jubilee*, using 115 performers, played to packed houses 72 times in 1769 and 152 times all told in three seasons, regaining his losses fourfold. To serious Shakespeare lovers the whole phenomenon was a sad demonstration of English taste. The young Boswell was an enthusiastic actor and recorder of the proceedings, but Johnson ignored it, and to Horace Walpole it all seemed preposterous. Writing to George Montagu on 16 October 1769, Walpole protested at this 'total extinction of all taste': 'I have blushed at Paris when the papers came over crammed with ... Garrick's insufferable nonsense about Shakespeare. As that man's writings will be preserved by his name, who will believe that he was a tolerable actor?'[35]

As an actor, despite his advancing age (he was 57 when he acted his *Hamlet*), Garrick continued to dominate the English theatre. His fame was considerable, and his audience included many foreign visitors, such as Rousseau, and the German polymath Lichtenberg, who has left some marvellously graphic accounts of what he saw.[36] There are fewer discussions of Garrick's acting in this period than in the previous one, perhaps because he was off the stage (partly through illness, and partly due to his trip to France and Italy), and perhaps because he performed less often: in the 1772–3 season he appeared only 29 times, compared with 101 times 10 years earlier.[37] But also the main features of his acting style were well known, and he was no longer a controversial figure, but a celebrity. There are enthusiastic appreciations in this volume by Francis Gentleman (No. 227), and George Steevens (No. 234), in which he wishes that Garrick as Hamlet were younger, yet concedes the retention of some of his powers: 'no Actor ever *saw* a Ghost like Garrick'.

After the panegyric, the denigration. The *Theatrical Monitor*, a short-lived journal, carried several pieces in the winter of 1767 attacking Garrick for unnatural stresses ('nobody ever repeated his starts so *often*, or continued his pauses so *long*, as Mr. G—'), for introducing 'stage tricks and gestures' to the serious stage that belong to the harlequins, 'to make the people laugh' (no. II, 24 October, pp. 4f.). In a later issue the author mocked Garrick's 'high heeled shoes, big looks, and stuffed garments, as introduced in order to make a hero of a pigmy', and repeated a charge often made, that Garrick had kept out actors who by stature or abilities might have rivalled him in tragic roles (no. V, 21 November, p. 1). This writer also gives us an explanation of Garrick's increasingly infrequent performances in the tragic roles:

It has long been observed by the judicious that he no longer plays in tragedy with the same fire and spirit that he did fifteen or sixteen years

15

ago. G— in *Lear* or *Hamlet* now is no longer the same G— that once excited the admiration of the Town. When I saw him about seven or eight years ago play the character of Richard, I could hardly believe that he was the same man whose performance almost raised astonishment when he appeared for the first time in that part at Goodman's Fields. The decline of his abilities in Tragedy is indeed visible to the most superficial observer, and naturally accounts for his playing it so seldom, for a man generally grows tired of that he is unfit for! (no. III, 7 November, p. 8)

There is a touch of malice about that last sentence which one deplores, but the amount of adulation and flattery that Garrick received far exceeded criticism. The problem for the next biographer of Garrick, now that so much more material is available, will be to strike a just balance.

In one area Garrick's Shakespearian activities were entirely admirable, and that is as a collector of old plays. With his great fortune as an actor-manager ('he was, even without his further earnings as playwright, certainly the wealthiest working man of his time')[38] Garrick systematically collected sixteenth- and seventeenth-century drama, amassing a unique library which was to be presented to the British Museum after his death. During his lifetime he generously made it available to a wide range of scholars: Peter Whalley editing Jonson, Thomas Hawkins (No. 241), Edward Capell (Nos 220, 242), Thomas Warton, for his history of English poetry (see Vol. 6 of this collection). He certainly lent some books to Dr Johnson, since he wrote to his brother on 23 August 1764, 'let Johnson have ye Vols' (*Letters*, II, p. 423), and Johnson promised to return some books to Garrick on 10 October 1766.[39] Yet in the Preface to his edition Johnson comments sourly that he had collated 'such copies' of early Shakespeare Quartos 'as I could procure, and wished for more, but have not found the collectors of these rarities very communicative'. This was immediately understood as a rebuke to Garrick (see Colman, p. 181 below), and Boswell once took up the matter with Johnson:

I told him, that Garrick had complained to me of it, and had vindicated himself by assuring me, that Johnson was made welcome to the full use of his collection, and that he left the key of it with a servant, with orders to have a fire and every convenience for him. I found Johnson's notion was, that Garrick wanted to be courted for them, and that, on the contrary, Garrick should have courted him, and sent him the plays of his own accord. But, indeed, considering the slovenly and careless manner in which books were treated by Johnson, it could not be expected that scarce and valuable editions should have been lent to him. (*Life*, II, p. 192)

Johnson's careless treatment of books is well documented, but another account of his failure to collate the Quartos is given by Edmond Malone, a close and respected friend of both Johnson and Boswell. In his copy of Johnson's edition (Bodleian: Malone 140) Malone wrote:

The truth is Dr Johnson was not very fond of examining the old Quartos. Mr Garrick was possessed of almost all of them, and often *offered* to lend them to his old acquaintance;—but he never availed himself of a treasure, which was not perhaps any where else to be found.

George Steevens, who made frequent use of Garrick's library for his editions (Nos 212, 240), went out of his way to state his indebtedness publicly in the Prefaces, writing to Garrick on 3 December 1772 that 'I have taken the liberty to introduce your name, because *I have found* no reason to say that the possessors of the old quartos were not sufficiently communicative'.[40] When we consider the extent to which Garrick's collection acted as an unofficial Shakespeare library, and the number of writers included in this series who had personal connections with him, then it must be said that in the history of Shakespeare studies in the eighteenth century Garrick holds a key position, off-stage for once, but none the less important.

IV

In the texts presented here the central place is fittingly held by Dr Johnson's Shakespeare (No. 205), and the reactions it provoked. The number of issues raised by this edition is so large, and Johnson's stature as critic is so great, that I can only hope to touch on a few points in the space available. It is a major edition, of great interest to anyone interested in literature, or life, yet, paradoxically, it does not show Johnson's abilities at anything like their best. Contemporary reviewers expressed disappointment— Colman (No. 206), Kenrick (No. 207), Guthrie (No. 208), even James Barclay (No. 209), who had set out to defend it—and the best modern account of Johnson as editor has also recorded disappointment.[41] There is much to compensate for this negative balance, yet I believe that it is pointless for apologists (such as Bernard Bronson and Arthur Eastman)[42] to attempt to explain away its deficiencies. Johnson is great enough not to need his weaknesses hushed up.

A major cause of the disappointment was the time it had taken Johnson to produce it. In 1745 he had issued, anonymously, his *Miscellaneous Observations on the Tragedy of 'Macbeth'* (Vol. 3, No. 105),[43] at the end of which is a single leaf of *Proposals For Printing a New Edition of the Plays of William Shakespear, With Notes Critical and Explanatory, In Which The Text will be corrected: The Various Readings remarked: The Conjectures of former Editions examin'd, and their Omissions supply'd*, including a specimen page and notes. It was to be printed in 'Ten small volumes', at a 'Price to Subscribers' of 'one Pound five Shillings in Sheets', to be published by Edward Cave. The copyright in Shakespeare, however, was claimed by Tonson, and whether or not Johnson was ready to start an edition at this time, Cave's plans were blocked by Tonson, and it was not until June 1756 that Johnson issued, with Tonson, concrete *Proposals For Printing, by Subscription, The Dramatick Works of William Shakespeare, Corrected and Illustrated by Samuel Johnson* (Vol. 4, No. 160). Johnson had conceived of two great projects in the 1740s, the *Dictionary* (the *Plan* for which was issued in 1747), and the *Shakespeare*, and it would seem as if the *Dictionary* (1755) won. If we consider Johnson's output in the 20 years between the first essay and the completed edition, we can hardly accuse him of indolence. Yet, however much he managed to overcome his habitual lethargy in other areas, the edition made very slow progress.[44] He had made the tactical mistake of accepting subscriptions and announcing publication by Christmas 1757 (Vol. 4, p. 268). He worked with some application between 1756 and 1758, completing the editing of several plays, but as he failed to keep first one, and then another deadline, his energy seems to have petered out. He turned instead to the *Idler*, which he ran from 1758 to 1760; for three years after that he did next to nothing (he was then in his early fifties). His increased activity from 1763 on may have been due to a sense of shame occasioned by the jibe in Book Three of Charles Churchill's poem *The Ghost*, published in September 1762. Boswell's account is well known, but deserves to be quoted (*Life*, I, pp. 319f.):

His throes in bringing [the edition] forth had been severe and remittent; and at last we may almost conclude that the Caesarian operation was performed by the knife of Churchill, whose upbraiding satire, I dare say, made Johnson's friends urge him to dispatch.

> He for subscribers bates his hook,
> And takes your cash; but where's the book?
> No matter where; wise fear, you know,
> Forbids the robbing of a foe;
> But what, to serve our private ends,
> Forbids the cheating of our friends?

Johnson received the proofs of the final play, *Othello*, in July 1764, and then only had the Appendix and the Preface to see to. But by 20 July 1765 'not a Line of the Preface' had been written, as Tonson complained to Capell, and publication had to be postponed; Johnson managed to complete the Preface by September, and the edition was finally published on 10 October.

This prolonged gestation affected the printing in a number of ways, and although we do not yet have a full bibliographical study it is evident that Johnson's *Shakespeare* had an erratic career in the printing-house. He wrote to Warton on 21 June 1757, 'I am printing my new edition', and by 14 April 1758 he could tell him that some notes Warton had supplied were 'on plays already printed', and would thus have to appear in the Appendix (*Life*, I, pp. 322, 335–6). The printer, William Strahan, noted in his ledger for December 1761 that vols I–VI had been printed, and recorded in September 1765 that vols VII–VIII were completed. But D. J. Fleeman's analysis reveals several discrepancies between the computations and the finished edition,[45] and Strahan's note of additional printing costs—'Extra for Corrections, Alterations, Matter lost, and Appendix in these two vols.'—suggest some chaotic last-minute changes ('Matter lost' is a particularly intriguing category). The finished volumes show many signs of disorder: 'hasty bindings—e.g., gatherings omitted in some copies; additional gatherings added in others, canceled leaves tipped in at the wrong places', the signature 'placed above the footnotes'.[46] Some leaves in the volumes printed in 1761 were not in fact completed until 1765 (Sherbo, *Johnson, Editor*, p. 12), while a great many interpolated notes, replete with asterisks and obelisks, are inserted throughout.[47] As A. M. Eastman has conceded, 'Almost everything in Johnson's Shakespeare points to irregular and uneven work.'[48] Although he had undertaken, in 1756, to make a completely fresh collation of the texts Johnson did no such thing, but, like other eighteenth-century editors, printed from his predecessors' texts, notably Warburton's 1747 edition and the 1757 reissue of Theobald. Yet he moved from one to the other on no rational principle, and at one point even went back to Theobald's first (and superseded) edition.[49] Johnson's editing was spasmodic, erratic, inconsistent. The fact that the work had been carried out over some time, as evidenced by the Appendix containing a number of corrections and second thoughts, was not lost on the contemporary reviewers. Nor did the most searching of them, William Kenrick, fail to note that in a number of places Johnson had cancelled the first-printed text, as we now know, in order to tone down some of his criticisms of William Warburton, Bishop of Gloucester.[50]

I have gone into this much detail about the genesis of Johnson's edition since it may explain why the work failed to meet his own standards, publicly set out in the 1756 *Proposals*. He had stated that he would correct the text by 'a careful collation of the oldest copies', and that his edition 'will exhibit *all* the observable varieties of *all* the copies that can be found' (Vol. 4, p. 271; my italics), that is, list all variant readings. He did neither of these things. He promised to 'read the books which the authour read, to trace his knowledge to its source and compare his copies with their originals' (p. 272): he signally failed to do this.[51] He promised to explain 'obsolete or peculiar diction', gloss *'any* obscurity' arising from the 'allusion to some other book', explain *'any* forgotten custom' by reference to contemporary sources: he did not keep these promises. He had promised to adopt *'all* that is valuable . . . from *every* commentator, that posterity may consider it as including *all the rest* and exhibiting *whatever is hitherto known* of the great father of the English drama' (p. 273). I have italicized the expansive gestures, the reckless offers to perform any and every task which could be expected from an editor of Shakespeare. Johnson set himself the ideal goal, far beyond his own abilities, or indeed those of any other editor of his day, or ours. It is not surprising that he did not perform all that he had promised; but, as even his friendly critics observed,[52] the discrepancy was glaring.

One of Johnson's greatest difficulties was that in the 20 years since he first projected an edition the English literary world had become enormously conscious of the unsettled nature of Shakespeare's text. Suggesting emendations was almost a national pastime, for which everyone felt himself to be qualified. A great impetus to this text-consciousness was given by a series of controversial works attacking editors for their textual errors, as exemplified by Theobald, Upton, Holt, Grey, Edwards, Heath, and others. The rage for emendation was not confined to printed books, for almost any literary journal of the period has its quota, while the columns of the *Gentleman's Magazine* or the *St. James's Chronicle* were filled with correspondence on the great cruxes ('making the green, one red', 'unhouseld, unaneled', for instance),[53] controversies which continued over years. In May 1765 a correspondent to the *Gentleman's Magazine* (xxxv, p. 229) is in the full swing of fashion:

While almost every body is making emendations, annotations, or illustrations, of some part or other of *Shakespeare*, with the principal of which your Magazine is enriched, give me leave to take this opportunity of throwing one mite into the treasury, which I accidentally cast my eye upon the other day.

That textual criticism had been pursued with enormous energy and controversy was obvious to Johnson. 'The part of criticism . . . which has occasioned the most arrogant ostentation and excited the keenest acrimony, is the emendation of corrupted passages', he wrote in the Preface (p. 93 below). His discussion of his own work as a textual critic is curiously defensive, as if designed to anticipate and deflect criticism. His statement that conjecture should not be wantonly or licentiously indulged is correct, albeit truistic, and his belief 'that the reading of the ancient books is probably true' is both generally acceptable yet false in a thousand instances. Throughout this section Johnson is placing himself in the light of a judicious editor, who has not allowed himself to be rushed into error. His caution about conjectural emendation ('As I practised conjecture more I learned to trust it less', 1765; 'It were to be wished that we all explained more and amended less', 1773) would be endorsed, in general, by modern bibliography, but it will not do to make Johnson a hero in the reestablishment of Shakespeare's authentic text. He left unchanged many passages in Shakespeare which were evidently corrupt, and changed others which were correct; he explained some passages incorrectly, and failed to explain others. Sometimes he is honest about his incapacity, sometimes he is silent. He claimed to have collated the Folios but did not, and made very sparing use of the Quartos. On the other side he sometimes restored the true text by reference to early editions (as in No. 205 below, Notes 69, 81, 84, 130, 133, 136, 159, 167, 210, 224); he explained the sense of many words by his knowledge of Elizabethan English; and he wrote admirable paraphrases of difficult passages, some of which, indeed, have never been improved on (see, for instance, Notes 11, 134, 143, 179, 202, 213). Johnson certainly had the ability to produce an edition which would have improved on its predecessors, but in the field of textual criticism he simply did not do the work, and his powers were applied only intermittently.

As a Shakespeare critic Johnson makes an equally divided impression. There is a great difference between the Preface and the Notes, to begin with. The Notes were written over a period of years, mostly between 1756 and 1764, although those on *Macbeth* are reprinted, with some alterations, from the 1745 pamphlet;[54] the Preface he wrote in August-September 1765. The Notes were produced in a variety of moods, discursive, expansive, laconic, indifferent, bored, disapproving; but whatever the mood they are the result of Johnson's direct engagement with the text, derive from first-hand reading and go into detailed exposition, analysis, and criticism. The Preface is written from a distance, refuses, almost scorns to make direct reference to the text (Johnson's analogy with the pedant in Hierocles, who offered to sell his house and peddled one brick as a specimen, is a rhetorical self-defence of his decision not to go into detail which makes a curiously forbidding impact). This decision has the bad effect of allowing Johnson to be too abstract, taking many points too far, too fast, so that his criticisms of Shakespeare, unsupported, insupportable, flourish as inventions or extensions of a basic idea (as in the contrast between Shakespeare's excellence in comedy and mediocrity in tragedy, or the paragraph on the quibble), uncorrected by any reference back to the object they are meant to describe. In the Notes praise or blame, whether enlightened or not, are at least referable to specific contexts; in the Preface, as his reviewers complained, all is general and undefined. The Notes, various in mood, are written in Johnson's ordinary, everyday range of styles; the Preface, however, although there are lapses, and a deal of repetition in the later stages discussing (and defending) the editor's own practice, is mostly written in Johnson's highest style, as if he were giving a formal oration at a centenary gathering, making a definitive statement for posterity. So he is, of course, yet while this sense of an occasion to which he must rise produces much memorable writing it is also responsible for over-writing, for a sense of strain, for judgments which are simply extreme. I lack space at this time to illustrate my conclusion, but I believe that it is impossible to justify by rational argument and quotation either Johnson's praise or his blame of Shakespeare, that he over-topples on the one side into the splendid but vapid idolatry produced by many of his contemporaries, and on the other into the violent denigration which we associate with such 'anti-Shakespearians' as Rymer, Dennis, Smollett, Mrs Lennox, and Voltaire. A balanced estimate in the Preface seems hardly possible, even when discussing previous editors; Warburton is treated far too kindly, Edwards and Heath far too harshly, while Johnson's treatment of Theobald is a deplorable instance of the workings of his prejudices, which, once fixed, were aggravated, not placated, when they discovered any virtue in their butts. In sum, the Preface is a curiously unsatisfying document, highly finished, polished indeed in the proof-reading,[55] 'admirable for the fineness of thread and work, but of little substance or profit'.

Yet Johnson is a critic to whom we return year after year for pleasure and insight. The paradox is sometimes resolved by arguing that whatever is good in Johnson is original to him, whatever is bad derives from his times. That is too crude, however: many of the most unsatisfying parts of the Preface are due to Johnson's own style and argument, while the critical tradition offered him some fruitful possibilities, notably in its concern with dramatic character and with moral judgment, both areas, as a fuller study could show, in which Johnson far excelled his predecessors. Without begging the question of the relative value of each, it is important to discriminate in Johnson's Shakespeare criticism between (to use Saussure's terminology), *langue*, the inherited critical tradition, and *parole*, his individual judgments. In these terms the Preface is almost entirely traditional in content, though unique and idiosyncratic in expression. Johnson's debts to his predecessors have been well set out by D. Nichol Smith, Arthur Sherbo, and R. D. Stock,[56] and in the annotations below I have cited more instances in which Johnson rephrases traditional ideas. As his reviewers said, Johnson conceded too much to Rymer, Dennis, and Voltaire; and despite his dispute on one or two points, it is evident that he is in fundamental agreement with them on many more. Johnson's affinities are, in fact, with a group of critics who had worked at the time when he first proposed an edition, at least a generation before he finally came to write his Preface. The best statement of this fact known to me comes from a contemporary, no less an authority than Malone. In his copy of the 1773 edition, now in the Bodleian (Malone 140), he noted several parallels between Johnson and Dennis, and when he came to Johnson's borrowing from Guthrie, he wrote: 'Dr Johnson sat down to write this admirable preface with a mind fraught with all that had been written by Dennis, Gildon, Rymer, Guthrie &c on the same subject; whose pamphlets he had recently read.' Whoever studies the Shakespeare criticism in this collection will see how strongly Johnson identifies himself with the orthodox school, and how he resists or ignores the newer developments which are to be associated with such writers as Theobald, Upton, Hurd, Roderick, Webb, or Kames.

The one sequence in the Preface where *parole*, rather than *langue*, dominates is the discussion of the Unities, still thought in some areas to be Johnson's major critical achievement. Yet T. M. Raysor[57] showed in 1927 that attacks on the Unities had been made at least 60 years before Johnson wrote, and that these had become increasingly frequent in the 1750s and 1760s, as the preceding volumes in this series will testify.[58] It will no longer do to cite the presence of this attack as proof of Johnson's 'sturdy common sense and independence of judgment'.[59] The turn it takes, however, is independent, though not necessarily good. Where the liberal tradition, as seen in such critics as Farquhar, Stubbes, Upton, and Kames, had defended the dramatist's rejection of literalist conceptions of time and place by his appeal to dramatic illusion, Johnson disposes of the whole issue in these brusque terms: 'The necessity of observing the Unities of time and place arises from the supposed necessity of making the drama credible'. Where the liberal tradition had stressed the willing co-operation of the imagination Johnson rejects the concept of illusion on

24

matter-of-fact, not imaginative grounds. After two paragraphs
mocking rigid critics' objection to the 'impossible' elements in
drama, Johnson diverts the argument from imagination to literal
truth: 'It is false that *any* representation is mistaken for reality;
that *any* dramatick fable in its materiality was *ever* credible, or,
for a single moment, was *ever credited*.' Johnson's position is given
the appearance of weight by its absoluteness, in the words which
I have italicized, but it must be noted that he has deflected the
traditional issue of whether poets lie to an epistemological or
psychological crisis in the audience. If, when the play opens, 'the
spectator *really imagines* himself at Alexandria, and *believes* that
his walk to the theatre has been a voyage to Egypt, and that he
lives in the days of Antony and Cleopatra'—anyone familiar with
Johnson's style or thought will detect the sarcasm there, will feel
the bubble being inflated only to be burst—then 'Surely he that
imagines this may imagine more'. If he is silly, or crazy enough—
I bring out Johnson's latent meaning—to 'take the stage at one
time for the palace of the Ptolemies', then he can equally easily
'take it half an hour later for the promontory of Actium'. Either
way he has lost contact with reality, since he has given in to
'delusion', which Johnson defines in the *Dictionary* as 'A cheat;
guile; treachery; falsehood; A false representation; illusion;
error; a chimerical thought' ('chimerical' is defined as 'imaginary',
i.e. 'remote from reality', 'wildly, vainly, or fantastically conceived'). The imagination, Johnson believed in company with
many of his contemporaries, was a subversive agent needing
constant supervision by the reason,[60] and 'Delusion, if delusion be
admitted'—spectator beware!—'has no certain limitations'. That
is the starting point for a superb flourishing of Johnson's fantasy
at the expense of the spectator who allows his imagination to
co-operate with fiction, and who thus, Johnson suggests, loses
contact with reality, flies 'above the reach of reason, or of truth',
his mind 'wandering in extasy', suffering from a 'calenture of the
brains'. As I have indicated by my annotation below, reference
to Johnson's *Dictionary* is essential to grasp the pejorative associa-
tions of those words, indeed probably for most of us even to
understand the rare term 'calenture', a form of delirium experienced by sailors in the tropics, 'wherein they imagine the sea to be
green fields, and will throw themselves into it, if not restrained'.
This is an awful fate to be risked for a mere play! Johnson's

account of the state of mind of someone who cannot tell fantasy from reality might indeed be supported by modern clinical psychiatry; but what has it to do with the experience of drama?

Johnson's argument may be put concisely in this form: the Unities were invented in order to make the drama credible, but anyone who were to credit the drama would be out of his mind. (Everything depends on the sense given to 'credit'.) 'The truth is', he goes on, having burst the bubble to his own satisfaction, the spectators 'are always in their senses', know that 'the stage is only a stage, and that the players are only players'. That reductivist position turns into a dismissive account of the theatre as a whole: a play is merely 'a certain number of lines recited with just gesture and elegant modulation.... A dramatic exhibition is a book recited with concomitants that encrease or diminish its effect.... A play read affects the mind like a play acted'. Here Johnson's life-long prejudice against actors seems to be the cause of his down-grading drama to the level of a text recited which derives nothing more from the representation than the reader can gain for himself in a solitary reading. No one who has ever experienced the drama can endorse that position. When we say that Johnson dismisses the Unities, we must add that he dismisses many more important things as well. He rejects dramatic illusion, he rejects the imagination's co-operation with fiction, he rejects the actors, he seems finally to reject the theatre as a whole. This ought to be clear to all readers, and much as I admire Johnson I cannot join his apologists in excusing, or even praising this sequence. The best modern comments are in the brief note by J. H. Adler,[61] concluding that Johnson reduces the imagination to 'the least possible function, severely limits—indeed very nearly abolishes—illusion as an element in stagecraft, and takes a position almost totally unempathic'.

The best contemporary account is that by William Kenrick (No. 207), which starts by showing Johnson's fundamental error in assuming that the 'dramatic fable' is meant to be believed 'in its materiality': 'The dramatic unities, if necessary, are necessary to support the *apparent probability*, not the *actual credibility* of the drama'. Whatever 'deception' is involved in the presentation of a play is of the passions, not the reason: 'it affects our sensibility but not our understanding; and is by no means so powerful a delusion as to affect our *belief*'. Kenrick's argument is superior to Johnson's not only in its logic but in its grasp of the fundamentals of theatrical experience. Kenrick sees that the audience in the theatre are emotionally involved in the action represented. They know that 'the stage is only a stage' but 'they are often so intent on the scene as to be absent with regard to everything else. A spectator properly affected by a dramatic representation makes no reflection about the fiction or the reality of it' since 'his attention' is 'fully engaged to the fable and his passions affected by the distress of the characters'. Whatever reservations we may have about Kenrick's manners in polemic, or his subsequent career, his refutation of Johnson is both intelligent and responsive to the nature of drama.

Johnson's individual contribution to critical discussion in the Preface is hardly a happy one. The Notes, if they offer less polished writing, also offer less idiosyncrasy. Their make-up can be most fairly described as a blend of traditional and personal criticism. I have only been able to print a representative selection of them here, but it is enough to show both aspects. Johnson endorses most orthodox Neo-classical attitudes, not all of them sympathetic to Shakespeare. When Shakespeare offers a moral attitude which can be easily extrapolated, and is in line with orthodox beliefs, he is praised in such Notes as 50 ('a very just and moral reason'), 93 ('The moral to be drawn from this representation is . . .'), 145 ('a very powerful warning'), and 218 ('ought to be deeply impressed on every reader').[62] Where no moral is visible, or where Shakespeare differs from orthodox beliefs, Johnson uses such words as 'horrible', 'blameable', 'unsuitable'.[63] On at least one occasion Johnson attributes to Shakespeare a view which belongs to a character in the play, and takes it as an instance of what he several times[64] sneeringly refers to as Shakespeare's pandering to the taste of the audience, to the low social level of which he himself belonged ('I am afraid our Varlet Poet intended to inculcate . . .': Note 17; cf. Kenrick's reply, p. 209). Johnson evaluates plots according to typical Neo-classical criteria: they should be probable,[65] unified, preferably single,[66] and characters should be well discriminated and coherent. Like most Neo-classic critics Johnson was offended by Shakespeare's faults of language, such as violations of decorum,[67] puns, quibbles,[68] and what he describes as Shakespeare's 'counteracting' his own pathos.[69] (It is worth observing how closely Johnson resembles Francis Gentleman on such points.) The epithets used show his feelings of contempt for these failings: 'harsh', 'very poor', 'childish prattle', 'trifling', 'far-fetched and unaffecting', 'this toil of antithesis'. The passages which Johnson singles out for praise are, consistently enough, those in which the emotions are simple, brought to a climax without distracting variations in style, and are often sententious or gnomic. It is significant that the plays thus singled out for praise are either early (*Two Gentlemen*) or late (*Henry VIII*), and are most often histories, where the components of style are easily separable, not as densely interwoven as in the mature tragedies. These are expressions of period, rather than of individual taste.

Johnson's individuality is always perceptible in the style of these notes, never conventional, and often strikingly laconic in expression; especially in the caustic mode. Individuality of thought and response is found within notes which use conventional Neo-classical categories, but emerges on its own in many notes where Johnson's critical tradition seems to fall away, and he writes simply as a man caught up in the experience of reading. There would be little in Neo-classical theory, for instance, to justify the delight Johnson takes in the low-life characters of the *Henry IV* plays, a delight which makes him record the last appearance of each of the characters on-stage: Falstaff himself (Note 99), Bardolph (Note 101), and Pistol (Note 107), a note which becomes the cue for a valedictory, almost elegiac note on the passing of this world. He writes of *Henry IV*: 'Perhaps no author has ever in two plays afforded so much delight' (Note 93). Again, Johnson pronounces what for him is one of the highest praises that can be given to a work of literature, that 'no man wished it shorter',[70] not of a tragedy, nor of a romantic, nor an aristocratic comedy, but of *The Merry Wives of Windsor*. The end-note, which he added for the 1773 edition, concludes with this paragraph:

The conduct of this drama is deficient; the action begins and ends often before the conclusion, and the different parts might change places without inconvenience; but its general power, that power by which all works of genius shall finally be tried, is such that perhaps it never yet had reader or spectator who did not think it too soon at an end. (No. 240 below, Note 10)

The moments when Johnson responds directly to Shakespeare are when he is emotionally moved, or when the play echoes his own experience of life. His well-known difficulty in moving from contemplation to action is revealed in response to a speech in *Measure for Measure* (Note 14: 'When we are young we busy ourselves in forming schemes for succeeding time ...'), a topic also appealed to by Biron's warning against vows (Note 23). When a passage 'comes home to his bosom' Johnson is moved to write, in his moral-reflective vein, generalizations about life which are often expressed in the present tense, such as the note on Don John's claim to being unable to dissimulate (Note 46). The reflective present-tense generalization appears in the marvellously intuitive response to Falstaff's remark on Prince John, this 'sober-blooded Boy':

Falstaff speaks here like a veteran in life. The young prince did not love him, and he despaired to gain his affection, for he could not make him laugh. Men only become friends by community of pleasures. He who cannot be softened into gayety cannot easily be melted into kindness. (Note 89)

As Johnson tends to prefer passages of verse where a single topic is presented, so here he responds to emotional states which are shown at some length, held long enough to be felt in extension, such as the generalizations provoked by the remorse of Leontes (Note 21), the grief of Constance (Note 56), the guilt of Whitmore (Note 115), the virtue of Posthumus (Note 169), and others.[71]

Johnson reacts to specific characters in specific situations. While he shares the general Neo-classical interest in characters as totalities who are to be kept distinct and coherent, his concern is not so much aesthetic as moral,[72] or, perhaps better, human. Johnson evaluates behaviour as he would in real life, finding qualities worthy of praise in Celia (Note 22) or Timon (Note 142), being rather cool about Viola (Notes 30, 31), indignant about Angelo and Bertram (Notes 17, 51), contemptuous of Parolles (Note 51), and more concerned at Hotspur (Note 71). Johnson judges behaviour for the effect it would have on society, and the note on Falstaff (93), the beginning of which is often quoted on its own by modern critics who wish to celebrate Falstaff as a god of misrule, and imagine that Johnson agrees with them, concludes with a warning:

The moral to be drawn from this representation is that no man is more dangerous than he that with a will to corrupt hath the power to please;

and that neither wit nor honesty ought to think themselves safe with such a companion when they see *Henry* seduced by *Falstaff*.

In the end-notes Johnson has more room to develop and sum up his response to the play. The end-notes on the early comedies often use the conventional categories of Neo-classicism, yet at times say important things through them. The notes on the mature comedies and histories become more individual, the critical ones on *Measure for Measure* and *Henry V* raising problems that defenders of those plays must still cope with. The most memorable are the end-notes on *Hamlet*, *King Lear*, and *Othello*. Here Johnson's attitude is complex, responding to the variety and bustle of the first while making some important reservations about the function of Hamlet's madness and the relation of the catastrophe to the main action. Johnson's emotional response to the death of Ophelia (Note 215) is as touching as that to the death of Cordelia (Note 141), yet we cannot share his wish to preserve these heroines by the workings of poetic justice (compare Francis Gentleman). These are tributes to his sensitivity, at least. Johnson is just as upset by the death of Desdemona (Note 224), but since he does not in this case wish for poetic justice that must mean that he thinks it just. While the *Lear* note gives, in its first paragraph, an admirable account of Johnson's involvement in the experience of the play, and surveys some traditions in the criticism of it, that on *Othello* concentrates on giving brief sketches of the main characters, wonderfully pregnant observations which reveal an intellectual and emotional response:

The fiery openness of *Othello*, magnanimous, artless, and credulous, boundless in his confidence, ardent in his affection, inflexible in his resolution, and obdurate in his revenge; the cool malignity of Iago, silent in his resentment, subtle in his designs, and studious at once of his interest and his vengeance; the soft simplicity of *Desdemona*, confident of merit, and conscious of innocence, her artless perseverance in her suit, and her slowness to suspect that she can be suspected, are such proofs of *Shakespeare*'s skill in human nature as, I suppose, it is vain to seek in any modern writer. (Note 226)

No critic has ever said so much about *Othello* in such few words. The thumbnail sketches of Cassio, Roderigo, and Emilia are equally penetrating, and the authority with which Johnson judges from experience here is so much more impressive than the dutiful remarks on 'scenes' and 'narrative' that follow.

Johnson does have some original and penetrating notes on the design of the plays, but they are not expressed through the conventional critical categories. Here he moves from his own response to the characters towards grasping Shakespeare's intentions in controlling his, and the audience's reactions. So he notes the two-part structure of *Richard II*, for instance:

It seems to be the design of the poet to raise *Richard* to esteem in his fall, and consequently to interest the reader in his favour. He gives him only passive fortitude, the virtue of a confessor rather than of a king. In his prosperity we saw him imperious and oppressive, but in his distress he is wise, patient, and pious. (Note 63)

And a few notes later: 'This pathetick denunciation shews that *Shakespeare* intended to impress his auditors with dislike of the deposal of *Richard*' (Note 66). Where previous commentators, such as Warburton, had noted that a speech was 'confused' in its expression Johnson goes on to enquire what Shakespeare meant by such an effect. The speech of Decius is confused because it 'is intentionally pompous' (Note 163); of a speech by Juliet he writes: 'This speech is confused and inconsequential, according to the disorder of *Juliet*'s mind' (Note 191). Although Johnson shared the Neo-classical distrust of soliloquies he made exceptions for two which to him expressed genuine feeling. Hamlet's 'To be or not to be' he described (perhaps as a deliberate defence of it against the criticisms of Smollett)[73] as 'this celebrated soliloquy, which bursting from a man distracted with contrariety of desires and overwhelmed with the magnitude of his own purposes, is connected rather in the speaker's mind than on his tongue', and therefore he offered a paraphrase in order 'to shew how one sentiment produces another' (Note 202). Similarly he approved of the speech by Posthumus in the last act of *Cymbeline*, using again a psychological approach, diagnosing the emotional state of the speaker:

This is a soliloquy of nature, uttered when the effervescence of a mind agitated and perturbed spontaneously and inadvertently discharges itself in words. The speech, throughout all its tenour, if the last conceit be excepted, seems to issue warm from the heart. (Note 176)

It is the sensitivity and warmth of response shown here or in the acute 1745 note on the 'Artifice and Dissimulation' conveyed by

the 'forced and unnatural Metaphors' used by Macbeth to describe
the murder of Duncan (Vol. 3, p. 176) that makes one bitterly regret
that Johnson did not apply his talents more fully to commenting
on Shakespeare.

V

Johnson's labours on Shakespeare extended from 1745, or earlier,
to 1765. The labours of Edward Capell, he tells us in the introduction to his edition (No. 220), began in 1745, extended to 1768,
when his edition was published, work on the *Notes* continuing
right up to his death in 1781. Yet while Johnson picked up
Shakespeare and put him down again, edited the *Dictionary*, wrote
the *Rambler*, the *Idler* and many smaller pieces, wasted much time
and spent much time regretting the waste of time, Capell did
nothing else but edit Shakespeare, with prodigious dedication and
industry. He is said to have transcribed the whole of Shakespeare
10 times over; since he dated his manuscript transcriptions
(bequeathed to the library of Trinity College, Cambridge) it is
possible to reconstruct his life's work year by year. Capell deserved
to have produced a great edition, and what he did produce represented in many ways the best scholarship of the century. Yet the
edition as a whole never achieved the recognition it deserved in
its own day, although the recent evaluation by Alice Walker[74] has
won it far greater respect.

Capell made a number of unfortunate decisions concerning the
physical make-up of his edition. He evolved an idiosyncratic
punctuation scheme, to understand which it is necessary to consult
(if we can find it) his *Prolusions: select pieces of ancient poetry* (1760).
A stickler for typographical elegance, he resented the beauty of the
printed textpage being disfigured with footnotes; nor could he
manage to space them out equally (I, pp. 23f.). So he announced
that the variant readings would be published in subsequent
volumes, 'together with the Notes' (I, p. 49). To these he planned
to add an enormous collection of historical parallels designed to
show Shakespeare's reading, *The School of Shakespeare*. Unfortunately, the labour of preparing all the ancillary materials took
far longer than he had expected. It was, I believe, only as the result
of a spiteful campaign in the *St. James's Chronicle* for 1772–3,
apparently led by George Steevens,[75] that he was persuaded to part

with the first instalment of his *Notes* (No. 242). Transcription of the remainder was unfinished at his death, and they were finally published posthumously by his friend John Collins, in 1783. Even today the use of the 10 small octavo volumes of the edition together with the three large folio volumes of notes is an inconvenience unmatched by hardly any other enterprise of such merit. In his own day Capell's critics crowed mercilessly over the awkwardness of his edition.

Although few of his contemporaries realized the fact, Capell revolutionized both the theory and practice of editing Shakespeare. In the Preface to his 1725 edition Pope had destroyed the status of the early printed texts, Quartos and Folios, by his account of the damage that Shakespeare's plays were supposed to have received at the hands of the actors. The 1623 Folio, he supposed, was printed from texts which had been progressively deteriorating in the theatre, 'cut or added to arbitrarily' over the years, and then botched up by the editors, the actors Heminge and Condell (Vol. 2, pp. 410ff.). The erroneousness of Pope's account was exposed by John Roberts (Vol. 2, pp. 454ff.) and Lewis Theobald (Vol. 2, pp. 484ff.), but it was accepted, and even imaginatively embroidered on, both by Dr Johnson in the 1756 *Proposals* (Vol. 4, pp. 269) and the 1765 Preface (p. 83 below), and by George Steevens in 1766 (No. 212). Capell succeeded in clearing the actors, and the early texts, from these false suppositions by showing that the Quartos are 'the Poet's own copies, however they were come by', and that the Folio does not derive solely from playhouse manuscripts but from previously printed editions, where available. This revolution in theory was made possible by a revolution in practice, for Capell was the first editor to collate variant texts systematically. By a line-by-line, word-by-word, comma-by-comma comparison he was able to show that the Folio text, in copying the Quartos, introduced many errors, and that since the text degenerated in successive reprints the earliest edition was in general the best. By the same technique of collation Capell showed that the first modern editor, Rowe in 1709, had based his text on the fourth Folio of 1685; that Pope in 1725 based his text on Rowe, Theobald in 1733 based his on Pope, Warburton in 1747 based his on Theobald, and Dr Johnson in 1765 based his on Warburton (and, as we now know, on the 1757 Theobald). Thus all the modern editions descended from Rowe, and the fourth

Folio, although the editors supplemented their texts, with varying degrees of thoroughness, by reference to the first Folio and various Quartos. It was to break with this tradition that Capell began from the early texts and transcribed his edition afresh by hand, rather than transmit the errors of the printed editions. Alice Walker has said that 'the result of this return to the substantive editions was the restoration of hundreds of authoritative readings. On this account we may allow him the title of "the Restorer of Shakespeare"' (Walker, 'Edward Capell and his edition of Shakespeare', pp. 137–8).

In other departments of the editor's task Capell is also impressive. On Shakespeare's learning he gave one of the best-informed accounts. On the question of authorship he defended the authenticity of the three parts of *Henry VI*, *Love's Labour's Lost*, *The Taming of the Shrew*, and *Titus Andronicus*, and modern scholarship would endorse his findings on almost every point. Some of his arguments take the traditional and relatively inarticulate form (2 *Henry VI* has 'beauties . . . and grandeurs' in it 'of which no other author but Shakespeare was capable'), but for the *Shrew* he applied his admirable grasp of Shakespeare's chronology, noting its stylistic affinities with another early play, *Love's Labour's Lost*, while for *Titus Andronicus* Capell extended the historical argument out into Elizabethan drama as a whole, relating the play to its proper context in style, subject-matter, and attitude, the 'tragedy of blood' of the decade on either side of 1590. Although brief, this discussion is a model of the union of scholarship and criticism. On the sources Capell is even better, not only giving the most complete and accurate account that had yet appeared (I, pp. 49–71), which alone would have been enough to establish him as a major scholar,[76] but stressing how completely Shakespeare has integrated the materials into his design. Capell concludes the introduction by noting two urgent desiderata for the study of Shakespeare, a proper biography, and an accurate chronology, so that Shakespeare's artistic development could be studied: both suggestions were taken up by Edmond Malone, who devoted most of his life to them. In this way Capell can be said to have helped programme the future of Shakespeare studies.

Capell's realization of the importance of collation was shared by two other textual critics of his day. Thomas Tyrwhitt, a distinguished classical scholar and editor of Chaucer, produced a brief essay on Shakespeare's text (1766: No. 210) in response to Johnson's edition, and observed that Johnson would have done better if he had consulted the early editions properly: 'Collating is certainly dull work; but I doubt whether, upon the whole, an Editor would not find it the shortest and easiest, as well as the surest method of discharging his duty.' The same belief was held by Charles Jennens, who produced editions of five of Shakespeare's tragedies between 1770 and 1774 as part of a projected complete edition. In the first of these, *King Lear* (No. 225), Jennens states that 'no fair and exact collation of *Shakespeare* hath yet been presented to the public', due to Capell's edition appearing without the variant readings, and that he has now begun to fill that gap. This is in effect the first edition of a Shakespeare text which approaches anything near modern standards in textual criticism, and it is vastly more scholarly than anything that had yet appeared. As well as listing text variants Jennens defends his readings in notes which show how well he could unite textual and literary criticism. He was an independent scholar of no mean ability,[77] but he was attacked with savagery in a series of anonymous reviews, which contemporaries had no difficulty in identifying as the work of George Steevens.[78]

Consideration of the work of Steevens himself as an editor starts most appropriately from his activities as a polemicist, for the whole of his career as a Shakespearian, from 1765 to 1800, was disfigured by an unending output of abuse, mockery, scandal, and malicious practical jokes, directed against friend and enemy alike. Garrick described him as 'a pest to society' (*Private Correspondence*, II, p. 361), indeed Steevens was unhappy unless causing somebody anxiety and unease, exploiting to the full his access to the anonymity of the journals and magazines, often playing a double role. His attacks on rival Shakespeare editors and critics show him trying to safeguard his own career by destroying other people's, but unfortunately in the process he showed up his own poor grasp of the principles of textual criticism. He sneered at Capell's accuracy, both privately (writing to Garrick on 27 December 1765: 'I do not pretend to the exactness of [Capell], for should a flea break its chain I declare myself utterly incapable of mending it', *Private Correspondence*, I, p. 217), and publicly, in the Preface to his 1773 edition (No. 240). Yet while criticizing Capell he was busy plagiarizing him, as Capell's friend John Collins showed[79] in one of those remarkably thorough pieces of textual polemic that the eighteenth century excelled in. Collins commented on the absurdity of criticizing an editor for being too accurate—'surely correctness is an essential quality in an editor' (p. 10)—and showed that in Capell's edition of 2 *Henry VI* (which Steevens had cited as an instance of gross inaccuracy) of the 199 differences between Capell's text and Steevens's, two-thirds are due to Capell having in fact given the authentic reading of the Folio or Quarto text, with all other insertions or emendations faithfully recorded. Steevens, however, failed to use the authentic texts, took many of his readings from Warburton's unscholarly and eccentric edition, and did not draw the reader's attention to the textual alterations which he had made. Steevens, being unable to deny the charge, had a petty revenge on Collins (who was a clergyman), in subsequent editions by writing notes on Shakespeare's bawdy and signing them with his adversary's name.

Charles Jennens, the other editor abused by Steevens, defended himself in a pamphlet[80] which also pointed out the absurdity of Steevens criticizing editors for being '*too exact*': 'it is the duty of every editor who pretends to collate, to give all the different readings of the several editions of his work' (p. 8), whatever their significance. Jennens showed that in his reprint, *Twenty Quartos* (No. 211), Steevens is 'a wretched collator, who frequently omits material readings, and at other times is very exact in giving the most trifling ones ...' (p. 40), and his exposure of Steevens's editorial performance is devastating. A modern authority has judged Steevens's work in this edition to be 'slapdash', 'not ... an advance on Pope's methods' (Walker, *op. cit.*, p. 145), and the pedigree is just. Steevens's acceptance of Pope's theory of the progressive corruption of Shakespeare's text in the playhouse is seen in the introduction, and is taken still further in the 1766 *Proposals* (No. 212), with the amazing suggestion that Shakespeare's plays were constantly altered by

casual additions ... in the Playhouse Copy. These, we may suppose, were preserved only in the memory of the performer to whose lot they might fall; and being ecchoed from one to another would easily grow more corrupt at every inaccurate transmission.

By the time he had finished his revision of Johnson in 1773 (No. 240), Capell's edition had appeared, and Steevens could now refer scornfully to previous suppositions 'that Shakespeare was originally an author correct in the utmost degree, but maimed and interpolated by the neglect or presumption of the players': so much for his own theories! Now he derived his account of the text from Capell, stating that the Quartos 'published in Shakespeare's lifetime' should be followed 'in preference to the folio' (Note 38). At least Steevens recognized the force of Capell's demonstration, even though he neither acknowledged nor acted on it.

Steevens's great achievement as an editor lies in the illustration of the text by quotations from sixteenth- and seventeenth-century books. It is as if he had taken for his goal in life the paragraph in Johnson's Preface on the difficulty of reclaiming information about the 'minute customs of the past'. Already in 1766 he had announced that 'from a diligent perusal of the comedies of contemporary authors, I am persuaded that the meaning of many expressions in SHAKESPEARE might be retrieved', and 'as words and phrases are only understood by comparing them in different places, the lower writers must be read for the explanation of the highest' (No. 211). In the formal *Proposals* of that year Steevens observed, justly enough, that 'A perfect edition of the Plays of Shakespeare requires at once the assistance of the Antiquary, the Historian, the Grammarian, and the Poet' (No. 212), and he himself filled the first two roles. The full extent of his learning is not seen until the 1778 edition, but already in 1765 we find such examples of out-of-the-way historical knowledge as the gloss of '*frothing* beer and *liming* sack' (No. 205, Note 242), while the 1773 edition brings us such glosses as that on 'stewed prunes' (No. 240, Note 37), which attracted much derisory criticism in the press, 'deprive' (Note 56), on 'bodkin' in *Hamlet* (Note 64), and the 'Pontick sea' in *Othello* (Note 73). Steevens also alludes to relevant passages in contemporary authors, such as Lyly (Note 20), Chapman (Note 54), and Beaumont and Fletcher (Note 63). In his *Proposals* Steevens had advertised in order to solicit notes from all and sundry, proposing a 'Notes and Queries' section in 'the public prints' (the newspapers). The later volumes, especially the Appendix, include a number of valuable notes by such friends as Warton (Note 78), Sir John Hawkins (Note 79), Dr James (Note 81), and above all Farmer, who wrote a long letter, 41 pages of notes and observations (X, Sig. $O_0 2^v$-$Q_q 6$). For all of his close friends Steevens seems to have been careful to acknowledge debts, but a fuller study could show that in other cases he is not so scrupulous.

As a literary critic Steevens is a strange mixture of independent good sense and violent orthodoxy. Of his notes in the 1773 edition several are modelled on Johnson's style and taste, although in a heavier, pompous manner. But he also shows independence, as in his sensible defence of *Othello* from the 'double time' theory of Rymer and Johnson (Note 77), or his objection to Warburton's claim that Edmund's 'Thou, Nature, art my goddess' makes him an atheist (Note 55). Steevens has a good eye for dramatic consistency (Note 17), for Shakespeare's alterations to sources in order to kill off his heroines (Notes 42, 60), and for the dramatic function of a soliloquy (Note 50). Like many eighteenth-century critics he is alert to character contrast, as in the distinction between Banquo's attitude to sleep and temptation and Macbeth's (Note 24), while he acutely observes Lady Macbeth's suppression of 'human feelings' in order to manipulate her husband, as seen in her greeting, 'Great Glamis! Worthy Cawdor!':

She meets him here on his return from an expedition of danger with such a salutation as would have become one of his friends or vassals; a salutation apparently fitted rather to raise his thoughts to a level with her own purposes than to testify her joy at his return, or manifest an attachment to his person,

whereas Macbeth continues to show tenderness to her throughout his horrible deeds (Note 23). That note echoes specific passages in Steevens's theatre-criticism, as does his long note on Cloten (Note 53).

Evidently Steevens is no mean critic. Yet the other overlap between his theatre criticism and his editorial capacities shows a quite different attitude. In two of the notes that I have reprinted here he attacks *Hamlet* so violently that orthodox Neo-classicism seems to be submerged by a personal animus. The play, and the character of Hamlet, he finds, lose all interest after Act III (Note 67); far from being a hero, Hamlet is by turns irresolute, dilatory, vicious, cruel, unfeeling, dishonest, and self-seeking (Note 70). Steevens claims that he is the first 'to point out the immoral tendency of Hamlet's character', and although some parts of his criticism can be found previously it is original in the force with which it is expressed, and in its thorough-going refusal to consider any positive features of the play. It is remarkable, too, for the range of publications in which these ideas are expressed: in the letter to Garrick approving of his alteration of the play (No. 235), and in a whole series of theatre-reviews which I ascribe to Steevens, in the *St. James's Chronicle* in 1772 (Nos 234c, d, f; 237e), and the *General Evening Post* of 1772–3 (Nos 237b, c, d, g, h; 238a, b). Steevens, always a forceful writer, reiterates his points with increasing venom: the later Acts contain 'Scenes of no Action or Interest to the play', and the spectator should quit the theatre; '*Hamlet* cannot sustain any[!] change derogatory to the character of its celebrated author'. When he complains that neither the instruction to the players nor the gravediggers' scene is relevant to the plot (No. 237g, 238b), and applies the term 'Buffoonery' to the gravediggers (234c, 237c), we seem to hear the tones of Rymer, Dennis, and Voltaire. Yet on a number of points Steevens anticipates what has come to be thought of as an essentially Romantic preoccupation with Hamlet's delay.[81] Starting from the orthodox Neo-classic concern for the unity of character and fable, Steevens protests that Hamlet knows that he ought to take revenge for his father's murder, says so, but does not do it (Nos 234c, 237b, 238a). The discrepancy between speech and action is viewed sometimes in terms of design (No. 238a), sometimes as belonging to the 'moral Part' of drama (No. 234c), and therefore Steevens can utter moral denunciations of Hamlet for being 'irresolute, unnatural, inconstant, and brutal' (No. 238a). Neither the structural nor the moral criticisms were to be taken up in quite those terms, but all the materials are available for the re-evaluation of Hamlet's delay as an essentially psychological problem.

VI

Turning finally to Shakespearian scholarship in this period, several aspects have necessarily been touched on in discussing the main editions. The biggest step forward was in the historical explanation of Shakespeare's language and his allusions to contemporary customs and affairs. One notable example of this interest outside the editions is the Shakespeare glossary of Richard Warner (No. 219), product of an industry matching that of Capell or Steevens. (There is something heroic in the sight of so many able men devoting their whole lives to the better understanding of Shakespeare. The status he enjoyed justified their dedication: the idolatry had some useful results.) Like them, Warner is committed to explaining all rare or obsolete words, and achieves some remarkable successes, notably with the cant sense of 'occupy'. The systematic reclamation of low-level Elizabethan language is one of the great achievements of this period, although the critic was open to mockery for his pains.

It is not possible to study the Shakespeare scholarship of the late eighteenth century without becoming embroiled in controversies. Many of these are personal, trivial, and unrewarding. But one was of major importance, involving many of the writers collected in this volume, namely the dispute over Shakespeare's knowledge of other languages and literatures. The central document is Richard Farmer's *An Essay on the Learning of Shakespeare* (No. 214), a work which has been much praised since Dr Johnson accepted Farmer's own estimate of it as 'an Answer to everything that shall hereafter be written on the Subject'.[82] Farmer set out to show that the claims which had been made in the previous half-century concerning Shakespeare's learning were flimsy. All the instances cited, he claimed, were capable of other explanations: Shakespeare had read the texts concerned in English translations, the allusion was common property, or the suggested borrowing was patently absurd. Some of the parallels were indeed ridiculous, such as Tyrwhitt's attempt to link *Twelfth Night* and 'the *Arabian Tales*', or Upton's derivation of 'Truepenny' from the Greek. Farmer is completely convincing in his demonstrations, from close verbal parallels, that Shakespeare read Plutarch in English, used Golding's translation of Ovid for Prospero's speech in *The Tempest*, Lydgate's *Troy booke* for *Troilus and Cressida*, and Gascoigne's *Supposes* for *The Taming of the Shrew*. But in other places he is simply too absolute: *Macbeth* undoubtedly derives from Holinshed, but William Guthrie's claim that the play is also indebted to Buchanan is not without probability.[83] Farmer is too absolute in denying that *Hamlet* draws on the Latin history of Saxo Grammaticus, while his own candidate, the black-letter romance *The Hystorie of Hamblet*, is in fact later than Shakespeare's play.

As a polemicist Farmer has the great art of placing quotations within the argument to give them a conclusive force, and the almost off-hand way in which he uses his learning suggests that he has much more in reserve. He is undoubtedly better informed than almost anyone else of his age, yet his book is an essentially negative exercise, which falls into the trap of one-sidedness. In his anxiety to refute less well informed scholars Farmer ends up by denying Shakespeare any classical knowledge at all:

He remembered perhaps enough of his *school-boy* learning to put the *Hig, hag, hog*, into the mouth of *Sir Hugh Evans*; and might pick up in the Writers of the time or the course of his conversation a familiar phrase or two of *French* or *Italian*: but his *Studies* were most demonstratively confined to *Nature* and *his own Language*.

Or, as he put it at the end of his letter to Steevens, 'one may remark once for all that *Shakespeare* wrote for the *people*; and could not have been so absurd to bring forward any allusion which had not been familiarized by some accident or other' (No. 240, Note 86). Dr Johnson, who had dismissed the whole question briefly in his Preface, on grounds very similar to those of Farmer (whom he had visited in February 1765), declared on reading the *Essay* that 'The Question is *now* for ever decided'. Yet other scholars were of a different opinion, and disagreement soon came from Guthrie, Kenrick, Capell, Warner, and Colman.

None of Farmer's critics denied the evidence of Shakespeare having used Golding's Ovid, or Gascoigne, or Lydgate, or Gower, but they discovered a number of holes in the argument. Guthrie (No. 215) gave the correct historical context for the seventeenth-century tributes to Shakespeare's 'Nature', which Farmer makes so much of: these writers 'never meant to say positively that Shakespeare was entirely illiterate', but that his learning was less than his genius. Farmer had proved that Shakespeare *could* have used translations, not that he *did* so, and Guthrie doubts whether Farmer has established Shakespeare's 'total ignorance of ancient learning': 'we know what a rapid progress a great genius passionate for knowledge, and sensible of its own defects, may make in a short time'. George Colman (No. 217) accepts much of Farmer's argument, accepts the evidence concerning Shakespeare's knowledge of school-texts, but then neatly turns the tables:

Still, however, Shakespeare's total ignorance of the learned languages remains to be proved; for it must be granted that such books are put into the hands of those who are learning those languages, in which

41

class we must necessarily rank Shakespeare, or he could not even have quoted Terence from Udall or Lilly. . . .

In the same year Richard Warner (No. 219) argued that a writer might know a foreign language yet still use translations, for various reasons.

The great weakness in Farmer's argument was his failure to consider the nature of grammar-school education in Elizabethan England, a deficiency supplied in our time by the massive study of T. W. Baldwin.[84] Some evidence of Shakespeare's schooling was given by Capell, who expressed the 'firm belief' that he 'was very well grounded, at least in *Latin*, at school', for the biographical reason, first, that his father was a prosperous businessman who would follow the practice of his class in sending his son to a grammar school. Then Capell cites the evidence of his first-published works, *Venus and Adonis*, and *The Rape of Lucrece*, with the quotation from Ovid's *Amores* as the epigraph to the former, and their evident 'acquaintance with some of the Latin classicks'. Gildon had made this point in 1710 (Vol. 2, p. 218), and it is suspicious that Farmer should ignore both poems. Capell argues 'that such a mind as' Shakespeare's would never 'lose the tincture of any knowledge it had once been imbu'd with', and it is this remembered 'school-learning' which accounts for the Latin in many of his plays, 'and most plentifully in those that are most early'. Capell's good sense of the chronology of Shakespeare's plays makes an essential point there, one lost on his contemporaries, and he is also unique in noting how Shakespeare has used his Latin, integrating it into the dramatic design and verbal texture:

Every several piece of it is aptly introduc'd, given to a proper character, and utter'd upon some proper occasion; and so well cemented, as it were, and join'd to the passage it stands in as to deal conviction to the judicious that the whole was wrought up together, and fetch'd from his own little store upon the sudden and without study.

That observation could have raised the whole discussion to a new and more valuable level, if anyone had taken notice of it. But it was Capell's fate to be dismissed by influential critics, who had either not read him or were too indebted to him to be able to acknowledge the fact, lampooning or insulting him instead.

May the presentation of his work in this volume bring him a more deserved recognition.

VII

It is difficult to sum up this, or any other period in the history of Shakespeare's reception. Older ideas and methods carry on side by side with those designed to replace them; new ideas are developed using older methods, and so on. It is far too early to speak of the demise of Neo-classicism. Dr Johnson is perhaps the last major exponent of it as a complete system, but some of its attitudes and methodologies are to persist for many years yet, and certainly the theatre has little new to offer. But in any case the historian ought to resist the dangerous aspects of trend-spotting, especially that of encouraging the belief that whatever is new in a period is necessarily good. It is possible to apply traditional methods to yield new insights, if the critic has intelligence and the ability to think himself into a dramatic situation witness Johnson, and some acute observations by writers as dissimilar as Mrs Montagu, Francis Gentleman, Edward Capell, and George Steevens. On balance it seems as if the greatest energies of this period went into scholarship rather than criticism, into the fundamental tasks of establishing and understanding the meaning of Shakespeare's text.

In 'pure' literary criticism this volume may show a rather static picture, especially after the contributions of Murphy, Roderick, Hurd, Kames, and Webb in the preceding one. While there are, properly speaking, no innovations in idea or method represented here, we can see an intensification of elements already existing. Shakespeare's genius had been celebrated before, but is now done so with increasing conviction; his ability to move the passions had always been praised, but is elevated still higher by the newer sensibility of a William Duff (No. 226 on Shakespeare's power 'to penetrate and to melt the heart'), or a Henry Mackenzie.[85] One epithet which partly sums up the direction to be taken by literary criticism is the word 'creative': it had been applied to Shakespeare previously, but many more calls are made upon it here, by T. W. (No. 216: Shakespeare's 'creative power of imagination'), by the 1769 orator (No. 223), by Duff ('creative Genius', 'creative power' of Shakespeare's imagination), and by Paul Hiffernan (No. 228: 'creative power'). Critics of the next generation, both German and English, had their tastes formed in reading the criticism of this one.

NOTES

1 *The Dramatic Censor* (1770), II, p. 76.
2 See Arthur Sherbo, 'Warburton and the 1745 *Shakespeare*', *Journal of English and Germanic Philology*, 51 (1952), pp. 71–82, which establishes that whoever was responsible for this edition (designed to expose Hanmer's silent adoption of previous editors' emendations) it was not Warburton.
3 *Critical Review*, xxxvi (November 1773), pp. 345–58; (December 1773), pp. 401–16; *Monthly Review*, xlix (December 1773), pp. 419–24. Identification of the reviewers in the *Monthly* derives from Griffiths's marked-up set, now in the Bodleian, expertly edited by Benjamin C. Nangle, *The Monthly Review. First Series*, 1749–1789. *Indexes of Contributors and Articles* (Oxford, 1934).
4 See *Shakespeare: The Critical Heritage*, Vol. 3, pp. 2ff.; Vol. 4, pp. 1ff.
5 See R. W. Babcock, *The Genesis of Shakespeare Idolatry*, 1766–1799 (Chapel Hill, N. C., 1931).
6 Capell's edition (No. 220), vol. I, Sig. a_2-a_4.
7 Some contemporaries took exception to Duff's bracketing of Ossian with Homer and Shakespeare: the *Critical Review* described it as 'poetical blasphemy' (xxx, p. 23).
8 Ogilvie, *Poems on Several Subjects* (1762), pp. 8–15 (1764: pp. 75–82).
9 In the *London Magazine* for March 1771; p. 169.
10 See Vol. 3, p. 2.
11 Schoenbaum, *Shakespeare's Lives* (Oxford, 1970), pp. 160, 317ff., notes that it was itself derivative from the *Biographia Britannica* (1763), but became the source of the accounts of Shakespeare in, for example, D. E. Baker, *Biographica Dramatica* (1782, 1812,), John Berkenhout, *Biographia Literaria* (1777), and the second edition of *Encyclopedia Britannica* (1783).
12 *Monthly Review*, xlix, p. 421, note (reviewing Johnson-Steevens, 1773).
13 Mrs Montagu also found the Porter's scene 'absurd and improper' (No. 221), while the fact that T. W. can rate *Macbeth* above the other tragedies for having 'no mixture of buffoonery or low humor' (No. 216) must mean that he read the play in an edition which omitted the scene.
14 See Vol. 1, pp. 191ff., and Vol. 2, pp. 29f.
15 *The London Stage, 1747–1776* (Carbondale, Ill., 1968), pp. clxiiff.
16 See Leo Hughes, *The Drama's Patrons. A Study of the Eighteenth-Century London Audience* (Austin, 1971), pp. 124ff., on the bowdlerization of Restoration comedy; on *The Beggar's Opera* see R.D. Stock, *Samuel Johnson and Neoclassical Dramatic Theory* (Lincoln, Nebr.,

1973), pp. 106f., citing A. S. Turberville (ed.), *Johnson's England* (2 vols, Oxford, 1933), II, p. 174.

17 *Monthly Review*, xxxviii, p. 245; *Critical Review*, xxv, pp. 148–9 (by Guthrie).

18 Victor, *The History of the Theatres of London. From the Year* 1760 *to the present Time* (1771), pp. 119–20.

19 Price, *Theatre in the Age of Garrick* (Oxford, 1973), p. 147.

20 *Critical Review*, xxxii, p. 470; *Monthly Review*, xlv, pp. 507–8.

21 Stone, 'Garrick's long lost alteration of *Hamlet*', *PMLA*, 49 (1934), pp. 890–921.

22 Available most conveniently in *Voltaire on Shakespeare*, ed. Theodore Besterman (Geneva, 1967), pp. 63–76.

23 *Ibid.*, pp. 57f.; translated by Arthur Murphy in the *Gray's-Inn Journal*: see Vol. 4 of this collection, pp. 90ff.

24 Wilkes, *A General View of the Stage* (1759), p. 41.

25 Garrick restored 629 lines, according to Stone, 'Garrick's long lost alteration of *Hamlet*', pp. 897ff. However, I cannot agree with Professor Stone that with the restoration of these theatre-cuts (which may lessen the impact of a character but do not fundamentally distort it) 'every character in the play is made richer by restorations', since although that may be true up to Act V what happens thereafter is a total distortion of Shakespeare. Professor Stone praises Garrick's care with the text, 'seldom found among the tamperers with Shakespeare', and concludes with this remarkable eulogy: the adaptation

> is worth study, for in it Garrick has made an effective play, has lost as few 'drops of that immortal man' as was consistent with his scheme, has restored hundreds of lines to enrich every part, has with care adopted Shakespeare's text in many cases, and has added but thirty-seven lines of his own. (p. 902)

This is to avoid the issue altogether. In his introduction to *The London Stage* volumes which he so magnificently edited (1958) Professor Stone even down-grades Shakespeare in order to elevate Garrick: 'The combined palaver of the grave diggers, Hamlet, and Horatio, in the cut scene, entertaining as it is, amounts to but one-third of the number of lines restored' (p. xciv). 'Palaver' is good.

26 *The Letters of David Garrick*, ed. D. M. Little and G. M. Kahrl (3 vols, 1963), II, pp. 845f. Cited hereafter as Garrick, *Letters*.

27 *Ibid.*, II, pp. 840, 841. The editors of the *Letters* share Professor Stone's high estimate of Garrick's performance: 'Garrick actually restored a great many lines not found in the acting version. . . .' The adaptation 'reveals a handling very much to Garrick's credit both in his devotion to the text of Shakespeare and his abilities as

an actor-manager' (p. 846, note). 'Devotion to the text' of the passages retained, that is.

28 *London Chronicle*, xxxii, no. 592 (17–19 December 1772):

> Last night the Tragedy of *Hamlet*, with alterations, was performed at the Theatre in Drury-Lane to a very crouded house. Mr. Garrick played the Danish Prince with uncommon spirit. The old scenes of low humour (particularly that of the Grave Diggers) were omitted. Hamlet does not go to England, but fights with Laertes soon after his scene with the King. The Queen, at the encounter, runs off, and an account is at the conclusion given of her death. Polonius's advice to his son, a fine lesson for young travellers, is restored, with the description of Fortinbras's army, and many other fine passages, which have been hitherto over-looked. In short, the play makes a very respectable figure in its present state, and the alterations seem to have been produced by the hand of a master.

29 *Horace Walpole's Correspondence*, ed. W. S. Lewis *et al.*, xxviii (New Haven, Conn., 1955), p. 58.

30 Besterman, *op. cit.*, p. 192: 'Enfin on les avait retranchées sur le théâtre de Londres le plus accredité'. Voltaire goes on to quote Marmontel's introduction to his *Chefs-d'œuvre dramatiques* (1773):

> 'On abrége tous les jours Shakespeare', dit-il, 'on le châtie; le célèbre Garrick vient tout nouvellement de retrancher sur son théâtre la scène des fossoyeurs et presque tout le cinquième acte. La pièce et l'auteur n'en ont été que plus applaudis.'

That is just the right word for Garrick's attitude to *Hamlet*: 'châtie'.

31 If one instance of the flattery of Garrick may represent many others, in the *Theatrical Review; or, Annals of the Drama* a correspondent wrote to Garrick:

> YOU, Sir, are *The* SHAKESPEARE *of Acting*. HE stands unrivalled above all Dramatic authors; YOU, as eminently conspicuous above all dramatic performers. I only lament you have not equal advantages to eternize your fame. The works of that great genius will be lasting testimonies of HIS superiority; but when YOU are gone, posterity can have no just idea of YOURS.... None will be ever truly sensible of your amazing excellence in acting, but those who have *seen* and *experienced* its power. It may be *felt*, but can never be *told*.—In a word, SHAKESPEARE, and YOU are both legitimate and favourite sons of NATURE. Ye are *Twin-brothers*, HE the oldest. SHAKESPEARE was born a *poet*,

YOU an actor. HE to write, YOU to illustrate what he wrote. (i (1763), p. 107)

The myth of Garrick re-discovering Shakespeare is well expressed in the *London Chronicle*, xxvi (31 August–2 September 1769), pp. 221–2.

32 *The Interview; or Jack Falstaff's Ghost. A Poem Inscribed to David Garrick, Esq.* (1766), p. 12.

33 See C. Oman, *David Garrick* (London, 1958), pp. 285–306; Martha W. England, *Garrick's Jubilee* (Columbus, Ohio, 1964), which collects material previously published in *Shakespeare Survey* 9 (1956), pp. 90–100, and *Bulletin of the New York Public Library* 63 (1959), pp. 117–33 and 66 (1962), pp. 73–92, 178–204, 261–72, these last three articles having been previously collected as *Garrick at Stratford* (New York, 1962); Johanne M. Stochholm, *Garrick's Folly. The Shakespeare Jubilee of 1769 at Stratford and Drury Lane* (London, 1964); and Christian Deelman, *The Great Shakespeare Jubilee* (London, 1964). The widest historical survey is by England; the most searching critical evaluation by Deelman. The topic has been sufficiently studied.

34 A scathing review of the *Ode* appeared in the *London Museum* (1770), pp. 48–9; the *Warwickshire Journal* (9 September 1769), and the *Gentleman's Magazine*, xxxix, pp. 446–7, carried slightly more temperate reviews. Warburton praised the *Ode* to Garrick's face but wrote to Bishop Hurd on 23 September 1769:

> Garrick's *portentous* ode, as you truly call it, had but one line of truth in it, which is where he calls Shakespeare the *God of our Idolatry*: for *sense* I will not allow it.... The ode itself is below any of Cibber's. Cibber's nonsense was something like sense; but this man's sense, whenever he deviates into it, is much more like nonsense. (*Letters from a Late Eminent Prelate to One of his Friends*, ed. Hurd (Kidderminster, 1808), p. 327; quoted Deelman, *op. cit.*, p. 266)

Mr Deelman has some caustic notes on the poem, pp. 139ff., 201, 217ff., and refers to a full analysis by Frank Hedgcock, *David Garrick and his French Friends* (London, 1912). Garrick wrote a lengthy defence of his *Ode* against the criticism of Charles Macklin: see James Boaden (ed.), *The Private Correspondence of David Garrick* (2 vols, London, 1831: cited hereafter as *Private Correspondence*), II, pp. 343–6; Garrick, *Letters*, II, pp. 670–4. This defence is very revealing of Garrick's ideas about poetry.

35 *Horace Walpole's Correspondence*, x, pp. 287, 298.

36 See M. L. Mare and W. H. Quarrell (ed. and tr.), *Lichtenberg's Visits*

to England as described in his Letters and Diaries (Oxford, 1938), pp. 6–17, 30f. Lichtenberg did not approve of the *Hamlet* adaptation:

> Voltaire has, however, gained one victory at Drury Lane. The gravediggers' scene is omitted. They retain it at Covent Garden. Garrick should not have done this. To represent so ancient and superb a piece in all its characteristic rude vigour in these insipid times, when even in this country the language of nature is beginning to yield to fine phrases and conventional twaddle, might have arrested this decline, even if it could not put a stop to it. (p. 17)

37 Margaret Barton, *Garrick* (London, 1948), p. 233.
38 Deelman, *op. cit.*, p. 82; Kalman Burnim, *David Garrick, Director* (Pittsburgh, Pa., 1961), p. 4.
39 Johnson, *Letters*, ed. R. W. Chapman (3 vols, Oxford, 1952), no. 186: I, p. 191. See Boswell's *Life of Johnson*, ed. G. B. Hill, revised L. F. Powell (6 vols, Oxford, 1934), II, pp. 192–3 and notes; this edition will be subsequently referred to as '*Life*'. On Whalley's use of Garrick's collection see Edward Jacob (ed.), *Arden of Feversham* (1770), p. iii.
40 *Private Correspondence*, I, p. 501. For other letters recording Steevens's use of Garrick's library see *ibid.*, I, pp. 216–17, 449–52, 581, 582, 586–8, 589–90, 591–4, 595–8, 606–8; II, pp. 122, 129f.; and Garrick, *Letters*, II, pp. 780f., 907f., 913, 914; III, pp. 919, 944f., 982.
41 See Arthur Sherbo, *Samuel Johnson, Editor of Shakespeare* (Urbana, Ill., 1956: *Illinois Studies in Language and Literature*, XLII; hereafter cited as 'Sherbo, *Johnson, Editor*'), on 'Johnson's seeming distaste for the editorial labours upon which he had perhaps too casually embarked' (pp. 44).
42 Bronson (ed.), Introduction to Arthur Sherbo, *Johnson on Shakespeare* (vols VII and VIII of the Yale Edition of the Works of Samuel Johnson; New Haven, Conn., and London, 1968; paginated consecutively, and hereafter cited as 'Sherbo, *Johnson on Shakespeare*', with single page-references), pp. xiii-xxxviii; Eastman, 'In defense of Dr. Johnson', *Shakespeare Quarterly*, 8 (1957), pp. 493–500. For two searching reviews of Bronson's apologia see J. P. Hardy in *Review of English Studies*, n.s., 21 (1970), pp. 86–8, and D. J. Fleeman in *Notes and Queries*, n.s., 215 (November 1970), pp. 437–9.
43 In the head-note to this item I wrote, in a fit of absentmindedness, that it 'reads like a preliminary essay towards an edition' (Vol. 4, p. 165). Let there be no mistake: it *is* a preliminary to an edition. 'Knowledge is not always present.' The specimen page is reproduced in Sherbo, *Johnson on Shakespeare*, following p. 46.

44 The best account of the progress of Johnson's editing remains Sherbo, *Johnson, Editor,* chapter one. See also Fleeman, *op. cit.* in n. 42, p. 438, and correspondence in the *Times Literary Supplement* for 1974 by Tom Davies (19 April, p. 419) and D. J. Fleeman (17 May, p. 528).

45 Fleeman, *op. cit.* in note 42 above.

46 D. D. Eddy, 'Samuel Johnson's editions of Shakespeare (1765)', *Papers of the Bibliographical Society of America,* 56 (1962), pp. 428–44, at 429; also G. B. Evans, 'The text of Johnson's *Shakespeare,* 1765', *Philological Quarterly,* 28 (1949), pp. 425–8.

47 B. H. Bronson (in Sherbo, *Johnson on Shakespeare,* pp. xxii f.) computes that in volume I there are 82 additional, unnumbered notes, while the Appendix adds a further 44 notes that belong in sequence to volume I; for the remaining volumes the figures are: II, 105 and 58; III, 39 and 36; IV, 132 and 32; V, 101 and 19; VI, 93 and 32; VII, 7 and 12; VIII, 11 and 45, a total of 722 late additions.

48 Eastman, 'In defense of Dr. Johnson', p. 499.

49 Eastman, *ibid.,* and 'The texts from which Johnson printed his Shakespeare', *Journal of English and Germanic Philology,* 49 (1950), pp. 182–91.

50 See A. T. Hazen, 'Johnson's Shakespeare, a study in cancellation', *Times Literary Supplement,* 24 December 1938, p. 820, and Sherbo, *Johnson on Shakespeare,* p. xliii and illustrations at pp. 962, 975.

51 See Karl Young, 'Samuel Johnson on Shakespeare, One Aspect', *University of Wisconsin Studies in Language and Literature,* No. 18 (Madison, 1924), pp. 147–227.

52 For the judgments of his biographers see Sir John Hawkins, *The Life of Samuel Johnson, Ll. D.,* abridged, ed. B. H. Davis (London, 1962), pp. 151 f., 196, excerpts in *Johnsonian Miscellanies,* ed. G. B. Hill (2 vols, Oxford, 1897; New York, 1966: hereafter cited as *Miscellanies*), II, p. 107; Arthur Murphy, *Miscellanies,* II, p. 473; and Thomas Tyers (*ibid.,* II, pp. 357 f.).

53 See, for example, *Gentleman's Magazine,* xxxiii (1763), pp. 12–15 (text of *Macbeth*), 160 ff. (*Othello*); xxxv, pp. 65–7, 110 f., 229, and many more; *St. James's Chronicle,* e.g. letters in 1771, issues numbered 1668 (31 Oct.–2 Nov.), 1674 (14–16 Nov.), 1678 (23–6 Nov.); 1680 (28–30 Nov.); 1681 (30 Nov.–3 Dec.); 1682 (3–5 Dec.); etc. For textual criticism in a novel see Smollett, *The Expedition of Humphry Clinker,* ed. L. M. Knapp (London, 1966), p. 200.

54 See Arthur Sherbo, 'Dr. Johnson on *Macbeth*: 1745 and 1765', *Review of English Studies,* n.s., 2 (1951), pp. 40–7. In 'Sanguine expectations: Dr. Johnson's *Shakespeare*', *Shakespeare Quarterly,* 9 (1958), pp. 426–8, Professor Sherbo lists 19 notes which he believes Johnson wrote before 1745.

55 See Arthur Sherbo, 'The proof-sheets of Dr. Johnson's Preface to Shakespeare', *Bulletin of the John Rylands Library*, 35 (1952–3), pp. 206–10.

56 Smith, *Shakespeare in the Eighteenth Century* (Oxford, 1928); Sherbo, *Johnson, Editor*, chapter 3 and Appendix B makes a detailed analysis of Johnson's debts to previous editors and textual critics. His account of Johnson's borrowings from Heath is open to some of the objections made by Arthur Eastman, in an all too melodramatic style ('In defense of Dr. Johnson', *op. cit.*), yet Mr Eastman refuses to acknowledge any debt, which seems too absolute. Sherbo, chapters 4–6 and Appendix C, considers Johnson's debt to the critical tradition, a topic explored more fully, but reaching much the same conclusion (i.e. it was considerable), by R. D. Stock, *op. cit.* in note 16.

57 Raysor, 'The downfall of the three Unities', *Modern Language Notes*, 42 (1927), pp. 1–9. See also C. C. Green, *The Neo-Classic Theory of Tragedy in England during the Eighteenth Century* (Cambridge, Mass., 1934; New York, 1966), pp. 194–218; E. N. Hooker (ed.), *The Critical Works of John Dennis*, 2 vols, II (Baltimore, 1943), pp. 453–4; R. D. Stock, *op. cit.*, pp. 72–103, 176–9, 195–6; and a discussion in *Notes and Queries*, n.s., 207 (1962), between R. K. Paul (pp. 261–4), J. P. Hardy (pp. 350f.), and G. Sorelius (pp. 466f.).

58 See the introduction to Vol. 4, pp. 10–16; and for discussions of the Unities included in this collection see, for example, Farquhar (Vol. 2, pp. 185ff.), Dennis (Vol. 2, pp. 350f.), Stubbes (Vol. 3, pp. 64–6), Foote (Vol. 3, p. 222), Upton (Vol. 3, pp. 292f., 295f.), Fielding (Vol. 4, p. 11), an anonymous writer in 1750 (Vol. 3, pp. 366f.), Johnson himself in 1751 (Vol. 3, p. 434), Murphy (Vol. 3, p. 450), the author of *Miscellaneous Observations on Hamlet* (Vol. 3, pp. 452f.), Berkenhout (Vol. 4, pp. 11f.), Orrery (Vol. 4, pp. 353f.), Lloyd (Vol. 4, pp. 420f.), Kames (Vol. 4, pp. 495ff.), Webb (Vol. 4, pp. 519f.), Langhorne (Vol. 4, p. 14), and Heath (Vol. 4, p. 558).

59 D. N. Smith, *Eighteenth Century Essays on Shakespeare* (Glasgow, 1903; Oxford, 1963, p. xx). The second edition of this pioneering collection, posthumously completed by F. P. Wilson and Herbert Davis, corrected some of the factual errors in the first, but made no attempt to take notice of the transformations of critical awareness made in the 60 years since it was first published. The section on Johnson was rendered obsolete by Nichol Smith's own book of 1928 (cited in note 56). There are still extremely few valuable assessments of Johnson's work as a Shakespeare critic.

60 See, for example, *Rasselas*, chapter xliv, 'The dangerous prevalence of imagination', and R. D. Havens, 'Johnson's distrust of the imagination', *ELH*, 10 (1943), pp. 243–55.

61 Adler, 'Johnson's "He That Imagines This"', *Shakespeare Quarterly*, 11 (1960), pp. 225–8.

62 Approval of Shakespeare's morals: Notes 1, 12, 14, 22, 23, 27, 40, 51, 60, 70, 97, 138, 155, 174, 182, 190, 193, 198, 215.

63 Disapproval of Shakespeare's morals: Notes 13, 22, 34, 52, 54, 88, 91, 120, 208, 209, 214, 215.

64 See the Preface, p. 66 (hastening to the end 'to snatch the profit'), p. 75 ('He knew how he should most please'), p. 82 (when his plays 'were such as would satisfy the audience, they satisfied the writer'), and, for example, Notes 37, 73, 75, 92, 100, 101, 118.

65 On 'probability' see, for example, Notes 19, 22, 34, 54, 85, 93, 122, 124, 155, 178, 195, 215, 220.

66 On plot unity see, for example, Notes 19, 37, 45, 62, 82, 109, 215; complex plots accepted: Notes 20, 42, 141, and 1773, No. 240 below, Note 10.

67 On Shakespeare's offences against decorum see Vol. 3, pp. 436–8, and, for example, Notes 28, 94, 205 below.

68 Against word-play: Notes 36, 61, 80, 81, 90, 112, 134, 152, 165, 170, 186, 189.

69 See Notes 57, 64, 123, 166, 177, 195, 223.

70 Cf., for example, in the *Life of Dryden*:

> Works of imagination excel by their allurement and delight, by their power of attracting and detaining the attention. That book is good in vain which the reader throws away. . . . By his pro-portion of this predomination I will consent that Dryden be tried—of this which, in . . . defiance of criticism, continues Shakespeare the sovereign of the drama. (*Lives of the Poets*, ed. G. B. Hill (3 vols, Oxford, 1905), I, p. 454)

71 For reflective generalizations see also Notes 58, 76, 97, 117, 131, 136, 142, 199, 218.

72 See the valuable essay by J. P. Hardy, 'The "Poet of Nature" and self-knowledge: one aspect of Johnson's moral reading of Shake-speare', *University of Toronto Quarterly*, 36 (1967), pp. 141–60.

73 For Smollett's attack on Hamlet's soliloquy see Vol. 4, pp. 7, 44–5, 266, 498–502.

74 Walker, 'Edward Capell and his edition of Shakespeare', *Proceedings of the British Academy*, 46 (1960), pp. 131–45; repr. and cit. from *Studies in Shakespeare*, ed. P. Alexander (London, 1964), pp. 132–48.

75 See *St. James's Chronicle*, 1773, nos 1980 (21–23 Oct.), 1997 (30 Nov.–2 Dec.), 2004 (16–18 Dec.)—these two particularly nasty letters—2009 (28–30 Dec.), etc.

76 The contemporary reaction to Capell was disappointing: neither

the *Monthly Review* (Langhorne: xxxix, pp. 271ff.) nor the *Critical* (Guthrie: xxvi, pp. 321ff.) understood his scholarship, while the triumvirate of Johnson, Malone, and Steevens expressed contempt and animus in various ways. The only just assessment came from Richard Farmer, who described Capell as 'the most able of all men to give information' on Shakespeare's reading (No. 214), 'a very curious [that is, accurate] and intelligent Gentleman, to whom the lovers of Shakespeare will some time or other owe great obligations' (*Essay*, in Nichol Smith, *Essays, ed. cit.* in note 59, pp. 185–6).

77 A brief but favourable assessment by Gordon Crosse, 'Charles Jennens as editor of Shakespeare', appeared in the *Library*, 4th series, 16 (1936), pp. 236–40. The traditionally derogatory view of Jennens, deriving from Steevens, has been unfortunately repeated recently by S. Schoenbaum, *op. cit.*, p. 284.

78 See the *Critical Review*, xxx, pp. 436–9; xxxi, pp. 82–4; xxxiv, pp. 475–9; xxxv, p. 230; xliii, pp. 348–53. Steevens has as yet had no biographer; the extant authorities are John Nichols, *Literary Anecdotes of the Eighteenth Century* (7 vols, 1813), II, pp. 650–63, III, pp. 121–3; Garrick, the *Letters* and *Private Correspondence, ed. cit.*; Boswell's *Life of Johnson*; Walpole's *Letters*; Isaac D'Israeli, 'On Puck the Commentator', *The Curiosities of Literature*, 3 vols (in his *Works*, ed. Benjamin D'Israeli, 7 vols, 1859), III, pp. 296–303; and the *DNB* article by Sir Sidney Lee. See now Evelyn Wenner, 'George Steevens and the Boydell Shakespeare', Ph.D. dissertation, George Washington University, 1951, pp. 1–99, drawing on much unpublished material.

79 Collins, *A Letter to George Hardinge, Esq., on the Subject of a Passage in Mr. Steevens's Preface to his Impression of Shakespeare*. Published in 1777, this pamphlet was written in 1774. For an instance of Steevens's malice towards Capell, in which he posthumously ascribed to Dr Johnson a vicious dismissal of Capell's scholarship (which Steevens had previously applied to Jennens in an anonymous article in the *Critical Review*), see my note 'Steevens as a reporter of Johnson', *Notes and Queries*, n.s. 25 (February, 1978), pp. 58–9.

80 Jennens, *The Tragedy of King Lear, as Lately Published, Vindicated from the Abuse of The Critical Reviewers* . . . (1772).

81 C. C. Williamson, in his collection, *Readings on the Character of Hamlet 1661–1947* (London, 1950), pp. 20f., prints a short excerpt from the *St. James's Chronicle* papers (No. 234), while P. S. Conklin, in *A History of Hamlet Criticism 1601–1821* (New York, 1957, 1968), pp. 65–6, quotes Steevens's long note from the 1773 edition (No. 240, Note 70), which D. Nichol Smith had actually cited as the origin of the 'Hamlet problem': see *Shakespeare in the Eighteenth Century* (Oxford, 1928), p. 88.

82 Recently Samuel Schoenbaum has described it as 'casually brilliant ... remarkable' (*op. cit.*, p. 150). Nichol Smith found it
'convincing' as an attack on the arguments hitherto advanced, yet
noted that 'Farmer is apt to think he has proved his own case when
he has merely destroyed the evidence of his opponents' (*Eighteenth
Century Essays on Shakespeare*, pp. xxvi f.).

83 See Geoffrey Bullough (ed.), *Narrative and Dramatic Sources of
Shakespeare*, vol. 7, *Major Tragedies* (London, 1973), pp. 438–40,
509–17.

84 Baldwin, *William Shakespeare's Small Latine and Lesse Greeke* (2 vols,
Urbana, Ill., 1944).

85 See Mackenzie, *The Man of Feeling* (1771), ed. Brian Vickers (Oxford,
1967), pp. ix ff., 137.

Note on the Text

The texts in this collection are taken from the first printed edition, unless otherwise stated. The date under which a piece is filed is that of the first edition, with two exceptions: plays, for which, usually, the first performance is used (for such information I have relied on *The London Stage* for the period 1660 to 1800); and those works for which the author gives a date of composition substantially earlier than its first printing. The place of publication is London, unless otherwise indicated.

Spelling and punctuation are those of the original editions except where they seemed likely to create ambiguities for the modern reader. Spelling has, however, been standardized for writers' names (Jonson not Johnson, Rymer not Rhimer), for play titles, and for Shakespearian characters.

Omissions in the text are indicated by three dots: [...].

Footnotes intended by the original authors are distinguished with an asterisk, dagger, and so on; those added by the editor are numbered. Editorial notes within the text are placed within square brackets.

Act-, scene-, and line-numbers have been supplied in all quotations from Shakespeare, in the form 2.1.85 (Act II, scene 1, line 85). The text used for this purpose was the *Tudor Shakespeare*, ed. P. Alexander (Collins, 1951).

Classical quotations have been identified, and translations added, usually those in the Loeb library.

205. Samuel Johnson, edition of Shakespeare

1765

From *The Plays of William Shakespeare, in Eight Volumes, with the Corrections and Illustrations of Various Commentators; To which are added Notes by Sam. Johnson* (1765).

This edition appeared on 10 October 1765, reprinting shortly after 4 November; it was reissued in 1768, and in an enlarged version by Johnson and Steevens in 1773 (No. 240 below). In annotating the Preface I am partly indebted to Arthur Sherbo, *Samuel Johnson, Editor of Shakespeare*, chapter 3 and Appendix C.

PREFACE.

That praises are without reason lavished on the dead, and that the honours due only to excellence are paid to antiquity, is a complaint likely to be always continued by those who, being able to add nothing to truth, hope for eminence from the heresies of paradox; or those who, being forced by disappointment upon consolatory expedients, are willing to hope from posterity what the present age refuses, and flatter themselves that the regard which is yet denied by envy, will be at last bestowed by time.

Antiquity, like every other quality that attracts the notice of mankind, has undoubtedly votaries that reverence it, not from reason, but from prejudice. Some seem to admire indiscriminately whatever has been long preserved, without considering that time has sometimes co-operated with chance; all perhaps are more willing to honour past than present excellence; and the mind contemplates genius through the shades of age, as the eye surveys the sun through artificial opacity. The great contention of criticism is to find the faults of the moderns, and the beauties of the ancients.[1]

---

[1] Cf. Gildon (*Shakespeare: The Critical Heritage*, Vol. 2, pp. 216–17. In subsequent footnotes, page-references to earlier volumes of *Shakespeare: The Critical Heritage* will appear in the form: 2.216–17. Document-references are given in the form: Vol. 2, No. 50).

While an authour is yet living we estimate his powers by his worst performance, and when he is dead we rate them by his best.

To works, however, of which the excellence is not absolute and definite, but gradual and comparative; to works not raised upon principles demonstrative and scientifick, but appealing wholly to observation and experience, no other test can be applied than length of duration and continuance of esteem. What mankind have long possessed they have often examined and compared, and if they persist to value the possession it is because frequent comparisons have confirmed opinion in its favour. As among the works of nature no man can properly call a river deep or a mountain high, without the knowledge of many mountains and many rivers; so in the productions of genius nothing can be stiled excellent till it has been compared with other works of the same kind. Demonstration immediately displays its power, and has nothing to hope or fear from the flux of years; but works tentative and experimental must be estimated by their proportion to the general and collective ability of man, as it is discovered in a long succession of endeavours. Of the first building that was raised, it might be with certainty determined that it was round or square, but whether it was spacious or lofty must have been referred to time. The Pythagorean scale of numbers was at once discovered to be perfect; but the poems of *Homer* we yet know not to transcend the common limits of human intelligence, but by remarking that nation after nation, and century after century, has been able to do little more than transpose his incidents, new name his characters, and paraphrase his sentiments.

The reverence due to writings that have long subsisted arises therefore not from any credulous confidence in the superior wisdom of past ages, or gloomy persuasion of the degeneracy of mankind, but is the consequence of acknowledged and indubitable positions, that what has been longest known has been most considered, and what is most considered is best understood.

The Poet, of whose works I have undertaken the revision, may now begin to assume the dignity of an ancient, and claim the privilege of established fame and prescriptive veneration. He has long outlived his century, the term commonly fixed as the test of literary merit. Whatever advantages he might once derive from personal allusions, local customs, or temporary opinions, have for many years been lost;[1] and every topick of merriment or motive of sorrow, which the modes of artificial life afforded him, now only obscure the scenes which they once illuminated. The effects of favour and competition are at an end; the tradition of his friendships and his enmities has perished; his works support no opinion with arguments, nor supply any faction with invectives; they can neither indulge vanity nor gratify malignity, but are read without any other reason than the desire of pleasure, and are therefore praised only as pleasure is obtained. Yet, thus unassisted by interest or passion, they have past through variations of taste and changes of manners, and as they devolved from one generation to another have received new honours at every transmission.

But because human judgment, though it be gradually gaining upon certainty, never becomes infallible; and approbation, though long continued, may yet be only the approbation of prejudice or fashion; it is proper to inquire by what peculiarities of excellence *Shakespeare* has gained and kept the favour of his countrymen.

Nothing can please many, and please long, but just representations of general nature. Particular manners can be known to few, and therefore few only can judge how nearly they are copied. The irregular combinations of fanciful invention may delight a-while, by that novelty of which the common satiety of life sends us all in quest; but the pleasures of sudden wonder are soon exhausted, and the mind can only repose on the stability of truth.

Shakespeare is above all writers, at least above all modern writers, the poet of nature; the poet that holds up to his readers a faithful mirrour of manners and of life. His characters are not modified by the customs of particular places, unpractised by the rest of the world; by the peculiarities of studies or professions, which can operate but upon small numbers; or by the accidents of transient fashions or temporary opinions: they are the genuine progeny of common humanity, such as the world will always supply, and observation will always find. His persons act and speak by the influence of those general passions and principles by which all minds are agitated, and the whole system of life is continued in motion. In the writings of other poets a character is too often an individual; in those of *Shakespeare* it is commonly a species.

It is from this wide extension of design that so much instruction is derived. It is this which fills the plays of *Shakespeare* with practical

[1] Cf. Whalley (3.278).

axioms and domestick[1] wisdom. It was said of *Euripides* that every verse was a precept; and it may be said of *Shakespeare* that from his works may be collected a system of civil and œconomical prudence.[2] Yet his real power is not shown in the splendor of particular passages, but by the progress of his fable and the tenour of his dialogue; and he that tries to recommend him by select quotations will succeed like the pedant in *Hierocles*,[3] who, when he offered his house to sale, carried a brick in his pocket as a specimen.

It will not easily be imagined how much *Shakespeare* excells in accommodating his sentiments to real life, but by comparing him with other authours. It was observed of the ancient schools of declamation that the more diligently they were frequented, the more was the student disqualified for the world, because he found nothing there which he should ever meet in any other place. The same remark may be applied to every stage but that of *Shakespeare*. The theatre, when it is under any other direction, is peopled by such characters as were never seen, conversing in a language which was never heard, upon topicks which will never arise in the commerce of mankind. But the dialogue of this authour is often so evidently determined by the incident which produces it, and is pursued with so much ease and simplicity that it seems scarcely to claim the merit of fiction, but to have been gleaned by diligent selection out of common conversation, and common occurrences.

Upon every other stage the universal agent is love,[4] by whose power all good and evil is distributed, and every action quickened or retarded. To bring a lover, a lady and a rival into the fable; to entangle them in contradictory obligations, perplex them with oppositions of interest,[5] and harrass them with violence of desires inconsistent with each other; to make them meet in rapture and part in agony; to fill their mouths with hyperbolical joy and outrageous sorrow; to distress them as nothing human ever was

---

1 'Domestick': 1. 'Belonging to the house; not relating to things publick'. 2. 'Private; done at home; not open' (Johnson, *Dictionary*, 1755. Quoted meanings of words in subsequent footnotes to Johnson's edition are from Johnson's *Dictionary*).

2 'Civil': 'Relating to the community; political; relating to the city or government'; 'Oeconomical': 'Pertaining to the regulation of an household'; 'Prudence': 'wisdom applied to practice'.

3 A Stoic philosopher of the second century A. D.; see *Hieroclis Commentarius in Aurea Carmina*, ed. Needham (1709), p. 462.

4 Cf. Dennis (2.282, 350).

5 'Interest': 3. 'Share; part in anything'. 4. 'Regard to private profit'.

distressed; to deliver them as nothing human ever was delivered, is the business of a modern dramatist. For this, probability is violated, life is misrepresented, and language is depraved. But love is only one of many passions, and as it has no great influence upon the sum of life it has little operation in the dramas of a poet who caught his ideas from the living world, and exhibited only what he saw before him. He knew that any other passion, as it was regular or exorbitant, was a cause of happiness or calamity.

Characters thus ample and general were not easily discriminated and preserved, yet perhaps no poet ever kept his personages more distinct from each other. I will not say with *Pope* that every speech may be assigned to the proper speaker,[1] because many speeches there are which have nothing characteristical; but perhaps, though some may be equally adapted to every person it will be difficult to find any that can be properly transferred from the present possessor to another claimant. The choice is right, when there is reason for choice.

Other dramatists can only gain attention by hyperbolical or aggravated characters, by fabulous and unexampled excellence or depravity, as the writers of barbarous romances invigorated[2] the reader by a giant and a dwarf; and he that should form his expectations of human affairs from the play, or from the tale, would be equally deceived. *Shakespeare* has no heroes; his scenes are occupied only by men, who act and speak as the reader thinks that he should himself have spoken or acted on the same occasion. Even where the agency is supernatural the dialogue is level with life.[3] Other writers disguise the most natural passions and most frequent incidents; so that he who contemplates them in the book will not know them in the world. *Shakespeare* approximates the remote, and familiarizes the wonderful; the event which he represents will not happen, but if it were possible its effects would be probably such as he has assigned,[4] and it may be said that he has not only shewn human nature as it acts in real exigences, but as it would be found in trials to which it cannot be exposed.

This therefore is the praise of *Shakespeare*, that his drama is the

[1] See 2.404; also Dennis (2.282).
[2] 'Invigorate': 'To endure with vigour; to strengthen; to animate; to enforce'.
[3] Cf. Dryden (1.260), Rowe (2.197); Addison, *Spectator*, cdxix (2.280); Stubbes (3.41); Guthrie (3.195); Upton (3.298).
[4] Cf. Addison (2.280) and Stubbes (3.41); Upton, *Critical Observations on Shakespeare*, 1748 ed., pp. 91–2.

mirrour of life; that he who has mazed[1] his imagination in following the phantoms which other writers raise up before him, may here be cured of his delirious extasies[2] by reading human sentiments in human language; by scenes from which a hermit may estimate the transactions of the world, and a confessor predict the progress of the passions.

His adherence to general nature has exposed him to the censure of criticks, who form their judgments upon narrower principles. *Dennis*[3] and *Rymer*[4] think his *Romans* not sufficiently Roman; and *Voltaire* censures his kings as not completely royal. *Dennis* is offended that *Menenius*, a senator of *Rome*, should play the buffoon; and *Voltaire* perhaps thinks decency violated when the *Danish* usurper is represented as a drunkard.[5] But *Shakespeare* always makes nature predominate over accident; and if he preserves the essential character is not very careful of distinctions superinduced and adventitious. His story requires Romans or kings, but he thinks only on men. He knew that *Rome*, like every other city, had men of all dispositions; and, wanting a buffoon, he went into the senate-house for that which the senate-house would certainly have afforded him. He was inclined to shew an usurper and a murderer not only odious but despicable: he therefore added drunkenness to his other qualities, knowing that kings love wine like other men, and that wine exerts its natural power upon kings. These are the petty cavils of petty minds; a poet overlooks the casual distinction of country and condition, as a painter satisfied with the figure neglects the drapery.[6]

The censure which he has incurred by mixing comick and tragick scenes, as it extends to all his works, deserves more consideration. Let the fact be first stated, and then examined.

Shakespeare's plays are not in the rigorous and critical sense either tragedies or comedies, but compositions of a distinct kind;[7]

---

[1] 'To maze': 'To bewilder; to confuse'.
[2] 'Delirious': 'Light-headed; raving; doting'. 'Ecstasy': 'Any passion by which the thoughts are absorbed and in which the mind is for a time lost'.
[3] See 2.283.
[4] See 2.55ff.
[5] See *Dissertation sur la tragédie ancienne et moderne* (1748), in *Voltaire on Shakespeare*, ed. Theodore Besterman (Geneva, 1967), p. 57. The passage is translated by Arthur Murphy in 4.91.
[6] See Upton, 1748 ed., p. 93.
[7] Cf. Dryden (1.137); Dryden (1.201); Rowe (2.198); Pope (2.406); Upton (3.298); Johnson, *Rambler*, clvi (3.434f.); Percy (4.545).

exhibiting the real state of sublunary nature, which partakes of good and evil, joy and sorrow, mingled with endless variety of proportion and innumerable modes of combination; and expressing the course of the world, in which the loss of one is the gain of another; in which, at the same time, the reveller is hasting to his wine, and the mourner burying his friend; in which the malignity of one is sometimes defeated by the frolick of another; and many mischiefs and many benefits are done and hindered without design.

Out of this chaos of mingled purposes and casualties the ancient poets, according to the laws which custom had prescribed, selected some the crimes of men, and some their absurdities; some the momentous vicissitudes of life, and some the lighter occurrences; some the terrours of distress, and some the gayeties of prosperity. Thus rose the two modes of imitation known by the names of *tragedy* and *comedy*, compositions intended to promote different ends by contrary means, and considered as so little allied that I do not recollect among the *Greeks* or *Romans* a single writer who attempted both.[1]

Shakespeare has united the powers of exciting laughter and sorrow not only in one mind but in one composition. Almost all his plays are divided between serious and ludicrous[2] characters,[3] and, in the successive evolutions of the design, sometimes produce seriousness and sorrow, and sometimes levity and laughter.

That this is a practice contrary to the rules of criticism will be readily allowed; but there is always an appeal open from criticism to nature. The end of writing is to instruct; the end of poetry is to instruct by pleasing.[4] That the mingled drama may convey all the instruction of tragedy or comedy cannot be denied, because it includes both in its alternations[5] of exhibition, and approaches nearer than either to the appearance of life by shewing how great machinations and slender designs may promote or obviate one another, and the high and the low co-operate in the general system by unavoidable concatenation.

It is objected that by this change of scenes the passions are inter-

---

[1] Cf. Dryden, *Essay of Dramatic Poesy*, ed. G. Watson, I, p. 38; and Warton (4.262f).

[2] 'Ludicrous': 'Burlesque; merry; sportive; exciting laughter'.

[3] Cf. Upton (3.298f.).

[4] Horace, *Ars Poetica*, 343–4.

[5] The printed editions read 'alterations', the proofs have 'vicissitudes'; the emendation was made by Malone.

rupted in their progression, and that the principal event, being not advanced by a due gradation of preparatory incidents, wants at last the power to move, which constitutes the perfection of dramatick poetry. This reasoning is so specious[1] that it is received as true even by those who in daily experience feel it to be false. The interchanges of mingled scenes seldom fail to produce the intended vicissitudes of passion.[2] Fiction cannot move so much but that the attention may be easily transferred; and though it must be allowed that pleasing melancholy be sometimes interrupted by unwelcome levity, yet let it be considered likewise that melancholy is often not pleasing, and that the disturbance of one man may be the relief of another;[3] that different auditors have different habitudes; and that, upon the whole, all pleasure consists in variety.

The players, who in their edition divided our authour's works into comedies, histories, and tragedies, seem not to have distinguished the three kinds by any very exact or definite ideas.

An action which ended happily to the principal persons, however serious or distressful through its intermediate incidents, in their opinion constituted a comedy. This idea of a comedy continued long amongst us, and plays were written which, by changing the catastrophe, were tragedies to-day and comedies to-morrow.[4]

Tragedy was not in those times a poem of more general dignity or elevation than comedy; it required only a calamitous conclusion, with which the common criticism of that age was satisfied, whatever lighter pleasure it afforded in its progress.

History was a series of actions, with no other than chronological succession, independent of each other, and without any tendency to introduce or regulate the conclusion. It is not always very nicely distinguished from tragedy.[5] There is not much nearer approach to unity of action in the tragedy of *Antony and Cleopatra* than in the history of *Richard the Second.* But a history might be continued through many plays; as it had no plan, it had no limits.[6]

---

[1] 'Specious': 'Plausible; superficially, not solidly right; striking at first view'.
[2] Cf. Dryden, *Essay of Dramatic Poesy*, I, pp. 58–61, 279.
[3] Upton, 1748 ed., p. 96.
[4] Such as Suckling's *Aglaura* (1637–8) and Howard's *Vestal Virgin* (1665). See also Downes on Howard's adaptation of *Romeo and Juliet*, 'Tragical one Day, and Tragicomical another' (2.189).
[5] Cf. Pope (2.406).
[6] Cf. Gildon (2.222f., 245, 249).

Through all these denominations of the drama *Shakespeare*'s mode of composition is the same; an interchange of seriousness and merriment, by which the mind is softened at one time and exhilarated at another.[1] But whatever be his purpose, whether to gladden or depress, or to conduct the story without vehemence or emotion through tracts of easy and familiar dialogue, he never fails to attain his purpose; as he commands us, we laugh or mourn, or sit silent with quiet expectation, in tranquillity without indifference.

When *Shakespeare*'s plan is understood, most of the criticisms of *Rymer* and *Voltaire* vanish away. The play of *Hamlet* is opened without impropriety by two sentinels; *Iago* bellows at *Brabantio*'s window without injury to the scheme of the play,[2] though in terms which a modern audience would not easily endure; the character of *Polonius* is seasonable and useful; and the Gravediggers themselves may be heard with applause.[3]

Shakespeare engaged in dramatick poetry with the world open before him; the rules of the ancients were yet known to few; the publick judgment was unformed; he had no example of such fame as might force him upon imitation, nor criticks of such authority as might restrain his extravagance. He therefore indulged his natural disposition, and his disposition, as *Rymer*[4] has remarked, led him to comedy. In tragedy he often writes with great appearance of toil and study, what is written at last with little felicity; but in his comick scenes he seems to produce without labour what no labour can improve. In tragedy he is always struggling after some occasion to be comick, but in comedy he seems to repose, or to luxuriate, as in a mode of thinking congenial to his nature. In his tragick scenes there is always something wanting, but his comedy often surpasses expectation or desire. His comedy pleases by the thoughts and the language, and his tragedy for the greater part by incident and action. His tragedy seems to be skill, his comedy to be instinct.

The force of his comick scenes has suffered little diminution

---

[1] 'Soften': 'To make easy; to compose; to make placid'. 'Exhilarate': 'To make cheerful; to fill with mirth; to enliven'.
[2] See 2.31f. (Rymer); and *Voltaire on Shakespeare, ed. cit.*, pp. 77f., 94f.
[3] See *Voltaire on Shakespeare, ed. cit.*, pp. 64f. (the sentinels); 67f., 70 (Polonius); 45, 57, 70f., 192 (the gravediggers); and on the gravediggers see Garrick's adaptation of *Hamlet*, No. 236 below, and the comments of Horace Walpole, pp. 484f.
[4] See 2.58, and Colman's comments, No. 206 below.

from the changes made by a century and a half, in manners or in words.[1] As his personages act upon principles arising from genuine passion, very little modified by particular forms, their pleasures and vexations are communicable to all times and to all places; they are natural, and therefore durable; the adventitious peculiarities of personal habits are only superficial dyes, bright and pleasing for a little while, yet soon fading to a dim tinct, without any remains of former lustre; but the discriminations of true passion are the colours of nature; they pervade the whole mass, and can only perish with the body that exhibits them. The accidental compositions of heterogeneous modes are dissolved by the chance which combined them; but the uniform simplicity of primitive qualities neither admits increase nor suffers decay. The sand heaped by one flood is scattered by another, but the rock always continues in its place. The stream of time, which is continually washing the dissoluble fabricks of other poets, passes without injury by the adamant of *Shakespeare*.

If there be, what I believe there is, in every nation a stile which never becomes obsolete, a certain mode of phraseology so consonant and congenial to the analogy[2] and principles of its respective language as to remain settled and unaltered;[3] this stile is probably to be sought in the common intercourse of life, among those who speak only to be understood, without ambition of elegance. The polite are always catching modish innovations, and the learned depart from established forms of speech in hope of finding or making better; those who wish for distinction forsake the vulgar, when the vulgar is right; but there is a conversation above grossness and below refinement, where propriety resides, and where this poet seems to have gathered his comick dialogue. He is therefore more agreeable to the ears of the present age than any other authour equally remote, and among his other excellencies deserves to be studied as one of the original masters of our language.

These observations are to be considered not as unexceptionably constant, but as containing general and predominant truth. *Shakespeare*'s familiar dialogue is affirmed to be smooth and clear, yet not wholly without ruggedness or difficulty; as a country may

[1] Cf. Dennis (2.282).
[2] 'Analogy': '1. Resemblance between things with regard to some circumstances or effects'; 3. 'By grammarians, it is used to signify the agreement of several words in one common mode; as, from *love* is formed *loved* ... '.
[3] Cf. Dryden (1.164f.); Dennis (2.282).

be eminently fruitful, though it has spots unfit for cultivation. His characters are praised as natural, though their sentiments are sometimes forced, and their actions improbable; as the earth upon the whole is spherical, though its surface is varied with protuberances and cavities.

Shakespeare with his excellencies has likewise faults, and faults sufficient to obscure and overwhelm any other merit. I shall shew them in the proportion in which they appear to me, without envious malignity or superstitious veneration. No question can be more innocently discussed than a dead poet's pretensions to renown; and little regard is due to that bigotry which sets candour[1] higher than truth.

His first defect is that to which may be imputed most of the evil in books or in men. He sacrifices virtue to convenience, and is so much more careful to please than to instruct that he seems to write without any moral purpose. From his writings indeed a system of social duty may be selected, for he that thinks reasonably must think morally; but his precepts and axioms drop casually from him; he makes no just distribution of good or evil,[2] nor is always careful to shew in the virtuous a disapprobation of the wicked; he carries his persons indifferently through right and wrong, and at the close dismisses them without further care, and leaves their examples to operate by chance. This fault the barbarity of his age cannot extenuate; for it is always a writer's duty to make the world better, and justice is a virtue independant on time or place.

The plots are often so loosely formed that a very slight consideration may improve them, and so carelessly pursued that he seems not always fully to comprehend his own design.[3] He omits opportunities of instructing or delighting which the train of his story seems to force upon him, and apparently rejects those exhibitions which would be more affecting for the sake of those which are more easy.

It may be observed that in many of his plays the latter part is evidently neglected.[4] When he found himself near the end of his

---

[1] 'Candour': 'Sweetness of temper; purity of mind; openness; ingenuity; kindness'. It often has the sense of 'generosity' in this period.
[2] Cf. Dennis (2.147, 284f., 294ff.), and Addison's objections (2.272–4); Mrs Lennox (4.110ff.).
[3] Cf. Dryden (1.145, 255); Rowe (2.198); Dennis (2.351); Whalley (3.275ff.); Warton (4.60); Lennox (4.110ff.).
[4] Cf. Dryden (1.250); Rymer (2.54); Whalley (3.272).

work, and in view of his reward, he shortened the labour to snatch the profit. He therefore remits his efforts where he should most vigorously exert them, and his catastrophe is improbably produced or imperfectly represented.

He had no regard to distinction of time or place, but gives to one age or nation, without scruple, the customs, institutions, and opinions of another, at the expence not only of likelihood but of possibility. These faults *Pope* has endeavoured, with more zeal than judgment, to transfer to his imagined interpolators.[1] We need not wonder to find *Hector* quoting *Aristotle*, when we see the loves of *Theseus* and *Hippolyta* combined with the *Gothick* mythology of fairies.[2] *Shakespeare*, indeed, was not the only violator of chronology, for in the same age *Sidney*, who wanted not the advantages of learning, has in his *Arcadia* confounded the pastoral with the feudal times, the days of innocence, quiet and security with those of turbulence, violence and adventure.

In his comick scenes he is seldom very successful when he engages his characters in reciprocations of smartness and contests of sarcasm; their jests are commonly gross, and their pleasantry licentious;[3] neither his gentlemen nor his ladies have much delicacy, nor are sufficiently distinguished from his clowns by any appearance of refined manners. Whether he represented the real conversation of his time is not easy to determine; the reign of *Elizabeth* is commonly supposed to have been a time of stateliness, formality and reserve, yet perhaps the relaxations of that severity were not very elegant. There must, however, have been always some modes of gayety preferable to others, and a writer ought to chuse the best.

In tragedy his performance seems constantly to be worse, as his labour is more. The effusions of passion which exigence forces out are for the most part striking and energetick; but whenever he solicits his invention, or strains his faculties, the offspring of his throes is tumour,[4] meanness,[5] tediousness, and obscurity.[6]

---

[1] See 2.410; also Dennis (2.286), Upton (3.300).

[2] Cf. Seward (3.386f.); Hurd (4.542f.).

[3] Cf. Dryden (1.144f., 149f.); Rymer (2.31f.); Stubbes (3.57ff.); Seward (3.387).

[4] 'Tumour': 'Affected pomp; false magnificence; puffy grandeur; swelling mien; unsubstantial greatness'.

[5] 'Meanness': 'Want of excellence'; 'Want of dignity; low rank; poverty'.

[6] Cf. Dryden (1.138, 149, 263); Rymer (2.30); Addison (2.272); Dennis (2.293); Stubbes (3.63f.); Pope (3.70); Warburton (3.225); Kames (4.477, 479ff., 481ff.).

In narration he affects a disproportionate pomp of diction and a wearisome train of circumlocution, and tells the incident imperfectly in many words, which might have been more plainly delivered in few. Narration in dramatick poetry is naturally tedious, as it is unanimated and inactive, and obstructs the progress of the action; it should therefore always be rapid, and enlivened by frequent interruption. *Shakespeare* found it an encumbrance, and instead of lightening it by brevity endeavoured to recommend it by dignity and splendour.

His declamations or set speeches are commonly cold and weak, for his power was the power of nature; when he endeavoured, like other tragick writers, to catch opportunities of amplification, and instead of inquiring what the occasion demanded, to show how much his stores of knowledge could supply, he seldom escapes without the pity or resentment of his reader.

It is incident to him to be now and then entangled with an unwieldy sentiment, which he cannot well express, and will not reject; he struggles with it a while, and if it continues stubborn comprises it in words such as occur, and leaves it to be disentangled and evolved by those who have more leisure to bestow upon it.[1]

Not that always where the language is intricate the thought is subtle, or the image always great where the line is bulky; the equality of words to things is very often neglected, and trivial sentiments and vulgar ideas disappoint the attention, to which they are recommended by sonorous epithets and swelling figures.[2]

But the admirers of this great poet have[3] never less reason to indulge their hopes of supreme excellence than when he seems fully resolved to sink them in dejection, and mollify them with tender emotions by the fall of greatness, the danger of innocence, or the crosses of love.[4] He is not long soft and pathetick without some idle conceit, or contemptible equivocation.[5] He no sooner begins to move than he counteracts himself; and terrour and pity, as they are rising in the mind, are checked and blasted by sudden frigidity.

A quibble is to *Shakespeare* what luminous vapours are to the

---

[1] Cf. Upton (3.300); Warburton (3.224f.).
[2] Cf. Dryden (1.138, 263).
[3] In the 1778 edition Johnson substituted: 'have most reason to complain when he approaches nearest to his highest excellence, and seems full resolved . . . '.
[4] 1778 adds: 'What he does best, he soon ceases to do.'
[5] Cf. Dryden (1.138); Kames (4.479ff.).

traveller; he follows it at all adventures, it is sure to lead him out of his way, and sure to engulf him in the mire. It has some malignant power over his mind, and its fascinations are irresistible. Whatever be the dignity or profundity of his disquisition, whether he be enlarging knowledge or exalting affection, whether he be amusing attention with incidents or enchaining it in suspense, let but a quibble spring up before him and he leaves his work unfinished. A quibble is the golden apple for which he will always turn aside from his career, or stoop from his elevation. A quibble, poor and barren as it is, gave him such delight that he was content to purchase it by the sacrifice of reason, propriety and truth. A quibble was to him the fatal *Cleopatra* for which he lost the world, and was content to lose it.[1]

It will be thought strange that, in enumerating the defects of this writer, I have not yet mentioned his neglect of the unities,[2] his violation of those laws which have been instituted and established by the joint authority of poets and of cricks.

For his other deviations from the art of writing I resign him to critical justice, without making any other demand in his favour than that which must be indulged to all human excellence, that his virtues be rated with his failings. But from the censure which this irregularity may bring upon him I shall, with due reverence to that learning which I must oppose, adventure to try how I can defend him.

His histories, being neither tragedies nor comedies, are not subject to any of their laws;[3] nothing more is necessary to all the praise which they expect than that the changes of action be so prepared as to be understood, that the incidents be various and affecting, and the characters consistent, natural and distinct. No other unity is intended, and therefore none is to be sought.

In his other works he has well enough preserved the unity of action. He has not, indeed, an intrigue regularly perplexed and regularly unravelled; he does not endeavour to hide his design only to discover it, for this is seldom the order of real events, and *Shakespeare* is the poet of nature. But his plan has commonly what

---

[1] Compare Theobald on Shakespeare's '*Clinches, false wit*, and descending beneath himself', signs of 'Deference ... to the then *reigning Barbarism*': 'He was a *Sampson* in Strength, but he suffer'd some such *Dalilah* to give him up to the *Philistines*' (2.477).

[2] On Johnson's place in the critical tradition attacking the Unities see pp. 24ff. above, and the Introduction to Vol. 4, pp. 10ff. For Kenrick's criticism see pp. 188ff. below.

[3] Cf. Rowe (2.194f.); Percy (4.545).

Aristotle requires, a beginning, a middle, and an end; one event is concatenated with another, and the conclusion follows by easy consequence. There are perhaps some incidents that might be spared, as in other poets there is much talk that only fills up time upon the stage; but the general system makes gradual advances, and the end of the play is the end of expectation.

To the unities of time and place he has shewn no regard, and perhaps a nearer view of the principles on which they stand will diminish their value, and withdraw from them the veneration which from the time of *Corneille*[1] they have very generally received, by discovering that they have given more trouble to the poet than pleasure to the auditor.

The necessity of observing the unities of time and place arises from the supposed necessity of making the drama credible. The criticks hold it impossible that an action of months or years can be possibly believed to pass in three hours; or that the spectator can suppose himself to sit in the theatre while ambassadors go and return between distant kings, while armies are levied and towns besieged, while an exile wanders and returns, or till he whom they saw courting his mistress shall lament the untimely fall of his son. The mind revolts from evident falsehood, and fiction loses its force when it departs from the resemblance of reality.

From the narrow limitation of time necessarily arises the contraction of place. The spectator who knows that he saw the first act at *Alexandria* cannot suppose that he sees the next at *Rome*, at a distance to which not the dragons of *Medea* could in so short a time have transported him; he knows with certainty that he has not changed his place; and he knows that place cannot change itself, that what was a house cannot become a plain, that what was *Thebes* can never be *Persepolis*.

Such is the triumphant language with which a critick exults over the misery of an irregular poet, and exults commonly without resistance or reply. It is time therefore to tell him, by the authority of *Shakespeare*, that he assumes as an unquestionable principle a position which, while his breath is forming it into words, his understanding pronounces to be false. It is false that any representation is mistaken for reality; that any dramatick fable in its materi-

[1] See especially *Discours dramatiques* (1660), § iii: 'Discours des trois unités', reprinted with useful notes in H. T. Barnwell (ed.), Pierre Corneille, *Writings on the Theatre* (Oxford, 1965).

ality was ever credible, or, for a single moment, was ever credited.

The objection arising from the impossibility of passing the first hour at *Alexandria*, and the next at *Rome*, supposes that when the play opens the spectator really imagines himself at *Alexandria*, and believes that his walk to the theatre has been a voyage to *Egypt*, and that he lives in the days of *Antony* and *Cleopatra*. Surely he that imagines this may imagine more. He that can take the stage at one time for the palace of the *Ptolemies* may take it in half an hour for the promontory of *Actium*. Delusion,[1] if delusion be admitted, has no certain limitation.[2] If the spectator can be once persuaded that his old acquaintance are *Alexander* and *Cæsar*, that a room illuminated with candles is the plain of *Pharsalia* or the bank of *Granicus*, he is in a state of elevation above the reach of reason, or of truth, and from the heights of empyrean poetry may despise the circumscriptions of terrestrial nature. There is no reason why a mind thus wandering[3] in extasy should count the clock, or why an hour should not be a century in that calenture[4] of the brains that can make the stage a field.

The truth is, that the spectators are always in their senses, and know from the first act to the last that the stage is only a stage, and that the players are only players. They come to hear a certain number of lines recited with just gesture and elegant modulation. The lines relate to some action, and an action must be in some place; but the different actions that compleat a story may be in places very remote from each other; and where is the absurdity of allowing that space to represent first *Athens* and then *Sicily*, which was always known to be neither *Sicily* nor *Athens*, but a modern theatre?

By supposition, as place is introduced time may be extended; the time required by the fable elapses for the most part between the acts; for, of so much of the action as is represented the real and poetical duration is the same. If in the first act preparations for war against *Mithridates* are represented to be made in *Rome*, the event

---

[1] 'Delusion': 'A cheat; guile; treachery'; 'A false representation; illusion; error'. 'Illusion': 'Mockery; false show; counterfeit appearance'.

[2] Cf. Stubbes (3.64f.); *Rambler*, 156 (3.434); the Introduction to Vol. 4, pp. 10–16, and above, pp. 25ff.

[3] 'Wandering': 'Uncertain peregrination'; 'Aberration; mistaken way'. For 'extasy' see p. 60 above, note 2.

[4] 'Calenture': 'A distemper peculiar to sailors, in hot climates; wherein they imagine the sea to be green fields, and will throw themselves into it, if not restrained. *Quincy*' (*Dictionary*).

of the war may, without absurdity, be represented in the catastrophe as happening in *Pontus*; we know that there is neither war,
nor preparation for war; we know that we are neither in *Rome* nor
Pontus; that neither *Mithridates* nor *Lucullus* are before us. The
drama exhibits successive imitations of successive actions, and
why may not the second imitation represent an action that happened years after the first, if it be so connected with it that nothing
but time can be supposed to intervene? Time is, of all modes of
existence, most obsequious to the imagination; a lapse of years is as
easily conceived as a passage of hours. In contemplation we easily
contract the time of real actions, and therefore willingly permit
it to be contracted when we only see their imitation.

It will be asked how the drama moves, if it is not credited. It is
credited with all the credit due to a drama. It is credited, whenever
it moves, as a just picture of a real original; as representing to the
auditor what he would himself feel, if he were to do or suffer what
is there feigned to be suffered or to be done. The reflection that
strikes the heart is not that the evils before us are real evils, but that
they are evils to which we ourselves may be exposed. If there be
any fallacy, it is not that we fancy the players but that we fancy
ourselves unhappy for a moment; but we rather lament the possibility than suppose the presence of misery, as a mother weeps over
her babe when she remembers that death may take it from her.
The delight of tragedy proceeds from our consciousness of fiction;
if we thought murders and treasons real they would please no more.

Imitations produce pain or pleasure not because they are mistaken for realities but because they bring realities to mind. When
the imagination is recreated by a painted landscape, the trees are
not supposed capable to give us shade or the fountains coolness;
but we consider how we should be pleased with such fountains
playing beside us, and such woods waving over us. We are agitated
in reading the history of *Henry the Fifth*, yet no man takes his book
for the field of *Agincourt*. A dramatick exhibition is a book recited
with concomitants that encrease or diminish its effect. Familiar
comedy is often more powerful on the theatre than in the page;
imperial tragedy is always less.[1] The humour of *Petruchio* may be
heightened by grimace, but what voice or what gesture can hope
to add dignity or force to the soliloquy of *Cato*?

[1] Compare *Rambler*, lx, and Johnson, *Letters*, p. 233; for Colman's comments see p. 179
below.

71

A play read affects the mind like a play acted. It is therefore evident that the action is not supposed to be real, and it follows that between the acts a longer or shorter time may be allowed to pass, and that no more account of space or duration is to be taken by the auditor of a drama than by the reader of a narrative, before whom may pass in an hour the life of a hero or the revolutions of an empire.

Whether *Shakespeare* knew the unities, and rejected them by design, or deviated from them by happy ignorance it is, I think, impossible to decide, and useless to inquire. We may reasonably suppose that when he rose to notice he did not want the counsels and admonitions of scholars and criticks, and that he at last deliberately persisted in a practice which he might have begun by chance. As nothing is essential to the fable but unity of action, and as the unities of time and place arise evidently from false assumptions, and by circumscribing the extent of the drama lessen its variety, I cannot think it much to be lamented that they were not known by him, or not observed. Nor, if such another poet could arise, should I very vehemently reproach him that his first act passed at *Venice*, and his next in *Cyprus*.[1] Such violations of rules merely positive become the comprehensive genius of *Shakespeare*, and such censures are suitable to the minute and slender criticism of *Voltaire*:

> *Non usque adeo permiscuit imis*
> *Longus summa dies, ut non, si voce Metelli*
> *Serventur leges, malint a Cæsare tolli.*[2]

Yet when I speak thus slightly of dramatick rules, I cannot but recollect how much wit and learning may be produced against me; before such authorities I am afraid to stand, not that I think the present question one of those that are to be decided by mere authority, but because it is to be suspected that these precepts have not been so easily received but for better reasons than I have yet been able to find. The result of my enquiries, in which it would be ludicrous to boast of impartiality, is that the unities of time and place are not essential to a just drama, that though they may some-

---

[1] See Rymer (2.35); Voltaire also objected to this change of scene: *Voltaire on Shakespeare, ed. cit.*, p. 77.

[2] Lucan, *Pharsalia*, 3.138ff.: 'The course of time has not wrought such confusion that the laws would not rather be trampled on by Caesar than saved by Metellus.'

times conduce to pleasure they are always to be sacrificed to the nobler beauties of variety and instruction; and that a play written with nice observation of critical rules is to be contemplated as an elaborate curiosity, as the product of superfluous and ostentatious art, by which is shewn rather what is possible than what is necessary.

He that without diminution of any other excellence shall preserve all the unities unbroken, deserves the like applause with the architect who shall display all the orders of architecture in a citadel without any deduction from its strength; but the principal beauty of a citadel is to exclude the enemy, and the greatest graces of a play are to copy nature and instruct life.

Perhaps what I have here not dogmatically but deliberatively[1] written may recal the principles of the drama to a new examination. I am almost frighted at my own temerity; and when I estimate the fame and the strength of those that maintain the contrary opinion, am ready to sink down in reverential silence; as *Æneas* withdrew from the defence of *Troy* when he saw *Neptune* shaking the wall, and *Juno* heading the besiegers.

Those whom my arguments cannot persuade to give their approbation to the judgment of *Shakespeare* will easily, if they consider the condition of his life, make some allowance for his ignorance.

Every man's performances, to be rightly estimated, must be compared with the state of the age in which he lived and with his own particular opportunities; and though to the reader a book be not worse or better for the circumstances of the authour, yet as there is always a silent reference of human works to human abilities, and as the enquiry how far man may extend his designs, or how high he may rate his native force, is of far greater dignity than in what rank we shall place any particular performance, curiosity is always busy to discover the instruments as well as to survey the workmanship, to know how much is to be ascribed to original powers, and how much to casual and adventitious help. The palaces of *Peru* or *Mexico* were certainly mean and incommodious habitations, if compared to the houses of *European* monarchs; yet who could forbear to view them with astonishment, who remembered that they were built without the use of iron?

---

[1] This is the reading of the first edition, as corrected in proof by Johnson. The second edition, and subsequent ones, alter the word to 'deliberately'.

The *English* nation, in the time of *Shakespeare*, was yet struggling to emerge from barbarity.[1] The philology of *Italy* had been transplanted hither in the reign of *Henry* the Eighth; and the learned languages had been successfully cultivated by *Lilly*, *Linacre*, and *More*; by *Pole*, *Cheke*, and *Gardiner*; and afterwards by *Smith*, *Clerk*, *Haddon*, and *Ascham*. Greek was now taught to boys in the principal schools; and those who united elegance with learning read with great diligence the *Italian* and *Spanish* poets. But literature[2] was yet confined to professed scholars, or to men and women of high rank. The publick was gross and dark; and to be able to read and write was an accomplishment still valued for its rarity.

Nations, like individuals, have their infancy.[3] A people newly awakened to literary curiosity, being yet unacquainted with the true state of things, knows not how to judge of that which is proposed as its resemblance. Whatever is remote from common appearances is always welcome to vulgar, as to childish credulity;[4] and of a country unenlightened by learning the whole people is the vulgar. The study of those who then aspired to plebeian learning was laid out upon adventures, giants, dragons, and enchantments. *The Death of Arthur* was the favourite volume.[5]

The mind which has feasted on the luxurious wonders of fiction has no taste of the insipidity of truth. A play which imitated only the common occurrences of the world would, upon the admirers of *Palmerin* and *Guy of Warwick*, have made little impression; he that wrote for such an audience was under the necessity of looking round for strange events and fabulous transactions, and that incredibility by which maturer knowledge is offended was the chief recommendation of writings to unskilful curiosity.[6]

Our authour's plots are generally borrowed from novels, and it is reasonable to suppose that he chose the most popular, such as were read by many and related by more; for his audience could not have followed him through the intricacies of the drama had they not held the thread of the story[7] in their hands.

1 Cf. Rowe (2.198); Theobald (2.477); Stubbes (3.43); Guthrie (3.192f.); Anon., 1752 (3.452).
2 'Literature': 'Learning; skill in letters', i.e. often 'literacy'.
3 Cf. Dryden (1.145); Warburton (3.225).
4 Cf. Pope (2.405); Guthrie (3.192f.); Whalley (3.275f.); Upton (3.293).
5 Cf. Thomas Warton, *Observations on the Fairy Queen* (1762 ed., I, p. 27).
6 Cf. Pope (2.405).
7 Cf. Pope (2.406); Whalley (3.275); Upton (3.296).

The stories which we now find only in remoter authours were in his time accessible and familiar. The fable of *As you like it*, which is supposed to be copied from *Chaucer*'s Gamelyn,[1] was a little pamphlet of those times; and old Mr. *Cibber* remembered the tale of *Hamlet* in plain *English* prose,[2] which the criticks have now to seek in *Saxo Grammaticus*.

His *English* histories he took from *English* chronicles and *English* ballads; and as the ancient writers were made known to his countrymen by versions, they supplied him with new subjects; he dilated some of *Plutarch*'s lives into plays,[3] when they had been translated by *North*.

His plots, whether historical or fabulous, are always crouded with incidents, by which the attention of a rude people was more easily caught than by sentiment or argumentation; and such is the power of the marvellous, even over those who despise it, that every man finds his mind more strongly seized by the tragedies of *Shakespeare* than of any other writer; others please us by particular speeches, but he always makes us anxious for the event, and has perhaps excelled all but *Homer* in securing the first purpose of a writer, by exciting restless and unquenchable curiosity, and compelling him that reads his work to read it through.

The shows and bustle with which his plays abound have the same original. As knowledge advances pleasure passes from the eye to the ear, but returns, as it declines, from the ear to the eye. Those to whom our authour's labours were exhibited had more skill in pomps or processions than in poetical language, and perhaps wanted some visible and discriminated events as comments on the dialogue.[4] He knew how he should most please; and whether his practice is more agreeable to nature, or whether his example has prejudiced the nation, we still find that on our stage something must be done as well as said,[5] and inactive declamation is very coldly heard, however musical or elegant, passionate or sublime.

[1] Theobald, Upton, and Zachary Grey had made this (erroneous) judgment; Farmer showed the true source to be Lodge's *Rosalynde*: see p. 270 below.
[2] This is the prose work, *History of Hamblet*, which was printed in 1608 and is thus later than Shakespeare's play.
[3] Cf. Rowe (2.200); Gildon (2.251); Dennis (2.286f.); Pope (2.407); Theobald (2.517, 536f.). Johnson was the first to point to North's translation.
[4] Cf. Guthrie (3.192f.); Whalley (3.276).
[5] Cf. Dennis (2.162).

Voltaire[1] expresses his wonder that our authour's extravagances are endured by a nation which has seen the tragedy of *Cato*. Let him be answered, that *Addison* speaks the language of poets, and *Shakespeare* of men. We find in *Cato* innumerable beauties which enamour us of its authour, but we see nothing that acquaints us with human sentiments or human actions; we place it with the fairest and the noblest progeny which judgment propagates by conjunction with learning, but *Othello* is the vigorous and vivacious offspring of observation impregnated by genius. *Cato* affords a splendid exhibition of artificial and fictitious manners, and delivers just and noble sentiments in diction easy, elevated and harmonious, but its hopes and fears communicate no vibration to the heart; the composition refers us only to the writer; we pronounce the name of *Cato* but we think on *Addison*.[2]

The work of a correct and regular writer is a garden accurately formed and diligently planted, varied with shades and scented with flowers; the composition of *Shakespeare* is a forest, in which oaks extend their branches and pines tower in the air, interspersed sometimes with weeds and brambles, and sometimes giving shelter to myrtles and to roses; filling the eye with awful pomp, and gratifying the mind with endless diversity. Other poets display cabinets of precious rarities, minutely finished, wrought into shape, and polished unto brightness. *Shakespeare* opens a mine which contains gold and diamonds in unexhaustible plenty, though clouded by incrustations, debased by impurities, and mingled with a mass of meaner minerals.[3]

It has been much disputed whether *Shakespeare* owed his excellence to his own native force, or whether he had the common helps of scholastick education, the precepts of critical science, and the examples of ancient authours.

There has always prevailed a tradition that *Shakespeare* wanted learning, that he had no regular education nor much skill in the dead languages. *Jonson*, his friend, affirms that *he had small Latin, and no Greek*;[4] who, besides that he had no imaginable temptation to falsehood, wrote at a time when the character and acquisitions of *Shakespeare* were known to multitudes. His evidence ought

---

[1] In his *Appel à toutes les nations de l'Europe* (1761): *Voltaire on Shakespeare, ed. cit.*, p. 73.
[2] Cf. Guthrie (3.201f.), and Edward Young, *Conjectures on Original Composition* (1759), pp. 87–96.
[3] Cf. Fuller (1.12); Pope (2.415); Theobald (2.475); Morris (3.129).
[4] In the 1773 edition Johnson corrected this to 'less Greek': for Jonson's text see 1.24.

therefore to decide the controversy, unless some testimony of equal force could be opposed.

Some have imagined that they have discovered deep learning in many imitations of old writers; but the examples which I have known urged were drawn from books translated in his time;[1] or were such easy coincidences of thought as will happen to all who consider the same subjects; or such remarks on life or axioms of morality as float in conversation, and are transmitted through the world in proverbial sentences.

I have found it remarked[2] that in this important sentence, *Go before, I'll follow*, we read a translation of *I prae, sequar*. I have been told that when *Caliban*, after a pleasing dream, says *I cry'd to sleep again*, the author imitates *Anacreon*, who had, like every other man, the same wish on the same occasion.

There are a few passages which may pass for imitations, but so few that the exception only confirms the rule; he obtained them from accidental quotations or by oral communication, and as he used what he had, would have used more if he had obtained it.

The *Comedy of Errors* is confessedly taken from the *Menæchmi* of *Plautus*, from the only play of *Plautus* which was then in *English*.[3] What can be more probable than that he who copied that would have copied more, but that those which were not translated were inaccessible?

Whether he knew the modern languages is uncertain. That his plays have some *French* scenes proves but little; he might easily procure them to be written, and probably, even though he had known the language in the common degree, he could not have written it without assistance. In the story of *Romeo and Juliet* he is observed[4] to have followed the *English* translation where it deviates from the *Italian*; but this on the other part proves nothing against his knowledge of the original. He was to copy, not what he knew himself, but what was known to his audience.

It is most likely that he had learned *Latin* sufficiently to make him acquainted with construction, but that he never advanced to an

---

[1] Cf. Whalley (3.389); Hurd (4.305f.); Farmer, No. 214 below.
[2] By Zachary Grey, *Critical, Historical, and Explanatory Notes on Shakespeare* (1754), II, p. 53.
[3] Langbaine was the first to make this (erroneous) claim: see 1.419. (Warner's translation, published 1595, is later than Shakespeare's play.) It was repeated by Rowe (2.194), Gildon (2.218), Dennis (2.290ff.), Pope (2.408), and Mrs Lennox.
[4] By Mrs Lennox in *Shakespeare Illustrated*, I, p. 90.

easy perusal of the *Roman* authours.[1] Concerning his skill in modern languages I can find no sufficient ground of determination; but as no imitations of *French* or *Italian* authours have been discovered, though the *Italian* poetry was then high in esteem, I am inclined to believe that he read little more than *English*, and chose for his fables only such tales as he found translated.

That much knowledge is scattered over his works is very justly observed by *Pope*,[2] but it is often such knowledge as books did not supply. He that will understand *Shakespeare* must not be content to study him in the closet, he must look for his meaning sometimes among the sports of the field, and sometimes among the manufactures of the shop.[3]

There is however proof enough that he was a very diligent reader,[4] nor was our language then so indigent of books but that he might very liberally indulge his curiosity without excursion into foreign literature. Many of the *Roman* authours were translated, and some of the *Greek*; the reformation had filled the kingdom with theological learning; most of the topicks of human disquisition had found *English* writers; and poetry had been cultivated not only with diligence but success. This was a stock of knowledge sufficient for a mind so capable of appropriating and improving it.

But the greater part of his excellence was the product of his own genius. He found the *English* stage in a state of the utmost rudeness;[5] no essays either in tragedy or comedy had appeared from which it could be discovered to what degree of delight either one or other might be carried. Neither character nor dialogue were yet understood. *Shakespeare* may be truly said to have introduced them both amongst us, and in some of his happier scenes to have carried them both to the utmost height.

By what gradations of improvement he proceeded is not easily known; for the chronology of his works is yet unsettled. *Rowe* is of opinion that *perhaps we are not to look for his beginning, like those of other writers, in his least perfect works; art had so little, and nature so large a share in what he did, that for ought I know*, says he, *the perfor-*

---

[1] Cf. Rowe (2.191); Gildon (2.240); Dennis (2.291).
[2] See 2.407f.
[3] Cf. Dryden, *Essay of Dramatic Poesy*, ed. Watson (II, p. 74); Pope (2.407); Whalley (3.279).
[4] Cf. Pope (2.407); Theobald (2.475f.).
[5] Cf. Dryden, *Essay of Dramatic Poesy* (II, p. 73); Rowe (2.198); Stubbes (3.43); Hanmer (3.119); Anon. 1752 (3.452); Upton, 1748 ed., p. 98.

mances of his youth, as they were the most vigorous, were the best.[1] But the power of nature is only the power of using to any certain purpose the materials which diligence procures, or opportunity supplies. Nature gives no man knowledge, and when images are collected by study and experience can only assist in combining or applying them. *Shakespeare*, however favoured by nature, could impart only what he had learned; and as he must increase his ideas, like other mortals, by gradual acquisition he, like them, grew wiser as he grew older, could display life better as he knew it more, and instruct with more efficacy as he was himself more amply instructed.[2]

There is a vigilance of observation and accuracy of distinction which books and precepts cannot confer; from this almost all original and native excellence proceeds. *Shakespeare* must have looked upon mankind with perspicacity, in the highest degree curious and attentive.[3] Other writers borrow their characters from preceding writers, and diversify them only by the accidental appendages of present manners; the dress is a little varied but the body is the same.[4] Our authour had both matter and form to provide; for except the characters of *Chaucer*, to whom I think he is not much indebted,[5] there were no writers in *English*, and perhaps not many in other modern languages, which shewed life in its native colours.

The contest about the original benevolence or malignity of man had not yet commenced. Speculation had not yet attempted to analyse the mind, to trace the passions to their sources, to unfold the seminal principles of vice and virtue, or sound the depths of the heart for the motives of action. All those enquiries which from that time that human nature became the fashionable study have been made sometimes with nice[6] discernment, but often with idle subtilty,[7] were yet unattempted. The tales with which the infancy of learning was satisfied exhibited only the

[1] See 2.192.
[2] Cf. Dryden (1.250); Pope (2.406); Gildon (2.236, 242).
[3] Cf. Dryden (1.138); Pope (2.407f.).
[4] Cf. Pope (2.403f.).
[5] Johnson seems here to mean to contradict Dryden (1.250), Pope (2.408), and Mrs Lennox (4.132ff.).
[6] 'Nice': 'Accurate in judgement to minute exactness; superfluously exact. It is often used to express a culpable delicacy'.
[7] 'Idle': 'Useless; vain; ineffectual'; 'Worthless; barren; not productive of good'. 'Subtilty': 'Nicety'; 'Refinement; too much acuteness'.

superficial appearances of action, related the events but omitted the causes, and were formed for such as delighted in wonders rather than in truth. Mankind was not then to be studied in the closet; he that would know the world was under the necessity of gleaning his own remarks by mingling as he could in its business and amusements.

Boyle congratulated himself upon his high birth, because it favoured his curiosity by facilitating his access. *Shakespeare* had no such advantage; he came to *London* a needy adventurer, and lived for a time by very mean employments. Many works of genius and learning have been performed in states of life that appear very little favourable to thought or to enquiry; so many, that he who considers them is inclined to think that he sees enterprise and perseverance predominating over all external agency, and bidding help and hindrance vanish before them. The genius of *Shakespeare* was not to be depressed by the weight of poverty, nor limited by the narrow conversation to which men in want are inevitably condemned; the incumbrances of his fortune were shaken from his mind, *as dewdrops from a lion's mane.*[1]

Though he had so many difficulties to encounter, and so little assistance to surmount them, he has been able to obtain an exact knowledge of many modes of life and many casts of native dispositions, to vary them with great multiplicity, to mark them by nice distinctions, and to shew them in full view by proper combinations. In this part of his performances he had none to imitate, but has himself been imitated by all succeeding writers; and it may be doubted whether from all his successors more maxims of theoretical knowledge, or more rules of practical prudence, can be collected than he alone has given to his country.

Nor was his attention confined to the actions of men; he was an exact surveyor of the inanimate world; his descriptions have always some peculiarities, gathered by contemplating things as they really exist. It may be observed that the oldest poets of many nations preserve their reputation, and that the following generations of wit, after a short celebrity, sink into oblivion. The first, whoever they be, must take their sentiments and descriptions immediately from knowledge; the resemblance is therefore just, their descriptions are verified by every eye, and their sentiments acknowledged by every breast. Those whom their fame invites

[1] *Troilus and Cressida*, 3.3.224.

to the same studies copy partly them and partly nature, till the books of one age gain such authority as to stand in the place of nature to another, and imitation, always deviating a little, becomes at last capricious and casual. *Shakespeare*, whether life or nature be his subject, shews plainly that he has seen with his own eyes; he gives the image which he receives, not weakened or distorted by the intervention of any other mind; the ignorant feel his representations to be just, and the learned see that they are compleat.[1]

Perhaps it would not be easy to find any authour, except *Homer*,[2] who invented so much as *Shakespeare*, who so much advanced the studies which he cultivated, or effused so much novelty upon his age or country. The form, the characters, the language, and the shows of the *English* drama are his. *He seems*, says Dennis,[3] *to have been the very original of our* English *tragical harmony, that is, the harmony of blank verse, diversified often by dissyllable and trissyllable terminations. For the diversity distinguishes it from heroick harmony, and by bringing it nearer to common use makes it more proper to gain attention, and more fit for action and dialogue. Such verse we make when we are writing prose; we make such verse in common conversation.*

I know not whether this praise is rigorously just. The dissyllable termination, which the critick rightly appropriates to the drama, is to be found, though I think not in *Gorboduc*, which is confessedly before our author, yet in *Hieronymo*,[4] of which the date is not certain, but which there is reason to believe at least as old as his earliest plays. This however is certain, that he is the first who taught either tragedy or comedy to please, there being no theatrical piece of any older writer of which the name is known, except to antiquaries and collectors of books, which are sought because they are scarce, and would not have been scarce had they been much esteemed.

To him we must ascribe the praise, unless *Spenser* may divide it with him, of having first discovered to how much smoothness and harmony the *English* language could be softened. He has speeches, perhaps sometimes scenes, which have all the delicacy of *Rowe*

---

[1] Cf. Young (4.407).
[2] Cf. Dryden (1.139); Dennis (2.282); Theobald (2.353); Pope (2.403); Akenside (3.190); Guthrie (3.195); Whalley (3.274); Upton, 1748 ed., p. 135; Hurd (3.430f.); Colman (4.59); Warton (4.61); Murphy (4.92); Shebbeare (4.185); Wilkes (4.356); Colman (4.447); Anon. (4.464).
[3] See 2.282f.
[4] Kyd, *The Spanish Tragedy* (c. 1592).

without his effeminacy. He endeavours indeed commonly to strike by the force and vigour of his dialogue, but he never executes his purpose better than when he tries to sooth by softness.

Yet it must be at last confessed that as we owe every thing to him, he owes something to us; that if much of his praise is paid by perception and judgement, much is likewise given by custom and veneration. We fix our eyes upon his graces, and turn them from his deformities, and endure in him what we should in another loath or despise. If we endured without praising, respect for the father of our drama might excuse us; but I have seen in the book of some modern critick a collection of anomalies which shew that he has corrupted language by every mode of depravation, but which his admirer has accumulated as a monument of honour.[1]

He has scenes of undoubted and perpetual excellence, but perhaps not one play which, if it were now exhibited as the work of a contemporary writer, would be heard to the conclusion.[2] I am indeed far from thinking that his works were wrought to his own ideas of perfection; when they were such as would satisfy the audience, they satisfied the writer. It is seldom that authours, though more studious of fame than *Shakespeare*, rise much above the standard of their own age; to add a little to what is best will always be sufficient for present praise, and those who find themselves exalted into fame are willing to credit their encomiasts, and to spare the labour of contending with themselves.

It does not appear that *Shakespeare* thought his works worthy of posterity, that he levied any ideal tribute upon future times, or had any further prospect than of present popularity and present profit. When his plays had been acted his hope was at an end; he solicited no addition of honour from the reader. He therefore made no scruple to repeat the same jests in many dialogues, or to entangle different plots by the same knot of perplexity, which may be at least forgiven him by those who recollect that of *Congreve*'s four comedies two are concluded by a marriage in a mask, by a deception which perhaps never happened, and which, whether likely or not, he did not invent.

So careless was this great poet of future fame that, though he

---

[1] John Upton, *Critical Observations on Shakespeare* (1746, 1748): see 3.307–17. This important demonstration of Shakespeare's grammatical practice was taken further by Richard Hurd: see 4.297ff.
[2] Cf. Dennis (2.350–1) and Goldsmith (4.373).

retired to ease and plenty while he was yet little *declined into the vale of years*,[1] before he could be disgusted with fatigue or disabled by infirmity, he made no collection of his works, nor desired to rescue those that had been already published from the depravations that obscured them, or secure to the rest a better destiny by giving them to the world in their genuine state.

Of the plays which bear the name of *Shakespeare* in the late editions, the greater part were not published till about seven years after his death, and the few which appeared in his life are apparently thrust into the world without the care of the authour, and therefore probably without his knowledge.

Of all the publishers, clandestine or professed, their[2] negligence and unskilfulness has by the late revisers been sufficiently shown. The faults of all are indeed numerous and gross, and have not only corrupted many passages perhaps beyond recovery, but have brought others into suspicion which are only obscured by obsolete phraseology, or by the writer's unskilfulness and affectation. To alter is more easy than to explain, and temerity is a more common quality than diligence. Those who saw that they must employ conjecture to a certain degree, were willing to indulge it a little further. Had the authour published his own works we should have sat quietly down to disentangle his intricacies, and clear his obscurities; but now we tear what we cannot loose, and eject what we happen not to understand.

The faults are more than could have happened without the concurrence of many causes. The stile of *Shakespeare* was in itself ungrammatical, perplexed, and obscure;[3] his works were transcribed for the players by those who may be supposed to have seldom understood them; they were transmitted by copiers equally unskilful, who still multiplied errours; they were perhaps sometimes mutilated by the actors for the sake of shortening the speeches; and were at last printed without correction of the press.[4]

In this state they remained, not as Dr. *Warburton* supposes[5] because they were unregarded, but because the editor's art was

---

[1] *Othello*, 3.3.269f.

[2] Malone emended to 'the'; accepted by Sherbo, *Johnson on Shakespeare*, p. 92.

[3] 'Perplex': 'To make intricate; to involve; to complicate'; 'to entangle; ... to puzzle'. 'Obscure': 'Not easily intelligible; abstruse; difficult'.

[4] Cf. Pope (2.410ff.); Theobald (2.484ff.); Johnson (3.269ff.); Upton, 1748 ed., p. 177; Dodd (3.466f.).

[5] Preface to his edition of Shakespeare, 1747; in Nichol Smith, *Essays*, p. 89.

not yet applied to modern languages, and our ancestors were accustomed to so much negligence of *English* printers that they could very patiently endure it. At last an edition was undertaken by *Rowe*; not because a poet was to be published by a poet,[1] for *Rowe* seems to have thought very little on correction or explanation, but that our authour's works might appear like those of his fraternity, with the appendages of a life and recommendatory preface.[2] *Rowe* has been clamorously blamed for not performing what he did not undertake, and it is time that justice be done him, by confessing that though he seems to have had no thought of corruption beyond the printer's errours, yet he has made many emendations, if they were not made before, which his successors have received without acknowledgement, and which, if they had produced them, would have filled pages and pages with censures of the stupidity by which the faults were committed, with displays of the absurdities which they involved, with ostentatious expositions of the new reading, and self congratulations on the happiness of discovering it.

Of *Rowe*,[3] as of all the editors, I have preserved the preface, and have likewise retained the authour's life, though not written with much elegance or spirit; it relates however what is now to be known, and therefore deserves to pass through all succeeding publications.

The nation had been for many years content enough with Mr. *Rowe*'s performance, when Mr. *Pope* made them acquainted with the true state of *Shakespeare*'s text, shewed that it was extremely corrupt, and gave reason to hope that there were means of reforming it. He collated the old copies, which none had thought to examine before, and restored many lines to their integrity; but by a very compendious criticism he rejected whatever he disliked, and thought more of amputation than of cure.[4]

I know not why he is commended by Dr. *Warburton*[5] for distinguishing the genuine from the spurious plays. In this choice he exerted no judgement of his own; the plays which he received

1 Warburton, in Nichol Smith, *op. cit.*, p. 90.

2 See 2.15, 190ff.

3 Johnson in fact reprinted Rowe's preface in the revised and abridged version made by Pope for his 1725 edition; this became the standard version of Rowe in the eighteenth century.

4 See 2.15f., 403ff.

5 Warburton, in Nichol Smith, *op. cit.*, p. 90.

were given by *Hemings* and *Condel*, the first editors; and those which he rejected, though, according to the licentiousness of the press in those times, they were printed during *Shakespeare*'s life with his name, had been omitted by his friends, and were never added to his works before the edition of 1664, from which they were copied by the later printers.

This was[1] a work which *Pope* seems to have thought unworthy of his abilities, being not able to suppress his contempt of *the dull duty of an editor*.[2] He understood but half his undertaking. The duty of a collator is indeed dull, yet like other tedious tasks is very necessary; but an emendatory critick would ill discharge his duty without qualities very different from dulness. In perusing a corrupted piece he must have before him all possibilities of meaning, with all possibilities of expression. Such must be his comprehension of thought, and such his copiousness of language. Out of many readings possible he must be able to select that which best suits with the state, opinions, and modes of language prevailing in every age, and with his authour's particular cast of thought and turn of expression. Such must be his knowledge, and such his taste. Conjectural criticism demands more than humanity possesses, and he that exercises it with most praise has very frequent need of indulgence. Let us now be told no more of the dull duty of an editor.

Confidence is the common consequence of success. They whose excellence of any kind has been loudly celebrated are ready to conclude that their powers are universal. *Pope*'s edition fell below his own expectations, and he was so much offended when he was found to have left any thing for others to do that he passed the latter part of his life in a state of hostility with verbal criticism.

I have retained all his notes,[3] that no fragment of so great a writer may be lost; his preface, valuable alike for elegance of composition and justness of remark, and containing a general criticism on his authour so extensive that little can be added, and so exact that little can be disputed, every editor has an interest to suppress, but that every reader would demand its insertion.

---

[1] The 1778 edition emended to 'is'.
[2] See 2.414.
[3] Johnson did not in fact reprint all of Pope's notes (Sherbo, *Johnson on Shakespeare*, p. 95, note).

Pope was succeeded by *Theobald*,[1] a man of narrow comprehension and small acquisitions, with no native and intrinsick splendour of genius, with little of the artificial light of learning, but zealous for minute accuracy, and not negligent in pursuing it. He collated the ancient copies, and rectified many errours. A man so anxiously scrupulous might have been expected to do more, but what little he did was commonly right.

In his reports of copies and editions he is not to be trusted without examination. He speaks sometimes indefinitely of copies, when he has only one. In his enumeration of editions he mentions the two first folios as of high, and the third folio as of middle authority;[2] but the truth is that the first is equivalent to all others, and that the rest only deviate from it by the printer's negligence. Whoever has any of the folios has all, excepting those diversities which mere reiteration of editions will produce. I collated them all at the beginning, but afterwards used only the first.

Of his notes I have generally retained those which he retained himself in his second edition, except when they were confuted by subsequent annotators, or were too minute to merit preservation. I have sometimes adopted his restoration of a comma, without inserting the panegyrick in which he celebrated himself for his atchievement. The exuberant excrescence of his diction I have often lopped, his triumphant exultations over *Pope* and *Rowe* I have sometimes suppressed, and his contemptible ostentation I have frequently concealed; but I have in some places shewn him as he would have shewn himself, for the reader's diversion, that the inflated emptiness of some notes may justify or excuse the contraction of the rest.

Theobald, thus weak and ignorant, thus mean and faithless, thus petulant and ostentatious, by the good luck of having *Pope* for his enemy[3] has escaped, and escaped alone with reputation from this undertaking. So willingly does the world support those who solicite favour against those who command reverence; and so easily is he praised whom no man can envy.

---

[1] See 2.16ff., 426ff., 471ff.; and on Johnson's prejudice against Theobald see the Introduction above, p. 23. Nearly all eighteenth-century critics (with the obvious exception of Warburton) rate Theobald well above Pope: cf., for example, Stubbes (3.41f.), Seward (3.388), Dodd (3.466f.), and Kenrick below, pp. 198f.

[2] See 2.527f.

[3] See Vol. 2, No. 74; Vol. 3, No. 84.

Our authour fell then into the hands of Sir *Thomas Hanmer*,[1] the *Oxford* editor, a man in my opinion eminently qualified by nature for such studies. He had what is the first requisite to emendatory criticism, that intuition by which the poet's intention is immediately discovered, and that dexterity of intellect which despatches its work by the easiest means. He had undoubtedly read much; his acquaintance with customs, opinions, and traditions seems to have been large; and he is often learned without shew. He seldom passes what he does not understand without an attempt to find or to make a meaning, and sometimes hastily makes what a little more attention would have found. He is solicitous to reduce to grammar what he could not be sure that his authour intended to be grammatical. *Shakespeare* regarded more the series of ideas than of words, and his language, not being designed for the reader's desk, was all that he desired it to be if it conveyed his meaning to the audience.

Hanmer's care of the metre has been too violently censured.[2] He found the measure reformed in so many passages by the silent labours of some editors, with the silent acquiescence of the rest, that he thought himself allowed to extend a little further the license which had already been carried so far without reprehension; and of his corrections in general it must be confessed that they are often just, and made commonly with the least possible violation of the text.

But by inserting his emendations, whether invented or borrowed, into the page, without any notice of varying copies, he has appropriated the labour of his predecessors and made his own edition of little authority. His confidence indeed, both in himself and others, was too great; he supposes all to be right that was done by *Pope* and *Theobald*; he seems not to suspect a critick of fallibility, and it was but reasonable that he should claim what he so liberally granted.

As he never writes without careful enquiry and diligent consideration, I have received all his notes, and believe that every reader will wish for more.

Of the last editor[3] it is more difficult to speak. Respect is due to

[1] See 3.14f., 118ff., and 184f.
[2] By Warburton: in Nichol Smith, *op. cit.*, pp. 92f.
[3] William Warburton: see 2.17ff., 475ff., 529ff.; 3.15ff., 81ff., 223ff., 323, 346ff., 351ff., 388, 390ff., 467, 475; 4.147ff., 331ff., 551ff., 566ff.

high place, tenderness to living reputation, and veneration to genius and learning; but he cannot be justly offended at that liberty of which he has himself so frequently given an example, nor very solicitous what is thought of notes, which he ought never to have considered as part of his serious employments, and which, I suppose, since the ardour of composition is remitted he no longer numbers among his happy effusions.

The original and predominant errour of his commentary is acquiescence in his first thoughts; that precipitation which is produced by consciousness of quick discernment; and that confidence which presumes to do by surveying the surface, what labour only can perform by penetrating the bottom. His notes exhibit sometimes perverse interpretations, and sometimes improbable conjectures; he at one time gives the authour more profundity of meaning than the sentence admits, and at another discovers absurdities where the sense is plain to every other reader. But his emendations are likewise often happy and just; and his interpretation of obscure passages learned and sagacious.

Of his notes I have commonly rejected those against which the general voice of the publick has exclaimed, or which their own incongruity immediately condemns, and which, I suppose, the authour himself would desire to be forgotten. Of the rest, to part I have given the highest approbation by inserting the offered reading in the text; part I have left to the judgment of the reader as doubtful, though specious; and part I have censured without reserve, but I am sure without bitterness of malice, and I hope without wantonness of insult.

It is no pleasure to me, in revising my volumes, to observe how much paper is wasted in confutation. Whoever considers the revolutions of learning, and the various questions of greater or less importance upon which wit and reason have exercised their powers, must lament the unsuccessfulness of enquiry and the slow advances of truth, when he reflects that great part of the labour of every writer is only the destruction of those that went before him. The first care of the builder of a new system is to demolish the fabricks which are standing. The chief desire of him that comments an authour is to shew how much other commentators have corrupted and obscured him. The opinions prevalent in one age as truths above the reach of controversy are confuted and rejected in another, and rise again to reception in remoter times. Thus the human mind is kept in motion without progress. Thus sometimes truth and errour, and sometimes contrarieties of errour, take each other's place by reciprocal invasion. The tide of seeming knowledge which is poured over one generation retires and leaves another naked and barren; the sudden meteors of intelligence which for a while appear to shoot their beams into the regions of obscurity on a sudden withdraw their lustre, and leave mortals again to grope their way.

These elevations and depressions of renown, and the contradictions to which all improvers of knowledge must for ever be exposed, since they are not escaped by the highest and brightest of mankind, may surely be endured with patience by criticks and annotators, who can rank themselves but as the satellites of their authours. How canst thou beg for life, says *Achilles* to his captive, when thou knowest that thou art now to suffer only what must another day be suffered by *Achilles*?

Dr. *Warburton* had a name sufficient to confer celebrity on those who could exalt themselves into antagonists, and his notes have raised a clamour too loud to be distinct. His chief assailants are the authours of *The Canons of Criticism*,[1] and of the *Review of* Shakespeare's *text*;[2] of whom one ridicules his errours with airy petulance, suitable enough to the levity of the controversy; the other attacks them with gloomy malignity, as if he were dragging to justice an assassin or incendiary. The one stings like a fly, sucks a little blood, takes a gay flutter, and returns for more; the other bites like a viper, and would be glad to leave inflammations and gangrene behind him. When I think on one, with his confederates, I remember the danger of *Coriolanus*, who was afraid that *girls with spits, and boys with stones, should slay him in puny battle* [4.4.5]; when the other crosses my imagination, I remember the prodigy in *Macbeth*,

> *A falcon tow'ring in his pride of place,*
> *Was by a mousing owl hawk'd at and kill'd.* [2.4.12]

Let me however do them justice. One is a wit, and one a scholar. They have both shewn acuteness sufficient in the discovery of faults, and have both advanced some probable interpretations of obscure passages; but when they aspire to conjecture and emen-

---

[1] Thomas Edwards: see 3.16ff., 390ff.; 4.40, 331ff.
[2] Benjamin Heath: for his *The Revisal of Shakespeare's Text* see Vol. 4, No. 203.

dation it appears how falsely we all estimate our own abilities, and the little which they have been able to perform might have taught them more candour to the endeavours of others.

Before Dr. *Warburton*'s edition, *Critical Observations on Shakespeare* had been published by Mr. *Upton*,[1] a man skilled in languages and acquainted with books, but who seems to have had no great vigour of genius or nicety of taste. Many of his explanations are curious[2] and useful, but he likewise, though he professed to oppose the licentious confidence of editors, and adhere to the old copies, is unable to restrain the rage of emendation, though his ardour is ill seconded by his skill. Every cold empirick,[3] when his heart is expanded by a successful experiment, swells into a theorist, and the laborious collator at some unlucky moment frolicks in conjecture.

Critical, Historical, and Explanatory Notes have been likewise published upon *Shakespeare* by Dr. *Grey*,[4] whose diligent perusal of the old *English* writers has enabled him to make some useful observations. What he undertook he has well enough performed, but as he neither attempts judicial nor emendatory criticism he employs rather his memory than his sagacity. It were to be wished that all would endeavour to imitate his modesty who have not been able to surpass his knowledge.

I can say with great sincerity of all my predecessors, what I hope will hereafter be said of me, that not one has left *Shakespeare* without improvement, nor is there one to whom I have not been indebted for assistance and information. Whatever I have taken from them it was my intention to refer to its original authour,[5] and it is certain that what I have not given to another I believed when I wrote it to be my own. In some perhaps I have been anticipated; but if I am ever found to encroach upon the remarks of any other commentator, I am willing that the honour, be it more or less, should be transferred to the first claimant, for his right, and his alone, stands above dispute. The second can prove his pretensions only to himself, nor can himself always distinguish invention with sufficient certainty from recollection.

---

[1] See 3.5ff., 290ff.
[2] 'Curious': 'Accurate; careful not to mistake'; 'Exact; nice; subtle'.
[3] 'Empirick': 'A trier of experiments; such persons as have no true education in, or knowledge of physical practice; but venture upon hearsay and observation only. *Quincy*'.
[4] See 4.40f., 147ff.
[5] For the extent of Johnson's borrowings see Sherbo, *Johnson, Editor*, pp. 28–45, 122–4.

They have all been treated by me with candour, which they have not been careful of observing to one another. It is not easy to discover from what cause the acrimony of a scholiast can naturally proceed. The subjects to be discussed by him are of very small importance; they involve neither property nor liberty; nor favour the interest of sect or party. The various readings of copies, and different interpretations of a passage, seem to be questions that might exercise the wit without engaging the passions. But, whether it be that *small things make mean men proud*,[1] and vanity catches small occasions; or that all contrariety of opinion, even in those that can defend it no longer, makes proud men angry; there is often found in commentaries a spontaneous strain of invective and contempt, more eager and venomous than is vented by the most furious controvertist in politicks against those whom he is hired to defame.

Perhaps the lightness of the matter may conduce to the vehemence of the agency; when the truth to be investigated is so near to inexistence as to escape attention, its bulk is to be enlarged by rage and exclamation. That to which all would be indifferent in its original state may attract notice when the fate of a name is appended to it. A commentator has indeed great temptations to supply by turbulence[2] what he wants of dignity, to beat his little gold to a spacious surface, to work that to foam which no art or diligence can exalt to spirit.

The notes which I have borrowed or written are either illustrative, by which difficulties are explained; or judicial, by which faults and beauties are remarked; or emendatory, by which depravations are corrected.[3]

The explanations transcribed from others, if I do not subjoin any other interpretation, I suppose commonly to be right, at least I intend by acquiescence to confess that I have nothing better to propose.

After the labours of all the editors I found many passages which appeared to me likely to obstruct the greater number of readers, and thought it my duty to facilitate their passage. It is impossible for an expositor not to write too little for some and too much for others. He can only judge what is necessary by his own ex-

[1] 2 *Henry VI*, 4.1.106 (Johnson writes 'mean' instead of 'base').
[2] 'Turbulence': 'Tumult, confusion', i.e. ostentatious and unnecessary activity.
[3] Cf. Pope (2.414); Theobald (2.487ff.); Warburton (3.223ff.).

perience; and how long soever he may deliberate will at last explain many lines which the learned will think impossible to be mistaken, and omit many for which the ignorant will want his help. These are censures merely relative, and must be quietly endured. I have endeavoured to be neither superfluously copious nor scrupulously reserved, and hope that I have made my authour's meaning accessible to many who before were frighted from perusing him, and contributed something to the publick by diffusing innocent and rational pleasure.

The compleat explanation of an authour not systematick and consequential but desultory and vagrant,[1] abounding in casual allusions and light hints, is not to be expected from any single scholiast. All personal reflections, when names are suppressed, must be in a few years irrecoverably obliterated; and customs too minute to attract the notice of law, such as modes of dress, formalities of conversation, rules of visits, disposition of furniture, and practices of ceremony, which naturally find places in familiar dialogue, are so fugitive and unsubstantial that they are not easily retained or recovered. What can be known will be collected by chance, from the recesses of obscure and obsolete papers, perused commonly with some other view. Of this knowledge every man has some, and none has much; but when an authour has engaged the publick attention those who can add any thing to his illustration communicate their discoveries, and time produces what had eluded diligence.

To time I have been obliged to resign many passages which, though I did not understand them, will perhaps hereafter be explained; having, I hope, illustrated some which others have neglected or mistaken, sometimes by short remarks or marginal directions, such as every editor has added at his will, and often by comments more laborious than the matter will seem to deserve; but that which is most difficult is not always most important, and to an editor nothing is a trifle by which his authour is obscured.

The poetical beauties or defects I have not been very diligent to observe.[2] Some plays have more, and some fewer judicial

---

[1] 'Desultory': 'Roving from thing to thing; unsettled; immethodical; unconstant'. 'Vagrant': 'wandering; unsettled, vagabond'.
[2] Compare the announcement in Johnson's 1756 *Proposals* for an edition: 4.272f.; and cf. Rowe (2.194); Pope (2.403); Theobald (2.481); Warburton (2.486); Upton (3.321); Dodd (3.464ff.).

observations, not in proportion to their difference of merit, but because I gave this part of my design to chance and to caprice. The reader, I believe, is seldom pleased to find his opinion anticipated; it is natural to delight more in what we find or make than in what we receive. Judgement, like other faculties, is improved by practice, and its advancement is hindered by submission to dictatorial decisions, as the memory grows torpid by the use of a table book. Some initiation is however necessary; of all skill part is infused by precept, and part is obtained by habit; I have therefore shewn so much as may enable the candidate of criticism to discover the rest.

To the end of most plays I have added short strictures,[1] containing a general censure of faults or praise of excellence; in which I know not how much I have concurred with the current opinion; but I have not, by any affectation of singularity, deviated from it. Nothing is minutely and particularly examined, and therefore it is to be supposed that in the plays which are condemned there is much to be praised, and in these which are praised much to be condemned.

The part of criticism in which the whole succession of editors has laboured with the greatest diligence, which has occasioned the most arrogant ostentation and excited the keenest acrimony, is the emendation of corrupted passages, to which the publick attention having been first drawn by the violence of the contention between *Pope* and *Theobald*, has been continued by the persecution which, with a kind of conspiracy, has been since raised against all the publishers of *Shakespeare*.

That many passages have passed in a state of depravation through all the editions is indubitably certain; of these the restoration is only to be attempted by collation of copies or sagacity of conjecture. The collator's province is safe and easy, the conjecturer's perilous and difficult. Yet as the greater part of the plays are extant only in one copy the peril must not be avoided, nor the difficulty refused.

Of the readings which this emulation of amendment has hitherto produced, some from the labours of every publisher I have advanced into the text; those are to be considered as in my opinion sufficiently supported; some I have rejected without mention, as evidently erroneous; some I have left in the notes without censure

[1] 'Stricture': 'A slight touch upon a subject; not a set discourse'.

or approbation, as resting in equipoise between objection and defence; and some, which seemed specious but not right, I have inserted with a subsequent animadversion.

Having classed the observations of others I was at last to try what I could substitute for their mistakes, and how I could supply their omissions. I collated such copies as I could procure, and wished for more, but have not found the collectors of these rarities very communicative. Of the editions which chance or kindness put into my hands I have given an enumeration, that I may not be blamed for neglecting what I had not the power to do.

By examining the old copies I soon found that the later publishers, with all their boasts of diligence, suffered many passages to stand unauthorised, and contented themselves with *Rowe*'s regulation of the text, even where they knew it to be arbitrary, and with a little consideration might have found it to be wrong. Some of these alterations are only the ejection of a word for one that appeared to him more elegant or more intelligible. These corruptions I have often silently rectified; for the history of our language, and the true force of our words, can only be preserved by keeping the text of authours free from adulteration. Others, and those very frequent, smoothed the cadence or regulated the measure; on these I have not exercised the same rigour; if only a word was transposed, or a particle inserted or omitted, I have sometimes suffered the line to stand; for the inconstancy of the copies is such as that some liberties may be easily permitted. But this practice I have not suffered to proceed far, having restored the primitive diction wherever it could for any reason be preferred.

The emendations which comparison of copies supplied I have inserted in the text; sometimes, where the improvement was slight, without notice, and sometimes with an account of the reasons of the change.

Conjecture, though it be sometimes unavoidable, I have not wantonly nor licentiously indulged.[1] It has been my settled principle that the reading of the ancient books is probably true, and therefore is not to be disturbed for the sake of elegance, perspicuity, or mere improvement of the sense. For though much credit is not due to the fidelity, nor any to the judgment of the first publishers, yet they who had the copy before their eyes were more likely to read it right than we who read it only by imagination.

[1] For the next two paragraphs compare Upton, 1748 ed., pp. 133-4.

But it is evident that they have often made strange mistakes by ignorance or negligence, and that therefore something may be properly attempted by criticism, keeping the middle way between presumption and timidity.

Such criticism I have attempted to practise, and where any passage appeared inextricably perplexed have endeavoured to discover how it may be recalled to sense with least violence. But my first labour is always to turn the old text on every side, and try if there be any interstice through which light can find its way; nor would *Huetius*[1] himself condemn me as refusing the trouble of research for the ambition of alteration. In this modest industry I have not been unsuccessful. I have rescued many lines from the violations of temerity, and secured many scenes from the inroads of correction. I have adopted the *Roman* sentiment that it is more honourable to save a citizen than to kill an enemy, and have been more careful to protect than to attack.

I have preserved the common distribution of the plays into acts, though I believe it to be in almost all the plays void of authority. Some of those which are divided in the later editions have no division in the first folio, and some that are divided in the folio have no division in the preceding copies. The settled mode of the theatre requires four intervals in the play, but few, if any, of our authour's compositions can be properly distributed in that manner. An act is so much of the drama as passes without intervention of time or change of place. A pause makes a new act. In every real, and therefore in every imitative action, the intervals may be more or fewer, the restriction of five acts being accidental and arbitrary.[2] This *Shakespeare* knew, and this he practised; his plays were written and at first printed in one unbroken continuity, and ought now to be exhibited with short pauses, interposed as often as the scene is changed or any considerable time is required to pass. This method would at once quell a thousand absurdities.

In restoring the authour's works to their integrity I have considered the punctuation as wholly in my power;[3] for what could be their care of colons and commas who corrupted words and sentences? Whatever could be done by adjusting points is therefore silently performed, in some plays with much diligence,

---

[1] Pierre Daniel Huet (1630–1721): Johnson owned a copy of his *De Interpretatione* (1661).
[2] Cf. *Rambler*, clvi (3.434).
[3] Cf. Theobald (2.488).

in others with less; it is hard to keep a busy eye steadily fixed upon evanescent atoms, or a discursive mind upon evanescent truth.[1]

The same liberty has been taken with a few particles, or other words of slight effect. I have sometimes inserted or omitted them without notice. I have done that sometimes which the other editors have done always, and which indeed the state of the text may sufficiently justify.

The greater part of readers, instead of blaming us for passing trifles, will wonder that on mere trifles so much labour is expended, with such importance of debate and such solemnity of diction. To these I answer with confidence, that they are judging of an art which they do not understand; yet cannot much reproach them with their ignorance, nor promise that they would become in general, by learning criticism, more useful, happier, or wiser.

As I practised conjecture more I learned to trust it less; and after I had printed a few plays resolved to insert none of my own readings in the text. Upon this caution I now congratulate myself, for every day encreases my doubt of my emendations.

Since I have confined my imagination to the margin,[2] it must not be considered as very reprehensible if I have suffered it to play some freaks in its own dominion. There is no danger in conjecture, if it be proposed as conjecture; and while the text remains uninjured, those changes may be safely offered which are not considered even by him that offers them as necessary or safe.

If my readings are of little value they have not been ostentatiously displayed or importunately obtruded. I could have written longer notes, for the art of writing notes is not of difficult attainment. The work is performed, first by railing at the stupidity, negligence, ignorance, and asinine tastelessness of the former editors, and shewing from all that goes before and all that follows, the inelegance and absurdity of the old reading; then by proposing something which to superficial readers would seem specious, but which the editor rejects with indignation; then by producing the true reading, with a long paraphrase, and concluding with loud acclamations on the discovery, and a sober wish for the advancement and prosperity of genuine criticism.

All this may be done, and perhaps done sometimes without

---

[1] 'Evanescent': 'Vanishing; imperceptible; lessening beyond the perception of the senses'. 'Discursive': 'moving here and there; roving'.

[2] That is, to footnotes recording conjectures, rather than just emending the text.

impropriety. But I have always suspected that the reading is right which requires many words to prove it wrong; and the emendation wrong that cannot without so much labour appear to be right. The justness of a happy restoration strikes at once, and the moral precept may be well applied to criticism, *quod dubitas ne feceris*.[1]

To dread the shore which he sees spread with wrecks is natural to the sailor. I had before my eye so many critical adventures ended in miscarriage that caution was forced upon me. I encountered in every page Wit struggling with its own sophistry, and Learning confused by the multiplicity of its views. I was forced to censure those whom I admired, and could not but reflect, while I was dispossessing their emendations, how soon the same fate might happen to my own, and how many of the readings which I have corrected may be by some other editor defended and established.

> *Criticks I saw, that other's names efface,*
> *And fix their own, with labour, in the place;*
> *Their own, like others, soon their place resign'd,*
> *Or disappear'd, and left the first behind.*
>
> POPE.

That a conjectural critick should often be mistaken cannot be wonderful, either to others or himself, if it be considered that in his art there is no system, no principal and axiomatical truth that regulates subordinate positions.[2] His chance of errour is renewed at every attempt; an oblique view of the passage, a slight misapprehension of a phrase, a casual inattention to the parts connected, is sufficient to make him not only fail but fail ridiculously; and when he succeeds best he produces perhaps but one reading of many probable, and he that suggests another will always be able to dispute his claims.

It is an unhappy state, in which danger is hid under pleasure. The allurements of emendation are scarcely resistible. Conjecture has all the joy and all the pride of invention, and he that has once started a happy change is too much delighted to consider what objections may rise against it.

Yet conjectural criticism has been of great use in the learned world; nor is it my intention to depreciate a study that has exercised

---

[1] Pliny, *Epistles*, 1.18: 'when in doubt do nothing'.
[2] 'System': 'A scheme which reduces many things to regular dependence or co-operation'. 'Axiom': 'A proposition, evident at first sight, that cannot be made any plainer by demonstration'.

so many mighty minds from the revival of learning to our own age, from the bishop of *Aleria* to English *Bentley*.[1] The criticks on ancient authours have, in the exercise of their sagacity, many assistances which the editor of *Shakespeare* is condemned to want. They are employed upon grammatical and settled languages, whose construction contributes so much to perspicuity that *Homer* has fewer passages unintelligible than *Chaucer*. The words have not only a known regimen but invariable quantities, which direct and confine the choice. There are commonly more manuscripts than one; and they do not often conspire in the same mistakes. Yet *Scaliger* could confess to *Salmasius* how little satisfaction his emendations gave him. *Illudunt nobis conjecturæ nostræ, quarum nos pudet, posteaquam in meliores codices incidimus.*[2] And *Lipsius* could complain that criticks were making faults by trying to remove them, *Ut olim vitiis, ita nunc remediis laboratur.*[3] And indeed, where mere conjecture is to be used the emendations of *Scaliger* and *Lipsius*, notwithstanding their wonderful sagacity and erudition, are often vague and disputable, like mine or *Theobald*'s.

Perhaps I may not be more censured for doing wrong than for doing little; for raising in the publick expectations which at last I have not answered. The expectation of ignorance is indefinite, and that of knowledge is often tyrannical. It is hard to satisfy those who know not what to demand, or those who demand by design what they think impossible to be done. I have indeed disappointed no opinion more than my own; yet I have endeavoured to perform my task with no slight solicitude. Not a single passage in the whole work has appeared to me corrupt, which I have not attempted to restore; or obscure, which I have not endeavoured to illustrate. In many I have failed like others; and from many, after all my efforts I have retreated, and confessed the repulse. I have not passed over with affected superiority what is. equally difficult to the reader and to myself, but where I could not instruct him have owned my ignorance. I might easily have accumulated a mass of seeming learning upon easy scenes; but it ought not to be imputed to negligence that, where nothing was necessary, nothing

---

[1] Giovanni Andrea, a fifteenth-century librarian and editor; Dr Richard Bentley, the most distinguished English textual critic up to Johnson's time.
[2] *Epistolae* (1627), p. 534: 'Our conjectures make fools of us, putting us to shame, when later we hit upon better manuscripts' (tr. Sherbo).
[3] Preface to his edition of Tacitus (1581).

has been done, or that where others have said enough I have said no more.

Notes are often necessary, but they are necessary evils. Let him that is yet unacquainted with the powers of *Shakespeare*, and who desires to feel the highest pleasure that the drama can give, read every play from the first scene to the last, with utter negligence of all his commentators. When his fancy is once on the wing, let it not stoop at correction or explanation. When his attention is strongly engaged, let it disdain alike to turn aside to the name of *Theobald* and of *Pope*. Let him read on through brightness and obscurity, through integrity and corruption; let him preserve his comprehension of the dialogue and his interest in the fable. And when the pleasures of novelty have ceased let him attempt exactness; and read the commentators.

Particular passages are cleared by notes, but the general effect of the work is weakened. The mind is refrigerated by interruption; the thoughts are diverted from the principal subject; the reader is weary, he suspects not why; and at last throws away the book which he has too diligently studied.

Parts are not to be examined till the whole has been surveyed; there is a kind of intellectual remoteness necessary for the comprehension of any great work in its full design and its true proportions; a close approach shews the smaller niceties, but the beauty of the whole is discerned no longer.

It is not very grateful to consider how little the succession of editors has added to this authour's power of pleasing. He was read, admired, studied, and imitated, while he was yet deformed with all the improprieties which ignorance and neglect could accumulate upon him; while the reading was yet not rectified, nor his allusions understood; yet then did *Dryden* pronounce that *Shakespeare* 'was the man, who, of all modern and perhaps ancient poets, had the largest and most comprehensive soul. All the images of nature were still present to him, and he drew them not laboriously, but luckily. When he describes any thing, you more than see it, you feel it too. Those who accuse him to have wanted learning, give him the greater commendation: he was naturally learned: he needed not the spectacles of books to read nature; he looked inwards, and found her there. I cannot say he is every where alike; were he so, I should do him injury to compare him with the greatest of mankind. He is many times flat and insipid;

his comick wit degenerating into clenches, his serious swelling into bombast. But he is always great, when some great occasion is presented to him. No man can say, he ever had a fit subject for his wit, and did not then raise himself as high above the rest of poets,

Quantum lenta solent inter viburna cupressi.[1]

It is to be lamented that such a writer should want a commentary; that his language should become obsolete, or his sentiments obscure. But it is vain to carry wishes beyond the condition of human things; that which must happen to all has happened to *Shakespeare*, by accident and time; and more than has been suffered by any other writer since the use of types has been suffered by him through his own negligence of fame, or perhaps by that superiority of mind which despised its own performances when it compared them with its powers, and judged those works unworthy to be preserved which the criticks of following ages were to contend for the fame of restoring and explaining.

Among these candidates of inferior fame I am now to stand the judgment of the publick; and wish that I could confidently produce my commentary as equal to the encouragement which I have had the honour of receiving. Every work of this kind is by its nature deficient, and I should feel little solicitude about the sentence were it to be pronounced only by the skilful and the learned. [I, Sigs. A^r-E$_5$^{r}]

[From the NOTES]

[1] [On *The Tempest*, 1.1.26: *Gonzalo*. I have great comfort from this fellow]
It may be observed of *Gonzalo* that, being the only good Man that appears with the King, he is the only Man that preserves his Cheerfulness in the Wreck, and his Hope on the Island. (I, 4)

[2] [*Ibid.*, 1.2.321ff.: Caliban's curses]
Whence these criticks[2] derived the notion of a new language appropriated to *Caliban* I cannot find. They certainly mistook brutality

---

[1] See 1.138.
[2] This critical tradition derives from Dryden (1.260), Rowe (2.197), and many others, including Warburton (3.227). Johnson follows Holt (3.346) and Heath (4.552) in rejecting it.

of sentiment for uncouthness of words. *Caliban* had learned to speak of *Prospero* and his daughter, he had no names for the sun and moon before their arrival, and could not have invented a language of his own without more understanding than *Shakespeare* has thought it proper to bestow upon him. His diction is indeed somewhat clouded by the gloominess of his temper and the malignity of his purposes; but let any other being entertain the same thoughts and he will find them easily issue in the same expressions. (I, 21)

[3] [On *A Midsummer Night's Dream*, 1.2: *Enter Quince the carpenter*. . . .]
In this Scene *Shakespeare* takes advantage of his knowledge of the theatre to ridicule the prejudices and competitions of the Players. *Bottom*, who is generally acknowledged the principal Actor, declares his inclination to be for a tyrant, for a part of fury, tumult, and noise, such as every young man pants to perform when he first steps upon the Stage. The same *Bottom*, who seems bred in a tiring-room, has another histrionical passion. He is for engrossing every part, and would exclude his inferiors from all possibility of distinction. He is therefore desirous to play *Pyramus*, *Thisbe* and the *Lyon* at the same time. (I, 100)

[4] [*Ibid.*, 1.2.82; Bottom's list of beards]
Here *Bottom* again discovers a true genius for the Stage by his solicitude for propriety of dress, and his deliberation which beard to chuse among many beards, all unnatural. (I, 103)

[5] [*Ibid.*, 2.1.130ff.: 'with pretty and with swimming gait/ Following' Warburton reads 'Follying']
The foregoing Note is very ingenious, but since *follying* is a word of which I know not any example, and the Fairy's favourite might, without much licentiousness of language, be said to *follow* a ship that sailed in the direction of the coast, I think there is no sufficient reason for adopting it. The coinage of new words is a violent remedy, not to be used but in the last necessity. (I, 113)

[6] [*Ibid.*, 3.1.156: 'the fiery glow-worm's eyes']
I know not how *Shakespeare*, who commonly derived his knowledge of nature from his own observation, happened to place the

101

glow-worm's light in his eyes, which is only in his tail. (I, 132)

[7] [On *The Two Gentlemen of Verona*: Pope had found the style of this play to be 'less figurative and more natural than most' (2.415); Theobald found it one of Shakespeare's 'worst plays', yet 'less corrupted than any other'; Upton had denied Shakespeare's authorship (3.307)]
When I read this play I cannot but think that I discover, both in the serious and ludicrous scenes, the language and sentiments of *Shakespeare*. It is not indeed one of his most powerful effusions, it has neither many diversities of character, nor striking delineations of life, but it abounds in γνωμαὶ[1] beyond most of his plays, and few have more lines or passages which, singly considered, are eminently beautiful. I am yet inclined to believe that it was not very successful, and suspect that it has escaped corruption only because being seldom played it was less exposed to the hazards of transcription. (I, 179-80)

[8] [End-note to *The Two Gentlemen of Verona*]
In this play there is a strange mixture of knowledge and ignorance, of care and negligence. The versification is often excellent, the allusions are learned and just; but the authour conveys his heroes by sea from one inland town to another in the same country; he places the Emperour at *Milan* and sends his young men to attend him, but never mentions him more; he makes *Proteus*, after an interview with *Silvia*, say he has only seen her picture, and if we may credit the old copies he has by mistaking places left his scenery inextricable. The reason of all this confusion seems to be that he took his story from a novel which he sometimes followed, and sometimes forsook, sometimes remembred, and sometimes forgot. [2] (I, 259)

[9] [On *Measure for Measure;* Dramatis Personae ... Varrius, *a Gentleman*]
Varrius might be omitted, for he is only once spoken to, and says nothing. (I, 262)

---

[1] Sententiae, or quotable sayings.
[2] Cf. Mrs Lennox (4.130f.).

[10] [Head-note to *Measure for Measure*:]
There is perhaps not one of *Shakespeare*'s plays more darkened than this by the peculiarities of its Authour and the unskilfulness of its Editors, by distortions of phrase or negligence of transcription. (I, 263)

[11] [On *Measure for Measure*, 1.1.52: *Duke*. We have with a leaven'd and prepared choice/Proceeded to you.] [Warburton emended 'leaven'd' to 'leavel'd']
No emendation is necessary. *Leaven'd choice* is one of *Shakespeare*'s harsh[1] metaphors. His train of ideas seems to be this. *I have proceeded to you with choice* mature, concocted, fermented, *leaven'd*. When Bread is *leaven'd* it is left to ferment: a *leaven'd* choice is therefore a choice not hasty but considerate, not declared as soon as it fell into the imagination, but suffered to work long in the mind. Thus explained, it suits better with *prepared* than *levelled*. (I, 268)

[12] [*Ibid.*, 3.1.13ff.:

> *Duke.*   Thou art not noble;
> For all th'accommodations, that thou bear'st,
> Are nurs'd by baseness:]

Dr. *Warburton* is undoubtedly mistaken in supposing that by *baseness* is meant *self-love*, here assigned as the motive of all human actions. *Shakespeare* meant only to observe that a minute analysis of life at once destroys that splendour which dazzles the imagination. Whatever grandeur can display, or luxury enjoy, is procured by *baseness*, by offices of which the mind shrinks from the contemplation. All the delicacies of the table may be traced back to the shambles and the dunghill, all magnificence of building was hewn from the quarry, and all the pomp of ornaments dug from among the damps and darkness of the mine. (I, 313)

[13] [*Ibid.*, 3.1.17ff.:

> *Duke.*   Thy best of Rest is sleep,
> And that thou oft provok'st; yet grosly fear'st
> Thy death, which is no more.]

---

[1] Far-fetched, indecorous.

[Warburton claimed that this was an imitation of Cicero, but that Shakespeare had omitted 'the Epicurean insinuation ... , with great judgment'.]

Here Dr. *Warburton* might have found a sentiment worthy of his animadversion. I cannot without indignation find *Shakespeare* saying that *death is only sleep*, lengthening out his exhortation by a sentence which in the *Friar* is impious, in the reasoner is foolish, and in the poet trite and vulgar. (I, 314)

[14] [*Ibid.*, 3.1.32ff.:

> *Duke.* Thou hast nor youth, nor age;
> But as it were an after-dinner's sleep,
> Dreaming on both;]

This is exquisitely imagined. When we are young we busy ourselves in forming schemes for succeeding time, and miss the gratifications that are before us; when we are old we amuse the languour of age with the recollection of youthful pleasures or performances; so that our life, of which no part is filled with the business of the present time, resembles our dreams after dinner, when the events of the morning are mingled with the designs of the evening. (I, 314)

[15] [*Ibid.*, 3.1.114ff.:

> *Claudio.* If it were damnable, he being so wise,
> Why would he for the momentary trick
> Be perdurably fin'd?]

Shakespeare shows his knowledge of human nature in the conduct of *Claudio*. When *Isabella* first tells him of *Angelo*'s proposal he answers with honest indignation, agreeably to his settled principles, *thou shalt not do't*. But the love of life being permitted to operate, soon furnishes him with sophistical arguments: he believes it cannot be very dangerous to the soul since *Angelo*, who is so wise, will venture it. (I, 319–20)

[16] [*Ibid.*, 3.1.140ff.: *Isabella*. Is't not a kind of incest, to take life/From thine own sister's shame?]

In *Isabella*'s declamation there is something harsh, and something forced and far-fetched. But her indignation cannot be thought violent when we consider her not only as a virgin but as a nun.[1] (I, 321)

---

[1] Johnson is here disagreeing with Mrs Lennox: cf. 4.114f.

[17] [*Ibid.*, 5.1.444ff.:]

The *Duke* has justly observed that *Isabel* is *importuned against all sense* to solicit for *Angelo*, yet here *against all sense* she solicits for him. Her argument is extraordinary.

> *A due sincerity govern'd his deeds,*
> *'Till he did look on me; since it is so,*
> *Let him not die.*

That *Angelo* had committed all the crimes charged against him, as far as he could commit them, is evident. The only *intent* which *his act did not overtake* was the defilement of *Isabel*. Of this *Angelo* was only intentionally guilty.

Angelo's crimes were such as must sufficiently justify punishment, whether its end be to secure the innocent from wrong, or to deter guilt by example; and I believe every reader feels some indignation when he finds him spared.[1] From what extenuation of his crime can *Isabel*, who yet supposes her brother dead, form any plea in his favour? *Since he was good 'till he looked on me, let him not die.* I am afraid our Varlet Poet intended to inculcate that women think ill of nothing that raises the credit of their beauty, and are ready, however virtuous, to pardon any act which they think incited by their own charms. (I, 377–8)

[18] [From the end-note to *Measure for Measure*]

Of this play the light or comick part is very natural and pleasing,[2] but the grave scenes, if a few passages be excepted, have more labour than elegance. The plot is rather intricate than artful. The time of the action is indefinite; some time, we know not how much, must have elapsed between the recess of the *Duke* and the imprisonment of *Claudio*; for he must have learned the story of *Mariana* in his disguise, or he delegated his power to a man already known to be corrupted.[3] The unities of action and place are sufficiently preserved.[4] (I, 382)

[19] [On *The Merchant of Venice*, 2.7.78f.:]

The old quarto Edition of 1600 has no distribution of acts, but proceeds from the beginning to the end in an unbroken tenour.

---

1 Cf. Mrs Lennox (4.110f., 116f.).
2 Contra-Lennox: cf. 4.110, 112.
3 Cf. Mrs Lennox (4.112f.).
4 Contra-Lennox: cf. 4.111f.

This play therefore, having been probably divided without authority by the publishers of the first folio, lies open to a new regulation if any more commodious division can be proposed. The story is itself so wildly incredible, and the changes of the scene so frequent and capricious, that the probability of action does not deserve much care; yet it may be proper to observe that by concluding the second act here time is given for *Bassanio's* passage to *Belmont*. (I, 422)

[20] [From the end-note to *The Merchant of Venice*]
   Of *The Merchant of Venice* the stile is even and easy, with few peculiarities of diction or anomalies of construction. The comick part raises laughter, and the serious fixes expectation. The probability of either one or the other story cannot be maintained. The union of two actions in one event is in this drama eminently happy. *Dryden* was much pleased with his own address in connecting the two plots of his *Spanish Friar*, which yet, I believe, the critick will find excelled by this play. (I, 488)

[21] [On *As You Like It*, 3.2.137: 'Atalanta's better part']
I know not well what could be the better part of *Atalanta* here ascribed to *Rosalind*. Of the *Atalanta* most celebrated, and who therefore must be intended here, where she has no epithet of discrimination the *better part* seems to have been her heels, and the worse part was so bad that *Rosalind* would not thank her lover for the comparison. There is a more obscure *Atalanta*, a Huntress and a Heroine, but of her nothing bad is recorded, and therefore I know not which was the better part. *Shakespeare* was no despicable Mythologist, yet he seems here to have mistaken some other character for that of *Atalanta*. (II, 54)

[22] [End-note to *As You like It*]
   Of this play the fable is wild and pleasing. I know not how the ladies will approve the facility with which both *Rosalind* and *Celia* give away their hearts. To *Celia* much may be forgiven for the heroism of her friendship. The character of *Jaques* is natural and well preserved. The comick dialogue is very sprightly, with less mixture of low buffoonery than in some other plays; and the graver part is elegant and harmonious. By hastening to the end of his work *Shakespeare* suppressed the dialogue between the usurper

and the hermit, and lost an opportunity of exhibiting a moral lesson in which he might have found matter worthy of his highest powers. (II, 108)

[23] [On *Love's Labour's Lost*, 1.1.147 ff.:

> *Biron.* Necessity will make us all forsworn
> Three thousand times within this three years' space:]

Biron, amidst his extravagancies, speaks with great justness against the folly of vows. They are made without sufficient regard to the variations of life, and are therefore broken by some unforeseen necessity. They proceed commonly from a presumptuous confidence, and a false estimate of human power. (II, 117–18)

[24] [*Ibid.*, 5.1.2.: *Nathaniel.* I praise God for you, Sir, your reasons at dinner have been sharp and sententious;]
I know not well what degree of respect *Shakespeare* intends to obtain for this vicar, but he has here put into his mouth a finished representation of colloquial excellence. It is very difficult to add anything to this character of the school-master's table-talk, and perhaps all the precepts of *Castiglione* will scarcely be found to comprehend a rule for conversation so justly delineated, so widely dilated, and so nicely limited.

It may be proper just to note that *reason* here, and in many other places, signifies *discourse*; and that *audacious* is used in a good sense for *spirited, animated, confident. Opinion* is the same with *obstinacy* or *opiniâtreté.* (II, 181)

[25] [End-note to *Love's Labour's Lost*]
In this play, which all the editors have concurred to censure, and some have rejected as unworthy of our Poet, it must be confessed that there are many passages mean, childish, and vulgar; and some which ought not to have been exhibited, as we are told they were, to a maiden queen. But there are scattered, through the whole, many sparks of genius; nor is there any play that has more evident marks of the hand of *Shakespeare*.[1] (II, 224)

[26] [On *The Winter's Tale*, 3.1.1f.: *Cleomenes.* The climate's delicate, the air most sweet,/Fertile the isle] [Warburton (2.501)

---

[1] Cf. Gildon (2.242).

emended *isle* to *soil*, since the temple of Apollo was inland.]
Shakespeare is little careful of geography. There is no need of this emendation in a play of which the whole plot depends upon a geographical errour, by which *Bohemia* is supposed to be a maritime country. (II, 273)

[27] [*Ibid.*, 3.2.150ff.: the remorse of Leontes]
This vehement retraction of *Leontes*, accompanied with the confession of more crimes than he was suspected of, is agreeable to our daily experience of the vicissitudes of violent tempers, and the eruptions of minds oppressed with guilt. (II, 280)

[28] [*Ibid.*, 4.4.21f.: *Perdita.* How would he look, to see his work, so noble/Vilely bound up!]
It is impossible for any man to rid his mind of his profession. The authourship of *Shakespeare* has supplied him with a metaphor, which rather than he would lose it he has put with no great propriety into the mouth of a country maid. Thinking of his own works his mind passed naturally to the Binder. I am glad that he has no hint at an Editor. (II, 298)

[29] [End-note to *The Winter's Tale*]
This play, as Dr. *Warburton* justly observes, is, with all its absurdities, very entertaining. The character of *Autolycus* is very naturally conceived, and strongly represented. (II, 349)

[30] [On *Twelfth Night*, 1.2.41f.: *Viola.* O, that I serv'd that lady ...]
... *Viola* seems to have formed a very deep design with very little premeditation: she is thrown by shipwreck on an unknown coast, hears that the prince is a batchelor, and resolves to supplant the lady whom he courts. (II, 357)

[31] [*Ibid.*, 1.2.55: *Viola.* I'll serve this Duke]
Viola is an excellent schemer, never at a loss; if she cannot serve the lady she will serve the Duke. (II, 358)

[32] [*Ibid.*, 2.3.25: *Clown.* I did impeticos thy gratility]
This, Sir T. *Hanmer* tells us, is the same with *impocket thy gratuity.* He is undoubtedly right; but we must read, *I did* impeticoat *thy*

gratuity. The fools were kept in long coats, to which the allusion is made. There is yet much in this dialogue which I do not understand. (II, 380)

[33] [*Ibid.*, 2.5.55: *Malvolio.* wind up my watch]
In our authour's time watches were very uncommon. When *Guy Faux* was taken it was urged as circumstance of suspicion that a watch was found upon him. (II, 395)

[34] [End-note to *Twelfth Night*]
    This play is in the graver part elegant and easy, and in some of the lighter scenes exquisitely humorous. *Ague-cheek* is drawn with great propriety, but his character is in a great measure that of natural fatuity, and is therefore not the proper prey of a satirist. The soliloquy of *Malvolio* is truly comick; he is betrayed to ridicule merely by his pride. The marriage of *Olivia* and the succeeding perplexity, though well enough contrived to divert on the stage, wants credibility, and fails to produce the proper instruction required in the drama, as it exhibits no just picture of life. (II, 448)

[35] [On *The Merry Wives of Windsor*, 3.4.13f.; *Fenton.* ... thy father's wealth/Was the first motive that I woo'd thee, *Anne*:]
Some light may be given to those who shall endeavour to calculate the encrease of *English* wealth by observing that *Latymer*, in the time of *Edward* VI., mentions it as a proof of his father's prosperity *That though but a yeoman, he gave his daughters five pounds each for her portion.* At the latter end of *Elizabeth* seven hundred pounds were such a temptation to courtship as made all other motives suspected. *Congreve* makes twelve thousand pounds more than a counterbalance to the affectation of *Belinda.* No poet would now fly his favourite character at less than fifty thousand. (II, 514)

[36] [*Ibid.*, 3.5.133: *Ford.* ... If I have horns to make one mad, let the proverb go with me, I'll be horn-mad.]
There is no image which our authour appears so fond of as that of cuckold's horns. Scarcely a light character is introduced that does not endeavour to produce merriment by some allusion to horned husbands. As he wrote his plays for the stage rather than the press he perhaps reviewed them seldom, and did not observe this repetition; or finding the jest, however frequent, still successful did not think correction necessary. (II, 522)

[37] [*Ibid.*, 4.1]
This is a very trifling scene, of no use to the plot, and I should think of no great delight to the audience; but *Shakespeare* best knew what would please. (II, 523)

[38] [*Ibid.*, 4.2.171: *Evans. I spy a great peard under her muffler.*]
As the second stratagem by which *Falstaff* escapes is much the grosser of the two, I wish it had been practised first. It is very unlikely that *Ford*, having been so deceived before, and knowing that he had been deceived, would suffer him to escape in so slight a disguise. (II, 531)

[39] [*Ibid.*, 4.3.10: *Host. I have turn'd away my other guests; they must come off*]
To come off signifies in our authour sometimes *to be uttered with spirit and volubility.* In this place it seems to mean what is in our time expressed by *to come down*, to pay liberally and readily. These accidental and colloquial senses are the disgrace of language, and the plague of commentators. (II, 533)

[40] [*Ibid.*, 4.5.115f.: 'serve heaven . . . cross'd']
The great fault of this play is the frequency of expressions so profane that no necessity of preserving character can justify them. There are laws of higher authority than those of criticism. (II, 541)

[41] [On *The Taming of the Shrew*, 1.2.109: *Grumio* . . . an' he begin once, he'll rail—In his rope tricks]
This is obscure. Sir *Thomas Hanmer*[1] reads *he'll rail in his* rhetorick; *I'll tell you*, &c. Rhetorick agrees very well with *figure* in the succeeding part of the speech, yet I am inclined to believe that *Rope-tricks* is the true word. (III, 27)

[42] [From the end-note to *The Taming of the Shrew*]
   Of this play the two plots are so well united that they can hardly be called two without injury to the art with which they are interwoven. The attention is entertained with all the variety of a double plot, yet is not distracted by unconnected incidents.
   The part between *Catharine* and *Petruchio* is eminently spritely and diverting. At the marriage of *Bianca* the arrival of the real

[1] The emendation was in fact Theobald's: see 2.458.

father perhaps produces more perplexity than pleasure. The whole play is very popular and diverting. (III, 99)

[43] [On *The Comedy of Errors*, 3.1.82: *Dromio of Ephesus.* Am I so round with you as you with me,/That like a football you do spurn me thus?]
He plays upon the word *round*, which signified *spherical* applied to himself, and *unrestrained*, or *free in speech* or *action* spoken of his mistress. So the king in *Hamlet* bids the queen be *round* with her son. (III, 115)

[44] [*Ibid.*, 3.2.121f.: 'Where *France?*'—'In her forehead; arm'd and reverted, making war against her hair.' Theobald chose the Folio reading, 'Heir', suggesting an allusion to the dispute over the accession to the French throne in 1589, when Henry IV was the heir to Henry III.]
With this correction and explication Dr. *Warburton* concurs, and Sir *T. Hanmer* thinks an equivocation intended, though he retains *hair* in the text. Yet surely they have all lost the sense by looking beyond it. Our authour, in my opinion, only sports with an allusion in which he takes too much delight, and means that his mistress had the *French* disease. The ideas are rather too offensive to be dilated.[1] By a forehead *armed*, he means covered with incrusted eruptions: by *reverted*, he means having the hair turning backward. An equivocal word must have senses applicable to both the subjects to which it is applied. Both *forehead* and *France* might in some sort make war against their *hair*, but how did the *forehead* make war against its *heir*? The sense which I have given immediately occurred to me and will, I believe, arise to every reader who is contented with the meaning that lies before him, without sending out conjecture in search of refinements. (III, 135–6)

[45] [*Ibid.*, 4.2.39f.:

> *Dromio of Syracuse.* A hound that runs counter, and yet draws
> dry-foot well;
> One, that, before the judgment, carries poor souls to hell.]

To *run counter* is to *run backward*, by mistaking the course of the animal persued; to *draw dry-foot* is, I believe, to persue by the *track*

---
[1] 'Dilate': 'To speak largely and copiously'; here, 'to discuss in detail'.

111

or *prick of the foot*; to *run counter* and *draw dry-foot well* are, therefore, inconsistent. The jest consists in the ambiguity of the word *counter*, which means the *wrong way in the chase*, and a *prison* in *London*. The officer that arrested him was a serjeant of the *counter*. For the congruity of this jest with the Scene of action, let our authour answer. (III, 144)

[46] [On *Much Ado About Nothing*, 1.3.11: *Don John*. I cannot hide what I am: I must be sad when I have cause, and smile at no man's jests.]
This is one of our authour's natural touches. An envious and unsocial mind, too proud to give pleasure, and too sullen to receive it, always endeavours to hide its malignity from the world and from itself under the plainness of simple honesty, or the dignity of haughty independence. (III, 186)

[47] [*Ibid.*, 2.1.42ff.]
Of the two next speeches Mr. *Warburton* says *All this impious nonsense thrown to the bottom is the players, and foisted in without rhyme or reason.* He therefore puts them in the margin. They do not deserve indeed so honourable a place, yet I am afraid they are too much in the manner of our authour, who is sometimes trying to purchase merriment at too dear a rate. (III, 190)

[48] [*Ibid.*, 2.1.286: *Beatrice*. Thus goes every one to the world but I, and I am sun-burn'd;]
What is it, *to go to the world?* perhaps, to enter by marriage into a settled state: but why is the unmarry'd lady *sunburnt?* I believe we should read, *Thus goes every one to the* wood *but I, and I am sunburnt*. Thus does every one but I find a shelter, and I am left exposed to wind and *sun. The nearest way to the* wood, is a phrase for the readiest means to any end. It is said of a woman who accepts a worse match than those which she had refused that she has passed through the *wood*, and at last taken a crooked stick. But conjectural criticism has always something to abate its confidence. *Shakespeare*, in *All's well that ends well*, uses the phrase *to go to the world* for *marriage*. So that my emendation depends only on the opposition of *wood* to *sunburnt*. (III, 199)

[49] [On *All's Well That Ends Well*, 2.3.11ff.]

> *Parolles.* So I say, both of *Galen* and *Paracelsus.*
> *Lafeu.*   Of all the learned and authentick fellows—
> *Parolles.* Right, so I say.

As the whole merriment of this scene consists in the pretensions of *Parolles* to knowledge and sentiments which he has not, I believe here are two passages in which the words and sense are bestowed upon him by the copies, which the author gave to *Lafeu.* I read this passage thus,

> *Laf.* To be relinquished of the artists—
> *Par.* So I say.
> *Laf.* Both of *Galen* and *Paracelsus*, of all the
>   learned and authentick fellows—
> *Par.* Right, so I say.   (III, 318)

[50] [*Ibid.*, 4.3.30ff.: 1 *Lord.* I would gladly have him [*Bertram*] see his [*Parolles'*] company anatomiz'd; that he might take a measure of his own Judgment, wherein so curiously he hath set this counterfeit.]
This is a very just and moral reason. *Bertram*, by finding how erroneously he has judged, will be less confident, and more easily moved by admonition. (III, 364)

[51] [*Ibid.*, 5.2.50: *Lafeu* [to Parolles]. tho' you are a fool and a knave, you shall eat.]
Parolles has many of the lineaments of *Falstaff*, and seems to be the character which *Shakespeare* delighted to draw, a fellow that had more wit than virtue. Though justice required that he should be detected and exposed, yet his *vices sit so fit in him* that he is not at last suffered to starve. (III, 384)

[52] [*Ibid.*, 5.3.21: *King.* We're reconcil'd, and the first view shall kill/All repetition]
The first interview shall put an end to all recollection of the past. Shakespeare is now hastening to the end of the play, finds his matter sufficient to fill up his remaining scenes, and therefore, as on other such occasions, contracts his dialogue and precipitates his action. Decency required that *Bertram*'s double crime of cruelty and disobedience, joined likewise with some hypocrisy, should raise more resentment; and that though his mother might easily forgive him, his king should more pertinaciously vindicate his own

authority and *Helen*'s merit; of all this *Shakespeare* could not be ignorant, but *Shakespeare* wanted to conclude his play. (III, 386)

[53] [*Ibid.*, 5.3.294ff.]
This dialogue is too long, since the audience already knew the whole transaction; nor is there any reason for puzzling the king and playing with his passions; but it was much easier than to make a pathetical interview between *Helen* and her husband, her mother, and the king. (III, 397)

[54] [End-note to *All's Well That Ends Well*]
   This play has many delightful scenes, though nor sufficiently probable, and some happy characters, though not new not produced by any deep knowledge of human nature. *Parolles* is a boaster and a coward, such as has always been the sport of the stage, but perhaps never raised more laughter or contempt than in the hands of *Shakespeare*.
   I cannot reconcile my heart to *Bertram*; a man noble without generosity, and young without truth; who marries *Helen* as a coward, and leaves her as a profligate: when she is dead by his unkindness, sneaks home to a second marriage, is accused by a woman whom he has wronged, defends himself by falshood, and is dismissed to happiness.
   The story of *Bertram* and *Diana* had been told before of *Mariana* and *Angelo*, and, to confess the truth, scarcely merited to be heard a second time.
   The story is copied from a novel of *Boccace*, which may be read in *Shakespear Illustrated*, with remarks not more favourable to *Bertram* than my own. (III, 399)

[55] [On *King John*, 1.1.27f.:

> *K. John.* So, hence! Be thou the trumpet of our wrath,
> And sullen presage of your own decay.]

By the epithet *sullen*, which cannot be applied to a trumpet, it is plain that our authour's imagination had now suggested a new idea. It is as if he had said, be a *trumpet* to alarm with our invasion, be a *bird* of *ill omen* to croak out the prognostick of your own ruin. (III, 405)

[56] [*Ibid.*, 3.1.68f.: *Constance*. To me, and to the state of my great grief,/Let kings assemble.]

In *Much Ado about Nothing* the father of Hero, depressed by her disgrace, declares himself so subdued by grief that *a thread may lead him*. How is it that grief in *Leonato* and lady *Constance* produces effects directly opposite, and yet both agreeable to nature? Sorrow softens the mind while it is yet warmed by hope, but hardens it when it is congealed by despair. Distress, while there remains any prospect of relief, is weak and flexible, but when no succour remains is fearless and stubborn; angry alike at those that injure and at those that do not help; careless to please where nothing can be gained, and fearless to offend when there is nothing further to be dreaded. Such was this writer's knowledge of the passions. (III, 440)

[57] [*Ibid.*, 3.4.61f.:

> *King Philip*. Bind up those tresses: Oh, what love I note
> In the fair multitude of those her hairs! ...]

It was necessary that *Constance* should be interrupted, because a passion so violent cannot be born long. I wish the following speeches had been equally happy; but they only serve to shew how difficult it is to maintain the pathetick long. (III, 459)

[58] [*Ibid.*, 4.2.231ff.: King John's wish that Hubert had refused to carry out his orders to murder Arthur]

There are many touches of nature in this conference of *John* with *Hubert*. A man engaged in wickedness would keep the profit to himself, and transfer the guilt to his accomplice. These reproaches vented against *Hubert* are not the words of art or policy, but the eruptions of a mind swelling with consciousness of a crime, and desirous of discharging its misery on another.

This account of the timidity of guilt is drawn *ab ipsis recessibus mentis*, from an intimate knowledge of mankind, particularly that line in which he says that *to have bid him tell his tale* in *express* words would have *struck him dumb*; nothing is more certain than that bad men use all the arts of fallacy upon themselves, palliate their actions to their own minds by gentle terms, and hide themselves from their own detection in ambiguities and subterfuges. (III, 477)

[59] [From the end-note to *King John*]

The tragedy of *King John*, though not written with the utmost power of *Shakespeare*, is varied with a very pleasing interchange of incidents and characters. The Lady's grief is very affecting, and the character of the *Bastard* contains that mixture of greatness and levity which this authour delighted to exhibit. ... (III, 503)

[60] [On *Richard II*, 1.3.227f.:

> *Gaunt*. Shorten my days thou canst with sullen sorrow,
> And pluck nights from me, but not lend a morrow.]

It is matter of very melancholy consideration, that all human advantages confer more power of doing evil than good. (IV, 21)

[61] [*Ibid.*, 1.3.272ff.: a journeyman to grief]
I am afraid our authour in this place designed a very poor quibble, as *journey* signifies both *travel* and a *day's work*. However, he is not to be censured for what he himself rejected.[1] (IV, 22)

[62] [*Ibid.*, 2.4: *Enter* Salisbury, *and a Captain*.]
Here is a scene so unartfully and irregularly thrust into an improper place that I cannot but suspect it accidentally transposed; which, when the scenes were written on single pages, might easily happen in the wildness of *Shakespeare*'s drama. This dialogue was, in the authour's draught, probably the second scene of the ensuing act, and there I would advise the reader to insert it, though I have not ventured on so bold a change. My conjecture is not so presumptuous as may be thought. The play was not, in *Shakespeare*'s time, broken into acts; the two editions published before his death exhibit only a sequence of scenes from the beginning to the end, without any hint of a pause of action. In a drama so desultory and erratick, left in such a state, transpositions might easily be made. (IV, 49)

[63] [*Ibid.*, 3.2.93ff.: *Richard*. The worst is worldly loss thou canst unfold]
It seems to be the design of the poet to raise *Richard* to esteem in his fall, and consequently to interest the reader in his favour. He gives him only passive fortitude, the virtue of a confessor rather

---

[1] This passage was supplied by Theobald from the Quarto text, since it is not in the Folio. Johnson therefore imagines that it was 'expunged in the revision' by Shakespeare.

than of a king. In his prosperity we saw him imperious and oppressive, but in his distress he is wise, patient, and pious. (IV, 55)

[64] [*Ibid.*, 3.3.155–70: Richard's thought of being buried 'in the king's high way ... where subject's feet/May hourly trample [*] on their sovereign's head' ...]
Shakespeare is very apt to deviate from the *pathetick* to the *ridiculous*. Had the speech of *Richard* ended at this line [*] it had exhibited the natural language of submissive misery, conforming its intention to the present fortune, and calmly ending its purposes in death. (IV, 66)

[65] [*Ibid.*, 4.1.181ff.: *Richard*. Now is this golden crown like a deep well,/That owes two buckets ...]
This is a comparison not easily accommodated to the subject, nor very naturally introduced. The best part is this line, in which he makes the usurper the *empty* bucket. (IV, 79)

[66] [*Ibid.*, 4.1.322f.: Carlisle's prediction, 'The woe's to come']
This pathetick denunciation shews that *Shakespeare* intended to impress his auditors with dislike of the deposal of *Richard*. (IV, 83)

[67] [*Ibid.*, 5.1.46ff.: Richard's conceit of 'the senseless brands' weeping in sympathy]
The poet should have ended this speech with the foregoing line, and have spared his childish prattle about the fire. (IV, 86)

[68] [From the end-note to *Richard II*]
This play is one of those which *Shakespeare* has apparently revised; but as success in works of invention is not always proportionate to labour, it is not finished at last with the happy force of some other of his tragedies, nor can be said much to affect the passions or enlarge the understanding. (IV, 105)

[69] [On 1 *Henry IV*, 1.1.5f.:

> *King Henry*. No more the thirsty entrance of this Soil
> Shall *damp* her lips with her own children's blood.]

[Rowe read 'damp'; Warburton:[1] 'This nonsense should be read, *shall* TREMPE, *i.e.* moisten']

[1] See 3.237

117

That these lines are absurd is soon discovered, but how this nonsense will be made sense is not so easily told; surely not by reading *trempe*, for what means he that says *the thirsty* entrance *of this* Soil *shall no more* trempe *her lips with her children's blood*, more than he that says *it shall not* damp *her lips*? To suppose the *entrance of the soil* to mean the *entrance* of a King upon *Dominion*, and King *Henry* to predict that *Kings shall enter hereafter without bloodshed*, is to give words such a latitude of meaning that no nonsense can want a congruous interpretation.

The antient copies neither have *trempe* nor damp; the first 4to of 1599, that of 1622, the Folio of 1623, and the 4to of 1639, all read,

> *No more the thirsty entrance of this soil*
> *Shall* daube *her lips with her own children's blood.*

The Folios of 1632 and 1664 read, by an apparent errour of the press, *Shall* damb *her lips*, from which the later editors have idly adopted *damp*. The old reading helps the editor no better than the new, nor can I satisfactorily reform the passage. I think that *thirsty entrance* must be wrong, yet know not what to offer. We may read, but not very elegantly,

> *No more the thirsty* entrails *of this soil*
> *Shall* daubed be *with her own childrens' blood.*

The relative *her* is inaccurately used in both readings; but to regard sense more than grammar is familiar to our authour.

We may suppose a verse or two lost between these two lines. This is a cheap way of palliating an editor's inability; but I believe such omissions are more frequent in *Shakespeare* than is commonly imagined. (IV, 110)

[70] [*Ibid.*, 1.2.201ff.: *Prince Henry*. So, when this loose behaviour I throw off . . .]
. . . This speech is very artfully introduced to keep the Prince from appearing vile in the opinion of the audience; it prepares them for his future reformation; and, what is yet more valuable, exhibits a natural picture of a great mind offering excuses to itself, and palliating those follies which it can neither justify nor forsake. (IV, 123)

[71] [*Ibid.*, 1.3.201ff.:

Hotspur. By heaven, methinks, it were an easy leap,
To pluck bright honour from the pale-fac'd moon]

Though I am very far from condemning this speech with *Gildon* and *Theobald*, as *absolute madness*, yet I cannot find in it that profundity of reflection and beauty of allegory which the learned commentator has endeavoured to display.[1] This sally of *Hotspur* may be, I think, soberly and rationally vindicated as the violent eruption of a mind inflated with ambition and fired with resentment; as the boasted clamour of a man able to do much, and eager to do more; as the hasty motion of turbulent desire; as the dark expression of indetermined thoughts. (IV, 133–4)

[72] [*Ibid.*, 1.3.209: He apprehends a world of figures here]
Figure is here used equivocally. As it is applied to *Hotspur*'s speech it is a *rhetorical mode*; as opposed to *form*, it means *appearance* or *shape*. (IV, 134)

[73] [*Ibid.*, 2.4: *Enter Francis the drawer.*]
This scene, helped by the distraction of the drawer and grimaces of the prince, may entertain upon the stage, but affords not much delight to the reader. The authour has judiciously made it short. (IV, 152)

[74] [*Ibid.*, 2.4.375: *Falstaff*. I will do it in King *Cambyses'* vein]
I question if *Shakespeare* had ever seen this tragedy; for there is a remarkable peculiarity of measure which, when he professed to speak in *King* Cambyses' *vein*, he would hardly have missed if he had known it. (IV, 166)

[75] [*Ibid.*, 2.4.482: *Prince Henry*. Go, hide thee behind the arras]
The bulk of *Falstaff* made him not the fittest to be concealed behind the hangings, but every poet sacrifices something to the scenery; if *Falstaff* had not been hidden he could not have been found asleep, nor had his pockets searched. (IV, 170)

[76] [*Ibid.*, 3.3.26: *Falstaff* [to Bardolph]. thou art the knight of the burning lamp.]
This is a natural picture. Every man who feels in himself the pain

[1] See Warburton (3.237f.).

119

of deformity however, like this merry knight, he may affect to make sport with it among those whom it is his interest to please, is ready to revenge any hint of contempt upon one whom he can use with freedom. (IV, 188)

[77] [*Ibid.*, 3.3.112f.: *Falstaff*. There's no more faith in thee than in a stew'd prune; no more truth in thee than in a drawn Fox]
The propriety of these similies I am not sure that I fully under-stand.[1] A *stewed prune* has the appearance of a prune, but has no taste. A *drawn fox*, that is, an *exenterated fox* has the form of a fox without his powers. I think Dr. *Warburton*'s explication wrong, which makes a *drawn fox* to mean a fox *often hunted*; though to *draw* is a hunter's term for persuit by the track. My interpretation makes the *fox* suit better to the *prune*. These are very slender disquisitions, but such is the task of a commentator. (IV, 191)

[78] [*Ibid.*, 4.1.97ff.: All furnish'd, all in arms ...]
... A more lively representation of young men ardent for enter-prize perhaps no writer has ever given. (IV, 198–9)

[79] [*Ibid.*, 4.2.11: *Falstaff*. I am a sowc'd gurnet.]
I believe a *sowced gurnet* is a *pickled anchovy*. Much of *Falstaff*'s humour consists in comparing himself to somewhat little.[2] (IV, 201)

[80] [*Ibid.*, 5.1.89ff.: *Prince Henry*. More active valiant, or more valiant-young]
Sir *T. Hanmer* reads more *valued* young. I think the present gingle has more of *Shakespeare*. (IV, 213)

[81] [*Ibid.*, 5.4.107: *Prince Henry*. Death hath not struck so fair a Deer to day]
This is the reading of the first edition, and of the other quartos. The first folio has *fat*, which was followed by all the editors.

There is in these lines a very natural mixture of the serious and ludicrous produced by the view of *Percy* and *Falstaff*. I wish all play on words had been forborn. (IV, 226)

---

[1] See Steevens's explanation in the 1773 edition: No. 240 below, Note 37.
[2] Johnson corrected this definition in the Appendix, Note 232 below. The note was omitted in the 1773 edition.

[82] [On 2 *Henry IV*, Induction 1ff.:

> *Rumour.* Open your ears; for which of you will stop
> The vent of hearing, when loud Rumour speaks?]

This speech of *Rumour* is not inelegant or unpoetical, but is wholly useless, since we are told nothing which the first scene does not clearly and naturally discover. The only end of such prologues is to inform the audience of some facts previous to the action, of which they can have no knowledge from the persons of the drama. (IV, 233)

[83] [Head-note to 2 *Henry IV*]

Mr. *Upton* thinks these two plays improperly called the *First* and *Second parts* of *Henry* the *fourth.* The first play ends, he says, with the peaceful settlement of *Henry* in the kingdom by the defeat of the rebels.[1] This is hardly true, for the rebels are not yet finally suppressed. The second, he tells us, shews *Henry* the *fifth* in the various lights of a good-natured rake, till on his father's death he assumes a more manly character. This is true; but this representation gives us no idea of a dramatick action. These two plays will appear to every reader who shall peruse them without ambition of critical discoveries to be so connected that the second is merely a sequel to the first; to be two only because they are too long to be one. (IV, 235)

[84] [*Ibid.*, 2.1.57f.: *Falstaff.* Away, you scullion, you rampallion, you fustilarian! I'll tickle your catastrophe.]
This speech is given to the *Page* in all the editions to the folio of 1664. It is more proper for *Falstaff*, but that the boy must not stand quite silent and useless on the stage. (IV, 259)

[85] [*Ibid.*, 2.2.163ff.: Hal and Poins's plot to disguise as drawers]
This was a plot very unlikely to succeed where the *Prince* and the drawers were all known, but it produces merriment, which our authour found more useful than probability. (IV, 269)

[86] [*Ibid.*, 2.4.44ff.: *Falstaff.* ... the Diseases, *Dol*, we catch of you. ... Your brooches, pearls, and owches]
I believe *Falstaff* gives these splendid names as we give that of

[1] See 3.294.

carbuncle, to something very different from gems and ornaments, but the passage deserves not a laborious research. (IV, 275)

[87] [*Ibid.*, 3.2.272ff.: *Shallow*. . . . (I was then Sir *Dagonet* in *Arthur*'s Show)]
The story of Sir *Dagonet* is to be found in *La Mort d' Arthure*, an old romance much celebrated in our authour's time, or a little before it. . . . In this romance Sir *Dagonet* is King *Arthur*'s fool. *Shakespeare* would not have shewn his *justice* capable of representing any higher character. (IV, 300–1)

[88] [*Ibid.*, 4.1.122f.: *Lancaster*. Some guard these traitors to the block of death.]
It cannot but raise some indignation to find this horrible violation of faith passed over thus slightly by the poet, without any note of censure or detestation.[1] (IV, 317)

[89] [*Ibid.*, 4.3.86ff.: *Falstaff*. Good faith, this same young sober-blooded Boy doth not love me; nor a man cannot make him laugh.]
Falstaff speaks here like a veteran in life. The young prince did not love him, and he despaired to gain his affection, for he could not make him laugh. Men only become friends by community of pleasures. He who cannot be softened into gayety cannot easily be melted into kindness. (IV, 320)

[90] [*Ibid.*, 4.5.129: *King Henry*. *England* shall double gild his treble guilt] [Warburton pronounced this 'Evidently the nonsense of some foolish player'.]
I know not why this commentator should speak with so much confidence what he cannot know, or determine so positively what so capricious a writer as our poet might either deliberately or wantonly produce. This line is indeed such as disgraces a few that precede and follow it, but it suits well enough with the *daggers hid in thought, and whetted on the flinty hearts*; [4.5.107f.] and the answer which the prince makes, and which is applauded for wisdom, is not of a strain much higher than this ejected line. (IV, 331)

[91] [*Ibid.*, 5.5.64ff.: *King Henry V*. Till then I banish thee, on pain of death. . . .]

[1] Cf. Heath (4.556f.).

Mr. *Rowe* observes that many readers lament to see *Falstaff* so hardly used by his old friend.[1] But if it be considered that the fat knight has never uttered one sentiment of generosity, and with all his power of exciting mirth has nothing in him that can be esteemed, no great pain will be suffered from the reflection that he is compelled to live honestly, and maintained by the king with a promise of advancement when he shall deserve it.

I think the poet more blameable for *Poins*, who is always represented as joining some virtues with his vices, and is therefore treated by the prince with apparent distinction. Yet he does nothing in the time of action, and though after the bustle is over he is again a favourite, at last vanishes without notice. *Shakespeare* certainly lost him by heedlessness, in the multiplicity of his characters, the variety of his action, and his eagerness to end the play. (IV, 353)

[92] [*Ibid.*, 5.5.92f.]
I do not see why *Falstaff* is carried to the Fleet. We have never lost sight of him since his dismission from the king; he has committed no new fault, and therefore incurred no punishment. But the different agitations of fear, anger, and surprise in him and his company made a good scene to the eye; and our authour, who wanted them no longer on the stage, was glad to find this method of sweeping them away. (IV, 354)

[93] [End-note to 2 *Henry IV*]
I fancy every reader, when he ends this play, cries out with *Desdemona, O most lame and impotent conclusion!* As this play was not, to our knowledge, divided into acts by the authour, I could be content to conclude it with the death of *Henry* the Fourth: '*In that* Jerusalem *shall* Harry *dye.*' [4.5.241] These scenes which now make the fifth act of *Henry the Fourth* might then be the first of *Henry the Fifth*; but the truth is that they do unite very commodiously to either play. When these plays were represented I believe they ended as they are now ended in the books; but *Shakespeare* seems to have designed that the whole series of action, from the beginning of *Richard the Second* to the end of *Henry the Fifth*, should be considered by the reader as one work, upon one plan, only broken into parts by the necessity of exhibition.

None of *Shakespeare*'s plays are more read than the *First* and

[1] See 2.195.

Second Parts of *Henry the Fourth.* Perhaps no authour has ever in two plays afforded so much delight. The great events are interesting, for the fate of kingdoms depends upon them; the slighter occurrences are diverting, and, except one or two, sufficiently probable; the incidents are multiplied with wonderful fertility of invention, and the characters diversified with the utmost nicety of discernment, and the profoundest skill in the nature of man.

The prince, who is the hero both of the comick and tragick part, is a young man of great abilities and violent passions, whose sentiments are right, though his actions are wrong; whose virtues are obscured by negligence, and whose understanding is dissipated by levity. In his idle hours he is rather loose than wicked, and when the occasion forces out his latent qualities he is great without effort, and brave without tumult. The trifler is roused into a hero, and the hero again reposes in the trifler. This character is great, original, and just.

Percy is a rugged soldier, cholerick and quarrelsome, and has only the soldier's virtues, generosity and courage.

But *Falstaff* unimitated, unimitable *Falstaff*, how shall I describe thee? Thou compound of sense and vice; of sense which may be admired but not esteemed, of vice which may be despised, but hardly detested. *Falstaff* is a character loaded with faults, and with those faults which naturally produce contempt. He is a thief and a glutton, a coward and a boaster, always ready to cheat the weak, and prey upon the poor; to terrify the timorous and insult the defenceless. At once obsequious and malignant, he satirises in their absence those whom he lives by flattering. He is familiar with the prince only as an agent of vice, but of this familiarity he is so proud as not only to be supercilious and haughty with common men, but to think his interest of importance to the Duke of *Lancaster.* Yet the man thus corrupt, thus despicable, makes himself necessary to the prince that despises him by the most pleasing of all qualities, perpetual gaiety, by an unfailing power of exciting laughter, which is the more freely indulged as his wit is not of the splendid or ambitious kind, but consists in easy escapes and sallies of levity, which make sport but raise no envy. It must be observed that he is stained with no enormous or sanguinary crimes, so that his licentiousness is not so offensive but that it may be borne for his mirth.

The moral to be drawn from this representation is that no man is more dangerous than he that with a will to corrupt hath the power to please; and that neither wit nor honesty ought to think themselves safe with such a companion when they see *Henry* seduced by *Falstaff*. (IV, 355–6)

[94] [On *Henry V*, 1 *Prol*.12: *Chorus*. ... *or may we cram,/Within this wooden O*. ...]
Nothing shews more evidently the power of custom over language, than that the frequent use of calling a circle an *O* could so much hide the meanness of the metaphor from *Shakespeare* that he has used it many times where he makes his most eager attempts at dignity of stile. (IV, 361)

[95] [*Ibid.*, 1 *Prol*. 24:

> *Chorus. Into a thousand parts divide one man,*
> *And make imaginary puissance.*]

This passage shews that *Shakespeare* was fully sensible of the absurdity of shewing battles on the theatre, which indeed is never done but tragedy becomes farce. Nothing can be represented to the eye but by something like it, and *within a wooden O* nothing very like a battle can be exhibited. (IV, 362)

[96] [*Ibid.*, 1.1.47: *Canterbury*. ... when he speaks,/The air, a charter'd libertine, is still.]
This line is exquisitely beautiful. (IV, 365)

[97] [*Ibid.*, 2.2.126ff.: *King Henry*. Oh, how hast thou with jealousy infected/The sweetness of affiance! ....]
Shakespeare urges this aggravation of the guilt of treachery with great judgment. One of the worst consequences of breach of trust is the diminution of that confidence which makes the happiness of life, and the dissemination of suspicion, which is the poison of society. (IV, 392)

[98] [*Ibid.*, 2.3.16: *Quickly*. ... his nose was as sharp as a pen, and a' babbled of green fields.]
Upon this passage Mr. *Theobald* has a note[1] that fills a page, which I omit in pity to my readers, since he only endeavours to prove

[1] See 2.435ff.

what I think every reader perceives to be true, that at this time no *table* could be wanted. Mr. *Pope*, in an appendix to his own edition in 12*mo*, seems to admit *Theobald*'s emendation, which we would have allowed to be uncommonly happy had we not been prejudiced against it by a conjecture[1] with which, as it excited merriment, we are loath to part. (IV, 396)

[99] [*Ibid.*, 2.3.22ff.: *Quickly*. I put my hand into the bed, and felt them, and they were as cold as a stone; then I felt to his knees, and so upward, and upward, and all was as cold as any stone.]

Such is the end of *Falstaff*, from whom *Shakespeare* had promised us in his epilogue to *Henry IV* that we should receive more entertainment. It happened to *Shakespeare* as to other writers, to have his imagination crowded with a tumultuary confusion of images which, while they were yet unsorted and unexamined, seemed sufficient to furnish a long train of incidents and a new variety of merriment; but which, when he was to produce them to view, shrunk suddenly from him, or could not be accommodated to his general design. That he once designed to have brought *Falstaff* on the scene again we know from himself; but whether he could contrive no train of adventures suitable to his character, or could match him with no companions likely to quicken his humour, or could open no new vein of pleasantry and was afraid to continue the same strain, lest it should not find the same reception, he has here for ever discarded him and made haste to dispatch him, perhaps for the same reason for which *Addison* killed Sir *Roger*, that no other hand might attempt to exhibit him.

Let meaner authours learn from this example, that it is dangerous to sell the bear which is yet not hunted, to promise to the publick what they have not written.

This disappointment probably inclined Queen *Elizabeth* to command the poet to produce him once again, and to shew him in love or courtship. This was indeed a new source of humour, and produced a new play from the former characters.

I forgot to note in the proper place, and therefore note here that Falstaff's courtship, or *The Merry Wives of Windsor*, should be read between *Henry IV* and *Henry V*. (IV, 397)

---

1 That is, as Johnson writes in the 1773 edition, 'Mr. *Pope*'s first note', for which see 2.413, 416.

[100] [*Ibid.*, 3.4: the 'French scene', which Warburton wished to reject]

Sir *T. Hanmer* has rejected it. The scene is indeed mean enough when it is read, but the grimaces of two *French* women, and the odd accent with which they uttered the *English*, made it divert upon the stage. It may be observed that there is in it not only the *French* language but the *French* spirit. *Alice* compliments the princess upon her knowledge of four words, and tells her that she pronounces like the *English* themselves. The princess suspects no deficiency in her instructress, nor the instructress in herself. Throughout the whole scene there may be found *French* servility, and *French* vanity.

I cannot forbear to transcribe the first sentence of this dialogue from the edition of 1608, that the reader who has not looked into the old copies may judge of the strange negligence with which they are printed.

> Kate. Alice *venecia, vous aves cates en, vou parte fort*
> *bon Angloys englatara, Coman sae palla vou la main en francoy.* (IV, 414)

[101] [*Ibid.*, 3.6.96ff.: *Fluellen.* . . . one *Bardolph* . . . his face is all bubukles, and whelks, and knobs, and flames of fire . . . but his nose is executed, and his fire's out.]

This is the last time that any sport can be made with the red face of *Bardolph*, which, to confess the truth, seems to have taken more hold on *Shakespeare*'s imagination than on any other. The conception is very cold to the solitary reader, though it may be somewhat invigorated by the exhibition on the stage. This poet is always more careful about the present than the future, about his audience than his readers. (IV, 423)

[102] [*Ibid.*, 4.1.263ff.:

> K. Henry. Not all these, laid in bed majestical,
> Can sleep so soundly as the wretched slave . . .
> Who . . . like a lacquey, from the rise to set,
> Sweats in the eye of *Phoebus*; and all night
> Sleeps in *Elysium*.]

These lines are exquisitely pleasing. *To sweat in the eye of* Phoebus, and *to sleep in* Elysium, are expressions very poetical. (IV, 443)

[103] [*Ibid.*, 4.3.57ff.:

> King Henry. And *Crispin Crispian* shall ne'er go by,
> From this day to the ending of the world,
> But we in it shall be remembered.]

It may be observed that we are apt to promise to ourselves a more lasting memory than the changing state of human things admits. This prediction is not verified; the feast of *Crispin* passes by without any mention of *Agincourt*. Late events obliterate the former: the civil wars have left in this nation scarcely any tradition of more ancient history. (IV, 450)

[104] [*Ibid.*, 4.3.66f.: the Crispin's Day speech]
This speech, like many others of the declamatory kind, is too long. Had it been contracted to about half the number of lines it might have gained force and lost none of the sentiments. (IV, 450)

[105] [*Ibid.*, 4.3.76: *King Henry*. Why, now hast thou unwish'd five thousand men.]
By wishing only thyself and me, thou hast wished five thousand men away. *Shakespeare* never thinks on such trifles as numbers. In the last scene the *French* are said to be *full threescore thousand*, which *Exeter* declares to be *five to one;* but by the King's account they are twelve to one. (IV, 451)

[106] [*Ibid.*, 4.7.60ff.: *King Henry*. Besides, we'll cut the throats of those we have.]
The King is in a very bloody disposition. He has already cut the throats of his prisoners, and threatens now to cut them again. No haste of composition could produce such negligence; neither was this play, which is the second draught of the same design, written in haste. There must be some dislocation of the scenes. If we place these lines at the beginning of the twelfth scene [i.e. 4.6], the absurdity will be removed, and the action will proceed in a regular series. This transposition might easily happen in copies written for the players. Yet it must not be concealed that in the imperfect play of 1608 the order of the scenes is the same as here. (IV, 461)

[107] [*Ibid.*, 5.1.81ff.: *Pistol*. To *England* will I steal, and there I'll steal:]

The comick scenes of *The History of Henry the Fourth* and *Fifth* are now at an end, and all the comick personages are now dismissed. *Falstaff* and Mrs. *Quickly* are dead; *Nym* and *Bardolph* are hanged; *Gadshill* was lost immediately after the robbery; *Poins* and *Peto* have vanished since, one knows not how; and *Pistol* is now beaten into obscurity. I believe every reader regrets their departure. (IV, 474)

[108] [*Ibid.*, 5.2.121ff.: King Henry's wooing scene]
I know not why *Shakespeare* now gives the king nearly such a character as he made him formerly ridicule in *Percy*. This military grossness and unskilfulness in all the softer arts does not suit very well with the gaieties of his youth, with the general knowledge ascribed to him at his accession, or with the contemptuous message sent him by the *Dauphin*, who represents him as fitter for the ball room than the field, and tells him that he is not *to revel into dutchies* or win provinces *with a nimble galliard*. The truth is that the poet's matter failed him in the fifth act, and he was glad to fill it up with whatever he could get; and not even *Shakespeare* can write well without a proper subject. It is a vain endeavour for the most skilful hand to cultivate barrenness, or to paint upon vacuity. (IV, 479)

[109] [End-note to *Henry V*]
This play has many scenes of high dignity, and many of easy merriment. The character of the King is well supported, except in his courtship, where he has neither the vivacity of *Hal* nor the grandeur of *Henry*.[1] The humour of *Pistol* is very happily continued; his character has perhaps been the model of all the bullies that have yet appeared on the *English* stage.

The lines given to the Chorus have many admirers; but the truth is that in them a little may be praised, and much must be forgiven; nor can it be easily discovered why the intelligence given by the Chorus is more necessary in this play than in many others where it is omitted. The great defect of this play is the emptiness and narrowness of the last act, which a very little diligence might have easily avoided. (IV, 487)

[110] [On 1 *Henry VI*, 3.3.85: *Joan La Pucelle*. Done like a Frenchman: turn, and turn again!]

[1] Cf. Mrs Lennox (4.137).

The inconstancy of the *French* was always the subject of satire. I have read a dissertation written to prove that the index of the wind upon our steeples was made in form of a cock to ridicule the *French* for their frequent changes. (IV, 548)

[111] [*Ibid.*, 4.5.16f.:

> *John Talbot.* The world will say, he is not Talbot's blood,
> That basely fled, when noble Talbot stood.]

For what reason this scene is written in rhyme I cannot guess. If *Shakespeare* had not in other plays mingled his rhymes and blank verses in the same manner I should have suspected that this dialogue had been a part of some other poem which was never finished, and that being loath to throw his labour away he inserted it here. (IV, 563)

[112] [On 2 *Henry VI*, 1.1.116f.:

> *Warwick.* And are the cities, that I got with wounds,
> Deliver'd up again with peaceful words?]

The indignation of *Warwick* is natural, and I wish it had been better expressed; there is a kind of jingle intended in *wounds* and *words*. (V, 7)

[113] [*Ibid.*, 3.2.160ff.: the description of the corpse of Duke Humphrey: *Warwick.* See, how the blood is settled in his face. ...] ... I cannot but stop a moment to observe that this horrible description is scarcely the work of any pen but *Shakespeare*'s. (V, 64)

[114] [*Ibid.*, 3.3: the death of the guilty Cardinal Beaufort]
This is one of the scenes which have been applauded by the criticks, and which will continue to be admired when prejudice shall cease, and bigotry give way to impartial examination. These are beauties that rise out of nature and of truth; the superficial reader cannot miss them, the profound can image nothing beyond them. (V, 73)

[115] [*Ibid.*, 4.1.1ff.:

> *Captain Whitmore.* The gaudy, blabbing, and remorseful day
> Is crept into the bosom of the sea.]

The epithet *blabbing* applied to the day by a man about to commit murder is exquisitely beautiful. Guilt is afraid of light, considers darkness as a natural shelter, and makes night the confidante of those actions which cannot be trusted to the *tell-tale day*. (V, 74)

[116] [On 3 *Henry VI*, 2.5.21ff.:

> *King Henry.* O God! methinks it were a happy life,
> To be no better than a homely swain]

This speech is mournful and soft, exquisitely suited to the character of the king, and makes a pleasing interchange by affording, amidst the tumult and horrour of the battle, an unexpected glimpse of rural innocence and pastoral tranquillity. (V, 156)

[117] [*Ibid.*, 3.2.165ff.: *Gloucester.* Then, since this earth affords no joy to me ...]
Richard speaks here the language of nature. Whoever is stigmatised with deformity has a constant source of envy in his mind, and would counter-ballance by some other superiority these advantages which they feel themselves to want. *Bacon* remarks that the deformed are commonly daring, and it is almost proverbially observed that they are ill-natured. The truth is that the deformed, like all other men, are displeased with inferiority, and endeavour to gain ground by good or bad means, as they are virtuous or corrupt. (V, 173–4)

[118] [*Ibid.*, 4.6.67ff.: King Henry's blessing on Henry, Earl of Richmond]
He was afterwards *Henry* VII., a man who put an end to the civil war of the two houses, but not otherwise remarkable for virtue. *Shakespeare* knew his trade. *Henry* VII was grandfather to Queen *Elizabeth*, and the King from whom *James* inherited. (V, 198)

[119] [*Ibid.*, 5.2.24: *Warwick.* My parks, my walks, my manors that I had,/Even now forsake me.]

> *Cedes coemptis saltibus, et domo, Villâque.* Hor.[1]

This mention of his *parks* and *manours* diminishes the pathetick effect of the foregoing lines. (V, 211)

[120] [*Ibid.*, 5.5.65ff.: Queen Margaret's lament at the murder of her son]

[1] Horace, *Odes*, 2.3.17f.: 'Thou shalt leave thy purchased pastures, thy house, and thy estate ... '

The condition of this warlike queen would move compassion could it be forgotten that she gave *York*, to wipe his eyes in his captivity, a handkerchief stained with his young child's blood. (V, 218)

[121] [End-note to 3 *Henry VI*]

The three parts of *Henry VI* are suspected by Mr. *Theobald* of being supposititious,[1] and are declared by Dr. *Warburton* to be *certainly not Shakespeare*'s. Mr. *Theobald*'s suspicion arises from some obsolete words; but the phraseology is like the rest of our authour's stile, and single words, of which however I do not observe more than two, can conclude little.

Dr. *Warburton* gives no reason, but I suppose him to judge upon deeper principles and more comprehensive views, and to draw his opinion from the general effect and spirit of the composition, which he thinks inferior to the other historical plays.

From mere inferiority nothing can be inferred; in the productions of wit there will be inequality. Sometimes judgment will err, and sometimes the matter itself will defeat the artist. Of every authour's works one will be the best, and one will be the worst. The colours are not equally pleasing, nor the attitudes equally graceful, in all the pictures of *Titian* or *Reynolds*.

Dissimilitude of stile and heterogeneousness of sentiment may sufficiently show that a work does not really belong to the reputed authour. But in these plays no such marks of spuriousness are found. The diction, the versification, and the figures are *Shakespeare*'s. These plays, considered without regard to characters and incidents, merely as narratives in verse, are more happily conceived and more accurately finished than those of *King John*, *Richard II*, or the tragick scenes of *Henry IV* and *V*. If we take these plays from *Shakespeare* to whom shall they be given? What authour of that age had the same easiness of expression and fluency of numbers?

Having considered the evidence given by the plays themselves, and found it in their favour, let us now enquire what corroboration can be gained from other testimony. They are ascribed to *Shakespeare* by the first editors, whose attestation may be received in questions of fact, however unskilfully they superintended their edition. They seem to be declared genuine by the voice of

[1] See 2.503

Shakespeare himself, who refers to the second play in his epilogue to *Henry V.* and apparently connects the first act of *Richard III.* with the last of the third part of *Henry VI.* If it be objected that the plays were popular, and therefore he alluded to them as well known, it may be answered, with equal probability, that the natural passions of a poet would have disposed him to separate his own works from those of an inferior hand. And indeed if an authour's own testimony is to be overthrown by speculative criticism no man can be any longer secure of literary reputation.

Of these three plays I think the second the best. The truth is that they have not sufficient variety of action, for the incidents are too often of the same kind; yet many of the characters are well discriminated. King *Henry*, and his queen, King *Edward*, the duke of *Gloucester*, and the earl of *Warwick*, are very strongly and distinctly painted.

The old copies of the two latter parts of *Henry VI* and of *Henry V* are so apparently imperfect and mutilated that there is no reason for supposing them the first draughts of *Shakespeare*. I am inclined to believe them copies taken by some auditor who wrote down, during the representation, what the time would permit, then perhaps filled up some of his omissions at a second or third hearing, and when he had by this method formed something like a play, sent it to the printer. (V, 224–5)

[122] [On *Richard III*, 4.4.198ff.: Richard's wooing of Queen Elizabeth]
On this dialogue 'tis not necessary to bestow much criticism: part of it is ridiculous, and the whole improbable. (V, 329)

[123] [*Ibid.*, 5.3.177ff.: *King Richard.* Give me another horse,— bind up my wounds,— /Have mercy, Jesu! ...]
There is in this, as in many of our authour's speeches of passion, something very trifling and something very striking. *Richard*'s debate whether he should quarrel with himself is too long continued, but the subsequent exaggeration of his crimes is truly tragical. (V, 353)

[124] [The end-note to *Richard III*]
This is one of the most celebrated of our authour's performances; yet I know not whether it has not happened to him as to others, to

be praised most when praise is not most deserved. That this play has scenes noble in themselves, and very well contrived to strike in the exhibition, cannot be denied. But some parts are trifling, others shocking, and some improbable. (V, 362)

[125] [On *Henry VIII*, 4.2: the death-scene, and vision, of the dowager Queen Katharine]
This scene is above any other part of *Shakespeare*'s tragedies, and perhaps above any scene of any other poet, tender and pathetick, without gods, or furies, or poisons, or precipices, without the help of romantick circumstances, without improbable sallies of poetical lamentation, and without any throes of tumultuous misery. (V, 462)

[126] [End-note to *Henry VIII*]
The play of *Henry the Eighth* is one of those which still keeps possession of the stage, by the splendour of its pageantry. The coronation, about forty years ago, drew the people together in multitudes for a great part of the winter. Yet pomp is not the only merit of this play. The meek sorrows and virtuous distress of *Catherine* have furnished some scenes which may be justly numbered among the greatest efforts of tragedy. But the genius of *Shakespeare* comes in and goes out with *Catherine*. Every other part may be easily conceived, and easily written. (V, 491)

[127] [From the end-note to the histories]
The historical Dramas are now concluded, of which the two parts of *Henry the Fourth* and *Henry the Fifth* are among the happiest of our authour's compositions; and *King John*, *Richard the Third*, and *Henry the Eighth*, deservedly stand in the second class. Those whose curiosity would refer the historical scenes to their original, may consult *Holinshed*, and sometimes *Hall*: from *Holinshed Shakespeare* has often inserted whole speeches with no more alteration than was necessary to the numbers of his verse. To transcribe them into the margin was unnecessary, because the original is easily examined, and they are seldom less perspicuous in the poet than in the historian. .... (V, 493)

[128] [On *King Lear*, 1.1]
There is something of obscurity or inaccuracy in this preparatory

scene. The King has already divided his kingdom, and yet when he enters he examines his daughters to discover in what proportions he should divide it. Perhaps *Kent* and *Gloucester* only were privy to his design, which he still kept in his own hands, to be changed or performed as subsequent reasons should determine him. (VI, 3)

[129] [*Ibid.*, 1.1.35: *Lear.* Mean time we shall express our darker purpose.]
This word may admit a further explication. *We shall express our darker purpose*: that is, we have already made known in some measure our design of parting the kingdom; we will now discover what has not been told before, the reasons by which we shall regulate the partition.

This interpretation will justify or palliate the exordial dialogue. (VI, 5)

[130] [*Ibid.*, 1.1.146ff.: Johnson quotes the Folio text]
I have given this passage according to the old folio, from which the modern editions have silently departed for the sake of better numbers, with a degree of insincerity which, if not sometimes detected and censured, must impair the credit of antient books. One of the editors, and perhaps only one, knew how much mischief may be done by such clandestine alterations. ... (VI, 10)

[131] [*Ibid.*, 1.1.171: *Lear.* Which nor our nature, nor our place, can bear;]
... *Lear*, who is characterized as hot, heady and violent, is, with very just observation of life, made to entangle himself with vows upon any sudden provocation to vow revenge, and then to plead the obligation of a vow in defence of implacability. (VI, 12)

[132] [*Ibid.*, 1.1.178: *Lear.* Away! By *Jupiter*.]
Shakespeare makes his *Lear* too much a mythologist: he had *Hecate* and *Apollo* before. (VI, 12)

[133] [*Ibid.*, 1.2.137ff.: *Edmund.* I promise you, the effects, he writes of, succeed unhappily.] [Johnson notes that here the Quarto has the complete, the Folio an abridged text.]
It is *easy* to remark that in this speech, which ought, I think, to

be inserted in the text, *Edmund*, with the common craft of fortune-tellers, mingles the past and future, and tells of the future only what he already foreknows by confederacy or can attain by probable conjecture. (VI, 27–8)

[134] [*Ibid.*, 1.3.20f.:

> *Goneril.* Old Fools are Babes again; and must be us'd
> With Checks, as flatteries when they're seen abus'd.]

These lines hardly deserve a note, though Mr. *Theobald* thinks them *very fine*. Whether *fools* or *folks* should be read is not worth enquiry. The controverted line is yet in the old quarto, not as the editors represent it, but thus:

> *With checks as flatteries when they are seen abus'd.*

I am in doubt whether there is any errour of transcription. The sense seems to be this: *Old men must be treated with checks*, when as *they are seen to be deceived with flatteries*: or, *when they are weak enough to be* seen abused by flatteries, they are then weak enough to be *used with checks*. There is a play of the words *used* and *abused*. To *abuse* is, in our authour, very frequently the same as to *deceive*. This construction is harsh and ungrammatical; *Shakespeare* perhaps thought it vitious and chose to throw away the lines rather than correct them, nor would now thank the officiousness of his editors, who restore what they do not understand. (VI, 30–1)

[135] [*Ibid.*, 2.4.255:

> *Lear.* Those wicked creatures yet do look well-favour'd,
> When others are more wicked.]

[Warburton proposed 'wrinkled ... wrinkled' for 'wicked ... wicked',[1] but Johnson thinks 'the old reading best' despite 'this elaborate and ostentatious remark'.]
The commentator's only objection to the lines as they now stand is the discrepancy of the metaphor, the want of opposition between *wicked* and *well-favoured*. But he might have remembered what he says in his own preface concerning *mixed modes*.[2] *Shakespeare*, whose mind was more intent upon notions than words, had in his

---

[1] See 3.239f. [2] See 3.224f.

thoughts the pulchritude of virtue and the deformity of wickedness; and though he had mentioned *wickedness* made the correlative answer to *deformity*. (VI, 74)

[136] [*Ibid.*, 3.4.26f.:

> *Lear.* In, boy; go first. [*To the Fool*] You houseless poverty—
> Nay, get thee in; I'll pray, and then I'll sleep]

These two lines were added in the authour's revision, and are only in the folio. They are very judiciously intended to represent that humility, or tenderness, or neglect of forms, which affliction forces on the mind. (VI, 88)

[137] [*Ibid.*, 3.6.18: *Fool. He's mad that trusts in the tameness of a wolf, a horse's health*]
Shakespeare is here speaking not of things maliciously treacherous, but of things uncertain and not durable. A horse is above all other animals subject to diseases. (VI, 96)

[138] [*Ibid.*, 4.1.68ff.: Gloucester's attack on 'the superfluous and lust-dieted man']
Lear has before uttered the same sentiment, which indeed cannot be too strongly impressed, though it may be too often repeated. (VI, 110)

[139] [*Ibid.*, 4.1.69: *Gloucester.* That slaves your ordinance.]
[Warburton proposed 'braves' for 'slaves'.]
The emendation is plausible, yet I doubt whether it be right. The language of *Shakespeare* is very licentious, and his words have often meanings remote from the proper and original use. To *slave* or *beslave* another is to *treat* him *with terms of indignity*; in a kindred sense to *slave the ordinance* may be *to* slight *or* ridicule *it*. (VI, 110)

[140] [*Ibid.*, 4.6.11ff.: *Edgar.* How fearful/And dizzy 'tis, to cast one's eyes so low!]
This description has been much admired since the time of *Addison*,[1] who has remarked, with a poor attempt at pleasantry, that *he who can read it without being giddy has a very good head, or a very bad one.* The description is certainly not mean, but I am far from thinking

[1] *Tatler*, cxvii.

it wrought to the utmost excellence of poetry. He that looks from a precipice finds himself assailed by one great and dreadful image of irresistible destruction. But this overwhelming idea is dissipated and enfeebled from the instant that the mind can restore itself to the observation of particulars, and diffuse its attention to distinct objects. The enumeration of the choughs and crows, the samphire-man and the fishers, counteracts the great effect of the prospect as it peoples the desert of intermediate vacuity, and stops the mind in the rapidity of its descent through emptiness and horrour. (VI, 123)

[141] [End-note to *King Lear*]

The Tragedy of *Lear* is deservedly celebrated among the dramas of *Shakespeare*. There is perhaps no play which keeps the attention so strongly fixed; which so much agitates our passions and interests[1] our curiosity. The artful involutions of distinct interests, the striking opposition of contrary characters, the sudden changes of fortune, and the quick succession of events fill the mind with a perpetual tumult of indignation, pity, and hope. There is no scene which does not contribute to the aggravation of the distress or conduct of the action, and scarce a line which does not conduce to the progress of the scene. So powerful is the current of the poet's imagination that the mind which once ventures within it is hurried irresistibly along.

On the seeming improbability of *Lear*'s conduct it may be observed that he is represented according to histories at that time vulgarly received as true. And perhaps, if we turn our thoughts upon the barbarity and ignorance of the age to which this story is referred, it will appear not so unlikely as while we estimate *Lear*'s manners by our own. Such preference of one daughter to another, or resignation of dominion on such conditions, would be yet credible if told of a petty prince of *Guinea* or *Madagascar*. *Shakespeare*, indeed, by the mention of his Earls and Dukes has given us the idea of times more civilised, and of life regulated by softer manners; and the truth is that though he so nicely discriminates, and so minutely describes the characters of men he commonly neglects and confounds the characters of ages, by mingling customs ancient and modern, *English* and foreign.

---

[1] 'Interest': 'To affect; to move; to touch with passion; to gain the affections; as, this is an *interesting* story'.

My learned friend Mr. *Warton*, who has in the *Adventurer*[1] very minutely criticised this play, remarks that the instances of cruelty are too savage and shocking, and that the intervention of *Edmund* destroys the simplicity[2] of the story. These objections may, I think, be answered by repeating that the cruelty of the daughters is an historical fact, to which the poet has added little, having only drawn it into a series by dialogue and action. But I am not able to apologise with equal plausibility for the extrusion of *Gloucester*'s eyes, which seems an act too horrid to be endured in dramatic exhibition, and such as must always compel the mind to relieve its distress by incredulity. Yet let it be remembered that our authour well knew what would please the audience for which he wrote.

The injury done by *Edmund* to the simplicity of the action is abundantly recompensed by the addition of variety, by the art with which he is made to co-operate with the chief design, and the opportunity which he gives the poet of combining perfidy with perfidy and connecting the wicked son with the wicked daughters, to impress this important moral, that villany is never at a stop, that crimes lead to crimes, and at last terminate in ruin.

But though this moral be incidentally enforced, *Shakespeare* has suffered the virtue of *Cordelia* to perish in a just cause, contrary to the natural ideas of justice, to the hope of the reader, and, what is yet more strange, to the faith of chronicles.[3] Yet this conduct is justified by the *Spectator*, who blames *Tate* for giving *Cordelia* success and happiness in his alteration, and declares that in his opinion *the tragedy has lost half its beauty*.[4] *Dennis* has remarked, whether justly or not, that to secure the favourable reception of *Cato*, *the town was poisoned with much false and abominable criticism*, and that endeavours had been used to discredit and decry poetical justice. A play in which the wicked prosper, and the virtuous miscarry, may doubtless be good because it is a just representation of the common events of human life: but since all reasonable beings naturally love justice, I cannot easily be persuaded that the observation of justice makes a play worse; or that if other excellencies are equal the audience will not always rise better pleased from the final triumph of persecuted virtue.

[1] See Vol. 4, No. 139 c-e, especially p. 83.
[2] That is, makes it a double rather than a single, or simplex plot.
[3] Cf. Mrs Lennox (4.144) and Theobald (2.509f.).
[4] *Spectator*, xl: see 2.273.

In the present case the publick has decided. *Cordelia*, from the time of *Tate*, has always retired with victory and felicity. And, if my sensations could add any thing to the general suffrage, I might relate that I was many years ago so shocked by *Cordelia*'s death that I know not whether I ever endured to read again the last scenes of the play till I undertook to revise them as an editor.

There is another controversy among the criticks concerning this play. It is disputed whether the predominant image in *Lear*'s disordered mind be the loss of his kingdom or the cruelty of his daughters. Mr. *Murphy*, a very judicious critick,[1] has evinced by induction of particular passages, that the cruelty of his daughters is the primary source of his distress, and that the loss of royalty affects him only as a secondary and subordinate evil. He observes with great justness that *Lear* would move our compassion but little did we not rather consider the injured father than the degraded king.

The story of this play, except the episode of *Edmund*, which is derived, I think, from *Sidney*,[2] is taken originally from *Geoffry* of *Monmouth*, whom *Holinshed* generally copied. ... [Johnson now prints excerpts from 'an old historical ballad', 'A lamentable SONG of the Death of King Leir and his Three Daughters', as a possible source,[3] and argues that it was written before the play, since 'the ballad has nothing of *Shakespeare*'s nocturnal tempest, which is too striking to have been omitted', and that 'it has the rudiments of the play, but none of its amplifications: it first hinted *Lear*'s madness, but did not array it in circumstances'.] (VI, 158–60)

[142] [On *Timon of Athens*, 4.2.1: *Enter* Flavius, *with two or three servants.*]
Nothing contributes more to the exaltation of *Timon*'s character than the zeal and fidelity of his servants. Nothing but real virtue can be honoured by domesticks; nothing but impartial kindness can gain affection from dependants. (VI, 231)

---

[1] See 4.95ff.
[2] Cf. Mrs Lennox (4.144f.).
[3] See Mrs Lennox (4.145f.) for this (post-Shakespearian) ballad, and for a very similar argument as to its priority.

[143] [*Ibid.*, 4.3.157ff.:

> *Timon.*   ... take the bridge quite away
> Of him, that his particular to foresee
> Smells from the gen'ral weal.]

The metaphor is apparently incongruous, but the sense is good. To *foresee his particular* is *to provide for his private advantage*, for which *he leaves the right scent of publick good*. In hunting, when hares have cross'd one another it is common for some of the hounds *to smell from the general weal, and foresee their own particular*. *Shakespeare*, who seems to have been a skilful sportsman and has alluded often to falconry, perhaps alludes here to hunting.

To the commentator's emendation[1] it may be objected that he used *forefend* in the wrong meaning. To *forefend* is, I think, never to *provide for* but to *provide against*. The verbs compounded with *for* or *fore* have commonly either an evil or negative sense. (VI, 242–3)

[144] [*Ibid.*, 4.3.274f.:

> *Timon.* If thou hadst not been born the worst of men,
> Thou hadst been knave and flatterer.]

Dryden has quoted two verses of *Virgil* to shew how well he could have written satires. *Shakespeare* has here given a specimen of the same power by a line bitter beyond all bitterness, in which *Timon* tells *Apemantus* that he had not virtue enough for the vices which he condemns. (VI, 249)

[145] [End-note to *Timon of Athens*]

The play of *Timon* is a domestick Tragedy, and therefore strongly fastens on the attention of the reader. In the plan there is not much art, but the incidents are natural and the characters various and exact. The catastrophe affords a very powerful warning against that ostentatious liberality which scatters bounty but confers no benefits, and buys flattery but not friendship.

In this Tragedy are many passages perplexed, obscure, and probably corrupt, which I have endeavoured to rectify or explain with due diligence; but having only one copy, cannot promise myself that my endeavours will be much applauded. (VI, 276)

[1] Warburton read 'to forefend' for 'to foresee'.

[146] [End-note to *Titus Andronicus*]

All the editors and criticks agree with Mr. *Theobald* in supposing this play spurious. I see no reason for differing from them; for the colour of the stile is wholly different from that of the other plays, and there is an attempt at regular versification and artificial closes, not always inelegant yet seldom pleasing. The barbarity of the spectacles and the general massacre which are here exhibited can scarcely be conceived tolerable to any audience; yet we are told by *Jonson*[1] that they were not only borne but praised. That *Shakespeare* wrote any part, though *Theobald* declares it *incontestable*, I see no reason for believing.

The chronology of this play does not prove it not to be *Shakespeare*'s. If it had been written twenty-five years, in 1614, it might have been written when *Shakespeare* was twenty-five years old. When he left *Warwickshire* I know not, but at the age of twenty-five it was rather too late to fly for deer-stealing.

Ravenscroft,[2] who, in the reign of *Charles* II. revised this play and restored it to the stage, tells us in his preface, from a theatrical tradition I suppose, which in his time might be of sufficient authority, that this play was touched in different parts by *Shakespeare*, but written by some other poet. I do not find *Shakespeare*'s touches very discernible. (VI, 364–5)

[147] [On *Macbeth*, 1.5.35: *Lady Macbeth*. The raven himself is hoarse] [Warburton: 'himself's not hoarse']

The reading proposed by the learned commentator is so specious that I am scarcely willing to oppose it; yet I think the present words may stand. The messenger, says the servant, had hardly breath *to make up his message*; to which the lady answers mentally that he may well want breath, such a message would add hoarseness to the raven. That even the bird whose harsh voice is accustomed to predict calamities could not *croak the entrance of* Duncan but in a note of unwonted harshness. (VI, 393–4)

[148] [*Ibid.*, 1.6.1ff.:

> *King Duncan.* This Castle hath a pleasant seat; the air
> Nimbly and sweetly recommends itself
> Unto our gentle senses.]

---

[1] See 3.307 (Upton citing Theobald and Jonson); 4.560 (Heath).
[2] See 1.239.

[Warburton complained that the air could only 'recommend itself' to 'the sight and hearing'; so he read 'general sense'.] All this coil is to little purpose. *Senses* are nothing more than *each man's sense*, as *noses* would have been each man's nose. *Gentle senses* is very elegant, as it means *placid, calm, composed*, and intimates the peaceable delight of a fine day. (VI, 396)

[149] [*Ibid.*, 1.7.6f.: *Macbeth*. But *here*, upon this Bank and Shoal of time,/We'd jump the life to come.]
This is *Theobald's* emendation[1], undoubtedly right. The old edition has *School*, and Dr. *Warburton Shelve*. (VI, 398)

[150] [*Ibid.*, 2.1.1.]
Macbeth's *Castle*. The place is not mark'd in the old edition, nor is it easy to say where this encounter can be. It is not in the *hall*, as the editors have all supposed it, for *Banquo* sees the sky; it is not far from the bedchamber, as the conversation shews: it must be in the inner court of the castle, which *Banquo* might properly cross in his way to bed. (VI, 402)

[151] [*Ibid.*, 2.2.37: *Macbeth*. Sleep that knits up the ravell'd sleeve of care]
A skein of silk is called a *sleeve* of silk, as I learned from Mr. *Seward*,[2] the ingenious editor of *Beaumont* and *Fletcher*. (VI, 408)

[152] [*Ibid.*, 2.2.55ff.:

> Lady Macbeth. If he do bleed,
> I'll gild the faces of the grooms withal,
> For it must seem their guilt.]

Could *Shakespeare* possibly mean to play upon the similitude of *gild* and *guilt*? (VI, 409)

[153] [*Ibid.*, 2.4.15ff.: *Rosse*. And Duncan's horses, ... the minions of their race.]
Theobald reads, *minions of the race*, very probably, and very poetially. (VI, 420)

---

[1] See 2.512.
[2] See Vol. 3, No. 126, and 4.561 (Heath).

[154] [*Ibid.*, 5.5.17f.:

> *Macbeth.* She should have dy'd hereafter;
> There would have been a time for such a word]

[In 1745 Johnson had proposed reading: 'for—such a *world!*—':
see Vol. 3, p. 182.]
Such was once my conjecture, but I am now less confident.
Macbeth might mean that there would have been a more convenient
time for such a *word*, for such *intelligence*, and so fall into the following reflection. We say we send *word* when we give intelligence.
(VI, 476-7)

[155] [End-note to *Macbeth*]
This play is deservedly celebrated for the propriety of its
fictions, and solemnity, grandeur, and variety of its action; but
it has no nice discriminations of character, the events are too
great to admit the influence of particular dispositions, and the
course of the action necessarily determines the conduct of the
agents.

The danger of ambition is well described; and I know not
whether it may not be said in defence of some parts which now
seem improbable that in *Shakespeare*'s time it was necessary to
warn credulity against vain and illusive predictions.

The passions are directed to their true end. Lady *Macbeth* is
merely detested; and though the courage of *Macbeth* preserves
some esteem yet every reader rejoices at his fall. (VI, 484)

[156] [On *Coriolanus*, 1.3.14: *Volumnia.* .... his brows bound with
oak.]
The crown given by the *Romans* to him that saved the life of a
citizen, which was accounted more honourable than any other.
(VI, 501)

[157] [*Ibid.*, 2.1.151f.:

> *Volumnia.* Death, that dark Spirit, in's nervy arm doth lie;
> Which being advanc'd, declines, and then men die.]

Volumnia, in her boasting strain, says that her son, to kill his
enemy, has nothing to do but to lift his hand up and let it fall.
(VI, 526)

[158] [*Ibid.*, 3.3.129ff.: Coriolanus' parting speech to the citizens of Rome as they expel him, which Johnson paraphrases:]
Still retain the power of banishing your defenders, till your undiscerning folly, which can foresee no consequences, leave none in the city but yourselves, who are always labouring your own destruction.

It is remarkable that among the political maxims of the speculative *Harrington* there is one which he might have borrowed from this speech. *The people,* says he, *cannot see, but they can feel.* It is not much to the honour of the people that they have the same character of stupidity from their enemy and their friend. Such was the power of our authour's mind that he looked through life in all its relations private and civil. (VI, 575)

[159] [*Ibid.*, 4.1.7ff.:

> *Coriolanus.*   Fortune's blows,
> When most struck home, being gentle wounded, craves
> A noble cunning.]

This is the ancient and authentick reading. The modern editors have, for *gentle wounded*, silently substituted *gently warded*, and Dr. *Warburton* has explained *gently* by *nobly*. It is good to be sure of our authour's words before we go about to explain their meaning.

The sense is, When fortune strikes her hardest blows, to be wounded, and yet continue calm, requires a generous policy. He calls this calmness *cunning*, because it is the effect of reflection and philosophy. Perhaps the first emotions of nature are nearly uniform, and one man differs from another in the power of endurance as he is better regulated by precept and instruction.

They bore as heroes, but they felt as man.[1] (VI, 577)

[160] [*Ibid.*, 4.2.16ff.: *Sicinius.* Are you mankind?]
The word *mankind* is used maliciously by the first speaker, and taken perversely by the second. A *mankind* woman is a woman with the roughness of a man, and in an aggravated sense a woman ferocious, violent, and eager to shed blood. In this sense *Sicinius* asks *Volumnia* if she be *mankind.* She takes *mankind* for a *human creature,* and accordingly cries out 'Note but this fool./Was not a Man my Father?' (VI, 580)

---

[1] *Iliad,* 24.646, in Pope's translation, as Arthur Sherbo has noted.

[161] [*Ibid.*, 5.3.64: *Coriolanus*. The noble sister of *Poplicola*] *Valeria*, methinks, should not have been brought only to fill up the procession without speaking. (VI, 614)

[162] [End-note to *Coriolanus*]
The Tragedy of *Coriolanus* is one of the most amusing[1] of our authour's performances. The old man's merriment in *Menenius*; the lofty lady's dignity in *Volumnia*; the bridal modesty in *Virgilia*; the patrician and military haughtiness in *Coriolanus*; the plebeian malignity, and tribunitian insolence in *Brutus* and *Sicinius*, make a very pleasing and interesting[2] variety: and the various revolutions of the hero's fortune fill the mind with anxious curiosity. There is, perhaps, too much bustle in the first act, and too little in the last. (VI, 627)

[163] [On *Julius Caesar*, 2.2.88f.: *Decius*. Great Men shall press/ For tinctures, stains, relicks, and cognisance.] [Warburton thought that some lines had been lost.]
I am not of opinion that any thing is lost, and have therefore marked no omission. The speech, which is intentionally pompous, is somewhat confused. There are two allusions; one to coats armorial, to which princes make additions, or give new *tinctures* and new marks of *cognisance*; the other to martyrs, whose reliques are preserved with veneration. The *Romans*, says *Decius*, all come to you as to a saint for reliques, as to a prince for honours. (VII, 42)

[164] [End-note to *Julius Caesar*]
Of this tragedy many particular passages deserve regard, and the contention and reconcilement of *Brutus* and *Cassius* is universally celebrated; but I have never been strongly agitated in perusing it, and think it somewhat cold and unaffecting compared with some other of *Shakespeare*'s plays; his adherence to the real story, and to *Roman* manners, seems to have impeded the natural vigour of his genius. (VII, 102)

[165] [On *Antony and Cleopatra*, 3.13.126ff.:

> *Antony.*　　　　O that I were
> Upon the hill of *Basan*, to out-roar
> The horned herd, for I have savage cause!]

[1] 'Amuse': 'to fill with thoughts that engage the mind, without distracting it'.
[2] 'Interesting': affecting, moving.

146

It is not without pity and indignation that the reader of this great
Poet meets so often with this low jest, which is too much a favourite
to be left out of either mirth or fury. (VII, 198)

[166] [*Ibid.*, 4.9.15ff.:

    Enobarbus.   Throw my heart
Against the flint and hardness of my fault,
Which, being dried with grief, will break to powder,
And finish all foul thoughts.]

The pathetick of *Shakespeare* too often ends in the ridiculous. It is
painful to find the gloomy dignity of this noble scene destroyed
by the intrusion of a conceit so far-fetched and un-affecting.
(VII, 214)

[167] [*Ibid.*, 4.15.71ff.:

    Iras.   Royal *Egypt*! Empress!
    Charmian. Peace, Peace, *Iras.*
    Cleopatra. No more but in a woman.]

... *Hanmer* had proposed another emendation, not injudiciously.
He reads thus ... *No more but a meer woman*, &c. That is, *No more
an Empress, but a meer woman.*

It is somewhat unfortunate that the words, *meer woman*, which
so much strengthen the opposition to either *Empress* or *Isis*, are
not in the original edition, which stands thus

        No more but in a *woman.*

Meer woman was probably the arbitrary reading of *Rowe.* I suppose,
however, that we may justly change the ancient copy thus, *No more,
but* e'en a *woman*—which will well enough accommodate either
of the editors.

I am inclined to think that she speaks abruptly, not answering
her woman, but discoursing with her own thoughts.

      No more—but e'en a *woman*

I have no more *of my wonted greatness,* but am even a woman, *on the
level with other women; were I what I once was,*

          It were for me
      To throw my scepter, *&c.*

If this simple explanation be admitted, how much labour has been thrown away. *Peace, peace,* IRAS is said by *Charmian* when she sees the Queen recovering, and thinks speech troublesome. (VII, 230)

[168] [End-note to *Antony and Cleopatra*]

This Play keeps curiosity always busy, and the passions always interested. The continual hurry of the action, the variety of incidents, and the quick succession of one personage to another, call the mind forward without intermission from the first Act to the last. But the power of delighting is derived principally from the frequent changes of the scene; for except the feminine arts, some of which are too low, which distinguish *Cleopatra*, no character is very strongly discriminated. *Upton*, who did not easily miss what he desired to find, has discovered that the language of *Antony* is, with great skill and learning, made pompous and superb according to his real practice. But I think his diction not distinguishable from that of others: the most tumid[1] speech in the Play is that which *Caesar* makes to *Octavia*.

The events, of which the principal are described according to history, are produced without any art of connection or care of disposition. (VII, 254)

[169] [On *Cymbeline*, 1.1.46f.: 1 *Gentleman*. ... liv'd in Court,/ (Which rare it is to do) most prais'd, most lov'd.]

This encomium is high and artful. To be at once in any great degree *loved* and *praised* is truly *rare*. (VII, 260)

[170] [*Ibid.*, 1.1.100f.:

Posthumus. And with mine eyes I'll drink the words you send,
Though ink be made of gall.]

Shakespeare, even in this poor conceit, has confounded the vegetable *galls* used in ink with the animal *gall*, supposed to be bitter. (VII, 262)

[171] [*Ibid.*, 1.4.40f.: *Posthumus*. I was then a young traveller; rather shun'd to go even with what I heard]

---

[1] 'Tumid': 'Pompous; boastful; puffy; falsely sublime'. Presumably Johnson means 3.6.42ff.

This is expressed with a kind of fantastical perplexity. He means, I was then willing to take for my direction the experience of others, more than such intelligence as I had gathered myself. (VII, 273)

[172] [*Ibid.*, 1.5.33ff.:

> *Cornelius.* [*Solus*] I do not like her. She doth think, she has
> Strange ling'ring poisons; I do know her spirit,
> And will not trust one of her malice with
> A drug of such damn'd nature.]

This soliloquy is very inartificial. The speaker is under no strong pressure of thought; he is neither resolving, repenting, suspecting, nor deliberating, and yet makes a long speech to tell himself what himself knows. (VII, 279)

[173] [*Ibid.*, 2.4.70ff.:

> *Iachimo.* Proud *Cleopatra*, when she met her *Roman*,
> And *Cydnus* swell'd above the banks, or for
> The press of boats, or pride.]

[Warburton said that here Shakespeare was ridiculing Enobarbus' description of Cleopatra, while at the same time Iachimo was 'mocking the credulity' of Posthumus by the 'poetical exaggeration' of his language.]

It is easy to sit down, and give our authour meanings which he never had. *Shakespeare* has no great right to censure poetical exaggeration, of which no poet is more frequently guilty. That he intended to ridicule his own lines [in *Antony and Cleopatra*] is very uncertain, when there are no means of knowing which of the two plays was written first. The commentator has contented himself to suppose that the foregoing play in his book was the play of earlier composition. Nor is the reasoning better than the assertion. If the language of *Iachimo* be such as shews him to be mocking the credibility of his hearer, his language is very improper when his business was to deceive. But the truth is that his language is such as a skilful villain would naturally use, a mixture of airy triumph and serious deposition. His gayety shews his seriousness to be without anxiety, and his seriousness proves his gayety to be without art. (VII, 306)

[174] [*Ibid.*, 3.3.35f.: *Arviragus.* What whould we speak of,/When we are old as you?

This dread of an old age unsupplied with matter for discourse and meditation is a sentiment natural and noble. No state can be more destitute than that of him who, when the delights of sense forsake him, has no pleasures of the mind. (VII, 320)

[175] [*Ibid.*, 4.2.106f.: *Belarius.* ... the snatches in his voice,/And burst of speaking, were as his.]
This is one of our authour's strokes of observation. An abrupt and tumultuous utterance very frequently accompanies a confused and cloudy understanding. (VII, 349)

[176] [*Ibid.*, 5.1.1ff.:

> *Posthumus.* Yea, bloody cloth, I'll keep thee; for I wisht,
> Thou shouldst be colour'd thus. ...]

This is a soliloquy of nature, uttered when the effervescence of a mind agitated and perturbed spontaneously and inadvertently discharges itself in words. The speech, throughout all its tenour, if the last conceit be excepted, seems to issue warm from the heart. He first condemns his own violence; then tries to disburden himself, by imputing part of the crime to *Pisanio*; he next sooths his mind to an artificial and momentary tranquillity by trying to think that he has been only an instrument of the gods for the happiness of *Imogen.* He is now grown reasonable enough to determine that having done so much evil he will do no more; that he will not fight against the country which he has already injured; but as life is not longer supportable he will die in a just cause, and die with the obscurity of a man who does not think himself worthy to be remembered. (VII, 368)

[177] [*Ibid.*, 5.4.27f.:

> *Posthumus.* If you will take this audit, take this life,
> And cancel those cold bonds.]

This equivocal use of *bonds* is another instance of our authour's infelicity in pathetick speeches. (VII, 377)

[178] [End-note to *Cymbeline*]
This Play has many just sentiments, some natural dialogues, and some pleasing scenes, but they are obtained at the expence of much incongruity.

To remark the folly of the fiction, the absurdity of the conduct, the confusion of the names and manners of different times, and the impossibility of the events in any system of life, were to waste criticism upon unresisting imbecillity, upon faults too evident for detection and too gross for aggravation.[1] (VII, 403)

[179] [On *Troilus and Cressida*, 4.5.79: *Aeneas*. Valour and pride excel themselves in *Hector* ...] [Warburton had described 'excel' as 'an high absurdity' and emended to 'parcell'.]
I would not petulantly object that *excellence* may as well be *little* as *absurdity* be *high*, but to direct the reader's attention rather to sense than words. *Shakespeare's* thought is not exactly deduced. Nicety[2] of expression is not his character. The meaning is plain. *Valour*, says *Aeneas*, *is in* Hector *greater than valour in other men, and pride in* Hector *is less than pride in other men. So that* Hector *is distinguished by the excellence of having pride less than other pride, and valour more than other valour.* (VII, 508)

[180] [*Ibid.*, 5.1.16ff.: *Thersites*. Now the rotten diseases of the south, guts-griping, ruptures, catarrhs, loads o'gravel i'the back, letharges, cold palsies, raw eyes, dirt-rotten livers, wheezing lungs, bladders full of imposthume, sciatica's, lime-kilns i'th'palme, incurable bone-ach, and the rivell'd fee-simple of the tetter, take and take again such preposterous discoveries.]
This catalogue of loathsome maladies ends in the folio at *cold palsies*. This passage, as it stands, is in the quarto; the retrenchment was in my opinion judicious.

It may be remarked, though it proves nothing, that of the few alterations made by *Milton* in the second edition of his wonderful poem, one was an enlargement of the enumeration of diseases. (VII, 519)

[181] [*Ibid.*, 5.1.28ff.: *Thersites*. ... thou idle immaterial skein of slev'd silk, thou green sarcenet flap for a sore eye, thou tassel of a prodigal's purse, thou.]
All the terms used by *Thersites* of *Patroclus* are emblematically expressive of flexibility, compliance, and mean officiousness. (VII, 519)

[1] Cf. Mrs Lennox (4.121f.). [2] Accuracy.

[182] [End-note to *Troilus and Cressida*]

This play is more correctly written than most of *Shakespeare*'s compositions, but it is not one of those in which either the extent of his views or elevation of his fancy is fully displayed. As the story abounded with materials he has exerted little invention; but he has diversified his characters with great variety, and preserved them with great exactness. His vicious characters sometimes disgust, but cannot corrupt, for both *Cressida* and *Pandarus* are detested and contemned. The comick characters seem to have been the favourites of the writer; they are of the superficial kind, and exhibit more of manners than nature; but they are copiously filled and powerfully impressed.

Shakespeare has in his story followed, for the greater part, the old book of *Caxton*, which was then very popular; but the character of *Thersites*, of which it makes no mention, is a proof that this play was written after *Chapman* had published his version of *Homer*.[1] (VII, 547)

[183] [On *Romeo and Juliet*, 1.1.174: *Romeo*. Why then, O brawling love! O loving hate!]

Of these lines neither the sense nor occasion is very evident. He is not yet in love with an enemy, and to love one and hate another is no such uncommon state as can deserve all this toil of antithesis. (VIII, 12)

[184] [*Ibid.*, 1.2.24ff.:

> *Capulet*. At my poor house, look to behold this night
> Earth-treading stars that make dark heaven light.]

[Warburton proposed to reform 'this nonsense' by reading 'even' for 'heaven'.] But why nonsense? Is any thing more commonly said than that beauties eclipse the sun? Has not *Pope* the thought and the word?

> *Sol though white curtains shot a tim'rous ray,*
> *And ope'd those eyes that must eclipse the day.*

Both the old and the new reading are philosophical nonsense, but they are both, and both equally, poetical sense. (VIII, 16)

---

[1] Cf. Mrs Lennox (4.132–4). Johnson will not allow Chaucer as one of the sources: see the Preface above, p. 79.

[185] [*Ibid.*, 2.4.25ff.: *Mercutio.* Ah, the immortal passado, the punto reverso, the hay!—]
All the terms of the modern fencing-school were originally Italian; the rapier, or small thrusting sword, being first used in *Italy.* The *hay* is the word *hai,* you *have* it, used when a thrust reaches the antagonist, from which our fencers on the same occasion, without knowing I suppose any reason for it, cry out *ha!* (VIII, 49)

[186] [*Ibid.*, 2.4.128ff.: *Mercutio.* No hare, Sir, unless a hare, Sir, in a lenten pye, that is something stale and hoar ere it be spent.

An old hare hoar, ...]
Mercutio having roared out *So ho!* the cry of the sportsmen when they start a hare; *Romeo* asks *what he has found.* And *Mercutio* answers No *hare*; &c. The rest is a series of quibbles unworthy of explanation, which he who does not understand needs not lament his ignorance. (VIII, 53)

[187] [*Ibid.*, 3.1.1ff.:

Benvolio. I pray thee, good *Mercutio,* let's retire;
The day is hot, the *Capulets* abroad]

It is observed that in *Italy* almost all assassinations are committed during the heat of summer. (VIII, 60)

[188] [*Ibid.*, 3.1.173f.:

Lady Capulet. He is a kinsman to the *Montagues,*
Affection makes him false, he speaks not true.]

The charge of falshood on *Benvolio,* though produced at hazard, is very just. The authour, who seems to intend the character of *Benvolio* as good, meant perhaps to shew how the best minds, in a state of faction and discord, are detorted to criminal partiality. (VIII, 67)

[189] [*Ibid.*, 3.5.85f.:

Juliet. Ay, Madam, from the Reach of these my hands:
'Would, none but I might venge my Cousin's Death!]

Juliet's equivocations are rather too artful for a mind disturbed by the loss of a new lover. (VIII, 86)

153

[190] [*Ibid.*, 4.3.1ff.:

> *Juliet.* But, gentle Nurse,
> I pray thee, leave me to myself to-night;
> For I have need of many Orisons]

Juliet plays most of her pranks under the appearance of religion: perhaps *Shakespeare* meant to punish her hypocrisy. (VIII, 98)

[191] [*Ibid.*, 4.3.145ff.: *Juliet.* Alas, alas! is it not like, that I ...] This speech is confused and inconsequential, according to the disorder of *Juliet's* mind. (VIII, 100)

[192] [*Ibid.*, 5.1, Stage direction: *Enter* ROMEO] The acts are here properly enough divided, nor did any better distribution than the editors have already made occur to me in the perusal of this play; yet it may not be improper to remark that in the first folio, and I suppose the foregoing editions are in the same state, there is no division of the acts, and therefore some future editor may try whether any improvement can be made by reducing them to a length more equal, or interrupting the action at more proper intervals. (VIII, 108)

[193] [*Ibid.*, 5.1.3ff.:

> *Romeo.* My bosom's Lord sits lightly on his throne;
> And, all this day, an unaccustom'd spirit
> Lifts me above the ground with chearful thoughts.]

These three lines are very gay and pleasing. But why does *Shakespeare* give *Romeo* this involuntary cheerfulness just before the extremity of unhappiness? Perhaps to shew the vanity of trusting to those uncertain and casual exaltations or depressions which many consider as certain foretokens of good and evil. (VIII, 109)

[194] [*Ibid.*, 5.3.228ff.:

> *Friar Lawrence.* I will be brief, for my short date of breath
> Is not so long as is a tedious tale.]

It is much to be lamented that the Poet did not conclude the dialogue with the action, and avoid a narrative of events which the audience already knew. (VIII, 122)

[195] [End-note to *Romeo and Juliet*]

This play is one of the most pleasing of our Author's performances. The scenes are busy and various, the incidents numerous and important, the catastrophe irresistibly affecting, and the process of the action carried on with such probability, at least with such congruity to popular opinions, as tragedy requires.

Here is one of the few attempts of *Shakespeare* to exhibit the conversation of gentlemen, to represent the airy sprightliness of juvenile elegance. Mr. *Dryden* mentions[1] a tradition, which might easily reach his time, of a declaration made by *Shakespeare* that *he was obliged to kill* Mercutio *in the third act, lest he should have been killed by him.* Yet he thinks him *no such formidable person, but that he might have lived through the play, and died in his bed,* without danger to a poet. *Dryden* well knew, had he been in quest of truth, that in a pointed sentence more regard is commonly had to the words than the thought, and that it is very seldom to be rigorously understood. *Mercutio*'s wit, gaiety, and courage will always procure him friends that wish him a longer life; but his death is not precipitated, he has lived out the time allotted him in the construction of the play; nor do I doubt the ability of *Shakespeare* to have continued his existence, though some of his sallies are perhaps out of the reach of *Dryden*, whose genius was not very fertile of merriment nor ductile to humour, but acute, argumentative, comprehensive, and sublime.

The Nurse is one of the characters in which the Authour delighted: he has, with great subtilty of distinction, drawn her at once loquacious and secret, obsequious and insolent, trusty and dishonest.

His comick scenes are happily wrought, but his pathetick strains are always polluted with some unexpected depravations. His persons, however distressed, *have a conceit left them in their misery, a miserable conceit.*[2] (VIII, 124–5)

[196] [On *Hamlet*, 1.1.108: *Bernardo*. I think, it be no other; but even so/Well may it sort]

These, and all other lines printed in the *Italick* letter throughout this play, are omitted in the folio edition of 1623. The omissions leave the play sometimes better and sometimes worse, and seem made only for the sake of abbreviation. (VIII, 135)

---

[1] See 1.150.
[2] Dryden, Preface to *Fables* (ed. G. Watson, II, p. 279): an attack on Ovid's wordplay.

[197] [*Ibid.*, 1.2.89f.:

> *King Claudius.* . . . your father lost a father;
> That father lost, lost his.]

[Pope and Warburton wished to emend the text to avoid repeating 'lost'.][1]

I do not admire the repetition of the word, but it has so much of our authour's manner that I find no temptation to recede from the old copies. (VIII, 142)

[198] [*Ibid.*, 1.2.125: *King Claudius.* No jocund health, that *Denmark* drinks to-day]

The King's intemperance is very strongly impressed; every thing that happens to him gives him occasion to drink. (VIII, 144)

[199] [*Ibid.*, 2.1.114ff.:

> *Polonius.* It seems, it is as proper to our age
> To cast beyond ourselves in our opinions,
> As it is common for the younger sort
> To lack discretion.]

This is not the remark of a weak man. The vice of age is too much suspicion. Men long accustomed to the wiles of life *cast* commonly *beyond themselves*, let their cunning go further than reason can attend it. This is always the fault of a little mind, made artful by long commerce with the world. (VIII, 177)

[200] [*Ibid.*, 2.2.86ff., on Polonius; for Warburton's note see 3.247–9.]

This account of the character of *Polonius*, though it sufficiently reconciles the seeming inconsistency of so much wisdom with so much folly, does not perhaps correspond exactly to the ideas of our authour. The commentator makes the character of *Polonius* a character only of manners, discriminated by properties superficial, accidental, and acquired. The poet intended a nobler delineation of a mixed character of manners and of nature. *Polonius* is a man bred in courts, exercised in business, stored with observation, confident of his knowledge, proud of his eloquence, and declining into dotage. His mode of oratory is truly represented as designed

---

[1] For Theobald's defence of the original reading see 2.428f.

to ridicule the practice of those times, of prefaces that made no introduction, and of method that embarrassed rather than explained. This part of his character is accidental, the rest is natural. Such a man is positive and confident, because he knows that his mind was once strong, and knows not that it is become weak. Such a man excels in general principles, but fails in the particular application. He is knowing in retrospect, and ignorant in foresight. While he depends upon his memory and can draw from his repositories of knowledge he utters weighty sentences, and gives useful counsel; but as the mind in its enfeebled state cannot be kept long busy and intent, the old man is subject to sudden dereliction of his faculties, he loses the order of his ideas and entangles himself in his own thoughts, till he recovers the leading principle, and falls again into his former train. This idea of dotage encroaching upon wisdom will solve all the phænomena of the character of *Polonius*. (VIII, 182–3)

[201] [*Ibid.*, 2.2.320: *Hamlet.* . . . the humorous man shall end his part in peace.]
['After these words the *folio* adds, *the clown shall make those laugh whose lungs are tickled o' th' sere.*' Warburton]
This passage I have omitted, for the same reason, I suppose, as the other editors. I do not understand it. (VII, 194)

[202] [*Ibid.*, 3.1.56–88: *Hamlet.* To be, or not to be? that is the question . . .]
Of this celebrated soliloquy, which bursting from a man distracted with contrariety of desires and overwhelmed with the magnitude of his own purposes, is connected rather in the speaker's mind than on his tongue, I shall endeavour to discover the train, and to shew how one sentiment produces another.

  Hamlet, knowing himself injured in the most enormous and atrocious degree, and seeing no means of redress but such as must expose him to the extremity of hazard, meditates on his situation in this manner: *Before I can form any rational scheme of action under this pressure of distress*, it is necessary to decide whether, *after our present state, we are* to be or not to be. That is the question which, as it shall be answered, will determine *whether 'tis nobler* and more suitable to the dignity of reason *to suffer the outrages of fortune* patiently, or to take arms against *them*, and by opposing end them, *though perhaps* with the loss of life. If *to die* were *to sleep, no more, and by a sleep to end* the miseries of our nature, such a sleep were *devoutly to be wished*; but if *to sleep* in death be *to dream*, to retain our powers of sensibility, we must *pause* to consider *in that sleep of death what dreams may come.* This consideration *makes calamity* so long endured; *for who would bear* the vexations of life, which might be ended *by a bare bodkin*, but that he is afraid of something in unknown futurity? This fear it is that gives efficacy to conscience, which by turning the mind upon *this regard* chills the ardour of *resolution*, checks the vigour of *enterprise*, and makes the *current* of desire stagnate in inactivity.

We may suppose that he would have applied these general observations to his own case, but that he discovered *Ophelia*. (VIII, 207)

[203] [*Ibid.*, 3.1.59: *Hamlet.* Or to take arms against a sea of troubles]
Mr. *Pope* proposed *siege*. I know not why there should be so much solicitude about this metaphor. *Shakespeare* breaks his metaphors often, and in this desultory speech there was less need of preserving them. (VIII, 208)

[204] [*Ibid.*, 3.1.70: *Hamlet.* For who would bear the whips and scorns of time]
... It may be remarked that *Hamlet* in his enumeration of miseries forgets, whether properly or not, that he is a prince, and mentions many evils to which inferior stations only are exposed. (VIII, 209)

[205] [*Ibid.*, 3.1.77: *Hamlet.* To groan and sweat under a weary life.]
All the old copies have *to* grunt *and sweat*. It is undoubtedly the true reading, but can scarcely be borne by modern ears. (VIII, 209)

[206] [*Ibid.*, 3.1.89f.: *Hamlet.* Nymph, in thy orisons/Be all my sins remembered.]
This a touch of nature. *Hamlet*, at the sight of *Ophelia*, does not immediately recollect that he is to personate madness, but makes her an address grave and solemn, such as the foregoing meditation excited in his thoughts. (VIII, 209)

[207] [*Ibid.*, 3.2.124f.: *Hamlet*.... nay, then let the Devil wear black, for I'll have a suit of sables.] [Hanmer emended 'sables' to 'ermine'; Warburton ridiculed Hanmer's suggestion violently, and proposed instead 'fore I'll have a suit of sable': see 3.250f.]

I know not why our editors should, with such implacable anger, persecute their predecessors. Οἱ νεκροὶ μὴ δάκνουσιν ['The dead do not bite'], the dead, it is true, can make no resistance, they may be attacked with great security; but since they can neither feel nor mend, the safety of mauling them seems greater than the pleasure; nor perhaps would it much misbeseem us to remember, amidst our triumphs over the *nonsensical* and the *senseless*, that we likewise are men; that *debemur morti*, and as Swift observed to Burnet, shall soon be among the dead ourselves.

I cannot find how the common reading is nonsense, nor why *Hamlet*, when he laid aside his dress of mourning, in a country where it was *bitter cold* and the air was *nipping and eager*, should not have a *suit of sables*. I suppose it is well enough known that the fur of sables is not black. (VIII, 219)

[208] [*Ibid.*, 3.3.93f.:

> *Hamlet.* Then trip him, that his heels may kick at heav'n;
> And that his soul may be as damn'd and black
> As hell, whereto it goes.]

This speech, in which *Hamlet*, represented as a virtuous character, is not content with taking blood for blood but contrives damnation for the man that he would punish, is too horrible to be read or to be uttered. (VIII, 236)

[209] [*Ibid.*, 4.4.53ff.; Hamlet's speech on honour]
The sentiment of *Shakespeare* is partly just, and partly romantick:

> —*Rightly to be great,*
> *Is not to stir without great argument,*

is exactly philosophical.

> *But greatly to find quarrel in a straw,*
> *When Honour is at stake,*

is the idea of a modern hero. *But then*, says he, *honour is an argument, or subject of debate, sufficiently* great, *and* when honour is at stake we must *find cause of quarrel in a straw*. (VIII, 256)

[210] [*Ibid.*, 4.5.81: *King Claudius*. In hugger-mugger to inter him]
All the modern editions that I have consulted give it, *In* private
to inter him;— That the words now replaced are better I do not
undertake to prove; it is sufficient that they are *Shakespeare*'s. If
phraseology is to be changed as words grow uncouth by disuse,
or gross by vulgarity, the history of every language will be lost;
we shall no longer have the words of any authour; and, as these
alterations will be often unskilfully made, we shall in time have
very little of his meaning. (VIII, 260)

[211] [*Ibid.*, 4.7.154: *King Claudius*. If this should blast in proof.]
This, I believe, is a metaphor taken from a mine, which in the
proof or execution sometimes breaks out with an ineffectual
blast. (VIII, 276)

[212] [*Ibid.*, 5.2.38ff.: And stand a Comma 'tween their amities]
[Warburton proposed 'commere', a 'procuress' or 'trafficker in
love': see 3.251f.]
Hanmer reads, *And stand a* cement—
   I am again inclined to vindicate the old reading. That the word
Commere is *French* will not be denied; but when or where was it
English?
   The expression of our authour is, like many of his phrases,
sufficiently constrained and affected, but it is not incapable of
explanation. The *Comma* is the note of *connection* and continuity
of sentences; the *Period* is the note of *abruption* and disjunction.
Shakespeare had it perhaps in his mind to write That unless *England*
complied with the mandate *war should put a* period *to their amity*;
he altered his mode of diction, and thought that, in an opposite
sense, he might put that *Peace should stand a* Comma *between their
amities*. This is not an easy style; but is it not the style of *Shakespeare*?
(VIII, 293–4)

[213] [*Ibid.*, 5.2.187ff.: *Hamlet*. . . . and do but blow them to their
trials, the bubbles are out.]
These men of show, without solidity, are like bubbles raised from
soap and water, which dance, and glitter, and please the eye, but
if you extend them by blowing hard, separate into a mist; so if you
oblige these specious talkers to extend their compass of conver-

sation, they at once discover the tenuity[1] of their intellects. (VIII, 301)

[214] [*Ibid.*, 5.2.218: *Hamlet.* Give me your pardon, Sir. I have done you wrong.]
I wish *Hamlet* had made some other defence; it is unsuitable to the character of a good or a brave man to shelter himself in falsehood. (VIII, 303)

[215] [End-note to *Hamlet*]

If the dramas of *Shakespeare* were to be characterised, each by the particular excellence which distinguishes it from the rest, we must allow to the tragedy of *Hamlet* the praise of variety. The incidents are so numerous that the argument of the play would make a long tale. The scenes are interchangeably diversified with merriment and solemnity; with merriment that includes judicious and instructive observations, and solemnity not strained by poetical violence above the natural sentiments of man. New characters appear from time to time in continual succession, exhibiting various forms of life and particular modes of conversation. The pretended madness of *Hamlet* causes much mirth,[2] the mournful distraction of *Ophelia* fills the heart with tenderness, and every personage produces the effect intended, from the apparition that in the first act chills the blood with horror, to the fop in the last that exposes affectation to just contempt.

The conduct is perhaps not wholly secure against objections. The action is indeed for the most part in continual progression, but there are some scenes which neither forward nor retard it. Of the feigned madness of *Hamlet* there appears no adequate cause, for he does nothing which he might not have done with the reputation of sanity.[3] He plays the madman most when he treats *Ophelia* with so much rudeness, which seems to be useless and wanton cruelty.

Hamlet is, through the whole play, rather an instrument than an agent. After he has, by the stratagem of the play, convicted the King he makes no attempt to punish him, and his death is at last effected by an incident which *Hamlet* has no part in producing.[4]

The catastrophe is not very happily produced; the exchange of

---

[1] 'Tenuity': 'Thinness; exility; smallness; minuteness'.
[2] Cf. Mrs Lennox (4.129). [3] Cf. Mrs Lennox (4.129f.). [4] Cf. Steevens, p. 488 below.

weapons is rather an expedient of necessity than a stroke of art. A scheme might easily have been formed to kill *Hamlet* with the dagger, and *Laertes* with the bowl.

The poet is accused of having shewn little regard to poetical justice, and may be charged with equal neglect of poetical probability.[1] The apparition left the regions of the dead to little purpose; the revenge which he demands is not obtained but by the death of him that was required to take it; and the gratification which would arise from the destruction of an usurper and a murderer is abated by the untimely death of *Ophelia*, the young, the beautiful, the harmless, and the pious. (VIII, 311)

[216] [On *Othello*, 1.3.140ff.:

> *Othello.* Wherein of antres vast, and desarts idle,
> Rough quarries, rocks, and hills, whose heads touch heav'n]

[For their ridicule of this passage see Rymer, 2.28, 33f.: Shaftesbury, 2.264f.]
Whoever ridicules this account of the progress of love shews his ignorance,[2] not only of history but of nature and manners. It is no wonder that in any age, or in any nation, a lady, recluse, timorous, and delicate, should desire to hear of events and scenes which she could never see, and should admire the man who had endured dangers and performed actions which, however great, were yet magnified by her timidity. . . .
[Pope proposed 'desarts wild'] Every mind is liable to absence and inadvertency, else *Pope* could never have rejected a word so poetically beautiful. (VIII, 342)

[217] [*Ibid.*, 3.3.91: *Othello*. Excellent Wretch!]
The meaning of the word *wretch* is not generally understood. It is now, in some parts of *England*, a term of the softest and fondest tenderness. It expresses the utmost degree of amiableness, joined with an idea which perhaps all tenderness includes, of feebleness, softness, and want of protection. *Othello*, considering *Desdemona* as excelling in beauty and virtue, soft and timorous by her sex, and by her situation absolutely in his power, calls her *Excellent Wretch*! It may be expressed, *Dear, harmless, helpless Excellence.* (VIII, 391)

---

[1] Cf. Dennis (2.285) and Mrs Lennox (4.128f.).
[2] The exact words of Warburton's attack on Rymer and Shaftesbury, see 3.257f.

[218] [*Ibid.*, 3.3.210ff.:

>   *Iago.* She did deceive her father, marrying you;
> And when she seem'd to shake, and fear your looks,
> She lov'd them most.]

This and the following argument of *Iago* ought to be deeply impressed on every reader. Deceit and falsehood, whatever conveniences they may for a time promise or produce, are in the sum of life obstacles to happiness. Those who profit by the cheat distrust the deceiver, and the act by which kindness was sought puts an end to confidence.

The same objection may be made with a lower degree of strength against the imprudent generosity of disproportionate marriages. When the first heat of passion is over, it is easily succeeded by suspicion that the same violence of inclination which caused one irregularity may stimulate to another; and those who have shewn that their passions are too powerful for their prudence will, with very slight appearances against them, be censured as not very likely to restrain them by their virtue. (VIII, 397)

[219] [*Ibid.*, 3.3.266f.:

>   *Othello* I'd whistle her off, and let her down the wind
> To prey at fortune.]

The falconers always let fly the hawk against the wind; if she flies with the wind behind her she seldom returns. If therefore a hawk was for any reason to be dismissed she was *let down the wind,* and from that time shifted for herself and *prey'd at fortune.* This was told me by the late Mr. *Clark.* (VIII, 400)

[220] [*Ibid.*, 3.4.104: *Emilia.* 'Tis not a year, or two, shews us a man]
From this line it may be conjectured that the authour intended the action of this play to be considered as longer than is marked by any note of time. Since their arrival at *Cyprus*, to which they were hurried on their wedding-night, the fable seems to have been in one continual progress, nor can I see any vacuity into which a *year or two*, or even a month or two, could be put. On the night of *Othello*'s arrival a feast was proclaimed; at that feast *Cassio* was degraded, and immediately applies to *Desdemona* to get him re-

stored. *Iago* indeed advises *Othello* to hold him off a while, but there is no reason to think that he has been held off long. A little longer interval would increase the probability of the story, though it might violate the rules of the drama. (VIII, 416)

[221] [*Ibid.*, 4.1.39: *Othello*. Nature would not invest herself in such shadowing passion without some instruction.] [Warburton suggested emending 'instruction' to 'induction'; see 4.563f. for Heath's comments.]
This is a noble conjecture, and whether right or wrong does honour to its authour. Yet I am in doubt whether there is any necessity of emendation. There has always prevailed in the world an opinion that when any great calamity happens at a distance notice is given of it to the sufferer by some dejection or perturbation of mind, of which he discovers no external cause. This is ascribed to that general communication of one part of the universe with another which is called sympathy and antipathy; or to the secret monition, *instruction*, and influence of a superior Being, which superintends the order of Nature and of life. *Othello* says *Nature could not invest herself in such shadowing passion without* instruction. *It is not words that shakes me thus.* This passion which spreads its clouds over me is the effect of some agency more than the operation of words; it is one of those notices which men have of unseen calamities. (VIII, 425)

[222] [*Ibid.*, 5.1.11f.:

    Iago. I've rubbed this young quat almost to the sense,
And he grows angry.]

This is a passage much controverted among the editors. Sir *T. Hanmer* reads *Quab*, a *Gudgeon*; not that a Gudgeon can be *rubbed* to much *sense*, but that a man grossly deceived is often called a *Gudgeon.* Mr. *Upton* reads *Quail*, which he proves by much learning to be a very choleric bird. Dr. *Warburton* retains *Gnat*, which is found in the early quarto. Theobald would introduce *knot*, a small bird of that name. I have followed the text of the folio, and third and fourth quartos.

A *Quat* in the midland counties is a *pimple*, which by rubbing is made to smart, or is *rubbed to sense*. *Roderigo* is called a *Quat* by the same mode of speech, as a low fellow is now termed in low language a *Scab*. *To rub to the sense*, is *to rub to the quick*. (VIII, 449)

[223] [*Ibid.*, 5.2.21f.:

> *Othello*. This Sorrow's heavenly;
> It strikes, where it doth love.]

This tenderness, with which I lament the punishment which justice compels me to inflict, is a holy passion.

I wish these two lines could be honestly ejected. It is the fate of *Shakespeare* to counteract his own pathos. (VIII, 456)

[224] [*Ibid.*, 5.2.66ff.:

> *Othello*. Oh perjur'd woman! thou dost stone my heart,
> And mak'st me call, what I intend to do,
> *A murder, which I thought a sacrifice.*]

This line is difficult. *Thou hast hardened my heart, and makest me* kill thee with the rage of a *murderer*, when *I thought to have sacrificed* thee to justice with the calmness of a priest striking a victim.

It must not be omitted that one of the elder quartos reads *thou dost stone* thy *heart*; which I suspect to be genuine. The meaning then will be *thou forcest me* to dismiss thee from the world in the state of the *murdered* without preparation for death, *when I intended* that thy punishment should have been *a sacrifice* atoning for thy crime.

I am glad that I have ended my revisal of this dreadful scene. It is not to be endured. (VIII, 458)

[225] [*Ibid.*, 5.2.214f.:

> *Othello*. That she with *Cassio* had the act of shame
> A thousand times committed.]

This is another passage which seems to suppose a longer space comprised in the action of this play than the scenes include. (VIII, 464)

[226] [End-note to *Othello*]

The beauties of this play impress themselves so strongly upon the attention of the reader that they can draw no aid from critical illustration. The fiery openness of *Othello*, magnanimous, artless, and credulous, boundless in his confidence, ardent in his affection, inflexible in his resolution, and obdurate in his revenge; the cool malignity of *Iago*, silent in his resentment, subtle in his designs, and studious at once of his interest and his vengeance; the soft simplicity of *Desdemona*, confident of merit, and conscious of innocence, her artless perseverance in her suit, and her slowness to suspect that she can be suspected, are such proofs of *Shakespeare*'s skill in human nature as, I suppose, it is vain to seek in any modern writer. The gradual progress which *Iago* makes in the Moor's conviction, and the circumstances which he employs to inflame him are so artfully natural that though it will perhaps not be said of him as he says of himself, that he is *a man not easily jealous*, yet we cannot but pity him when at last we find him *perplexed in the extreme*.

There is always danger lest wickedness, conjoined with abilities, should steal upon esteem, though it misses of approbation; but the character of *Iago* is so conducted that he is from the first scene to the last hated and despised.

Even the inferiour characters of this play would be very conspicuous in any other piece, not only for their justness but their strength. *Cassio* is brave, benevolent, and honest, ruined only by his want of stubbornness to resist an insidious invitation. *Roderigo*'s suspicious credulity and impatient submission to the cheats which he sees practised upon him, and which by persuasion he suffers to be repeated, exhibit a strong picture of a weak mind betrayed, by unlawful desires, to a false friend; and the virtue of *Emilia* is such as we often find, worn loosely but not cast off, easy to commit small crimes, but quickened and alarmed at atrocious villanies.

The Scenes from the beginning to the end are busy, varied by happy interchanges, and regularly promoting the progression of the story; and the narrative in the end, though it tells but what is known already, yet is necessary to produce the death of *Othello*.

Had the scene opened in *Cyprus*, and the preceding incidents been occasionally related, there had been little wanting to a drama of the most exact and scrupulous regularity. (VIII, 472–3)

APPENDIX

In the prosecution of this work I received many remarks from learned Friends, which came sometimes too late for insertion, and some of my own remarks either more mature reflection or better information has disposed me to retract. An Appendix therefore became necessary, that I might omit nothing which could contribute to the explanation of my authour. I do not always concur with my friends in their opinion, but their abilities are such as make me less confident when I find myself differing from them, and the publick might justly complain if I suppressed their sentiments either by pride or timidity. From the *Revisal* of *Shakespeare* lately published, I have selected some just remarks, and from Dr. *Grey* some valuable illustrations. I am far at last from supposing my work perfect, but do not think any thing which I am likely to add to it of value enough to justify longer delay. (VIII, Sig. Hh$_6^r$)

[227] [End-note to *The Tempest*]
It is observed of the *Tempest* that its plan is regular; this the *Revisal* thinks, what I think too, an accidental effect of the story, not intended or regarded by the authour.[1] (Sig. Hh$_6^v$)

[228] [End-note to *A Midsummer Night's Dream*]
Of this play, wild and fantastical as it is, all the parts in their various modes are well written, and give the kind of pleasure which the authour designed. Fairies in his time were much in fashion; common tradition had made them familiar, and *Spenser*'s poem had made them great. (Sig. Hh$_7^v$)

[229] [On *Measure for Measure*, 5.1.233ff.:

> *Angelo*   I do perceive,
> These poor informal women are no more
> But instruments of some more mightier member.]

I think, upon further enquiry, that *informal* signifies *incompetent, not qualified to give testimony.*

Of this use I think there are precedents to be found, though I cannot now recover them. (Sig. Ii^r)

[230] [On *Love's Labour's Lost*, 4.2.26ff.:

> *Sir Nathaniel.* And such barren plants are set before us, that we thankful should be,
> Which we taste and feeling are for those parts that do fructify in us, more than He.]

[1] For Heath's note in his *Revisal of Shakespeare's Text* see 4.558.

167

The length of these lines was no novelty on the *English* stage. The moralities afford scenes of the like measure. (Sig. Ii$_2$^{v})

[231] [On *All's Well That Ends Well*, 4.2.25ff.: *Diana*. If I should swear by *Jove's* great Attributes]

In the print of the old folio it is doubtful whether it is *Jove's* or *Love's*, the characters being not distinguishable. If it is read *Love's*, perhaps it may be something less difficult. I am still at a loss. (Sig. Ii$_8$^{r})

[232] [On 1 *Henry IV*, 4.2.11; cf. note 79 above.]

Gurnet, as I am informed, is a fish, not large, but considerably larger than an anchovy, and we may suppose was commonly eaten when sous'd or pickled, in our authour's time. (Sig. Kk^{r-v})

[233] [On 2 *Henry IV*, 4.1.32ff.:

> *Westmorland.*　　　　　If that Rebellion
> Came like itself, in base and abject routs,
> Led on by bloody youth]

[Johnson had suggested 'moody' (i.e. 'furious') 'youth', IV, 304]

Bloody youth, with which I puzzled myself in the note, is only *sanguine* youth, or youth full of blood, and of those passions which blood is supposed to produce and incite or nourish. (Sig. Kk$_2$^{r})

[234] [On *Henry VIII*, 2.4.1., stage direction: '*Sennet*']

Sennet was an instrument of musick, as appears from other places of this authour, but of what kind I know not. (Sig. Kk$_4$^{v})

[235] [On *Hamlet*, 1.5.80: *Ghost*. Oh, horrible! oh, horrible! most horrible!]

It was very ingeniously hinted to me by a learned lady that this line seems to belong to *Hamlet*, in whose mouth it is a proper and natural exclamation, and who, according to the practice of stage, may be supposed to interrupt so long a speech. (Sig. Ll$_2$^{v})

[236] [*Ibid.*, 3.4.71f.: *Hamlet*. Sense, sure, you have,/Else could you not have notion.]

For *notion*, which the note of Dr. *Warburton* had persuaded me to admit into the text, I would now replace the old reading *motion*;

for though the emendation be elegant, it is not necessary. (Sig. Ll$_3^r$)

[237] [*Ibid.*, 5.1.3: 2 *Clown*. make her Grave straight.] [Johnson had glossed 'straight' as meaning to 'make her grave from east to west in a direct line parallel to the church; not from north to south, athwart the regular line': VIII, 278.]

Some, for whose opinions I have great regard, think that *straight* is only *immediately*. My interpretation I have given with no great confidence, but the longer I consider it the more I think it right. (Sig. Ll$_3^v$)

[238] I have endeavoured to enumerate the Editions of *Shakespeare*'s Plays, but finding that I have paid too much regard to inaccurate catalogues, I think it necessary to subjoin the following list given me by Mr. *Steevens*. (Sig. Ll$_7^r$)
[A list of the Quartos is given, concluding with this sentence:][1]
Of all the other plays, the only authentick edition is the folio of 1623, from which the subsequent folios never vary, but by accident and negligence. (Sig. Ll$_8^r$)

[Notes by other commentators]

[239] [On *Two Gentlemen of Verona*, 2.1.94]
Oh! excellent motion, &c.] I think this passage requires a note, as every reader does not know that *motion*, in the language of *Shakespeare*'s days, signifies *puppet*. In *Ben. Jonson*'s *Bartholomew Fair*, it is frequently used in that sense, or rather, perhaps, to *signify* a puppet shew; the master whereof may properly be said to be an interpreter, as being the explainer of the inarticulate language of the actors: the speech of the servant is an allusion to that practice, and he means to say, that *Silvia* is a puppet, and that *Valentine* is to interpret to, or rather, *for* her.

Mr. HAWKINS. (Sig. Hh$_7^v$–Hh$_8^r$)

[240] [On *The Winter's Tale*, 4.4.392: *Polixenes* [to Florizel]. Is not your father grown incapable/Of reasonable affairs? Can he ... *dispute his own estate*?]
[Johnson had suggested '*compute*'; or that the phrase meant 'talk

---

[1] This sentence is, however, printed in the smaller type used for Steevens's note, and may therefore be by him. It tallies with Johnson's views in the Preface above.

over his affairs' (II, 312).] *Dispute his own estate.*] Does not this allude to the next heir sueing for the estate in cases of imbecillity, lunacy, *&c.*

Mr. CHAMIER. (Sig. Ii₄ᵛ)

[241] [On *Twelfth Night*, 2.3.113: *Sir Toby* [to Malvolio]. Go, Sir, rub your *chain* with crumbs.]
[Johnson suggested '*chin*', since Malvolio 'was only a steward, and consequently dined after his lady' (II, 384).] The steward might in these days wear a *chain* as a badge of office, or mark of dignity; and the method of cleaning a chain, or any gilt plate, is by rubbing it with crums.

Mr. STEEVENS. (Sig. Ii₄ᵛ)

[242] [On *The Merry Wives of Windsor*, 1.3.14]
Let me see thee froth and live.] This passage has passed through all the editions without suspicion of being corrupted; but the reading of the old quartos of 1602, and 1619, *Let me see the froth and lyme*, I take to be the true one. The host calls for an immediate specimen of *Bardolph*'s abilities, as a tapster; and *frothing* beer and *liming* sack were tricks in practice in *Shakespeare*'s time; the one was done by putting soap into the bottom of the tankard, when they drew the beer; the other, by mixing *lime* with the sack (*i.e.* sherry) to make it sparkle in the glass. *Froth* and *live* is sense; but a little forced; and to make it so, we must suppose the host could guess, by his skill in doing the former, how he would succeed in the world. *Falstaff* himself complains of *limed* sack.

Mr. STEEVENS. (Sig. Ii₅ᵛ)

[243] [On *The Taming of the Shrew*, 4.1.49f.]
Be the Jacks *fair within, the* Jills *fair without.*]
Dr. *Warburton* seems to have made one blunder here, while he is censuring Sir *T. H.* for another. *Warburton* explains it thus, Are the drinking vessels clean, and the maids drest? *Hanmer* alters the text thus, *Are the* Jacks *fair without, the* Jills *fair within?* This seems to mean, Are the men, who are waiting without the house, for my master, dress'd, and the maids, who are waiting within, dress'd too?

The joke here intended is only a play upon the words of *Jack* and *Jill*, which signify *two drinking measures*, as well as *men* and *maids*; the distinction made in the question concerning them was owing to this; the *jacks* being made of leather, could not be made to appear beautiful on the outside, but were very apt to contract foulness within; whereas the *jills*, being of pewter, were to be kept bright on the outside, and, as they were of metal, were not liable to dirt on the inside, like the leather.

Mr. STEEVENS. (Sig. Ii₇ʳ)

[244] [On *All's Well that Ends Well*, 4.3.256: Bertram on Parolles: *Pox on him he is a cat still.*] Mr. *Johnson* has explained this passage thus, *Throw him how you will, he lights upon his legs.* [III, 372]

Bertram means no such thing. In a speech or two before, he declares his aversion to a cat, and now only continues of the same opinion, and says, he hates *Parolles* as much as a cat. The other meaning will not do, as *Parolles* could not be meant by the cat which lights always on its legs, for he is now in a fair way to be totally disconcerted.

Mr. STEEVENS.

I am still of my former opinion. [JOHNSON] (Sig. Ii₈ʳ)

[245] [On *Henry V*, 2.3.12: Mistress Quickly on Falstaff's death: —*chrisom child.*] The old quarto has it *crisomb'd child. The* chrysom *was no more than the white cloth put on the new baptised child.* See *Johnson's Canons of Eccles. Law*, 1720. And not a cloth anointed with holy unguent, as described under that article in *Johnson's Dictionary*, that of the *chrism* being a separate operation, and was itself no more than a composition of oil and balsam blessed by the bishop.

I have somewhere (but cannot recollect where) met with this farther account of it; that the *chrysom* was allow'd to be carried out of the church, to enwrap those children which were in too weak a condition to be borne thither, the *chrysom* being supposed to make every place holy. This custom would rather strengthen the allusion to the weak condition of *Falstaff*.

Mr. STEEVENS. (Sig. Kk₂ʳ)

[246] [On *Henry V*, 4.4.16]
   French Soldier. *Est il impossible d' eschapper la force de ton bras.*
   Pistol. *Brass, cur?*] Either *Shakespeare* had very little knowledge in the *French* language, or his over-fondness for punning led him in this place, contrary to his judgment, into an error. Almost any

one knows that the *French* word *bras* is pronounced *brau*; and what resemblance of sound does this bear to *brass*, that *Pistol* should reply, *Brass, cur?* The joke may appear to a reader but would scarce be discovered in the performance of the play.

Mr. HAWKINS.

If the pronounciation of the *French* language be not changed since *Shakespeare*'s time, which is not unlikely, it may be suspected some other man wrote the *French* scenes. [JOHNSON] (Sig. Kk$_3$^{r})

[247] [On *Richard III*, 4.2.115f., Richard III to Buckingham]
[Johnson had written, 'This passage, though I do not believe it corrupted, I do not understand' (V, 320).] *Because that like a jack thou keep'st the stroke between thy begging and my meditation.*] An image like those at *St. Dunstan*'s church in *Fleet-street*, and at the market-houses of several towns in this kingdom, was usually called *a jack of the clock-house.* See Cowley's *Discourse on the Government of* Oliver Cromwel. *Richard* resembles *Buckingham* to one of these automatons, and bids him not suspend the stroke on the clock bell, but strike, that the hour may be past, and himself be at liberty to pursue his meditations.

Mr. HAWKINS. (Sig. Kk$_4$^{r})

[248] [On *King Lear*, 2.4.7: the Fool on Kent in the stocks]
He wears cruel *garters.*] I believe a quibble was here intended. *Crewel* signifies *worsted*, of which stockings, garters, night caps, *&c.* are made, and is used in that sense in *Beaumont* and *Fletcher*'s *Scornful Lady*, act ii.

> For who that had but half his wits about him,
> Would commit the counsel of a serious sin
> To such a *crewel night-cap.*

Mr. STEEVENS. (Sig. Kk$_5$^{r})

[249] [*Ibid.*, 3.4.135: 'Poor Tom''s diet]
> —*Mice and rats and such small deare*
> *Have been my food for seven long year*—]

Warburton, instead of *deare*, proposes *geare*; but I have discovered that these two lines are taken from an old black letter'd romance of *St. Bevys* of *Hampton*, 4to. printed for *William Copland*, in which occurs this passage, stated within *ratts*, &c.

Mr. PERCY. (Sig. Kk$_5$^{r})

[250] [On *Macbeth*, 2.1.56]

— *thou sound and firm-set earth.*] A corrupt reading will sometimes direct us to find out the true one. The first folio has it.

— *thou* sowre *and firm-set* earth.

This brings us very near the right word, which was evidently meant to be,

— *thou* sure *and firm-set* earth.   Mr. STEEVENS.

Certainly right. [JOHNSON]   (Sig. Kk$_6^v$)

[251] [*Ibid.*, 5.1.36]

— *hell is murky.*] Lady *Macbeth* is acting over, in a dream, the business of the murder, and encouraging her husband, as when awake. She, therefore, would never have said any thing of the terrors of hell to one whose conscience she saw was too much alarmed already for her purpose. She certainly imagines herself here talking to *Macbeth*, who (she supposes) has just said *hell is murky*, (*i.e.* hell is a dismal place to go to, in consequence of such a deed) and repeats his words in contempt of his cowardice.

> *Hell is murky!* — *Fie, fie, my lord*, &c.

This explanation, I think, gives a spirit to the passage, which, for want of being understood, has always appeared languid on the stage.[1]

                                      Mr. STEEVENS. (Sig. Kk$_6^v$)

[252] [On *Romeo and Juliet*, 2.1.12ff.]

> — (Venus) *purblind son and heir,*
> *Young* Adam Cupid, *he that shot so true*
> *When King* Cophetua *lov'd the beggar-maid.*]

As the commentators are agreed that *Cupid* is here called *Adam* in allusion to the famous archer *Adam Bell*, the hero of many an ancient ballad: — So I believe, I can refer you to the ballad of King *Cophetua*, &c. In the first of the 3 vols. [of his *Reliques of Ancient Poetry*, 1765] 12mo. p. 141. is an old song of a king's falling in love with a beggar maid, which I take to be the very ballad in question, altho' the name of the king is no longer found in it, which will be no objection, to any one who has compared old copies of ballads with those now extant.

The third stanza begins thus:

[1] In the 1773 edition this sentence ends 'appeared languid, being perhaps misapprehended by those who placed a full point at the conclusion of it' (IV, 513).

> The blinded boy that shoots so trim,
> Did to his closet window steal,
> And drew a dart and shot at him,
> And made him soon his power feel, &c.

I should rather read as in *Shakespeare, The purblind boy.*

If this is the song alluded to by *Shakespeare*, these should seem to be the very lines he had in his eye; and therefore I should suppose the lines in *Romeo and Juliet, &c.* were originally.

> —Her *purblind* son and heir,
> Young *Adam Cupid*, he that shot so *trim*,
> When, &c. —

This word *trim*, the first editors, consulting the general sense of the passage, and not perceiving the allusion, would naturally alter to *true*: yet the former seems the more humourous expression, and, on account of its quaintness, more likely to have been used by the droll *Mercutio*.

Mr. PERCY. (Sig. Kk_8^v–Ll^r)

[253] [On *Hamlet*, 4.5: Ophelia's mad-scene]

Oph. *How should I*, &c.—] There is no part of this play, in its representation on the stage, is more pathetic than this scene, which, I suppose, proceeds from the utter insensibility she has to her own misfortune.

A great sensibility, or none at all, seem to produce the same effect; in the latter, the audience supply what she wants, and in the former, they sympathise.

Mr. REYNOLDS. (Sig. Ll_3^r)

[254] [On *Othello*, 1.3.218f.: *Brabantio*. I never yet did hear/That the bruis'd heart was pierced through the ear.]

Shakespeare was continually changing his first expression for another, either stronger or more uncommon, so that very often the reader, who has not the same continuity or succession of ideas, is at a loss for its meaning. Many of *Shakespeare*'s uncouth strained epithets may be explained, by going back to the obvious and simple expression which is most likely to occur to the mind in that state. I can imagine the first mode of expression that occurred to *Shakespeare* was this:

The troubled heart was never cured by words:

To give it poetical force, he altered the phrase;

> *The* wounded *heart was never reached through the ear:*

Wounded heart he changed to *broken*, and that to *bruised*, as a more uncommon expression. *Reach*, he altered to *touched*, and the transition is then easy to *pierced*, i.e. thoroughly touched. When the sentiment is brought to this state, the commentator, without this unraveling clue, expounds *piercing the heart*, in its common acceptation, *wounding the heart*, which making in this place nonsense, is corrected to *pieced the heart*, which is very stiff, and as *Polonius* says, is a *vile phrase*.

Mr. Reynolds. (Sig. Ll₄ʳ⁻ᵛ)

[255] [*Ibid.*, 2.1.303: Iago on Roderigo]

> —*If this poor brach of* Venice, *whom I trace*
> *For his quick hunting, stand the putting on.*]

The old reading was *trash*, which Dr. *Warburton* judiciously turned into *brach*. But it seems to me, that *trash* belongs to another part of the line, and that we ought to read *trash* for *trace*. To *trash a hound*, is a term of hunting still used in the North, and perhaps elsewhere; i.e. to correct, *to rate*. The sense is, 'If this hound *Roderigo*, whom I rate for *quick hunting*, for over-running the scent, will but *stand the putting on*, will but have patience to be properly and fairly put upon the scent, *&c.*' The context and sense is nothing if we read *trace*. This very hunting-term, to *trash*, is metaphorically used by *Shakespeare* in the *Tempest*, act i. sc. ii.

> *Pro.* Being once perfected how to grant suits,
> How to deny them; whom t'advance, and whom
> To *trash* for *overtopping*.   [1.2.79ff.]

To trash for overtopping; i.e. 'what suitors to check for their too great forwardness.' To *overtop* is when a hound gives his tongue, above the rest, too loudly or too readily; for which he ought to be *trash'd* or rated. *Topper*, in the good sense of the word, is a common name for a hound, in many parts of *England*. *Shakespeare* is fond of allusions to hunting, and appears to be well acquainted with its language.

Mr. Warton. (Sig. Ll₄ᵛ)

[256] [*Ibid.*, 3.3.214: Iago on Desdemona's deceits: 'To seal her father's eyes up close as oak'.]

[Johnson had found 'little relation between *eyes* and *oak*', and proposed to emend to '*owls*': '*As blind as an owl* is a proverb' (VIII, 397).] *To seal her father's eyes up* close as oak.] The *oak* is (I believe) the most *close-grained* wood of the growth of *England*. *Close as oak*, means *close as the grain of the oak*.

Mr. STEEVENS.

I am still of my former opinion. [JOHNSON]   (Sig. Ll$_5$^{r})

[257] [*Ibid.*, 4.1.39; Warburton proposed 'induction': see Johnson's note 221 above.]

Nature could not invest herself in such shadowing passions without some instruction.] However ingenious Dr. *Warburton*'s note may be, it is certainly too forced and farfetch'd. *Othello* alludes only to *Cassio*'s dream, which had been invented and told him by *Iago*, when many confused and very interesting ideas pour in upon the mind all at once, and with such rapidity, that it has not time to shape or digest them. If the mind does not relieve itself by tears, which we know it often does, whether for joy or grief, it produces stupefaction and fainting.

Othello, in broken sentences and single words, all of which have a reference to the cause of his jealousy, shews, that all the proofs are present at once to his mind, which so overpowers it, that he falls in a trance, the natural consequence.

Mr. REYNOLDS. (Sig. Ll$_5$^{r})

206. George Colman, Johnson's edition reviewed

1765

From the *St. James's Chronicle*, October 1765, pp. 8–10, 10–12, and 12–15; Colman reprinted a shortened version in his *Prose on Several Occasions* (3 vols, 1787), II, pp. 59–69.

On Colman (1732–94) see the head-notes to Nos 138 (Vol. 4, pp. 56–9) and 187 (*ibid.*, pp. 440–9). Colman was one of the first proprietors of the *St. James's Chronicle*, together with Bonnell Thornton and David Garrick (see R. P. and M. N. Bond, 'The Minute Books of the *St. James's Chronicle*', *Studies in Bibliography*, 28 (1975), pp. 17–40), and his series of essays 'The Genius' in 1761–2 was one of its early successes. Colman subsequently became a member of the Literary Club with Johnson, Boswell, and their circle, and together with Reynolds, Burke, and Sir John Hawkins was one of the pall-bearers at Johnson's funeral in 1784.

'Johnson's Shakespeare! published! When?' 'This Morning'—'What, at last!'—'*Vix tandem*,[1] 'egad! He has observed Horace's Rule of *nonum in annum*.[2] *Keep the Piece nine years*, as Pope says—I know a Friend of mine that subscribed in Fifty-six'—&c. &c. &c.

Such perhaps is the Language of some little Witling, who thinks his satirical Sallies extremely poignant and severe; but the Appearance of any Production of Mr. Johnson cannot fail of being grateful to the literary World; and, come when they will, like an agreeable Guest, we are sure to give them a hearty Welcome, though perhaps we may have betrayed some little Impatience at their not coming sooner. Nor have the Public in general been deceived. None but Subscribers have a Right to complain; and

[1] Terence, *Phormio*, 234; 'at last!' (Also *Andria*, 470, etc.)
[2] *Ars Poetica*, 388f.: 'Put your parchment in the closet and keep it back till the ninth year'.

they, I suppose, in general meant to shew their Respect for Mr. Johnson rather than to give themselves a Title of becoming clamorous Creditors.

But granting our Editor to be naturally indolent—and naturally indolent we believe him to be—we cannot help wondering at the Number, Vastness, and Excellence of his Productions. A Dictionary of our Language; a Series of admirable Essays in the *Rambler*, as well as, if we are not misinformed, several excellent ones in the *Adventurer*; an Edition of Shakespeare; besides some less considerable Works, all in the Space of no very great Number of Years! and all these the productions of a mere Idler!—We could wish there were a few more of such indolent Men in these Kingdoms.

Of the general Merit of this new Edition of Shakespeare we cannot now be expected to give any Account. It was published but this Morning; but as we obtained a Sight of the Editor's valuable Preface a few Days ago, we shall now oblige our Readers with Extracts from it, together with some Remarks which we have taken the Liberty to subjoin; for the Freedom of which we make no Apology, as Mr. Johnson need not now be told, that notwithstanding 'the Tenderness due to living Reputation, and Veneration to Genius and Learning, he cannot be justly offended at that Liberty of which he has himself so frequently given an Example.'

After some introductory Matter concerning the Degree of Merit, which we may suppose to be stamped on Works by the Suffrage of Antiquity, the Writer proceeds thus:

'*Shakespeare* is above all Writers, at least above all modern Writers, the Poet of Nature ... '. [Quotes pp. 57–60, including Dennis's complaint that Menenius in *Coriolanus* is a buffoon.]

Has not Mr. Johnson here made too liberal a concession to Dennis? and on an Examination of the Play of *Coriolanus*, would it not appear that the Character of Menenius, though marked with the Peculiarities of an hearty old Gentleman, is by no Means that of a Buffoon? Many have defended Polonius, who is much less respectable than Menenius.

The editor then enters into a very sensible and spirited vindication of the mingled drama of Shakespeare, and the interchange of serious and comick scenes in the same play. His reflections on this subject he closes in the following terms. [Quotes pp. 60–3, including Rymer's judgment that Shakespeare's genius was for comedy, not tragedy.]

This Opinion, in which Mr. J. concurs with the Arch Zoilus of our Author, is however very disputable; and we cannot help thinking, that what is said in this Place, as well as what is afterwards thrown out on this head, in speaking of his Faults, is infinitely too strong. A good Comment on Parts of *Othello, Hamlet, Lear, Macbeth,* and other tragick Scenes of Shakespeare, or perhaps a mere Perusal of them, would be the best Method of confuting these Assertions.

'But the Admirers of this great Poet have never less Reason to indulge their Hopes of supreme Excellence, than when he seems fully resolved to sink them in Dejection, and mollify them with tender Emotions by the Fall of Greatness, the Danger of Innocence, or the Crosses of Love. He is not long, soft, and pathetick, without some idle conceit, or contemptible Equivocation.' [p.67]

Does Mr. J. mean to refer his readers to the Fall of Wolsey, the Distresses of Lear, the Murders of Duncan and Desdemona, &c. &c. or was his Mind wholly occupied by some quibbling Scenes in *Romeo and Juliet,* and the *Midsummer's Night's Dream?*

'A Quibble was to him the fatal Cleopatra for which he lost the World, and was content to lose it.' [p. 68]

Has not Mr. J. been as culpably fond of writing upon Quibble, as Shakespeare in pursuing it? and is not this laboured Paragraph upon Quibble as puerile as a Remnant of a School-boy's Declamation? Besides, was it not a Vice common to all the Writers of that Age?

'Familiar Comedy is often more powerful on the Theatre, than in the page; Imperial Tragedy is always less.' [p. 71]

Imperial Tragedy, such at least as is attended with these Effects, is of all others the coldest; and that Tragick Writer has but very ill effected the Purposes of that Species of Drama whose Productions are more powerful in the Page than on the Theatre. *Cato,* perhaps, may possess more Dignity and Force in the Closet; but we know that *Richard, Lear, Othello,* &c. have most Power on the Stage.

[Quotes Johnson's discussion of the Unities.] There is much good Sense, sound Criticism, and fine Writing in these Observations on the Unities; and it is certain that a strict Observation of the Unities of Time and Place have not only 'given more Trouble to the Poet, than Pleasure to the Auditor,' but have perhaps created as many Absurdities as they have prevented. Yet it were to have been wished that Mr. J. had in this, as in all other Instances, rather maintained the Character of a Reasoner than assumed that of a Pleader. All Liberties may be carried to an Excess, and the Violation of these Unities may be so gross as to become unpardonable. Shakespeare himself seems to have been sensible of this; and therefore introduced the Chorus into *Henry the Fifth* to waft us from Shore to Shore; and for the same Reason he brings in the Personage of Time in the Character of Chorus in the *Winter's Tale* to apologise for the Lapse of sixteen Years, the Distance between the supposed Birth of Perdita and her Appearance as the Nymph beloved by Florizel.[1] It might have been worth while therefore to have endeavoured in some Measure to ascertain how far these Unities may allowably be transgressed. Such an Investigation by Mr. J. would have still enhanced the Value of this excellent Preface, and must have been agreeable to all readers.

'There has always prevailed a Tradition, that Shakespeare wanted Learning, that he had no regular Education, nor much Skill in the dead Languages. Jonson, his Friend, affirms, that *he had small Latin, and no Greek.*' [p. 76]

Mr. J. certainly quotes from Memory in this Place. The affirmation of Ben Jonson is that Shakespeare 'had *small* Latin, and LESS Greek,' which implies his having some Share of both. Even in our Times, a Man who has *some* Greek has commonly a pretty competent Knowledge of Latin.

In *The Taming of the Shrew* our Author very familiarly quotes both Ovid and Terence in the Original; and some Passages of the Plot, as has lately been observed,[2] are borrowed from the *Trinummus* of Plautus, of which we know of no Translation extant in those Times.

After having finished the critical Examen of his Author Mr. Johnson next proceeds to a Recapitulation of his several Editors, accompanied with Remarks on their various Merits and Demerits. Of Rowe and Pope he speaks very candidly and justly; of Theobald, (hitherto undoubtedly the most meritorious Editor

[1] Cf. Gildon (2.222f., 248).
[2] By Colman himself, in the preface to his translation of Terence, 1765: quoted by Farmer, p. 275 below.

of Shakespeare) we think that he speaks too hardly; and of Hanmer much too favourably. Of the last Right Rev. Annotator on our Author he speaks respectfully, though freely; and to atone for the Liberties taken with him Mr. Johnson sacrifices to his Resentment the Authors of the *Canons of Criticism*, and *The Revisal of Shakespeare's Text*. In short, Mr. J. treats Dr. W. as termagant Wives do their Husbands, who will let nobody call them to Account but themselves.

Lastly, Mr. J. apologizes for his own Labours. The Examination of these, though we should even attempt it hereafter, we cannot enter upon at present. We cannot however but express our Concern at his Declaration in the Preface, where he says that 'the Poetical Beauties or Defects I have not been very diligent to observe.' Such Observations might have been expected from Mr. Johnson; and Mr. Pope has declared, though he avoided a Criticism upon our Author himself, that 'to do it effectually, and not superficially, would be the best Occasion that any just Writer could take to form the Judgment and Taste of our Nation.'[1] Theobald also (in whose Preface there is much valuable Matter) professed that he left that Part of an Editor 'open to every willing Undertaker'.[2] Would to Heaven that Mr. J. had been that willing Undertaker!

Speaking of the old Copies, Mr. Johnson says that he 'collected such as he could procure, and wished for more, but did not find the Collectors of these Rarities very communicative'. We are much surprized at this. Mr. Garrick, we all know, is one of the principal Collectors of these Rarities; and as his Cabinet has, we all know too, been thrown open to every other Editor of old English Authors, we cannot imagine that it has been partially shut against Mr. Johnson.

On the whole this Preface, as it is an elaborate, so it is also a fine Piece of Writing. It possesses all the Virtues and Vices of the peculiar Stile of its Author. It speaks, perhaps, of Shakespeare's Beauties too sparingly, and of his Faults too hardly; but it contains, nevertheless, much Truth, good sense, and just Criticism.

[1] Cf. 2.403.
[2] Cf. 2.481.

207. William Kenrick, Johnson attacked

1765

Texts: (a) on the *Preface*, from the *Monthly Review*, xxxiii, pp. 285–301 and 374–89 (October, November 1765); (b) on the *Notes*, from Kenrick, *A Review of Doctor Johnson's New Edition of Shakespeare: in which the Ignorance, or Inattention, of that Editor is exposed, and the Poet defended from the Persecution of his Commentators* (1765).

William Kenrick (1725?–79), miscellaneous writer, translated Rousseau (*Eloisa*, 1761; *Emile*, 1763; *Miscellaneous Works*, 5 vols, 1767). In 1759 he succeeded Goldsmith on the *Monthly Review*, mainly reporting on foreign literature, but ceased to be a contributor after 1765, as a result of his attacks on Johnson. The editor, Ralph Griffiths, himself reviewed Kenrick's *Review* (xxxiii, pp. 457–67) and while acknowledging the justness of several of his criticisms deplored the manner of the attack: 'Mr. Kenrick is, in controversy, what the North-American Indians are in war; and comes armed with the tomahawk and scalping-knife, to slay, and to strip the slain, with the barbarity of a *Mohawk* or a *Cherokee*' (p. 458). Kenrick subsequently issued *A Defence of Mr. Kenrick's Review. By a Friend* (1766).

A prolific journalist, Kenrick contributed to Griffin's *Gentleman's Journal* from 1768 on, and in 1775 founded his own *London Review of English and Foreign Literature*, which was carried on after his death by his son, William Shakespeare Kenrick. His play *Falstaff's Wedding*, a 'sequel' to *The Merry Wives of Windsor*, was performed once only at Drury Lane (12 April 1766), but Kenrick managed to have it printed four times between 1766 and 1781. He was notorious for the violence and scurrility with which he abused Goldsmith, Johnson, Boswell, Colman, Garrick, and others. Yet as a critic he was often shrewd and intelligent.

[a] On Johnson's *Preface*. October 1765

It is a circumstance very injurious to the productions even of the best writers that the public prepossession is up in their favour before they make their appearance; especially if such prepossession hath been kept any considerable time in a state of expectation and suspense: delay being in itself a kind of disappointment, which prepares the mind for a still greater mortification, and even disposes us to conceive ourselves disappointed if we are not gratified with something superior to what we had at first a right to expect. A number of apologies are ready, and various are the pleas admitted in justification of a precipitated performance. Errour and inadvertence are imputed, as natural effects, to haste; and even ignorance itself finds a convenient shelter under the pretence of rapidity of composition. A very different fate attends on those works whose publication, having been long promised and frequently deferred, is supposed to be delayed only to render them by so much the more valuable when they appear, as their appearance may have been procrastinated.

Under this disadvantage lies the present edition of Shakespeare; a poet who least requires, and most deserves a comment, of all the writers his age produced. We cannot help thinking it, therefore, a misfortune almost as singular as his merit that, among so many ingenious scholiasts that have employed themselves in elucidating his writings, hardly one of them hath been found in any degree worthy of him. They all seem to have mistaken the route in which only they could do honour to themselves, or be useful to the reader. Engaged in the piddling task of adjusting quibbles and restoring conundrums, they have neglected the illustration of characters, sentiments and situations. Instead of aspiring to trim the ruffled bays that have a little obscured his brow they have been laboriously and servilely employed in brushing the dirt from his shoes. Instead of strewing flowers and planting fresh laurels on his tomb, they have been irreverently trampling down the turf that had otherwise covered his dust with perpetual verdure. From the present Editor, it is true, we hoped better things. But what shall we say? when he himself confesses that, as to 'the poetical beauties or defects of his author, he hath not been very diligent to observe them: having given up this part of his design to chance and caprice.' This is surely a strange concession to be made by the author of the proposals[1] for printing this work by subscription! We were by them given to understand that the Editor would proceed in a manner very different from his predecessors; and were encouraged to hope that Shakespeare would no longer be commented on like a barren or obsolete writer, whose works were of no other use than to employ the sagacity of antiquarians and philologers. But perhaps our Editor found the task of commenting on Shakespeare as a *poet* much more difficult than he had conceived it to be. It might sound as harsh in the ear of the public to tax a writer whom it hath so much honoured by its approbation with want of capacity for writing such a commentary, as it doubtless would, in the ears of Dr. Johnson, to hear himself charged with want of application to it, when he acknowledges the great encouragement he has had the honour of receiving for that purpose. We should be very tender, be the occasion what it would, of laying any writer of acknowledged merit under the necessity of pleading guilty either to the charge of ignorance or indolence. But we cannot help subscribing to the opinion of a very ingenious critic* when he affirms that 'every writer is justly chargeable with want of knowledge when he betrays it on the subject he is treating of, let him be ever so capable of treating other subjects, or however justly founded may be his reputation for learning in general.' It hath been observed in some remarks already published † on this occasion that our Editor's notes, few and exceptionable as they are, lay claim to our admiration if we reflect on the extreme indolence of the Writer, who is naturally an *idler*. How far such a plea may be satisfactory to the purchasers of this edition we know not; but we have too high an opinion of the Editor's character to think he will more readily acquiesce under the imputation of ingratitude than under that of incapacity. At the same time, however, we cannot but express our apprehensions that every judicious reader who may accompany us through a fair and impartial review of his preface and commentary will think, with us, that there are many evident marks of the want of ingenuity or industry in the Commentator.

---

[1] See Vol. 4, No. 160. There, however, Johnson made it quite clear that he did not intend to illustrate 'faults and beauties' in the conventional manner (pp. 272f.).

* The author of the *Canons of Criticism* [i.e. Thomas Edwards: see Vol. 3, No . 127 and Vol. 4, No. 168].

† In the *St. James's Chronicle* [i.e. George Colman, in the previous item].

We find little in the first five pages of our Editor's preface but trite and common-place reflections, on our veneration for antiquity, and on the general talents of Shakespeare; delivered in that pompous style which is so peculiar to himself, and is so much admired by some kind of readers. In some places, however, he is less verbose; and then he is generally sensible, instructive and entertaining. (285–7) [Quotes from 'Shakespeare' to 'passions', pp. 57–60.] After bestowing this just elogium on Shakespeare our editor proceeds to exculpate him from the censures of Rymer, Dennis, and Voltaire; entering particularly into a defence of the tragi-comedy, or that mixed kind of drama, which hath given such great offence to the minor critics. He states the fact, and considers it thus (289). [Quotes from 'Shakespeare's' to 'variety', pp. 60–2.]

We do not feel the force of this reasoning; though we think the critics have condemned this kind of drama too severely. What follows also is to us a little problematical. Dr. Johnson prefers Shakespeare's comic scenes to his tragic: in the latter, he says, 'there is always something wanting, while the former often surpasses expectation or desire. His tragedy seems to be skill, and his comedy instinct.' As this is a general assertion, unsupported by any particular examples, we cannot very easily controvert it; but we are apt to suspect it is founded in a great degree on the preference which the Editor himself may possibly be disposed to give to comedy in general. Different auditors, as he observes, have different habitudes; so that, were we to put this assertion to the proof by particular applications, we should possibly find *quot homines tot sententiæ*.[1]

After having enumerated the various excellencies of this great poet, our Editor proceeds to mention his faults; faults, says he, '*sufficient to obscure and overwhelm any other merit.*' The first defect he charges him with is indeed a very capital one; from which we should be glad, and shall endeavour, to exculpate him.

[Quotes from 'His first' to 'place', p. 65.] 'No question,' says our Editor in another place, 'can be more innocently discussed than a dead poet's pretensions to renown.' But tho' this be true some tenderness surely should be felt for his probity. Shakespeare is here charged with 'sacrificing virtue to convenience,' for no

---

[1] Terence, *Phormio*, 454: 'So many men so many minds', i.e. opinions.

other reason than that he seemed 'more careful to please than instruct,' and 'to write without any moral purpose'. But if it be admitted, as our Editor actually admits, that a system of social duty may be selected from his writings, and that his precepts and axioms were virtuous; we may justly ask whether they are less so for dropping casually from him? Must a writer be charged with making a sacrifice of virtue because he does not professedly inculcate it? Is every writer *ex professo* a parson or a moral philosopher? It is doubtless always the *moralist*'s duty to strive at least to make the world better, but we should think it no inconsiderable merit in a *comic-poet* to be able to divert and amuse the world without making it worse; especially if he should occasionally drop such virtuous precepts and axioms as would serve to form a system of social duty. We are, for these reasons, so far from thinking that the barbarity of his age cannot extenuate the fault here censured that we think he stands in need of no other excuse than our Editor hath on another occasion made for him, viz. his ignorance of poetical composition. He did not know that the rules of criticism required the drama to have a particular moral; nor did he conceive himself bound, as a *poet*, to write like a *philosopher*. He carries his persons, therefore, indifferently through right and wrong for the same reason as he makes them laugh and cry in the same piece, and is justifiable on the same principles: it is a strict imitation of nature, and Shakespeare is the Poet of Nature. Were our Poet now living, and possessed of Dr. Johnson's critical knowledge, we presume he would make no more nor greater sacrifices of *virtue* to *convenience* than his Editors may have done. Shakespeare, it is true, hath depicted none of

Those faultless monsters which the world ne'er saw.

He did not presume to limit the designs of providence to the narrow bounds of poetical justice; but hath displayed the sun shining, as it really does, both on the just and the unjust. . . .

Shakespeare is said to be seldom very successful in his comic scenes when he engages his characters in raillery or repartée, or as Dr. Johnson more quaintly expresses it, 'reciprocations of smartness and contests of sarcasm.' Their jests, we are told, are commonly gross and their pleasantry licentious: nor will, it seems, the barbarity of his age excuse our Poet with regard to this defect, any more than the former. For our part, however, we think that Shakespeare is sometimes peculiarly happy in hitting off that kind of sheer wit for which some modern writers, particularly Congreve and Farquhar, have been so generally admired. The reciprocations of smartness between Benedick and Beatrice in *Much Ado About Nothing* are scarce inferior to any thing of the kind; and tho' we cannot pretend that the dialogue of his gentlemen and ladies is so delicate and refined as that of Cibber and some other writers, it is full as witty, and not a jot more licentious than what we frequently find in Vanbrugh and Congreve, who had not the barbarity of the age to plead in excuse.

As to the quirks and quibbles of Shakespeare's clowns, which sometimes infect the graver parts of his writings, we cannot be of Dr. Johnson's opinion. [Quotes from 'A quibble' to 'lose it', pp. 67f.]

Quaintly as all this is expressed,* and boldly as it is asserted, we cannot be persuaded that Shakespeare's native genius was not too sublime to be so much captivated with the charms of so contemptible an object. How poorly soever it might descend to trifle with an *ignis fatuus* by owl-light, we cannot think an eagle, soaring in the direct beams of the meridian sun, could be allured to look down with pleasure on the feeble glimmerings of a rush-light. It is not impossible, indeed, that the necessity of accommodating himself in this particular so frequently to the humour and taste of the times had rendered a practice habitual to him, which his own better taste and judgment could not fail to condemn. We do therefore readily adopt Sir Thomas Hanmer's defence of Shakespeare with regard to this point. It must be remembered, says that judicious Editor, that 'our poet wrote for the stage, rude and unpolished as it then was' [Quotes to 'taste and judgment as a writer': Vol. 3, pp. 119f.]

In speaking of our poet's faults in tragedy the Editor says 'his performance seems constantly to be worse as his labour is more . . . ' [Quotes to 'pity or resentment of his reader', pp. 66–7.] It is a pity our Editor does not refer us to the particular passages that justify these general assertions. For, admitting the truth of

---

* Doth not this whole paragraph serve egregiously to prove that altho' our Editor may not be fond of down-right punning, he takes full as much delight in starting and hunting down a poor conceit as he affirms Shakespeare did? We will venture to assert, indeed, that this is a species of quibbling which, barren and pitiful as it is, seems to give the critic himself so much delight that he is 'content to purchase it by the sacrifice of reason, propriety and truth.'

them, yet if it be very seldom, as we will venture to say it is, that Shakespeare appears reduced to the necessity of straining his faculties; if he be hardly ever endeavouring, like other tragic poets, at amplification, or to make an impertinent display of his knowledge, what shall we say to the candour of that commentator who lays hold of a few defects, *ubi plura nitent*,[1] on which to found a general charge against his author? Were we disposed to be as harsh and severe on the learned Annotator as the Annotator himself hath been on his GREAT, INIMITABLE Author, we might here appeal to the public to decide which of them most demands our *pity* or merits our *resentment*.

He goes on: 'It is incident to Shakespeare to be now and then entangled with an unwieldy sentiment, which he cannot well express ...'. We know not whether this *incident* might not be called with more propriety a misfortune rather than a fault, and be imputed with greater justice to the then imperfect state of our language than to Shakespeare. ...

Having thus endeavoured to prove the faults of Shakespeare 'sufficient to obscure and *overwhelm any other merit*,' our Editor attempts dexterously to change sides, and to stand up in his defence against those who have accused him of violating those laws which have been instituted and established by the joint authority of poets and of critics; we mean, the unities of action, place and time. ... It happens, however, very unluckily for our Editor, that in spite of that respect which he is so notoriously ready to pay to his opponents he shews himself to be as indifferent a pleader *for* Shakespeare as he hath proved *against* him. Nay, we entertain some suspicion that the critical Reader will, on a due consideration of what is hereafter advanced, be apt to think Dr. Johnson too little acquainted with the nature and use of the drama to engage successfully in a dispute of so much difficulty as that which relates to the breach or observation of the dramatic unities.

To begin with the first. If we except the historical plays of Shakespeare, where these unities are never looked for; in his other works, our Editor says, he has well enough preserved the *unity* of *action*. ... 'Shakespeare is the poet of nature: but his plan has commonly what Aristotle requires, a beginning, a middle and an end ...'. All this, however, might be said of many simple

[1] *Ars Poetica*, 351: 'when the beauties in a poem are more in number'.

histories, that make no pretences to unity of action. Their merely having a beginning, middle, and end, is not sufficient. Aristotle's meaning is more distinctly explained by Bossu, thus: 'The causes and design of any action constitute the beginning of it: the effect of such causes, and the difficulties attending the execution of such design, are the middle of it; and the unravelling or obviating these difficulties are the end of it.' It is not our business here to contend whether Shakespeare be or be not defensible in this particular; it is enough for us to enquire how far our Editor hath actually defended him. Laying authorities, however, aside we cannot, on the principles of commonsense, conceive how any dramatic Writer can be justly said to have preserved the unity of action who hath confessedly shewn no regard to those of time and place,* with which we apprehend it to be very strictly connected. Certain at least it is that if any considerable time should elapse between, or space divide, the two parts of an action we should be more apt to consider them as two distinct and different actions than as united parts of one and the same action. This will be made more evident by our enquiry into the nature of these unities, and their essentiality to the drama. Before we enter on this point, however, we shall make some remarks on the supposed necessity on which, Dr. Johnson conceives, the observation of these unities is founded. To enable the Reader fully to comprehend the subject in dispute, we shall quote the whole of what our Editor hath advanced on this curious topic; which we are the more readily led to do, on account of his own suggestion, that it is 'not dogmatically but deliberatively, written, and may recall the principles of the drama to a new examination.' (290–6) [Quotes pp. 68 to 73.]

Plausible as these arguments may at first sight appear, we will venture to say there is hardly one of them that does not seem false, or foreign to the purpose. We apprehend that the assumption on which our Editor proceeds is not true. The observation of these unities may be necessary without requiring the dramatic fable in its *materiality* (as this writer terms it) to be either credited or credible. It is not requisite, in order to justify the necessity of such observation, that the Spectator should *really imagine* himself one hour in Alexandria and the next at Rome; or that he should actually *believe* the transactions of months and years to pass in a

---

* Our editor admits that Shakespeare hath shewn no regard to the unities of time and place.

few hours. The dramatic unities, if necessary, are necessary to support the *apparent probability*, not the *actual credibility* of the drama. Our learned Editor may not probably distinguish the difference; but Cicero will tell him *nihil est tam* INCREDIBILE, *quod non dicendo fiat* PROBABILE:[1] and if such be the power of oratory, can we doubt that a similar effect is produced by theatrical representation? Now, it is the senses and the passions, and not the imagination and understanding, that are in both these cases immediately affected. We do not pretend to say that the spectators are not always in their senses; or that they do not know (if the question were put to them) that the stage is only a stage, and the players only players. But we will venture to say they are often so intent on the scene as to be absent with regard to every thing else. A spectator properly affected by a dramatic representation makes no reflections about the fiction or the reality of it, so long as the action proceeds without grossly offending or palpably imposing on the senses. It is very true that a person going to Drury-lane to see the Tragedy of *Venice Preserved* knows, when he places himself in the pit, that he is in the theatre at London and not in Venice. But the curtain is no sooner drawn up than he begins to be interested in the business of the scene, the orchestra vanishes, and the views of St. Mark and the Rialto dispose him (not to think how *he* came *there* but) to see and hear what is to be *done* and *said* there. When his attention is fully engaged to the fable, and his passions affected by the distress of the characters, he is still farther removed from his own character and situation; and may be conceived *quatenus* a spectator to be rather at Venice than at London. The image of Mr. Garrick, it is true, is painted on the retina of his eye, and the voice of Mrs. Cibber mechanically affects the tympanum of his ear: but it is as true also that he sees only the transports of Jaffier and listens only to the ravings of Belvidera. And yet there is no frenzy, no calenture in the case; the man may be as much in his senses as Horace, when he supposed the same deception might happen to himself under the like influence of theatrical magic [Quotes *Epistles*, 2.1.210ff.][2]

---

[1] *Paradoxa Stoicorum*, Pref. 3: 'nothing is so difficult to believe that oratory cannot make it acceptable'.

[2] 'Methinks that poet is able to walk a tight rope, who with airy nothings wrings my heart, inflames, soothes, fills it with vain alarms like a magician, and sets me down now at Thebes, now at Athens.'

The spectator is unquestionably deceived, but the deception goes no farther than the passions, it affects our sensibility but not our understanding; and is by no means so powerful a delusion as to affect our *belief.* There is a species of probability which is necessary to be adhered to, even to engage the attention of the senses and affect our passions; but this regards the *representation* and not the *materiality* of the fable. The *incredulus odi* of Horace hath been cited with too great latitude of construction. It can hardly be supposed that the poet should stigmatize himself for incredulity merely because he could not believe that Progne was metamorphosed into a bird, or Cadmus into a serpent. Or, supposing he might, why should he use the verb *odi*? Why should he *hate* or *detest* a thing merely because he thought it incredible? It is natural indeed to hate whatever offends, or is shocking to, the senses. The truth is, these terms are directly applied to the *form* or *representation*, and not to the materiality of the fable; as is evident on perusing the context. The whole passage runs thus;

Aut agitur res in Scenis, aut acta refertur. ...[1]

We find no objection made to the credibility of these fables in themselves (for on this the auditor may not give himself the trouble to bestow a single reflection), but to the unseemliness or improbability that must necessarily attend their representation on the stage: by which means the senses would be offended with a palpable absurdity, not the understanding be imposed on by a falsehood. For he allows that the very same things may be agreeably related which will not bear to be represented.

—But to return to our Editor. That the judgment never mistook any dramatic representation we readily admit; but that our senses frequently do is certain from the effect it hath on our passions. Nay, Dr. Johnson himself, after all the pains he takes to prove the drama *absolutely incredible*, is reduced, for want of making this necessary distinction, to confess that it really is *credited*. ... The method he takes to evade this evident contradiction is by adopting the sophistry of those philosophers who strive to account for the emotions of pity, gratitude, generosity and all the nobler

[1] Horace, *Ars Poetica*, 179ff.: 'Either an event is acted on the stage, or the action is narrated ... you will not bring upon the stage what should be performed behind the scenes', such as acts of atrocity. 'Whatever you thus show me, I discredit and abhor.'

passions, from a retrospect to that of self-love. [Quotes from 'The drama is credited' to 'exposed', p. 71.] Now nothing is more certain than that those spectators who are most affected by dramatic representation are usually the least capable of making a comparison between the picture and the original. There are also few auditors that can put themselves in the place of the characters represented; and we believe still fewer who are moved because they reflect that they themselves are exposed to the evils represented on the stage. The audience are moved by mere mechanical motives; they laugh and cry from mere sympathy at what a moment's reflection would very often prevent them from laughing or crying at all. 'If there be any fallacy', continues our Editor, 'it is not that we fancy the players, but that we fancy ourselves unhappy for a moment ...' In reply to this it may be safely affirmed that we neither fancy the players nor ourselves unhappy: our imagination hath nothing to do with the immediate impressions whether of joy or sorrow; we are in this case merely passive, our organs are in unison with those of the players on the stage, and the convulsions of grief or laughter are purely involuntary. As to the delight we experience from Tragedy, it no more proceeds directly from a consciousness of fiction than the pleasure we reap from Comedy; but is the physical consequence of having the transient sense of pain or danger excited in us by sympathy, instead of actually and durably feeling it ourselves. Hence that diminution of pain which gives rise to the pleasing sensation, to which the ingenious Author of the *Enquiry into the Origin of our ideas of the Sublime and Beautiful* gives the name of *delight*. And hence it is that such persons who are most affected with the distress of a Tragedy are generally most delighted with its representation.

But we shall here take leave of this performance for the present; deferring our farther remarks on the Editor's misapprehension of the dramatic unities to another opportunity. (298–301)

[November, 1765] It is presumed the distinction we endeavoured to establish in our former article, respecting the effects of dramatic representation, is too obviously supported by facts to be called in question by even the most scrupulous reader. It is not a little surprising, therefore, to find the critics implicitly adopting each other's sentiments in this particular, and successively maintaining the necessity of our being so far deceived as to believe the distress

of a tragedian to be real, before we can possibly be affected by it. . . .
It is notorious, however, as hath already been observed, that the
spectator is affected and yet believes nothing at all of the actual
distress of the scene, or as our Editor calls it, the *materiality* of
the fable. It is, also, no less certain that the interest we take in the
representation of the drama doth by no means depend on those
retrospective refinements of intellect to which Dr. Johnson
imputes it. We are moved by sympathy, and to this end the appearance, the imitation of distress, even though we are conscious
on reflection that it is no more than imitation, is yet sufficient:

> Ut ridentibus arrident, ita flentibus adsunt
> Humani vultus. — [1]

. . . It does not appear to us that either Aristotle or Horace,
from whom we seem to derive the 'necessity of observing the
unities of time and place,' had any such notion, as the moderns
entertain, of 'the necessity of making the drama credible;' at
least in such a manner as Dacier, Bossu, Rapin, Le Blanc, and
Dr. Johnson would have us believe. The defective manner in
which the plays of the ancients were represented rendered indeed
such an attempt to impose on the audience still more impractic-
able than we even find it at present, with all the advantage of
moving scenes and perspective paintings. . . .

It is observed by the French academy, in their strictures on
the *Cid* of Corneille, that 'it is essential to the probable, whether
it be of the ordinary or extraordinary kind, that when it is presented
to the audience, either the *immediate impression it makes on the
mind*, or their reflections on its parts and consistency, should
excite them to believe what is represented to have been true, as
they find nothing in such representation repugnant to that belief.'
Here we see the probable is defined to be that which is generally
conceived possible, and carries with it an apparent proof of such
possibility.

We come now to consider how far the observation of the dramatic unities may be necessary to support the apparent proofs of
this possibility; and how far Shakespeare hath broken through
them. To begin, as usual, with that of action. The unity of action
is sufficiently observed when a single end is proposed, to which

---

[1] *Ars Poetica*, 101f.: 'As men's faces smile on those who smile, so they respond to those
who weep'.

all the means made use of in the piece effectually tend. These means, consisting of subordinate actions, may accordingly be few or many provided their several directions converge to one point, in which they unite and are concentrated. There is one circumstance, however, to be particularly observed with regard to the unities in general; and this is that those of action, time and place, should never break into that of character. It were needless indeed to mention this to critics who maintain the necessity of observing these unities in the strictest manner, as described by Boileau,

> Qu'en un lieu, qu'en un jour, un seul fait accomplé
> Tienne jusqu' à la fin le theatre rempli:

because it would be impossible for them to err in this particular. But the case is different with regard to those who may affirm with Dr. Johnson that 'because the drama exhibits successive imitations of successive actions, the second imitation may represent an action that happened years after the first.' It is absolutely essential to dramatic representation that the persons of the drama should be known and fixed. Now, though it is not to be supposed that in the space of twenty-four hours any great revolution can happen in the personality of the characters, so great a change is naturally produced in a term of years that the apparent proofs of the dramatic possibility required would necessarily be wanting in the representation. For instance, when Leontes in *The Winter's Tale* is looking at the imaginary statue of Hermione, and says to Paulina

> ——But yet, Paulina,
> Hermione was not so much wrinkled, nothing
> So aged as this seems: [5.3.27f.]

It is impossible for the spectator not to be offended with the palpable affront which is here offered to his senses*. For if the features of the player be not artificially disguised, since she was seen about an hour before sixteen years younger, in the first and second act, it is a most glaring imposition on his eye-sight; and though her features should be a little begrimed with charcoal to help the deceit, her shape, air, and manner are the same, and it is plain she was too recently in his company to pass upon him so soon again for an old acquaintance that had been sixteen years

* Not merely to his understanding, for his imagination might possibly have salved the absurdity from the reflection of its being a fiction.

absent. The imposition is still more gross with respect to the personality of Perdita, in the same play; whom Paulina presents in the second act in swaddling cloaths—

> —Behold, my Lords,
> Altho' the print be little, the whole matter
> And copy of the father; eye, nose, lip—   [2.3.97ff.]

Can any thing be more improbable than to see the same Perdita in the fourth act a marriageable young shepherdess? Whatever liberties Shakespeare hath taken with the unities in other plays, he knew too well to attempt an imposition of this kind. He hath, therefore, introduced the chorus at the end of the third act, by which means he hath in fact divided the drama into two parts, each part having different *dramatis personae*.

Dr. Johnson questions whether Shakespeare knew the unities and rejected them by design, or deviated from them by happy ignorance. It is impossible perhaps to determine this point; but we think it pretty clear that whether he learned the rules of the drama from the writings of the ancients or not, he was better versed in them than any of his successors that did. What should hinder Shakespeare from drinking knowledge at the fountain-head as well as the ancients? Must all knowledge be called *ignorance* that is not obtained at second-hand, by means of books? It is proper for those who cannot go alone to be led by others; but Shakespeare was the fondling of Nature, and needed not the leading-strings of Aristotle. It does not follow, however, that the practice of the one and the precepts of the other are incompatible. It is by no means necessary that Nature's strong and vigorous offspring should be confined to that strict regularity of diet and regimen which is requisite to support the weak and puny nurslings of art. They both, however, pursue the same objects, and attain them nearly by the same means. Hence, though it should be true that Shakespeare was

> above the critic's law,
> And but from Nature's fountains scorn'd to draw,

he might not deviate essentially from the general law of the Stagyrite, although he did not servilely adopt his particular rules. Indeed the point is almost universally given up with regard to the unity of *place*, the preservation of which gives rise to more improbabilities than the breach of it.—But to return to that of action. There is no doubt but Shakespeare hath taken many exceptionable liberties in this respect for want of a due attention to the mechanical part of composition. And this he hath done in common with the first dramatic poets among the ancients*. Nor is he, in this particular, to be justified by any thing his Editor hath advanced: for the unity of action must not only be so far observed as to preserve the unity of character but also so far as to preserve an apparent unity of design in the fable.

As to the unity of time, Dr. Johnson is also strangely mistaken with regard to its essentiality in the drama. 'A play read (says he) affects the mind like a play acted. . . .' Here again our Editor seems to betray a want of acquaintance with the conduct and effects of the drama. It is very certain that a longer or shorter time may be allowed to pass between the acts, provided the union of character be preserved, and nothing intervene between the two parts of the action but the lapse of time; there is yet a wide difference between the auditor of a drama and the reader of a narrative. Few things can be represented in the same time they are related; so that it would be impossible to *represent* the whole life of an hero, or the revolutions of an empire, in the same time as the history of them might be read. It is indeed impossible for the action represented to seem to be longer than the actual time of representation; for as we before observed it is the senses, and not the imagination, that is immediately employed on the representation.

Dr. Johnson indeed says that '. . . In contemplation we easily contract the time of real actions, and therefore willingly permit it to be contracted when we only see their imitation.'

In this argument, however, as in almost all his other reasoning on the subject, the conclusion hath little to do with the premises. During the actual representation of an action we are not *contemplating* but *observing*; and it is impossible for us either to shorten or to prolong the time of such representation: but when it ceases, as at the end of an act or even in shifting the scene, the attention of the senses being taken off, the imagination is at liberty to act during the interval,[1] which, however short, is sufficient for the purpose. And hence we see that the frequent shifting of the scenes, though it may break in upon the restrictions of action and place,

---

* See Aristotle's *Poetics*, Chap. VI.
[1] This is, in fact, what Johnson had argued: p. 72 above.

it affords an opportunity of preserving that of time together with the first and grand rule of probability. It is pleasant enough to see how the French critics, who affect to abide by the strictest observance of the unities, perplex themselves to excuse Corneille for the multiplicity of incidents in the *Cid*; the hero of which fights two duels, marches against the enemy, returns, is brought to a solemn trial; fights again, and finds means to reconcile himself to his mistress, whose father he had slain; and all this in the space of four and twenty hours. Now it is certain that all these actions, if properly disposed in succession, and judiciously divided, might be so represented as never to break in upon dramatic probability.

The French, indeed, in support of the unity of place, maintain that the stage never should be empty during the act; in consequence of their observance of this rule, however, they are guilty of much greater absurdities than would arise from shifting the scene. It is mentioned as an instance of consummate skill in Corneille that he hath provided, in one of his plays, for keeping the stage full while one of the characters goes to the field to fight, and returns conqueror. Now had this supposed combat passed during the interval between the acts, or even during the shifting of the scene, it had not transgressed the bounds of dramatic probability, because it then had passed during the interlude of the imagination; but the audience would not fail of perceiving the improbability of a combat's being fought while they had been listening to some twenty or thirty lines spoken by the persons of the stage. The unity of time is, indeed, so far essential to the drama that the successive actions represented must be confined to the time of actual representation; although the intervals between them may be as long as the poet pleases, consistent with the preservation of the unity of character, and that of the design of the fable.

In respect to the unity of place it appears more than probable that the pretended necessity of it originally arose from the imperfect state of the ancient theatres, as it is plain that the French poets have absurdly involved themselves in the most ridiculous perplexities by adopting it to an unnecessary degree. There can be no doubt, however, that it is so far essential to the drama as it is necessary to preserve the unity of action: for as the interval of time may in some cases be so great as to vary the personality, or

197

destroy the unity of character, so the transition of place may be so great as to destroy the unity of the action. We should not be more vehement, indeed, than Dr. Johnson in reproaching a poet who should make his first act pass in Venice and his next in Cyprus, provided they were both so nearly related as when Shakespeare wrote his *Othello*; but we should have[1] no great opinion of the dramatic conduct of a piece the first scene of which should be laid in England, and the last in China. In any other respect, however, it is certain that the unity of place is unnecessary to the modern drama, as the attention of the spectator is always diverted from the action of the piece, and the imagination is at liberty during the change of the scene.

It appears, on the whole, that the unities are essential to the drama, though not in that degree as hath been asserted by the critics; so that the result of Dr. Johnson's enquiries concerning them is as erroneous as his supposition of the necessity on which they were founded. (374–81).

Having treated of the character and abilities of the poet Dr. Johnson proceeds to consider those of his editors (384)....
[Quotes the accounts of Rowe and Pope, pp. 84f.] Dr. Johnson proceeds: 'Pope was succeeded by Theobald, a man of narrow comprehension and small acquisitions, with no native and intrinsic splendour of genius, with little of the artificial light of learning, but zealous for *minute accuracy*, and not negligent in pursuing [it]. He collated the ancient copies, and *rectified many errours*. A man so anxiously scrupulous might have been expected to do more, but what *little he did* was commonly right.'—Is our Editor here altogether consistent? Is Theobald's *doing little* compatible with his having been zealously and diligently attached to minute accuracy; with his having collated the ancient copies and *rectified many errours*?

Dr. Johnson indeed proceeds to treat poor Theobald with great severity, summing up his character, as an Editor, with the following reflections. 'Theobald, thus weak and ignorant....'
It is very true, as Dr. Johnson observes, that Theobald hath escaped alone with reputation from the task of commenting on Shakespeare; we cannot impute it, however, to the motives assigned by the present Editor. On the contrary, we are well

---

[1] The word 'have' is inserted in the margin by the editor of the *Monthly Review*, Ralph Griffiths, whose copy is now in the Bodleian.

convinced that the object of praise is generally the object of envy, and *vice versa*; although it is certain that in notorious cases the public prepossession sometimes gives way to public justice. At the same time the writer must content himself with a very slender pittance of fame, indeed, who derives it only from the public compassion. Fame, like other strumpets, may be sometimes bullied into compliance, but the fondest of her lovers may pine himself into a consumption ere he obtains any substantial favour from her pity. (385–6)

Our Editor proceeds next to give an account of what he hath done, or attempted to do himself, and to apologize for what he hath not done, or confessedly found himself unable to do. We cannot help being somewhat apprehensive, however, that the readers of this part of Dr. Johnson's preface will be apt to think he hath, in more places than one, betrayed a consciousness of the want of application in his pretended endeavours, as well as of the ill success attending them. There runs, indeed, through the whole of this preface such a mixed and inconsistent vein of praise and censure respecting others, and of boasting and excuse regarding himself, that we think we discover it to be the production of a wavering pen, directed by a hand equally wearied and disgusted with a task injudiciously undertaken and as indolently pursued. We shall take our leave of it therefore with one more quotation, which may serve farther to confirm what is here advanced [Quotes from 'Perhaps I may not be more censured' to 'I have said no more' pp. 98–9.]

As to the work itself; the present Editor hath prefixed the several prefaces. .... Of Mr. Pope's notes the Editor hath retained the whole; in order, as he says, that no fragment of so great a writer may be lost. With Dr. Johnson's leave, however, as Mr. Pope's attempts on Shakespeare do so little honour to his memory, a future editor who affected to revere that memory ought to have suppressed them, at least those of them which were the most exceptionable.—Of Theobald's notes, the *weak, ignorant, mean, faithless, petulant, ostentatious* Theobald, the present Editor hath generally retained those which he retained *himself* in his second edition; and these, we must acquaint our Readers, are not a few nor unimportant.—Of Sir Thomas Hanmer's notes Dr. Johnson professes, and we find no reason to disbelieve him, that he hath inserted them all.—To Dr. Warburton he is still more obliged than to any of the preceeding commentators, at least in point of quantity.—To the author of *The Canons of Criticism* he is also equally obliged in point of quality; but we know not to what cause we must impute it, that the Editor is so extremely sparing of confessing his obligations from this quarter.[1]

As to the Editor's own notes, it possibly will not be expected they should be so numerous or so important as those he had an opportunity of borrowing from his predecessors: the Reader will meet with some of them, however, here and there interspersed among the rest, and like the rest *bona quædam, mala, mediocra*. If the Reader should complain that these are too few and insignificant, we can only impute their paucity and want of importance to a notion entertained by the Editor (the most unfortunate, sure that ever entered into the head of a commentator!) that the Reader is more and better pleased with what he finds out himself than with what the most sagacious scholiast can point out to him. But this plea, if admitted, would of course be urged too far, and even supersede the talk of any commentator at all. Indeed Dr. Johnson seems full as little solicitous about the success of his annotations as he could possibly be about the composing them; it is to be wished, however, for the sake of his own reputation, that he had always treated the poet with the same candour as he *professes* to have observed toward his brother commentators.

[b] [From *A Review of Dr. Johnson's New Edition of Shakespeare*]

PREFACE

[Kenrick explains '1. The design or intent' of his piece, being 'to defend the text of Shakespeare from the *persecution* of his commentators' (p. i).]
With regard to the *second* division of our prefatory sermon, respecting the manner in which this Review is written; the author can readily foresee that he shall be thought to have treated both Dr. Johnson and Dr. Warburton with an ill-becoming levity, if not with unmerited severity: at least, this he conceives will be the opinion of those whom an innate consciousness of their own weakness inspires with a *timidity* which they miscall, and flatter themselves to be, CANDOUR. The Reviewer confesses indeed he

[1] On Johnson's debt to Edwards see Sherbo, *Johnson, Editor*, pp. 30f., 39–41, 123.

should have been glad to have had, on this occasion, less to do with the commentary of the reverend gentleman last mentioned. And this, he hath reason to think, would have been the case had not Dr. Johnson been prevailed on by his printer prudentially to cancel several annotations, in which he had strongly expressed his dissent from that learned scholiast.[1] But having on second thoughts judged it expedient to shelter himself, as it were, under the wing of the bishop of Gloucester, it is hoped the justice due to Shakespeare will excuse the Reviewer, tho' he should be sometimes obliged, in correcting his present editor, to ruffle and expose an irreverend feather or two of the Bishop's.

[Kenrick affirms that he has no personal resentment against either Johnson or Warburton, and will not be deterred by the prestige or position of either.] The republic of letters is a perfect democracy where, all being equal, there is no respect of persons but every one hath a right to speak the truth of another, to censure without fear, and to commend without favour or affection. . . . (iii–x)

To detain the reader but a moment longer.—Dr. Johnson having acted, in the outrage he hath committed on Shakespeare, just like other sinners, not only by doing those things he ought not to have done, but by leaving undone those things he ought to have done; his sins of omission are not less important, though much more numerous, than those of commission. Indeed, nothing is more usual with commentators in general than to display their own sagacity on obvious passages, and to leave the difficult ones to be explained by the sagacity of their readers. The Reviewer, however, cannot be supposed here to have given a compleat commentary himself; indeed he hath been able only to include in the following sheets some few remarks on the most glaring blunders and defects that occur in this new edition, of which such wonderful things were promised and expected, and to which, having seen the prophecy fulfilled, we may apply with as much justice as ever it was applied to any thing that well-known quotation from Horace.

---

[1] In the margin of his copy (Bodleian, Mal. 142) Malone has written 'This is true'. The cancellations are preserved in Bishop Percy's copy, also in the Bodleian. See A. T. Hazen, 'Johnson's Shakespeare, a study in cancellation', *TLS*, 24 December 1938, p. 820, and A. Sherbo, *Johnson on Shakespeare*, pp. 962, 975, for illustrations of two of the cancels.

Quid dignum tanto feret hic promissor hiatu?
Parturiunt montes: nascetur ridiculus mus![1]

(xv–xvi)

[On *The Tempest*, 2.2.30ff.: There would this monster make a man.]
'That is, make a man's fortune. So in *Midsummer Night's
Dream*.—We are all made men.'

Our editor might also have added, in *The Winter's Tale* too,
Act III. Scene 7. where the clown tells the shepherd that he is a
made old man. I have no fault to find with this note, except that I
think Dr. Johnson might have confessed his obligation to the
author of the *Canons of Criticism*; who gave this meaning, after
having exposed the absurdity of Dr. Warburton's very learned and
ridiculous note on this passage.—This is not the only instance,
however, by many, as the reader will find in the perusal of these
sheets, wherein Dr. Johnson adopts the opinion of that ingenious
critic without mentioning either his name, or his book. But perhaps, after treating this gentleman so scurvily as he has done in his
preface, he might be ashamed to have it known that his sentiments
so frequently coincided with so indifferent a critic. Or perhaps he
might think that, after having knocked him fairly on the head, the
law of arms gave him a right to plunder him at pleasure. (12) ...

[On *Measure for Measure*, 3.1.6ff.

DUKE. —Reason thus with life;
If I do lose thee, I do lose a thing
That none but fools would keep:]

Dr. Warburton, in order I presume to lay hold of an occasion for
altering the text, excepts against this passage as being a direct
persuasive to *suicide*. The absurdity, however, of supposing that
the speaker intended it as such is obvious, since he is endeavouring
to instil into a condemned prisoner a resignation to his sentence.
Dr. Johnson observes that the meaning seems plainly this, that
'none but fools would wish to keep life; or, none but fools would
keep it, if choice were allowed.' A sense which, whether true or
not, he remarks, is certainly innocent. But though our editor is

[1] *Ars Poetica*, 138f.: 'What will this boaster produce in keeping with such mouthing?
Mountains will labour, to birth will come a laughter-rousing mouse!'

graciously pleased to exculpate Shakespeare in this particular, it appears to be only that he may fall upon him with the greater violence in a page or two after; where Dr. Warburton vouchsafes to pay the poet a compliment. This passage is in the same speech as the foregoing;

> Thy best of rest is sleep,
> And that thou oft provok'st; yet grosly fear'st
> Thy death, which is no more.

[Quotes Johnson's Note 13 above, p. 104: 'I cannot, without indignation, find Shakespeare saying, that *death is only sleep* . . .'.] —Nor can I, Dr. Johnson, without equal indignation find you misrepresenting Shakespeare, and thence taking occasion to condemn him for what he is not culpable; lengthening out your censure with imputations that, being false in themselves, appear as invidious in the *man* as they are contemptible in the *critic*. Would not one imagine, from the warmth with which Dr. Johnson speaks of this passage, that it militates against the doctrine of the immortality of the soul, insinuating that in death we close our eyes and sleep for ever? Nothing, however, can be more foreign from the plain intent of the speaker and the obvious meaning of the passage. The duke, in the assumed character of a friar, is endeavouring to persuade Claudio to acquiesce in the sentence of death passed on him, and to prepare himself for launching into eternity. To this end he advises him to think altogether on death; and to excite him to do so he enumerates the several foibles of humanity and the calamities incident to human life, evidently intending by this means to wean his affections from the world and render him less averse to part with it, and less apprehensive of the pain of dying. *Thou oft provokest sleep*, says he, yet absurdly fear to die; which, with regard to the painful and perplexing vigil of life, is only to go to sleep. For that he only speaks of the mere *sense of death*, the parting of the soul from the body, and that Claudio understood him so, is very evident by the reply which the latter makes to his harangue; notwithstanding the very last words of it seem to be full as exceptionable as those objected to.

> DUKE.   . . . in this life
> Lie hid a thousand deaths; yet death we fear,
> That makes these odds all even.

> CLAU. I humbly thank you.
> To sue to live, I find, I seek to die;
> And, seeking death, find *life*: let it come on.

If any thing further be necessary to corroborate what is here advanced we might instance the duke's exhorting him, in scene III. of the same act, *to go to his knees* and prepare for death. It is highly inconsistent to think such a piece of advice should come from one who conceived death to be a perpetual sleep. Prayers must seem as superfluous to him as the advice must appear impertinent to the prisoner. But that Claudio had the strongest notions of a future state after death is not to be doubted since, speaking of the sin of debauching his sister, and Angelo's design to commit it, he says

> If it were damnable, he being so wise,
> Why would he for the *momentary* trick
> Be *perdurably* fin'd?   [3.1.114ff.]

Again, when his fears recurring, he tells his sister that 'Death is a fearful thing', [117] it is plain he doth not confine the meaning of the word, as the Duke did, to the mere act or circumstance of dying. For when she retorts upon him, 'And shamed life a hateful,' he goes on, 'Ay, but to die, and go we know not where.' As if he had said, I do not mean the mere pain of dying; it is what is to come after death that I fear, when we are to

> go we know not where;
> To lie in cold obstruction, and to rot;
> This sensible warm motion to become
> A kneeded clod; and the delighted spirit
> To bathe in fiery floods, or to reside
> In thrilling regions of thick-ribbed ice:
> To be imprison'd in the viewless winds,
> And blown with restless violence round about
> The pendant world; or to be worse than worst
> Of those, that lawless and incertain thoughts
> Imagine howling; 'tis too horrible!   [3.1.119ff.]

Can we think that Shakespeare could so far forget himself as to be here so very explicit regarding the notion of a future state, if but two or three pages before he had been inculcating a contrary doctrine!—What then must we think of his commentator, who affects to be moved with indignation and in effect presumes to charge him on this account with vulgarity, folly and impiety!

Shakespeare appears to have had such a regard, even for his mortal part*, as to bestow a curse on the person who should disturb his ashes; what a severe malediction, then, would he not have bestowed on that sacrilegious hand which hath thus mangled his immortal reputation, could he have penetrated the womb of time, or anticipated the temerity of a modern critic! (26–9) . . .

[*Ibid.*, 5.1.156ff.:

> PETER.———and what he with his oath
> By all probation will make up full clear,
> Whenever he's *convented*. First, for this woman.]

Dr. Johnson hath here inserted the word *convented*, instead of *convened*, which was the common reading. *Convented*, indeed, was the reading of the first folio, which Dr. Warburton insists upon to be right†, giving his reasons for it in the following arrogant and foolish note, which is as impertinently and sillily adopted by our editor. 'The first folio reads *convented*, and this is right; for to *convene* signifies to assemble; but *convent*, to cite or summons. Yet, because *convented* hurts the measure, the Oxford editor sticks to *convened*, though it be *nonsense*, and signifies, *whenever he is assembled together*. But thus it will be, when the author is thinking of one thing, and his critic of another. The poet was attentive to his sense, and the editor, quite throughout his performance, to nothing but the measure; which Shakespeare having entirely neglected, like all the dramatic writers of that age, he has spruced him up with all the exactness of a modern measurer of syllables.'

I should be glad to know how either Dr. Warburton or Dr. Johnson came to know that Shakespeare *entirely neglected measure*?[1] Shakespeare had a poetical ear; and though he might not stand to count his fingers, as probably these gentlemen do when they write verses, he wrote in general much more melodiously than any of the dramatic writers of his own age, or perhaps of the present. The

---

* At least if he wrote the verses, said to be put on his grave-stone:

Good friend, for Jesus' sake, forbear
To dig the dust inclosed here.
Blest be the man that spares these stones,
And curst be he who moves my bones.

† And yet Dr. Warburton, as the author of the *Revisal* shrewdly remarks, calls that edition, on another occasion, 'the old blundering folio.'

[1] For Heath's criticism of this point see 4.555.

Oxford editor did very wisely, therefore, in abiding by the measure, as he could do it without any injury to the sense. For to *convene*, as the author of the *Revisal* justly observes, means not only to *assemble together* but to *cite* or *cause to appear*; and is rendered in Latin by *cito, cieo.*—To this I may add also that *cito* does not mean simply to *cite* or *summons* in general, but also to summons or produce as a witness, exactly agreeable to the case before us. Thus CICERO, *in hâc re te testem citabo.*[1] But perhaps these learned gentlemen will object to all this, because the verb *convene* is not derived from *cito, cieo*, but from *convenio*: they will profit little, however, by this evasion; for the verb *convenio* itself is used in the sense of giving a citation or summons. Thus PLAUTUS, *illum in jus conveniam.*[2] But supposing these quotations to be, as learned quotations generally are, nothing at all to the purpose, I may safely borrow a phrase from Scripture on this occasion, and say to Dr. Johnson, *Out of thy own mouth will I judge thee, thou* CARELESS COMMENTATOR! The author of the *Revisal* seems a little unhappy that, having kept no common-place-book, he cannot produce an example of the use of the word *convene* in the sense contended for: but if he had turned to Dr. Johnson's common-place-book, i.e. his folio dictionary, he would have there found that this sense is properly authorized. To *convene*, says the lexicographer, is *to summon judicially*; as a proof of which he quotes the following passage from AYLIFFE; *By the papal canon law, clerks, in criminal and civil causes, cannot be* CONVENED *before any but an ecclesiastical judge.*—What a pity it is there should be so little connection between Samuel Johnson, M. A. the lexicographer, and Dr. Johnson the commentator? But so it is; nor is it any thing new; people are apt to forget themselves as they rise to preferment. (39–41) ...

[*Ibid.*, 5.1.331ff.:

> LUCIO. Do you so, Sir? and was the duke a flesh-monger, a fool, and a coward, as you then reported him to be?]

Dr. Johnson, who seems constantly on the watch to catch Shakespeare tripping, observes here that 'Lucio had not, in the former conversation, mentioned *cowardice* among the faults of the duke.' But, says he, very graciously, 'such failures of memory are incident

[1] *Pro Publio Quinctio*, xi. 37: 'on this point I will call you ... as a witness'.
[2] *Mostellaria*, 1089: modern editions, however, read *si veniam* (Oxford) or *sine inveniam* (Loeb).

to writers more diligent than this poet.'—On this occasion I cannot help remarking that it is somewhat singular to find our editor so extremely remiss and negligent in illustrating the beauties of Shakespeare, and so very diligent in discovering his faults. This carping critic is in this particular, however, egregiously mistaken; there being no grounds for charging the poet in this place with want of attention to his plot. It is true that Lucio does not expresly call the duke a coward, in that part of their conversation which passed on the stage, in scene VI. act 3. Our editor might have observed, however, that he hath a farther conversation with him in scene XI. act 4. where he begins again to talk of the *old fantastical duke of dark corners*; and when the duke wants to shake him off by bidding him farewel and telling him his *company is fairer than honest*, Lucio will not be thus got rid of, but follows him, saying, *By my troth, I'll go with thee to the lane's end. If bawdy talk offend you, we'll have very little of it. Nay, friar, I am a kind of bur, I shall stick*. [4.3.153–74] Is it not very natural to suppose that Lucio might afterwards call the duke a *coward*, considering the many opprobrious names he had already given him? and is the poet to be censured because he hath made the Duke charge Lucio with a single word of detraction which was not actually spoken before the audience? If this be not hypercriticism, I know not what is. But, to make the matter worse on the part of our unfortunate editor, the Duke doth not charge Lucio with calling him a coward at the time when he runs on enumerating his other vices. For this was in the open street, through which the officers passed in carrying the bawds to prison: but the time is particularly specified when he called him *coward*, which was when the duke met him in the prison and, as I above remarked, could not get rid of him. This is plain from the context.

LUCIO. Come hither, goodman bald-pate; do you know me?

DUKE. I remember you, Sir, by the sound of your voice: I met you AT THE PRISON in the absence of the duke.

LUCIO. Oh, did you so? and do you remember what you said of the duke?

DUKE. Most notedly, Sir.

LUCIO. Do you so, Sir? and was the duke a fleshmonger, a fool, a coward, as you THEN reported him to be?

DUKE. You must, Sir, change persons with me, ere you make that my report: *you* spoke so of him, and much *more*, much WORSE. [5.1.323ff.]

Surely Dr. Johnson must have *invidiously sought* occasion to depreciate the merit of Shakespeare, or he could never have laid hold of so groundless a pretext to cavil either at his inattention or want of memory. (44–5) . . .

[*Ibid.*, 5.1.441ff.:

> ISAB. A due sincerity govern'd his deeds
> Till he did look on me; since it is so,
> Let him not die.]

Dr. Johnson hath, in my opinion, a very exceptionable note on this passage. I shall quote it therefore entire, and make my observations on it afterwards. [Quotes Note 17 above, p. 105.]

To expose the several fallacies suggested throughout the above note, I shall observe first that it was very natural for Mariana to solicit Isabel's intercession for her husband, the man she so much loved. I cannot think also that it is in any respect out of character for Isabel, after repeated solicitations, to be moved to oblige Mariana, who had already obliged her, so far at least as to prevent the apparent necessity of prostituting herself to Angelo: especially if we reflect on the tranquil state of mind she seems to be in with regard to her brother, in whose supposed death she appears to have acquiesced, either from principles of religion or philosophy. For when the Duke, in the foregoing page, speaking of her brother, says

> Peace be with him!
> That life is better life, past fearing death,
> Than that which lives to fear: make it your comfort.
> So, happy is your brother. [5.1.394ff.]

Isabel answers 'I do, my lord'. [397] From a principle of philosophy she must be very conscious that the death of Angelo could not bring her brother to life again; and if to this reflection we suppose her religion might add the suggestion of Christian charity and forgiveness, I do not see any impropriety in Isabel's soliciting Angelo's pardon.

As to the argument she makes use of, and which Dr. Johnson thinks so very extraordinary, it is to be observed that she does not make use of it as a positive plea, but introduces it with 'I PARTLY THINK/A due sincerity', &c. Again, Dr. Johnson says, 'the only *intent* which *his act did not overtake* was the defilement of Isabel.'

Surely Dr. Johnson forgets the intended execution of Claudio! There is no doubt that Angelo's guilty intentions fully deserved punishment; but as the principal of them failed of being carried into execution I do not see why the reader should feel so much indignation at his being pardoned, especially as he must perceive the propriety of doing poetical justice to the injured Mariana; which would not be the case if her new-made husband were to be immediately punished with the severity due to his wicked designs.

As to the sinister meaning he imputes to the poet of intending a covert satire on the fair sex, I think enough is already said to exculpate him; I wish, therefore, Dr. Johnson were equally excusable for giving Shakespeare the appellation of *varlet* poet. Our editor can hardly intend here to confine that term to its simple and ancient meaning: for where is the jest or propriety of calling Shakespeare a yeoman or servant, agreeably to the old meaning of the word *varlet*; which like *fur* in Latin, it is allowed, originally conveyed no base or opprobrious idea?—And yet, if Dr. Johnson did not use the word in this limited and antiquated sense, what can he mean by calling Shakespeare a mean, sorry, or rascally poet? For this is the modern sense of the word; and in this sense the word *varletry* is inserted in a certain folio dictionary, on the authority of Shakespeare himself.—Perhaps, indeed, Dr. Johnson only meant here to express himself in a strain of wit and pleasantry. If so, let him beware how he attempts to be witty again: for surely never was such an aukward attempt made before! It is not in his nature. (46–8) . . .

[On *Twelfth Night*, 1.3.121.: *Sir Toby*. I would not so much as make water but in a *sink-a-pace*.]

I know not how many, or if all, the editions authorize this reading of *sink-a-pace*. Our editor adopts it and passes it over in silence, like the rest of the commentators. I have ever looked upon it, however, as so vile a blot in this admirable piece of raillery of Sir Toby's that I cannot help imputing it to the interpolation of some transcriber, who imagined there was an excellent joke in *making water into a* SINK-A-PACE. The conceit, however, is so low and vile that I cannot give into the notion that Shakespeare, fond as he seems of punning and playing upon words, was the author of it. I am confirmed in this opinion also by reflecting that the attention of the reader is diverted from the real humour of the passage by this horrid conundrum. Sir Toby, in carrying his ridicule of poor Ague-cheek's dancing-accomplishments to the highest pitch, proceeds so far as to tell him he would not stand still on the most necessary occasion, even to make water; but that he might not betray himself, even to this fool, by talking of absolute impossibilities he fixes on a grave, slow, and even hobbling kind of dance, the *cinque-pace*, for this suspicious occasion*.

I could wish, therefore, the authority of the copies would bear me out in discarding this miserable pun, and restoring the words to its genuine and original spelling. (96)

[On *The Taming of the Shrew*, 1.1.156f.:

> TRANIO. If love hath touch'd you, nought remains but so,
> *Redime te captum quam queas minimô.*]

'Dr. Warburton tells us, that the line here quoted from Terence shews that we should read, in the preceding, "*If love hath* TOYL'D *you,*" i.e. taken you in his toils, his nets. Alluding to the *captus est, habet*, of the same author.'

Dr. Johnson, however, without even deigning to adopt any thing that might do the least honour to Shakespeare's learning, takes upon him boldly to assure us that 'our author had this line from Lilly, which I mention,' says he, 'that it may not be brought as an argument of his learning.'

But pray, Dr. Johnson, how can you take upon you to say that Shakespeare had this line from Lilly, and not from Terence?[1] Is it because the line is to be found in Lilly? And is this your whole authority?—You can have no other. It appears by the application, however, that Shakespeare knew the meaning of this line; and if he knew it in Lilly why might he not know it in the original author from whom it was taken? Is it because you have so often quoted

---

* The gravity and interruptions of this dance are, indeed, particularly pointed out by Shakespeare on another occasion. 'Wooing, wedding, and repenting, is a Scotch jigg, a measure, and a cinque-pace. The first suit is hot and hasty like a Scotch jigg, and full as fantastical; the wedding mannerly and modest, as a measure full of state and gravity; and then comes repentance, and, with his bad legs, falls into the cinque-pace.' [*Much Ado About Nothing*, 2.1.61ff.]

[1] In Terence, however, the line is: 'quid agas? nisi ut te redimas captum quam queas/ minimo' (*Eunuchus*, 74f.: 'But I do. Ransom yourself from captivity [sc., being in love] as cheaply as you can'). Shakespeare indeed quotes from the version given in Lily's Latin syntax: see Farmer below, pp. 261, 275f.

words and passages in languages *you* do not understand that you suspect Shakespeare of a similar practice? You should never measure others' corn by your own bushel. You have been already reprehended in public for misrepresenting in your preface the testimony of your predecessor Ben Jonson; who tells us that Shakespeare had *small* LATIN *and less* GREEK. This you converted into *small Latin and* NO *Greek*. The ingenious critic who reminded you of this error was *candid* enough to impute it to your quoting from memory only*; but supposing that in this case such a method of quotation was excusable it appears, I think, too plainly from your constant and repeated endeavours to depreciate both the natural and acquired abilities of Shakespeare that this was not the case. Your perseverance in these endeavours at least give great reason to suspect the mistake was wilful, as the supposition of his having any Greek at all would not have suited with your darling project, or answered your end of invidiously representing him as a *varlet*, one of the illiterate vulgar. (105–6)

208. William Guthrie, Johnson reviewed

1765–6

From the *Critical Review*, xx, pp. 321–32, 401–11 (November, December 1765), and xxi, pp. 13–26, 81–8 (January, February 1766).

William Guthrie (1708–70), author of *An Essay upon English Tragedy* (1747) (No. 107 in Vol. 3, pp. 191–205), which was reissued in 1749 and 1757, translated Quintilian and Cicero, and contributed to various journals. For the ascription to Guthrie, see the Preface above.

[November 1765]

After Dr. Warburton's edition of our great poet appeared many

* In the *St. James's Chronicle* [i.e. Colman: see above, p. 180].

were of opinion that, supposing the labours of his great, middling, and little commentators, critics, and editors to be skilfully concentrated something might be produced that would approximate to perfection, if the editor possessed those funds of science and learning which could furnish him with the means of rendering that new birth of the press less violent and unnatural than all those which had preceded it.— Mr. Johnson offered his assisting hand, and was approved of. From him was expected something more satisfactory than had fallen from the pen of Rowe; something more elegantly characteristical of Shakespeare than Mr. Pope had produced; the learning of Warburton without his temerity; the sagacity of Hanmer, void of his singularities; and the application of Theobald, destitute of his groveling.— Mr. Johnson has at last brought the child to light; but alas! in the delivery it has received so many unhappy squeezes, pinches, and wrenches that the healthful constitution of the parent alone can prevent it from being lame and deformed for ever.

To what can this be owing?— To what shall we impute it?— Surely not to *a hope for eminence* (to use Mr. Johnson's words in the first paragraph of his preface) *from the heresies of paradox*.

We cannot help thinking that Mr. Johnson has run into the vulgar practice by estimating the merits of Shakespeare according to the rules of the French academy, and the *little* English writers who adopted them, as the criterions of *taste*. We have often been surprized how that word happens to be applied in Great-Britain to poetry, and can account for it only by the servility we shew towards every thing which is French.[1] Of all our sensations *taste* is the most variable and uncertain: Shakespeare is to be tried by a more sure criterion, that of *feeling*, which is the same in all ages and all climates. To talk of trying Shakespeare by the rules of *taste* is speaking like the spindle-shanked beau who *languished* to thresh a brawny coachman.

Shakespeare proceeds by storm. He knows nothing of regular approaches to the fort of the human heart. He effects his breach by the weight of his metal, and makes his lodgment though the enemy's artillery is thundering round him from every battery of criticism, learning, and even probability. He is invulnerable to them all by that enchanted armour in which the hand of heaven

[1] Cf. Guthrie's 1747 *Essay*: 3.191, 204f.

has cased him, and on whose powerful influence reasoning, reflection, and observation have always proved to be like the serpent's tongue licking the file.

Criticism (especially on such an author as Shakespeare) has, we believe, like other liberal arts, its foundation in simplicity of observation, which is the parent of sagacity. All the reading in the Vatican and Bodleian libraries is not half so useful to an editor of Shakespeare as the conversation of an old woman in the north of England or south of Scotland, where his language is understood. It is there, and not in dictionaries or cotemporary authors, nay, such is his peculiar cast, not even from his own works we are to look for a satisfactory explanation of many terms that occur in his writings. It is more than probable that a hundred and fifty years hence the language of Middlesex and Oxfordshire will be spoken in Cumberland and Westmoreland, and in about half a century more it may cross the Frith of Forth. But we have already† touched upon this subject, and are sorry the publication before us has obliged us to resume it.

To what we have said of the public expectation on this head, we must add the conviction it entertained that if Mr. Johnson attempted the character of his great author, he would *execute* it with that glow of genius, that native sublimity, those tender graces, and with that amiable simplicity which characterize his original. Shakespeare is too great for pomp, too knowing for books, too learned in human nature to require the assistance, and too exalted in his ideas to dread the criticism either of an enemy or an editor.

We would not, however, be thought to insinuate that Mr. Johnson's preface is without merit; we think some parts of it are well wrote, and if the reader will indulge us in a pun, with a *truely* critical spirit tho' not in the *true* spirit of criticism. — Our editor observes that Shakespeare's works *supply no faction with invectives.* Yet whoever knows the state of political writing for these forty years past, or remembers the existence of the *Champion*, a political Paper carried on by Fielding and Ralph against Sir Robert Walpole, must be sensible that they have supplied *all* factions with invectives, and those too of a more spirited and acrimonious kind than the authors who used them could furnish from their own wit or abilities.

† *Crit. Rev.* Vol. XIX. p. 165 [see Vol. 4, No. 204].

213

Mr. Johnson, after introducing Shakespeare as an ancient, proceeds *to enquire by what peculiarities of excellence he has gained and kept the favour of his countryman.* This he accounts for from his author's just representations of general nature. 'Shakespeare (says he) is above all writers, at least above all modern writers, the poet of nature . . .' [quotes p. 57 above, to 'commonly a species'].

We were inclinable to dismiss this paragraph without any animadversion; but we cannot pass it without observing that it is by no means descriptive of Shakespeare. For the truth of this we are ready to appeal to common sense and common observation. Shakespeare has succeeded better in representing the oddities of nature than her general properties, which characterise a Menander, a Terence, or an Addison. The characters of Terence are those that our editor has ascribed to Shakespeare; and never perhaps were the manners of two writers, though both excellent in the drama, so dissimilar. Can a Falstaff, a Malvolio, a Benedick, a Caliban; in short, can any of Shakespeare's successful characters in comedy be termed a species? or rather, do they not please by being oddities, or, if Mr. Johnson pleases, individuals? But it may be asked, From what qualities then do they please? We answer, By the command which its author has over the affections and passions; over the tender, the rational, and risible faculties of mankind. It may be again asked, Could these powers arise from any other source than that of general nature? They arise from the genius of the poet, which is so strong that it converts even absurdity into nature; for the objects that Shakespeare presents us with are compounds of peculiarities that never existed till he created them. This remark is confirmed by Mr. Pope, who says with equal discernment and justice, *The poetry of Shakespeare was inspiration indeed: he is not so much an imitator, as an instrument of nature; and 'tis not so just to say that he speaks from her, as that she speaks through him.*[1]

'Shakespeare's real power (says Mr. Johnson) is not shewn in the splendour of particular passages, but by the progress of his fable, and the tenour of his dialogue. . . .' We are afraid that Mr. Johnson here is unjust and unhappy in his illustration; perhaps, we may add, inconsistent with himself. The *progress* of Shakespeare's *fable* is an excellency, we believe, never before appropriated to that great writer; but perhaps we are ignorant of the

[1] See 2.403f.; and 3.194f. for Guthrie's (unacknowledged) earlier quotation.

meaning Mr. Johnson annexes to that expression, as well as to that of the *tenour of his dialogue.* We know the warmest friends of Shakespeare have thought most of his fables faulty in every sense of the drama, and his dialogue unequal in every mode of speaking: all, however, have agreed in the *splendour of his particular passages*; and we are of opinion that if they were committed to loose papers, and like the Sybilline leaves scattered about, they would be picked up wherever sentiment and feeling took place, and each of them *worn as the immediate jewel of the soul.*

We wish Mr. Johnson had not meddled with that unhappy pedantic brick, which he has so painfully dragged into this period ['like the Pedant in Hierocles . . .', p. 58]. It surely had no business there. . . .

But, to pursue Mr. Johnson's allusion: the bricks with which Shakespeare built did not owe their mould but their substance (as workmen call it) to him. The moulds of his tragedy are, if we mistake not, borrowed from historians and novelists; but he filled them with a clay which the Promethean fire alone could render fit for use, and a divine intelligence employ in building. If a coarser clay or grosser earth sometimes casually dropt into the mould, and from thence went to the kiln, these inadvertencies ought to give an editor very little trouble when they are compensated by the noble fabric of the whole.

At the same time, we cannot carry our veneration so far as to say with Mr. Johnson that real life is to be found upon no stage but that of Shakespeare. We can, indeed, admit that no stage exhibits so much true genius, wit, and nature; but there is a wide difference between drawing nature and painting life. If Mr. Johnson means (as he certainly does, or he means nothing at all) that we shall find common life in Shakespeare's characters and plays, we apprehend he will be puzzled to bring many specimens to prove his assertion; and yet we believe Shakespeare to have been more successful than any other poet in representing both life and nature. He did not draw a Polonius as he was formed by nature, but as he grew up in habit; for good sense is not naturally addicted to stiffness, pedantry, or affectation. . . .

We wish Mr. Johnson had not descended to any observations upon the minor critics, a Dennis, a Rymer, or one who in that capacity is more contemptible than both, a Voltaire. He says that Shakespeare made the Danish usurper a drunkard, 'knowing that kings love wine like other men, and that wine exerts its natural power upon kings.' We are ashamed that so uncritical an apology for the conduct of Shakespeare should fall from the pen of his editor. According to Mr. Johnson's rule a king may lie with a strumpet, pick a pocket, or play at taw upon the stage, because *kings love* whoring, money, and diversion *as well as other men*. He tells us at the same time that Shakespeare was inclined to shew an usurper and a murderer, not only odious but despicable. We should have been obliged to Mr. Johnson if he had pointed out the particular passages in which the king's drunkenness is exhibited. If he means the fencing-scene, in which the bowls of wine are brought upon the stage, we must be of opinion that his observation is very ill grounded. The reason why they are introduced is plain, to poison Hamlet; and the king drinks but twice. The truth is, Shakespeare is so far from representing the king as a drunkard that he leaves him more sober than he found him; for Saxo Grammaticus, if we remember right, has put him and all his courtiers to death at a drunken bout. Drinking in the northern countries till lately was scarcely esteemed a vice; and if we look into Homer and other ancients we shall perhaps find Achilles, and even the *pious* Æneas, on solemn occasions as great drunkards as his Danish majesty appears to be on the stage.

One of the passages that can justify Mr. Johnson in supposing the Danish usurper to have been exposed in the scene as a drunkard is that wherein Hamlet wishes to kill him when he is dead drunk; but this cannot amount to a proof that Shakespeare, as Mr. Johnson alledges, intended to render the tyrant contemptible by bringing him upon the stage in a state of intoxication. It expresses only Hamlet's desire to cut the monster off *should* he find him in such a condition. It is true that in the seventh scene of the first act Hamlet accuses him of drunkenness, but Horatio, who we must suppose to be acquainted with the manners of the court, asks him whether it is a custom. Hamlet replies it is, and common to the nation. If so, the king is a drunkard in a political compliance with the manners of his people in the same sense as our kings of England, before the present reign, may be called gamesters because they used to play at hazard every Twelfth-night.

Mr. Johnson informs us that Shakespeare, wanting a buffoon, went into the senate house for one, and that Dennis is offended that Menenius, a Roman senator, should play the buffoon. The editor gives his poet up on this head; and the only apology he makes for him is that 'these are the petty cavils of petty minds,' a most Laconic apology, and such as may be urged in answer to any question. But the truth is, Menenius is no buffoon. He is a good patriot, with a warm heart to his friend as well as country; and was remarkable for having a peculiar method of accosting the Roman people in their own language. His family was plebeian, and being a man of sense, the senate thought him the most proper agent to bring the people off from their secession; which he actually did by his plain humorous manner of speaking. Shakespeare has not perhaps in all his plays stuck closer to the truth of history than he has in the character of Menenius. *Intromissus* (says Livy, speaking of him) *in castra, prisco illo dicendi & horrido modo, nihil aliud, quam hoc narrasse fertur.*[1] Mr. Johnson is too good a classical scholar to be ignorant that the word *horridus* is of a very different signification from *horrens* or *horrendus*, and that it signifies plain, rough, homely, artless; in short, the very character that Shakespeare exhibits in Menenius. He was the Sir Thomas More of Rome. . . .

Mr. Johnson says that 'Shakespeare's plays are not, in the rigorous and critical sense, either tragedies or comedies, but compositions of a distinct kind.' Tho' we admit this position, yet we cannot agree with the editor as to the sources of that immense pleasure which the works of Shakespeare afford. Any man of common understanding, if Mr. Johnson's character is just, might have been as happy in the drama as Shakespeare. He needed only take a walk from Hyde-Park Corner to Limehouse; visit the undertakers, the coffee-houses, the taverns, and brothels in his way; look in at the Royal Exchange, the Alley, and Lombard-street; and after passing through Wapping, have reduced all that he had seen and heard into a drama. We can safely appeal to every candid reader whether the Shakespeare the editor has described has done more. Has he combined his dialogue with those secret charms of wit and humour which the most accurate observations in life cannot communicate, and which have their source in genius alone? Is the page of Shakespeare to be treated like that of a daily news-paper, as containing little more than a series of births and deaths, marriages, murders and misfortunes, bankruptcies and executions?

[1] Livy, 2.32.8: 'Admitted to the deserters' camp, he is said to have told them, in the rugged style of those far-off days, the following story' (tr. A. de Selincourt, Penguin).

'Shakespeare's tragedy, says Mr. Johnson, seems to be skill, and his comedy instinct.' Let the next of kin to Shakespeare's poetry lodge an appeal at the tribunal of human feeling against the first part of this partial sentence. We imagine we see the public indignation backing the appeal, and bringing all the great characters in Shakespeare's tragedies as evidences in its support. Our limits will not admit our expatiating on this head, yet we think we can safely leave Shakespeare's cause to the verdict of any man who has not read himself out of a true taste for nature, and who has not studied himself into a disregard of the human passions. Such a reader smothers the glow of passion under the embers of learning.

'Shakespeare, continues our editor, sacrifices virtue to convenience, and is so much more careful to please than to instruct, that he seems to write without any moral purpose.' If Shakespeare was so itinerant and desultory a writer as Mr. Johnson describes him how could he do otherwise? If where he most excels, to use Mr. Johnson's words, 'the successive evolutions of the design sometimes produce seriousness and sorrow, and sometimes levity and laughter,' what are we to expect but that effect which our editor has made a capital article in the impeachment, we had almost said indictment, of his original? Mr. Johnson's succeeding articles in the same charge are so much beyond what the greatest enemies of his author have ever urged to his dispraise that we cannot think him in earnest.—That Shakespeare has meannesses, which we now-a-days call faults, cannot be denied; but even those meannesses have often their *acumina*, and are so incorporated with the character that what in others would appear flat, in him becomes laughable. Even those quibbles, to which his editor says he sacrificed every thing, serve at least, like humorous prints, to hide the bare places in a wall elsewhere covered with the noblest and most pleasing images that painting can produce. But this we only speak in general; for we shall not much differ with Mr. Johnson if he should think that nakedness would in his author be sometimes preferable to such ornaments; that he himself condemned them; and that he used them only either in complaisance to the taste of the times, or to fill up vacancies where he was exhausted by a waste of more valuable spirit.—It is with reluctance we review the questionable parts of a preface which has many excellencies to recommend it; but we think Mr. Johnson, to preserve the character of impartiality, has often thrown the blemishes of his author in too odious a light, as some divines have given so much strength to the arguments of the atheist that their own reasoning appears weak when they attempt to confute them.

Though Mr. Johnson, in characterizing his author, has been *immoderately* moderate, yet it is with pleasure we give our readers the following quotations from his preface. [Quotes the passage on the Unities, pp. 69ff.]

Though these quotations are worthy of Mr. Johnson's pen, yet we cannot so readily assent to what follows. 'Familiar comedy is often more powerful on the theatre, than in the page; imperial tragedy is always less.' [p. 71] We shall not animadvert on the word *imperial* opposed to *familiar*; and we agree with Mr. Johnson that the soliloquy in *Cato* is not to be meliorated by action. We think, however, the editor to be defective in precision when he brings his example from Addison instead of Shakespeare; and are of opinion that many characters of his *imperial* tragedy may be meliorated, nay that they are explained by action. To give an instance out of a thousand equally pertinent: Can any reader imagine that when Iago is endeavouring to convince Othello of his wife's disloyalty, he peruses the scene with as much pleasure as he could have felt in seeing Booth act it? When Othello catches Iago by the throat that inimitable actor's voice went through all the scale of rage, first choaked, low and tremulous, then rising by just gradations; but when it came to a climax, or what we may call the diapason of passion, his modulations brought forth feelings unknown to reading. They who have seen Booth, if they are judges, can bear testimony to the truth of our assertion; nor are we afraid to pronounce that Shakespeare's Lear and Macbeth would receive great beauties from an actor who could join Booth's judgment to his execution.

Mr. Johnson's distinction between Shakespeare and Addison is not new. A certain writer, thirty years ago, observed that the famous soliloquy of Cato 'is that of a scholar, a philosopher, and a man of virtue: all the sentiments of such a speech are to be acquired by instruction, by reading, by conversation; Cato talks the language of the porch and academy. Hamlet, on the other hand, speaks that of the human heart.'* We think the

---

* *Essay on English Tragedy* [by William Guthrie, author of this review: see 3.201f. The *Essay* was published in 1747].

editor might have opposed Hamlet with more propriety than Othello to Cato.

Did Ben Jonson really say that Shakespeare 'had small Latin, and as little Greek?' If he did, we do not believe him. The evidences that can be brought from his works are too numerous and too strong to convince us that Jonson's testimony of Shakespeare, in this respect, cannot be relied on.[1] Perhaps it would be no difficult matter to prove from unexceptionable cotemporary evidence that a *liver* towards Shakespeare was rankling in Ben Jonson's breast, even when he was most profuse in his praises.

Few objections lie to the remaining part of this preface. Perhaps Mr. Johnson is mistaken in pronouncing so peremptorily that before *Shakespeare* no English writer, except Chaucer, shewed life in its natural colours; but this is a fact easily ascertained. We cannot embrace the opinion which Mr. Johnson seems to adopt that a high birth and affluent circumstances would have been of service to his author. ... We must likewise differ from Mr. Johnson, and all the modern editors of Shakespeare, as to the corruption of the antient editions of his works; for we firmly believe that a true knowledge of his language would prove them to be less faulty than any which have appeared since, of which we can produce many undeniable specimens. (xx, 321–2)

[December 1765]

Having in our last Number reviewed Mr. Johnson's preface, and differed from him who differs from (we believe) all Englishmen in their ideas of Shakespeare's genius and merit, we now proceed to investigate his edition of that great poet as to particular passages, and the emendations he has either introduced or admitted, by which the service he has done the literary world as an editor of Shakespeare must stand or fall. (xx, 401)

[On *The Tempest*, 4.1.3, 64]

We have already (see vol. xix, p. 166.) given our reason, which is very different from Mr. Johnson's, why the word *third* ought to stand in Prospero's speech, act iv. scene 1. and we cannot conceive to what species of obstinacy it must be owing that he did not replace the word *twilled*, if he saw our observations on the

[1] Cf. Guthrie (3.198f.).

word (ibid.)[1] To this day, where the undulations of the waves produce those small ridges that are often discernible on the sands of the shore, they are called the *twill'd sands*: our editor tells us in his note that he does not understand the word.

In scene iv. of the last act of the same play, where Ferdinand and Miranda are discovered at chess, the latter says that she would suffer him to play her false 'for a score of kingdoms,' [5.1.174f.] which Mr. Johnson and Dr. Grey very sagaciously interpret to be *twenty* kingdoms—we have no idea why Miranda should confine herself to the number *twenty*. Every one knows what it is to *score* up at play—yes (says she) if every *score* was a kingdom I would suffer you. (xx, 402) . . .

[On *As You Like It*, 1.2.249ff.]

In the seventh scene of the same act, Orlando says,

> My better parts
> Are all thrown down; and that, which here stands up,
> Is but a quintaine, a meer lifeless block.

Mr. Johnson gives us Dr. Warburton's note upon this passage, who observes that a '*Quintaine* was a *post* or *butt* set up for several kinds of martial exercises, against which they threw their darts, and exercised their arms.' This is but an imperfect (to call it no worse) explanation of a beautiful passage. The *quintaine* was not the object of the darts and arms: it was a stake driven into a field, upon which were hung a shield and other trophies of war at which they shot, darted, or rode with a lance. When the shield and the trophies were all thrown down the quintaine remained. Without this information how could the reader understand the allusion of 'my better parts/Are all thrown down'? This quintaine seems to have been of very old standing; Virgil, in describing the trophies of Mezentius, says,

> *Ingentem quercum, decisis undique ramis,*
> *Constituit tumulo, fulgentiaque induit arma.*[2]   (xx, 407)

---

[1] See 4.569.

[2] *Aeneid*, 11.5f.: 'A mighty oak, its branches lopped all about, he plants on a mound, and arrays in the gleaming arms . . . a trophy'. In the 1773 Johnson-Steevens edition this paragraph is quoted and signed CRITICAL REVIEW (III, p. 246); in the 1778 edition it is signed GUTHRIE (III, p. 281).

[*Ibid.*, 3.2.37]

In scene the third, act the third, says the clown 'thou art damn'd, like an ill roasted egg, all on one side.' Says Mr. Johnson, 'of this jest, I do not fully comprehend the meaning.' Then let him ask the first cook-maid he meets, and she will tell him that when an egg is roasting, and not turned before the fire, it is ill-roasted, for one side is too hard and t'other too soft. (xx, 408)

[*Ibid.*, 3.2.144ff.]

[Quotes Johnson's Note 21, that Shakespeare 'seems here to have mistaken some other character for that of Atalanta.'] On the contrary, we believe that honest Shakespeare, in the dictionaries of his times, met with one Atalanta who was Jason's daughter, and who after wounding the Calydonian boar vowed perpetual virginity. The poet had just before mentioned two lewd characters, Helen and Cleopatra, and he contrasts their wantonness with *Atalanta's better part, chastity,* and Lucretia's *modesty.* Some, perhaps, may think that *Atalanta's better part* alludes to Rosalind's quickness in repartee; as a page or two after, Jaques says to Orlando, 'You have a nimble wit, I think it was made of Atalanta's heels;' alluding to the well known story of the other Atalanta's swiftness. (xx, 408)

[*Ibid.*, 3.5.64]

'Here comes Sir Oliver—Sir Oliver Mar-text,' says the clown, in the same act. Mr. Johnson's note upon this passage is so curious that it is worth transcribing:

'He that has taken his first degree at the University is, in the academical stile, called *Dominus,* and in common language was heretofore termed *Sir.* This was not always a word of contempt; the graduates assumed it in their own writings; so Trevisa, the historian, writes himself *Syr* John de Trevisa.'

Had Mr. Johnson been more of an antiquarian he would have been a much better editor of Shakespeare. He would then have known that this is no academical but a pontifical stile. The popes, not to be behind-hand with our kings before the Reformation, arrogated to themselves a power of knighthood both in England and Scotland; and the honour was sold by their legates or agents to churchmen who could pay for it, which great numbers did in both kingdoms.'[1] (xx, 408–9)

[On *Love's Labour's Lost*, 4.2.126ff.]

As we do not propose to animadvert upon Mr. Johnson's performance in the disputes he has with Shakespeare's other editors concerning his author's meaning, on which much may generally be said on both sides, and both may be in the wrong, we shall confine ourselves to the passage[s] where nothing, or next to nothing, can be said for the alterations which our editor has admitted or introduced. In the same play he adopts the following criticism and emendation from Theobald:

'*So doth the hound his master, the ape his keeper, the* tired *horse his rider*'. [Johnson emended to 'tried', trained, obedient.]

As we have said on other occasions, had we found the word *tried* in former copies we should scarcely have dreamed of an emendation, but surely the word *tired* is much better. Where was our editor's sagacity, when he joined with Mr. Theobald in the idea that a tired horse was the same as a *weary* or *fatigued* horse? Every one acquainted with the nature of that noble animal knows how stately, how proud, how fond he is of his master when he is *tired*, that is, *caparisoned, drest out* with his *tires* of ribbands, knots, embossments, buckles and his other Phalaræ; and if we mistake not there exists at this very day such a trade as that of a horse-milliner, whose business is to *tire* or *dress out* horses. If we consult ancient prints and pictures, our ancestors were far more ingenious and costly in this branch of millinery, than the present age. (xx, 410)

[*Ibid.*, 4.3.341f.]

In the last scene of the same act, Mr. Johnson give[s] admittance to a very whimsical alteration of the two following lines:

> And when love speaks, the voice of all the gods
> *Makes* heav'n drowsy with the harmony!

Dr. Warburton, instead of *make*, reads *mark*, 'that is (says he) in the voice of love alone, is included the voice of all the gods.

[1] This note is referred to by Steevens in the 1773 edition as being by 'the late Mr. Guthrie' (VII, p. 124; 1778 edition, VII, p. 139).

Alluding to the ancient theogony, that love was the parent and support of all the gods. . . .'

Though we entertain an uncommon opinion of Shakespeare's learning, yet we dare assert that when he wrote the two lines in question, he had no such authors as Suidas or Palcephatus in his eye. Suidas, it is true, does speak of one Palæphatus (not Palce-phatus) who, he says, composed five thousand verses upon the language and discourse of Venus and Cupid; but we cannot find out the least authority why the learned doctor should suppose it to be a cosmogony, the harmony of which is so great that it calms and allays all disorders. We are therefore inclined to believe that he trusted too much to his memory on this occasion; and that he mistook this cosmogony for the *cosmopœia* which this same author composed, and which was no more than a poem on the creation of the world. One Antimachus, an Egyptian, according to Suidas wrote on the same subject.—Upon the whole we entirely agree with the author of *The Beauties of Shakespeare*[1] that our poet's meaning is to shew that when Love speaks, were all the rest of the gods to speak after him *heaven* would be *drowsy*. We scarcely think that the alteration of *make* into *makes* is here needful, as mention is made of many voices forming but one. (xx, 410–11)

[January 1766]

It is with no small pleasure we reflect that neither the criticisms hazarded, nor the corrections and emendations proposed in the various reviews we have undertaken of Shakespeare's commentators, have hitherto engaged us in any literary dispute worth mentioning; an uncommon piece of good-fortune, which we ascribe solely to the principles we have adopted in vindicating the text of that great poet.—We appeal to one-half of the united kingdom for the meanings we have affixed to his words; we call upon the vernacular modes of speech to justify our interpretations; we have even found it necessary to descend into what some may term the vulgarity of language to heal up the wounds which assassin-pens have inflicted on the Dictator of poetry:

> Look! in this place, ran Hanmer's dagger through;
> See, what a rent the envious Theobald made;
> Through this, the well-beloved Johnson stabb'd.

[1] Dodd: cf. 3.471.

We readily allow that the last-mentioned gentleman has, in some passages, vindicated the original of Shakespeare from the mutilations of his former editors; though we cannot but think him deficient in many qualifications of an editor. (xxi, 13–14)

[On *The Taming of the Shrew*, Ind. 1.1]

We suspect Mr. Johnson introduces his third volume with a note that indicates him to be above consulting the vernacularity of our language, though it is by that chiefly we can understand Shakespeare.

'*I'll pheeze you,*—] To *pheeze* or *fease*, is to separate a twist into single threads. In the figurative sense it may well enough be taken, like *teaze* or *toze*, for to *harrass*, to *plague*. Perhaps *I'll pheeze you*, may be equivalent to *I'll comb your head*, a phrase vulgarly used by persons of *Sly*'s character on like occasions.' [Johnson, III, 3]

Had Mr. Johnson visited the parts of this island to which Shakespeare's language has migrated, he would have known that to *pheese* differs but little from to *screw*. To *pheese* on the lid of a box is the same as to *screw* it on. 'I'll pheese you' is no more than *I'll make you fast—lay you by the heels*; and this sense of the word makes the tinker's wife reply very naturally, 'A pair of stocks, you rogue!'—The word *pheese* seems to be the corruption of *vice*, a common instrument which works by a screw,[1] and is made use of to fasten or secure a piece of work.

[*Ibid.*, 1.1.3]

'—*from fruitful* Lombardy.] So Mr. Theobald. The former editions, instead of *from*, had *for*.' So says Mr. Johnson; but has he removed any difficulty? has he not fallen into a gross absurdity? We shall not contend for the propriety of the phrase as it stood in the old editions to signify 'I am arrived from fruitful Lombardy,' tho' we believe it may be established; but surely it must be a gross blunder in Shakespeare to make Lucentio say *I am arrived from Great Britain that I may see the city of Bristol*, for Padua actually is a city of Lombardy. Had Mr. Johnson bestowed ever so little

---

[1] The *OED* defines *feeze v.*[1] as 1. *trans.* To drive; to drive off or away. 2. To frighten. 3a. *vaguely* To 'do for' a person (quoting this passage); *v.*[2] *dial. trans.* To turn, as a screw. 2 *intr.* for *refl.* To wind in and out; to hang off and on.

attention upon this passage he would have seen that Lucentio arrived from Pisa, which was a republic and is still a city in Tuscany.

Having finished the above observation we turned to Mr. Johnson's Appendix, where he surlily tells his reader, without the least apology for oscitancy or ignorance, that the old reading may stand. (xxi, 14–15)

[On *Much Ado About Nothing*, 3.3.186f.]

In Act III. Scene V. of the same play Mr. Johnson suffers Dr. Warburton's note to stand, which supposes Shakespeare to mean Samson to be the *shaven Hercules* mentioned there. We are of opinion he had no such meaning and that he alludes to the well-known story of Hercules and Omphale, especially as mention is made in the same speech of the club of Hercules, which surely was no attribute of Samson. (xxi, 17) . . .

As we have already extended this article much beyond our usual limits we are obliged to confine our future observations to passages only of the utmost consequence to Shakespeare's sense and language; and therefore we shall omit many remarks of less importance, though we can by no means perceive the propriety of our editor's transcribing so copiously from prior editors long notes, only that he may have the pleasure of rejecting their contents, or treating them as insignificant. (xxi, 18)

[On *Timon of Athens*, 4.3.439]

Mr. Johnson gives us a long note upon the following passage.

> The sea's a thief, whose liquid surge resolves
> The moon into salt tears.

In this note is crowded the theory of the moon and the sea, and other curious matters; but our editor might have spared all his long display of physical learning if he had reflected that the whole of Timon's speech here is no other than a very humorous parody of one of Anacreon's odes, in which he proves all the great bodies of nature to be drunkards by the same philosophy that Timon proves them to be thieves. That Shakespeare had Anacreon's ode before him, is self-evident; but where he found a translation of it we are uncertain.[1] It is possible his friend Ben Jonson, who was himself a toper, might help him to one.

We think the parade of learning in the first note to *Macbeth* might have been omitted with great propriety if our editor had informed his reader of a simple fact, that Shakespeare hardly deviates in the plan of his play from the narrative given by Hector Boece, a Scotch historian who wrote before Buchanan, and who took the facts from historians prior to him. Shakespeare, we will venture to assert, had neither Olympiodorus, Photius, Chrysostom, nor any great name, antient or modern, in his eye. In Macbeth's witches he follows Boece, as he does Plutarch and other historians in Cæsar's apparition to Brutus.[2] Mr. Johnson's learned dissertation would have been more proper to have prefaced *The Tempest*, where Shakespeare seems to have followed no history, than *Macbeth*, a play as strictly historical as any of the tragedies he takes from the English chronicles. (xxi, 21)

[On *Macbeth*, 2.2.33ff.]

[Warburton, whose note Johnson prints with silent approval, read 'The *birth* of each day's life': see Vol. 3, p. 241.]

We are almost tempted to be guilty of a Theobaldism, that is, an unmannerly, illiberal insult upon former critics; upon Dr. Warburton who penned, and upon Mr. Johnson who admitted, this note upon one of the most beautiful passages in Shakespeare. The whole is as follows:

> the innocent sleep;
> Sleep that knits up the ravell'd sleeve of care,
> The death of each day's life, sore labour's bath,
> Balm of hurt minds, great nature's second course,
> Chief nourisher in life's feast.

How could they imagine that our immortal poet called *sleep, the death of each day's life?* how could they be blind to the beautiful transition here between the didactic and the pathetic strain? It is not *sleep*, but *care*, that Shakespeare calls *the death of each day's life*; an observation equally just as elegant. *Life* means the enjoyment of *life*, of which *care* is undoubtedly the *death*. (xxi, 23–4) . . .

---

[1] Farmer solved this problem: see pp. 267f. below. The parallel was first pointed out by William Dodd, and was repeated by Christopher Smart: see 4.205.
[2] Cf. Guthrie (3.199).

[Ibid., 2.3.114f.]

Mr. Johnson[1] gives us several notes upon 'unmannerly breech'd with gore;' and he himself most sagaciously concludes, 'that Dr. Warburton has perhaps rightly put the word *reech'd* for *breech'd.*' We must here refer our reader to this curious collection of conjectures (which would contaminate our page) upon one of the plainest passages in Shakespeare. To *breech* is to *clothe* or to *cover*, and *unmannerly* is neither more nor less than *unseemly.* The reader has Shakespeare's idea, if he can form the disagreeable one of *a dagger covered with blood* (xxi, 24)

[February 1766]

The reverence owing to the name of Shakespeare, and the attention due to a work of the greatest expectation, have detained us longer than we intended upon the article before us, which we now propose to finish. (xxi, 81) . . .

[On *Julius Cæsar*, 3.1.47f.]

Mr. Johnson has studiously avoided the famous bull, as we may call it, which Ben Jonson[2] blames in Shakespeare:

> Cæsar did never wrong but with just cause.

This passage seems to have been given up by all the editors and commentators upon Shakespeare, by their admitting the modern emendations into the text. We are, perhaps, singular in thinking that even Ben Jonson's observation is a hypercriticism, and that Shakespeare is not guilty of such a bull as is commonly thought, supposing Ben Jonson's reading to be Shakespeare's, as we make no doubt it was. What does Cæsar do more than paraphrase the words of the poet? *Decipimur specie recti;*[3] that is, if he did wrong he was *misled by the appearances of justice*, or, *he thought he had just cause for what he did.* (xxi, 82) . . .

---

[1] See the 1745 *Observations* (3.176); and the expanded note for 1765 in Sherbo, *Johnson on Shakespeare*, p. 774.

[2] See 1.23.

[3] Horace, *Ars Poetica*, 24f.: 'most of us poets . . . deceive ourselves by the semblance of truth'.

[On *Antony and Cleopatra*, 4.12.25]

Mr. Johnson observes in the same scene that by *this* grave *charm* is meant, *this sublime, this majestick beauty.* We most *gravely* believe that Shakespeare makes Antony here use the word *grave* in the same sense Mercutio does in *Romeo and Juliet.* 'Ask for me to-morrow, and you shall find me a *grave* man.' [3.1.98]—*This grave charm.*—'This charm that has brought my glory to the *grave.*' In this sense, the expression is natural. (xxi, 84)

[On *Troilus and Cressida*, 3.2.52ff.]

Mr. Johnson has admitted a very contemptible note of Theobald's on the following expression: 'The faulcon as the tercel, for all the ducks i'th' river;' without recollecting that Pandarus says it, and that it contains a double entendre, which may not be quite decent to explain. . . .

Mr. Johnson tells us that in a speech of Thersites, the beginning of the fifth act, he does 'not well understand what is meant by *loving quails,*' [5.1.57] and we wish we could help him to a better meaning than the following. The French, whose proverbs Shakespeare very often adopts, have a notion that a *quail* is a very hot bird; hence *Chaud comme une Caille,* that is, *hot as a quail* is a common proverb among them; and Rabelais mentions the *Cailles coiphees* as being the same as the *lac'd mutton.* Gentle reader, *si quid novisti rectius—candidus imperti.*[1] (xxi, 86) . . .

Our limits will not permit us to pursue Mr. Johnson's notes through the most fertile fields of criticism; we mean in *Hamlet* and *Othello.* We cannot, however, applaud his management in stifling difficulties when he cannot remove them. Of this we have a pregnant instance in *Othello,* where the Moor is made to say,

> Oh thou weed!
> Who art so lovely fair, and smell'st so sweet. [4.2.67f.]

Dr. Warburton says, 'The old quarto reads, O thou *blache* weed, who art so lovely fair, &c. which the editors not being able to set right, altered as above. Shakespeare wrote, O thou *bale* weed, &c.

---

[1] Horace, *Epistles,* 1.6.67f.: 'If you know something better than these precepts, pass it on, my good fellow'.

Bale, i.e. *deadly, poisonous.*' Mr. Steevens's edition[1] reads, O thou *black* weed; and Mr. Johnson, contrary to all authorities we know of, retains O *thou weed*, and takes no notice of any farther doubts or difficulties, tho' the scene teems with both. We believe it would be no difficult matter to prove that *blache* weed is the true reading, and that a *blache* flower, in Shakespeare's and Sir Henry Spelman's time, was a common expression.[2]

We shall now take our leave of this work. The remarks and emendations we have laid before the public are but a few of a number too great for our plan to admit of. Mr. Johnson's chief defect as an editor seems to consist in his being too much of a Martinet (if we may use the expression) in learning. He consults only the academy and the portico, without deviating into the narrow turns and lanes where Shakespeare's words now lie obscure, tho' undeformed and unaltered. But notwithstanding his defects he has the merit of rescuing Shakespeare's meaning, in a multitude of passages, from the pragmatical efforts of preceding editors, who have most sacrilegiously presumed to alter his text according to their own groundless conjectures. We wish Mr. Johnson had stuck to his own discernment of Shakespeare's meaning, without attempting any alteration in the reading. He may perhaps, upon a review of his own notes, be of our opinion; but as his edition now stands, with the help of Dr. Warburton's notes, Shakespeare appears in it more himself than in any other which has appeared since that of Mr. Rowe. (xxi, 87–8)

---

[1] In his reprint of twenty Shakespearian quartos, No. 211 below, reviewed by Guthrie in the *Critical Review*, xxi (January 1766), pp. 26–33.
[2] In the 1773 edition Steevens rejects this suggestion: No. 240 below, Note 74.

209. James Barclay, Johnson defended

1766

From *An Examination of Mr. Kenrick's Review of Dr. Johnson's Edition of Shakespeare* (1766).

James Barclay (*c.* 1747–*c.* 1770) was an undergraduate at Balliol when he published this defence. Boswell recorded that 'Johnson was at first angry that Kenrick's attack should have the credit of an answer. But afterwards, considering the young man's intention, he kindly noticed him, and probably would have done more, had not the young man died' (*Life*, I, p. 498; see also *ibid.*, V, pp. 273, 549–50).

PREFACE.

Literary reputation, says a certain elegant moralist, is bestowed by the joint applauses of the generality, and destroyed by the malignity of individuals. Forbidding as this opinion may be to every eager candidate for literary fame, yet I am afraid the late attack upon Mr. Johnson's character will in some measure verify the observation.

Indeed a charge urged with such confidence, and backed with such delusive sophistry, can scarce fail of hurting him with the ignorant and unwary; with the learned and ingenious his reputation must for ever remain unshaken.—The reader, I suppose, is ready to anticipate me in my declaration concerning the design of the following Examination. He will easily conclude that to rescue injured merit from the hands of presuming arrogance is the sole end of the performance before him.

Before I proceed, I must observe that the parties attacking and attacked are equally unknown to me, and that I sat down to examine the extraordinary claims of the former, divested of any predilection for the one or prejudice against the other.

Upon the publication of Mr. Johnson's Shakespeare the expectations of the generality, it must be owned, were greatly disappointed. They had been induced to expect from his avowed learning and ingenuity a compleat commentary upon the works of their immortal bard, but through the concurring circumstances of inattention in the Editor and sanguine expectation in the reader the performance, I am afraid, has incurred the public censure.

This being a true state of the case, the injured party has certainly a right to complain, and an open declaration of the general sense would not have been unjust. But let me add, the manner in which it is conveyed to Mr. Johnson is UNJUST AND UNWARRANTABLE. (iii–iv)

[Barclay argues that Kenrick imitates the critics of Warburton:] Edwards and the author of the *Revisal* both urge their claims with personal abuse, only with this difference, the former cuts the Bishop's throat with a feather, the latter brains him with a club; the one wrote for the sake of LAUGHTER, the other to gratify malignant spleen. Edwards teizes him, but Heath assaults with all the indications of gloomy resentment. The Reviewer in his present attack upon Mr. Johnson blends both these different modes of dispute together, and *storms* and *grins* at one and the same time; like the savage Frenchman he laughs over murder, and is when most desperate in his incisions, then more particularly liberal of his gibes, and his pribbles, and his prabbles.

It must however be acknowledged that Mr. Kenrick has 'nor wit nor argumentation' enough to be the ape either of Edwards or Heath. He is clumsy in his anticks, and boisterous in his attacks. He first sneers, then gives you the reason for his raillery, and knocks down his adversary before he produces his warrant: whereas the opposite conduct is observable in his two ORIGINALS. (viii–ix) . . .

[On *The Tempest*, 1.2.28f.:

      Prospero. I have with such provision in mine art
    So safely order'd, that there is no soul—]

. . . Mr. Kenrick, in one part of his pamphlet, proposes a different mode of investigation, and advises a commentator to criticise upon his author as a POET, not as a PHILOLOGER. Why, O Reviewer, did you not continually comment as a poet! for a poet you certainly are if we believe yourself; if you had done so you would never have dwindled into the PHILOLOGISING SCHOLIAST whom you affect so much to despise.

But let us pay a little attention to Mr. Kenrick's emendation: 'If the passage, says he, must be altered' (but why must it be altered, can you give no why for this wherefore?) 'Let us at least make English of it. Shakespeare very probably wrote ILL, a word easily corrupted by the transcribers into SOUL.' Now in the name of common sense where lies the probability of the blunder? And why must *you* join the other scholiasts in exclaiming against the unlucky transcribers? Was it because you wanted to foist in a corruption of your own? Fie upon this correcting, Mr. Kenrick, it has done great hurt to YOUR Shakespeare's text! REVERE THE TEXT OF SHAKESPEARE!

But now let us see whether sense, and that too beautiful in the highest degree, cannot be *elicited* from the words as they stand in the old edition. Miranda, in *The Tempest*, is earnest to be informed by her father of the fortune of the vessel which she had seen labouring under the storm. Now I know not, Mr. K., whether you are a father, but I should think your poetical, if not your paternal, feelings would make you sensible of a father's impatience to disburden a beloved child of any oppressive fear.

Now let us re-peruse the passage in question. Prospero, the father, says to Miranda the daughter,

> I have with such provision in mine art
> So safely order'd, that there is no soul — &c.

That is, *I have so safely ordered* every thing *that there is no soul* — passionate impatience suppresses the necessary LOST. A common figure in rhetorick, the APOSIOPESIS, gave him leave to drop the word, and by that means add most beautifully to the sentiment, by representing the father so eager to ease the daughter of her fears as to pay no regard to the order of words.

But perhaps I have to do with a writer who is none of the most open to conviction; with such, quotation will better do the business than reason. In the beginning of this conference between Prospero and Miranda the latter expresses her fears lest the FRAIGHTING SOULS within the vessel did meet with any mischance; and again, some lines higher, she says, POOR SOULS, THEY PERISHED, speaking of the ship's crew. Here then appears an insurmountable reason for Prospero's use of *soul*.

233

MIR. *Poor* SOULS, *they perish'd!*   [1.2.9]
PROS. I have so safely order'd that there is *no soul*— &c.

Now, Mr. Kenrick, was there any occasion for your emendation, ushered in so pompously with groundless accusations? I believe not; your reading merely saves the poet harmless, while the other discovers his intimacy with the workings of the human soul. (2–4)

[On *A Midsummer Night's Dream*]

None of the most boasted compositions of learned antiquity afford a more noble scope for liberal criticism than the exquisite performance we are now entering upon. Through the medium of it we may contemplate the unbounded imagination of *our wonderful bard*, which could carry him beyond the limits of the natural world, into regions to which the poetry of Homer and Virgil was an absolute stranger: and experience has shewn, by the bad success of imitators, that he *alone* could wave the powerful rod, or walk within the magick circle. Criticks therefore who can fix their attention upon *words* instead of *sentiment* and *expression*, in such an effort of the fancy as the *Midsummer-night's Dream*, derogate from the dignity of their employment, and I had almost said, justly incur the sarcasm of petulant raillery. But as the Reviewer has thought fit to tread in the same paths, it is our duty as his examiner to toil through *his* verbal criticisms.

> PHILIST.——I have heard it over,
> And it is nothing, nothing in the world;
> Unless you can find sport in their intents,
> Extremely stretch'd and conn'd with cruel pain,
> To do you service.   [5.1.77ff.]

The old or partial use of the word *conn'd*, the singular sense of *intents*, together with the quaint expression of *extremely stretch'd* when applied to *intents*, so obscured the meaning of these lines that the Editor ingenuously owns himself at a loss for an explanation. It is much better to acknowledge our ignorance than to persist and blunder in the interpretation of any author.

Mr. Johnson, I am confident, knew as much of the matter as his Zoïlus; but whenever Shakespeare's meaning is dark enough to admit doubt it is much more advisable to let the reader com-

ment for himself, than hazard the danger of misleading his sense.
(14–15) . . .

[On *Measure for Measure*, 3.2.41]

Page 33 [of Kenrick's book] holds forth to us as surprising an
instance of scholiastic perverseness as is to be met with in any
wrong-headed scholiast whatever. Lucio in *Measure for Measure*
asks the clown, 'What is there none of Pygmalion's images, newly
made woman, to be had now, for putting the hand in the pocket and
extracting it clutched'? Would a person of *common* reading imagine
this passage stood in any need of a commentator? would he not
at first sight think the fop's meaning to be, is there no virgin to
be had now for money, or to speak in the loose phrase, no maiden-
head? The Reviewer's objection to this is, 'Procuresses seldom
deal in such commodities'; true, and for that reason, Lucio asks,
is there no possibility of lighting upon such an uncome-at-able thing? to
use his own most elegant phrase. As to the argument urged by
him in corroboration of his meaning, that dramatic writers use the
saying *to make a woman of her* for *to deflower a virgin*, it may be true
but has nothing to do here; for the words *newly made woman* merely
have reference to the immediate transformation of Pygmalion's
statue. This therefore is certainly the right meaning, and the one
advanced by Mr. Kenrick of *newly made woman*, for girls just de-
bauched, is as certainly wrong. I shall only add by way of advice to
him that the language of the stews has nothing to do with the
language of criticism. *Verbum sapienti.* (28)

As Mr. Kenrick, in this and the following page [pp. 54–5] has
treated Mr. Johnson with the most illiberal, outrageous and
arrogant language; I shall take no notice at present of his criticism,
but . . . I cannot pass over in silence his cruel raillery upon bodily
infirmity. 'The publick, says the raving Reviewer, will never be
prevailed upon to grace his *waving noddle* with a wreath, irreverently
torn from the brows of Shakespeare.'

Peradventure, reader, in the words *waving noddle* there lurks a
shrewd biting piece of wit with which thou mayest not be acquainted. Mr. Johnson, through the fault of a sedentary life, has contracted a paralytic disorder which affects his head in such a manner
as to give it an involuntary motion, which Mr. K. wittily expresses

by *waving noddle*: Now, dost thou perceive the smartness of the allusion? Thou dost—and smilest at the contemptible author of such an abuse of HUMANITY, DECENCY, and COMMON SENSE.

The *self-sufficient*, the *arrogant* Kenrick may possibly imagine that the zeal with which the very name of Johnson inspires me is counterfeited. By no means; tho' I have not the least personal connexion with him, *quanquam O!* yet I revere his character as a scholar and a *christian*. Towards the end of this extraordinary note Mr. Kenrick tells his reader, he 'is ready to crush a myriad of cockle-shell criticks in the cause, and under the banners of Shakespeare!' Giving him credit for his puissance, who can destroy a whole myriad of——cockle-shell criticks. I must tell him, Shakespeare disclaims such a factious servant; he is not qualified to fight under his command.—Shakespeare can defend himself!

> NON TALI AUXILIO, NON DEFENSORIBUS ISTIS
> ——EGET.——[1]   (34–5)

As Mr. Kenrick is so very waspish in defence of his Shakepeare, what encomiums upon the immortal Bard may we not expect in *his* intended edition? Doubtless, he will be extremely liberal with his apostrophes of admiration! Notes and text will swarm with *marks* of his approbation. Not content with adopting the method of Pope and Warburton*, in conveying their sense of the poet's beauties to the reader, he will quadruple their inverted commas, and exhaust the whole tribe of daggers†, asterisks*, double daggers‡, sections§, and parallels‖. For a sample of his dexterity in multiplying notes, I shall refer the reader to his annotations upon a BARBER'S FORFEITS, page 43–4. So that the sanguine admirers of Shakespeare may expect, in a short time, a man of their *own kidney* for his commentator; one who seems resolved to keep them agape from Act I. Scene I. of the first Play, to Act V. Scene the last of the last Play.

In fact, nothing has done more hurt to our great poet than these admirers in the gross; for ignorant of the principles of criticism,[2] an indifferent reader is apt to mistake their liberal praises for blind

---

[1] Virgil, *Aeneid*, 2.521f.: 'not such the aid nor these the defenders the hour craves'.
* Mr. Pope, in his Shakespeare, pointed out the beautiful passages with single inverted commas. Dr. Warburton doubled them in his edition.
[2] Cf. Johnson, p. 93 above.

adulation, and conclude that as they give no reason for their approbation, there is no foundation for it in the nature of things. Hence the petulant raillery of a flimsy Voltaire, and the dogmatical assertions of a Rymer. But we have no reason to lament the want of a *professed* commentary upon Shakespeare: The author[1] of the ELEMENTS OF CRITICISM has sufficiently rescued him from the hands of his worst enemies, his implicit adorers, and settled his beauties upon the stable foundation of manly principled criticism.

But to return from this digression; Mr. Kenrick is so very imprudent as to extend his inveteracy to *names*, and rakes sacrilegiously into the ashes of the immortal Jonson. The Reviewer in very positive terms insinuates that this honour of the British nation was himself a maligner of his cotemporary Shakespeare. This I know has been said, but he should have known that it has been refuted too; for what is the foundation of this silly charge? Will the unacquainted reader believe me, when I tell him that the enemies of Ben Jonson have only his *own* words to urge against him, and those too far from carrying any invidious reflections along with them? What envy is discoverable in saying Shakespeare had *little Latin and less Greek*, or wishing that among all his works he had blotted out *a thousand lines?* Mr. Kenrick speaks in the most contemptuous terms of all scholiasts; but if it be not a scholiast's trick to defend an author in every thing, especially one who writ almost merely through the light of nature, I am very much mistaken. Every true friend to Shakespeare, however, whose admiration is founded not on hearsay but mature consideration, will still continue to wish, *maugre* all the Reviewer's blind adulation, that he had blotted out *two* thousand;—then would he have defied the shafts of the most sharp-sighted examiner, and presided in a more eminent degree, if that indeed is possible, at the head of human wit! (71–3) . . .

The meaning of Shakespeare is like a variegated landskip; it will have more or less beauties according to the point of view in which the spectator is placed. To fix it then is an impossible task; all the critick can do is to give his sense; if it is wrong, the fault is not so much to be imputed to him as to his notions, which have no coincidence with those of the poet. For this reason, I am far from being wedded to the interpretation above given. It appears

[1] Henry Home, Lord Kames: see No. 193 in Vol. 4.

plausible to me; but still I may have considered the meaning in a wrong light. (82–3)

210. Thomas Tyrwhitt, on editing Shakespeare

1766

From *Observations and Conjectures upon Some Passages of Shakespeare* (Oxford, 1766). Although dated 1766, this pamphlet was in fact published in December 1765, and reviewed in the *Critical Review* for that month (by Guthrie), and in the *Gentleman's Magazine* (xxxv, pp. 528–33, 616–17; December 1765).

Thomas Tyrwhitt (1730–86), Oxford classicist, had an early career in politics (1756–62: deputy secretary at war; 1762-8: clerk of the House of Commons), but spent the greater part of his life as a scholar and editor. In classical literature he edited Babrius's *Aesop*, the Orphic poems, and made conjectures and emendations on the text of Aeschylus, Sophocles, Euripides, Aristophanes, Strabo, and Suidas, enjoying a high reputation in both England and Germany. In English literature he made an outstanding edition of Chaucer's *Canterbury Tales* (4 vols, 1775; vol. 5, with Glossary, 1778), and edited Chatterton's Rowley poems in 1777, identifying them as modern, not medieval, in an appendix published in 1778, with a *Vindication* of it in 1782, a decisive contribution to this controversy. In addition to these *Observations* he contributed notes on the text of Shakespeare to the Steevens editions of 1773 and 1778, to Malone's *Supplement* in 1780, and Reed's edition of 1785. His contemporaries regarded him as one of the leading scholars of the century.

The publication of Mr. *Johnson*'s long-expected Edition of *Shakespeare*'s Plays threw a temptation in my way, which I had no desire to resist, of looking over once more the enchanting scenes of that admirable Poet. As I had formerly read Him with more attention to his text than is usually given to the works of a modern Author, I had some curiosity to see how far my conjectures upon certain passages would be approved and confirmed by the judgment of Mr. *Johnson*; and I was not without hopes that other passages of which I had despaired might still be restored by the happier efforts of a more penetrating acuteness, with the assistance of the old copies. I confess freely that my vanity has not been gratified with many instances of the first sort; and of the latter I think the instances are indeed very few. However, I do not mean to enter into the merits of Mr. *Johnson*'s performance. Be they what they are. My intention is merely to set down my own observations and conjectures upon some passages of *Shakespeare* which have either been passed over in silence, or attempted, in my opinion, without success by former Commentators. (1–2) . . .

[On *Cymbeline*, 3.2.38]

At the bottom of this page there is a long note of Mr. *Johnson*'s, with some conjectures; all which, I believe, he would have spared if he had observed that the reading of the *Folio* Edition 1632 is (not *forfeitures* but) *forfeitours*, that is, *persons forfeiting*. Collating is certainly dull work; but I doubt whether, upon the whole, an Editor would not find it the shortest and easiest, as well as the surest method of discharging his duty.

The reading of the old Copies, though corrupt, is generally nearer to the truth than that of the later Editions, which for the most part adopt the orthography of their respective ages. An instance occurrs in the Play of CYMBELINE, in the last Scene. *Belarius* says to the King,

> Your pleasure was my NEAR offence, my punishment
> Itself, and all my treason.—   [5.5.334f.]

Mr. *Johnson* would read *dear* offence. In the *Folio* it is *neere*; which plainly points out to us the true reading, MEERE, as the word was then spelt. (12–3) . . .

But the old Copies do not only assist us to find the true reading by conjecture. I will give an instance from the second *Folio* of a reading (incontestably the true one) which has escaped the laborious researches of the many most diligent Criticks who have favoured the world with Editions of *Shakespeare*, from *Theobald* to Mr. *Johnson*. In TITUS ANDRONICUS, Act iv. Scene 1. *Marcus* says,

> My Lord, kneel down with me; *Lavinia*, kneel;
> And kneel, sweet boy, the *Roman Hector*'s hope;
> And swear with me, as, with the woeful *Peer*,
> And father of that chaste dishonour'd dame,
> Lord *Junius Brutus* sware for *Lucrece*' rape.—   [4.1.88ff.]

What meaning has hitherto been annexed to the word *Peer* in this passage I know not. The reading of the second Folio is FEERE, which signifies a *companion*, and here metaphorically a *husband*. The proceeding of *Brutus* which is alluded to is described at length in our Author's *Rape of Lucrece* as putting an end to the lamentations of *Collatinus* and *Lucretius*, the husband and father of *Lucretia*.

As I shall hardly have occasion to mention this Play of *Titus Andronicus* again I will take this opportunity of producing an authority for ascribing it to *Shakespeare* which I think a decisive one, though not made use of, as I remember, by any of his Commentators. It is given to him, among other Plays which are undoubtedly his, in a little book called *Palladis Tamia, or, the second Part of Wit's Commonwealth*, written by —— Maisier,[1] and printed at *London* in 1598. The other Tragedies enumerated as his in that book are *King John*, *Richard the second*, *Henry the fourth*, *Richard the third*, and *Romeo and Juliet*. The Comedies are the *Midsummer Night's Dream*, the *Gentlemen of Verona*, the *Errors*, the *Love's labour lost*, the *Love's labour won*, and the *Merchant of Venice*. I have given this list as it serves so far to ascertain the date of these Plays; and also as it contains a notice of a Comedy of *Shakespeare*, the *Love's labour won*, not included in any collection of his works nor, as far as I know, attributed to him by any other authority. If there should be a Play in being with that title, though without *Shakespeare*'s name, I should be glad to see it; and I think the Editor would be sure of the publick thanks even if it should prove no better than the *Love's labour lost*.

But to return to my Conjectures. . . . (pp. 14–16)

---

[1] By Francis Meres: see Johnson's reply in the 1773 edition, Note 47, p. 532 below.

In Act i. Scene 11 of CORIOLANUS he speaks thus;

> —— When drums and trumpets shall
> I' th' field prove flatterers, let courts and cities
> Be made all of false fac'd soothing! when steel grows
> Soft as the Parasite's silk, let HIM be made
> An OVERTURE for the wars!   [1.9.42ff.]

The first part of the passage has been altered, in my opinion unnecessarily, by Dr. *Warburton*; and the latter not so happily, I think, as he often conjectures. However, both his alterations have had the good luck to be admitted into Mr. *Johnson's* text of *Shakespeare*. In the latter part, which only I mean to consider, instead of *him* (an evident corruption) he substitutes *hymns*; which perhaps may palliate but certainly has not cured the wounds of the sentence. I would propose an alteration of two words.

> —— When steel grows
> Soft as the Parasite's silk, let THIS (i.e. silk) be made
> A COVERTURE for the wars!

The sense will then be apt and complete. *When* steel *grows soft as* silk *let armour be made of* silk *instead of* steel.

The mistake of *overture* for *coverture* has been made in Act iii. Scene 3. of the *third part of Henry the sixth*, at least in Mr. *Johnson's* Edition; and he has well corrected it in a note. To the arguments which he has there used in support of his conjecture I will add that *coverture* is actually the reading of the only two Editions which I have, the second *Folio* and *Theobald's*. It should seem by this that not only *the laborious Collator*, as Mr. *Johnson* expresses it in his Preface, but also the negligent Collator *at some unlucky moment frolicks in conjecture.*

The expression is indeed a happy one; for conjectural Criticism is properly a frolick of the understanding. It is pleasant enough to the Critick himself, and may serve to amuse a few readers, as long as it only professes to amuse. When it pretends to any thing higher, when it assumes an air of gravity and importance, a decisive and dictatorial tone, the acute Conjecturer becomes an object of pity, the stupid one of contempt. (18–20) . . .

In HENRY THE FIFTH, Act iv. Scene 6. the King says

O God of battles! steel my Soldiers hearts;
Possess them not with fear; take from them now
The sense of reckoning OF th' opposed numbers,
Pluck their hearts from them.   [4.1.285ff.]

Mr. *Theobald* reads

—— *lest* th'opposed numbers
Pluck their hearts from them.

And his alteration is admitted by Dr. *Warburton* and approved by Mr. *Johnson*. It certainly makes a very good sense; but I think we might read, with less deviation from the present text,   .

—— IF th'opposed numbers
Pluck their hearts from them.——

In conjectural Criticism, as in Mechanics, the perfection of the art, I apprehend, consists in producing a given effect with the least possible force. (43–4)

[On *Troilus and Cressida*, 1.3.66f.]

Of the rest of this passage Mr. *Johnson* says nothing. If he has no more conception than I have of

—— *a bond of* air, *strong as the axle-tree*
On which the heavens ride;——

he will perhaps excuse me for hazarding a conjecture that the true reading may possibly be,

——*a bond of* AWE.

After all, the construction of this passage is very harsh and irregular; but with that I meddle not, believing it was left so by the Author. Mr. *Johnson*, in his definitive sentence at the end of this Play, has pronounced it to be more *correctly* written than most of *Shakespeare*'s compositions: I presume he does not mean in point of *Style**.

---

* There are more hard, bombastical phrases in the serious part of this Play than, I believe, can be picked out of any other six Plays of *Shakespeare*. Take the following specimens in this Scene:—*Tortive,—persistive,—protractive,—importless,—insisture,—deracinate,—dividable*. And in the next Act,—*past-proportion,—unrespective,—propugnation,—self-assumption,—self-admission,—assubjugate,—kingdom'd*, &c.

But I begin to be tired, as I am afraid the Reader has been for some time, with these disquisitions; and therefore I will only offer two or three more corrections which I believe will not be disputed, and then conclude. (47–8) . . .

211. George Steevens, on Shakespearian scholarship

1766

From the Preface to *Twenty of the Plays of Shakespeare, being the whole Number printed in Quarto, during his Life-time, or before the Restoration; collated where there were different Copies, and published from the Originals* (4 vols, 1766).

George Steevens (1736–1800), began his long career as Shakespearian commentator with this collection. He had contributed 49 notes to the Appendix, and a list of the Quartos, to the last volume of Johnson's edition, and was to collaborate in an extensive revision of it in 1773 (see next item and No. 240 below), with further large additions in 1778, and again in 1785 (this time edited by Isaac Reed). As a result of a quarrel with Malone, Steevens embarked on a new edition, published in 15 volumes in 1793, and reissued in 21 volumes in 1803, by Reed, which included unpublished notes: thus Steevens's activities as a Shakespeare commentator stretched across nearly 40 years. He was a diligent user of libraries and archives, and became extraordinarily widely read in Elizabethan literature. But he also had an uncontrollable need for controversy and abuse, alienating almost every friend he had, which not only made him an impossible companion ('He came to live the life of an outlaw', Johnson said: *Life*, II, p. 375), but affected his scholarship for the worse. For his activities as a journalist see Nos 234, 237, and 238 below.

The plays of SHAKESPEARE have been so often republished, with every seeming advantage which the joint labours of men of the first abilities could procure for them, that one would hardly imagine they could stand in need of any thing beyond the illustration of some few dark passages. Modes of expression must remain in obscurity, or be retrieved from time to time, as chance may throw the books of that age into the hands of critics who shall make a proper use of them. Many have been of opinion that his language will continue obscure to all those who are unacquainted with the provincial expressions which they suppose him to have used,[1] but for my own part, I cannot believe but that those which are now local may once have been universal, and must have been the language of those persons before whom his plays were represented. However, it is certain that the instances of obscurity from this source are very few.

Some have been of opinion that even a particular syntax prevailed in the time of SHAKESPEARE;[2] but, as I do not recollect that any proofs were ever brought in support of that sentiment, I own I am of the contrary opinion.

In his time indeed a different arrangement of syllables had been introduced in imitation of the Latin, as we find in ASCHAM; and the verb was very frequently kept back in the sentence. But in SHAKESPEARE no marks of it are discernible; and though the rules of syntax were more strictly observed by the writers of that age than they have been since, He of all the number is perhaps the most ungrammatical. To make his meaning intelligible to his audience seems to have been his only care, and with the ease of conversation he has adopted its incorrectness.

The past editors, eminently qualified as they were by genius and learning for this undertaking, wanted industry; to cover which they published catalogues, transcribed at random, of a greater number of old copies than ever they can be supposed to have had in their possession; when at the same time they never examined

---

[1] Cf. Guthrie's reviews of Heath (4.567) and Johnson (above, No. 208).
[2] Cf. Guthrie (4.567); in his review of this collection by Steevens in the *Critical Review* for January 1766, pp. 27–8, Guthrie repeated his point, but with only one example.

the few which we know they had, with any great degree of accuracy. The last Editor alone has dealt fairly with the world in this particular; he professes to have made use of no more than he had really seen, and has annexed a list of such to every play, together with a complete one[1] of those supposed to be in being, at the conclusion of his work, whether he had been able to procure them for the service of it or not.

For these reasons I thought it would not be unacceptable to the lovers of SHAKESPEARE to collate all the Quartos I could find, comparing one copy with the rest where there were more than one of the same play; and to multiply the chances of their being preserved, by collecting them into volumes, instead of leaving the few that have escaped to share the fate of the rest, which was probably hastened by their remaining in the form of pamphlets, their use and value being equally unknown to those into whose hands they fell.

Of some I have printed more than one copy; as there are many persons who, not contented with the possession of a finished picture of some great master, are desirous to procure the first sketch that was made for it, that they may have the pleasure of tracing the progress of the artist from the first light colouring to the finishing stroke. To such the earlier editions of KING JOHN, HENRY THE FIFTH, HENRY THE SIXTH, THE MERRY WIVES OF WINDSOR, and ROMEO AND JULIET will, I apprehend, not be unwelcome; since in these we may discern as much as will be found in the hasty outlines of the pencil, with a fair prospect of that perfection to which He brought every performance He took the pains to retouch. (5–7)

[Quotes Pope's account of the Folio text: see Vol. 2, p. 411.] To this I must add that I cannot help looking on the Folio as having suffered other injuries from the licentious alteration of the players; as we frequently find in it an unusual word changed into one more popular; sometimes to the weakening the sense, which rather seems to have been their work who knew that plainness was necessary for the audience of an illiterate age, than that it was done by the consent of the author: for he would hardly have unnerved a line in his written copy, which they pretend to have transcribed, however he might have permitted many to have been familiarized in the representation. Were I to indulge my own private conjecture I should suppose that his blotted manuscripts were read over by one

---

[1] This list was in fact prepared by Steevens himself.

to another among those who were appointed to transcribe them; and hence it might easily happen that words of similar sounds, though of senses directly opposite, might be confounded with each other. They themselves declare that SHAKESPEARE's time of blotting was past, and yet half the errors we find in their edition could not be merely typographical. Many of the Quarto's (as our own printers assure me) were far from being unskilfully executed, and some of them were much more correctly printed than the Folio, which was published at the charge of the same proprietors whose names we find prefixed to the older copies: and I cannot join with Mr. POPE in acquitting that edition of more literal errors than those which went before it. The particles in it seem to be as fortuitously disposed, and proper names as frequently undistinguished by Italic or capital letters from the rest of the text. The punctuation is equally accidental; nor do I see on the whole any greater marks of a skilful revisal, or the advantage of being printed from unblotted originals in the one, than in the other. One reformation indeed there seems to have been made, and that very laudable; I mean the substitution of more general terms for a name too often unnecessarily invoked on the stage;[1] but no jot of obscenity is omitted: and their caution against prophaneness is, in my opinion, the only thing for which we are indebted to the judgment of the editors of the Folio.

How much may be done by the assistance of the old copies will now be easily known; but a more difficult task remains behind, which calls for other abilities than are requisite in the laborious collator.

From a diligent perusal of the comedies of contemporary authors I am persuaded that the meaning of many expressions in SHAKESPEARE might be retrieved; for the language of conversation can only be expected to be preserved in works which in their time assumed the merit of being pictures of men and manners. The stile of conversation we may suppose to be as much altered as that of books; and in consequence of the change we have no other authorities to recur to in either case. Should our language ever be recalled to a strict examination, and the fashion become general of striving to maintain our old acquisitions instead of gaining new

---

[1] That is, 'God': for a comment on the effect on *Othello* in the Folio text of James I's statute of 1606 against profanity in stage-plays see the note by Sir John Hawkins, No. 240 below, p. 544, Note 76.

ones, which we shall be at last obliged to give up or be incumbered with their weight; it will then be lamented that no regular collection was ever formed of the old ENGLISH books; from which, as from antient repositories, we might recover words and phrases as often as caprice or wantonness should call for variety; instead of thinking it necessary to adopt new ones, or barter solid strength for feeble splendor, which no language has long admitted and retained its purity ... (9–11)

It is not merely to obtain justice to SHAKESPEARE that I have made this collection, and advise others to be made. The general interest of ENGLISH literature, and the attention due to our own language and history, require that our ancient writings should be diligently reviewed. There is no age which has not produced some works that deserved to be remembered; and as words and phrases are only understood by comparing them in different places, the lower writers must be read for the explanation of the highest. No language can be ascertained and settled but by deducing its words from their original sources, and tracing them through their successive varieties of signification; and this deduction can only be performed by consulting the earliest and intermediate authors.

Enough has been already done to encourage us to do more. Dr. HICKES, by reviving the study of the SAXON language, seems to have excited a stronger curiosity after old ENGLISH writers than ever had appeared before. Many volumes which were mouldering in dust have been collected; many authors which were forgotten have been revived; many laborious catalogues have been formed; and many judicious glossaries compiled: the literary transactions of the darker ages are now open to discovery; and the language in its intermediate gradations, from the Conquest to the Restoration, is better understood than in any former time.

To incite the continuance, and encourage the extension of this domestic curiosity, is one of the purposes of the present publication. In the plays it contains the poet's first thoughts as well as words are preserved; the additions made in subsequent impressions distinguished in italics, and the performances themselves make their appearance with every typographical error, such as they were before they fell into the hands of the player-editors. The various readings, which can only be attributed to chance, are set down among the rest, as I did not chuse arbitrarily to determine for others which were useless or which were valuable. And many words differing only by the spelling, or serving merely to shew the difficulties which they to whose lot it first fell to disentangle their perplexities must have encountered, are exhibited with the rest. I must acknowledge that some few readings have slipped in by mistake which can pretend to serve no purpose of illustration, but were introduced by confining myself to note the minutest variations of the copies, which soon convinced me that the oldest were in general the most correct. Though no proof can be given that the poet super-intended the publication of any one of these himself, yet we have little reason to suppose that he who wrote at the command of ELIZABETH and under the patronage of SOUTHAMPTON was so very negligent of his fame as to permit the most incompetent judges, such as the players were, to vary at their pleasure what he had set down for the first single editions; and we have better grounds for a suspicion that his works did materially suffer from their presumptuous corrections after his death. ... (13-15)

At the end of the last volume I have added a tragedy of KING LEIR, published before that of SHAKESPEARE, which it is not improbable he might have seen,[1] as the father kneeling to the daughter, when she kneels to ask his blessing, is found in it; a circumstance two poets were not very likely to have hit on separately; and which seems borrowed by the latter with his usual judgment, it being the most natural passage in the old play; and is introduced in such a manner as to make it fairly his own. (16)

It is to be wished that some method of publication most favourable to the character of an author were once established; whether we are to send into the world all his works without distinction, or arbitrarily to leave out what may be thought a disgrace to him. The first editors, who rejected PERICLES, retained TITUS ANDRONICUS; and Mr. POPE, without any reason, named THE WINTER'S TALE, a play that bears the strongest marks of the hand of SHAKESPEARE, among those which he supposed to be spurious. Dr. WARBURTON has fixed a stigma on the three parts of HENRY THE SIXTH, and some others; and all have been willing to plunder SHAKESPEARE, or mix up A BREED OF BARREN METAL with his purest ore. (17) ...

There is perhaps sufficient evidence that the plays in question, unequal as they may be to the rest, were written by SHAKESPEARE;

[1] Lewis Theobald was the first to draw attention to this play: cf. 2.510f.

but the reason generally given for publishing the less correct pieces of an author, that it affords a more impartial view of a man's talents or way of thinking than when we only see him in form and prepared for our reception, is not enough to condemn an editor who thinks and practises otherwise. For what is all this to shew but that every man is more dull at one time than another; a fact which the world would have easily admitted without asking any proofs in its support that might be destructive to an author's reputation. . . .

As I have only collected materials for future artists, I consider what I have been doing as no more than an apparatus for their use. If the public is inclined to receive it as such I am amply rewarded for my trouble; if otherwise I shall submit with chearfulness to the censure which should equitably fall on an injudicious attempt; having this consolation, however, that my design amounted to no more than a desire to encourage others to think of preserving the oldest editions of the ENGLISH writers, which are growing scarcer every day; and to afford the world all the assistance or pleasure it can receive from the most authentic copies extant of its NOBLEST POET. (19–20)

212. George Steevens, proposals for a new edition of Shakespeare

1766

Four-page broadsheet, as issued.

FEBRUARY 1, 1766.

TO THE PUBLIC.

Had the last Editor of the Plays of Shakespeare met with the assistance he had reason to expect from the Public in aid of his own great abilities, all further attempts at the illustration of that Author had been as unnecessary as vain. I shall not pretend to ask whether the world has not hitherto imposed on itself by the expectation of a work more perfect than is consistent with the nature of the thing undertaken. This, at least, I am sure of, that no edition with notes critical and explanatory can be furnished by the application of one man but what will be found defective in as many particulars. The caution of an individual is frequently overwatched, and we find by daily experience that the attention of various readers is fixed on as many different parts of the page; and that no two will produce the same comment, or confine their observations to the same point. Hence it is that there is scarce a reader of Shakespeare but is in possession of some knowledge which another will continue to want; and is able to illustrate from his profession or track of reading what may have escaped the researches of the most industrious commentator. For these reasons it is become necessary to apply to the Public to send in their Remarks, and afford that assistance without which the task they wish to have well executed can be performed but in an imperfect manner. It is impossible to say where we are to look for information, nor are the books of that age in every hand. It cannot be gleaned entirely by industry, which stands itself in need of a guide; nor be supplied from any single library. In respect of the punctuation of the text, the least arduous part of the undertaking, the Editor has no rule to decide by, but will be more or less happy in proportion to his taste for dramatic performances, or his general knowlege of the manner of the Poet. But it cannot always be expected that he will be equally successful in the discovery of the local jest or personal allusion that once gave a poignancy to the passage; or that he shall be able as often to justify the expression which, though familiarized at that time by daily conversation, is now totally forgotten, unless something similar to it is to be found in the scenes of contemporary dramatic writers. There are some books we are already acquainted with by which many sources of this transient pleasantry may be traced, and have therefore reason to suppose there are more to be found in the repositories of the curious.

To intreat a general assistance is the purpose of the present Advertisement. It is not desired with a lucrative view to the Editor, but to engage the attention of the literary world. He will no more trust to his own single judgment in the choice of the notes he shall admit or reject than he would undertake the work in confidence of his own abilities. These shall in their turn be subjected to other eyes and other opinions; and he has reason to hope, from such precautions, that he shall bid fairer for success than from any single reliance. He is happy to have permission to enumerate Mr. GARRICK among those who will take such a trouble on themselves; and is no less desirous to see him attempt to transmit some part of that knowlege of Shakespeare to posterity without which he can be his best commentator no longer than he lives. The Editor will likewise assure those who may think proper to assist him that their contributions shall appear with or without their names, as they shall direct, though he will always take care to acknowlege the obligation; and will gladly pay those whose situation in life will not admit of their making presents of their labours, in such a proportion as Mr. Tonson shall think to be adequate to their merits. A perfect edition of the Plays of Shakespeare requires at once the assistance of the Antiquary, the Historian, the Grammarian, and the Poet. When their favours are solicited by one who is neither a writer by profession, nor hopes the least gain from the undertaking; who is neither obliged to publish in a limited time, nor depends on resources merely to be found in himself, it is hoped they will not be backward in complying with a request made for such a purpose as to procure justice to the immortal Author.

251

The characters of living or dead commentators, in the edition proposed, shall not be wantonly traduced, and no greater freedom of language be made use of than is necessary to convince, without any attempts to render those ridiculous whose assertions may seem to demand a confutation. An error in a quotation, or accidental misrepresentation of a fact, shall not be treated with the severity due to a moral crime; nor as the breach of any other laws than those of literature, lest the reputation of the Critic should be obtained at the expence of humanity, justice and good manners; and by multiplying notes on notes, we should be reduced at last, 'To fight for a spot whereon the numbers cannot try the cause.' The ostentation of bringing in the commentaries of others, merely to declare their futility, shall be avoided; and none be introduced here but such as tend to the illustration of the Author. Many notes were admitted into the last edition (which seems to have been published on the plan of the *Variorum* Classics) out of compliment to the acuteness with which a false reading or inter-pretation is sometimes defended; and were considered as a decoration proper to the page, though they afforded no oppor-tunity of conviction to the reader. It is true that decision is frequently expected where, from the nature of the point contested, it is not to be had; and in such a case, out of a variety of opinions, we must be left to form our own. But mistakes are still mistakes, however ingenious; nor is there any reason why we should mislead where we cannot convince, or offer splendid imposition for want of substantial proof. Should the retrenchment of notes that bear such a character be regretted by those who look for general amusement as much as a particular knowledge of the Author, it is hoped the omission will not be disagreeably supplied by parallel passages from the *Greek* and *Roman* poets. They will not be produced on a supposition that Shakespeare borrowed his ideas from them; but as a fresh argument that writers of the most distant ages, who were unread in the works of each other, must sometimes have thought and expressed themselves alike on the same occasions. And above all, because they are ornaments better becoming an Editor to furnish than refinements without founda-tion, or malicious though faithful records of the errors of his predecessors.

It should be remembered that there is no single text of

Shakespeare that can be depended on; and they are strangely mistaken who talk of restoring it to a state in which it never was. Among the alterations to be found in the earlier copies it is difficult to say with precision which were made by himself; or if any underwent his revisal. Shakespeare, who was a Poet as well as a Player, had a right to indulge himself in casual additions to what was set down originally in the Playhouse Copy. These, we may suppose, were preserved only in the memory of the performer to whose lot they might fall; and being ecchoed from one to another would easily grow more corrupt at every inaccurate transmission. The text we now receive has been gradually regulated from the old quarto's, and the folio in 1623; and as constantly has stood in need of some auxiliary syllables to restore it sometimes to sense, and sometimes to measure.—It is unnecessary to point out to the reader such of these as are trifling; nor would it be justifiable, by the omission of them, to reduce the Poet to the condition in which Mr. Rowe alone had found him. Where any thing has been injudiciously added it shall be silently removed; or if absolutely requisite, be continued with the name of the person who first introduced it; but the distinction will be only made where the passage is of consequence, and the liberty which has been taken with it great.

At the conclusion of the work shall be added a glossary, with examples of the usage of every word taken from more ancient or contemporary writers; with references sufficient to make it serviceable in respect of every other edition. The proposer of this scheme wishes, in aid of it, that it was the fashion to appropriate a part of some of the public prints for the use of asking and communicating information in regard to difficult passages in Shakespeare. Many gentlemen have conveyed their thoughts this way, but being scattered over several newspapers we must either daily examine the whole number or lose the benefit of their observations. Should he who now appears as a candidate for the public favour find himself unable to continue the work, or be disappointed of the expected aid, he will throw whatever he may be so happy to collect into the next edition that shall make its appearance. This too he heartily wishes may proceed from the late Editor, who will thereby have an opportunity of retracting his former errors; and by printing the additional notes and emendations at a cheap rate, and in a separate manner, do no injustice to the subscribers to the first edition of his book. It is not an uncommon thing to find many treasuring up those remarks which, if communicated in time, might have saved an Editor from mistakes, to make a more considerable figure in strictures on his work when it is too late for it to be benefited by them. But I should hope there are but few of such a disposition, and that even they will be convinced by comparing this trifling attempt with things of greater consequence, how little success we should meet with in general but for the mutual assistance our wants oblige us to bestow on each other.

The Editor must repeat that he will not lay himself under any obligations to prepare his work in a limited time, nor offers it by way of subscription; and if at last he should do no more than correct a few of the errors of others, and remove such notes as the judgment of the public has fully reprobated, he will still think he has performed something for which a future Editor will, in proportion, be as much obliged to him as he confesses himself to have been to those who preceded him in the undertaking. He cannot raise expectation by promises, as he does not depend on himself; and his success will be more certain as his coadjutors are more numerous. All he has to declare respecting his own part of the work amounts to this, that the little he may be able to supply towards its completion shall be executed with as much attention as he can bestow on it; and he heartily wishes his abilities were as equal to the task as his desire is ardent to have it performed, that when it comes to stand the test of censure it might prove to be deserving the acceptance of the Public, as well as adequate to the reputation of the Poet.

It is impossible, he is convinced, for him to say any thing relative to the difficulty of the undertaking but what has been better said already; nor does he flatter himself that the assistance which has been withheld from others will be as readily imparted to him. His pretence is to revive, not enforce the subject; and his hopes for indulgence are less founded on the efficacy of his own solicitations than on the conviction which the Public must have received, that none can escape with credit from the undertaking but such as are honoured with the assistance of a *literary subscription*.

That the Editor may not appear to be ashamed of what he has undertaken, or think it below him to solicit a literary contribution, he must now acquaint those who may be inclined to assist him, that their favours will be conferred on

GEORGE STEEVENS.

It is desired that all letters may be directed to be left at Mr. Tonson's in the Strand.

Since these proposals were drawn up I have been informed that more than one person[1] means to address the Public on the same subject; it is therefore necessary for me to declare that this Advertisement was communicated both to Mr. Garrick and Mr. Tonson many months ago, before any observations on the late edition had made their appearance, or the old copies of Shakespeare were published. Such an assertion, and having furnished others with materials which I might have kept in my own hands, will rescue me from the imputation of having produced these proposals in opposition to those of any other gentlemen.

213. Richard Hurd, Shakespeare's pastorals

1766

From his edition and commentary on Horace, *Epistola ad Pisones* (2 vols, 1766, I, pp. 205–11); this text from Hurd's *Works* (8 vols, 1811).

On Hurd (1720–1808) see the head-note to No. 120 in Vol. 3, pp. 362–4; also No. 128 (*ibid.*, pp. 420–31), No. 162 (Vol. 4, pp. 297–308), and No. 200 (*ibid.*, pp. 542–3). Gibbon wrote that there were 'few writers more deserving of the great, though prostituted, name of the critic' than Hurd. For Gibbon's long 1762 essay on Hurd's *Horace* see *The English Essays of Edward Gibbon*, ed. P. B. Craddock (Oxford, 1972), pp. 27–53.

---

[1] William Kenrick had announced his intention of editing Shakespeare, but never did so.

244. Sylvis deducti caveant[1] &c.) Having before (v. 232) settled the true idea of the satyric style in general, he now treats of the peculiar language of the satyrs themselves. This common sense demands to be in conformity with their sylvan character, neither affectedly tender and gallant on the one hand; nor grossly and offensively obscene on the other. The *first* of these cautions seems leveled at a false improvement which, on the introduction of the Roman satyr was probably attempted on the simple, rude plan of the Greek, without considering the rustic extraction and manners of the fauns and satyrs. The *latter* obliquely glances at the impurities of the Atellane, whose licentious ribaldry, as hath been observed, would of course infect the first essays of the Roman satyr.

But these rules so necessary to be followed in the *satyric* are (to observe it by the way) still more essential to the Pastoral poem: the fortunes and character of which (though numberless volumes have been written upon it) may be given in few words.

The prodigious number of writings, called Pastoral, which have been current in all times and in all languages, shews there is something very taking in this poem. And no wonder, since it addresses itself to Three leading principles in human nature, the love of ease, the love of beauty, and the moral sense: such pieces as these being employed in representing to us the tranquillity, the innocence, and the scenery of the rural life. But though these ideas are of themselves agreeable, good sense will not be satisfied unless they appear to have some foundation in truth and nature. And even then their impression will be but faint if they are not, further, employed to *convey instruction* or *interest the heart*.

Hence the different *forms* under which this poem hath appeared. Theocritus thought it sufficient to give a *reality* to his pictures of the rural manners. But in so doing it was too apparent that his draught would often be coarse and unpleasing. And in fact we find that his shepherds, contrary to the poet's rule,

——*immunda crepent ignominiosaque dicta.*[2]

[1] *Ars Poetica*, 244ff.: 'When the Fauns [satyrs] are brought from the forest, they should, methinks, beware of behaving as though born at the crossways and almost as dwelling in the Forum'.
[2] *Ars Poetica*, 247: 'cracking their bawdy and shameless jokes'.

Virgil avoided this extreme. Without departing very widely from the simplicity of rustic nature his shepherds are more decent, their lives more serene, and in general the scene more inviting. But the refinements of his age not well agreeing to these simple delineations, and his views in writing not being merely to *entertain*, he saw fit to allegorize these agreeable fancies, and make them the vehicles of *historical*, and sometimes even of *philosophic* information.

Our SPENSER wanted to engross all the beauties of his masters: and so, to the artless and too natural drawing of the *Greek* added the deep allegoric design of the *Latin*, poet.

One easily sees that this ænigmatic cast of the pastoral was meant to give it an air of instruction, and to make it a reasonable entertainment to such as would nauseate a sort of writing,

> Where pure description held the place of sense.

But this refinement was out of place, as not only inconsistent with the simplicity of the pastoral character, but as tending to rob us in a good degree of the *pleasure* which these amusing and picturesque poems are intended to give.

Others therefore took another route. The famous TASSO, by an effort of genius which hath done him more honour than even his epic talents, produced a new kind of pastoral by engrafting it on the drama. And under this form pastoral poetry became all the vogue. The charming AMINTAS was even commented by the greatest scholars and critics. It was read, admired, and imitated by all the world.

There is no need to depreciate the fine copies that were taken of it in Italy. But those by our own poets were by far the best. SHAKESPEARE had, indeed, set the example of something like pastoral dramas in our language; and in his *Winter's Tale*, *As ye like it*, and some other of his pieces has enchanted every body with his natural sylvan manners, and sylvan scenes. But FLETCHER set himself in earnest to emulate the Italian, yet still with an eye of reverence towards the English poet. In his *Faithful Shepherdess* he surpasses the *former* in the variety of his paintings and the beauty of his scene; and only falls short of the *latter* in the truth of manners, and a certain original grace of invention which no imitation can reach. The fashion was now so far established that every poet of the time would try his hand at a pastoral. Even surly BEN, though he found no precedent for it among his ancients was

257

caught with the beauty of this novel drama, and, it must be owned, has written above himself in the fragment of his *Sad Shepherd*.— The scene, at length, was closed with the *Comus* of MILTON, who in his rural paintings almost equalled the simplicity and nature of Shakespeare and Fletcher, and in the purity and splendor of his expression outdid TASSO.

In this new form of the pastoral what was childish before is readily admitted and excused. A simple *moral* tale being the ground-work of the piece, the charms of description and all the embellish-ments of the scene are only subservient to the higher purpose of picturing the manners, or touching the heart.

But the good sense of Shakespeare, or perhaps the felicity of his genius, was admirable. Instead of the deep tragic air of Tasso (which has been generally followed) and his continuance of the pastoral strain, even to satiety, through *five* acts, he only made use of these playful images to enrich his comic scenes. He saw, I suppose, that pastoral subjects were unfit to bear a tragic distress. And besides, when the distress rises to any height the wantonness of pastoral imagery grows distasteful. Whereas the genius of comedy admits of humbler distresses; and leaves us at leisure to recreate ourselves with these images, as no way interfering with the draught of characters or the management of a comic tale. But to make up in *surprize* what was wanting in *passion* Shakespeare hath, with great judgment, adopted the popular system of Faeries; which, while it so naturally supplies the place of the old sylvan theology, gives a wildness to this sort of pastoral painting which is perfectly inimitable.

In a word; if Tasso had the honour of inventing the *pastoral drama*, properly so called, Shakespeare has shewn us the just application of *pastoral poetry*; which, however amusing to the imagination, good sense will hardly endure except in a short dialogue or in some occasional dramatic scenes; and in *these* only as it serves to the display of characters and the conduct of the poet's plot.

And to confirm these observations on pastoral poetry, which may be thought too severe, one may observe that such, in effect, was the judgment passed upon it by that great critic as well as wit, CERVANTES. He concludes his famous adventures with a kind of project for his knight and squire *to turn shepherds*: an evident ridicule on the turn of that time for pastoral poems and romances that were beginning to succeed to their books of heroic knight-errantry. (I, 213–17)

214. Richard Farmer, Shakespeare's lack of classical learning

1767

From *An Essay on the Learning of Shakespeare* (Cambridge, 1767); this text from 'The Second Edition, with Large Corrections' (1767). In the copy which Farmer presented to him, now in the Bodleian, Malone has written 'The first edition was published at London in Jany 1767. It was written in the preceding year, and printed at Cambridge in Octr 1766, as the Author told me'.

Richard Farmer (1735–97), Master of Emmanuel College, Cambridge from 1775 on, also Vice-Chancellor and University Librarian, was a classicist and antiquarian, who built up an outstanding library. A friend of Johnson and a member of the Literary Club, he moved much in London literary society, twice declined a bishopric offered him by Pitt as a reward for his Tory principles, and was much respected as a scholar and an academic. In annotating the *Essay* I am partly indebted to D. Nichol Smith's edition of it in his collection *Eighteenth Century Essays on Shakespeare* (Glasgow, 1903; rev. ed., Oxford, 1963), which, however, does not include the errata slip found in Malone's copy in the Bodleian.

PREFACE to the SECOND EDITION.

The Author of the following Essay was sollicitous only for the honour of *Shakespeare*: he hath however, in *his own* capacity, little reason to complain of *occasional* Criticks or Criticks *by profession*.

The very FEW who have been pleased to controvert any part of his Doctrine have favoured him with better manners than arguments; and claim his thanks for a further opportunity of demonstrating the futility of *Theoretick* reasoning against *Matter of Fact*. It is indeed strange that any *real* Friends of our immortal POET should be still willing to force him into a situation which is not tenable: treat him as a *learned* Man, and what shall excuse the most gross violations of History, Chronology, and Geography?

Οὐ πείσεις, οὐδ' ἢν πείσῃς[1] is the Motto of every *Polemick*: like his Brethren at the *Amphitheatre*, he holds it a merit to *die hard*; and will not say *Enough*, though the Battle be decided. 'Were it shewn,' says some one,[2] 'that the old Bard borrowed *all* his allusions from *English* books then published, our *Essayist* might have possibly established his System.'—In good time!—This had scarcely been attempted by *Peter Burman* himself, with the Library of *Shakespeare* before him.—'Truly,' as Mr. *Dogberry* says, 'for *mine own* part, if I were as tedious as a King, I could find in my heart to bestow it all on this Subject:' [*Much Ado*, 3.5.22] but where should I meet with a Reader?—When the main Pillars are taken away the whole Building falls in course. Nothing hath been, or can be pointed out which is not easily removed; or rather, which was not *virtually* removed before: a very little *Analogy* will do the business. I shall therefore have no occasion to trouble myself any further; and may venture to call my Pamphlet, in the words of a pleasant Declaimer against *Sermons on the thirtieth of January*, 'an Answer to every thing that shall hereafter be written on the Subject.'

But 'this method of reasoning will prove any one ignorant of the Languages, who hath written when Translations were extant.'[3]—*Shade* of *Burgersdicius!*—does it follow, because *Shakespeare*'s early life was incompatible with a course of Education—whose Contemporaries, Friends and Foes, nay and himself likewise agree in his want of what is usually called *Literature*—whose mistakes from equivocal Translations and even typographical Errors cannot possibly be accounted for otherwise,—

---

[1] Aristophanes, *Ploutos*, 600: 'You will not alter my conviction, even if you should convince me' (tr. Burkert).

[2] William Guthrie in the *Critical Review*: see below, p. 281. (It might be noted that Farmer often re-words the authors he cites or runs several passages together.)

[3] Guthrie's review is alluded to throughout this paragraph.

that *Locke*, to whom not one of these circumstances is applicable, understood no *Greek*?—I suspect, *Rollin*'s Opinion of our Philosopher was not founded on this argument.

Shakespeare wanted not the Stilts of Languages to raise him above all other men. The quotation from *Lilly* in the *Taming of the Shrew*,[1] if indeed it be his, strongly proves the extent of his reading: had he known *Terence* he would not have quoted erroneously from his *Grammar*. Every one hath met with men in common life who, according to the language of the *Water-poet*, 'got only from *Possum* to *Posset*,' and yet will throw out a line occasionally from their *Accidence* or their *Cato de Moribus* with tolerable propriety. If, however, the old Editions be trusted in this passage our Author's memory somewhat failed him in point of *Concord*.

The rage of *Parallelisms* is almost over, and in truth nothing can be more absurd. 'THIS was stolen from *one* Classick,—THAT from *another*;'—and had I not stept in to his rescue poor *Shakespeare* had been stript as naked of ornament as when he first *held Horses* at the door of the Playhouse. . . .

Malvolio in the *Twelfth-Night* of *Shakespeare* hath some expressions very similar to *Alnaschar* in the *Arabian Tales*:[2] which perhaps may be sufficient for *some* Criticks to prove his acquaintance with *Arabic*!

It seems however, at last, that '*Taste* should determine the matter.' This, as *Bardolph* expresses it, is a *word of exceeding good command* [2 *Henry IV*, 3.2.84]: but I am willing that the Standard itself be somewhat better ascertained before it be opposed to demonstrative Evidence.

Upon the whole I may consider myself as the *Pioneer* of the *Commentators*: I have removed a deal of *learned Rubbish*, and pointed out to them *Shakespeare*'s track in the ever-pleasing *Paths of Nature*. This was necessarily a previous Inquiry; and I hope I may assume with some confidence, what one of the first Criticks of the Age* was pleased to declare on reading the former Edition, that 'The Question is *now* for ever decided.'

---

[1] See Johnson's note, cit. Farmer below (p. 276); also Kenrick's (p. 210), and Colman, below (pp. 291f.).

[2] Thomas Tyrwhitt had suggested this parallel, *Observations and Conjectures* (1766), p. 27.

* 'Dr. Johnson' [Malone's note in his copy: Bodleian Library, Mal. 142].

An Essay on the Learning of Shakespeare:

'SHAKESPEARE, says a Brother of the *Craft*,* is a vast garden of criticism:' and certainly no one can be favoured with more weeders *gratis*.

But how often, my dear Sir, are weeds and flowers torn up indiscriminately?—the ravaged spot is re-planted in a moment, and a profusion of critical thorns thrown over it for security. 'A prudent man therefore would not venture his fingers amongst them.'

Be however in little pain for your friend, who regards himself sufficiently to be cautious:—yet he asserts with confidence that no improvement can be expected whilst the natural soil is mistaken for a hot-bed, and the Natives of the banks of *Avon* are scientifically choked with the culture of exoticks.

Thus much for metaphor; it is contrary to the *Statute* to fly out so early: but who can tell whether it may not be demonstrated by some critick or other that a deviation from rule is peculiarly happy in an *Essay* on *Shakespeare*!

You have long known my opinion concerning the literary acquisitions of our immortal Dramatist; and remember how I congratulated myself on my coincidence with the last and best of his Editors.[†] I told you however, that his *small Latin and less Greek* would still be litigated, and you see very assuredly that I was not mistaken. The trumpet hath been sounded against 'the darling project of representing *Shakespeare* as one of the illiterate vulgar;'[1] and indeed to so good purpose that I would by all means recommend the performer to the army of the *braying Faction*, recorded by *Cervantes*. The testimony of his contemporaries is again disputed; constant tradition is opposed by flimsy arguments; and nothing is heard but confusion and nonsense. One could scarcely imagine this a topick very likely to inflame the passions: it is asserted by *Dryden* that 'those who accuse him to have wanted learning, give him the greatest commendation;'[2] yet an attack upon an article of faith hath been usually received with more

---

* Mr. *Seward* in his Preface to *Beaumont and Fletcher*, 1750 [see 3.390]. 'This had been said before by Lewis Theobald in the Introduction to his *Shakespeare Restored*, 4to. 1726' [Malone's note].

† 'Dr. Johnson' [Malone's note].

[1] W. Kenrick, *Review*: above, p. 211.

[2] *Essay of Dramatick Poesie* (1.138).

temper and complacence than the unfortunate opinion which I am about to defend.

But let us previously lament with every lover of *Shakespeare* that the Question was not fully discussed by Mr. *Johnson* himself: what he sees intuitively others must arrive at by a series of proofs; and I have not time to *teach* with precision. Be contented therefore with a few cursory observations as they may happen to arise from the Chaos of Papers you have so often laughed at, 'a stock sufficient to set up an *Editor in form.'*[1] I am convinced of the strength of my cause, and superior to any little advantage from sophistical arrangements.

General positions without proofs will probably have no great weight on either side, yet it may not seem fair to suppress them: take them therefore as their authors occur to me, and we will afterward proceed to particulars.

The testimony of *Ben.* stands foremost; and some have held it sufficient to decide the controversy.[2] In the warmest Panegyrick that ever was written he apologizes for what *he* supposed the only defect in his 'beloved friend,—

> ——————————————Soul of the age!
> Th' applause! delight! the wonder of our stage!—

whose memory he honoured almost to idolatry:'[3] and conscious of the worth of ancient literature, like any other man on the same occasion, he rather carries his acquirements *above* than *below* the truth. 'Jealousy! cries Mr. *Upton*; People will allow others any qualities, but those upon which they highly value *themselves.'*[4] Yes, where there *is* a competition, and the competitor formidable: but I think this Critick himself hath scarcely set in opposition the learning of *Shakespeare* and *Jonson*. When a superiority is universally granted it by no means appears a man's literary interest to depress the reputation of his Antagonist. In truth the received opinion of the pride and malignity of *Jonson*, at least in the earlier part of life, is absolutely groundless. At this time scarce a play or a poem appeared without *Ben*'s encomium, from the original *Shakespeare* to the translator of *Du Bartas*.

---

[1] Warburton's comment on Rowe: Nichol Smith, *op. cit.*, p. 90.
[2] Johnson: above, pp. 76f.
[3] For Jonson's tributes see 1.23–6.
[4] Upton, *Critical Observations* (1748) (3.290).

But *Jonson* is by no means our only authority. *Drayton*, the countryman and acquaintance of *Shakespeare*, determines his excellence to the *naturall Braine** only. *Digges*, a wit of the town before our Poet left the stage, is very strong to the purpose:

> Nature only helpt him, for looke thorow
> This whole book, thou shalt find he doth not borow
> One phrase from Greekes, not Latines imitate,
> Nor once from vulgar Languages translate.†

Suckling opposes his *easier strain* to the *sweat of learned Jonson*. [See Vol. 1, p. 12] *Denham* assures us that all he had was from *old Mother-wit*. [1.12] *His native wood-notes wild* every one remembers to be celebrated by *Milton*. [1.2] *Dryden* observes prettily enough that 'he wanted not the spectacles of books to read Nature.' [1.138] He came out of her hand, as some one else expresses it, like *Pallas* out of *Jove*'s head, at full growth and mature.[1]

The ever memorable *Hales of Eton* (who notwithstanding his Epithet is, I fear, almost forgotten), had too great a knowledge both of *Shakespeare* and the Ancients to allow much acquaintance between them, and urged very justly on the part of Genius in opposition to Pedantry that 'if he had not *read* the Classicks, he had likewise not *stolen* from them; and if any Topick was produced from a Poet of antiquity he would undertake to show somewhat on the same subject, at least as well written by *Shakespeare*.' [1.138, 341]

Fuller, a diligent and equal searcher after truth and quibbles, declares positively that 'his learning was very little, *Nature* was all the *Art* used upon him, as *he himself*, if alive, would confess.' [1.12] And may we not say he did confess it when he apologized for his *untutored lines* to his noble patron the Earl of *Southampton*?[2] —This list of witnesses might be easily enlarged; but I flatter myself I shall stand in no need of such evidence.

---

* In his *Elegie on Poets and Poesie*. p. 206. Fol. 1627. [See 1.11]

† From his Poem 'upon Master *William Shakespeare*,' intended to have been prefixed, with the other of his composition, to the Folio of 1623; and afterward printed in several miscellaneous Collections: particularly the spurious Edition of *Shakespeare*'s Poems, 1640. [1.27] Some account of him may be met with in *Wood's Athenæ*.

[1] Edward Young, *Conjectures on Original Composition* (1759) (4.406).

[2] In the dedication to *The Rape of Lucrece*.

One of the first and most vehement assertors of the learning of *Shakespeare* was the Editor of his Poems, the well-known Mr. *Gildon*;* and his steps were most punctually taken by a subsequent labourer in the same department, Dr. *Sewel* [2.421].

Mr. *Pope* supposed 'little ground for the common opinion of his want of learning:' [2.407] once indeed he made a proper distinction between *learning* and *languages*, as I would be understood to do in my Title-page; but unfortunately he forgot it in the course of his disquisition, and endeavoured to persuade himself that *Shakespeare*'s acquaintance with the Ancients might be actually proved by the same medium as *Jonson*'s.

Mr. *Theobald* is 'very unwilling to allow him so poor a scholar as many have laboured to represent him;' and yet is 'cautious of declaring too positively on the other side the question.'[1]

Dr. *Warburton* hath exposed the weakness of some arguments from *suspected* imitations; and yet offers others which I doubt not he could as easily have refuted.

Mr. *Upton* wonders 'with what kind of reasoning any one could be so far imposed upon, as to imagine that *Shakespeare* had no learning;' and lashes with much zeal and satisfaction 'the pride and pertness of dunces, who under such a name would gladly shelter their own idleness and ignorance.' [3.290]

He, like the learned Knight, at every anomaly in grammar or metre

> Hath hard words ready to shew why,
> And tell what *Rule* he did it by.

How would the old Bard have been astonished to have found that he had very skilfully given the *trochaic dimeter brachycatalectic*, COMMONLY called the *ithyphallic* measure, to the Witches in *Macbeth*!

---

* Hence perhaps the *ill-starr'd rage* between this Critick and his elder Brother, *John Dennis*, so pathetically lamented in the *Dunciad*. Whilst the former was persuaded, that 'the man who doubts of the Learning of *Shakespeare*, hath none of his own:' the latter, above regarding the attack in his *private* capacity, declares with great patriotic vehemence, that 'he who allows *Shakespeare* had Learning, and a familiar acquaintance with the Ancients, ought to be looked upon as a detractor from the Glory of *Great Britain*.' [2.293] *Dennis* was expelled his College for attempting to stab a man in the dark: *Pope* would have been glad of this anecdote.

[1] Preface to his edition: Nichol Smith, *op. cit.*, p. 70.

and that now and then a halting Verse afforded a most beautiful instance of the *Pes proceleusmaticus*![1]

'But, continues Mr. *Upton*, it was a learned age; [3.290] *Roger Ascham* assures us that Queen *Elizabeth* read more *Greek* every day than some *Dignitaries* of the Church did *Latin* in a whole week.'[2] This appears very probable; and a pleasant proof it is of the general learning of the times, and of *Shakespeare* in particular. I wonder he did not corroborate it with an extract from her injunctions to her Clergy, that 'such as were but *mean Readers* should peruse over before, once or twice, the Chapters and Homilies, to the intent they might read to the better understanding of the people.'

Dr. *Grey* declares that *Shakespeare*'s knowledge in the *Greek* and *Latin* tongues cannot *reasonably* be called in question.[3] Dr. *Dodd* supposes it *proved* that he was not such a novice in learning and antiquity as *some people* would pretend.[4] And to close the whole, for I suspect you to be tired of quotation, Mr. *Whalley*, the ingenious Editor of *Jonson*, hath written a piece expressly on this side the question.[5] Perhaps from a very excusable partiality he was willing to draw *Shakespeare* from the field of Nature to classick ground, where alone, he knew, his Author could possibly cope with him.

These criticks, and many others their coadjutors, have supposed themselves able to trace *Shakespeare* in the writings of the Ancients; and have sometimes persuaded us of their own learning, whatever became of their Author's. Plagiarisms have been discovered in every natural description and every moral sentiment. Indeed, by the kind assistance of the various *Excerpta, Sententiæ,* and *Flores* this business may be effected with very little expense of time or sagacity; as *Addison* hath demonstrated in his Comment on *Chevy-chace*, and *Wagstaff* on *Tom Thumb*: and I myself will engage to give you quotations from the elder *English* writers (for to own the truth, I was once idle enough to collect such) which shall carry with them at least an equal degree of similarity. But there can be no occasion of wasting any future time in this department: the world is now in possession of the *Marks of Imitation*.[6]

---

[1] Upton, *Critical Observations* (1748), pp. 381, 383.
[2] See Hurd, *Marks of Imitation* (1757), p. 24 (Vol. 4, No. 162b).
[3] Grey, *Notes on Shakespeare* (1754) (4.148).
[4] Dodd, *Beauties of Shakespeare* (1752) (Vol. 3, No. 136).
[5] Whalley, *An Enquiry into the Learning of Shakespeare* (1748) (Vol. 3, No. 113).
[6] Richard Hurd, *Marks of Imitation* (1757). See Vol. 4, No. 162.

'*Shakespeare* however hath frequent allusions to the *facts* and *fables* of antiquity.'[1] Granted:—and as *Mat. Prior* says, to save the effusion of more Christian ink, I will endeavour to shew how they came to his acquaintance. It is notorious that much of his *matter of fact* knowledge is deduced from *Plutarch*: but in what language he read him hath yet been the question. Mr. *Upton* is pretty confident of his skill in the Original, and corrects accordingly the *Errors of his Copyists* by the *Greek* standard. Take a few instances, which will elucidate this matter sufficiently.

In the third act of *Antony and Cleopatra*, *Octavius* represents to his Courtiers the imperial pomp of those illustrious lovers and the arrangement of their dominion:

> Unto her
> He gave the 'stablishment of Egypt, made her
> Of lower Syria, Cyprus, *Lydia*,
> Absolute Queen.   [3.6.8ff.]

Read *Libya*, says the critick *authoritatively*,[2] as is plain from *Plutarch*, Πρώτην μὲν ἀπέφηνε Κλεοπάτραν βασίλισσαν Αἰγύπτου καὶ Κύπρου καὶ ΛΙΒΥΗΣ, καὶ κοίλης Συρίας.

This is very true: Mr. *Heath* accedes to the correction, and Mr. *Johnson* admits it into the Text. But turn to the translation, from the French of *Amyot*, by *Thomas North*, in *Folio* 1579,*and you will at once see the origin of the mistake.

'First of all he did establish *Cleopatra* Queene of Ægypt, of Cyprus, of *Lydia*, and the lower Syria.' (1–11)

[Farmer then shows, from a series of verbal parallels, that Shakespeare had used North's Plutarch.]

... But matters may not always be so easily managed:—a plagiarism from *Anacreon* hath been detected!

> The Sun's a thief, and with his great attraction
> Robs the vast Sea. The Moon's an arrant thief,

---

[1] Hurd, *ibid.* (4.305).
[2] Upton, *Critical Observations*, p. 255.

* I find the character of this work pretty early delineated;

> 'Twas *Greek* at first, that *Greek* was *Latin* made,
> That *Latin French*, that *French* to *English* straid:
> Thus 'twixt one *Plutarch* there's more difference,
> Than i'th' same *Englishman* return'd from *France*.

And her pale fire she snatches from the Sun.
The Sea's a thief, whose liquid surge resolves
The Moon into salt tears. The Earth's a thief,
That feeds and breeds by a composture stol'n
From gen'ral excrements: each thing's a thief.

[*Timon of Athens*, 4.3.439 ff.]

'This, says Dr. *Dodd*, is a good deal in the manner of the celebrated *drinking Ode*, too well known to be inserted.'[1] Yet it may be alleged by those who imagine *Shakespeare* to have been generally able to think for himself, that the topicks are obvious and their application is different.—But for argument's sake, let the Parody be granted; and 'our Author, says some one,[2] may be puzzled to prove that there was a *Latin* translation of *Anacreon* at the time *Shakespeare* wrote his *Timon of Athens*.' This challenge is peculiarly unhappy: for I do not at present recollect any *other Classick* (if indeed, with great deference to *Mynheer De Pauw*, *Anacreon* may be numbered amongst them) that was *originally* published with *two Latin* translations.

But this is not all. *Puttenham* in his *Arte of English Poesie*, 1589, quotes some one of a 'reasonable good facilitie in translation, who finding *certaine* of *Anacreon's* Odes very well translated by *Ronsard* the French poet—comes our Minion, and translates the same out of *French* into *English*:' and his strictures upon him evince the publication. Now this identical Ode is to be met with in *Ronsard*! and as his works are in few hands I will take the liberty of transcribing it.

La terre les eaux va boivant,
L' arbre la boit par sa racine,
La mer salee boit le vent,
Et le Soleil boit la marine.
Le Soleil est beu de la Lune,
Tout boit soit en haut ou en bas:
Suivant ceste reigle commune,
Pourquoy donc ne boirons-nous pas?

Edit. Fol. p. 507. (16–17)

The only use of transcribing these things is to shew what absurdities men for ever run into when they lay down an

---

[1] Dodd, *Beauties of Shakespeare*, III, p. 285, note; also Christopher Smart (4.205).
[2] William Guthrie in the *Critical Review*: next item, p. 281.

Hypothesis, and afterward seek for arguments in the support of it. What else could induce this man, by no means a bad scholar, to doubt whether *Truepenny* might not be derived from Τρύπανον;[1] and quote upon us with much parade an old Scholiast on *Aristophanes?*—I will not stop to confute him, nor take any notice of two or three more Expressions in which he was pleased to suppose some learned meaning or other; all which he might have found in every Writer of the time, or still more easily in the vulgar Translation of the Bible, by consulting the Concordance of *Alexander Cruden.*

But whence have we the Plot of *Timon*, except from the *Greek* of *Lucian?*[2] The Editors and Criticks have been never at a greater loss than in their inquiries of this sort; and the source of a Tale hath been often in vain sought abroad which might easily have been found at home. My good friend, the very ingenious Editor of the *Reliques of ancient English Poetry*, hath shewn our Author to have been sometimes contented with a legendary *Ballad*.[3]

The Story of the *Misanthrope* is told in almost every Collection of the time; and particulary in two books with which *Shakespeare* was intimately acquainted, the *Palace of Pleasure*, and the *English Plutarch*. Indeed from a passage in an old Play called *Jack Drums Entertainement* I conjecture that he had before made his appearance on the Stage.

Were this a proper place for such a disquisition I could give you many cases of this kind. We are sent for instance to *Cinthio* for the Plot of *Measure for Measure*,[4] and *Shakespeare*'s judgement hath been attacked for some deviations from him in the conduct of it: when probably all he knew of the matter was from Madam *Isabella* in the *Heptameron* of *Whetstone*.* *Ariosto* is continually quoted for the Fable of *Much ado about Nothing*; but I suspect our Poet to have been satisfied with the *Geneura* of *Turberville*.† As

---

[1] Upton, *Critical Observations*, p. 26. [2] Cf. Gildon (2.254).

[3] The ballad of *King Leire and his Three Daughters* is to be dated after Shakespeare's play, however; Percy's mistake was often repeated.

[4] By Charlotte Lennox, *Shakespeare Illustrated*, 1753: see 4.110ff.

* Lond. 4to. 1582. She *reports* in the fourth dayes exercise, the rare *Historie of Promos and Cassandra*. A marginal note informs us that *Whetstone* was the Author of the *Commedie* on that subject; which likewise had probably fallen into the hands of *Shakespeare*.

† 'The tale is a pretie comicall matter, and hath bin written in *English* verse some few years past, learnedly and with good grace, by *M. George Turberuil*.' *Harrington's Ariosto*. Fol. 1591. p. 39.

you like it was *certainly borrowed*, if we believe Dr. *Grey* and Mr. *Upton*, from the *Coke's Tale of Gamelyn*; which by the way was not *printed* 'till a century afterward: when in truth the old Bard, who was no hunter of MSS. contented himself solely with *Lodge's Rosalynd* or *Euphues' Golden Legacye*, 4to. 1590. The Story of *All's well that ends well* or, as I suppose it to have been sometimes called, *Love's labour wonne*,* is originally indeed the property of *Boccace*, but it came immediately to *Shakespeare* from *Painter's Giletta of Narbon*.†
Mr. *Langbaine* could not conceive whence the Story of *Pericles* could be taken, 'not meeting in History with any such *Prince of Tyre*;[1] yet his legend may be found at large in old *Gower*, under the name of *Appolynus*. §

Pericles is one of the Plays omitted in the later Editions as well as the early Folio's, and not improperly; tho' it was published many years before the death of *Shakespeare*, with his name in the Title-page. *Aulus Gellius* informs us that some Plays are ascribed absolutely to *Plautus* which he only *retouched* and *polished*; and this is undoubtedly the case with our Author likewise. The revival of this performance, which *Ben. Jonson* calls *stale* and *mouldy*, was probably his earliest attempt in the Drama. (22–6)

But *to return*, as we say on other occasions.—Perhaps the Advocates for *Shakespeare's* knowledge of the *Latin* language may be more successful. Mr. *Gildon* takes the Van. 'It is plain, that He was acquainted with the *Fables* of antiquity very well: that some of the Arrows of *Cupid* are pointed with Lead, and others with Gold, he found in *Ovid*; and what he speaks of *Dido*, in *Virgil*: nor do I know any translation of these Poets so ancient as *Shakespeare's* time.'[2] The passages on which these sagacious remarks are made occur in the *Midsummer Night's Dream*, and exhibit, we see, a clear proof of acquaintance with the *Latin* Classicks. But we are not answerable for Mr. *Gildon's* ignorance; he might have been told of *Caxton* and *Douglas*, of *Surrey* and *Stanyhurst*, of *Phaer* and *Twyne*, of *Fleming* and *Golding*, of *Turberville* and *Churchyard!* But these *Fables* were easily known without the help of either the originals or the translations. The Fate of *Dido* had

* See *Meres's Wits Treasury*. 1598. p. 282 [and compare Tyrwhitt above, p. 240].
† In the first Vol. of the *Palace of Pleasure*. 4to. 1566.
[1] Langbaine, *An Account of the English Dramatick Poets* (1691) (Vol. 1, No. 27), p. 462.
§ *Confessio Amantis*, printed by T. *Berthelet*. Fol. 1532. p. 175, &c.
[2] In his *Remarks on the Plays of Shakespeare*, see Vol. 2, No. 50b; 'volume 7' of Rowe's edition (1710), p. 472; reprinted in 'volume 7' of Pope's edition (1725), pp. 358f.

been sung very early by *Gower*, *Chaucer*, and *Lydgate*; *Marlowe* had even already introduced her to the Stage: and *Cupid*'s arrows appear with their characteristick differences in *Surrey*, in *Sidney*, in *Spenser*, and every Sonetteer of the time. Nay, their very names were exhibited long before in the *Romaunt of the Rose*: a work you may venture to look into, notwithstanding Master *Prynne* hath so positively assured us, on the word of *John Gerson*, that the Author is most certainly damned if he did not care for a serious repentance.

Mr. *Whalley* argues in the same manner, and with the same success. He thinks a passage in the *Tempest*,

> High Queen of State,
> Great *Juno* comes; I know her by her *Gait*.   [4.1.101f.]

a remarkable instance of *Shakespeare*'s knowledge of ancient Poetick story; and that the hint was furnished by the *Divùm incedo Regina* of *Virgil*. [3.282]

You know, honest *John Taylor* the *Water-poet* declares that *he never learned his Accidence*, and that *Latin and French* were to him *Heathen-Greek*; yet by the help of Mr. *Whalley*'s argument I will prove him a *learned* Man in spite of every thing he may say to the contrary: for thus he makes a *Gallant* address his *Lady*,

'Most inestimable Magazine of Beauty —in whom *the Port and Majesty of Juno*, the Wisdom of *Jove*'s braine-bred Girle, and the Feature of *Cytherea*, have their domestical habitation.'

In the *Merchant of Venice* we have an oath 'By *two-headed Janus*;' and here, says Dr. *Warburton*, *Shakespeare* shews his knowledge in the Antique: and so again does the *Water-poet*, who describes *Fortune*, 'Like a *Janus* with a *double-face*.'

But *Shakespeare* hath somewhere a *Latin Motto*, quoth Dr. *Sewel*;[1] and so hath *John Taylor*, and a whole Poem upon it into the bargain.

You perceive, my dear Sir, how vague and indeterminate such arguments must be: for in fact this *sweet Swan of Thames*, as Mr. *Pope* calls him, hath more scraps of *Latin* and allusions to antiquity than are any where to be met with in the writings of *Shakespeare*. I am sorry to trouble you with trifles, yet what must be done when grave men insist upon them?

It should seem to be the opinion of some modern criticks that the personages of classick land began only to be known in *England*

---

[1] 'Mr. Gildon & not Dr. Sewell' (Malone's note): see Gildon (2.218).

in the time of *Shakespeare*; or rather, that he particularly had the honour of introducing them to the notice of his countrymen.

For instance, *Rumour painted full of tongues*, gives us a Prologue to one of the parts of *Henry the Fourth*; and, says Dr. *Dodd*, *Shakespeare* had doubtless a view to either *Virgil* or *Ovid* in their description of *Fame*. But why so? *Stephen Hawes* in his *Pastime of Pleasure* had long before exhibited her in the same manner,

> A goodly Lady envyroned about
> With *tongues* of fyre.—

and so had Sir *Thomas More* in one of his *Pageants*,

> *Fame* I am called, mervayle you nothing
> Though with *tonges* I am compassed all rounde.

not to mention her elaborate Portrait by *Chaucer* in the *Boke of Fame*; and by *John Higgins*, one of the Assistants in the *Mirour for Magistrates*, in his Legend of King *Albanacte*.

A very liberal Writer on the *Beauties of Poetry*, who hath been more conversant in the ancient Literature of other Countries, than his own, 'cannot but wonder, that a Poet, whose classical Images are composed of the finest parts, and breath the very spirit of ancient Mythology, should pass for being illiterate:'[1]

> See what a grace was seated on his brow!
> *Hyperion*'s curls: the front of *Jove* himself:
> An eye like *Mars* to threaten and command:
> A station like the herald *Mercury*,
> New lighted on a heaven-kissing hill.   *Hamlet*. [3.4.55]

Illiterate is an ambiguous term: the question is whether Poetick History could be only known by an Adept in *Languages*. It is no reflection on this ingenious Gentleman, when I say that I use on this occasion the words of a *better* Critick, who yet was not willing to carry the *illiteracy* of our Poet *too far*:—'They who are in such astonishment at the *learning* of *Shakespeare* forget that the Pagan Imagery was familiar to all the Poets of his time; and that abundance of this sort of learning was to be picked up from almost every *English* book, that he could take into his hands.'[2] For not to insist upon Stephen Bateman's *Golden booke of the leaden Goddes*,

---

[1] Daniel Webb, *Remarks on the Beauties of Poetry* (1762) (4.524).
[2] Hurd, *Marks of Imitation* (4.305f.).

1577, and several other laborious compilations on the subject, all this and much more Mythology might as perfectly have been learned from the *Testament of Creseide* and the *Faerie Queene*, as from a regular *Pantheon* or *Polymetis* himself. (32–7) ...

Thus likewise every word of antiquity is to be cut down to the classical standard. (38)

[Farmer shows that the names of the gates in the Prologue to *Troilus and Cressida* are derived from Lydgate's *Troy Book.*]

Our excellent friend Mr. *Hurd* hath born a noble testimony on our side of the question. '*Shakespeare*,' says this true Critick, 'owed the felicity of freedom from the bondage of classical superstition to the *want* of what is called the *advantage* of a learned Education. — This, as well as a vast superiority of Genius hath contributed to lift this astonishing man to the glory of being esteemed the most original *thinker* and *speaker*, since the times of *Homer*.'[1] And hence indisputably the amazing Variety of Style and Manner, unknown to all other Writers: an argument of *itself* sufficient to emancipate *Shakespeare* from the supposition of a *Classical training*. (40–1) ...

But to come nearer the purpose, what will you say if I can shew you that *Shakespeare* when, in the favourite phrase, he had a *Latin* Poet *in his Eye*,[2] most assuredly made use of a Translation?

Prospero in the *Tempest* begins the Address to his attendant *Spirits*,

Ye Elves of Hills, of standing Lakes, and Groves.

[5.1.33ff.]

This speech Dr. *Warburton* rightly observes to be borrowed from *Medea* in *Ovid*: and 'it proves,' says Mr. *Holt*, 'beyond contradiction, that *Shakespeare* was perfectly acquainted with the Sentiments of the Ancients on the Subject of Inchantments.' [3.358] The original lines are these.

> Auræque, & venti, montesque, amnesque, lacusque,
> Diique omnes nemorum, diique omnes noctis adeste.

It happens however that the translation by *Arthur Golding* is by no means literal, and *Shakespeare* hath closely followed it;

[1] Farmer runs together here two quotations from Hurd's commentary on Horace: for the original contexts see 3.364, 431.
[2] Cf. Whalley (3.281).

273

Ye Ayres and Winds; *Ye Elves of Hills*, of Brookes, of Woods alone,
Of standing Lakes, and of the Night approche ye everych one.

I think it is unnecessary to pursue this any further, especially
as more powerful arguments await us. (44–5) . . .

It is scarcely conceivable how industriously the puritanical
Zeal of the last age exerted itself in destroying, amongst better
things, the innocent amusements of the former. Numberless
Tales and *Poems* are alluded to in old Books which are now perhaps
no where to be found. Mr. *Capell* informs me (and he is in these
matters the most able of all men to give information) that our
Author appears to have been beholden to some *Novels* which he
hath yet only seen in *French* or *Italian*: but he adds, 'to say they are
not in some *English* dress, prosaic or metrical, and perhaps with
circumstances nearer to his stories, is what I will not take upon
me to do: nor indeed is it what I believe; but rather the contrary,
and that time and accident will bring some of them to light, if
not all.' —

W. Painter, at the conclusion of the second *Tome* of his *Palace of
Pleasure*, 1567, *advertises* the Reader 'bicause sodaynly (contrary to
expectation) this Volume is risen to greater heape of leaues, I doe
omit for this present time *sundry Nouels* of mery devise, reseruing
the same to be joyned with the rest of an other part, wherein shall
succeede the remnant of *Bandello*, specially sutch (suffrable) as the
learned French man *François de Belleforrest* hath selected, and the
choysest done in the *Italian*. Some also out of *Erizzo, Ser Giouanni
Florentino, Parabosco, Cynthio, Straparole, Sansouino*, and the best
liked out of the Queen of *Nauarre*, and other Authors. Take these
in good part, with those that haue and shall come forth.'—But I
am not able to find that a *third Tome* was ever published: and it is
very probable that the Interest of his Booksellers, and more especially the prevailing Mode of the time, might lead him afterward
to print his *sundry Novels* separately. If this were the case it is no
wonder that such *fugitive Pieces* are recovered with difficulty when
the *two Tomes*, which *Tom. Rawlinson* would have called *justa
Volumina*, are almost annihilated. Mr. *Ames*, who searched after
books of this sort with the utmost avidity, most certainly had not
seen them when he published his *Typographical Antiquities*, as
appears from his blunders about them; and possibly I myself might

have remained in the same predicament had I not been favoured with a Copy by my generous Friend, Mr. *Lort*.

Mr. *Colman*, in the Preface to his elegant Translation of *Terence*,[1] hath offered some arguments for the Learning of *Shakespeare* which have been retailed with much confidence since the appearance of Mr. *Johnson*'s Edition.

'Besides the resemblance of particular passages scattered up and down in different plays, it is well known that the *Comedy of Errors* is in great measure founded on the *Menæchmi* of *Plautus*; but I do not recollect ever to have seen it observed that the disguise of the *Pedant* in the *Taming of the Shrew*, and his assuming the name and character of *Vincentio*, seem to be evidently taken from the disguise of the *Sycophanta* in the *Trinummus* of the said Author; and there is a quotation from the *Eunuch* of *Terence* also, so familiarly introduced into the Dialogue of the *Taming of the Shrew* [1.1.167] that I think it puts the question of *Shakespeare*'s having read the Roman Comick Poets in the *original* language out of all doubt,

> Redime te captum, quam queas, minimo.'[2]

With respect to *resemblances*, I shall not trouble you any further. — That the *Comedy of Errors* is founded on the *Menæchmi* it is notorious: nor is it less so that a Translation of it by W. W. perhaps *William Warner*, the Author of *Albions England*, was extant in the time of *Shakespeare*;* tho' Mr. *Upton*, and some other advocates for his learning, have cautiously dropt the mention of it. Besides this (if indeed it were different), in the *Gesta Grayorum*, the Christmas Revels of the *Gray's-Inn* Gentlemen, 1594, 'a *Comedy of Errors* like to *Plautus* his *Menechmus* was played by the Players.' And the same hath been suspected to be the Subject of the *goodlie Comedie of Plautus* acted at *Greenwich* before the King and Queen in 1520; as we learn from *Hall* and *Holinshed*. *Riccoboni* highly compliments the *English* on opening their stage so well, but unfortunately *Cavendish* in his Life of *Wolsey*, calls it an *excellent Interlude in Latine*. About the same time it was exhibited in *German* at *Nuremburgh* by the celebrated *Hans Sachs*, the *Shoemaker*.

---

[1] 1765: for Colman's reply to Farmer in the second edition of his Terence see No. 217 below; and Farmer's further rejoinder in the 1773 Johnson-Steevens edition, p. 550 below.
[2] *Eunuchus*, 1.1.29: see the note to Kenrick above, p. 210.
* It was published in 4to. 1595. The Printer of *Langbaine*, p. 524. hath accidently given the date, 1515, which hath been copied implicitly by *Gildon*, *Theobald*, *Cooke*, and several others.

'But a character in the *Taming of the Shrew* is borrowed from the *Trinummus*, and no translation of *that* was extant.'

Mr. *Colman* indeed hath been better employ'd: but if he had met with an old Comedy called *Supposes*, translated from *Ariosto* by *George Gascoigne*, he certainly would not have appealed to *Plautus*. Thence *Shakespeare* borrowed this part of the Plot (as well as some of the phraseology), though *Theobald* pronounces it his own invention; there likewise he found the quaint name of *Petruchio*. My young Master and his Man exchange habits and characters, and persuade a *Scenæse*, as he is called, to personate the *Father*, exactly as in the *Taming of the Shrew*, by the pretended danger of his coming from *Sienna* to *Ferrara* contrary to the order of the government.

Still, *Shakespeare* quotes a line from the *Eunuch* of *Terence*: by memory too, and what is more, 'purposely alters it, in order to bring the sense within the compass of one line.'—This remark was previous to Mr. *Johnson*'s, or indisputably it would not have been made at all. 'Our Author had this line from *Lilly*; which I mention that it may not be brought as an argument of his learning.'[1]

But how, cries an unprovoked Antagonist,[2] can you take upon you to say that he had it from *Lilly*, and not from *Terence?* I will answer for Mr. *Johnson*, who is above answering for himself.— Because it is quoted as it appears in the *Grammarian*, and not as it appears in the *Poet*.—And thus we have done with the *purposed* alteration. *Udall* likewise in his '*Floures for Latin speaking*, gathered oute of *Terence*, 1560,' reduces the passage to a single line, and subjoins a Translation.

We have hitherto supposed *Shakespeare* the Author of the *Taming of the Shrew*, but his property in it is extremely disputable. I will give you my opinion, and the reasons on which it is founded. I suppose then the present Play not *originally* the work of *Shakespeare* but restored by him to the Stage, with the whole *Induction* of the *Tinker* and some other occasional improvements, especially in the Character of *Petruchio*. It is very obvious that the *Induction* and the *Play* were either the works of different hands or written at a great interval of time: the former is in our Author's *best* manner, and the greater part of the *latter* in his *worst*, or even below it. Dr. *Warburton* declares it to be *certainly* spurious: and without doubt, *supposing* it to have been written by *Shakespeare*, it must have been

[1] III, p. 20; Johnson on Shakespeare, p. 344.
[2] Kenrick, *Review*, p. 105: see above, p. 210.

one of his *earliest* productions; yet it is not mentioned in the List
of his Works by *Meres* in 1598. (59–66) ...

[On *Titus Andronicus*] I have not the least doubt but this *horrible*
piece was originally written by the Author of the *Lines* thrown into
the mouth of the *Player* in *Hamlet*, and of the *Tragedy of Locrine*
(69). ...

Thus much for the Learning of *Shakespeare* with respect to the
ancient languages: indulge me with an observation or two on his
supposed knowledge of the modern ones, and I will promise to
release you.

'It is *evident*', we have been told, 'that he was not unacquainted
with the *Italian*': but let us inquire into the *Evidence*.

Certainly some *Italian* words and phrases appear in the Works
of *Shakespeare*; yet if we had nothing else to observe, their Orthography might lead us to suspect them to be not of the *Writer*'s
importation. But we can go further, and prove this.

When *Pistol* 'chears up himself with ends of verse,' he is only
a copy of *Hanniball Gonsaga*, who ranted on yielding himself a
Prisoner to an *English* Captain in the *Low Countries*, as you may read
in an old Collection of Tales called *Wits, Fits, and Fancies*,

> Si Fortuna me tormenta,
> Il speranza me contenta.   [2 *Henry IV*, 2.4.171]

And Sir *Richard Hawkins*, in his Voyage to the South-Sea, 1593,
throws out the same jingling Distich on the loss of his Pinnace.
(78–9)

[Farmer shows that other Italian expressions used by Shakespeare were in common circulation.]

More hath been said concerning *Shakespeare*'s acquaintance with
the *French* language. In the Play of *Henry the fifth* we have a whole
Scene in it [3.4]: and in other places it occurs familiarly in the
Dialogue.

We may observe in general that the early Editions have not
half the quantity, and every sentence, or rather every word most
ridiculously blundered. These, for several reasons, could not

possibly be published by the Author,*and it is extremely probable that the *French* ribaldry was at first inserted by a different hand, as the many additions most certainly were after he had left the Stage.— Indeed, every friend to his memory will not easily believe that he was acquainted with the Scene between *Catharine* and the *old Gentlewoman*; or surely he would not have admitted such obscenity and nonsense. (pp. 84–6) . . .

I hope, my good Friend, you have by this time acquitted our great Poet of all piratical depredations on the Ancients, and are ready to receive my *Conclusion.*—He remembered perhaps enough of his *school-boy* learning to put the *Hig, hag, hog*, into the mouth of Sir *Hugh Evans* [*Merry Wives of Windsor*, 4.1.44]; and might pick up in the Writers of the time or the course of his conversation a familiar phrase or two of *French* or *Italian :* but his *Studies* were most demonstratively confined to *Nature* and *his own Language.*

In the course of this disquisition you have often smiled at 'all such reading, as was never read,' and possibly I may have indulged it too far: but it is the reading necessary for a Comment on *Shakespeare*. Those who apply solely to the Ancients for this purpose may with equal wisdom study the TALMUD for an Exposition of TRISTRAM SHANDY. Nothing but an intimate acquaintance with the Writers of the time, who are frequently of no other value, can point out his allusions and ascertain his Phraseology. The Reformers of his Text are for ever equally positive and equally wrong. The Cant of the Age, a provincial Expression, an obscure Proverb, an obsolete Custom, a Hint at a Person or a Fact no longer remembered, hath continually defeated the best of our *Guessers*. You must not suppose me to speak at random when I assure you that from

---

* Every writer on *Shakespeare* hath expressed his astonishment that his author was not solicitous to secure his Fame by a correct Edition of his performances. This matter is not understood. When a Poet was connected with a particular Playhouse he constantly sold his Works to the *Company*, and it was their interest to keep them from a number of Rivals. A favourite Piece, as *Heywood* informs us, only got into print, when it was copied *by the ear*, 'for a double sale would bring on a supicion of honestie.' *Shakespeare* therefore himself published nothing in the *Drama*: when he left the Stage his copies remained with his Fellow-Managers *Heminge* and *Condell*; who at their own retirement, about seven years after the death of the Author, gave the world the Edition now known by the name of the *first Folio*; and call the previous publications 'stolne and surreptitious, maimed and deformed by the frauds and stealths of injurious impostors'. But *this* was printed from the Playhouse Copies; which in a series of years had been frequently altered thro' convenience, caprice, or ignorance.

some forgotten book or other I can demonstrate this to you in many hundred Places; and I almost wish that I had not been persuaded into a different Employment.

Tho' I have as much of the *Natale Solum* about me as any man whatsoever, yct I own the *Primrose Path* is still more pleasing than the *Fosse* or the *Watling Street*:

> Age cannot wither it, nor custom stale
> It's infinite variety.—— [*Antony and Cleopatra*, 2.2.240]

And when I am fairly rid of the Dust of topographical Antiquity, which hath continued much longer about me than I expected, you may very probably be troubled again with the ever fruitful Subject of SHAKESPEARE and his COMMENTATORS. (93–5)

215. William Guthrie, Farmer reviewed

1767

From the *Critical Review*, xxiii, pp. 47–53 (January 1767).

This review of the first edition appeared before Farmer's enlarged second edition (the copy-text above, No. 214), in which Farmer was able to answer one of the points made here, the allusion to Anacreon in *Timon of Athens*. On Guthrie see the head-note to No. 208. This item can be ascribed to him since he twice refers to his own review of Johnson, and also to his earlier review of Heath (see the Preface above and Vol. 4, p. 568). The second edition was briefly noted by Guthrie in the *Critical* for November 1767, p. 400.

The public is much indebted to this writer for his ingenious researches into a subject which has long amused the critics.

Mr. Farmer cannot be refused the merit of having recovered to the present age many curious particulars which illustrate his principal proposition, viz. that Shakespeare was really destitute of what is generally understood by the word *learning*. Though we have already professed ourselves of a contrary opinion (see vol. XX p. 331)[1] yet we shall lay before our readers not only a candid but a favourable view of this author's arguments.

His first authority is the opinion of Mr. Johnson, which we omit because we have already fully canvassed that gentleman's merit as an editor of Shakespeare. The testimonies of Ben Jonson, Drayton the countryman and acquaintance of Shakespeare, and one Digges, who was a wit of the town before that bard left the stage, are next adduced; and then Mr. Farmer mentions the authorities of Suckling, Denham, Milton, and Dryden, who all favour his opinion.

Notwithstanding this, we are inclined to believe that those authors never meant to say positively that Shakespeare was entirely illiterate; at least, that they never imagined their words would be understood in that sense. The greatest friends of Shakespeare have been willing to acknowledge that his acquisitions in learning were undeserving notice when compared to the great, comprehensive, and intuitive genius with which nature endowed him. One might almost undertake to prove, upon Mr. Farmer's principles, that Locke was no more of a scholar than Shakespeare, for Locke shewed as inconsiderable an extent of learning in his philosophy as Shakespeare in his poetry. We should however deem that man very rash and adventurous who should dare to pronounce Mr. Locke was no scholar, merely because all the books he had occasion to make use of (which by the bye were very few) in his excellent essays were in his time translated into English. Several modern writers have, with some appearance of reason, maintained that Mr. Pope understood neither Latin nor Greek; and indeed, to confess the truth, it is almost certain that his critical knowledge of those languages was neither so universal nor extensive as to enable him to translate Homer, or imitate Horace; yet he succeeded in both.

Mr. Farmer (after quoting Fuller, who says that Shakespeare's learning was very little) proceeds as follows: [Quotes Farmer's

---

[1] In the review of Johnson above, p. 224.

summary of the claims made by previous commentators.]

Without pretending to defend the taste of Gildon and his coadjutor, the judgment of Pope, the learning of Theobald, the modesty of Warburton, the diffidence of Upton, or the literary qualifications of the three other reverend gentlemen abovementioned we think it would be no difficult matter to prove, from the criterions laid down by our author, that no writer of poetry in the English language understands Latin or Greek. Even the fine allusions drawn from Pindar and the lyric poets may be culled from translations; and the critic's hand may strip the bard as naked with respect to all literary merit as he was when he first went under the ferula.

Mr. Farmer's observations upon Shakespeare's using the old translations of Plutarch, and other ancient authors, seem to be very just, though we think they amount to no more than that Shakespeare was not such a proficient in Greek and Latin as to trust to his knowledge of the originals when he had the conveniency of translations. We likewise admit the merit of the discoveries this ingenious writer has made from those old translations and other publications in, or before, the time of Shakespeare; and had he proved that the poet borrowed *all* his allusions and translations of the classics from works then published, he might have established his system of the bard's total ignorance of ancient learning; but we apprehend our author will have great difficulty to bring Shakespeare to the bar of criticism for every petty larceny of this kind he may be suspected of having committed. Mr. Farmer may be puzzled to prove that there was a Latin translation of Anacreon at the time Shakespeare wrote his *Timon of Athens**. In his Tempest he even translates the expressions of Virgil; witness the *O dea certe*.[1] We think it almost impossible that any poet unacquainted with the Latin language (supposing his perceptive faculties to have been ever so acute) could have caught the characteristical madness of Hamlet, described by Saxo Grammaticus,[2] so happily as it is delineated by Shakespeare.[†] The

* See vol. XXI. p. 21 [in the review of Johnson above, pp. 226f.].

[1] *Aeneid*, 1.328: 'O goddess surely!'; cf. Guthrie, in his review of Heath (4.568).

[2] Cf. Guthrie (3.198f.) and Whalley (3.272). Guthrie reiterated his argument, referring back to this passage, in his review of Capell's edition in the *Critical Review*, xxvi (November 1768), p. 332.

[†] Falsitatis enim (Hamlethus) alienus haberi cupidus, ita astutiam veriloquio permiscebat, ut nec dictis veracitas deesset, nec acuminis modus verorum judicio proderetur.

same observation may be applied to his Macbeth's wife, which he draws from Buchanan. Shakespeare might have pored for years upon the *History of Hamblet* mentioned by our author (if such a history exists), and upon old Holinshed for facts, before he could have translated into his plays the very spirit, as well as words, of those elegant authors. We shall not, however, dispute this point with such an industrious antiquary as Mr. Farmer, who very possibly may produce such publications as may convict the poetical culprit of gross pilfering even in the instances we have mentioned.

We wish not to be thought strenuous advocates of Shakespeare's critical knowledge of the dead languages to such a degree as Mr. Upton (whom this writer very justly corrects) supposes. We do not even pretend to assert that Shakespeare had a classical education; but we know what a rapid progress a great genius passionate for knowledge, and sensible of its own defects, may make in a short time. . . . (47–51)

We shall conclude our review of this performance with acknowledging our obligations to the ingenious author, who has brought to light many curious circumstances relating to Shakespeare of which we believe the public were ignorant before this publication. (53)

216. T. W., on three Shakespearian tragedies

1767

From the *British Magazine*, viii (1767); the issues for February, September, October. Four more essays appeared later that year: on 'Shakespeare's merits as a comic writer'; on *Julius Caesar*, *Romeo and Juliet*, and *Richard the Third*.

In their enthusiastic but vague appreciation, their looseness of argument, and their lack of originality, these essays are typical of much Shakespeare criticism in the magazines of the period.

I. SHAKESPEARE VINDICATED from the IMPUTATION of wanting ART.

In criticism as well as philosophy, many opinions prevail for no other reason but because they were never examined: from being often repeated they come at last to be looked upon as axioms, and their truth is not so much as called in question. Thus it has been asserted that Shakespeare with all his genius was destitute of art; and this censure, re-echoed by every pretender to criticism, is now generally admitted, tho' it never was proved to be just. It is so far from being true, that many of Shakespeare's plays abound with the most masterly strokes of art; and the conduct of his pieces, tho' often irregular, is sometimes so skilfully managed that Ben Jonson himself, tho' justly admired for the incident and intrigue of his pieces, is not superior to Shakespeare in this article. In proof of what I have advanced I shall endeavour to shew with what admirable art the Ghost is introduced in the tragedy of *Hamlet*. Every circumstance of the appearance of this apparition is calculated to raise terror in the mind of the spectator; and the art of the poet is eminently conspicuous in the care he has taken to render each subsequent appearance of the spectre more terrible than the foregoing. The most picturesque imagination cannot conceive a finer night-piece than the scene in which the Ghost is first seen by Horatio, Marcellus, and the centinel. The time when this vision is seen is midnight; the place or platform before the palace; every circumstance that attends the appearance is so contrived as to raise terror and expectation in the minds of the audience. In how awful a manner is it introduced by the centinel's relation of its appearance on the night before!

> Last night of all, when yon same star
> Had made its course t'illume that part of heaven
> Where now it shines, the bell then beating one.
>
> [1.1.35 ff.]

Just at this moment the ghost enters. The circumstances of the star, and the clock's striking one, are admirably imagined, and greatly heighten the horror occasioned by this midnight phantom. The second appearance of the Ghost is still more striking, being preceded by a description of the various prodigies that happened after the murder of Cæsar, which for exquisite poetry is greatly superior to the admired one in Virgil's *Georgics*. It concludes with the following lines:

> And even the like precurse of fierce events,
> As harbingers preceding still the fates,
> And prologue to the omen'd coming on,
> Have heaven and earth together demonstrated
> Unto our climatures and countrymen.   [1.1.121 ff.]

Here the Ghost makes his second appearance, and the art with which the poet has contrived to render it more striking and terrible than the first, I think, cannot escape the most superficial observer. At the crowing of the cock it disappears; and these two scenes, in which it does not utter a word, prepare the spectator for the third, in which it appears to Hamlet himself and makes him a sign to go to some retired place in order to explain the reason of its appearance. At this third appearance it continues much longer on the stage than in the two former; and the terror of the beholders, which is worked up to a much higher pitch than before, is by a sympathetic feeling communicated to the breasts of the auditors in a much stronger manner than at the two former appearances. The spectator is led by the most natural gradation of circumstances from surprize to wonder, and from wonder to astonishment. The lines in which Horatio dissuades Hamlet from following the Ghost are so admirably picturesque that they are not to be matched by any author either ancient or modern:

> What if it tempt you to the flood, my lord,
> Or to the dreadful summit of the cliff ...   [1.4.69ff.]

But the fourth and last appearance of the Ghost, which the poet by an admirable stroke of art has deferred to the latter end of the piece, when it is almost forgotten by the audience, works up the mind to the highest pitch of terror and astonishment. It appears unexpectedly, just when Hamlet, who had been upbraiding his mother for her marriage with his uncle, is inveighing with the utmost bitterness against the latter. The prince is not prepared for a view of the apparition, as before, and every reader must have observed how much more strongly astonishment is expressed in his exclamation at this second appearance,

> Save me, and hover o'er me with your wings,
> You heavenly guards— [3.4.103f.]

than in that solemn invocation at the first, 'Angels and ministers of grace defend us!' [1.4.39]

It is in thus representing the gradual progress of the soul to the highest degree of passion that the art of the poet is chiefly displayed. The spectator, after having experienced a variety of emotions, at last finds his agitation at the height when Hamlet's astonishment is converted into a sort of phrenzy and he cries out like one raving,

> Why look you there—see how he stalks away—
> My father in his habit as he liv'd—
> See how he goes, even now, out at the portal! [3.4.134ff.]

The Ghost now disappears, and is never seen upon the stage again; and in this Shakespeare has shewn his judgment, since the terror excited by this last appearance was incapable of receiving any addition. Such scenes as these, at the same time that they prove Shakespeare's simple, plain sublime 'Can strike the soul with darted fire from heaven,' sufficiently evince that he was a consummate master of theatrical art, and thoroughly skilled in that most difficult part of the drama, which consists in working upon the mind of the spectators by well-imagined situations, sudden surprizes, and striking incidents. Neither Sophocles, Æschylus, or Euripides, whose well-conducted plots are the chief beauties of their works; nor their imitators, Corneille and Racine, who are so much admired for their judicious arrangement of incidents and artful unravelling of a catastrophe; can produce any thing superior to the above-cited scenes of Shakespeare's for art and contrivance. In the tragedy of *Othello* our poet has discovered equal skill; the gradation by which Iago conducts Othello from doubt to jealousy, and from jealousy to rage, till he ends in despair and self-murder; the several circumstances which naturally lead the unhappy Moor from one degree of guilt to another, are so happily imagined and so artfully introduced that this piece, when a few useless scenes are retrenched, must be allowed to be a masterpiece for conduct. But as I have already exceeded the bounds of an epistle, I shall not now enter upon this subject, but defer my remarks upon *Othello* to another opportunity. (57–9)

II. OBSERVATIONS on the TRAGEDY of *OTHELLO*.

GENTLEMEN, I some time ago sent you my observations upon the tragedy of *Hamlet*, in which I endeavoured to do justice to the character of Shakespeare as a dramatic author and to vindicate him from the imputation of wanting art. At the sequel of those observations I promised to vindicate him still farther in strictures upon the tragedy of *Othello*, which I now send you, not having before had an opportunity of performing my promise.

That there are some superfluous scenes in the tragedy of *Othello* must be allowed: as for example, the scene in which Bianca is introduced; that in which Desdemona sings the song of Willow; that in which the herald reads the proclamation; and some others. But these being retrenched what remains is a masterpiece of conduct; a plan for art and regularity equal to that of any of the celebrated Corneille's. In the *Cid* of the last-mentioned poet all the scenes between the infanta and her confidant, which turn upon her passion for Rodriguez, are considered as superfluous, and always retrenched at Paris in the representation; yet this play is, notwithstanding, considered by all the most judicious French critics as one of Corneille's best pieces for intrigue. I shall, however, make no scruple to prefer the plan of *Othello* to that of this famous tragedy, and even to that of the celebrated tragedy of the Horatii; concerning which the ingenious Mons. de Fontenelle, nephew to the great Corneille, justly observes that the three first acts of it are a master-piece of art and conduct unequalled by all the productions of the antients and moderns. Yet as this piece does not end with the conclusion of the combat between the Horatii and Curiatii and the murder of Horatius's sister, but is continued to two more acts, in which a new action, as it were, is commenced, it must be acknowledged that there is a material defect in the plan of this play. There is a fault equally visible in the catastrophe of the *Cid*, which always ends unsatisfactorily to the audience on account of the impossibility of Chimene's ever marrying Rodriguez, the murderer of her father, consistently with the laws of honour. For these reasons the plan of *Othello* will be always preferred by all judicious critics to either of these boasted master-pieces of French art.

The beginning of the chief action of *Othello*, I mean Iago's working him up to jealousy, is very judiciously deferred by the poet till the piece is far advanced, and the characters of all the principal personages of the play perfectly ascertained. The conjecture which the poet makes Iago avail himself of, in order to pour his first poison into Othello's ear, is admirably chosen; it is a stroke of art scarce to be matched in the works of the poets of our own or any other country. Cassio was just leaving Desdemona, whom he had sollicited to speak in his favour to her husband; Iago takes hold of this circumstance, and says in a low voice, 'Ha! I like not that.' Othello hereupon questions him, and Iago, by artfully deferring to give him any satisfaction, aggravates his suspicion to the highest pitch; but the passage is wrought up with such art that I make no doubt the reader will excuse me for here transcribing it at full length.

> *Iago.* Hah! I like not that—
> *Oth.* What dost thou say?
> *Iago.* Nothing, my lord, or if—I know not what.
> *Oth.* Was not that *Cassio* parted from my wife?
> *Iago. Cassio*, my lord?—no, sure, I cannot think it,
> That he would steal away so guilty-like,
> Seeing you coming.
> *Oth.* I think 'twas he—   [3.3.35ff.]

It is a circumstance admirably calculated to rouse the jealousy of Othello that Desdemona should speak in favour of the very man upon whom his suspicions had fallen.

The art of the poet is equally conspicuous in the next scene; it opens with a torrent and tempest of passion from Othello, who collars Iago and threatens him with death if he did not make good his accusation. This violent passion, upon its subsiding, puts him still more in the power of the villain, who avails himself of that opportunity to encrease the jealousy of Othello to the highest pitch, and make him resolute on the murder of Desdemona. As the gradation of steps by which Iago encreases the jealousy of Othello from bare surmise and suspicion to the highest pitch of rage is an admirable effect of art, the progress of Othello's behaviour to Desdemona, in proportion as his jealousy increases, is equally so. He begins by sullenness and dark expressions, proceeds to menaces, and ends by the most brutal treatment, and even blows. The murder of Roderigo and the attempt upon Cassio, with Iago's confusion at the approach of the catastrophe of his villainy, admirably introduce the last scene of the murder of Desdemona in her bed-chamber, which is introduced with the greatest solemnity imaginable. To this the circumstance of Othello's entering with a candle greatly contributes. The thought suggested by the taper he holds in his hand, has a beautiful propriety in it.

> Put out the light, and then—put out the light:
> If I quench thee, thou flaming minister ...   [5.2.7ff.]

The awful solemnity of this scene has an admirable effect in inhancing the horror and confusion of the catastrophe; it is like a calm preceding a storm: and this catastrophe I look upon as an example of what Longinus in his treatise upon the Sublime calls the terrible Graces, not to be matched by any other poet either antient or modern. (449–51)

III. OBSERVATIONS upon the TRAGEDY of *MACBETH*

There are no poetical beauties which so powerfully affect the imagination as those to which Longinus has given the appellation of the Terrible Graces. In these Shakespeare has surpassed all other poets; and in the tragedy of *Macbeth* he has even surpassed himself. If the chief end of tragedy be to excite terror and compassion, that of *Macbeth* must be allowed to surpass all others, whether antient or modern. Every circumstance preparatory to the murder of Duncan is admirably calculated to raise terror in the minds of the spectators; and their agitation is gradually increased till the perpetration of that execrable deed, by which it is raised to the highest pitch of horror.

In the soliloquy which precedes the murder, the poet with great judgment represents Macbeth so disordered in his imagination as to think he sees a dagger pointing to the apartment of Duncan and directing his foot-steps. There cannot be a more admirable representation of the state of mind of a man who has conceived a design replete with horror, and is meditating upon the means of putting it in execution. Nothing is more common at such a juncture than for the mind to hold a sort of conference with the instruments to be used in effecting the bloody purpose.

There cannot be a better comment upon the several scenes which precede the murder of the King, than the observation which our author puts into the mouth of Brutus, in his *Julius Cæsar*:

> Between the acting of a dreadful thing
> And the first motion, all the interim is
> Like a phantasma, or a hideous dream;
> The genius and the mortal instruments
> Are then in council, and the whole state of man
> Like to a little kingdom, suffers then
> The nature of an insurrection.
>
> [2.1.63 ff.]

There is an admirable contrast between the characters of Macbeth and his wife. Her harden'd insensibility makes his horrors and remorse more striking, and contributes to render the loss of her senses and her raving, upon the murder of Duncan in the last scene, in a particular manner affecting. Shakespeare has, in many of his pieces, represented the ravings of a disordered mind with great success; but I think in none so well as in this tragedy. The madness of Ophelia in *Hamlet*, and the songs which she sings are little suited to the dignity of tragedy; and that of Lear is continued too long, and of consequence in part loses its effect. But the madness of lady Macbeth, occasioned by her stings of conscience, is perfectly in nature and has in it something shocking, which greatly increases the horror raised by the sanguinary catastrophe of the piece. The circumstance of her constantly rubbing her hand in order to wipe out the stain made by Duncan's murder, is admirably imagined; and her exclamation, 'Who would have thought that there was so much blood in the old man's body!' [5.1.37f.] is a most natural representation of the state of a mind racked with the consciousness of having committed murder.

The madness of Orestes and Ajax are in comparison but weakly represented by Sophocles, though he surpassed all the other Greek tragedians in the art of moving the passions.

The appearance of the witches and Hecate have been censured by many critics as offending against probability; but this, in my opinion, is carrying criticism too far. The persuasion of the vulgar is a sufficient foundation for a poet to introduce marvellous events and imaginary personages; and if this reasoning was admitted it would be sufficient to make us condemn all the poetry of the antients, as their mythology is interwoven with it in such a manner that one cannot subsist without the other. The prophecy of the witches, 'that none of woman born should be able to hurt Macbeth, and that he need fear nothing till Birnam wood should come to Dunsinane,' have, when fulfilled in a sense different from what the words seemed to import, an excellent effect in rendering the fall of the bloody tyrant dreadful and shocking. The scene in which the Ghost of the murdered Banquo appears is an admirable picture; at each subsequent appearance Macbeth's horror and astonishment are increased by the most natural grada-tion, till at last he can contain no longer but exclaims, upon lady Macbeth's asking him, 'Are you a man?'

> Ay, and a bold one too,
> That dare look on that which might appal the devil.   [3.4.58ff.]

There is something sufficient to chill the blood with horror in the following speech, which Macbeth makes to the Ghost:

> Approach thou like the rugged Russian boar. . . .   [3.4.100ff.]

How admirably emphatical are the lines which follow soon after:

> Thy bones are marrowless, thy blood is cold;
> There is no speculation in those eyes
> Which thou dost glare with—   [3.4.94ff.]

It was such striking passages as these which extorted that acknowledgment from Mons. de Marmontel, that the latitude taken by the English tragic poets have given room to strokes which the French, who have tied themselves down to severer rules, can only envy and admire without aspiring to imitate them. I am, however, rather inclined to think that it is want of genius in the French poets, and not the strictness of the rules which they have prescribed to themselves, that has deprived their works of these beauties; for we find that Mons. de Voltaire attempted to follow the foot-steps of Shakespeare, and has introduced the ghost of Ninus in his tragedy of *Semiramis*; but the little success he met with sufficiently shews that only such a genius as Shakespeare's can succeed in describing objects like these, which require a creative power of imagination in the poet, as they have no existence in nature.

If the tragedy of *Macbeth* surpasses all the other tragedies of Shakespeare in exciting terror, it is likewise superior to them in having no mixture of buffoonery or low humour in it, and may, of consequence, be justly considered as the master-piece of that great poet. The several attempts made to alter this piece serve only to set the genius of Shakespeare in a stronger light, as they all shew the superiority of the original. (514–16)

217. George Colman, Farmer criticized

1768

The 'Appendix to the Second Edition of the Translation of the Comedies of Terence Published in the Year 1768': II, pp. 389–94; reprinted in Colman's *Prose on Several Occasions* (1787), II, pp. 173–8.

The reverend and ingenious Mr. Farmer, in his curious and entertaining *Essay on the Learning of Shakespeare*, having done me the honour to animadvert on some passages in the preface to this translation, I cannot dismiss this edition without declaring how far I coincide with that gentleman; although what I then threw out carelessly on the subject of his pamphlet was merely incidental, nor did I mean to enter the lists as a champion to defend either side of the question.

It is most true, as Mr. Farmer takes for granted, that I had never met with the old comedy called *The Supposes*, nor has it even yet fallen into my hands; yet I am willing to grant, on Mr. Farmer's authority, that Shakespeare borrowed part of the plot of *The Taming of the Shrew* from that old translation of Ariosto's play by George Gascoigne and had no obligations to Plautus. I will accede also to the truth of Dr. Johnson's and Mr. Farmer's observation that the line from Terence, exactly as it stands in Shakespeare, is extant in Lilly and Udall's *Floures for Latin Speaking*. Still, however, Shakespeare's total ignorance of the learned languages remains to be proved; for it must be granted that such books are put into the hands of those who are learning those languages, in which class we must necessarily rank Shakespeare, or he could not even have quoted Terence from Udall or Lilly; nor is it likely that so rapid a genius should not have made some further progress. 'Our author' (says Dr. Johnson, as quoted by Mr. Farmer) 'had this line from Lilly; which I mention, that it may not be brought as an argument of his learning.' It is, however, an argument that he read Lilly; and a few pages further it seems

291

pretty certain that the author of *The Taming of the Shrew* had at least read Ovid, from whose epistles we find these lines:

> *Hàc ibàt Simois; hic est Sigeia tellus;*
> *Hic steterat Priami regia celsa senis.*[1]

And what does Dr. Johnson say on this occasion? Nothing. And what does Mr. Farmer say on this occasion? Nothing.

In *Love's Labour's Lost* which, bad as it is, is ascribed by Dr. Johnson himself to Shakespeare, there occurs the word *thrasonical* [5.1.10]; another argument which seems to shew that he was not unacquainted with the comedies of Terence;[2] not to mention that the character of the Schoolmaster in the same play could not possibly be written by a man who had travelled no further in Latin than *hic, hæc, hoc*.

In *Henry the Sixth* we meet with a quotation from Virgil, *Tantæne animis cœlestibus iræ*?[3] [2 *Henry VI*, 2.1.24]

But this it seems proves nothing, any more than the lines from Terence and Ovid in *The Taming of the Shrew*; for Mr. Farmer looks on Shakespeare's property in the comedy to be extremely disputable; and he has no doubt but *Henry the Sixth* had the same author with *Edward the Third*, which hath been recovered to the world in Mr. Capell's *Prolusions*.

If any play in the collection bears internal evidence of Shakespeare's hand, we may fairly give him *Timon of Athens*. In this play we have a familiar quotation from Horace, *Ira furor brevis est* [1.2.28]. I will not maintain but this hemistich may be found in Lilly or Udall; or that it is not in the *Palace of Pleasure* or the *English Plutarch*; or that it was not originally foisted in by the players. It stands, however, in the play of *Timon of Athens*.[4]

The world in general, and those who purpose to comment on Shakespeare in particular, will owe much to Mr. Farmer, whose researches into our old authors throw a lustre on many passages, the obscurity of which must else have been impenetrable. No future Upton or Gildon will go further than North's translation for Shakespeare's acquaintance with Plutarch, or balance between Dares Phrygius and *the Troye booke of Lydgate*. The *Hystorie of*

---

[1] *The Taming of the Shrew*, 3.1.28f.; Ovid, *Heroides*, 1.33.
[2] But see Farmer in the 1773 edition, below, p. 550, Note 84.
[3] *Aeneid*, 1.11.
[4] But see Farmer's note below, p. 550.

Hamblet, in *black letter,* will for ever supersede Saxo Grammaticus; translated novels and ballads will perhaps be allowed the sources of *Romeo, Lear,* and *The Merchant of Venice;* and Shakespeare himself, however unlike Bayes in other particulars, will stand convicted of having *transversed* the prose of Holinshed; and at the same time, to prove 'that his *studies* lay in his own language,' the translations of Ovid are determined to be the production of Heywood.

'That his *studies* were most demonstratively confined to *nature,* and his *own language,*' I readily allow. But does it hence follow that he was so deplorably ignorant of every other tongue, living or dead, that he only 'remembered, perhaps, enough of his *schoolboy* learning to put the *hig, hag, hog,* into the mouth of Sir H. Evans; and might pick up in the writers of the time, or the course of his conversation, a familiar phrase or two of French or Italian?' In Shakespeare's plays both these last languages are plentifully scattered: but then, we are told, they might be impertinent additions of the players. Undoubtedly they might: but there they are, and perhaps few of the players had much more learning than Shakespeare.

Mr. Farmer himself will allow that Shakespeare began to learn Latin: I will allow that his *studies* lay in English; but why insist that he neither made any progress at school, nor improved his acquisitions there? The general encomiums of Suckling, Denham, Milton, *&c.* on his *native genius*,* prove nothing; and Ben Jonson's celebrated charge of Shakespeare's *small Latin, and less Greek*† seems absolutely to decide that he had *some* knowledge of both; and if we may judge by our own time a man who has any Greek is seldom without a very competent share of Latin; and yet such a man is very likely to study Plutarch in English, and to read translations of Ovid.

* Mr. Farmer closes these general testimonies of Shakespeare's having been only indebted to nature by saying, 'He came out of her hand, *as some one else expresses it,* like Pallas out of Jove's head, at full growth and mature.' It is whimsical enough, that this *some one else,* whose expression is here quoted to countenance the general notion of Shakespeare's want of literature, should be no other than myself.[1] Mr. Farmer does not chuse to mention where he met with this expression of *some one else;* and *some one else* does not chuse to mention where he dropt it.

† In defence of the various reading of this passage, given in the preface to the last edition of Shakespeare, 'small Latin, and *no* Greek,' Mr. Farmer tells us that 'it was adopted above a century ago by W. Towers, in a panegyrick on Cartwright.' Surely, Towers having said that Cartwright had *no* Greek is no proof that Ben Jonson said so of Shakespeare.

[1] But the passage occurs in Young (4.406), who, perhaps, plagiarized it from Colman.

218. George Colman, *King Lear* partly restored

1768

From *The History of King Lear. As it is performed at the Theatre Royal in Covent Garden*, published on 20 February 1768, the day of its first performance.

Colman's alteration was the least successful of all his productions, being performed only three times in its first season, and infrequently thereafter: 'he went too far to satisfy an eighteenth-century public' (E. R. Page, *George Colman the Elder* (New York, 1935), p. 171).

PREFACE.

[Colman begins by quoting Nahum Tate's account of his purpose in introducing a love-relationship between Edgar and Cordelia: see Vol. 1, p. 345.]

Now this very expedient of *a love* betwixt Edgar and Cordelia, on which Tate felicitates himself, seemed to me to be one of the capital objections to his alteration. For even supposing that it rendered Cordelia's indifference to her father more probable (an indifference which Shakespeare has no where implied), it assigns a very poor motive for it; so that what Edgar gains on the side of romantick generosity Cordelia loses on that of real virtue. The distress of the story is so far from being heightened by it that it has diffused a languor and insipidity over all the scenes of the play from which Lear is absent, for which I appeal to the sensations of the numerous audiences with which the play has been honoured. And had the scenes been affectingly written they would at least have divided our feelings, which Shakespeare has attached almost entirely to Lear and Cordelia in their parental and filial capacities; thereby producing passages infinitely more tragick than the embraces of Cordelia and the ragged Edgar, which would have appeared too ridiculous for representation had they not been mixed and incorporated with some of the finest scenes of Shakespeare.

Tate, in whose days *love* was the soul of Tragedy as well as Comedy, was, however, so devoted to intrigue that he has not only given Edmund a passion for Cordelia but has injudiciously amplified on his criminal commerce with Goneril and Regan, which is the most disgusting part of the original. The Rev. Dr. Warton has doubted 'whether the cruelty of the daughters is not painted with circumstances too savage and unnatural,'* even by Shakespeare. Still, however, in Shakespeare some motives for their conduct are assigned; but as Tate has conducted that part of the fable they are equally cruel and unnatural, without the poet's assigning any motive at all.

In all these circumstances it is generally agreed that Tate's alteration is for the worse, and his *King Lear* would probably have quitted the stage long ago had not the poet made 'the tale conclude in a success to the innocent distressed persons.' Even in the catastrophe he has incurred the censure of Addison: but 'in the present case', says Dr. Johnson, 'the publick has decided, and Cordelia, from the time of Tate, has always retired with victory and felicity.'[1]

To reconcile the catastrophe of Tate to the story of Shakespeare was the first grand object which I proposed to myself in this alteration, thinking it one of the principal duties of my situation to render every drama submitted to the Publick as consistent and rational an entertainment as possible. In this kind of employment one person cannot do a great deal; yet if every Director of the Theatre will endeavour to do a little the Stage will every day be improved, and become more worthy attention and encouragement. *Romeo, Cymbeline, Every Man in his Humour* have long been refined from the dross that hindered them from being current with the Publick, and I have now endeavoured to purge the tragedy of *Lear* of the alloy of Tate, which has so long been suffered to debase it.

'The utter improbability of Gloucester's imagining, though blind, that he had leaped down Dover Cliff,' has been justly censured by Dr. Warton†; and in the representation it is still more

---

* *Adventurer*, No. 132 [4.83].
[1] Johnson, Note 141 above, p. 140.
† *Adventurer*, No. 132 [4.83].

liable to objection than in print. I have therefore without scruple omitted it, preserving, however, at the same time that celebrated description of the Cliff in the mouth of Edgar. The putting out Gloucester's eyes is also so unpleasing a circumstance that I would have altered it, if possible; but upon examination it appeared to be so closely interwoven with the fable that I durst not venture to change it. I had once some idea of retaining the character of *the fool*, but though Dr. Warton has very truly observed† that the poet 'has so well conducted even the natural jargon of the beggar and the jestings of the fool, which in other hands must have sunk into burlesque, that they contribute to heighten the pathetick;' yet after the most serious consideration I was convinced that such a scene 'would sink into burlesque' in the representation, and would not be endured on the modern stage. (i–v)

219. Richard Warner, Shakespeare's language

1768

From *A Letter to David Garrick, Esq.*, *concerning a glossary to the plays of Shakespeare, On a more extensive Plan than has hitherto appeared, to which is annexed a Specimen* (1768).

Richard Warner (1713?–75) was a classical scholar who translated Plautus, a botanist, and a Shakespearian. Having inherited a large fortune he furthered his researches with a large botanical garden at his house; associated with Linnaeus, he was the first to make the Cape jasmine flower (a friend suggested it be named Warneria but he demurred, calling it Gardenia). His other main career, the study of Shakespeare, was first directed towards an edition, which he abandoned when Steevens's *Proposals* appeared, devoting the rest of his

† *Adventurer*, No. 116. [4.77]

life to collecting materials for a Shakespeare Glossary. Only this 'Specimen' appeared, but his manuscripts are in the British Library, comprising 51 quarto and 20 octavo volumes, with an interleaved edition of Shakespeare, and further notes on Beaumont and Fletcher.

... That Shakespeare was not what the world calls a scholar I readily admit. But is there no medium? must he, with Mr. Upton and some others, be as much master of the Greek language as perhaps they themselves were? or must he, with the ingenious author of the *Essay on his Learning* before-mentioned, be supposed just 'to remember enough of his school-boy learning to put the *Hig, hag, hog* into the mouth of Sir Hugh Evans? [above, p. 278]— As on the one hand I cannot by any means raise his learning to the first pitch, so neither can I bring it down so low as that gentleman would have it. His *Essay* is a very ingenious one; and he has put it beyond doubt that our author might, and undoubtedly did take many things, perhaps all, from translations—but this neither is or can be a proof that he might not have taken them from originals. At least if it is, it can be only proof *presumptive*; I can by no means allow it to be proof *positive*.—When style is not concern'd but only mere matters of fact from history, or information concerning antiquities or customs of particular nations, there is scarce an author, let him be ever so great an adept in languages, but might in order to save time and trouble consult a translation, if he had it at hand.

Where a man professes himself a translator, to *translate* from translations is, if he understands the original, inexcusable. To copy matters of fact is quite another affair: and I will venture to say there are few if any authors, let them understand Greek ever so well, who, if they wanted in the course of their writing to be inform'd of mere matters of fact in the lives of Julius Cæsar, Antony, and Coriolanus, would not lay aside their Greek Plutarch and turn to their Latin one, if they read that language with more fluency; nay even give up that and have recourse to one in French or in English: more especially if they wrote in as much haste as our author was obliged to do, and most evidently did.

Can we suppose that his natural genius, his fire of writing, would submit to this when he had it in his power to evade it by making use of auxiliaries nearer at hand, and to be come at with less trouble?

I will not however contend that he read Greek with any *tolerable fluency*; I most sincerely believe he did not. I really think he understood at least as much of the language as a school-boy, never suppos'd to be an idle one, might be allow'd to have done; and as to *Latin*, if no better authority can be produc'd than his having taken from *translations* it is inadequate to the point intended to be gain'd; and for what as yet appears *he might*, or *he might not* have had a tolerable at least, if not a competent knowledge of that language. (16–18) . . .

[Warner describes the contents of his Glossary.]

Where words of this class, I mean obsolete or uncommon, are omitted I shall endeavour to make up the deficiency, and insert them accordingly. One in particular I shall mention, and that is *Pillicock*. It occurs in *King Lear*, Act iii. Sc. 6. and is an expression of *Edgar*'s in his assum'd madness. '*Pillicock* sat upon *Pillicock* hill—loo! loo!' [3.4.75f.]

It is not improbable it was the burthen of some song, and seems to be either from the Italian *Pellicione* or *Pillicione*, or the French *Pendilloche*, which word we find in *Rabelais*; and therefore that might probably have been the word us'd by our Author, which the Editors not knowing the meaning of might thus give it more of an English termination. It being too the word in *Ozell*'s translation, shews it not unknown in that sense.—It is one of those few words in our Author which though on my plan it must be taken notice of, yet I think should not be explained. The reader that is of a different opinion may consult that facetious Author [Rabelais], Book I. Chap. 2;—or *Cinthio Giraldi*, Decad. IV. Novel. 4. (30–1)

Corinthian, when us'd for an inhabitant of *Corinth*, is obvious. But in the following passage it is quite another thing, and in cant language means an impudent, harden'd, brazen-fac'd fellow. Corinthian brass was famous among the antients; of which, among others, we find this instance in Martial, Book ix. Ep. 60: 'Consuluit nares, an olerent æra *Corinthen*'.[1] and from hence it is probable we have this sense of the word.

---

[1] 'He took counsel of his nose whether the bronzes smelt of Corinth' (ix.59.11).

They take it already upon their conscience, that though I be but Prince of Wales, yet I am the King of courtesie: telling me flatly, I am no proud Jack, like Falstaff, but a *Corinthian*, a lad of mettle, a good boy.

1 Henry IV. [2.4.10 ff.]

There are many senses in which the word *profane* is commonly us'd and as commonly known; such as, irreverent to sacred names or things, not sacred or secular, polluted or not pure, not purified by holy rites: but our author makes use of it in a sense not taken notice of in the dictionaries, that of *free of speech, using gross language*. Thus for example:

What *prophane* wretch art thou?   *Othello*. [1.1.115]

How say you, Cassio, is he not a most *profane*
And liberal counsellor   [2.1.163f.]

I have long dream'd of such a kind of man,
So surfeit-swell'd, so old and so *profane*.   2 *Henry IV*. [5.5.50f.]

In the following speech the sense of the word *occupy* is remarkable:

A Captain! these villains will make the word *Captain*, as odious as the word *occupy*; which was an excellent good word, before it was ill sorted; therefore Captains had need look to it.   2 *Henry IV*. [2.4.137ff.]

Dol Tear-sheet is not the only one that has complain'd of this abuse of the word. The author of *The Glossary to Gawin Douglas's Translation of The Æneis of Virgil* printed 1553—has observ'd the same. 'Occupy,' says he, 'signifies to employ, to be busy or taken up with any thing, to use. So in our version of the Bible:

If they bind me fast with new ropes that never were *occupy'd*, then shall I be weak and be as another man.

Judges, xvi. 11.

It also signifies to trade or merchandize:

The merchants of Sheba and Raamah they were thy merchants: they *occupied* in thy fairs with chief of all spices, and with all precious stones and gold.

Ezeckiel, xxvii.22.

—he called his ten servants, and delivered them ten pounds, and saith unto them, *occupy* till I come—

Luke, xix. 13.

Hence *occupation* for a trade:

It shall come to pass, when Pharaoh shall call you, and shall say, what is your *occupation?*
That ye shall say, thy servants *trade* hath been about cattle.

Genesis, xlvi. 33, 34.

But this signification of the word,' continues he, 'is much worn out, and a very *bad one* come in its place.'

Ben Jonson also mentions the same. Speaking of style; 'In picture,' says he, 'light is required no lesse than shadow; so in stile height as well as humbleness. But beware they be not too humble, as Pliny pronounc'd of Regulus's writing. You would thinke them written not on a child, but by a child. Many, out of their obscene apprehensions, refuse proper and fit words; as *occupie*, nature, and the like: so the curious industry in some of having all alike good, hath come nearer a vice than a virtue.' *Discoveries*, Folio Edition, 1640, page 112.

Sir John Harington, the ingenious translator of Ariosto's *Orlando Furioso*, hints at it likewise; and speaks of Chaucer's having also abus'd the word *occupyer* and us'd it in the sense he himself alludes to, *viz*. that of *Bawd, Procuress*. He wrote in the reign of Queen Elizabeth, and towards the end of it. It is in one of his epigrams, the eighth of his first book; I shall transcribe it, and then you will not be at a loss for the odious sense of the word the *virtuous* Mrs. Dol Tear-sheet complains of:

Of *Lesbia*, a great Ladie.
Lesbia doth laugh to heare sellers and buyers
Call'd by this name, substantial *occupyers:*
Lesbia, the word was good, while good folk us'd it;
You mar'd it, that with Chaucer's jest abus'd it:
But good or bad, how e'er the word be made,
Lesbia is loth perhaps to leave the trade.

You will, I think, Sir, acquiesce in this; but if you desire further authority, the following epigram of Ben Jonson will abundantly confirm what has been here observ'd:

On Groyne.
Groyne, come of age, his 'state sold out of hand,
For's whore: Groyne still doth *occupy* his land.

(52–5)

Besides, in a Glossary like this not only the present age but posterity are to be regarded. Words now but *little* us'd may probably ere long be *less* so; and the time may also come when they too may become obsolete. In this light the word *clean*, in the sense of *quite, perfectly, fully, compleatly*, may be consider'd: common indeed at this time in the Northern parts of England, but in this sense by no means generally known. It occurs, among others, in the following instances:

> Five summers have I spent in farthest Greece,
> Roaming *clean* through the bounds of Asia,
> And coasting homeward, came to Ephesus.
> *Comedy of Errors*, [1.1.133ff.]

> —men may construe things after their fashions,
> *Clean* from the purpose of the things themselves.
> *Julius Cæsar*, [1.3.34f.]

> ———famine,
> Ere *clean* it o'erthrow nature, makes it valiant.
> Plenty, and peace breeds cowards; hardness ever
> Of hardiness is mother.
> *Cymbeline*, [3.6.19ff.]

And our Bard found the word us'd in this sense in Scripture: 'Is his mercy *clean* gone for evermore?' (Psalm lxxvii. 8.)

In the following passage the use of the word *imperious* is remarkable:

> I thank thee, most *imperious* Agamemnon.
> *Troilus and Cressida*, [4.5.172]

The common meaning of it is *haughty, arrogant, overbearing*. Now we cannot suppose that at such a time, and on such an occasion, when Agamemnon had been bidding Hector welcome to his tent, and all kinds of civilities were passing between Trojans and Greeks, that he would reply to his compliments and expressions of friendship by giving him opprobrious terms. Can we then make the least doubt but our Bard uses the word for *imperial*, that is *royal, one of supreme rule and authority?* In which sense the Romans sometimes us'd their word *imperiosus*. (69–71)

It may in general be observ'd that in *Shakespeare* strict grammar is not always to be expected; he deviates from it perpetually. The energy of his language, the strength of his expression mount aloft, above the comprehension of the mere verbal critick;[1] and this in great measure accounts for many of those *anomalies* which his irregular way of writing naturally leads him into.

Authorities for Shakespeare's use of words in a particular sense will be taken from Authors, chiefly Poets, before or cotemporary with him. . . . (80-2)

Where authorities cannot be found, which will sometimes be the case, it is hoped Shakespeare will be accepted as an authority for himself. Thus, for instance:

I saw him break Schoggan's head at the Court gate, when he was a *Crack*, not thus high.

> 2 *Henry IV.* [3.2.28ff.]

—Indeed, la, 'tis a noble child,
A *Crack*, madam——

> *Coriolanus.* [1.3.67]

Now it is plain *Crack* here must mean a *smart child, boy,* or *girl.* But the word in this sense is not to be found in any of the dictionaries; nor have I been able to trace it in any other author.

To this I annex a few words of the Glossary in the manner it is design'd to be printed, as a Specimen of the whole; and which are taken from the first letter of the alphabet as they occur, without any particular choice; as culling them out from each letter would look like an intention of exhibiting the most striking figures by way of Specimen, in order to engage a more favourable attention to the work; which, should it be thought worthy to see the light and be so happy to meet with approbation from the Publick, my end will be abundantly answer'd; and I shall have the satisfaction of having thrown in my mite towards the further elucidation of our immortal Bard, and making the reading him more familiar to the generality of his admirers.

The number of his Plays said to be genuine (allowing *Titus Andronicus* to be one) is thirty-six. Of these I have gone through upwards of thirty with some care, and I hope with tolerable accuracy. In these I have met with upwards of fifty words the meaning of which, as they stand in our Author, I have not yet been able to discover with that precision I could wish. Should I not be so happy as to do it time enough to insert them in their proper places, they shall be printed by themselves and the explanation,

---

[1] Cf. Heath (4.553).

if I can trace it, inserted accordingly. In a work of this sort, and so extensive as it is intended to be, mistakes will, I fear, happen, and omissions too often occur. All I can say is that I shall, should this work ever see the light, think it a duty I owe the Publick and yourself to make it as accurate and compleat as my abilities, such as they are, will enable me to do.

Thus, Sir, I have submitted to you an account of my intended performance, and the manner in which I propose to execute it. A work, however slight and trifling it may appear to those who read merely for amusement, yet by the readers of our *Shakespeare* in general, and by yourself in particular I flatter myself may be look'd on in a more favourable light. The intimate acquaintance you have had with his writings, the very *minutiæ* of which you have made your study; the obligations his admirers with the warmest sense of gratitude profess to owe to you for your repeated revivals on the Stage of most of his Plays; the allow'd connexion of your name with that of our immortal Bard as the Guardian of his Fame, will, it is hop'd, induce you to give a sanction to a work not of Genius, Indeed, but of her handmaid Industry; without whose assistance even your Genius, as well as that of Shakespeare, must have appear'd with imperfect beauty. (89–92)

220. Edward Capell, introduction to Shakespeare

1768

From *Mr. WILLIAM SHAKESPEARE his Comedies, Histories, and Tragedies, set out by himself in quarto, or by the Players his Fellows in folio, and now faithfully republish'd from those Editions in ten Volumes octavo; with an INTRODUCTION; Whereunto will be added, in some other Volumes, NOTES, critical and explanatory, and a Body of VARIOUS READINGS entire* (10 vols, 1768).

Edward Capell (1713–81) was appointed deputy-inspector of plays in 1737, an official position which gave him both leisure and opportunity to study English drama. In 1760 he published *Prolusions; or select Pieces of antient Poetry*, including *Edward the third*, which he would not ascribe definitely to Shakespeare (*Preface*, pp. ix f.), and in 1766 *Reflections On Originality in Authors*, an attack on Hurd's *Letter ... on the Marks of Imitation* (Vol. 4, No. 162b), a detailed and scholarly refutation of Hurd's argument. His edition, the fruit of over 20 years' work, was completed by the *Notes and Various Readings*; the first volume of which appeared in 1774 (No. 242 below).

INTRODUCTION.

It is said of the ostrich that she drops her egg at random, to be dispos'd of as chance pleases; either brought to maturity by the sun's kindly warmth, or else crush'd by beasts and the feet of passers-by. Such at least is the account which naturalists have given us of this extraordinary bird; and admitting it for a truth, she is in this a fit emblem of almost every great genius. They conceive and produce with ease those noble issues of human understanding; but incubation, the dull work of putting them correctly upon paper and afterwards publishing, is a task they can not away with. If the original state of all such authors' writings, even from HOMER downward, could be enquir'd into and known they would yield proof in abundance of the justness of what is here asserted. But the Author now before us shall suffice for them all; being at once the greatest instance of genius in producing noble things, and of negligence in providing for them afterwards. This negligence indeed was so great, and the condition in which his works are come down to us so very deform'd that it has, of late years, induc'd several gentlemen to make a revision of them. But the publick seems not to be satisfy'd with any of their endeavours; and the reason of it's discontent will be manifest when the state of his old editions, and the methods that they have taken to amend them, are fully lay'd open, which is the first business of this Introduction.

Of thirty-six plays which SHAKESPEARE has left us, and which compose the collection that was afterwards set out in folio, thirteen only were publish'd in his life-time that have much resemblance to those in the folio; these thirteen are—*Hamlet, First* and *second Henry IV, King Lear, Love's Labour's lost, Merchant of Venice, Midsummer Night's Dream, Much Ado about Nothing, Richard II, Richard III, Romeo and Juliet, Titus Andronicus,* and *Troilus and Cressida.* Some others that came out in the same period bear indeed the titles of—*Henry V, King John, Merry Wives of Windsor,* and *Taming of the Shrew*; but are no other than either first draughts, or mutilated and perhaps surreptitious impressions of those plays, but whether of the two is not easy to determine. . . . (1–2)

As for the plays which, we say, are either the Poet's first draughts or else imperfect and stolen copies, it will be thought, perhaps, they might as well have been left out of the account. But they are not wholly useless: some *lacunæ* that are in all the other editions have been judiciously fill'd up in modern impressions by the authority of these copies; and in some particular passages of them, where there happens to be a greater conformity than usual between them and the more perfect editions, there is here and there a various reading that does honour to the Poet's judgment and should upon that account be presum'd the true one; in other respects they have neither use nor merit, but are meerly curiosities.

Proceed we then to a description of the other fourteen. They all abound in faults, though not in equal degree; and those faults are so numerous, and of so many different natures that nothing but a perusal of the pieces themselves can give an adequate conception of them; but amongst them are these that follow. Division of acts and scenes they have none, *Othello* only excepted, which is divided into acts. Entries of persons are extreamly imperfect in them (sometimes more, sometimes fewer than the scene requires) and their Exits are very often omitted; or when mark'd not always in the right place; and few scenical directions are to be met with throughout the whole. Speeches are frequently confounded and given to wrong persons, either whole or in part; and sometimes instead of the person speaking you have the actor who presented him. And in two of the plays, (*Love's Labour's lost,* and *Troilus and Cressida*) the same matter, and in nearly the same words, is set down twice in some passages; which who sees not to be only a negligence of the Poet, and that but one of them ought to have been printed? But the reigning fault of all is in the measure: prose is very often printed as verse and verse as prose, or where rightly printed verse, that verse is not always right divided, and in all these

305

pieces the songs are in every particular still more corrupt than the other parts of them. These are the general and principal defects: to which if you add transposition of words, sentences, lines, and even speeches; words omitted, and others added without reason; and a punctuation so deficient and so often wrong that it hardly deserves regard, you have, upon the whole, a true but melancholy picture of the condition of these first-printed plays: which, bad as it is, is yet better than that of those which came after, or than that of the subsequent folio impression of some of these which we are now speaking of. ... [Capell quotes the claim of Heminge and Condell, the editors of the Folio, that they presented Shakespeare's plays 'cur'd, and perfect of their limbes'.] Who now does not feel himself inclin'd to expect an accurate and good performance in the edition of these prefacers? But, alas, it is nothing less, for (if we except the six spurious ones, whose places were then supply'd by true and genuine copies) the editions of plays preceeding the folio are the very basis of those we have there; which are either printed from those editions or from the copies which they made use of: and this is principally evident in *First* and *second Henry IV*, *Love's Labour's lost, Merchant of Venice, Midsummer Night's Dream, Much Ado about Nothing, Richard II, Titus Andronicus*, and *Troilus and Cressida*; for in the others we see somewhat a greater latitude, as was observ'd a little above. But in these plays there is an almost strict conformity between the two impressions. Some additions are in the second, and some omissions; but the faults and errors of the quarto's are all preserv'd in the folio and others added to them; and what difference there is is generally for the worse on the side of the folio editors, which should give us but faint hopes of meeting with greater accuracy in the plays which they first publish'd. And, accordingly, we find them subject to all the imperfections that have been noted in the former. Nor is their edition in general distinguish'd by any mark of preference above the earliest quarto's, but that some of their plays are divided into acts, and some others into acts and scenes; and that with due precision, and agreable to the Author's idea of the nature of such divisions. (3–7) ...

Having premis'd thus much about the state and condition of these first copies it may not be improper, nor will it be absolutely a digression, to add something concerning their authenticity. In doing which it will be greatly for the reader's ease, and our own, to confine ourselves to the quarto's: which it is hop'd he will allow of, especially as our intended vindication of them will also include in it (to the eye of a good observer) that of the plays that appear'd first in the folio; which therefore omitting, we now turn ourselves to the quarto's. . . . (8–9)

[Capell defends the quartos from the charge that they are all 'stolne, and surreptitious copies', pirated and inauthentic texts produced from actors' parts.]

Let it then be granted that these quarto's are the Poet's own copies, however they were come by; hastily written at first, and issuing from presses most of them as corrupt and licentious as can any where be produc'd, and not overseen by himself nor by any of his friends. And there can be no stronger reason for subscribing to any opinion than may be drawn in favour of this from the condition of all the other plays that were first printed in the folio: for in method of publication they have the greatest likeness possible to those which preceeded them, and carry all the same marks of haste and negligence . . . . (10–11)

But to return to the thing immediately treated, the state of the old editions. The quarto's went through many impressions, as may be seen in the Table: and in each play the last is generally taken from the impression next before it, and so onward to the first. . . . And this further is to be observ'd of them, that generally speaking the more distant they are from the original the more they abound in faults; 'till in the end the corruptions of the last copies become so excessive as to make them of hardly any worth. The folio too had it's re-impressions, the dates and notices of which are likewise in the Table, and they tread the same round as did the quarto's. Only that the third of them has seven plays more, in which it is follow'd by the last; and that again by the first of the modern impressions, which come now to be spoken of.

If the stage be a mirror of the times, as undoubtedly it is, and we judge of the age's temper by what we see prevailing there, what must we think of the times that succeeded SHAKESPEARE? JONSON, favour'd by a court that delighted only in masques, had been gaining ground upon him even in his life-time; and his death put him in full possession of a post he had long aspir'd to, the empire of the drama. The props of this new king's throne, were FLETCHER, SHIRLEY, MIDDLETON, MASSINGER, BROOME, and others; and how unequal they all were, the monarch and his subjects too, to the

Poet they came after, let their works testify. Yet they had the vogue on their side during all those blessed times that preceded the civil war, and SHAKESPEARE was held in disesteem. The war, and medley government that follow'd swept all these things away: but they were restor'd with the king; and another stage took place, in which SHAKESPEARE had little share.[1] DRYDEN had then the lead and maintain'd it for half a century: though his government was sometimes disputed by LEE, TATE, SHADWELL, WYTCHERLEY and others, weaken'd much by *The Rehearsal,* and quite overthrown in the end by OTWAY and ROWE. What the cast of their plays was is known to every one. But that SHAKESPEARE, the true and genuine SHAKESPEARE was not much relish'd is plain from the many alterations of him that were brought upon the stage by some of those gentlemen, and by others within that period.

But from what has been said we are not to conclude that the Poet had no admirers. For the contrary is true; and he had in all this interval no inconsiderable party amongst men of the greatest understanding who both saw his merit, in despite of the darkness it was then wrapt up in, and spoke loudly in his praise; but the stream of the publick favour ran the other way. But this too coming about at the time we are speaking of, there was a demand for his works, and in a form that was more convenient than the folio's. In consequence of which the gentleman last mention'd was set to work by the booksellers, and in 1709 he put out an edition in six volumes octavo which, unhappily, is the basis of all the other moderns. For this editor went no further than to the edition nearest to him in time, which was the folio of 1685, the last and worst of those impressions. This he republish'd with great exactness; correcting here and there some of it's grossest mistakes, and dividing into acts and scenes the plays that were not divided before.

But no sooner was this edition in the hands of the publick than they saw in part its deficiences, and one of another sort began to be required of them; which accordingly was set about some years after by two gentlemen at once, Mr. POPE, and Mr. THEO-BALD. The labours of the first came out in 1725, in six volumes quarto: and he has the merit of having first improv'd his Author by the insertion of many large passages, speeches and single lines,

---

[1] This is not in fact true: see 1.5f., 2.12f., 2.20f. for details of the place held by Shakespeare on the post-Restoration stage.

taken from the quarto's; and of amending him in other places by readings fetch'd from the same. But his materials were few and his collation of them not the most careful; which, join'd to other faults and to that main one, of making his predecessor's the copy himself follow'd, brought his labours in disrepute and has finally sunk them in neglect.

His publication retarded the other gentleman, and he did not appear 'till the year 1733, when his work too came out in seven volumes, octavo. The opposition that was between them seems to have enflam'd him, which was heighten'd by other motives, and he declaims vehemently against the work of his antagonist. Which yet serv'd him for a model; and his own is made only a little better by his having a few more materials, of which he was not a better collator than the other, nor did he excel him in use of them. For in this article both their judgments may be equally call'd in question: in what he has done that is conjectural he is rather more happy; but in this he had large assistances.

But the gentleman that came next [Hanmer], is a critick of another stamp, and pursues a track in which it is greatly to be hop'd he will never be follow'd in the publication of any authors whatsoever. For this were in effect to annihilate them, if carry'd a little further, by destroying all marks of peculiarity and notes of time, all easiness of expression and numbers, all justness of thought, and the nobility of not a few of their conceptions. The manner in which his Author is treated excites an indignation that will be thought by some to vent itself too strongly; but terms weaker would do injustice to my feelings, and the censure shall be hazarded. Mr. POPE's edition was the ground-work of this over-bold one, splendidly printed at *Oxford* in six quarto volumes, and publish'd in the year 1744. The publisher disdains all collation of folio or quarto, and fetches all from his great self and the moderns his predecessors, wantoning in very licence of conjecture, and sweeping all before him (without notice or reason given) that not suits his taste or lies level to his conceptions. But this justice should be done him: as his conjectures are numerous they are oftentimes not unhappy; and some of them are of that excellence that one is struck with amazement to see a person of so much judgment as he shows himself in them, adopt a method of publishing that runs counter to all the ideas that wise men have hitherto entertain'd of an editor's province and duty.

The year 1747 produc'd a fifth edition, in eight octavo volumes, publish'd by Mr. WARBURTON; which though it is said in the title-page to be the joint work of himself and the second editor [Pope], the third [Theobald] ought rather to have been mention'd, for it is printed from his text. The merits of this performance have been so thoroughly discuss'd in two very ingenious books, *The Canons of Criticism*, and *Revisal of* SHAKESPEARE'*s Text*, that it is needless to say any more of it. This only shall be added to what may be there met with, that the edition is not much benefited by fresh acquisitions from the old ones, which this gentleman seems to have neglected. *

Other charges there are that might be brought against these modern impressions without infringing the laws of truth or candour either. But what is said will be sufficient, and may satisfy their greatest favourers that the superstructure cannot be a sound one which is built upon so bad a foundation as that work of Mr. ROWE's; which all of them, as we see, in succession have yet made their corner-stone. The truth is, it was impossible that such a beginning should end better than it has done: the fault was in the setting-out; and all the diligence that could be us'd, join'd to the discernment of a PEARCE or a BENTLEY, could never purge their Author of all his defects by their method of proceeding.

The editor now before you was appriz'd in time of this truth; saw the wretched condition his Author was reduc'd to by these late tamperings, and thought seriously of a cure for it, and that so long ago as the year 1745. For the attempt was first suggested by that gentleman's performance which came out at *Oxford* the year before, which when he had perus'd with no little astonishment, and consider'd the fatal consequences that must inevitably follow

---

* It will perhaps be thought strange, that nothing should be said in this place of another edition [Johnson's] that came out about a twelvemonth ago, in eight volumes, octavo; but the reasons for it, are these. There is no use made of it, nor could be, for the present was finish'd, within a play or two, and printed too in great part before that appear'd. The first sheet of this work (being the first of volume 2.) went to the press in September 1760: and this volume was follow'd by volumes 8, 4, 9, 1, 6, and 7; the last of which was printed off in August 1765. In the next place the merits and demerits of it are unknown to the present editor even at this hour: this only he has perceiv'd in it, having look'd it but slightly over, that the text it follows is that of it's nearest predecessor, and from that copy it was printed.[1]

[1] Capell seems never to have owned Johnson's edition, judging by the contents of his collection, now in the library of Trinity College, Cambridge.

the imitation of so much licence, he resolv'd himself to be the champion, and to exert to the uttermost such abilities as he was master of to save from further ruin an edifice of this dignity which *England* must for ever glory in. Hereupon he possess'd himself of the other modern editions, the folio's and as many quarto's as could presently be procur'd; and, within a few years after fortune and industry help'd him to all the rest, six only excepted; adding to them withal twelve more which the compilers of former tables had no knowledge of. Thus furnish'd, he fell immediately to collation, which is the first step in works of this nature, and without it nothing is done to purpose,—first of moderns with moderns, then of moderns with ancients, and afterwards of ancients with others more ancient. 'Till, at the last, a ray of light broke forth upon him by which he hop'd to find his way through the wilderness of these editions into that fair country the Poet's real habitation. He had not proceeded far in his collation before he saw cause to come to this resolution, to stick invariably to the old editions (that is, the best of them) which hold now the place of manuscripts, no scrap of the Author's writing having the luck to come down to us, and never to depart from them but in cases where reason, and the uniform practice of men of the greatest note in this art, tell him they may be quitted; nor yet in those, without notice. . . .

It is said a little before, that we have nothing of his in writing, that the printed copies are all that is left to guide us, and that those copies are subject to numberless imperfections, but not all in like degree. Our first business, then, was to examine their merit, and see on which side the scale of goodness preponderated; which we have generally found to be on that of the most ancient. It may be seen in the Table what editions are judg'd to have the preference among those plays that were printed singly in quarto; and for those plays the text of those editions is chiefly adher'd to. In all the rest the first folio is follow'd, the text of which is by far the most faultless of the editions in that form, and has also the advantage in three quarto plays, in 2. *Henry IV*, *Othello*, and *Richard III*. Had the editions thus follow'd been printed with carefulness from correct copies, and copies not added to or otherwise alter'd after those impressions, there had been no occasion for going any further. But this was not at all the case, even in the best of them; and it therefore became proper and necessary to look into the other old editions, and to select from thence whatever improves the Author

311

or contributes to his advancement in perfectness, the point in view throughout all this performance. That they do improve him, was with the editor an argument in their favour; and ... he does for the present acknowledge that he has every-where made use of such materials as he met with in other old copies which he thought improv'd the editions that are made the ground-work of the present text. And whether they do so or no the judicious part of the world may certainly know by turning to a Collection that will be publish'd, where all discarded readings are enter'd, all additions noted and variations of every kind, and the editions specify'd to which they severally belong.[1] (8–22) ...

[On act and scene division, punctuation, and the regulation of prose and verse.] The plays that are come down to us divided must be look'd upon as of the Author's own settling; and in them, with regard to acts we find him following establish'd precepts, or rather, conforming himself to the practice of some other dramatick writers of his time; for they, it is likely, and Nature were the books he was best acquainted with. His scene divisions he certainly did not fetch from writers upon the drama; for in them he observes a method in which perhaps he is singular, and he is invariable in the use of it. With him, a change of scene implies generally a change of place, though not always; but always an entire evacuation of it, and a succession of new persons. That *liaison* of the scenes which JONSON seems to have attempted, and upon which the *French* stage prides itself, he does not appear to have had any idea of. Of the other unities he was perfectly well appriz'd, and has follow'd them in one of his plays with as great strictness and greater happiness than can perhaps be met with in any other writer. The play meant is *The Comedy of Errors*, in which the action is one, the place one, and the time such as even ARISTOTLE himself would allow of—the revolution of half a day. But even in this play the change of scene arises from change of persons, and by that it is regulated. ... (25–6)

It remains now to speak of errors of the old copies which are here amended without notice, to wit the pointing, and wrong division of much of them respecting the numbers. And as to the first, it is so extreamly erroneous throughout all the plays, and in every old copy that small regard is due to it; and it becomes an

---

[1] Capell published separately his *Notes and Various Readings to Shakespeare*: part 1 in 1774 (No. 242 below), republished posthumously with parts 2 and 3 in 1783.

editor's duty (instead of being influenc'd by such a punctuation, or even casting his eyes upon it) to attend closely to the meaning of what is before him, and to new-point it accordingly. (27) ...

The other great mistake in these old editions, and which is very insufficiently rectify'd in any of the new ones, relates to the Poet's numbers, his verse being often wrong divided or printed wholly as prose, and his prose as often printed like verse. This, though not so universal as their wrong pointing, is yet so extensive an error in the old copies, and so impossible to be pointed out otherwise than by a note, that an editor's silent amendment of it is surely pardonable at least. For who would not be disgusted with that perpetual sameness which must necessarily have been in all the notes of this sort? Neither are they in truth emendations that require proving; every good ear does immediately adopt them, and every lover of the Poet will be pleas'd with that accession of beauty which results to him from them. It is perhaps to be lamented that there is yet standing in his works much unpleasing mixture of prosaic and metrical dialogue, and sometimes in places seemingly improper, as in *Othello* [2.1]; and some others which men of judgment will be able to pick out for themselves. But these blemishes are not now to be wip'd away (at least not by an editor, whose province it far exceeds to make a change of this nature), but must remain as marks of the Poet's negligence, and of the haste with which his pieces were compos'd. What he manifestly intended prose (and we can judge of his intentions only from what appears in the editions that are come down to us) should be printed as prose, what verse as verse; which it is hop'd is now done, with an accuracy that leaves no great room for any further considerable improvements in that way. (28–9) ...

[Capell announces that he will publish separately a work called *The School of Shakespeare*, consisting of extracts 'from books that may properly be call'd his school; as they are indeed the sources from which he drew the greater part of his knowledge in mythology and classical matters, his fable, his history, and even the seeming peculiarities of his language'. He then adds this note on Shakespeare's learning.]

Though our expressions, as we think, are sufficiently guarded in this place yet, being fearful of misconstruction, we desire to be heard further as to this affair of his learning. It is our firm belief, then, that SHAKESPEARE was very well grounded, at least in *Latin*, at school. It appears from the clearest evidence possible that his father was a man of no little substance, and very well able to give him such education; which perhaps he might be inclin'd to carry further by sending him to a university, but was prevented in this design (if he had it) by his son's early marriage; which, from monuments and other like evidence, it appears with no less certainty must have happen'd before he was seventeen, or very soon after. The displeasure of his father which was the consequence of this marriage, or else some excesses which he is said to have been guilty of, it is probable drove him up to town; where he engag'd early in some of the theatres, and was honour'd with the patronage of the earl of *Southampton*. His *Venus and Adonis* is address'd to that earl in a very pretty and modest dedication, in which he calls it '*the first heire of his invention*' and ushers it to the world with this singular motto,

> *Vilia miretur vulgus, mihi flavus Apollo*
> *Pocula Castalia plena ministret aqua*;

and the whole poem, as well as his *Lucrece* which follow'd it soon after, together with his choice of those subjects are plain marks of his acquaintance with some of the *Latin* classicks at least, at that time. The dissipation of youth, and when that was over, the busy scene in which he instantly plung'd himself, may very well be suppos'd to have hinder'd his making any great progress in them; but that such a mind as his should quite lose the tincture of any knowledge it had once been imbu'd with cannot be imagin'd. Accordingly we see that this school-learning (for it was no more) stuck with him to the last, and it was the recordations, as we may call it, of that learning which produc'd the *Latin* that is in many of his plays, and most plentifully in those that are most early. Every several piece of it is aptly introduc'd, given to a proper character, utter'd upon some proper occasion; and so well cemented, as it were, and join'd to the passage it stands in as to deal conviction to the judicious that the whole was wrought up together, and fetch'd from his own little store upon the sudden and without study.

The other languages which he has sometimes made use of, that is the *Italian* and *French*, are not of such difficult conquest that we should think them beyond his reach. An acquaintance with the first of them was a sort of fashion in his time; *Surrey* and the sonnet-writers set it on foot, and it was continu'd by SIDNEY and SPENSER.

All our poetry issu'd from that school, and it would be wonderful indeed if he whom we saw a little before putting himself with so much zeal under the banner of the muses, should not have been tempted to taste at least of that fountain to which of all his other brethren there was such continual resort. Let us conclude, then, that he did taste of it; but happily for himself, and more happy for the world that enjoys him now, he did not find it to his relish and threw away the cup. Metaphor apart, it is evident that he had some little knowledge of the *Italian*: perhaps just as much as enabl'd him to read a novel or a poem, and to put some few fragments of it with which his memory furnish'd him into the mouth of a pedant, or fine gentleman.

How or when he acquir'd it we must be content to be ignorant, but of the *French* language he was somewhat a greater master than of the two that have gone before. Yet, unless we except their novelists, he does not appear to have had much acquaintance with any of their writers; what he has given us of it is meerly colloquial, flows with great ease from him, and is reasonably pure. Should it be said he had travel'd for't, we know not who can confute us. In his days indeed, and with people of his station, the custom of doing so was rather rarer than in ours. Yet we have met with an example, and in his own band of players, in the person of the very famous Mr. KEMPE; of whose travels there is mention in a silly old play, call'd *The Return from Parnassus*, printed in 1606, but written much earlier in the time of queen *Elizabeth*. Add to this the exceeding great liveliness and justness that is seen in many descriptions of the sea and of promontories which, if examin'd, shew another sort of knowledge of them than is to be gotten in books or relations; and if these be lay'd together this conjecture of his travelling may not be thought void of probability.

One opinion, we are sure, which is advanc'd somewhere or other, is utterly so;—that this *Latin* and this *Italian*, and the language that was last mention'd, are insertions and the work of some other hand. There has been started now and then in philological matters a proposition so strange as to carry it's own condemnation in it, and this is of the number. It has been honour'd already with more notice than it is any ways entitl'd to, where the Poet's *Latin* is spoke of a little while before; to which answer it must be left, and we shall pass on to profess our entire belief of the genuineness of every several part of this work, and that he only was the Author of it. He might

315

write beneath himself at particular times, and certainly does in some places, but is not always without excuse; and it frequently happens that a weak scene serves to very good purpose, as will be made appear at one time or other.

It may be thought that there is one argument still unanswer'd, which has been brought against his acquaintance with the *Latin* and other languages; and that is that had he been so acquainted it could not have happen'd but that some imitations would have crept into his writings, of which certainly there are none. But this argument has been answer'd in effect when it was said that his knowledge in these languages was but slender, and his conversation with the writers in them slender too, of course. But had it been otherwise, and he as deeply read in them as some people have thought him, his works (it is probable) had been as little deform'd with imitations as we now see them. SHAKESPEARE was far above such a practice; he had the stores in himself, and wanted not the assistance of a foreign hand to dress him up in things of their lending. (31–9, notes) . . .

[On the authenticity of the plays.] This discourse is run out, we know not how, into greater heap of leaves than was any ways thought of, and has perhaps fatigu'd the reader equally with the penner of it. Yet can we not dismiss him, nor lay down our pen 'till one article more has been enquir'd into, which seems no less proper for the discussion of this place than one which we have inserted before. . . . As we there ventur'd to stand up in the behalf of some quarto's and maintain their authenticity, so mean we to have the hardiness here to defend some certain plays in this collection from the attacks of a number of writers who have thought fit to call in question their genuineness. The plays contested are— *The three Parts of Henry VI*; *Love's Labour's lost*; *The Taming of the Shrew*; and *Titus Andronicus*; and the sum of what is brought against them, so far at least as is hitherto come to knowledge, may be all ultimately resolv'd into the sole opinion of their unworthiness, exclusive of some weak surmises which do not deserve a notice. It is therefore fair and allowable, by all laws of duelling, to oppose opinion to opinion; which if we can strengthen with reasons and something like proofs, which are totally wanting on the other side, the last opinion may chance to carry the day. . . . (34–5)

The plays we are now speaking of [*Henry VI*, 1, 2, and 3] have been inconceivably mangl'd either in the copy or the press, or perhaps both. Yet this may be discover'd in them, that the alterations made afterwards by the Author are nothing near so considerable as those in some other plays, the incidents, the characters, every principal out-line in short being the same in both draughts; so that what we shall have occasion to say of the second [part] may in some degree, and without much violence, be apply'd also to the first. And this we presume to say of it; that, low as it must be set in comparison with his other plays, it has beauties in it and grandeurs, of which no other author was capable but SHAKESPEARE only. That extreamly-affecting scene of the death of young *Rutland*, that of his father which comes next it, and of *Clifford* the murtherer of them both; *Beaufort's* dreadful exit, the exit of king *Henry*, and a scene of wondrous simplicity and wondrous tenderness united, in which that *Henry* is made a speaker while his last decisive battle is fighting,—are as so many stamps upon these plays by which his property is mark'd, and himself declar'd the owner of them, beyond controversy as we think. And though we have selected these passages only, and recommended them to observation, it had been easy to name abundance of others which bear his mark as strongly; and one circumstance there is that runs through all the three plays by which he is as surely to be known as by any other that can be thought of, and that is, the preservation of character. All the personages in them are distinctly and truly delineated, and the character given them sustain'd uniformly throughout. The enormous *Richard's*, particularly, which in the third of these plays is seen rising towards it's zenith; and who sees not the future monster, and acknowledges at the same time the pen that drew it in these two lines only, spoken over a king who lies stab'd before him:

What, will the aspiring blood of *Lancaster*
Sink in the ground? I thought, it would have mounted

[3 *Henry VI*, 5.6.61f.]

let him never pretend discernment hereafter in any case of this nature.

It is hard to persuade one's self that the objecters to the play which comes next are indeed serious in their opinion; for if he is not visible in *Love's Labour's lost* we know not in which of his comedies he can be said to be so. The ease and sprightliness of the

317

dialogue in very many parts of it; it's quick turns of wit, and the humour it abounds in, and (chiefly) in those truly comick characters the pedant and his companion, the page, the constable, *Costard*, and *Armado*, seem more than sufficient to prove SHAKESPEARE the Author of it. And for the blemishes of this play, we must seek their true cause in it's antiquity, which we may venture to carry higher than 1598, the date of it's first impression. Rime, when this play appear'd, was thought a beauty of the drama, and heard with singular pleasure by an audience who but a few years before had been accustom'd to all rime; and the measure we call dogrel, and are so much offended with, had no such effect upon the ears of that time. But whether blemishes or no, or however this matter be which we have brought to exculpate him, neither of these articles can with any face of justice be alledg'd against *Love's Labour's lost*, seeing they are both to be met with in several other plays, the genuineness of which has not been question'd by any one. And one thing more shall be observ'd in the behalf of this play, that the Author himself was so little displeas'd at least with some parts of it that he has brought them a second time upon the stage. For who may not perceive that his famous *Benedick* and *Beatrice* are but little more than the counter-parts of *Biron* and *Rosaline?* All which circumstances consider'd, and that especially of the Writer's childhood (as it may be term'd) when this comedy was produc'd, we may confidently pronounce it his true off-spring and replace it amongst it's brethren.

That the *Taming of the Shrew* should ever have been put into this class of plays, and adjudg'd a spurious one, may justly be reckon'd wonderful when we consider it's merit, and the reception it has generally met with in the world. It's success at first, and the esteem it was then held in, induc'd FLETCHER to enter the lists with it in another play, in which *Petruchio* is humbl'd and *Catharine* triumphant; and we have it in his works under the title of *The Woman's Prize, or, the Tamer tam'd*. But by an unhappy mistake of buffoonery for humour and obscenity for wit, which was not uncommon with that author, his production came lamely off, and was soon consign'd to the oblivion in which it is now bury'd. Whereas this of his antagonist flourishes still, and has maintain'd it's place upon the stage (in some shape or other) from it's very first appearance down to the present hour. And this success it has merited by true wit and true humour; a fable of very artful construction, much business, and highly interesting; and by natural and well-sustain'd characters, which no pen but SHAKESPEARE's was capable of drawing. What defects it has are chiefly in the diction; the same (indeed) with those of the play that was last-mention'd, and to be accounted for the same way, for we are strongly inclin'd to believe it a neighbour in time to *Love's Labour's lost*, though we want the proofs of it which we have luckily for that.

But the plays which we have already spoke of are but slightly attack'd, and by few writers in comparison of this which we are now come to of *Titus Andronicus*. Commentators, editors, every one (in short) who has had to do with SHAKESPEARE, unite all in condemning it, as a very bundle of horrors, totally unfit for the stage, and unlike the Poet's manner and even the style of his other pieces. All which allegations are extreamly true, and we readily admit of them, but can not admit the conclusion that therefore it is not his; and shall now proceed to give the reasons of our dissent. ... (37–41)

[Capell dates the play *c.* 1589, then discusses its affinities with the drama of that period.]

The books of that time afford strange examples of the barbarism of the publick taste both upon the stage and elsewhere. A conceited one of *John* LYLY's set a nation a madding; and for a while every pretender to politeness 'parl'd Euphuism,' as it was phras'd, and no writings would go down with them but such as were pen'd in that fantastical manner. The setter-up of this fashion try'd it also in comedy, but seems to have miscarry'd in that, and for this plain reason: the people who govern theatres are the middle and lower orders of the world, and these expected laughter in comedies, which this stuff of LYLY's was incapable of exciting. But some other writers who rose exactly at that time succeeded better in certain tragical performances, though as outragious to the full in their way, and as remote from nature as these comick ones of LYLY's. For, falling in with that innate love of blood which has been often objected to *British* audiences, and choosing fables of horror which they made horrider still by their manner of handling them, they produc'd a set of monsters that are not to be parallel'd in all the annals of play-writing. Yet they were receiv'd with applause, and were the favourites of the publick for almost ten years together ending at 1595. Many plays of this stamp, it is probable, have perish'd; but those that are come down to us are as follows;—

The Wars of Cyrus; *Tamburlaine the great*, in two parts; *The Spanish Tragedy*, likewise in two parts; *Soliman and Perseda*; and *Selimus a tragedy*; which whoever has means of coming at, and can have the patience to examine will see evident tokens of a fashion then prevailing, which occasion'd all these plays to be cast in the same mold. Now SHAKESPEARE, whatever motives he might have in some other parts of it, at this period of his life wrote certainly for profit; and seeing it was to be had in this way (and in this way only, perhaps) he fell in with the current, and gave his sorry auditors a piece to their tooth in this contested play of *Titus Andronicus*; which as it came out at the same time with the plays above-mention'd is most exactly like them in almost every particular. Their very numbers, consisting all of ten syllables with hardly any redundant, are copy'd by this *Proteus*, who could put on any shape that either serv'd his interest or suited his inclination. And this, we hope, is a fair and unforc'd way of accounting for *Andronicus*; and may convince the most prejudic'd that SHAKESPEARE might be the writer of it, as he might also of *Locrine*, which is ascrib'd to him, a ninth tragedy, in form and time agreeing perfectly with the others.

But to conclude this article: however he may be censur'd as rash or ill-judging the editor ventures to declare that he himself wanted not the conviction of the foregoing argument to be satisfy'd who the play belongs to. For though a work of imitation, and conforming itself to models truly execrable throughout, yet the genius of it's Author breaks forth in some places, and to the editor's .eye SHAKESPEARE stands confess'd. The third act in particular may be read with admiration even by the most delicate, who, if they are not without feelings may chance to find themselves touch'd by it with such passions as tragedy should excite, that is, terror, and pity. The reader will please to observe that all these contested plays are in the folio, which is dedicated to the Poet's patrons and friends, the earls of *Pembroke* and *Montgomery*, by editors who are seemingly honest men, and profess themselves dependant upon those noblemen. To whom, therefore, they would hardly have had the confidence to present forgeries and pieces supposititious; in which, too, they were liable to be detected by those identical noble persons themselves as well as by a very great part of their other readers and auditors. Which argument, though of no little strength in itself, we omitted to bring before as having better (as we thought) and more forcible to offer; but it had behov'd those gentlemen who have question'd the plays to have got rid of it in the first instance, as it lies full in their way in the very entrance upon this dispute. (43–6) . . .

Origin of SHAKESPEARE's Fables

Antony and Cleopatra

This play, together with *Coriolanus*, *Julius Cæsar*, and some part of *Timon of Athens*, are form'd upon Plutarch's *Lives*, [in North's version of Amyot's translation]. As the language of this translation is pretty good for the time, and the sentiments which are PLUTARCH's breath the genuine spirit of the several historical personages, SHAKESPEARE has, with much judgment, introduc'd no small number of speeches into these plays in the very words of that translator, turning them into verse; which he has so well wrought up and incorporated with his plays, that what he has introduc'd cannot be discover'd by any reader 'till it is pointed out for him. (50) . . .

1 Henry IV.

In the eleven plays that follow,—*Macbeth*, *King John*, *Richard II*, *Henry IV 2 parts*, *Henry V*, *Henry VI 3 parts*, *Richard III*, and *Henry VIII*,—the historians of that time, HALL, HOLINSHED, STOW and others (and in particular, HOLINSHED) are pretty closely follow'd; and that not only for their matter but even sometimes in their expressions. The harangue of the archbishop of Canterbury in *Henry V*, that of queen Catharine in *Henry VIII* at her trial, and the king's reply to it, are taken from those chroniclers and put into verse. Other lesser matters are borrow'd from them; and so largely scatter'd up and down in these plays that whoever would rightly judge of the Poet must acquaint himself with those authors, and his character will not suffer in the enquiry . . . (53–4)

King Lear

Lear's distressful story has been often told in poems, ballads, and chronicles. But to none of these are we indebted for

SHAKESPEARE'S *Lear*, but to a silly old play which made it's first appearance in 1605, the title of which is as follows:—The |True Chronicle Hi-story of King LEIR, and his three|*daughters, Gonorill, Ragan,* |*and Cordella.* |As it hath bene divers and sundry times lately acted.| LONDON, |Printed by Simon Stafford for John |Wright, and are to bee sold at his shop at| Christes Church dore, next Newgate- | Market. 1605. (4°.I.4ᵇ.)—As it is a great curiosity, and very scarce, the title is here inserted at large: and for the same reason, and also to shew the use that SHAKESPEARE made of it, some extracts shall now be added.

The author of this LEIR has kept him close to the chronicles; for he ends his play with the re-instating king *Leir* in his throne, by the aid of *Cordella* and her husband. But take the entire fable in his own words. Towards the end of the play, at signature H₃, you find *Leir* in *France*, upon whose coast he and his friend *Perillus* are landed in so necessitous a condition that, having nothing to pay their passage the mariners take their cloaks, leaving them their jerkins in exchange. Thus attir'd they go up further into the country; and there, when they are at the point to perish by famine (insomuch that *Perillus* offers *Leir* his arm to feed upon), they light upon *Gallia* and his queen, whom the author has brought down thitherward, in progress, disguis'd. Their discourse is overheard by *Cordella*, who immediately knows them, but at her husband's persuasion forbears to discover herself a while, relieves them with food, and then asks their story; which *Leir* gives her in these words:

> *Leir*. Then know this first, I am a Brittayne borne,
> And had three daughters by one loving wife:
> And though I say it, of beauty they were sped;
> Especially the youngest of the three,
> For her perfections hardly matcht could be:
> On these I doted with a jelous love,
> And thought to try which of them lov'd me best,
> By asking of them, which would do most for me?
> The first and second flattred me with words,
> And vowd they lov'd me better then their lives:
> The youngest sayd, she loved me as a child
> Might do: her answere I esteem'd most vild,
> And presently in an outragious mood,
> I turnd her from me to go sinke or swym:

322

And all I had, even to the very clothes,
I gave in dowry with the other two:
And she that best deserv'd the greatest share,
I gave her nothing, but disgrace and care.
Now mark the sequell: When I had done thus,
I soiournd in my eldest daughters house,
Where for a time I was intreated well,
And liv'd in state sufficing my content:
But every day her kindnesse did grow cold,
Which I with patience put up well ynough
And seemed not to see the things I saw:
But at the last she grew so far incenst
With moody fury, and with causelesse hate,
That in most vild and contumelious termes,
She bade me pack, and harbour some where else.
Then was I fayne for refuge to repayre
Unto my other daughter for reliefe,
Who gave me pleasing and most courteous words;
But in her actions shewed her selfe so sore,
As never any daughter did before:
She prayd me in a morning out betime,
To go to a thicket two miles from the Court,
Poynting that there she would come talke with me:
There she had set a shaghayrd murdring wretch,
To massacre my honest friend and me.

And now I am constraind to seeke reliefe
Of her to whom I have bin so unkind;
Whose censure, if it do award me death,
I must confesse she payes me but my due:
But if she shew a loving daughters part,
It comes of God and her, not my desert.
    Cor. No doubt she will, I dare be sworne she will.

Thereupon ensues her discovery; and with it a circumstance of
some beauty, which SHAKESPEARE has borrow'd [4.7.57ff.], their
kneeling to each other,[1] and mutually contending which should
ask forgiveness. The next page presents us *Gallia*, and *Mumford*
who commands under him, marching to embarque their forces
to re-instate *Leir*; and the next a sea-port in *Britain*, and officers

---

[1] Steevens had pointed this out in 1766: above, p. 248. In his 1773 edition, as Collins
showed (*A Letter to George Hardinge*, pp. 29f.), Steevens plagiarized this passage (cf. p. 511
below). Both editors were borrowing early plays from Garrick's collection.

setting a watch, who are to fire a beacon to give notice if any ships approach, in which there is some low humour that is passable enough. *Gallia* and his forces arrive, and take the town by surprize: immediately upon which they are encounter'd by the forces of the two elder sisters and their husbands. A battle ensues, *Leir* conquers. He and his friends enter victorious, and the play closes thus:—

> Thanks (worthy Mumford) to thee last of all,
> Not greeted last, 'cause thy desert was small. ....
> Come, sonne and daughter, who did me advance,
> Repose with me awhile, and then for *Fraunce*.   [*Exeunt*.

Such is the *Leir* now before us. Who the author of it should be I cannot surmise, for neither in manner nor style has it the least resemblance to any of the other tragedies of that time. Most of them rise now and then, and are poetical; but this creeps in one dull tenour from beginning to end. ... But whoever he was SHAKESPEARE has done him the honour to follow him in a stroke or two. One has been observ'd upon above; and the reader who is acquainted with SHAKESPEARE's *Lear*, will perceive another in the second line of the concluding speech. And here is a third: 'Knowest thou these letters?' says *Leir* to *Ragan*, (sign. I.3^b.) shewing her hers and her sister's letters commanding his death; upon which she snatches at the letters, and tears them (v. *Lear*, [5.3.154ff.] &c.) Another, and that a most signal one upon one account, occurs at signature *C*. 3^b;

> But he, the myrrour of mild patience,
> Puts up all wrongs, and never gives reply:

Perillus says this of *Leir*, comprizing therein his character as drawn by this author. How opposite to that which SHAKESPEARE has given him, all know; and yet he has found means to put nearly the same words into the very mouth of his *Lear*;

> No, I will be the pattern of all patience,
> I will say nothing.

Lastly, two of SHAKESPEARE's personages, *Kent* and the steward, seem to owe their existence to the above-mention'd 'shag-hair'd wretch,' and the *Perillus* of this *Leir*.

The episode of *Gloster* and his two sons is taken from the *Arcadia*: in which romance there is a chapter thus intitl'd;—

'*The pitifull state, and storie of the* Paphlagonian *unkinde King, and his kind sonne, first related by the son, then by the blind father.*' (Arcadia. *p.* 142, Edit. 1590, 4⁰.) of which episode there are no traces in either chronicle, poem, or play wherein this history is handl'd. (55–9)

Measure for Measure

In the year 1578 was publish'd in a black-letter quarto a miserable dramatick performance, in two parts, intitl'd *Promos and Cassandra*; written by one George WHETSTONE, author likewise of the *Heptameron*, and much other poetry of the same stamp printed about that time. (60) [Capell quotes the Argument and passages from the first scene, concluding:]

And thus it proceeds, without one word in it that SHAKESPEARE could make use of, or can be read with patience by any man living. And yet, besides the characters appearing in the argument his Bawd, Clown, *Lucio*, *Juliet*, and the Provost, nay, and even his *Barnardine* are created out of hints which this play gave him; and the lines too that are quoted, bad as they are, suggested to him the manner in which his own play opens. (62–3) ...

Such are the materials out of which this great Poet has rais'd a structure, which no time shall efface, nor any envy be strong enough to lessen the admiration that is so justly due to it; which if it was great before cannot fail to receive encrease with the judicious when the account that has been now given them is reflected upon duly. Other originals have, indeed, been pretended; and much extraordinary criticism has, at different times and by different people, been spun out of those conceits. But, except some few articles in which the writer professes openly his ignorance of the sources they are drawn from, and some others in which he delivers himself doubtfully, what is said in the preceding leaves concerning these fables may with all certainty be rely'd upon.

How much is it to be wish'd that something equally certain, and indeed worthy to be intitl'd a Life of SHAKESPEARE, could accompany this relation, and compleat the tale of those pieces which the publick is apt to expect before new editions? But that nothing of this sort is at present in being may be said without breach of candour, as we think, or suspicion of over much niceness. An imperfect and loose account of his father and family; his own marriage, and the issue of it; some traditional stories, many of them triffling in themselves, supported by small authority and seemingly ill-grounded; together with his life's final period as gather'd from his monument, is the full and whole amount of historical matter that is in any of these writings, in which the critick and essayist swallow up the biographer, who yet ought to take the lead in them. The truth is, the occurrences of this most interesting life (we mean, the private ones) are irrecoverably lost to us. The friendly office of registring them was overlook'd by those who alone had it in their power, and our enquiries about them now must prove vain and thrown away.

But there is another sort of them that is not quite so hopeless; which besides affording us the prospect of some good issue to our endeavours do also invite us to them by the promise of a much better reward for them. The knowledge of his private life had done little more than gratify our curiosity, but his publick one as a writer would have consequences more important. A discovery there would throw a new light upon many of his pieces; and, where rashness only is shew'd in the opinions that are now current about them, a judgment might then be form'd which perhaps would do credit to the giver of it. When he commenc'd a writer for the stage, and in which play; what the order of the rest of them, and (if that be discoverable) what the occasion; and, lastly, for which of the numerous theatres that were then subsisting they were severally written at first,—are the particulars that should chiefly engage the attention of a writer of SHAKESPEARE's Life, and be the principal subjects of his enquiry.

To assist him in which the first impressions of these plays will do something, and their title-pages at large, which upon that account we mean to give in another work that will accompany the *School of* SHAKESPEARE; and something the *School* itself will afford that may contribute to the same service. But the cornerstone of all must be the works of the Poet himself, from which much may be extracted by a heedful peruser of them; and for the sake of such a peruser, and by way of putting him into the train when the plays are before him, we shall instance in one of them. The time in which *Henry V* was written is determin'd almost precisely by a passage in the chorus to the fifth act, and the concluding chorus of it contains matter relative to *Henry VI*. Other plays might be

mention'd, as *Henry VIII* and *Macbeth*; but this one may be sufficient to answer our intention in producing it, which was to spirit
some one up to this task in some future time,[1] by shewing the
possibility of it; which he may be further convinc'd of if he reflects
what great things have been done by cricks amongst ourselves
upon subjects of this sort, and of a more remov'd antiquity than
he is concern'd in.

A Life thus constructed, interspers'd with such anecdotes of
common notoriety as the writer's judgment shall tell him are
worth regard; together with some memorials of this Poet that are
happily come down to us, such as an Instrument in the Heralds'
Office confirming arms to his father, a Patent preserv'd in RYMER
granted by *James* the first, his last Will and Testament, extant now
at Doctors-Commons; his *Stratford* Monument, and a monument
of his daughter which is said to be there also: such a Life would
rise quickly into a volume, especially with the addition of one
proper and even necessary episode, a brief history of our Drama
from it's origin down to the Poet's death.[2] Even the stage he
appear'd upon, it's form, dressings, actors should be enquir'd
into, as every one of those circumstances had some considerable
effect upon what he compos'd for it. The subject is certainly a good
one and will fall (we hope) ere it be long into the hands of some
good writer, by whose abilities this great want may at length be
made up to us, and the world of letters enrich'd by the happy
acquisition of a masterly '*Life of* SHAKESPEARE.' (71–4)

---

[1] Edmond Malone's first publication was an *Attempt to ascertain the Order in which the Plays
of Shakespeare were written*, included in the second edition (1778) of Steevens's Shakespeare.
[2] An attempt at such a history was made by Thomas Hawkins: see No. 242 below.

221. Elizabeth Montagu, Shakespeare's genius

1769

From *An Essay on the Writings and Genius of Shakespeare, Compared with the Greek and French Dramatic Poets, with Some Remarks Upon the Misrepresentations of Mons. de Voltaire* (1769).

Mrs Elizabeth Montagu (1720–1800), first of the bluestockings, was a gifted woman who made her home one of the centres of London intellectual society for nearly 50 years, her regular guests including Lord Lyttelton, Horace Walpole, Johnson, Burke, Garrick, and Reynolds; she was a close friend of Elizabeth Carter, Mrs Thrale, Hannah More, and Fanny Burney. Her *Essay* was perfectly adapted to the taste of the age, and went through further editions in 1770, 1772, 1773, 1778, 1785, and 1810, with a French translation in 1777 and an Italian in 1828. Dr Johnson found 'not one sentence of true criticism in her book,' but it was praised by Boswell, Reynolds, and others, while Cowper admired its 'good sense, sound judgment', and wit; in the magazines and newspapers of the period it is treated with universal respect, and frequently plagiarized. Her introductory defence of Shakespeare against Voltaire owes much to Johnson, and many sections are commonplaces of the age; but the response to *Macbeth* is personal, and perceptive.

[From the Introduction] . . . Our Shakespeare, whose very faults pass here unquestioned, or are perhaps consecrated through the enthusiasm of his admirers, and the veneration paid to long-established fame, is by a great wit, a great critic, and a great poet of a neighbouring nation, treated as the writer of monstrous farces, called by him tragedies; and barbarism and ignorance are attributed to the nation by which he is admired. Yet if wits, poets, critics, could ever be charged with presumption, one might say there was some degree of it in pronouncing that in a country where Sophocles and Euripides are as well understood as in any in Europe the perfections of dramatic poetry should be as little comprehended as among the Chinese.

Learning here is not confined to ecclesiastics or a few lettered sages and academics; every English gentleman has an education which gives him an early acquaintance with the writings of the ancients. His knowledge of polite literature does not begin with that period which Mr. de Voltaire calls Le Siecle de Louis quatorze. Before he is admitted as a spectator at the theatre at London it is probable he has heard the tragic muse as she spoke at Athens, and as she now speaks at Paris, or in Italy; and he can discern between the natural language in which she addressed the human heart, and the artificial dialect which she has acquired from the prejudices of a particular nation, or the jargon caught from the tone of a court. To please upon the French stage every person of every age and nation was made to adopt their manners. (1–3) . . .

The editor of Corneille's works, in terms so gross as are hardly pardonable in such a master of fine raillery, frequently attacks our Shakespeare for the want of delicacy and politeness in his pieces: it must be owned that in some places they bear the marks of the unpolished times in which he wrote. . . . (4–5)

Shakespeare wrote at a time when learning was tinctured with pedantry, wit was unpolished and mirth ill-bred. The court of Elizabeth spoke a scientific jargon, and a certain obscurity of style was universally affected. James brought an addition of pedantry, accompanied by indecent and indelicate manners and language. By contagion, or from complaisance to the taste of the public, Shakespeare falls sometimes into the fashionable mode of writing. But this is only by fits, for many parts of all his plays are written with the most noble, elegant, and uncorrupted simplicity. Such is his merit that the more just and refined the taste of the nation has become the more he has encreased in reputation. He was approved by his own age, admired by the next, and is revered, and almost adored by the present. (10) . . .

Shakespeare's plays were to be acted in a paltry tavern, to an unlettered audience just emerging from barbarity. . . . The period when Sophocles and Euripides wrote was that in which the fine arts and polite literature were in a degree of perfection which succeeding ages have emulated in vain.

It happened in the literary as in the moral world; a few sages, from the veneration which they had obtained by extraordinary wisdom and a faultless conduct, rose to the authority of legislators. The practice and manner of the three celebrated Greek tragedians were by succeeding critics established as dramatic laws: happily for Shakespeare, Mr. Johnson, whose genius and learning render him superior to a servile awe of pedantic institutions, in his ingenious preface to his edition of Shakespeare has greatly obviated all that can be objected to our author's neglect of the unities of time and place.

Shakespeare's felicity has been rendered compleat in this age. His genius produced works that time could not destroy. But some of the lighter characters were become illegible; these have been restored by critics whose learning and penetration traced back the vestiges of superannuated opinions and customs. They are now no longer in danger of being effaced, and the testimonies of these learned commentators to his merit will guard our author's great monument of human wit from the presumptuous invasions of our rash critics, and the squibs of our witlings; so that the bays will flourish unwithered and inviolate round his tomb. . . . (14–15)

Shakespeare seems to have had the art of the Dervise in the Arabian tales, who could throw his soul into the body of another man, and be at once possessed of his sentiments, adopt his passions, and rise to all the functions and feelings of his situation.

Shakespeare was born in a rank of life in which men indulge themselves in a free expression of their passions, with little regard to exterior appearance. This perhaps made him more acquainted with the movements of the heart, and less knowing or observant of outward forms: against the one he often offends, he very rarely misrepresents the other. (37)

[From chapter 1, 'On the Historical Drama'] Those dramas of Shakespeare which he distinguishes by the name of his histories, being of an original kind and peculiar construction, cannot come within any rules which are prior to their existence. (55) . . .

[On the Tudor chronicles as sources for the history plays:] The patterns from whence he drew were not only void of poetical spirit and ornament but also of all historical dignity. The histories of these times were a mere heap of rude undigested annals, coarse in their style and crouded with trivial anecdotes. No Tacitus had investigated the obliquities of our statesmen, or by diving into the profound secrets of policy had dragged into light the latent motives, the secret machinations of our politicians: yet how does he enter into the deepest mysteries of state! There cannot be a stronger proof of the superiority of his genius over the historians of the times than the following instance.

The learned Sir Thomas More in his history of Crook'd-Back Richard tells, with the garrulity of an old nurse, the current stories of this king's deformity and the monstrous appearances of his infancy, which he seems with superstitious credulity to believe to have been the omens and prognostics of his future villainy. Shakespeare, with a more philosophic turn of mind, considers them not as presaging but as instigating his cruel ambition, and finely accounts in the following speeches for the asperity of his temper and his fierce and unmitigated desire of dominion, from his being by his person disqualified for the softer engagements of society. [Quotes 3 *Henry VI*, 3.2.146–71 and 5.6.74–83] (68–9) . . .

Our author by following minutely the chronicles of the times has embarrassed his drama's with too great a number of persons and events. The hurley-burley of these plays recommended them to a rude illiterate audience, who, as he says, loved a noise of targets. His poverty and the low condition of the stage (which at that time was not frequented by persons of rank) obliged him to this complaisance; and unfortunately he had not been tutored by any rules of art, or informed by acquaintance with just and regular drama's. (71) . . .

Shakespeare and Corneille are equally blamable for having complied with the bad taste of the age; and by doing so they have brought unmerited censures on their country. (74) . . .

Shakespeare's dramatis personæ are men, frail by constitution, hurt by ill habits, faulty and unequal. But they speak with human voices, are actuated by human passions and are engaged in the common affairs of human life. We are interested in what they do or say by feeling every moment that they are of the same nature as ourselves. Their precepts therefore are an instruction, their fates and fortunes an experience, their testimony an authority, and their misfortunes a warning. (81) . . .

[From chapter 3, 'On *The First Part of Henry IV*']

Our author is so little under the discipline of art that we are apt to ascribe his happiest successes, as well as his most unfortunate failings, to chance. But I cannot help thinking there is more of contrivance and care in his execution of this play than in almost any he has written. It is a more regular drama than his other historical plays, less charged with absurdities, and less involved in confusion. It is indeed liable to those objections which are made to tragicomedy. But if the pedantry of learning could ever recede from its dogmatical rules I think that this play, instead of being condemned for being of that species, would obtain favour for the species itself, though perhaps correct taste may be offended with the transitions from grave and important to light and ludicrous subjects, and more still with those from great and illustrious, to low and mean persons. . . .

We cannot but suppose that at the time it was written many stories yet subsisted of the wild adventures of this Prince of Wales and his idle companions. His subsequent reformation and his conquests in France rendered him a very popular character. It was a delicate affair to expose the follies of Henry V. before a people proud of his victories and tender of his fame, at the same time so informed of the extravagancies and excesses of his youth that he could not appear divested of them with any degree of historical probability. Their enormity would have been greatly heightened if they had appeared in a piece entirely serious and full of dignity and decorum. How happily therefore was the character of Falstaff introduced, whose wit and festivity in some measure excuse the Prince for admitting him into his familiarity and suffering himself to be led by him into some irregularities. There is hardly a young hero full of gaiety and spirits who, if he had once fallen into the society of so pleasant a companion, could have the severity to discard him or would not say, as the Prince does, 'He could better spare a better man.' [5.4.104]

How skilfully does our author follow the tradition of the Prince's having been engaged in a robbery, yet make his part in it a mere frolic to play on the cowardly and braggart temper of Falstaff! The whole conduct of that incident is very artful: he rejects the proposal of the robbery, and only complies with playing a trick on the robbers; and care is taken to inform you that the money is returned to its owners.—The Prince seems always diverted rather than seduced by Falstaff; he despises his vices while he is entertained by his humour, and though Falstaff is for a while a stain upon his character yet it is of a kind with those colours which are used for a disguise in sport, being of such a nature as are easily washed out without leaving any bad tincture. . . . (100–3)

Whether we consider the character of Falstaff as adapted to encourage and excuse the extravagancies of the Prince, or by itself, we must certainly admire it and own it to be perfectly original. The professed wit, either in life or on the stage is usually severe and satirical. But mirth is the source of Falstaff's wit. He seems rather to invite you to partake of his merriment than to attend to his jest; a person must be ill-natured as well as dull who does not join in the mirth of this jovial companion, who is in all respects the best calculated to raise laughter of any that ever appeared on a stage.

He joins the finesse of wit with the drollery of humour. Humour is a kind of grotesque wit, shaped and coloured by the disposition of the person in whom it resides, or by the subject to which it is applied. It is oftenest found in odd and irregular minds: but this peculiar turn distorts wit, and though it gives it a burlesque air which excites momentary mirth, renders it less just and consequently less agreeable to our judgments. Gluttony, corpulency, and cowardice are the peculiarities of Falstaff's composition; they render him ridiculous without folly, throw an air of jest and festivity about him, and make his manners suit with his sentiments without giving to his understanding any particular bias. As the contempt attendant on these vices and defects is the best antidote against any infection that might be caught in his society, so it was very skilful to make him as ridiculous as witty and as contemptible as entertaining. The admirable speech upon honour would have been both indecent and dangerous from any other person. We must every where allow his wit is just, his humour genuine, and his character perfectly original, and sustained through every scene in every play in which it appears.

As Falstaff, whom the author certainly intended to be perfectly witty, is less addicted to quibble and play on words than any of his comic characters, I think we may fairly conclude our author was sensible it was but a false kind of wit, which he practised from the hard necessity of the times: for in that age the professor quibbled in his chair, the judge quibbled on the bench, the prelate quibbled in the pulpit, the statesman quibbled at the council-board; nay even majesty quibbled on the throne.[1] (106–8)

[From chapter 4, 'On *The Second Part of Henry IV*']

I have before observed that Shakespeare had the talents of an orator as much as of a poet; and I believe it will be allowed the speeches of Westmorland and Lancaster are as proper on this occasion, and the particular circumstances are as happily touch'd as they could have been by the most judicious orator. I know not that any poet, ancient or modern, has shewn so perfect a judgment in rhetoric as our countryman. I wish he had employed his eloquence too in arraigning the baseness and treachery of John of Lancaster's conduct in breaking his covenant with the rebels.[2]

Pistol is an odd kind of personage, intended I suppose to ridicule some fashionable affectation of bombast language. When such characters exist no longer any where but in the writings in which they have been ridiculed they seem to have been monsters of the poet's brain. The originals lost and the mode forgot, one can neither praise the imitation nor laugh at the ridicule. Comic writers should therefore always exhibit some characteristic distinctions as well as temporary modes. Justice Shallow will for ever rank with a certain species of men; he is like a well painted portrait in the dress of his age. Pistol appears a mere antiquated habit, so uncouthly fashioned we can hardly believe it was made for any thing but a masquerade frolic. The poets who mean to please posterity should therefore work as painters, not as taylors, and give us peculiar features rather than fantastic habits. But where there is such a prodigious variety of well-drawn portraits as in this play we may excuse one piece of mere drapery, especially when exhibited to expose an absurd and troublesome fashion.

Mine hostess Quickly is of a species not extinct. It may be said the author there sinks from comedy to farce, but she helps to compleat the character of Falstaff, and some of the dialogues in which she is engaged are diverting. Every scene in which Doll Tearsheet appears is indecent, and therefore not only indefensible but inexcusable. There are delicacies of decorum in one age unknown to another age, but whatever is immoral is equally blamable in all ages, and every approach to obscenity is an offence for which

---

[1] Cf. Addison (2.278).
[2] Cf. Heath (4.557) and Dr Johnson (p. 122 above).

wit cannot atone, nor the barbarity or the corruption of the times excuse. (121–3) . . .

[From chapter 5, 'On the Praeternatural Beings']

. . . Shakespeare saw how useful the popular superstitions had been to the ancient poets: he felt that they were necessary to poetry itself (135). . . . Ghosts, fairies, goblins, elves, were as propitious, were as assistant to Shakespeare, and gave as much of the sublime and of the marvellous to his fictions as nymphs, satyrs, fawns, and even the triple Geryon to the works of ancient bards. Our poet never carries his præternatural beings beyond the limits of the popular tradition. It is true that he boldly exerts his poetic genius and fascinating powers in that magic circle, *in which none e'er durst walk but he*: but as judicious as bold, he contains himself within it (137). . . .

To all these beings our poet has assigned tasks and appropriated manners adapted to their imputed dispositions and characters; which are continually developing through the whole piece in a series of operations conducive to the catastrophe. They are not brought in as subordinate or casual agents, but lead the action and govern the fable; in which respect our countryman has entered more into theatrical propriety than the Greek tragedians. (139)

Shakespeare, in the dark shades of Gothic barbarism, had no resources but in the very phantoms that walked the night of ignorance and superstition, or in touching the latent passions of civil rage and discord; sure to please best his fierce and barbarous audience when he raised the bloody ghost or reared the warlike standard. His choice of these subjects was judicious if we consider the times in which he lived; his management of them so masterly that he will be admired in all times.

In the same age, Ben. Jonson, more proud of his learning than confident of his genius, was desirous to give a metaphysical air to his compositions. He composed many pieces of the allegorical kind established on the Grecian mythology, and rendered his play-house a perfect pantheon. Shakespeare disdained these quaint devices; an admirable judge of human nature, with a capacity most extensive and an invention most happy, he contented himself with giving dramatic manners to history, sublimity and its appropriated powers and charms to fiction; and in both these arts he is unequalled. The *Catiline* and *Sejanus* of Jonson are cold, crude, heavy pieces; turgid where they should be great; bombast where they should be sublime; the sentiments extravagant, the manners exaggerated, and the whole undramatically conducted by long senatorial speeches and flat plagiarisms from Tacitus and Sallust (150–1).

[From chapter 6, 'The Tragedy of *Macbeth*']

This piece is perhaps one of the greatest exertions of the tragic and poetic powers that any age or any country has produced. Here are opened new sources of terror, new creations of fancy. The agency of witches and spirits excites a species of terror that cannot be effected by the operation of human agency or by any form or disposition of human things. For the known limits of their powers and capacities set certain bounds to our apprehensions; mysterious horrors, undefined terrors are raised by the intervention of beings whose nature we do not understand, whose actions we cannot control, and whose influence we know not how to escape. Here we feel through all the faculties of the soul and to the utmost extent of her capacity. The apprehension of the interposition of such agents is the most salutary of all fears. It keeps up in our minds a sense of our connection with awful and invisible spirits to whom our most secret actions are apparent, and from whose chastisement innocence alone can defend us. (173–4) . . .

The dexterity is admirable with which the predictions of the witches (as Macbeth observes) prove true to the ear but false to the hope, according to the general condition of vain oracles. With great judgment the poet has given to Macbeth the very temper to be wrought upon by such suggestions. The bad man is his own tempter. Richard III. had a heart that prompted him to do all that the worst demon could have suggested, so that the witches had been only an idle wonder in his story. Nor did he want such a counsellor as Lady Macbeth: a ready instrument like Buckingham to adopt his projects and execute his orders was sufficient. But Macbeth, of a generous disposition and good propensities, but with vehement passions and aspiring wishes, was a subject liable to be seduced by splendid prospects and ambitious counsels. This appears from the following character given of him by his wife:

Yet do I fear thy nature;
It is too full o'th' milk of human kindness

> To catch the nearest way. Thou wouldst be great;
> Art not without ambition; but without
> The illness should attend it. What thou wouldst highly,
> That wouldst thou holily; wouldst not play false,
> And yet wouldst wrongly win.   [1.5.13ff.]

So much inherent ambition in a character without other vice, and full of the milk of human kindness, though obnoxious to temptation yet would have great struggles before it yielded, and as violent fits of subsequent remorse.

If the mind is to be medicated by the operations of pity and terror, surely no means are so well adapted to that end as a strong and lively representation of the agonizing struggles that precede and the terrible horrors that follow wicked actions. Other poets thought they had sufficiently attended to the moral purpose of the drama in making the furies pursue the perpetrated crime. Our author waives their bloody daggers in the road to guilt, and demonstrates that as soon as a man begins to hearken to ill suggestions terrors environ and fears distract him. Tenderness and conjugal love combat in the breasts of a Medea and a Herod in their purposed vengeance. Personal affection often weeps on the theatre while jealousy or revenge whet the bloody knife; but Macbeth's emotions are the struggles of conscience, his agonies are the agonies of remorse. They are lessons of justice, and warnings to innocence. I do not know that any dramatic writer except Shakespeare has set forth the pangs of guilt separate from the fear of punishment. Clytemnestra is represented by Euripides as under great terrors on account of the murder of Agamemnon; but they arise from fear, not repentance. It is not the memory of the assassinated husband which haunts and terrifies her but an apprehension of vengeance from his surviving son; when she is told Orestes is dead her mind is again at ease. It must be allowed that on the Grecian stage it is the office of the chorus to moralize, and to point out on every occasion the advantages of virtue over vice. But how much less affecting are their animadversions than the testimony of the person concerned! (176–9) ...

Our author has so tempered the constitutional character of Macbeth by infusing into it the milk of human kindness and a strong tincture of honour, as to make the most violent perturbation and pungent remorse naturally attend on those steps to which he is led by the force of temptation. Here we must commend the poet's judgment, and his invariable attention to consistency of character. But more amazing is the art with which he exhibits the movement of the human mind, and renders audible the silent march of thought; traces its modes of operation in the course of deliberating, the pauses of hesitation, and the final act of decision; shews how reason checks and how the passions impel; and displays to us the trepidations that precede and the horrors that pursue acts of blood. No species of dialogue but that which a man holds with himself could effect this. The soliloquy has been permitted to all dramatic writers; but its true use has been understood only by our author, who alone has attained to a just imitation of nature in this kind of self-conference.

It is certain men do not tell themselves who they are, and whence they came; they neither narrate nor declaim in the solitude of the closet, as Greek and French writers represent. Here then is added to the drama an imitation of the most difficult and delicate kind, that of representing the internal process of the mind in reasoning and reflecting; and it is not only a difficult but a very useful art, as it best assists the poet to expose the anguish of remorse, to repeat every whisper of the internal monitor, conscience, and upon occasion to lend her a voice *to amaze the guilty and appal the free*. As a man is averse to expose his crimes and discover the turpitude of his actions, even to the faithful friend and trusty confidant, it is more natural for him to breathe in soliloquy the dark and heavy secrets of the soul than to utter them to the most intimate associate. The conflicts in the bosom of Macbeth, before he committed the murder, could not by any other means have been so well exposed. He entertains the prophecy of his future greatness with complacency, but the very idea of the means by which he is to attain it shocks him to the highest degree.

> This supernatural solliciting
> Cannot be ill; cannot be good. . . .   [1.3.130ff.]

There is an obscurity and stiffness in part of these soliloquies which I wish I could charge entirely to the confusion of Macbeth's mind from the horror he feels at the thought of the murder; but our author is too much addicted to the obscure bombast much affected by all sorts of writers in that age. The abhorrence Macbeth feels at the suggestion of assassinating his king brings him back to this determination:

> If chance will have me king, why, chance may crown me,
> Without my stir. [1.3.143f.]

After a pause, in which we may suppose the ambitious desire of a crown to return so far as to make him undetermined what he shall do, and leave the decision to future time and unborn events, he concludes

> Come what come may,
> Time and the hour runs thro' the roughest day. [1.3.146f.]

By which I confess I do not with his two last commentators imagine is meant either the tautology of time and the hour, or an allusion to time painted with an hour-glass, or an exhortation to time to hasten forward, but rather to say *tempus & hora*, time and occasion will carry the thing through and bring it to some determined point and end, let its nature be what it will. (183–6) . . .

Macbeth, in debating with himself, chiefly dwells upon the guilt, and touches something on the danger of assassinating the king. When he argues with Lady Macbeth, knowing her too wicked to be affected by the one and too daring to be deterred by the other, he urges with great propriety what he thinks may have more weight with one of her disposition, the favour he is in with the king, and the esteem he has lately acquired of the people. In answer to her charge of cowardice he finely distinguishes between manly courage and brutal ferocity.

> I dare do all that may become a man;
> Who dares do more is none. [1.7.46f.]

At length, overcome rather than persuaded, he determines on the bloody deed.

> I am settled, and bend up
> Each corp'ral agent to this terrible feat. [1.7.79f.]

How terrible to him, how repugnant to his nature we plainly perceive when, even in the moment that he summons up the resolution needful to perform it, horrid phantasms present themselves: murder alarumed by his centinel, the wolf stealing towards his design, witchcraft celebrating pale Hecate's offerings, the midnight ravisher invading sleeping innocence, seem his associates, and bloody daggers lead him to the very chamber of the king. (188–9)

How natural is the exclamation of a person who from the fearless state of unsuspecting innocence is fallen into the suspicious condition of guilt, when upon hearing a knocking at the gate he cries out: 'How is it with me, when every noise appals me?' [2.2.58]

The poet has contrived to throw a tincture of remorse even into Macbeth's resolution to murder Banquo.—He does not proceed in it like a man who, impenitent in crimes and wanton in success, gaily goes forward in his violent career; but seems impelled on and stimulated to this additional villany by an apprehension that if Banquo's posterity should inherit the crown he has sacrificed his virtue and defiled his own soul in vain. [Quotes 3.1.63ff.] His desire to keep Lady Macbeth innocent of this intended murder, and yet from the fulness of a throbbing heart uttering what may render suspected the very thing he wishes to conceal, shews how deeply the author enters into human nature in general, and in every circumstance preserves the consistency of the character he exhibits.

How strongly is expressed the great truth that to a man of courage the most terrible object is the person he has injured, in the following address to Banquo's ghost. [Quotes 3.4.99ff.] It is impossible not to sympathize with the terrors Macbeth expresses in his disordered speech: 'It will have blood.—They say, blood will have blood. ...' [3.4.122ff.]

The perturbation with which Macbeth again resorts to the witches, and the tone of resentment and abhorrence with which he addresses them, rather expresses his sense of the crimes to which their promises excited him than any satisfaction in the regal condition those crimes had procured. (191–3) ...

Towards the conclusion of the piece his mind seems to sink under its load of guilt! Despair and melancholy hang on his words! We see he has griefs that press harder on him than his enemies, by his address to the physician: 'Canst thou not minister to a mind diseas'd' [5.3.40ff.] The alacrity with which he attacks young Siward, and his reluctance to engage with Macduff, of whose blood he says he has already had too much, compleat a character which is uniformly preserved from the opening of the fable, to its conclusion.—We find him ever answering to the first idea we were made to conceive of him.

The man of honour pierces through the traitor and the assassin. His mind loses its tranquillity by guilt, but never its fortitude in danger. His crimes presented to him, even in the unreal mockery of a vision or the harmless form of sleeping innocence, terrify him more than all his foes in arms. (194–5) . . .

There are many bombast speeches in the tragedy of *Macbeth*; and these are the lawful prize of the critic. But envy, not content to nibble at faults, strikes at its true object, the prime excellencies and perfections of the thing it would depreciate. [Voltaire's objections to the ghost-scenes are briefly refuted.]

The difference between a mind naturally prone to evil, and a frail one warped by force of temptations, is delicately distinguished in Macbeth and his wife. There are also some touches of the pencil that mark the male and female character. When they deliberate on the murder of the king the duties of host and subject strongly plead with him against the deed. She passes over these considerations; goes to Duncan's chamber resolved to kill him, but could not do it because, she says, he resembled her father while he slept. There is something feminine in this, and perfectly agreeable to the nature of the sex, who even when void of principle are seldom entirely divested of sentiment; and thus the poet who, to use his own phrase, had overstepped the modesty of nature in the exaggerated fierceness of her character, returns back to the line and limits of humanity, and that very judiciously, by a sudden impression which has only an instantaneous effect. Thus she may relapse into her former wickedness, and from the same susceptibility, by the force of other impressions, be afterwards driven to distraction. As her character was not composed of those gentle elements out of which regular repentance could be formed, it was well judged to throw her mind into the chaos of madness; and as she had exhibited wickedness in its highest degree of ferocity and atrociousness she should be an example of the wildest agonies of remorse. As Shakespeare could most exactly delineate the human mind in its regular state of reason so no one ever so happily caught its varying forms in the wanderings of delirium. . . .

This piece may certainly be deemed one of the best of Shakespeare's compositions, and though it contains some faulty speeches and one whole scene entirely absurd and improper,[1] which art might have corrected or lopped away; yet genius, powerful genius only (wild nature's vigour working at the root!), could have produced such strong and original beauties, and adapted both to

[1] The porter's scene.

341

the general temper and taste of the age in which it appeared. (199–203) . . .

[From chapter 8 'Upon the death of Julius Caesar'; Antony's funeral oration.] Is there any oration extant in which the topics are more skilfully selected for the minds and temper of the persons to whom it is spoken? Does it not by the most gentle gradations arrive at the point to which it was directed? (271) . . . The fickle humour of the people, and the influence of eloquence upon their minds, are truly exhibited; and I must own, as the imitation is so just, though the original may be called mean I think it is not to be entirely condemned: one might perhaps wish the part of the mob had been shorter. The miserable conceit of Cæsar's blood rushing out of the wound to ask who so unkindly knocked is indefensible. The repetition of the words 'honourable men' is perhaps too frequent.

The oration of Brutus in many parts is quaint and affected, an unhappy attempt, as the learned commentator observes,[1] to imitate that brevity and simplicity of expression of which this noble Roman was a professed admirer. Our author, who followed with great exactness every circumstance mentioned in Plutarch, would probably have attempted to give to Antony the pomp of Asiatic eloquence if his good sense had not informed him that to be pathetic it is necessary to be simple.

The quarrel between Brutus and Cassius does not by any means deserve the ridicule thrown upon it by the French critic. The characters of the men are well sustained; it is natural, it is interesting; but it rather retards than brings forward the catastrophe, and is useful only in setting Brutus in a good light. A sublime genius, in all its operations, sacrifices little things to great, and parts to the whole. Modern criticism dwells on minute articles. The principal object of our poet was to interest the spectator for Brutus; to do this he was to shew that his temper was the furthest imaginable from any thing ferocious or sanguinary, and by his behaviour to his wife, his friends, his servants, to demonstrate that out of respect to public liberty he made as difficult a conquest over his natural disposition as his great predecessor had done for the like cause over natural affection. Clemency and humanity add lustre to the greatest hero; but here these sentiments determine

[1] Warburton (3.244).

the whole character of the man and the colour of his deed. The victories of Alexander, Cæsar, and Hannibal, whether their wars were just or unjust, must obtain for them the laurel wreath which is the ambition of conquerors. But the act of Brutus in killing Cæsar was of such an ambiguous kind as to receive its denomination from the motive by which it was suggested; it is that which must fix upon him the name of patriot or assassin. Our author, therefore, shews great judgment in taking various opportunities to display the softness and gentleness of Brutus. The little circumstance of his forbearing to awaken the servant who was playing to him on the lute is very beautiful, for one cannot conceive that he whose tender humanity respected the slumber of his boy Lucilius would from malice or cruelty have cut short the important and illustrious course of Cæsar's life. (272–5) ...

As it was Shakespeare's intention to make Brutus his hero he has given a disadvantageous representation of Cæsar, and thrown an air of pride and insolence into his behaviour which is intended to create an apprehension in the spectator of his disposition to tyrannize over his fellow-citizens. In this haughty style he answers the petitions of Metellus Cimber and the other conspirators for the repeal of Publius Cimber's banishment. The speech suits the purpose of the poet, but is very blamable if compared with the historical character of the speaker, which ought certainly to have been more attended to. (277–8) ...

Mr. Voltaire, in all the comparisons he has made between these authors, has not taken into the account that Shakespeare has written the best comedy in our language: that the same man should have had such variety of talents as to have produced *Macbeth* and *The Merry Wives of Windsor* is astonishing. Where is there an instance among the ancients or moderns of one poet's uniting the sublime and pathetic, the boldest inventions of fiction and the most just and accurate delineation of characters; and also possessing the *vis comica* in its highest perfection? (284–5)

222. David Garrick, Jubilee *Ode* to Shakespeare

1769

An Ode upon Dedicating a Building and Erecting a Statue, to Shakespeare, at Stratford Upon Avon (1769).

The 'Building' was the Stratford Town Hall, which was to have been dedicated to Shakespeare during the 1769 Jubilee. The *Ode* was spoken by Garrick, as a recitative over string accompaniment, the airs and choruses sung (the music was by Thomas Arne). Garrick's model was William Havard's *Ode to the Memory of Shakespeare* (1756) (Vol. 4, pp. 289–91). For the background and for critical comment see C. Deelman, *The Great Shakespeare Jubilee* (1964), pp. 138–43, 214–25.

ADVERTISEMENT.

Could some gentlemen of approved ability have been prevailed upon to do justice to the subject of the following Ode,[1] the present apology would have been unnecessary;—but as it was requisite to produce something of this kind upon the occasion, and the lot having unluckily fallen on the person perhaps the least qualified to succeed in the attempt, it is hoped the candour of the public will esteem the performance rather as an act of duty, than vanity in the author.

As some news-paper writers have illiberally endeavoured to shake the poetic character of our immortal bard (too deeply indeed rooted in the heart to be affected by them) it is recommended to those who are not sufficiently established in their dramatic faith to peruse a work lately published called *An Essay on the Writings and Genius of* SHAKESPEARE, by which they will with much satisfaction be convinced that *England* may justly boast the honour of producing the greatest dramatic poet in the world.

[1] Garrick suggested this task to both Joseph and Thomas Warton, without success.

To strengthen and justify the general admiration of this astonishing Genius, it has been thought proper to subjoin to the Ode some undeniable Testimonies (both in prose and verse) of his unequalled original talents.[1]

If it shall be found that *speaking* that part of the Ode which has usually been conveyed in recitative produces a better effect, the Author flatters himself he may lay claim to some little merit on that account. As to the Ode itself, he presents it to the public as an object of their good-nature,—to his friends as an exercise of their partiality,—to his enemies as a lucky opportunity of venting their wit, humour, criticism, spleen or whatever else they please, should they think it worthy of their notice.

ODE

To what blest genius of the isle,
Shall Gratitude her tribute pay,
   Decree the festive day,
Erect the statue, and devote the pile?

Do not your sympathetic hearts accord,
   To own the 'bosom's lord?'
'Tis he! 'tis he!—that demi-god!
Who Avon's flow'ry margin trod,
   While sportive *Fancy* round him flew,
Where *Nature* led him by the hand,
   Instructed him in all she knew,
And gave him absolute command!
    'Tis he! 'tis he!
'The god of our idolatry!'
To him the song, the Edifice we raise,
He merits all our wonder, all our praise!
   Yet ere impatient joy break forth,
   To tell his name, and speak his worth,
   And to your spell-bound minds impart
   Some faint idea of his magic art;
   Let awful silence still the air!

---

[1] This, the first anthology of Shakespeare criticism, assembled many famous tributes, all of which are included in this present collection.

From the dark cloud, the hidden light
   Bursts tenfold bright!
  Prepare! prepare! prepare!
Now swell at once the choral song,
Roll the full tide of harmony along;
  Let Rapture sweep the trembling strings,
  And Fame expanding all her wings,
  With all her trumpet-tongues proclaim,
  The lov'd, rever'd, immortal name!
SHAKESPEARE! SHAKESPEARE! SHAKESPEARE!
   Let th' inchanting sound,
   From Avon's shores rebound;
    Thro' the Air,
    Let it bear,
The precious freight the envious nations round!

CHORUS.

  Swell the choral song,
Roll the tide of harmony along,
  Let Rapture sweep the strings,
  Fame expand her wings,
With her trumpet-tongues proclaim,
The lov'd, rever'd, immortal name!
SHAKESPEARE! SHAKESPEARE! SHAKESPEARE!

AIR.

I.

Sweetest bard that ever *sung,*
Nature's *glory,* Fancy's *child;*
Never sure did witching tongue,
Warble forth such wood-notes wild!

II.

Come each Muse, *and sister* Grace,
Loves *and* Pleasures *hither come;*

Well you know this happy place,
Avon's banks were once your home.

III.

Bring the laurel, bring the flow'rs,
Songs of triumph to him raise;
He united all your pow'rs,
All uniting, sing his praise!

Tho' *Philip*'s fam'd unconquer'd son,
Had ev'ry blood-stain'd laurel won;
He sigh'd—that his creative word,
    (Like that which rules the skies,)
Could not bid other nations rise,
To glut his yet unsated sword:

But when our SHAKESPEARE's matchless pen,
Like *Alexander*'s sword, had done with men;
  He heav'd no sigh, he made no moan,
    Not limited to human kind,
    He fir'd his wonder-teeming mind,
Rais'd other worlds, and beings of his own!

AIR.

When Nature, smiling, hail'd his birth,
To him unbounded pow'r was given;
The whirlwind's wing to sweep the sky,
  'The frenzy-rowling eye,
To glance from heav'n to earth,
  From earth to heav'n!'

O from his muse of fire
  Could but one spark be caught,
Then might these humble strains aspire,
  To tell the wonders he has wrought.
To tell,—how sitting on his magic throne,
    Unaided and alone,

In dreadful state,
The subject passions round him wait;
Who tho' unchain'd, and raging there,
He checks, inflames, or turns their mad career;
With that superior skill,
Which winds the fiery steel at will,
He gives the aweful word—
And they, all foaming, trembling, own him for their Lord.

With these his slaves he can controul,
Or charm the soul;
So realiz'd are all his golden dreams,
Of terror, pity, love, and grief,
Tho' conscious that the vision only seems,
The woe-struck mind finds no relief:
Ingratitude would drop the tear,
Cold-blooded age take fire,
To see the thankless children of old *Lear*,
Spurn at their king, and sire!
With *his* our reason too grows wild!
What nature had disjoin'd,
The poet's pow'r combin'd,
Madness and *age*, *ingratitude* and *child*.

Ye guilty, lawless tribe,
Escap'd from punishment, by art or bribe,
At *Shakespeare*'s bar appear!
No bribing, shuffling there—
His genius, like a rushing flood,
Cannot be withstood,
Out bursts the penitential tear!
The look appall'd, the crime reveals,
The marble-hearted monster feels,
Whose hand is stain'd with blood.

SEMI-CHORUS.

When law is weak, and justice fails,
The poet holds the sword and scales.

AIR.

Though crimes from death and torture fly,
The swifter muse,
Their flight pursues,
Guilty mortals more than die!
They live indeed, but live to feel
The scourge and wheel,
'On the torture of the mind they lie;'
Should harrass'd nature sink to rest,
The Poet wakes the scorpion in the breast,
Guilty mortals more than die!

When our *Magician*, more inspir'd,
By charms, and spells, and incantations fir'd,
Exerts his most tremendous pow'r;
The thunder growls, the heavens low'r,
And to his darken'd throne repair,
The *Demons* of the deep, and *Spirits* of the air!

But soon these horrors pass away,
Thro' storms and night breaks forth the day:
He smiles,—they vanish into air!
The buskin'd warriors disappear!
Mute the trumpets, mute the drums,
The scene is chang'd—*Thalia* comes,
Leading the nymph *Euphrosyne*,
Goddess of joy and liberty!
She and her sisters, hand in hand,
Link'd to a num'rous frolick band,
With roses and with myrtle crown'd,
O'er the green velvet lightly bound,
Circling the Monarch of th' inchanted land!

AIR.

I.

Wild, frantick with pleasure,
They trip it in measure,

349

To bring him their treasure,
    The treasure of joy.

II.

How gay is the measure,
How sweet is the pleasure,
How great is the treasure,
    The treasure of joy.

III.

Like roses fresh blowing,
Their dimpled-cheeks glowing,
His mind is o'erflowing;
    A treasure of joy!

IV.

His rapture perceiving,
They smile while they're giving,
He smiles at receiving,
    A treasure of joy.

With kindling cheeks, and sparkling eyes,
Surrounded thus, the Bard in transport dies;
    The little *Loves*, like bees,
    Clust'ring and climbing up his knees,
        His brows with roses bind;
    While *Fancy*, *Wit*, and *Humour* spread
    Their wings, and hover round his head,
        Impregnating his mind.
Which teeming soon, as soon brought forth,
    Not a tiny spurious birth,
        But out a mountain came,
    A mountain of delight!
LAUGHTER roar'd out to see the sight,
    And FALSTAFF was his name!

With sword and shield he, puffing, strides;
   The joyous revel-rout
   Receive him with a shout,
And modest *Nature* holds her sides:
No single pow'r the deed had done,
   But great and small,
Wit, Fancy, Humour, Whim, and *Jest,*
   The huge, mishapen heap impress'd;
   And lo—SIR JOHN!
   A compound of 'em all,
   A comic world in ONE.

AIR.

A world where all pleasures abound,
   So fruitful the earth,
   So quick to bring forth,
And the world too is wicked and round.

   As the well-teeming earth,
   With rivers and show'rs,
   Will smiling bring forth
   Her fruits and her flow'rs;
So FALSTAFF *will never decline;*
   Still fruitful and gay,
   He moistens his clay,
And his rain and his rivers are wine;
Of the world he has all, but its care;
   No load, but of flesh, will he bear;
   He laughs off his pack,
   Takes a cup of old sack,
And away with all sorrow and care.

Like the rich rainbow's various dyes,
Whose circle sweeps o'er earth and skies,
   The heav'n-born muse appears;
Now in the brighest colours gay,
Now quench'd in show'rs, she fades away,
   Now blends her smiles and tears.

Sweet *Swan of Avon!* ever may thy stream
Of tuneful numbers be the darling theme;
Not *Thames* himself, who in his silver course
  Triumphant rolls along,
 Britannia's riches and her force,
  Shall more harmonious flow in song.

O had those bards, who charm the list'ning shore
Of Cam and Isis, tun'd their classic lays,
 And from their full and precious store,
Vouchsaf'd to fairy-haunted *Avon* praise!
  (Like that kind bounteous hand*,
 Which lately gave the ravish'd eyes
   Of Stratford swains
   A rich command,
 Of widen'd river, lengthen'd plains,
   And opening skies)
Nor *Greek*, nor *Roman* streams would flow along,
More sweetly clear, or more sublimely strong,
Nor thus a shepherd's feeble notes reveal,
At once the weakest numbers, and the warmest zeal.

AIR.

I.

Thou soft-flowing Avon, *by thy silver stream,*
Of things more than mortal, sweet Shakespeare *would dream,*
The fairies by moonlight dance round his green bed,
For hallow'd the turf is which pillow'd his head.

II.

The love-stricken maiden, the soft-sighing swain,
Here rove without danger, and sigh without pain,

---

* The Duke of Dorset, [High Steward of the Borough], with the concurrence of Mr. Bradley [owner of the land], most generously ordered a great number of Trees to be cut down, to open the river *Avon* for the Jubilee.

The sweet bud of beauty, no blight shall here dread,
For hallow'd the turf is which pillow'd his head.

III.

Here youth shall be fam'd, for their love, and their truth,
And chearful old age, feel the spirit of youth;
For the raptures of fancy here poets shall tread,
For hallow'd the turf is that pillow'd his head.

IV.

Flow on, silver Avon, *in song ever flow,*
Be the swans on thy bosom still whiter than snow,
Ever full be thy stream, like his fame may it spread,
And the turf ever hallow'd which pillow'd his head.

Tho' bards with envy-aching eyes,
Behold a tow'ring eagle rise,
   And would his flight retard;
Yet each to *Shakespeare*'s genius bows,
Each weaves a garland for his brows,
   To crown th' heaven-distinguish'd Bard.
Nature had form'd him on her noblest plan,
And to the genius join'd the feeling man.
   What tho' with more than mortal art,
   Like *Neptune* he directs the storm,
Lets loose like winds the passions of the heart,
   To wreck the human form;
Tho' from his mind rush forth, the Demons to destroy,
His heart ne'er knew but love, and gentleness, and joy.

AIR.

More gentle than the southern gale,
Which softly fans the blossom'd vale,
And gathers on its balmy wing,
The fragrant treasures of the spring,

Breathing delight on all it meets,
'And giving, as it steals, the sweets.'

Look down blest SPIRIT from above,
With all thy wonted gentleness and love;
   And as the wonders of thy pen,
      By heav'n inspir'd,
      To virtue fir'd,
   The charm'd, astonish'd, sons of men!
With no reproach, even now, thou view'st thy work,
      To nature sacred as to truth,
   Where no alluring mischiefs lurk,
      To taint the mind of youth.
Still to thy native spot thy smiles extend,
And as thou gav'st it fame, that fame defend;
   And may no sacrilegious hand
   Near *Avon*'s banks be found,
   To dare to parcel out the land,
   And limit Shakespeare's hallow'd ground *.
For ages free, still be it unconfin'd,
As broad, and general, as thy boundless mind.

Can *British* gratitude delay,
   To him the glory of this isle,
   To give the festive day
The song, the statue, and devoted pile?
To him the first of poets, best of men?
'We ne'er shall look upon his like again!'

DUETT.

Shall the hero laurels gain,
For ravag'd fields, and thousands slain?
And shall his brows no laurels bind,
Who charms to virtue humankind?

* This alludes to a design of inclosing a large common field at *Stratford*.

CHORUS.

We will,—his brows with laurel bind,
Who charms to virtue human kind:
   Raise the pile, the statue raise,
   Sing immortal *Shakespeare*'s praise!
The song will cease, the stone decay,
     But his Name,
    And undiminish'd fame,
Shall never, never pass away.

223. Unsigned oration, *In honour of Shakespeare*

1769

This oration was printed in several newspapers at the time of the Stratford Jubilee, e.g. in *Lloyd's Evening Post*, 1–4 September 1769, as a piece 'intended to be spoken by Mr. Garrick'; subsequent writers believed that it had been spoken, or indeed written by Garrick, but Deelman (*op. cit*, pp. 231–2) shows that there is no evidence for either claim. This text is from R. B. Wheler, *History and Antiquities of Stratford-upon-Avon* (Stratford, n.d. [1806]), pp. 191–6. In her *Garrick's Jubilee* (Columbus, Ohio, 1964), pp. 127–42, M. W. England attributes it to Burke on stylistic grounds, but without any certainty; the same identification had been made by the Victorian critic, Charles Knight.

AN ORATION IN HONOUR OF SHAKESPEARE

'*The only science of mankind is man.*' This is the aphorism of an author who has been equally admired as a philosopher and a poet;

and if it is allowed that man is the fittest object of our study, the drama, which exhibits the passions and pursuits of man, stands in the first class of literary composition. Shakespeare is, above all others, allowed to be the poet of nature; and therefore as an author he stands highest in the highest class. The beings exhibited by the poet of nature are *men*. They are not creatures of the imagination, acting from principles by which human actions were never produced and suffering distress which human beings never suffered, but partakers of the same nature with ourselves, to whose hearts our own sensations are a clue; beings of like passions, impelled by the same hopes and fears, and sacrificing virtue to interest or interest to virtue as circumstances concur with disposition, and opinion connects present and immediate good and evil with future, either by necessary consequence or judicial determination.

But the contemplation of man, as exhibited by the poet upon the stage, is of more advantage than as passing before us in the scenes of life. In the world we see only the actions of mankind, and before we can infer any useful knowledge from them we must investigate their motives, and often suspend our judgment of the consequences till they appear in a distant event. But in the scenes where men are exhibited by the poet we see at once their action and its secret springs, which being thus connected, as effect and cause, we are afterwards able to refer conduct into passions and principles. We see also upon the stage the final events in which the whole concatenation of motive and action terminates; which enable us to look through life with a kind of prescient sagacity, and discover the effects of human action in their cause.

But Shakespeare does not only teach us what it is most our interest to know; for by the very manner in which he conveys the most important knowledge he gives us the most rational, refined, and exquisite delight. He has not delineated a chart but painted a picture. He shews us the path of life, not by geometrical line but by perspective and elevation. He does not personify human passions and exhibit them, either separate or combined, as they would appear abstracted from the modes of life; he '*catches the manners living as they rise.*' He paints character not merely as resulting from different turns of disposition and degrees of understanding, but from situation and habit. Their passions and principles are indeed general, but they act and speak with the peculiarities of a class, though not of an individual. Shallow and Falstaff differ as much in consequence of circumstances, that made one a justice and one a soldier, as of any radical and native turn of mind; and the originals in nature, from which these portraits were drawn, are as well known now as they were then. The difference which custom has produced in the language and modes of life is but like different dresses, in which the same air and features will always be distinguished. Justice Shallow is still to be found, though he has changed his coat; he still boasts of midnight frolics, though it is not now the custom of rakes to sleep in the windmill in St. George's Fields; and of familiarity with the great, though there is no object of puny ambition called John of Gaunt.

We get knowledge from Shakespeare, not with painful labour as we dig gold from the mine, but at leisure and with delight, as we gain health and vigour from the sports of the field. A picture frequently pleases which represents an object that in itself is disgustful. Teniers represents a number of Dutch boors, drunk and quarreling in a wretched hovel, and we admire the piece for a kind of relative beauty, as a just imitation of life and nature. With this beauty we are struck in Shakespeare; we know his originals, and contemplate the truth of his copy with delight.

It was happy for Shakespeare, and for us, that in his time there was no example by the imitation of which he might hope to be approved. He painted nature as it appeared to his own eye, and not from a transcript of what was seen in nature by another. The genius looks not *upon* nature but *through* it; not at the outline only but the differences, nice and innumerable within it: at all that the variation of tints, and the endless combinations of light and shade can express. As the power of perception is more, more is still perceived in the inexhaustible varieties of life; but to copy only what another has seen is to render superior perspicacity vain, and neither the painter nor the poet can hope to excel who is content to reflect a reflection, and to seek for nothing in nature which others have not found.

But there are beauties in Shakespeare not relative; powers that do not imitate, but create. *He was as another nature*: he represents not only actions that were not performed but beings that do not exist. Yet to these beings he assigns not only faculties but character; he gives them not only peculiar dispositions but characteristic modes of expressing them. They have character not merely from

357

the passions and understanding, but from situation and habit. Caliban and Ariel, like Shallow and Falstaff, are not more strongly distinguished in consequence of different natures, than of different circumstances and employments.

As there was no poet to seduce Shakespeare into imitation there was no critic to restrain his extravagance; yet we find the force of his own judgment sufficient to rein his imagination, and reduce to system the new world which he made.

Does any one now enquire whether Shakespeare was learned? Do they mean whether he knew how to call the same thing by several names? for learning, with respect to language, teaches no more. Learning in its best sense is only nature at the rebound, it is only the discovery of what is; and he who looks upon nature with a penetrating eye derives learning from the source. Rules of poetry have been deduced from examples, and not examples from rules. As a poet, therefore, Shakespeare did not need books; and in no instance in which he needed them as a philosopher or historian does he appear ignorant of what they teach.

His language, like his conceptions, is strongly marked with the characteristic of nature: it is bold, figurative, and significant. His terms, rather than his sentences, are metaphorical. He calls an endless multitude a sea, by a happy allusion to the perpetual succession of wave to wave; and he immediately expresses opposition by taking up arms; which, being fit in itself, he was not solicitous to accomodate to his first image. This is the language in which a figurative and rapid conception will always be expressed: this is the language both of the prophet and the poet, of native eloquence and divine inspiration.

It has been objected to Shakespeare that he wrote without any moral purpose, but I boldly reply that he has effected a thousand. He has not, indeed, always contrived a series of events from the whole of which some moral precept may be inferred, but he has conveyed some rule of conduct, some principle of knowledge, not only in almost every speech of his dialogue but in every incident, character, and event. Thus great was Shakespeare as he appears in his *works*; but in *himself* he was greater still. The genius in every art has an idea of perfection which he cannot attain: this idea, beyond what others can conceive, and a perpetual effort to reach it produce that excellence which distinguishes his works.

But Shakespeare appears to have despised his performances when he compared them not only with his ideas but his powers; for how else can we account for his taking no care to collect them? When he saw part of them corruptly published by others he neither amended the faults nor secured the rest from the same injury. It appears, therefore, 'that he judged those works unworthy to be preserved, by restoring and explaining which the critics of succeeding ages were to contend for fame.'

Thus, without the incentive of future reputation, without any other exertion of his powers than would satisfy an audience wholly unacquainted with the drama, he has excited universal admiration, as the sun becomes glorious by the spontaneous effusions of his rays.

Is there any here whose attention has been fixed, whose imagination filled and whose passions moved by other scenes, as they have been fixed, filled, and moved by the scenes of Shakespeare? 'If there be any, speak! for him have I offended.'

To feel the powers of Shakespeare is at once pleasure and praise; when we express this sensibility, therefore, by an act of homage to his memory, we erect a monument of honour to ourselves; to ourselves indeed, and to posterity, who may be stimulated to excellence by the hope of fame, all that we nominally offer to the manes of Shakespeare must eventually relate. In these fields where we are pleased with the notion of doing him honour *he* is mouldering into dust; 'Deaf the prais'd ear, and mute the tuneful tongue.' How awful is the thought!—Let me pause;—if I speak, it must be in my own character, and in your's. We are men; and we know that the hour approaches with silent but irresistible rapidity when *we* also shall be dust. We are now in health and at ease; but the hour approaches when we shall be sensible only to sickness and to pain; when we shall perceive the world gradually to fade from our sight, and close our eyes in perpetual darkness.

These truths we know to be indubitable and important, yet they are sometimes forgotten; and, stranger still, are sometimes remembered with indifference. Let me, by whom the Poet of Avon has so often touched the heart with imaginary woe, be now forgiven if, unassisted by his language or his thought, I have tried the force of reality and truth. If at this moment we not only know but feel that where Shakespeare is we shortly shall be, let us preserve the sacred sensibility which will never imbitter the enjoyments of life, if it effectually reminds us of its use.

224. Unsigned essay, on the deficiencies of English drama

1769

From the *Oxford Magazine*, iii (1769), pp. 249–50.

The lack of sympathy with popular or vernacular culture, and the persistence of the notion of 'Ancients versus Moderns' are perhaps representative of academic taste in this period.

Cursory Strictures on the English Drama

Human Improvement rises to a greater or less degree of excellence in proportion to the nobleness or meanness of the ruling principle which keeps the society together. A community that has acquired its greatness by conquest must naturally carry the more elevated passions of the mind to a higher pitch of elegance and perfection than nations that have derived their consequence and power from skill in manufactures and assiduity in commerce. Hence it is that, though we perhaps excel the Greeks and Romans in the conveniences which suit the ease of the body, we are far from equalling either in those productions of genius that do honour to the mind.

There is not one branch of liberal knowledge that we have carried to greater perfection than the ancients, excepting mathematicks; and that science depends more upon a high improvement of the vulgar arts than on an elevation of sentiment. In history, poetry, and rhetorick, we are left far behind them. In the first we are diffuse, inaccurate, and in-elegant; in the second turgid, conceited and unequal; and the popular government of this country, contrary to all others of the same kind, has substituted dry, unimpassioned, and incorrect declamation in the place of eloquence.

It has been often remarked by ourselves, with more partiality than truth, that theatrical entertainment is carried to a higher pitch with us than among the Greeks and Romans, that our poets have more genius, a more extensive knowledge of human nature, and in short that the English Drama is in every respect superior to that of the two most deservedly celebrated nations of antiquity. Though an assertion of this kind is apt to make a man of real taste smile, I believe more than ninety nine in an hundred, were we to collect the suffrage of the inhabitants of the dirty lanes of this city, would determine the question in favour of the present times. The great vulgar in this join issue with the small; and being strangers to elevation as well as elegance of sentiment, prefer the ribaldry of a clown in Shakespeare to the terse manner of Terence or the pathos of Euripides.

Theatrical amusements, when well conducted, are not only rational in themselves but have a great and good effect upon the genius of the people. When they are calculated to please the vicious appetites of the populace in order to fill the pockets of individuals, they are not only disgustful to men who amidst the general corruption have the misfortune of possessing a good taste, but they even render the mean manners of the times more depraved. A picture of human life in its most pleasing attitudes, or a transcript of the passions of the mind in their most elevated form, mend the manners of an age and exalt the national character. Language without wit, humour, or sentiment, and scenes without character in Comedy; mere rhodomontade instead of sublimity, antithetical conceits in the place of pathos in Tragedy, are a ridicule upon genius and vitiate the minds of an audience.

It was the misfortune of the English Drama that it had its origin in an age prior to the establishment of taste in modern Europe. In the reigns of Elizabeth and James conceit was wit, and absurdity humour. The nation having no formed idea of composition required none in their Poets. The irregularity and desultory manner of Shakespeare could not disgust a people whose taste had not been formed upon the correct model of the ancients; and his uncommon manner of expression and obsolete

361

phrases passed as good Poetry upon men who place its excellence in language far removed from what is called the *Soluta Oratio* by Horace. His many beauties, like gems strewed on mud, became obscured; and had they even retained their native lustre they must have remained unobserved by a Gothic age and nation.

When Dryden, who is justly called the great High Priest of all the Nine, began to write for the stage he found the current of manners too strong for him to attempt to stem it with rational and natural composition. His necessity obliged him to give way to the times; and he, the most capable to remove the stigma of absurdity from the English Drama, became an addition to its disgrace.

The men of genius in the beginning of the present age had either no turn for Dramatic composition, or did not chuse to trust their reputation to the judgment of a vitiated and mean audience. The pert wit of Congreve and the obscenity of Wycherley kept possession of the scene, and could not fail to please the frivolous and the vicious. The mass of an English audience, like a herd of cattle, excepting in a few rooted prejudices for favourite absurdities, were the dupes of some leading but shallow critics; till what they did not understand became their delight through the mere force of habit. Whilst our rivals in Letters as well as Arms, the French, adopted the pure simplicity of the ancients we, with peculiar perverseness, construed into real beauties the absurdities of our first Dramatic Writers and formed our judgment of excellence upon their manner.

It is scarcely thirty years since the Plays of Shakespeare emerged from the obscurity which our Dramatic Writers in the seventeenth century had thrown over them. Men of genius discovered those beauties which are sown up and down through the irregular chaos of his dramatic romances. They were lavish in his praise, and the bulk of the nation, who had no judgment of their own, received him in gross as a complete writer. Our Theatres have ever since resounded with his applause; and though his excellence consists in things which are by no means understood by such people as now frequent our theatres it is the fashion to clap, and the flock will invariably follow habit, their great bell-wether, both in praise and dislike. Where men of taste would admire the wit of Falstaff, the humour with the multitude lies in his stuffed belly, and the joke is literally in Ancient Pistol's great Jack Boots.

225. Charles Jennens, on editing *King Lear*

1770

From *King Lear. A tragedy. By Wm. Shakespeare. Collated with the old and modern editions* (1770).

Charles Jennens (1700–73) succeeded to his estate at Gospall, Leicester in 1747, where he lived in great state, to the amusement or disapproval of his contemporaries. He was a loyal friend of Handel, whom he supported in financial difficulties and defended from enemies. In 1740 he arranged Milton's *Allegro* and *Penseroso* to be set to music by Handel, also writing the texts for *Saul* (1735), *The Messiah* (1742), and *Belshazzar* (1745). Starting to edit Shakespeare late in life, after *Lear* he issued *Macbeth*, *Othello*, and *Hamlet* in 1773; *Julius Cæsar* appeared posthumously in 1774.

PREFACE.

It will appear to any one who will give himself the trouble of examination that no fair and exact collation of *Shakespeare* hath yet been presented to the public. Great were the hopes that Mr. *Capell*'s edition would have at length gratified their curiosity in giving them with his text the various readings of the old editions in one view, that every reader might be furnished with materials to judge, and that with ease and readiness, what might be *Shakespeare*'s and what not. But so far from such a desirable end being answered by his edition, we are only farther led in the dark thereby; and are held in trust for notes, which might much better have been inserted with the text. But he was afraid his notes placed with the text should spoil the beauty of the book. If they are good ones they would not: for that man must be greatly mistaken in his ideas of beauty who prefers the handsome appearance of a page in black and white to the quick and easy information of his readers in matters necessary to be known for their becoming proper judges of the sense of the author, and the goodness of the edition. Would not Mr. *Capell*'s readers have been much more obliged to him if with the text he had given his notes, which (supposing them valuable) would in such a situation have had additional value, in being easily perused without the trouble of turning over pages and interrupting, for a longer time than was necessary, their way through the author?—for this will be the case when his notes do appear.

His method in compiling the text was to print after what he thought the best edition of each play, with such alterations as he saw fit to make, giving notice what those alterations were. And he proposes hereafter, in his *School of Shakespeare*, to give his reasons for preferring the particular edition he makes use of. But this is far from being the best method; for it is evident that one edition, though the best, may be in many places corrected by another, though a worse edition; and the several editions are a mutual help to each other—or why do editors collate? And if they do collate, why do they not publish their collations so that their readers may be in possession of them? No editor that I know of has a right to impose upon every body his own favourite reading, or to give his own conjectural interpolation without producing the readings of the several editions. The editor who does so, though he may be a good critic, will not be looked upon as a fair dealer: for after all the public will be the judge, and will censure every editor according as he has abused or disabused it.

What the public is here presented with is only one play of *Shakespeare*, faithfully collated, line by line, with the old as well as modern editions; the different readings whereof are given with notes at the bottom of the page. ... This play is published as a specimen, which if approved of the work will be pursued (health and opportunity permitting) through the whole of *Shakespeare*'s dramatic works. 'Tis no doubt a slavish business to proceed through so many editions of so voluminous a writer in the slow and exact manner this editor hath done in *King Lear*, and proposes to do in the rest of *Shakespeare*'s plays; and though it is a work that seemed absolutely necessary, yet nothing but the merit of the author and the approbation of his admirers could inspire one with patience to undergo so laborious a task. (i–v) ...

[From the Notes]

[On *King Lear*, 1.1.123: 'Hence, and avoid my sight!']
'All the modern editions direct the words, *Hence, and avoid*

my sight, to be spoken to *Cordelia*; but they are undoubtedly addressed to *Kent*. For in the next words *Lear* sends for *France* and *Burgundy* in order to tender them his youngest daughter, if either of them would accept her without a dowry. At such a time therefore to drive her out of his presence would be a contradiction to his declared intention.' *Heath*.

And for that very reason I think, with submission, the words are spoken to *Cordelia*, and not to *Kent*. It is plain, *Cordelia* had raised his fury to the highest pitch; *Kent* was not yet so far advanced; he had but just begun to speak, and that in the most respectful terms, *Good my liege* [1.1.120].—*Lear*, with all his rage, still retained so much love and respect for him, and so much hope of diverting him from the attempt he saw he was beginning, to dissuade him from his resolution of disinheriting *Cordelia*, that he warns him of the danger of continuing it—*Come not between the dragon and his wrath* [121]; and even after proceeding in it, when *Kent* interrupted him a second time and resumed his addresses, *Lear* also continued his warning—*The bow is bent and drawn, make from the shaft* [142]. *Kent*, seeing that respectful behaviour had no effect, has recourse to rougher language: even after that *Lear* thinks to make him cease by a severe and passionate prohibition—*Kent, on thy life no more* [153]. *Kent* still persists, and urges his own inflexible loyalty as a reason for his being heard: *Lear* then first bids him *out of my sight* [156]; *Kent* further intreats, *Lear* swears, *Kent* returns the oath [159], and at last urges his reproaches with such vehemence that *Lear*, despairing of silencing him any other way, pronounces the final sentence of banishment upon him [166ff.]. This is the natural, not the designed gradation of *Lear*'s anger. It rises by degrees to its height, and at last falls with its full weight. These steps by which it advances shew a reluctance in the king to be so severe upon one for whom he had the greatest regard: whereas the imaginary breach of filial love and duty which he foolishly fancied he found in *Cordelia* had already extinguished all sparks of his *imaginary* love to her. The contradiction to his declared intention is the natural effect of his rage, which vented itself in sudden and contrary starts of passion. The whole scene, in this view, I take to be one of the most beautiful in all *Shakespeare*.—Neither Quartos nor Folios have any direction in this place. (8–9) . . .

[*Ibid.*, 1.1.220f.: 'or you for vouch'd affections/Fall'n into taint']
So the Quartos; the Folios read *Or your fore-voucht affection fall*

into taint, &c. Rowe, Pope and Hanmer read *Or your fore-voucht affection could not fall into taint*, &c. Theobald and Warburton, *Or your fore-vouch'd affection fall'n into taint*, &c. Johnson reads as the Folios, but interprets *or* before, because *or ever* signifies *before ever*; but does he remember where *or* had at any time this signification unless joined with *ever?* Rowe seems to make the best sense of all these readings, but then he is obliged to interpolate. But let us now try the old reading; and to make sense of it the best way perhaps will be to consider what was the real cause of the estrangement of *Lear's* love from *Cordelia*. It was the *vouch'd affections* of his three daughters: the two eldest vouch'd such affection to him as was beyond all nature and possibility to a father; but *Cordelia* vouched only such an affection as was natural and reasonable for a daughter to feel for her father. Now *Lear* was *fallen into taint*, i.e. his judgment was corrupted in preferring the extravagant and lying protestations of his eldest daughters to the sincere and just ones of his youngest. And if we ruminate a little, this is only the second reason for *Lear's* rejecting *Cordelia* that can with any probability be supposed to be guessed at by *France*: for it would be rude in *France* to charge *Lear* with vouching the dearest affections to one he did not really love; and it is absurd to suppose that so great a love should change to hate, without she had committed some very great crime, and which *France* could not be brought to believe; therefore this second guess becomes the only one, and the true one, viz. that *Regan* and *Goneril* had, by their superior art in coaxing, won all *Lear's* love from *Cordelia*. (16)

[*Ibid.*, 1.1.225f.]

> *Cordelia.* ... since what I well intend,
> I'll do't before I speak—that you may know ...

The Folios (followed by all the rest) read *that you make known*, to make it grammar with *I yet beseech your majesty*: but I am apt to think *Shakespeare* intended this as a broken speech, which should express the modest fear and bashful diffidence of *Cordelia*, heightened by her concern under her present pitiable circumstances. She begins speaking to the king in a broken interrupted manner; then to *France*, *that you may know*, &c. then, without making a period, to the king again. (17)

226. William Duff, Shakespeare's genius

1770

From *Critical Observations on the Writings of the Most Celebrated Original Geniuses in Poetry* (1770).

William Duff (1732–1815), Scottish minister (of Foveran, Aberdeenshire, from 1774 onwards), published *An Essay on Original Genius* in 1767 (which anticipates some of the ideas worked out here), an oriental tale, *The History of Rhedi, the Hermit of Mount Ararat* in 1773, two volumes of sermons in 1786, and *Letters on the Intellectual and Moral Character of Women* in 1807. As a Shakespeare critic he is typical of the vague enthusiasm which produced its responses in reaction to such concepts as 'taste' or 'genius'

SECT. III: OF SHAKESPEARE.

Having endeavoured, as far as the limited nature of our plan would allow, to point out and to exemplify the distinguishing characters of original Genius as they appear in Homer and Ossian, we shall next proceed to consider the merits of Shakespeare.

As the Genius of this extraordinary person was perfectly excentric and irregular, and his excellencies are of a very peculiar kind, it is indeed scarce possible to give a complete view of his character as a poet. ... His talent in the invention of incidents therefore is first to be considered by us.

Were we to estimate the Genius of Shakespeare by the number of incidents which he has really invented, we should not be apt to rank him among the most complete originals; nor could he bear to stand in competition with Homer, or even with poets of far inferior merit. But we ought not to form our opinion of his abilities in this way, by what he hath actually performed ... but on what we have reason to think, from a view of the extent of his Genius displayed in a higher species of *invention*, he could have performed had he chosen to employ the powers of his mind in the manner above mentioned.

We have already allowed that the invention of a variety of new and surprizing incidents is an indication of the exertion of original Genius in a very considerable degree, but we have also shewn that the invention and just exhibition of supernatural characters in particular, is a certain proof of a still higher exertion of this quality. If Shakespeare therefore excelled in the last more difficult effort of Genius, he might doubtless have excelled in the first if he had thought it proper to have attempted it. ... [Ossian, wishing to celebrate 'the most distinguished heroes of his own age', was limited to 'real facts'.] Shakespeare, on the other hand, acquainted with a much greater variety of surprizing events collected from history and tradition, set himself to work up an affecting representation of these in the drama, not thinking it necessary for the most part to invent others, as the incidents he had acquired in the manner above mentioned were in general very much adapted to please and to astonish the mind. In the exhibition of supernatural and ideal characters however the case is far otherwise. ... (126–9)

The fourth act of *Macbeth* opens with a scene calculated to produce an inexplicable kind of emotion, participating of dread and horror. It exhibits the witches in a dark cave marching round a burning cauldron, throwing in the ingredients of their charms and pronouncing their infernal incantations. [Quotes the witches' scene, 4.1.] Such ingredients, and such a composition, we are persuaded no man ever heard of before; but the Genius of Shakespeare delighted in the most uncommon and astonishing combinations of ideas, and it never appears with so much strength and advantage as when he bursts into the ideal world, and presents to our view the characters and offices of supernatural beings, in which highest exertion of Genius he hath in most instances indeed never been equalled.

The last sort of ideal characters to be considered by us is the fairy species, in the description of which Shakespeare hath given full scope to the exuberance of his creative Genius. [Quotes 'Over hill, over dale,' *Midsummer Night's Dream*, 2.1.2ff.] Every reader must observe that the above description which the fairy gives of his employment is distinguished by its vivacity and wildness. The lightness and volatility of these visionary beings seems to be imitated in the quick returns, and (if we may use the expression) brisk boundings of the verse.

How strangely picturesque and original is the description of the employments enjoined by Titania to her fairies, in the third scene of the third act! [Quotes 'Be kind and courteous to this gentleman', 3.1.150ff.] We observed in the section on original Poetic Genius in a preceding work that wildness of description was the pastime of a great Genius. In the above passage the imagination of Shakespeare seems to wanton and sport in exuberance. Who but this author ever thought of such fairy courtesies as stealing the honey bags from the bees, cropping their waxen thighs to make tapers, lighting them at the glow-worm's eyes, and plucking the wings of butterflies to fan the moon beams from the eyes of one asleep? These employments, so fanciful and so wild, are however at the same time perfectly apposite to the imagined nature and qualities of the fairy species.

These few examples will be sufficient to give us an idea of Shakespeare's creative Genius, discovered in the invention and exhibition of supernatural characters. We altogether omit the consideration of his great merit in the just representation of human characters because, though in his management of these he has discovered a surprizing degree of originality, it is in the display of ideal characters alone that he has discovered the full force of his Genius.

We shall next consider Shakespeare's talent in the invention and adaption of the images of Poetry.

A tragic Poet is not allowed to use the ornament of imagery so frequently as other classes of Poets, because his principal object is not to produce admiration but to excite terror and pity. Images therefore ought never to be introduced in tragedy when the affections are wrought up to a high pitch or motion; for then they have a bad effect by contributing to break or at least to divert the tide of passion. Though Shakespeare has in several instances violated this rule by admitting affected metaphors and similitudes very much out of time and place, yet for the most part he has used them with great propriety, efficacy and beauty. Let us adduce a few examples. The following image is remarkable for its justness, elegance, and resemblance in every point of similitude to the object with which it is compared.

> The charm dissolves apace,
> And as the morning steals upon the night,
> Melting the darkness, so their rising senses

> Begin to chase the ignorant fumes that mantle
> Their clearer reason.   *Tempest* [5.1.64ff.]

... Our sympathy for the wretched though worthless Cleopatra is strongly excited by a single image alluding to the manner of her death.

> Dost thou not see my baby at my breast,
> That sucks the nurse asleep?
>   *Ant. and Cleop.* [5.2.307f.]

The beauty of an image sometimes depends upon a contrariety of effect in the object with which it is compared, when there is at the same time a resemblance in some of the essential particulars. The above passage affords an example of this, as it is the contrast betwixt the effects of suckling a child and the effects of the asp's sucking the vital blood which renders the image peculiarly affecting. In the passage quoted below the reader will observe that the sentiment receives an additional dignity from the image in which it is conveyed. Patroclus exhorting Achilles to resume his valour, thus expresses his importunate request.

> O rouse yourself! and the weak wanton Cupid
> Shall from your neck unloose his am'rous fold,
> And like a dew-drop from the lion's mane
> Be shook to air.   *Troil. and Cress.* [3.3.222ff.]
>   (140-9)

... Let us next adduce some examples of pathetic sentiment. No Poet ever knew better how to penetrate and to melt the heart than Shakespeare. A few passages culled out from his writings will convince us of his power over the passions. Queen Margaret and her son prince Edward having been taken prisoners after the battle of Tewksbury; and the latter having been slain by the usurper Edward, and his brothers Clarence and Gloucester in his mother's presence, the unhappy queen addresses a speech to her dead son and to his murderers, animated with those abrupt and violent workings of passion which we may suppose naturally to have arisen in her mind upon such a dreadful occasion. The tender, but strong affections of the mother first discover themselves.

> Oh Ned! sweet Ned! speak to thy mother, boy.
> Canst thou not speak?   [3 *Henry VI*, 5.5.51ff.]

This is the language of nature. The first transport of grief allows her not time to reflect that he is dead, or to brand his murderers with the crime which they had committed. She utters her first sentiments in short exclamations to her son; but receiving no answer she as naturally vents the rage of her passion upon the perpetrators of the horrid deed, who were standing before her.

> O traitors! murderers! ...
> Butchers and villains, bloody cannibals,
> How sweet a plant have you untimely cropt?
> Have you no children, butchers? [52, 61ff.]

The epithets she bestows on the murderers of Edward are strongly expressive of their aggravated guilt, and the question 'Have you no children, butchers?' is peculiarly poignant and emphatical, as it serves at once to show the violence of queen Margaret's grief and rage, and to represent their crime as enormous in the highest degree by intimating an impossibility of conceiving any persons who had ever felt the emotions of parental affection capable of committing it. (153–5) ...

An irregular greatness, wildness, and enthusiasm of imagination were the last mentioned ingredients of an exalted and original Genius in Poetry. The compositions of Shakespeare, beyond those of any other author, are distinguished by the above mentioned properties to such a degree that they may be said to constitute their ruling character. ... [Quotes 'Is this a dagger which I see before me', *Macbeth*, 2.1.33ff.] It is impossible to read this soliloquy without feeling an emotion of horror arising in our minds, which is greatly heightened by the circumstances of the aerial dagger with drops of blood upon it appearing to Macbeth and pointing out to him the way he was to go. We can characterize this strangely horrific representation no way so properly as to say that it is irregularly great and wild, proceeding from a noble boldness and enthusiasm of imagination. (165–7) ...

[On the 'three greatest geniuses': Homer, Shakespeare, Ossian]
If I should be required to point out that single quality which appears most remarkably to predominate in the character of each of those divine bards respectively, I would say that ... Shakespeare discovers the strength of his Genius most signally in a

certain wild and picturesque manner of describing every object he intends to exhibit, which is indeed peculiar to himself. ... In Homer and Ossian this quality ['wildness of description'] breaks forth for the most part in sudden and interrupted flashes; but in Shakespeare it is one continued blaze, and shines forth with distinguished lustre in his *Tempest*, his *Midsummer Night's Dream*, in *Romeo and Juliet*, in *Hamlet*, and in *Macbeth*. If we were to distinguish the different species of this quality in which those divine bards severally excelled, I think we might observe that Homer in the *Odyssey* discovers the wildness of his fancy in that kind of description which wraps us in a pleasing and enchanting delirium, of which we have fine examples in his representation of the grotto of Calypso, the gardens of Alcinous, and the bower of Circe; that Ossian mixes the solemn with the wild, and impresses our minds with awe at the same time that he overwhelms them with astonishment; and that Shakespeare's wildness is principally characterized by a certain sportiveness of fancy, which delights to riot and wanton in its own exuberance. (184–9) ...

Shakespeare has been much happier in his fame than Ossian; but in this respect has been far inferior to Homer. His inferiority of reputation hath arisen more from the local prevalence of the English language, and the uncultivated taste of the age in which he lived, than from any real inferiority of merit. The age of queen Elizabeth, however justly renowned for the wisdom of her councils and the terror of her arms, was certainly not the æra of correct and refined taste; and it may not be amiss to observe that the writings of Shakespeare, with all their uncommon excellence, have taken a strong tincture of the antithesis, the witticisms, and the rudeness of the times; a circumstance which, if properly attended to, will account for and extenuate the far greatest part of the blemishes which have been imputed to him.

Want of learning or rather knowledge of the learned languages, hath been considered by many as a great disadvantage to Shakespeare; but it should seem to have been very improperly considered as such. For my own part I am persuaded that had Shakespeare's learning been greater his merit as a Poet had been less. Conscious of the greatness of his own powers, he had no occasion for the advantitious aid of books and the observations of others. He had nothing to do but to look upon nature and man, and he at one glance caught a perfect idea of every object and character which he viewed, of which his imagination enabled him to present a complete resemblance; as well as by its creative power to present objects and characters which never existed in nature, nor in any human imagination but his own. A constant attendance to the rigid rules of criticism would probably at least have damped the divine spirit which frequently breaks forth in his writings, and gives them their chief value. However much we may condemn his faults we are astonished and delighted with those Master-strokes of nature and character which are the efforts of the unaided strength of his own Genius.

The fame of Shakespeare was neither in his own time, nor has been since, equal to his distinguished merit, though in the present age his writings are very generally admired. The reputation which these have already required is daily increasing, and will increase; and being so justly founded, we may be assured that it will be as permanent as great. (194-6)

227. Francis Gentleman, Shakespeare the dramatist

1770

From *The Dramatic Censor; or, Critical Companion* (2 vols, 1770).

Francis Gentleman (1728–84), an Irishman who served for a time in the army, was an actor, appearing with Thomas Sheridan at Smock Alley, Dublin, with Macklin at Chester (where he produced an adaptation of *Sejanus*), with Simpson at Bath (adapting and producing *Richard II*), and with Samuel Foote. He wrote several plays, and supplied the introduction and notes to Bell's 'acting edition' of Shakespeare in 1774.

Of the nearly 1,000 pages of Gentleman's book some 300 are devoted to Shakespeare: in addition to the plays represented here he discusses *Richard III* (in Cibber's adaptation), *Othello*, *Romeo and Juliet*, *The Merchant of Venice*, *As You Like It*, *Julius Cæsar*, *Cymbeline*, *King John*, *Much Ado About Nothing*, *Henry V*, and 1 *Henry IV*.

Introduction

Criticism is undoubtedly the most elaborate and ungracious of all literary compositions. Passing censure must ever be painful to a liberal mind, and has no palliation, no balancing pleasure but contrasted praise. However, the general advantages arising from candid investigation, equally separated from partial indulgence or malevolent severity, deserve some degree of honest approbation, and strengthen the feelings to undertake with becoming resolution so hazardous a task. . . .

The hallowed shrine of Shakespeare every friend of intrinsic merit must approach with reverence. Yet why, amidst the meridian blaze of his brightness, should we decline discovering and pointing out those dark spots which his genius shares in common with the sun? Implicit admiration, as well as implicit faith, argues a narrowness or sycophancy of mind which we hope ourselves free from, and shall, as much as possible, follow that excellent maxim, *to extenuate nothing, nor to set down aught in malice*.

To pursue all the nice and intricate distinctions of classical criticism would occasion prolixity, appeal only to the judgments of learned readers, and therefore be totally incompatible with our design; which is merely to try each drama as a picture of nature, at the bar of nature; and the manners of those nations where the scene of each is laid.

Well knowing how insipid prefatory matter generally is, thus much only is offered by way of Introduction; and we hope the candid reader will from hence suggest whatever else may seem essential. (I, 1–3).

HAMLET

The opening of this tragedy is extremely well devised. The time of night, the place, the characters, and what they speak, all most naturally concur to raise an awful preparatory apprehension for the appearance of that supernatural agent on whom the main

374

action totally depends; and indeed so artfully has Shakespeare wrought upon his great patroness, nature, so powerfully does he engage our passions upon this occasion that even those who laugh at the idea of ghosts as old womens' tales cannot avoid lending an eye and ear of serious attention to this of Hamlet's father. . . .

The singularity of Hamlet's appearance as a mourner, when all the rest of the court are in a state of festivity and congratulation, raises our idea of his filial affection and concern; his indifferent, contemptuous replies to the King, and his catching so eagerly at the word *seems* used by his mother, are a happy commencement of his character. Laertes's soliciting leave to travel seems merely calculated to keep him out of the way, and to learn fencing against the fifth act.

The first soliloquy of Hamlet is particularly striking and essential, as it lays open in a pathetic, beautiful manner the cause of his melancholy, and paints his mother's frailty with strong feeling yet preserves a delicate respect.

The scene which introduces Horatio, &c. to communicate the circumstance of the preceding night succeeds naturally; and the broken mode of conversation, in lines and half-lines, is so artfully contrived, is executed in so masterly a manner that the spectators, tho' they previously know the subject, are yet agreeably lured on to hear it related and thoroughly sympathize in the transitions of Hamlet, whose interrogations concerning the awful ambassador of heaven are such as give us a stronger feeling of the Ghost than even his appearance does. On the prince's determination to watch, notwithstanding his violent agitation, he might have used a phrase less censurable than the following: 'I'll speak to it, tho' *hell* itself should gape.' [1.2.244]

Laertes's short advice to Ophelia is pregnant with affection and good sense. As Polonius is introduced to hasten his son on board we could wish those excellent maxims for youth in the first scene of the second act, and which are always omitted in representation, were transposed to this place and given personally by the father to his son; such a treasure of useful instruction should upon no account be lost to the stage. Polonius's observations to Ophelia are prudent, and descriptive of paternal affection.

The remarks of Hamlet and his friends, when entered upon the platform, are very politically thrown by the author upon a far different subject from what has brought them there; and with the intervention of a flourish of martial music, usher in the Ghost with as much, or more effect than at his first appearance.

The prince's address begins with becoming awe, yet we apprehend rises too suddenly into expressions ill applied to the venerable, well-known, beloved figure then before him. Terror does indeed confound reason, but seldom gives birth to a passionate, presumptive effusion; wherefore we must be hardy enough to offer an objection against the following lines, as to their import:

> Be thou a spirit of health, or *goblin damn'd*,
> Be thy intents *wicked*, or charitable.   [1.4.40f.]

Nor can we by any means acquiesce in opinion that a heart so fluttered and affected as Hamlet's is could possibly dictate multiplied images; most certainly we discover much more of the poet and fancy than suitable feeling in

> ——tell
> Why thy *bones*, hearsed in canonized earth,
> Have burst their searments? Why the sepulchre,
> Wherein we saw thee quietly interr'd,
> Hath op'd its ponderous and marble jaws,
> To cast thee up again?   [1.4.47ff.]

Besides, in the strictness of observation it is worthy notice that Hamlet in one line calls the appearance in view a *spirit*, and immediately materializes him by mentioning the corporeal appurtenance of *bones*. The conclusion of this scene is admirably composed of broken sentences, terror, passion, and assumed resolution.

In the succeeding scene a narration of a very affecting nature is delivered by the Ghost, in language worthy that inimitable author who created characters from the force of imagination, and from the same inexhaustible source furnished a peculiar mode of expression from each.

The Roman catholic opinion of purgatory is inculcated through the whole of this interview; and funeral rites, or preparatives thereto, particularly mentioned in this line: 'Unhousel'd, unanointed, unaneal'd.' [1.5.77] But whether Shakespeare may thence be deemed a favourer of popish principles remains a matter of much doubt, and the determination, could we come at it, would be of no consequence to our present purpose. However, let the religious bent be what it may, we must admit the Ghost's stimulation to revenge furnishes a very gross idea of immortality, which should be freed from the passions and remembrances of clay; nor does the palliative distinction, which forbids any violence against the Queen, take off the imputation of mortal frailty hanging about an existence merely spiritual. An abrupt departure, and those beautiful lines with which the Ghost disappears, are a very happy conclusion to the scene which, spun out to a greater length, would have lost much of its force and beauty.

Hamlet's ensuing soliloquy is very natural, and highly expressive of the impressions left upon him. His conversation with Horatio and Marcellus is judiciously evasive, for the circumstance just learned of his father's death does not admit in policy of communication, and if it did a repetition would pall the audience. However, tho' this scene altogether has the merit of pleasing propriety, we can by no means, unless Hamlet *here* assumes his frenzy, commend the light expressions to his father's shade—*Truepenny*—*working in the cellarage*—*old mole*—*worthy pioneer* [1.5.150ff.]—especially as he is calling upon his friends in a most solemn, sensible manner for a promise of secrecy.

Thus ends the first act, which is so full of business, and that of so important a nature, that perhaps no author but Shakespeare could have produced any thing after relative to the same story worthy of attention; yet what follows shews us the possibility and executive power. ... (37–41)

There could not be a more pregnant, rich, and philosophical dissertation upon the mode of his own mind, and the excellence of human nature, than the following elegant piece of poetical prose delivered by Hamlet: [Quotes 'What a piece of work is a man!' 2.2.302ff.] (42) ...

From the imagery of those speeches which the player repeats it appears plainly that they, and the scene in the third act, are not only intended as preparatory means to convict the King of guilt but are also meant to realize the characters of the main action. Therefore the matter, manner, and action are evidently proposed as a contrast of fiction to what it is necessary the audience should think truth. (43) ...

At the beginning of the soliloquy which concludes the second act Hamlet gives himself additional force and reality by alluding to the player's fictitious feelings, compared with his own substantial cause of grief. .... (44) His remarks that the spirit he has seen may be a devil and that the devil may have power to assume a pleasing shape favour very strongly of a weak, superstitious mind, and give us no exalted idea of the prince's head, however favourably we judge of his heart.

In the first scene of the third act ... the celebrated soliloquy— *To be, or not to be*—is here introduced, and exhibits a beautiful chain of moral reasoning. The objection thrown in against suicide, 'The dread of something after death', [3.1.78] is concise, persuasive, and highly consonant with the true principles of moral philosophy. Critics have with justice pointed out the inconsistence of that parenthesis which stiles the future world

An undiscover'd country, from whose bourne
No traveller returns, [79f.]

notwithstanding the master-spring of this very play is such a traveller, therefore a palpable, flat contradiction to the above assertion. The author no doubt meant a corporeal traveller, but it is stretching indulgence very far to admit such a latitude of expression.

The conversation between Hamlet and Ophelia is finely imagined to puzzle the spies who watch his words and actions, and tho' it exhibits madness yet, as Polonius remarks of a former scene—*there is method in it*. Shakespeare, in all his pieces, seems to have had great regard to the capital characters, both as to strength and variety. The feigned madness in this piece tends greatly to the latter and gives much scope, particularly in this scene, for powerful action.— The King's proposition of sending the prince to England, though a strange scheme, shews the apprehension which conscious guilt fixes on his mind. (44–5) ...

The King's soliloquy is a most finished piece of argumentative, pathetic contrition, and furnishes a very instructive picture of a guilty mind. Of Hamlet's, which immediately succeeds, we cannot speak favourably, as it greatly derogates not only from an amiable but even a common moral character. Revenge, when most provoked, rather violates human feelings; however, as in some instances, the heart cannot decline it, and what more provoking than the death of a father? Yet life for life is the utmost that can be required. For a mortal vice or failing premeditately to plunge the perpetrator into a state of infinite misery, had we power, would be giving nature a diabolical bent. Therefore, when Hamlet resolves upon taking his uncle in some peculiar act of sin that his heels may kick at heaven, he certainly forms a design and utters sentiments more suitable to an assassin of the basest kind than a virtuous prince and a feeling man.

In that excellent scene of the closet, where the Prince so beautifully and so powerfully remonstrates to his mother upon her guilty and shameful situation, there appears an incident which rather casts another shade upon our hero's character, that is the death of Polonius. It happens evidently through a mistake, supposing him the King; yet when the mistake is discovered he has not common humanity enough to regret taking the life of an innocent, inoffensive old man, nay the father of a lady too for whom he professes a regard, but by the following lines seems to hold the matter light: 'Thou wretched, rash, intruding fool, farewel ... ' [3.4.31ff.] In the conclusive speech of the act it is true he seems to feel, but we apprehend too slightly; and making himself the vindictive minister of heaven is arraigning providence for influencing punishment where no guilt has appeared. By the same mode of argument every rash or bad man may palliate the most inordinate actions. Indeed why Polonius should be killed, in flat contradiction to every degree of poetical justice, is rather mysterious. If meant merely as a cause for Laertes's resentment and Ophelia's madness, we must assert that both might have been brought about on a better principle, as will appear from some general strictures on the plot. (46–7) ...

The King's resolution of sending Hamlet to England seems justly precipitated by the unjustifiable event of Polonius's death. The scene in which the King enquires for the body contains some pointed expressions, and the Prince's departure is of that unaffecting nature that we doubt whether one spectator out of a thousand ever said I hope he will come again, though from such a voyage so late in the piece it seems very doubtful. (48) ...

Ophelia's second introduction relieves and gives some sparks of life to a conversation full of false fire and impotence, wherein one party appears a blustering fool and the other a dastard villain. As to the conspiracy against Hamlet's life, it seems the *ne plus ultra* of a forced catastrophe; a plan which, by approving it, shews Laertes to be as much an intentional murderer as the king. There is a degree of detestation mingled with contempt: and that disagreeable feeling both these characters raise. The Queen's account of Ophelia's mournful end is justly admired; and tho' the lady, while in her senses, said very little to affect us, yet here the poet teaches us to feel for the event which has deprived her of life.

Notwithstanding Mr. Voltaire's objections to the first scene of the fifth act as being inconsistent with the dignity and decorum of tragedy are in a great measure true, yet the characters are so finely drawn, such pointed satire and such instructive moral sentiments arise, as give it great estimation and raise it far above insipid propriety. Some expressions of the grave-digger in answer to Hamlet's question how long a corpse will be in the ground before it rots, however true, are offensively indelicate.

The funeral of Ophelia is indeed a maimed, and to me an irreconcileable piece of work. She is, we find, allowed Christian burial, is attended by the king, queen, and whole court. Yet the clergyman refuses funeral service, supposing her death doubtful, tho' the queen in the foregoing act imputes it without reservation to an accident; and we venture to presume there is no medium between admission to consecrated ground, with all usual ceremonies, and a total exclusion from the whole. But the author seems to have been in a state of difficulty; he would have a grave, and made the best apology for it he could.

The encounter of Hamlet and Laertes is supported with an excess of spirit on both sides; and, if we consider the real state of things, rather blameably on the part of the former. He has killed the father, and in consequence deprived the sister of her senses; yet when a grieving, injured brother and son vents an explanation, very excusable in his situation, the prince, even at the interment of a woman he pretends love for, indulges a most outrageous degree of passion, interrupts a sacred ceremony, and offers his lesson in stile of a challenge to Laertes; nay, after most insulting behaviour, when separated—he retorts accusation upon the challenged person in the following irritative taunt [Quotes 5.1.282–6].

There is indeed a palliative excuse made by Hamlet to Laertes, for this inconsistent behaviour at the beginning of the last scene— where he says ' ... I am punish'd/With a sore *distraction* ... *madness*' [5.2.221ff.]. Now if it be considered that this madness has been but *assumed*, this appears a mean prevarication to a man whom he has most deeply injured, and who, to his knowledge, never meant him

380

wrong. To say that this passion was put on to deceive the court weighs but little, as we find in the action: dishevelled hair, ungartered stockings &c. are laid aside for a composed appearance, and immediately after the bluster we perceive him not only regular in conversation with a coxcomb messenger of the king's but punctual in the terms of the challenge, and coolly sensible in fulfilling it *before the court* without any design more than the credit of victory in view.

Another faint apology is made in a scene with Horatio, where the prince seems to be sorry that the *bravery* of Laertes's grief should so far provoke him. But all this scene, except a very few lines, is left out in the representation; and indeed, tho' meant to account for Hamlet's coming back it draws such a strange picture of his getting at the king's dispatches and forging others to turn the design of his death upon Rosencranz and Gildenstern, that we may lament such low chicanery in a character of dignity, one who had no occasion, but much to the contrary, to appear a volunteer in his uncle's proposition of sending him to England. However, as the transaction of his speedy return should be accounted for, we wish somewhat more like a narrative was preserved in action. ...

The last scene, if there are two good fencers, (which by the bye seldom happens) must please the eye considerably. Yet such a slaughter of characters must cloy the most sanguine critic that ever thirsted for theatrical blood-shed, and pity must extend very far indeed to attend even the expiring hero of this piece with any degree of patience.

Having thus progressively delineated the plan it becomes necessary to make some general strictures upon the whole, to justify those occasional remarks which have been made.

At the opening of the play we find that a very remarkable apparition has been seen by the palace-guard two nights together, yet so resolute and secret have these soldiers been that no mention is made of it, except to Horatio, who disbelieves the story. But on his watch the third night is convinced by ocular demonstration, upon which he very naturally determines to mention it to Hamlet in particular, as seemingly most interested in the appearance. This, in conjunction with Bernardo and Marcellus, he does the next morning. Here it seems a little irreconcileable that Horatio, the particular and intimate friend of the prince, should be in Elsineur two days or more, as we must suppose from circumstances, before he paid respects to his royal patron. These, we confess, are minutiæ, yet claim notice in the strictness of criticism.

Hamlet's assumed madness might undoubtedly have been made the instrument of some important secret purpose relative to his father's murder and his own just resentment; yet as it now appears answers no other end than merely cajoling the King, distressing the Queen and Ophelia, bamming Polonius and the courtiers, and giving great scope for capital acting—which last article seems much more the author's intention through this piece than decorum and consistence.

The King not being able (either by his spies, or even condescending to be a listener himself) to find out the bottom of this frenzy which, through conscious guilt, to him looks terrible, forms a resolution of sending Hamlet to England under pretence of receiving tribute, but, as appears afterwards, that the complaisant English monarch should put to death the heir of the Danish crown upon mere request. Strange! that he who found means to destroy his own brother in the plenitude of power and popular esteem should take such a round-about method to dispose of a nephew he seems to fear; and full as strange is it that Hamlet, who has so much cause to suspect his uncle's intention and who has such powerful motives for staying at home, should tamely, without objection go upon the voyage.

On returning we do not find him taking any step towards punishing the murderer; nay, most politely undertakes to win a wager for him. How unworthily for him then does the catastrophe come about! When wounded with a poisoned weapon himself, when he hears of his mother's being poisoned, then and not before, urged by desperation not just revenge, he demolishes the king of shreds and patches, as he properly stiles his uncle in the third act.

From this view it is with all deference apprehended that after his detection at the play, if his majesty upon the principle of self-defence had formed a design of taking the prince off by instruments at home; if that design had been made known to the Queen; had she, through maternal affection put Hamlet on his guard; and had that prince taken measures worthy the motives of stimulation, a tyrant of some consequence and uniformity would have been shewn in Claudius; a tender mother in the Queen, and a hero in Hamlet. The innocent characters, Polonius and Ophelia, might have been saved; and death prevented from stalking without limitation at the catastrophe. As it stands no less than eight of the characters are disposed of that way, four in view at one time upon the stage.

In respect of characters we are to lament that the hero, who is intended as amiable, should be such an apparent heap of inconsistency: impetuous, tho' philosophical; sensible of injury, yet timid of resentment; shrewd, yet void of policy; full of filial piety, yet tame under oppression; boastful in expression, undetermined in action; and yet, from being pregnant with great variety, from affording many opportunities to exert sound judgment and extensive powers, he is as agreeable and striking an object as any in the English drama.

In the performance of this character we must, as in RICHARD, place Mr. GARRICK far before any other competitor. His reception of, and address to the Ghost; his natural, picturesque attitude, terror-struck features, low, tremulous expression, rising in harmonious gradation with the climax of his speech and feeling, all give us the most pleasing, we had almost said, astonishing sensibility. In all the pointed parts of the dialogue his matchless eyes anticipate his tongue, and impress the meaning upon us with double force. No man ever did, nor possibly ever will, speak hemistics, broken sentences, and make transitions with such penetrating effect. In this lies the indisputable superiority of our modern Roscius: that where other performers, and good ones too, pass unnoticed, he is frequently great; where an author is languid, he gives him spirit; where powerful, due support. ... (49–56)

Horatio is the only amiable man in the piece, yet, except his first scene, is very inconsiderable. ... The Queen should be an object of detestation, or pity, yet is neither, but an odd compound of both. (59) ...

As to the versification and dialogue of this piece, they are flowing without monotony, poetical without bombast, easy without flatness, and always speak to the heart where there is opportunity or occasion. To transcribe all the beautiful passages would seem a design to fill up; and to produce only few, where there is abundance, must be deemed partiality. Wherefore we refer to the reader's taste and the piece itself, presuming to conclude our remarks on it with one general observation, which is that no play can afford more entertainment on the stage or improvement in the closet, tho' abounding with superfluities and inconsistencies;

several of the former are omitted in performance, most of the latter must remain. All the moral we can deduce is that murder cannot lie hid, and that conscience ever makes a coward of guilt. (59) . . .

MACBETH

Preternatural beings afford the widest, most luxuriant field for genius to sport, and ideas to vegetate in. Of this, being truly sensible and willing to give his *muse of fire* unlimited scope, Shakespeare has in several pieces availed himself, but in none more powerfully than the tragedy now before us. However, though critically we must admire that characteristic peculiarity of sentiment and expression which distinguish the Witches, it is nevertheless necessary to remark that exhibiting such personages and phantoms as never had any existence but in credulous or heated imaginations tends to impress superstitious feelings and fears upon weak minds. For which reason we consider every dramatic piece which treats the audience with a ghost, fairy, or witch as improper for young, unexperienced spectators in particular. If, as is well known, old womens stories of such impress a timidity upon every child who hears their terrifying tales, a timidity which lasts to the conclusion of life, may we not infer apprehensions of their having a more forceable effect from being realized on the stage?

It may be said that interdicting such poetical auxiliaries would cramp genius, and deprive us of many unparalelled beauties. To this the answer is plain, that nothing which has not a good effect, or at least an inoffensive tendency, should be deemed beautiful or stand estimation.

From what is thus premised we hope no other charge will be laid against Shakespeare than the barbarous and credulous taste of the times in which he wrote, and to which he submitted, with possibly an oblique design of flattering the favourite opinion of James the first. Yet, allowing this to be really the case, it cannot exculpate his preternatural beings as such from rational censure, for the reasons assigned above, notwithstanding the author had historical tradition to countenance his introduction of them. After this general, and we hope, just objection against the weird sisters, we are to take the piece as it stands, and consider distinctly its several component parts.

Macbeth commences with all the apparatus of terror—a storm! a desart! and three withered hags of little less than infernal appearance. Their short conference is full of meaning, and a kind of oracular obscurity. Their sudden disappearance gains a desire in the spectators to see them again, and to know in what sort of business such extraordinary agents are to be employed. But we know not why they should *sink* under the stage, immediately after pronouncing these words, '*Hover* through the fog and filthy air.' ... (79–80)

Macbeth's feelings upon this unexpected acquisition [of the title of Cawdor], verifying in part the prediction which has been so lately pronounced to him, the dawnings of ambition which break out upon his unconnected mediation, are extremely natural; but his adverting to murther for obtaining the state of royalty in view shew him much too susceptible of villainous impressions.

There are many circumstances and events to bring about the most unthought-of changes in human affairs. Wherefore that man who premeditates the worst means at first must have by nature a deep depravation of heart; and such Macbeth will appear infected with from the whole of that speech which begins 'Two truths are told,' &c [1.3.127ff.] notwithstanding somewhat like palliation is offered in two or three lines. Indeed, his conclusion seems to banish what he beautifully stiles *fantastical murther*, but cannot banish from spectators his barbarous ideas so suddenly conceived. We have dwelt upon this circumstance to strengthen our opinion that the author meant to draw him a detestable monster, which some critics have rather disputed, allowing him a generous disposition which we find no instance of; even the conscientious struggles which we shall presently find him engaged with might arise in the most villainous nature. He who does a bad action precipitately, or without knowing it to be such, may stand in some measure excusable. But when a man has scrupulously weighed every relative circumstance in the nicest scale of reflection, and after all determines upon what nature, gratitude, and justice would avoid, he must be composed of the worst materials.

To corroborate the general idea of Macbeth's character which we have here offered and which will be enlarged upon when we go through the whole piece, let us view him in the very next scene, where, after a most cordial reception from the king, with unbounded promises of future favours, he is so possessed of his base

385

purpose that, void of even common gratitude, he replies upon Duncan's appointing Malcolm prince of Cumberland,

> The prince of Cumberland! that is a step   [*aside.*
> On which I must fall down, or else o'er leap:
> For in my way it lies—Stars hide your fires,
> Let not night see my black and deep desires;
> The eye wink at the end—yet let that be,
> Which the eye fears, when it is done, to see.   [1.4.47 ff.]

From this passage it appears that, not content with the simple idea of regicide he determines to cut off the whole family; in return for being loaded with honours by royal favour, and at the very instant when this unsuspecting monarch and friend places himself upon his hospitable reception. If this does not prove Macbeth an exception to the satirist's remark, *Nemo repente fuit turpissimus,*[1] we know not what can.

Lady Macbeth, and her husband's letter, are judiciously introduced. But sure such sympathetic barbarity was never in nature as suddenly, on the instant, breaks out in these words,

> Glamis thou art and Cawdor—and shalt be
> What thou art promised.   [1.5.12f.]

What follows accuses Macbeth of a milky softness in his nature, of which he does not seem at all possessed, for unsuccessful struggles of conscience cannot justly be called so. However, that he may not have the whole load of aggravated guilt to bear alone, our author has made this matchless lady—we lament so detestable, though a possible picture of the fair sex—exert uncommon talents of temptation. On hearing of the king's visit, with most unrelenting precipitation of thought she dooms the royal visitant. Her invocation to spirits of evil influence is worthy of a powerful imagination, and Macbeth's interruptive entrance extremely well timed; but we must offer some doubt whether the word *blanket* of the dark does not convey a low and improper idea.

Macbeth's mention of Duncan's approach without making any previous reply to his wife's cordial reception is a natural effect of what sits nearest his heart; and her coming to the main point at once is well devised for working him up to her great purpose. Her confining the sentiment of murther in less than a line, and

---

[1] Juvenal, *Satires,* 2.83: 'no one reaches the depths of turpitude all at once'.

warning him to disguise those looks which appear too intelligible, impress us with a strong idea of her policy, as does her second hint of Duncan's death, and promising to take a great part of the dreadful business on herself.

The short scene before the castle has nothing material in it, except the following truly poetical remark made by Banquo [quotes 'This guest of summer', 1.6.3ff.].

Lady Macbeth's strained compliment to the king has also merit as being natural, no truth being more certain than that treacherous hypocrisy ever strives to wear the fairest smiles.

In such a state of guilty perturbation as Macbeth now appears, no mode of expression could be so suitable as that of soliloquy. It were to be wished, however, that our great author, pursuing energy, had not in some sentences bordered upon obscurity, especially if we consider those passages as only repeated on the stage, where the ear must inevitably be too quick for reception. In an alteration of this play which has been often performed, there are some attempts to render the lines we speak of more intelligible; but, like most other paraphrases, they destroy the essential spirit.

The reflection that if he could but gain case even in this life he would jump the life to come is rather wildly impious; but the inevitable temporal punishment of a conscience loaded with guilt is very well and commendably inculcated. The arguments for declining the murther are so forcible that nothing but the most hardened heart, under such conviction, would proceed. Where he personifies pity, and mounts her astride on the *blast*, fancy takes a very vigorous flight, nor does expression fall beneath. Yet we are afraid they leave propriety behind; the following lines are in our opinion very exceptionable:

—I have no spur
To prick the sides of my intent, but only
Vaulting ambition, which o'er-leaps itself
And falls on the other—   [1.7.25ff.]

To embody *intention*, that *ambition* may be a *spur* to prick its sides, leans towards the burlesque; and then turning the *spur* into another body, that it may vault over, instead of gaining the *saddle* of *intent*, corroborates this idea; indeed this speech should always end at 'The deep damnation of his taking off.' [20] For 'pity'—'heaven's cherubim' and 'ambition', all upon the full gallop, are strained figures at least; not at all adapted to a man deliberating upon one of the foulest, most important murthers he could commit.

Lady Macbeth comes to speak in rather plainer terms. Yet, unless we allow great latitude of expression, what follows evidently admits of objection:

> ——Was the hope drunk
> Wherein you drest yourself? Hath it slept since,
> And wakes it now to look so pale and sickly.   [1.7.35ff.]

Suppose we pass over the literal acceptation of *hope* being drunk, surely we must blame a lady of high rank for descending to such a vulgar and nauseous allusion as the paleness and sickness of an inebriated state; nor is her comparison of the cat in the adage much more the effect of good breeding.

Macbeth's reply to the very gross rebuff he has just received is as concise, significant, and noble a one as ever was uttered; but his bloody-minded virago's next speech, towards the conclusion, wounds humanity with such a sentiment as no woman should utter, nor any rational being hear. Yet that strange, horrid picture of dashing a smiling infant's brains out, and laying a plan for complicated destruction, occasions Macbeth to say 'Bring forth men children only.' [1.7.72ff.] Should he not rather have said,

> Bring forth fierce tygers only,
> For thy relentless nature should compose
> Nothing but beasts.

If it should be urged that such characters have been, and may be, we still contend that they are among the frightful deformities and essential concealments of nature, which should be excluded from the stage.

The midnight interview of Macbeth and Banquo, at the beginning of the second act, very properly ushers in the dreadful business then in agitation. ... We could heartily wish this passage did not occur: 'There's husbandry in heaven,/Their *candles* are all out' [2.1.4f]. What a poverty of idea and expression! yet we also find the stars called *candles* by our author in his *Romeo and Juliet*. How much more worthy of himself, and of his subject, is what Lorenzo stiles them in *The Merchant of Venice*, *pattens of bright gold?* [5.1.59]

In Macbeth's soliloquy, where a visionary dagger strikes his mind's eye, the abrupt introduction of that alarming object is very judicious and beautiful. Nor can any thing be more natural than the effect it has on Macbeth, which is most admirably described and strongly impressed by a nervous succession of breaks, which, for a dozen or fourteen lines, rise into a powerful climax of confusion.

The momentary pause of unclouded reason, which relieves imagination from her painful load, and the quick return of coward conscience, diversify the sentiment and action in a most interesting manner. The picture of midnight, as favouring witchcraft, rapes and murther, concludes this inimitable soliloquy with a due solemnity of terror; a soliloquy of such unspeakable merit that, like charity, it may apologize for a multitude of faults.

Lady Macbeth's ... remark that a likeness of her father in Duncan's sleeping appearance prevented her from doing the business herself, lets in a gleam of humanity upon this female fiend. The entrance of Macbeth, his high-wrought confusion, and every syllable of the ensuing scene exhibit an unparalelled combination of judgment and genius, calculated to awake the drowsiest feelings, and to alarm the most resolute heart. The picture of the grooms crying out in disturbed dreams—one 'Heaven bless us,' and 'amen' the other [2.2.26ff.] with the inimitable description of sleep, and the idea of nature's general friend being murthered in that sleep, are astonishing efforts of mental ability, and for so much certainly place Shakespeare beyond any degree of comparative merit.

The refusal of Macbeth to go again into the scene of blood is an apt stroke of well-timed remorse; indeed, his bringing the daggers from the place they should have been left in is an extreme well-judged mark of confusion. However, we would rather have forfeited that instance of judgment than have heaped such savage inhumanity upon the female; her boast of having hands crimsoned like those of her husband carries the offensive colouring still higher. What succeeds, on the interruption of knocking, is expressed very characteristically.

To what end Shakespeare could introduce so incongruous a character as the porter, who is commendably omitted in representation, we believe no mortal can tell. At such an interesting period to turn the most serious feelings into laughter, or rather into distaste, by a string of strained quibbles is an insult upon judgment, and must fill the imagination with chaos of idea. Some more suitable pause might have been made to give Macbeth time for composing his ruffled figure. . . .

The successive entrances and exits of various characters, the real grief of some and the feigned sorrow of others, Macbeth's apology for his political stroke of killing the grooms by an affecting picture of Duncan's situation, and the rapid resolution of enquiring judicially into so unaccountable an event, are all well arranged and happily expressed. But the amazing precipitate flight of Malcolm and Donalbain, without any apology except the paltry one of instantaneous fear, places these sprigs of royalty in a contemptible light, and its effect on the stage proves the justice of this remark. For when one says, 'I'll to England,' and the other comically replies, 'To Ireland I,' [2.3.136f.] nine times out of ten the audience are thrown into a horse-laugh. — We could wish this circumstance was altered, as it easily might be, by giving a few speeches of spirit and dutiful affection to one or both the princes, expressive of their particular determination to discover and revenge their father's death; which might be overruled by Macduff's representation of the danger they stand exposed to, and that for their greater security it would be better to retire till the unavoidable convulsions of state were subdued, or till proper measures could be taken to establish the legal succession. This, we apprehend, would have carried them off with some grace, whereas in their present disposition they make such a wretched figure that we can scarce forget it when Malcolm appears to assert his right at the head of an army. . . .

Introducing the witches at the end of the second act is a very seasonable relief to a feeling mind from the painful weight of horror which some preceding scenes must have laid upon it; and, in suitable music, they continue the story predictively as a kind of chorus. Their rejoicing in the mischief already done, and that which yet lies in the womb of time, shews a disposition worthy such agents as the subordinate fiends of darkness. . . .

In respect of Macbeth's scene with the murderers, we apprehend he uses too much circumlocution, especially as we perceive, by what he says at their entrance, that those ruffians have been made acquainted with a main part of the affair, Banquo's oppression of them. . . .

What succeeds between Macbeth and his lady is well adapted to their unavoidable perturbation. .... Every thing he advances in this short conference shews a striking, poetical, yet natural picture of mental gloom and heart-felt agony; his invocation of night and description of its solemn approach are pleasing effusions of genius.

The scene of the murtherers, Banquo's fall, and Fleance's escape, is partly trifling, partly shocking, and seldom fails of proving laughable. We wish something better had been substituted, and the circumstance referred to a relation of it by the murtherer. We could also wish that decorum had not suffered by such a ragamuffin's entrance into a room of state amidst the whole court, and apprehend no necessity for this, therefore are induced to blame it.

Considering the place, hurry of spirits, &c. [we] are bold to censure all the following speech, except the first hemistich, and the last, marked in Italics. They are certainly as much as any man, so situated, would have said, therefore what comes between is superfluous.

> *Then comes my fit again*—(I had else been perfect,
> Whole as the marble, founded as the rock,
> As free and general as the easing air;
> But now I'm cabbin'd, cribb'd, confin'd, bound in
> To saucy doubts and fears.)—*But Banquo's safe*.   [3.4.21ff.]

... Banquo's ghost, which, without being too ludicrous, we may call the raw-head and bloody-bones of tragedy, is nevertheless well introduced to throw Macbeth into those violent agitations which nature must feel, and such as furnish extensive powers an almost unlimited scope to shew themselves. The words of both Macbeth and his lady are beautifully applicable through the whole scene, which concludes, so far as the ghost is concerned, with as forceable a climax of impassioned terror as ever any author penned. ... Macbeth's determination to consult the witches plainly indicates the agitation and weakness of a guilty heart and a superstitious head; we should be glad to know how he is so well acquainted with their places of rendezvous as to know exactly the spot of consultation. ...

That remarkable incantation which begins the fourth act, the mysterious ceremony practised, the emblematic ingredients

391

collected for enchantment, and the arrangement of them shew a more peculiar luxuriance of fancy than any other author ever compacted into such narrow bounds. The music also, as in two former scenes, has a very just and pleasing effect.

Macbeth's mode of addressing the witches seems too much of the compulsive.

... A number of strange, indeed very strange apparitions, or sucking ghosts, present themselves and deliver flattering, dubitable predictions, well calculated to mislead credulity; and Macbeth's eagerly catching at the most favourable interpretation shews coward conscience, like a drowning man, catching at every broken reed for support. The long train of shades, representing the succession of royalty, is well enough calculated to impress additional uneasiness upon the tyrant. But such a superabundance and variety of spectres palls even terror, fatigues imagination, and offends sight: a dance is very well introduced here to relieve attention. One would naturally suppose that Macbeth had enjoyed a full sufficiency of such agreeable company, yet we find him rather displeased that they are gone.

The intelligence of Macduff's flight to England is well thrown in to give spirit and an opening of business; his wife and children being devoted to destruction in consequence, we might reasonably expect from what has been already shewn of Macbeth's jealous, impatient cruelty. The next scene of Macduff's lady and son, where murtherers come and demolish the latter in view of the audience is, if we can be allowed the phrase, farcically horrid; as disgraceful an oddity as ever invaded Shakespeare's muse, and therefore with great justice omitted in representation. ...

A doctor, brought in merely to introduce mention of English Edward's power to cure by a touch—that very dubitable circumstance of tradition—is at best trifling, or a paltry compliment to the then reigning monarch, nothing at all to the matter in question, and only breaks in abruptly upon a very interesting continuation, we mean, the heart-felt intelligence that Rosse brings of the fatal tragedy acted in Macduff's family. His first speaking of general griefs, the miseries of Scotland, is a well judged preparative for a more confined and peculiar concern relative to one of the characters present. Indeed, Macduff's enquiry for Scotland, before his wife and children, shews great magnanimity of mind; and Rosse's diffident manner of revealing their lamentable fall is sensibly humane. Hence the scene, by degrees of most exact proportion, presents a climax of grief which never fails to work a general and suitable effect, and concludes with a pleasing, spirited denunciation of revenge against the blood-stained usurper. Thus the fourth act terminates, leaving, as every fourth act in particular should do, an impatient expectation impressed upon the audience for what must follow.

Lady Macbeth's physician, and one of the ladies of her bed-chamber, begin the fifth act with a few preparatory and pertinent speeches for a circumstance not expected, the tormenting effects of a thorny conscience galling that female fiend beyond all power of disguise or composure, a circumstance the more pleasing as it approaches us unawares, and beautifully vindicates the justice of providence, *even here upon this bank and shoal of time*. Walking and speaking while actually asleep has been verified by many hundred instances, therefore her ladyship is brought to view in as justifiable and affecting a situation as could possibly have been imagined. Her disjointed mode of speaking, the imaginary spot on her hand, the confused apprehensions of Macbeth's timidity, similar to what she expressed at the time the action was really committed, and the explanation thrown in by the attendants are admirably combined; we may also venture to pronounce the heavy sigh she vents on despairing to clear herself of blood a striking effusion of a guilty heart. Her departure is finely and most naturally precipitated by acting over again the confusion which arose from knocking at the gate. . . .

Macbeth's expressions, at his entrance, most plainly evince a disturbed brain and forced resolution. Flying for safety to the prediction of the witches is a well-timed additional proof of that superstitious weakness which, stimulated by ambition, has hurried him into all his guilt and consequent misfortunes. The expressions he uses to the servant or officer who enters with intelligence of the English army are low and gross, far beneath even a private gentleman; and why Shakespeare should make a monarch run into such vulgarisms is not easy to guess, for the rage or grief of a king should always preserve peculiar dignity, without which the author cannot boast a chaste preservation of character. The following speech, however, makes full amends for a thousand venial slips. The breaks in the two first lines afford a beautiful variety of action of tones of voice, and countenance—

those which succeed are as fine declamatory reflections arising from the consciousness of guilt and general dislike in a sensible man as the severest criticism could relish; nor is it easy to determine which claims preference, the sentiment or versification. [Quotes 5.3.19–28]

Macbeth's reply to the physician on hearing of his lady's strong mental indisposition, is no less worthy of capital genius, no less satisfactory in speaking, hearing, or reading: 'Canst thou not minister to a mind diseas'd' [5.3.40ff.] Nothing could be more happily introduced from the morals they inculcate, and the pause they give to Macbeth's rage, than the two foregoing speeches. They are a timely relief to the performer's expression, which otherwise must have been kept too much on the strain, and a delicious treat to every intelligent mind amongst an audience. (82–101) . . .

[Quotes 'She should have died hereafter . . .' 5.5.17–28.]

The foregoing speech has the first principle of intrinsic merit to an eminent degree, moral instruction. An equal number of lines never yet exhibited a fuller, more compleat picture of the vanity of human life; and our author has, with great address, again used the method of realizing his character by making Macbeth speak of the player as a fictitious, transitory representative. . . .

The business now encreases, and justly hurries on to a rapidity of material events. The tyrant is, as himself aptly expresses it, tied to a stake, and therefore through compulsion must fight. As to the combat, wherein that unfledged warrior young Siward falls, it seems to have very little business in the piece unless to encrease a torrent of blood already exceeding all due bounds.

Macduff's encounter with Macbeth raises expectation to the very top of its bent, and justice sits trembling in every humane bosom for so essential a sacrifice to her as the tyrant. The introduction of Macbeth's sole remaining hope, that of being invulnerable to any person born of a woman, shews great judgment, and his feelings on being told the fallacy of his charm are expressed in very apt terms.—Why the author chose to execute so great a culprit behind the scenes, thereby depriving the audience of a most satisfactory circumstance, is not easy to imagine. Death certainly is made in this instance too modest, and the bringing on a head defeats every trace of the author's new-born false delicacy. The present mode of representation is much better.[1]

What follows Macbeth's fall is, like the remainder of every tragedy when the plot is revealed and the principal characters are disposed of, a matter of very little consequence; therefore is confined, as it ought to be, within the bounds of judicious brevity. Malcolm, however, gives a piece of historic information concerning the first institution of earldoms in Scotland, which a tythe of every audience would not else know.

As Macbeth, in representation, dies before the audience, it appeared necessary according to dramatic custom to give him some conclusive lines; which Mr. GARRICK, as we have been told, has happily supplied,[2] as nothing could be more suitable or striking than to make him mention with dying breath his guilt, delusion, the witches, and those horrid visions of future punishment which must ever appall and torture the last moments of such accumulated crimes.

It has been already hinted, and may be laid down as an irrefragable maxim, that moral tendency is the first great and indispensible merit of any piece written for the stage. In which light I am afraid the tragedy before us, though a favourite child of genius, will not hold a very distinguished place. Fate, necessity or predestination, has embarrassed the most inquisitive philosophers, the most painful theologists, and still remains matter of much perplexity to those who endeavour to develope it. SHAKESPEARE, therefore, who was no doubt an able moralist, should have declined any subject which glanced an eye that way. Yet we find his *Macbeth* strongly inculcates power of prediction, even in the worst and most contemptible agents; inculcates a supernatural influence of one mortal being over another. It is but a very weak defence to say he only wrote according to the accepted notions of those times from whence he drew his plot.——Admitted, but whatever tends to weaken reason, to mislead the understanding and intimidate the heart, should not be used as a subject for dramatic composition, which adorns fiction with her most persuasive charms. Weak minds are ever more liable to receive prejudicial than advantageous impressions; wherefore any character, incidents, or sentiments which may work the former effect should be industriously avoided.

[1] Since the time of Garrick's adaptation, at least, Macbeth died on-stage.
[2] See 3.133f.

If the stage upon some occasions does not improve, it should at least leave an audience no worse than it finds them, equally avoiding vice and credulity. [Quotes two references to 'fate' (1.5.26; 3.1.70) to show Shakespeare 'promulging principles of fatalism'.]

The plot of *Macbeth*, though the unities of time and place are much infringed upon, does not strike in representation with any offensive ideas of improbability, but rises by very just degrees to a catastrophe which is well wrought up. The moral is the same as that of *Richard the Third*, shewing that a guilty conscience is a constant tormentor, and that a royal as well as a private murderer is obnoxious to punishment.

Among the natural characters, if Macbeth and his lady deserve such an epithet, there is very little variety or contrast; all the men, except the principal, are tolerably honest; as to the heroine, she stands alone.

To delineate Macbeth is not easy. The author seems, like Prometheus, to have made a man of his own, but to have stolen his animation rather from Hell than Heaven. By the account we hear of him previous to his entrance, magnanimity and courage appear conspicuous in his conduct. Yet no sooner does he present himself, but with all the weakness of unpractised youth he receives a strong impression from old women's prognostications; and with all the aptness of a studied villain suggests the most pernicious practices, which from that moment, with a very few slight intervals, take entire possession of his heart. From his future proceedings we perceive him more actuated by jealous apprehensions than sound policy, more influenced by rage and desperation than any degree of natural resolution; credulous, impatient, vindictive; ambitious without a spark of honour; cruel without a gleam of pity. In short, as compleat a tool for ministers of temptation to work upon as ever fancy formed, and too disgraceful for nature to admit amongst her works.

However, considered in the view of theatrical action, there is not one personage to be found in our English drama which more strongly impresses an audience, which requires more judgment and greater powers to do him justice. Many passages are intricate, some heavy, but for the greater part powerfully impassioned. The mental agitation he is thrown into requires expression peculiarly forcible of action, look, and utterance, even so far as to make the hearts of spectators shrink and to thrill their blood. Indeed, every assistance from externals is given the actor, such as daggers, bloody hands, ghosts, &c. but these must be treated judiciously or the effect, as we have sometimes seen it, may take a ludicrous turn.

Through all the soliloquies of anxious reflections in the first act; amidst the pangs of guilty apprehensions and pungent remorse in the second; through all the distracted terror of the third; all the impetuous curiosity of the fourth, and all the desperation of the fifth, Mr. GARRICK shews uniform, unabating excellence; scarce a look, motion, or tone but takes possession of our faculties and leads them to a just sensibility.

As SHAKESPEARE rises above himself in many places so does this his greatest and best commentator, who not only presents his beauties to the imagination but brings them home feelingly to the heart. Among a thousand other instances of almost necromantic merit let us turn our recollection only to a few in the character of Macbeth. Who ever saw the *immortal actor* start at, and trace the imaginary dagger previous to Duncan's murder, without embodying, by sympathy, unsubstantial air into the alarming shape of such a weapon? Who ever heard the low but piercing notes of his voice when the *deed is done*, repeating those inimitable passages which mention the sleeping grooms and murder of sleep, without feeling a vibration of the nerves? Who ever saw the guilty distraction of features he assumes on Banquo's appearance at the feast without sacrificing reason to real apprehension from a mimic ghost? Who has heard his speech after receiving his death wound, uttered with the utmost agony of body and mind, but trembles at the idea of future punishment and almost pities the expiring wretch, though stained with crimes of the deepest dye?

Theatrical performance to most spectators appears a mechanical disposition of limbs and a parotted mode of speech. So indeed it really is too often; but intrinsic merit soars far beyond such narrow, barren limits, she traces nature through her various windings, dives into her deepest recesses, and snatches ten thousand beauties which plodding method can never display. The dullest comprehension may be taught to enter on this side or that, to stand on a particular board, to raise the voice here and fall it there; but unless motion and utterance are regulated by a cultivated knowledge of life and self-born intelligent feelings, no greater degree of excellence can be attained than unaffecting propriety. Like a fair field whose native fertility of soil produces a beauteous luxuriant crop of spontaneous vegitation, which art can only regulate not enrich, Mr. GARRICK's matchless genius not only captivates our sportive senses but also furnishes high relished substantial food for our minds to strengthen by. (102-9) ...

Macbeth, for its boldness of sentiment, strength of versification, variety of passions and preternatural beings, deserves to be esteemed a first rate tragedy, containing a number of beauties never exceeded, with many blemishes very censurable; dangerous in representation, as has been said, to weak minds; unintelligible to moderate conceptions in several places, upon perusal; therefore chiefly calculated for sound understanding and established resolution of principles, either on the stage or in the study. (113) ...

KING LEAR. A TRAGEDY. Altered from Shakespeare, by Tate and Colman.

The person who enters upon dramatic alteration, without being a slave to his original, should nearly as possible confine himself to pruning luxuriances, correcting irregularity, rationalizing bombast, and elucidating obscurity; cautious of adding, unless where unavoidable gaps are made and connection consequently wanting. It is most allowable that SHAKESPEARE's *King Lear* very much wanted such assistance as we have mentioned.

TATE's opening of the play[1] we apprehend preferable to that adopted by COLMAN; for the Bastard makes us much better, that is much more decently acquainted with his illegitimacy in the soliloquy spoken by him than Gloster's account. ...

Where Lear divides his kingdom upon the childish principle of asking which daughter loves him best, COLMAN has preserved that unjustifiable, cynical roughness which SHAKESPEARE has stamped upon Cordelia, in the barren, churlish answer she gives her father; this TATE has considerably softened by making her attachment to Edgar the cause of such reply [1.349]. We think, however, that the whole affair might have been thrown into a much better light by making the old monarch divide his kingdom on the marriage of his daughters with those persons he approved. Cordelia's refusing the person of his choice from a secret inclination elsewhere would have rescued him from the extreme folly now chargeable against him, and the successful daughters might

1 See 1.346, 351ff.

have made professions equally flattering from a seeming gratitude
as they now do from affected duty. Lear's seeing into, and declaring
a knowledge of Cordelia's attachment would have furnished strong
additional reason for Edgar's flight. The rough, honest interposition of Kent is a circumstance extremely pleasing. In this, as well
as many other scenes of the play, TATE has enervated the versification by endeavouring to give it a smoother flow; wherefore
COLMAN has shewn greater judgment and more modesty by only
retrenching, not altering the original.

We can by no means agree with the last mentioned gentleman,
that the love episode of Edgar and Cordelia is superfluous or
unaffecting.[1] We must rather contend, in opposition to the frigidity of criticism, that natural and very pleasing sensations are raised
by it without any invasion upon the main distress of the piece. . . .
(I,352–4)

Mr. COLMAN objects to making the daughters entertain a criminal
passion for Edmund; but if we can once suppose them capable
of filial ingratitude all other vices, as Dr. YOUNG emphatically
has it, may seem virtues in them. For this reason we approve the
intimation TATE has furnished Regan with, of her prejudice in
favour of Edmund. When Kent and the Gentleman Usher appear
COLMAN has again judiciously preserved several passages which
the laureat strangely slipped over, or wretchedly metamorphosed.
We know not any scene written with more spirit and originality
than this; Kent's honest, sarcastical bluntness is finely contrasted
to the courtly water-fly's supple nothingness. However, decorum
is certainly intruded upon, for such language to be used in presence
of a joint ruler of the state is unpardonable; and we heartily agree
that Kent deserves some punishment, but much regret so farcical
an incident as a pair of moveable stocks, so conveniently placed in
a nobleman's castle as to be forth coming on the instant. (356) . . .

In Edgar's soliloquy as altered by TATE we find that he does
not fly his enemies, as in COLMAN, from a paltry fear of the danger
which hangs over his person, but from a generous, laudable motive
of waiting an opportunity of serving the woman he loves and who
has made so great a sacrifice on his account.[2] For this purpose he
has resolution to put on the wretchedest appearance, and to encounter a situation worse than death: this places him in a degree

[1] See pp. 294f. above.
[2] See 1.355.

of estimation with the audience which otherwise he could not have obtained.

The stocks again present themselves to view, merely as an object of inflammation to the old king, who being already nettled, fires at the treatment his messenger has met; and indeed well he may, not knowing what personal provocation that messenger had given. The appearance of Cornwall and Regan brings matters to a pathetic and striking explanation. SHAKESPEARE, in this scene, has particularly summoned the amazing powers of his genius to exert themselves. The transitions of Lear are beautiful; from passion he falls to condescension and tenderness, mingled with grief; then flames again, while the two unnatural hags, as he justly calls them, alternately stab a dagger in his aged heart. (357) . . .

[After the storm scenes] Cordelia is prettily introduced, and the sentiments she utters render her extremely amiable; so material an object of the plot as she is should not be left long unseen. Her filial duty is pleasingly displayed, and we wish that so meritorious a speech as what follows should have been overlooked by TATE, when he might have so much improved the acting merit of Cordelia, by putting it in her mouth. It . . . displays a most fanciful picture of Lear's deplorable situation; a few verbal altera- tions would suit it to the purpose we mention, and the introduc- tion of it is recommended to any lady who performs Cordelia— Suppose it run thus [transfers 3.1.4ff., 'the poor unhappy king,/ Contending with the fretful elements,' to Cordelia]. . . .

The great defect of SHAKESPEARE's Cordelia is that she makes too inconsiderable a figure, is too seldom in view, and has not matter for a capital actress to display extensive talents in. COLMAN has too implicitly maintained this poverty of character, and even TATE's improvement falls short of what might have been. Every alterer of SHAKESPEARE should remember there were no female performers in his days, and improve according to the present time such parts as necessity, not want of genius or knowledge, made him abbreviate. . . .

Lear and Kent again offer themselves to view; when it appears that an interval of calmness, a ray of reason breaks in upon the former, who after some very pregnant and affecting remarks upon his own condition and the shocking cause of it—filial ingratitude— submits to the persuasion of his trusty follower, and consents to take shelter in a hovel. Their approach to this wretched refuge for distressed royalty calls Edgar, in his bedlamite garb and expression, upon the stage. It was a most masterly thought of SHAKESPEARE to make the assumed madman cause an instantaneous return of Lear's frenzy: indeed, the beautiful distinction he has made between real and affected madness cannot be sufficiently admired. In all Edgar's flights we may plainly perceive a laboured diffusion of ideas, a methodical strain of images, and a studied wildness, adverting to no particular leading subject. In the execution of this our author has been amazingly successful, beyond imagination luxuriant. From Lear we have not a syllable but directs either to the original cause of his frenzy, or collaterally alludes to it. Among many other matchless beauties which occur in this scene we cannot find words to express our feelings of the king's supposing that nothing could reduce nature to so wretched a state as Edgar's, but unkind daughters; consequently that he, like himself, is an unhappy father. That speech which begins 'a serving man proud of heart,' [3.4.83ff.] we deem inimitable; as well as that of Lear which follows it.

The incident of Edgar's saving Cordelia from the Bastard's ruffians is not only, as we think, defencible, but worthy of praise as a happy thought and well calculated for action; as is the princess's cordial and becoming deportment to her exiled deliverer when he makes himself known.[1] This scene ever has, and ever will have, except upon unfeeling, stoical criticism a very engaging effect. It enriches and recommends both the characters so much that we must pronounce Mr. COLMAN's objection to it as the whimsical offspring of judgment too squeamishly chaste; especially where, in his preface, he sneers at Cordelia's embracing the ragged Edgar.[2] We are sorry for that gentleman's notions of love and gratitude, if he thinks they are confined to externals. If the princess, through false delicacy, had shunned Edgar merely on account of his mean attire, she must appear unworthy the regard of him or any other worthy man. The matter appears to us in so fair a point of view that we are bold to say if SHAKESPEARE, that competent and liberal judge of human nature, was alive he would consider this addition as an ornament also. Critics upon the drama should not only have good heads, but feeling hearts; if either requisite is

[1] See 1.360f.
[2] See pp. 294f. above.

401

wanting we should chuse to spare the former, and try nature at her own bar, without Aristotelian legislation.

We heartily wish that the insignificant, cruel, offensive scene where Gloster's eyes are put out had been left to narration. The subject of it, while in action, is shocking, and Cornwall's scuffle with his domestic ludicrous; both circumstances would have approached well in description, and so the stage would have been saved from very unbecoming transactions. However, both the alterers, through a reverence even for SHAKESPEARE's blemishes, or want of invention, have preserved what we thus object to. (359–62)

In the next scene, the description of Dover cliff engages and gratifies taste abundantly; though making Gloster fancy he has fallen down such a precipice is a bold, it is no unnatural stretch of imagination, where a mind is agonized like his by a combination of painful and distracting events, and wishes to put a period to woe by terminating existence. Splenatic persons we know, by a multitude of instances, conceive and credit [these] as great adsurdities; and why the mere matter of falling on the stage should be laughable we know not. Of this we are certain, that a Gloster otherwise respectable would never occasion even a critical smile. But Mr. COLMAN judges, perhaps, from some instances at Covent-Garden; and if these influenced him he would have been prudent in cutting out three fourths of the part. Besides, as the matter appears in his alteration, Gloster stands within a foot of the extreme verge of the cliff, yet upon hearing the king, whom he knows to be mad, he never mentions safer footing, nor ever after mentions the resolution of ending his life in such a manner. Now in the original and TATE there is a very good reason for not continuing such a determination; supposing himself preserved by a providential interposition, he resolves to bear his afflictions with a becoming resignation. If this incident was less defensible in point of probability it gives so fine a warning against the worst of crimes, suicide, and inculcates so useful, so moral a lesson of bearing up under temporal affliction that we cannot entertain any doubt of the propriety in retaining it.

Lear's madness is finely, though not quite so characteristically supported in this scene as in the third act. Though women have been the cause of his wretchedness, we wish what he says of them in the speech that begins in both the alterations: 'Behold yon simpering dame,' [4.6.118ff.] had been totally omitted. It is, indeed, considerably softened from SHAKESPEARE, but as raising fulsome ideas is its only tendency we wish it struck entirely out.

The encounter between Edgar and Goneril's gentleman-usher we by no means like: it brings an unnecessary death upon the stage. The lady's attachment to Edmund, and murderous designs upon her husband, might have been discovered in a much more suitable manner.

COLMAN's beginning the fifth act with Lear upon his couch is certainly better than making it end the fourth, as TATE has done. However, the scene is very much indebted to that gentleman[1] for the merit we find in it; nor do we remember one of more affecting nature upon the single feeling of pity. Mr. COLMAN certainly did right to adopt it. . . . (363–5)

The encounter between the two brothers is very spirited, and making Edgar the successful instrument of Edmund's punishment is a pleasing instance of poetical justice. We could have wished the ladies absent, for their contention about the Bastard is rather laughable; this COLMAN has prudently avoided.

Lear, in prison, attended by his faithful daughter, again calls upon our feelings; the attempt to assassinate him alarms human apprehension, and the happy effect of his desperation raises a degree of satisfactory astonishment.

Edgar's approach with Albany confirms the royal prisoners' safety, and different events fall in very naturally. We must not only give TATE great praise for bringing about a happy catastrophe by probable circumstance, but, in point of justice, endeavour to prove that his distribution of the characters is much better than that in the original, or that in Mr. COLMAN's supposed amendment of the alteration.

That Lear as a rash and rigid father deserves punishment is very obvious; this is sufficiently inflicted by his madness, therefore saving his life was undoubtedly just. Gloster comes under the same predicament of blame, for pursuing even the life of an innocent son. The ungrateful daughters deserve the rigour of justice, and could not fall more properly than by the barbarity of each other; and the Bastard loses his life most righteously by the hand of his injured brother. Cordelia's piety merits the highest reward of temporal

[1] That is, Tate. Gentleman does not appear to have consulted the original: Tate's version merely abridges Shakespeare, adding a few prosaic lines.

happiness, which TATE has given her by a connection with the man of her heart. The becoming a queen through France's generous behaviour, as we do not hear of any previous attachment in his favour, cannot be deemed so delicate or adequate a compensation for her virtues as bestowing her on Edgar, who is thereby also recompensed in a peculiar manner for both the love and loyalty he has manifested. The old king's consent, with Gloster's and Kent's hearty blessing, shed a brilliance on TATE's last scene highly pleasing to every good and tender mind. It adds great force to the old king's restoration and furnishes, to our apprehension, as satisfactory and compleat a catastrophe as any in the whole scope of dramatic composition.

We perfectly join in opinion that Lear should speak last, but think Mr. COLMAN might have avoided the trouble of patching up a concluding speech, when that we find in TATE,[1] preceding Edgar's, is sufficient without any alteration or addition. It is matter of no little surprize that the solicism of bringing Cordelia to view, as queen of France, without any mention of her royal consort or any attendance equal to her station, should not have struck Mr. COLMAN's critical observation. Upon the whole we must remark that in respect of the two alterations TATE had no guide but his own judgment, which, though very fallible in many places, has yet operated successfully upon the whole. Mr. COLMAN had his labours, as well as the original to work upon, and has shewed great modesty in avoiding additions, considerable merit in restoring so much of SHAKESPEARE; but has certainly weakened the piece, both for action and perusal, by rejecting so justifiable, pleasing, natural and relative an episode as the loves of Edgar and Cordelia. . . .

King Lear's character as a man we know nothing of, except from the concise picture of his being choleric and rash. There are no opportunities of displaying either virtues or vices; the impetuosity of his temper first makes him a very culpable father and afterwards, mingled with pride, runs him into distraction; the unnatural cruelty of his daughters renders him an object of pity, and SHAKESPEARE's irresistable genius has drawn him a character of admiration.

To enter upon the representation of this odd and violent old

[1] See 1.385.

monarch is a daring flight of theatrical resolution. A wide and various complication of requisites are essential to placing him in a proper and striking point of view, especially an imagination possessed of the same fine frenzy which first drew him into light. His situations, sentiments, and language being peculiar, so must his tones, looks and gestures be. Mechanical acting, which may pass agreeably enough in other smaller creations of the brain, must here flatten idea to a very palling degree.

Come forth the man whom nature has happily formed to animate with unrivalled excellence this her most favourite theatrical production—GARRICK come forth! fearless of severest criticism. We, who have singularly and repeatedly felt the most indescribable sensations from this gentleman's performance of King Lear, are obliged to confess that had he pleased us less, we should have been able to say more. There is a transcendant degree of merit which checks the boldest flight of praise, and here most certainly we have encountered it. But the more danger the more honour—therefore we rush fearless amidst an abundance of beauties, hoping we shall select with some judgment, though satisfaction is bewildered with variety.

It must be remembered that Lear is a monarch who amidst the infirmities of age has all the pride of royalty about him, and consequently aims at supporting external dignity as far as the decline of strength will admit. This natural struggle between vanity and debilitation is as happily displayed as possible in the consequential feebleness of Mr GARRICK's deportments. Strength and activity of spirit are by him most judiciously united to nerveless limbs. In the sudden starts of passion you perceive the quick flow of blood giving momentary firmness to his sinews, which passing off, an increase of languor succeeds. In his execration of Goneril at the end of the first act his face displays such a combination of painful, enraged feelings as scarce any countenance but his own could describe, though so happily pictured that the dullest mind must conceive and feel.

In the second act, where he parlies between Goneril and Regan who alternately reject him, rage and tenderness, suppressed fury and affectionate condescension are mingled happily till the conclusive speech, where his breaks of voice and variation of features surpass the finest conception that has not been impressed by him, and leave those who have seen him without words to describe.

405

At the beginning of the third act we plainly perceive the element-
ary conflict re-imaged in his distracted looks, while the eyes are
also feasted by a succession of expressive, striking attitudes. But
a peculiar beauty is the unparalleled force with which he speaks
'Have his daughters brought him to this pass', and many other
similar passages, which pass almost unnoticed from the mouth of
every other Lear we have seen. In short, through the whole of the
madness he cuts competition short by most evident superiority.
Through the fifth act, especially in the couch and prison scenes, his
critical judgment and happy powers unitedly exert themselves with
equal, though not such unparalleled success. However, where he
says, 'Pray do not mock me,' &c. to Cordelia, and 'Did I not fellow?' after demolishing the ruffians, we conceive his merit to reach
beyond all expectation. After these faint outlines of excellence
so strongly felt by the heart and so fully approved by the head,
permit us, reader, to prophecy that as no man will ever draw a
character of more importance and variety than SHAKESPEARE's
Lear, so we apprehend no person will ever shew a more powerful,
correct, affecting, original, and chaste piece of acting than Mr.
GARRICK's performance of him has done. (366–71) . . .

This tragedy in its original state exhibits a beautiful collection
of poetical flowers choaked up with a profusion of weeds, the un-
retrenched produce of luxuriant fertility; and it was an undertaking
of great merit to root up the latter without injuring the former.
How far TATE, the first adventurer, and COLMAN, his supervisor,
have succeeded, we hope the reader may collect from our animadversions.

The language of *King Lear* is of mixed nature, verse and prose;
where the former occurs, we find it bold, nervous, figurative and,
with some few exceptions, flowing; the latter is compact, pregnant
and spirited. The characters are various, and mostly very interesting, well grouped to shew each other. The plot is rather disjointed,
and the scenes frequently intrude upon the unities of time and place.
But the catastrophe, so happily conceived by TATE, atones for all
the unreformed irregularities; and we may venture to say that from
his hands the public have received a dramatic piece which appeals
so powerfully to the passions that when performed with suitable
abilities it proves rather a degree of painful pleasure, and shrinks
nature back upon herself.

In the closet it must furnish particular gratification to critical judgment, but will always be caviare to the generality of readers. (I, 376–7)

[From *A Summary View of the Most Known Dramatic Writers*]

SHAKESPEARE, who has by general consent been stiled father of the English drama, first presents himself. His characteristics in tragedy are supporting and pursuing all the passions which agitate, adorn, or disgrace human nature to their utmost extent; a strict and most praiseworthy adherence to uniformity of character, both in conduct and language. He never sinks an elevated personage in dialogue, nor raises a low one by improper dignity of phrase. Variety and strong contrasts seem always in his view: he well knew the force of his own genius, and sought subjects suitable. His choice of historical plots was highly judicious, as a more extensive field than any other, a field in which scarce any other author has ranged with success, except BANKES, whose well chosen subjects made the worst writing that ever escaped poetical pen bearable.

Though we should have been sorry to perceive the trammels of criticism on SHAKESPEARE's fire-eyed Pegasus, yet we rather wish that he had not shown so total a contempt for probable regularity. He certainly might have observed some bounds without any prejudice to his imagination, and we particularly lament those disgusting scraps of fashionable buffoonery which occur in, and disgrace, many of his best pieces. In comedy we find him fanciful and pleasant. His characters are rich and pleasing, though obsolete; his plots in general good, though irregular; most of his catastrophes satisfactory; his conversation nervous and pointed, but in some places rather stiff. Faults frequently occur, but they are hid amidst a blaze of beauties; and it may be truly said of this author that criticism reluctantly stumbles upon his blemishes, having so rich a fund for praise and admiration. (II, 459–60)...

BEN JONSON, though ranked so high in literary fame, does not appear to us deserving of so honourable a station. His tragedies are the most stiff, uncouth, laborious, unaffecting productions we know, spun out to an intolerable length by tedious, unessential, declamatory passages translated from the classics. Three of his comedies have justly received the stamp of general approbation: VOLPONE, SILENT WOMAN, and EVERY MAN in his HUMOUR; yet even in these nature seems rather carricatur'd, and there are many blamable intrusions upon delicacy of idea and expression. The remainder of his works might have dubbed any man less lucky, with the title of a bad writer, and we are perfectly of opinion that naming him with his great cotemporary is pairing authors as poulterers do rabbits, a fat and a lean one. (461)

[From *Theatrical Presentation and Performers*]

Mr. Garrick, whom we are to consider merely as an actor, is indebted to nature for an almost matchless significance of feature, enlivened with eyes peculiarly brilliant; from an amazing flexibility of countenance he can express the most contrast feelings; simplicity, mirth, rage, grief, despair, and horror, with nearly equal excellence. Hence his Abel Drugger, Benedick, Ranger, Hamlet, Macbeth, King Lear, and several other characters, have no equal, possibly never had; what may lie in the womb of time we know not, but think it would not be a very extravagant prophecy to set him up against any future excellencies taken in a general view. Great, no doubt, he is in both departments, the sock and buskin; however, though that eminent genius Sir Joshua Reynolds has placed him equally between both, we have no scruple to pronounce him most conspicuous in the latter. In light scenes he exhilirates, 'tis true, in a very peculiar manner; but in the graver and more impassioned ones he leads the heart captive as he pleases, and rouses feelings of a much more important, difficult nature, than can arise from comedy; with her he is very pleasingly sportive, but with her sister astonishingly powerful.

His peculiar excellencies are an harmonious, distinct, voluble, and extensive voice. Without any unnatural snaps the last word of all his periods is as intelligible as the loudest; in all sudden transitions his correctness, force, and judgment, are scarcely to be described; in his soliloquies he happily avoids that absurd method of speaking solitary meditation to the audience; he appears really alone.

His defects, for every light has its shade; is shortness of figure, which however by art he evades as much as possible, by not only disposing it to the greatest advantage, but also by taking care to shift situations so often that the eye can hardly have time to find out, and dwell upon the defect. Though graceful in motion, and very much so in attitude, he never could picture dignity, nor attain what is called the fine gentleman, a character indeed too languid for his active powers. Though generally correct in modulation, and almost invariably so in expressing the sense of his author, there is a respirative drag as if to catch breath, and some unnecessary pauzes, seemingly for the same purpose, which we have often been under a necessity of silently objecting to; and the same sort of censure should have sufficed still but that we set out with a positive resolution to be just, and having thus far maintained it we must continue to the end.

The leading figures should be more minutely investigated than those who have less advantages. We have often regretted an adulteration of language, by changing the *e* and *i* into *u*; this gentleman, and several after him, have pronounced *stern, sturn, mirth, murth, birth, burth*, which is really rendering our language, already sufficiently dissonant, still more so. Our English Roscius we could never admire in declamation, indeed he has kept pretty clear of it, and we heartily wish that for sake of his fame, Benedick, Ranger, Archer, Don Felix, or anything in that juvenile stile may not hereafter serve to show his advance in life. It is not enough to say he is *greater* than *any body else*; in the true cordiality of heart we form a hope that he will not in any future season appear *less* than *himself*.
(II, 482–4)

228. Paul Hiffernan, idolizing Shakespeare

1770

From *Dramatic Genius. In Five Books* (1770).

Paul Hiffernan (1719–77), an Irishman who studied medicine in Paris and practised it in Dublin, wrote dramatic criticism in the *Tuner*, 1754 (see Vol. 4, p. 46), had several farces performed, and published some miscellaneous verse. On the strength of this proposed national Shakespeare temple (Garrick had had his own private one at Hampton House since 1758) Garrick raised a subscription for him amounting to over £120. Hiffernan kept his place of lodging a complete secret.

THE FIRST BOOK

Delineates the PLAN of a permanent TEMPLE, to be erected to the Memory of SHAKESPEARE, in a Classical Taste; with INSCRIPTIONS and DECORATIONS, suitable to the Object chosen. (v)

INTRODUCTION.

The Title adopted for this Work arises with the greatest propriety from the subject in its two principal departments of *writing* and *acting*, theoretically and practically considered.

The foremost ornament in the latter article (as *Shakespeare* was in the former) England could ever boast, and at least equal to that of any other nation, having been afflicted with a severe fit of sickness in the spring of last year,[1] all ranks of tasteful and elegant life were stricken with an universal concern at the apprehension of such a loss; but which a wished-for recovery soon forced to give place to as general a satisfaction.

The interesting event was celebrated by several ingenious writers, and attempted by the Author of this Work in a short *Latin* Poem (to be introduced in the fourth Book), which proved so fortunate as to please those who are best qualified to judge of such compositions. That approbation encouraged him, on his hearing of the intended institution of a commemorative Jubilee in the honour of *Shakespeare*, to set about delineating the plan of a permanent Temple; which he humbly hopes to have executed in a manner that will not be judged unfavourably of by all admirers of theatric excellence.

It was thought proper that the inscriptions should be in *Latin*, as well as *English*; the one for the sake of learned Foreigners unacquainted with our language, and by whom we are now visited

---

[1] David Garrick was ill in 1769.

in greater numbers than usual heretofore: the other for the entertainment of our fellow-subjects, uninitiated in the poetic diction of ancient Rome. The leading thoughts in both are similar, but neither in the plain phrasing nor figurative expression strictly observant of each other, in order that an unfettered, free, and original air might prevail in both. They contain either an epitome of each piece in question or a confined allusion to one chief scene; where a narrative of the whole drama, however succinct and cursory, must be productive of intricacy and confusion.

The inscription over the Temple door, calculated to give the reader a just and reverential idea of the place, is to be farther illustrated by all the pictures within. To the entire design let those blest with ample fortunes employ our several eminent artists to give a practical existence which, through their merit, would probably not be deemed an unornamental addition to the other improvements of England's magnificent villas.

When entered into the Temple the first object for the curious spectator's attention is the great Poet; over whom is to be a sun, rising in all his glory after having dissipated and expelled from our British Theatre the long incumbent clouds of Gothic ignorance and barbarism that are to be seen flying from the victorious lustre; and underneath is to be read,

> *Barbaridûm exoriens scenæ Sol dissipat umbras.*
> *Dulness' dark shades fly* SHAKESPEARE's *solar Beams.*

Next to be considered is the painted representation of him who hath best felt, and best expressed what our transcendent *Author* wrote in the most towering efforts of his all-surpassing imagination. Over whom, as his most faithful copyist, let a rainbow return in the most striking manner all the vivid and various colourings which are imbibed from the great fountain of light; and within the sweep of the arch be read this happily apposite line from Virgil,

> *Mille trahens varios adverso sole colores.*   [*Aeneid*, 4.701]
> *All lively tints from yonder sun I draw.*

On the right hand side of SHAKESPEARE is to begin the series of chosen tragic exhibitions, which are

1° King LEAR in the storm.

2° MACBETH, with horror, confusion, and dismay on his countenance at MACDUFF's declaration that he had been untimely ript from his mother's womb.

3° Distracted CONSTANCE lamenting the loss of her son, prince ARTHUR.

4° RICHARD THE THIRD when fallen under the victorious sword of RICHMOND; he, with the gnashing of despair, upbraids Heaven for his disgrace.

5° HAMLET hearing his father's ghost as he relates how he had been poisoned.

6° ROMEO and JULIET in the tomb scene.

Over these MELPOMENE is to be displayed with all her attributes, and pointing to them with a scroll in her hand, bearing these words, *En mea progenies.* (*Behold my progeny.*)

OTHELLO has been purposely omitted for this reason; the blacking screens and renders incommunicable to spectators all impassioned working of the countenance.

The comic series is to be headed, from the left hand side of SHAKESPEARE, by

1° BENEDICK and BEATRICE in their most spirited encounter; to be followed by

2° CALIBAN between the two sailors.

3° TOUCHSTONE and ROSALIND, in the humourous scene of berhiming her name.

4° APEMANTUS and TIMON railing at each other.

5° SHYLOCK and PORTIA in the senate scene.

6° Cornuted FALSTAFF with THE MERRY WIVES OF WINDSOR and other spectators of his vicious folly.

Over these the *comic* muse, in contrast to the *tragic*, is to be seen with her attributes, and a scroll in her hand, as she points to them, bearing these words, *Hæc mea sunt.* (*These belong to me.*)

On the ceiling, APOLLO is to be painted looking affectionately towards SHAKESPEARE, as his favourite son; and upon the part opposite MERCURY, pointing to the Actor whose exertion alone could equal the fire of that superior and priviledged mortal whom APOLLO delights to behold.

Thus the composition will hold together, progressively unfolding and illustrating the inscription over the Temple door.

THE EXTERIOR INSCRIPTION FOR THE TEMPLE.

Nor gay THALIA's comic *Fane* stands here,
Nor solemn *Temple* of the TRAGIC MUSE;
But SHAKESPEARE's Shrine, they emulous have rais'd!

SHAKESPEARE.

Behold the prince of all dramatic bards;
Tho' *Greece* shou'd boast her *Æschylus*, and join
Euripides to *Sophocles*, with those
Of comic merit to support her claim.
   In competition less can dare to stand
Either the *Sock* or *Buskin* of old *Rome*;
Of *christian* date the *new* has no pretence.
   To him, proud *Gallia*, you must yield the palm,
And own, however great, your efforts short
Of his all-grasping comprehensive thought.
   Albion rejoice, and celebrate the name
That beams immortal honour on thine isle;
SHAKESPEARE of THEE, and THOU of SHAKESPEARE worthy!
   Who can th' extent of such a genius trace,
And who portray the features of his mind?
Vain were th' attempt, for when th' impulsive glow
Of energy divine inflames his soul,
He's more than mortal as he thinks and writes!
He tow'rs above the imagery of Nature,
That wond'ring stares at his creative power! (3–9) ...

The MERRY WIVES of WINDSOR.

A Braggart, liar, coward, and a knave,
All puff without, all worthlessness within;
Lo; *Falstaff* pants, a fluctuating waste
Of monstrous garbage, not of human flesh!
   Alien from honour, and bright glory's call,
He envies not the fame of yesterday,
To virtuous victims of the warring pow'r,
In brave defence of all that man holds dear.

413

Deprest with fat, with impotence, and age,
He'd fain be thought to feel love's am'rous flame,
And *Windsor's merry Wives*, with lewd display
Of wanton, loose, libidinous desires,
Incontinent assails. In sportive mood
They hear; resolving on their cumb'rous wooer,
Just and repeated punishment to have.

The first in *Buck-basket at Datchet-Mead*,
Where, from amidst foul linen closely pent,
And congregated stench of vapours rank,
Into the *Thames* ROTUNDITY is hurl'd,
With *Fat all melted! hissing hot!*—amaz'd,
The water starts from it's huge flouncing guest!
And were the river's bottom sunk to hell,
He down to hell precipitate had shot,
Alertly twinkling his alacrity in sinking!

The next in shape of *Brentford's* beldam swath'd.
The personage of spell-fraught witch, he suffer'd
Correctful bastinado, for vile scheme
Of making chaste young dames break marriage vows.

Their last device th' old lecher to entrap
Was, that he'd wear th' adornings of a buck—
Lo—what he meant on other heads to plant,
Our new *Actæon* brandisher of, horns;
The scoff, joke, scorn, and ridicule of all. (41–3)

[Shakespeare defended from Voltaire]

The following answer I gave to a French gentleman's remark,
as we were walking in the gardens of *Versailles*:—'Is it not surprising that so sensible a people as the *English* can be pleased with
Shakespeare's absurdities?'—'The *English*, sir, are not pleased with
Shakespeare's absurdities but bear with them (which they very
well knew before any strangers had attempted a discovery of) on
account of his excellencies, which every thing considered, the
æra he lived in, his narrow education, early marriage, deer-
stealing frolicks, &c. are really miraculous.'

But it were needless here to undertake the defence of that
Olympian *Jove* in dramatic writing, who has been so victoriously
defended by our English PALLAS* against the vain and impious

* An Essay on the Writings and Genius of SHAKESPEARE.

attempts of French giants in criticism, ENCELADUS VOLTAIRE
at their head; proving from his works

> Unde nil majus generatur ipso;
> Nec viget quicquam simile, aut secundum:
> Proximos illi tamen occupavit
> PALLAS HONORES.   HOR.[1]

[Imitated.]
Than him no greater bard was ever born;
None equal sang, or next in rank is nam'd;
Yet second honours let her brows adorn
Who in his cause will live for ever fam'd.

Shakespeare shines first on the list of our *tragic* writers, and is the
foremost on that of our *comic*; for as to him nature gave all the
power she could: so art gave to *Ben. Jonson* every resource.—
Therefore they are recommended as the best models to study;
in the most regular of *Shakespeare*'s comedies, *The merry wives of
Windsor*; with the *Silent Woman*, *The Alchymist*, and *The Fox*, by
the second father of our stage. ... (94–5)

---

[1] *Odes,* 1.12.17ff. (Praising Augustus): 'From whom is begotten nothing greater than
himself, nor doth aught flourish like or even next to him. Yet the glory nearest his Pallas ...
hath secured.'

229. Edward Burnaby Greene, rhetoric in Shakespeare

1770

From *Critical Essays* (1770), § I: 'Observations on the Sublime of Longinus. With Examples of Modern Writers, As of The Holy Scriptures, To illustrate the several Figures remarked throughout the Work'. Essays III, IV, and V are on the *Aeneid*.

Edward Burnaby Greene (*c.* 1735–88), a poet and translator of no great originality or accomplishment, published an essay on pastoral poetry in Francis Fawkes's translation of *The idylliums of Theocritus* (1767), and 'Occasional essays' added to his own translation of *The works of Anacreon and Sappho* (1768). He translated Pindar, Persius, the *Argonautica*, turned Gray's Latin odes into English and an English one into Latin. His associating of Shakespeare with Longinus derives from the tradition of Leonard Welsted in 1712 (see No. 57 in Vol. 2) and William Smith in 1739 (No. 91 in Vol. 3).

Prolixity in sudden transports of passion is unnatural, and conciseness pushes forward upon the soul a thought which is weakened, if not ruined, by description. ... Though our excellent Shakespeare (who from his admirable adherence to nature eclipses the rays of the ancient drama) expands his abilities more usually in a vein of sentiments which 'come home to men's bosoms,' he possesses a share of merit in the more *direct* road of conciseness. (28) ...

[Chapter 15] Shakespeare introduces images with admirable taste: but in this he is perhaps superior to any author, ancient or modern. Perhaps!—that is injustice to his merits. The* madness of Lear, the wild confusion of Macbeth preparing the murder of Duncan, and the singular distress of Timon upon his fall, are

* See the string of elegant examples represented by Mr. Smith [3.97f.].

copied only from nature. SHAKESPEARE's pen is the magician's wand commanding the soul of his reader; an AMALTHEA's horn, decorated with all the flowers of luxuriant genius. (65) ...

[Chapter 22: On the figure *Hyperbaton*]
The Hyperbaton has been usually construed 'a transposition of words, inverting the natural order of a sentiment, and calculated to describe the confusion arising from anger and impatience.' But this definition seems not so wholly to characterise the figure. I think that the following quotations will consistently express the real meaning of the *Hyperbaton* which, in addition to the above opinion, I should be tempted to call 'a repetition, or a series of repetitions gracefully introduced, which steals upon the attention by enlarging the thought and dwelling (in a degree) on the same expressions.' The first definition excludes the softer passions, which the latter may be judged to respect. May I venture to submit the following lines as an example of the Hyperbaton in its complete acceptation, conformably to the foregoing complex definition?

ANTONY addresses the Romans over the body of the *butchered* CÆSAR, in the play of SHAKESPEARE formed on the wild barbarism of his murder. The speech is a master-piece of judgement and poetic artifice, drawn from the source of eloquence.

> Friends, Romans, countrymen, lend me
>   your ears. ...
> But BRUTUS says, he was ambitious;
> And BRUTUS is an honorable man. ...   [3.2.73ff.]

The force and peculiar propriety of this repeated side-compliment to BRUTUS is evident when it is reflected that he was idolised by the people for assassinating CÆSAR (87–90) ...

[Chapter 31: that 'Simplicity is often a source of true sublimity']
Two exquisite proofs are produced by Mr. SMITH[1] from the plays *Romeo and Juliet*, and *Timon*. Another, not inferior, is remarked from the fall of Cardinal WOLSEY, who was, as his own conscience told him, justly punished with degradation, for prostituting himself to the capricious violence of a tyrant. [Quotes 'Farewell; a long farewell to all my greatness!' 3.2.351ff.] He then goes on in this expressive simile:

[1] See 3.101f.

417

I have ventur'd,
Like little wanton boys, that swim on bladders,
These many summers, on a sea of glory,
But far beyond my depth.   [358ff.]

... That comparisons drawn from an inferior object will not always be defective appears from SHAKESPEARE, where he paints 'Lowliness as young Ambition's ladder' in his tragedy of JULIUS CÆSAR. BRUTUS corroborates his innate aversion to kings, improved from the patriotic violence of a predecessor kinsman, by the ensuing enlargement on CÆSAR's principles. [Quotes 2.1.12ff.]

This comparison at first sight appears not labored, like that of VIRGIL: but nature pleads so strongly in its favor, that there had been little use in art.(121–4) ...

[Chapter 38] The author is here treating of *Hyperbole*, which means an expression above the ordinary course of reason or experience. Hyperbolical descriptions necessarily carry with them an air of dignity, till they come to be (which is too often the case) absolute incoherencies. An hyperbole in the hands of an unskilful author is extravagance painted to excess; and the reader cries out with the poet, 'Incredulus odi.' The quotation of the critic may serve as a proof of this: such an expression as that which he offers is not an hyperbole but an absurdity below confutation.

SHAKESPEARE has made use of a very striking hyperbole in his *Hamlet*.

Bow, stubborn knees; and hearts with strings of steel,
Be soft as sinews of the new-born babe.   [3.3.70f.]
                                                  (139–40) ...

[Chapter 38: on *Diasyrm*, the inverted hyperbole, which 'increases the Lowness of any Thing'.]

The *Diasyrm* (mentioned in the text) is more immediately characteristic of the speaker MERCUTIO, where he jests upon his wound— in *Romeo and Juliet*. 'It is not so deep as a well, or so wide as a church-door; but it will do.' [3.1.93f.]

A train of more solemn Diasyrms is to be met with in the following passage of SHAKESPEARE, in his tragedy of *Julius Cæsar*.

CÆSAR, addressing himself to ANTONY, speaks of CASSIUS.

Yond CASSIUS has a lean and hungry look;
He thinks too much. Such men are dangerous. ...   [1.2.192ff.]

These speeches flow from human nature, which evinces daily, that 'nugæ in seria ducant.'[1] (145–6)

[From Essay IV, on Virgil's *Æneid*, Book IV]

In Tragedy, the younger sister of Epic poetry, the wildest efforts, introduced with becoming dignity, are admitted if they shock not belief. The plays of our SHAKESPEARE are many of them formed on the plan of novels, and of novels more evidently romantic. The understanding disapproves them not, because *real* history is neglected; indeed fables are better adapted to the drama, as the author, by varying events at pleasure, may make a history of his own, and no critics can fall on him for the violation of truth. (226)

230. John Armstrong, Shakespeare and the Unities

1770

From *Sketches: or Essays on Various Subjects*, II (1770).

On Armstrong (1709–79) see the head-note to No. 164 (Vol. 4, pp. 313–15).

OF THE DRAMATIC UNITIES.

I suppose few architects will deny that walls, doors, windows, a roof and chimneys are necessary to a convenient habitation. In my opinion a strict adherence to the three Unities, as they are established upon the firm foundation of good sense, is not less necessary in the structure of both Tragedy and Comedy; which otherways, especially as represented upon the stage are irregular,

---

[1] Horace, *Ars Poetica*, 451: 'These trifles into serious mischiefs lead' (tr. Ben Jonson).

slovenly, blundering, absurd and improbable. And that even *we* are not shocked at the daily trespasses against them is owing to custom and Shakespeare. But it requires so much art to fill up five acts of a play with the business of one single interesting event; without one scene that is not necessary to forward it; without the least change of place; and without exceeding the time of representation, or even the compass of twelve hours, which is permitted by the courtesy of the critics; that it is no wonder most of our dramatic writers affect to despise rules so difficult to practise.

The three great French dramatic poets, Corneille, Racine and Moliere, have in this article been much more successful than the English: amongst whom, if you except Ben Jonson in three or four of his capital pieces, I am afraid we shall find very few who have built upon a regular plan; which is exactly the same thing to a play as composition is to a history in painting. Shakespeare indeed without one perfect plan has perhaps excelled all other dramatic poets as to detached scenes. But he was a wonder!— His deep knowledge of human nature, his prodigious variety of fancy and invention, and of characters drawn with the strongest, truest, and most exquisite strokes oblige you to forget his most violent irregularities. However, to compare two stupenduous geniuses in different departments; Shakespeare for this mere disregard of plan appears less perfect than Raphael: who has heightened the truest and most masterly expressions in his various characters by the advantages of a composition the most august and superb imaginable, where it was proper; and always the most elegant, easy, happy, and natural. (241–2)

231. J. R., Ode to Shakespeare

1771

From the *St. James's Chronicle*, no. 1559, 16–19 February 1771.

SHAKESPEARE

When Nature to Athens and Rome bid adieu,
To Britain the Goddess with Extasy flew:
So tempting she look'd, and so blooming her Charms,
Jove quitted his Sky, and indulg'd in her Arms.

On Avon's fair Banks, now the Subject of Fame,
She brought forth a Boy, and Will Shakespeare his Name:
Not Egg was to Egg more alike, than in Feature,
The smiling young Rogue to his Parent, Dame Nature.

Of all her sweet Prattlers she lov'd Willy best;
She nurs'd the young Smiler with Milk from her Breast:
And as he grew older, she nothing conceal'd,
But all, all her Secrets to Willy reveal'd.

She fed him with Honey from Hybla's sweet Shore,
The same which her Homer had tasted before;
A Swan on the Avon first taught him to sing,
Whilst the Loves and the Graces danc'd round in a Ring.

An Eaglet from Jove's fav'rite Hobby was given,
On which the young Genius oft frolick'd to Heaven;
And when Willy sung, all the Deities swore,
They ne'er heard such Warblings, such Wild-notes before.

With Envy just bursting, with impotent Lies,
And Sneers, Momus pelted the Bard of the Skies;

Jove kick'd the foul Critic from Heav'n's azure Round,
And, venting his Spleen, now at Ferney he's found*.

To govern, and lead as he pleas'd in a String,
Jove gave him the Passions, they hail'd Willy King;
The Muses, as Handmaids, were doom'd to attend him,
And Phœbus with Wit's brightest Ray did befriend him.

A Pow'r to create Jove to Willy assign'd;
This Pow'r, tho' to Fancy's bright Regions confin'd,
Or Willy all Chaos with Life had endo'd,
And Jove for Creations had wanted new Food.

Jove next gave the Boy from his Thunder a Shaft;
Will grasp'd it, and fearless play'd with it and laugh'd:
Not Jove could his Light'ning dispatch with more Art,
Or send the wing'd Vengeance more sure to the Heart.

The Deities all shew'd their Love to the Boy;
Minerva gave Wisdom, and Venus gave Joy;
But Juno, quite jealous, with insolent Pride,
To Jove's Love-begotten all Favours deny'd.

Fresh pluck'd from his Wing Cupid gave him a Quill,
Which Willy long flourish'd with magical Skill;
He penn'd with it Strains that enchanted the Spheres,
And drew from the Soul of stern Pluto salt Tears.

The Harp, when he sounded, Vice instant grew pale,
Whilst Virtue triumphant rose high on the Gale;
Each Note to our inmost of Cores found its Way,
Nor like mortal Notes on the Surface did play.

The light-tripping Fays still awaited his Nod,
Oft with them he danc'd on the green-circled Sod;
Sylphs, Demons and Witches, strait flew at his Call,
And his Magic the Mob of the Air could enthrall.

* Voltaire's Seat near Geneva.

Ye Bards of all Ages, yield Shakespeare the Bays,
What Star can be seen 'mid the Sun's dazzling Blaze?
Let Britons, enraptur'd, their Thanks swell on high,
One Shakespeare on Earth—and one Jove in the Sky.

York, Jan. 1.   J. R.

232. Richard Cumberland, adaptation of *Timon of Athens*

1771

From *Timon of Athens. A Tragedy altered from Shakespeare, by Richard Cumberland, Esq.* (1771).

Richard Cumberland (1732–1811), interspersed a political career with prolific output as a dramatist (over 30 plays), a novelist, and an essayist (his periodical the *Observer*, 1785–91, contains much literary criticism, and translations of Greek comedy). His two most successful plays were *The Brothers* (1769), and *The West Indian* (1771), which ran for 28 nights and sold 12,000 copies. In the *Critic* Sheridan had a personal revenge on him in the portrait of Sir Fretful Plagiary.

Cumberland cuts much of the Apemantus plot, including the first banquet; he removes most of Timon's curses; and he adds a female role, Evanthe, the daughter of Timon. She has been wooed for two years by Lucius, one of Timon's syco-phants, but he rejects her once Timon loses his fortune. Alcibiades, however, has fallen in love with her, and decides to help Timon: for this the Senate banishes him. When he returns for vengeance on Athens Evanthe persuades him to relent, then sets out to find her father. In the last two scenes, given here, Cumberland first applies poetic justice to the 'flattering lords' Lucullus and Lucius.

[Act V, Scene 2]

SCENE *changes to a Street in* Athens.

Enter Lucullus

    Lucul. Let the storm light upon improvident man!
I saw it in the wind. Let *Athens* blaze;
Let *Alcibiades* with brutal rage
Extinguish this fair scene, and these fam'd schools,
Towers, temples, palaces, convert to dust;
Lucullus built not on such sandy hopes;
But as the wary falcon hangs her nest
Where danger cannot reach it, so did I,
Prophetic of this hour, dispose my fortune
Where the sun never looks, within the womb
Of mother earth, deep hid, a mine of gold,
A magazine to save or sack a city,
The fruit of seven years bounty from this *Timon*
With all my thrift cou'd add—Good morrow, *Caphis.*
Enter Caphis
    Caph. Here's a sad change; all's lost—myself beheld
Your palace flaming.
    Lucul.   Knowing this, good *Caphis,*
I know the worst—What bring you from Lord *Timon?*
    Caph. Contempt and mockery; he's too proud to curse you.
    Lucul. Took he the gold I sent?
    Cap.   He took your gold
And scattered it like ashes; why 'twas nothing;
Breast high in coin he stands, I think the Gods
Have show'r'd it on him; never did I see
So vast a treasure.
    Lucul.   Hah! a treasure sayst thou?
Did I hear right; hath *Timon* found a treasure?
    Caph. He hath, my Lord; and such an one it seems
As betters his lost fortune.
    Lucul.   You confound me;
Where was this mine discover'd? Tell me, *Caphis.*
Canst thou describe the spot?
    Caph.   Know you the wood
West of the city, where Lord *Timon* keeps
His wild and savage haunt?

  Lucul.   Well, *Caphis*, well;
Proceed, I know it well; each brake and bramble;
Each little path that threads its winding way
Thro' the fantastic maze, I can unravel
Familiar as my garden.
  Caph.   On the skirts
Of this rude waste within a lonely dell,
With poplars and with aspins planted round,
Sacred to *Faunus* stands a Sylvan fane,
An antique structure.
  Lucul.   Did he find it there?
I am alive again.
  Caph.   Observe me well:
South of this fane, about an arrow's flight,
A solitary beech, whose upmost boughs,
Mould'ring with age, in leafless ruin hang,
The grandsire of the forest, stands—
  Lucul.   Enough.
It is my treasure; you've describ'd the spot—
It is my treasure; these providing hands
Dug the unfaithful soil and at the root
Of that old traitor buried all my hopes.
  Caph. Your treasure?—Fortune, how severe thou art!
  Lucul. These are your doings, ye vindictive Gods!
I see you rise against ingratitude,
And push us from the earth; I have deserv'd it.
Timon, thou art revenged—Death, be my refuge!

              [Exeunt.

Lucius *enters muffled.*
  Luc. Soft, who goes there? *Lucullus*, as I think;
I have no heart to speak. Where shall I hide?
What hill will cover, or what cave conceal
A wretch like me? Wou'd I were *Timon*'s dog
Rather than what I am—Egregious dotard!
Various Soldiers of Alcibiades *enter, carrying plate, treasure,* &c.
  How now, what's here? O poison to my sight!
These are my treasures—Lost, undone for ever.
See, see another yet, and yet another—
By heavens the very cup which I did worship
More reverently than the Gods—It was the work

Of antique *Melidorus*, fit to bear
Celestial *Nectar* from the ministring hand
Of *Hebe* to the lips of *Cretan Jove*.
Swallow me, earth—Oh, the unholy villains,
They pause for breath; they'll kill me if I speak to 'em.

[They pass over.

But soft! this man seems of a gentler sort:
He is a stranger of the General's train
And knows me not. I may accost him safely.
The good hour to you, Sir—I pray you now
Whence are these riches?
     Sold.   Do you live in *Athens*,
And ask that question? Know you not one *Lucius?*
     Luc. I've seen the man.
     Sold.   Then you have seen a villain,
A most dissembling, base, unmanly villain.
Wou'd I cou'd meet him—
     Luc.   Wou'd you slay him then?
     Sold. No, but the sight of these his treasures wou'd:
We've stript the knave to the skin; he did deny
Lord *Timon* certain vile and sorry drachms
In his distress; now *Timon*'s star prevails,
And justice wrings these treasures from the gripe
Of that perfidious, that ingrateful *Lucius*.
     Luc. Men in all ages have been found ingrateful.
     Sold. But none like him; society bleeds for it.
     Luc. Hath *Athens* then a law to try the heart?
     Sold. The order of the General is our law.
     Luc. But is there nothing sav'd?
     Sold.   All, all is swept
To the last drachm; pictures, statues, coins,
Rich hangings, couches, vestments wrought with gold,
And robes of *Tyrian* dye; plate, jewels, gems—
Is't not a pleasant jest? Why laugh you not?
You only seem of all men to be sad.
     Luc. I cry you mercy; I am wondrous merry—

[Feigns a laugh

I've heard he had a ring, a most rare jewel,
Is that gone too?
     Sold.   Behold!   [*Shewing the ring*

426

Luc.   Ay, 'tis the same.
Sold. Mark, what a play! 'tis a most perfect stone.
  Luc. Wou'd 'twere a basilisk!—must this away
To *Timon*'s with the rest?
  Sold.   Yes, and 'tis time
That it were there—Good morrow, gentle Sir.
  Luc. Curse on your courtesy!   [*aside.*
  Sold.   I'm glad you like
The ring so well: If you should meet the knave,
Tell him the prize we've got, and gird him well,
I know 'twill give you pleasure: All men loath him.
Be sure you wring him to the quick—remember.

                          [*Exit*

  Luc. Remember! yes: no fear but I'll remember.
You've giv'n me cause; the Gods, who deal in vengeance,
Reward you for it! I could dash my brains,
For that way only can I 'scape remembrance.
O nature, what a luckless piece of work was man!

                          [*Exit.*

[Act V, Scene 3]

The prospect of a rude wild country, to a considerable extent, with the ruins of a temple to Faunus. Timon *is discovered at the extremity of the stage led in by* Flavius: *At the same time* Evanthe *enters at the front, surveys him some time, and while he slowly advances, speaks.*

  Evan. O spectacle of sorrow! Mighty Gods,
Is that my father?—is that mournful ruin,
That bare and blasted trunk the spreading vine,
Beneath whose shade late a whole nation sat
And feasted from its branches? Hold, my heart:
Sink not, my knees, beneath your weight of woe,
But bear me to his feet—My Lord, my father!

                        [*She kneels.*

  Timon. Rise, rise, my daughter—do I once again
Enfold thee in my arms? Alas, my child,
I'm old and weak and smitten sore with grief.
Gods, how ingratitude lays waste your works!
Unkindness, like another deadly plague,
Strikes all below the moon; creation groans;

Nature with more than mother's pangs brings forth
Her thankless offspring man.
    Evan.   All shall be well.
    Timon. All, all is well, for thou art in my sight.
Mute as these scenes and calm as summer seas,
Here will we sit and meditate a while,
Then die and be at peace.
    Evan.   Oh! talk not thus.
    Timon. Give me your pardon; I have suffer'd much,
And much I fear sorrow has shook my wits;
But in the bitterest moments of affliction,
I have remember'd still to bless my child.
    Evan. O bless me not in part, compleat my joy,
Return to me, to *Athens*, to thyself,
And these base emblems of thy discontent
Like the *Nessean* garment cast away,
And be at peace with a repentant world.
    Tim. Can I, who from the depth of hell have call'd
Malignant spirits to ensnare mankind,
I, who each night upon the lonely strand
By the sea brink, or in this silent waste
Have stood and bandied curses to the moon,
Till the grey dawn look'd out; can I now teach
That voice, which execration has made hoarse,
The smooth soft notes of peace? will nature pardon,
That common mother, in whose patient bosom
I have stuck iron goads?—It will not be.
    Flav. Move him no more, dear Lady, 'tis in vain.
    Tim. Yet I had cause—Speak, *Flavius*, thou art honest,
And wilt not flatter, had I not full cause?
    Flav. May the just Gods, who know thy wrongs, revenge 'em!
    Tim. Hush, hush! no more of that—We must be calm;
Shatter'd with storms, at length I see my port,
And stretch for death's calm shore—Rejoice, my child,
Thy father's sufferings hasten to an end,
And life and care shall terminate together.
    Evan. Alas, my father, talk not in this strain;
Bright years of glory rise to crown thy hopes;
Great *Alcibiades* defends thy cause,
The suppliant Senate come to kiss thy feet,

Loaded with treasure, while repentant *Athens*
From all her gates pours forth unnumber'd crowds,
To hail thy glad return.
    Tim.   —Why, let them come!
Shou'd *Alcibiades* to please old *Timon*,
Burn *Athens* to a heap, crush the proud Senate,
And swallow that vile swarm of summer friends,
That left him bare to shame; shall *Timon* say
I thank thee, Sir, for this great courtesy?
Shall man say this to man, who in pure love
And singleness of heart ne'er stirs his hand
To aid his suffering fellow?
    Evan.   Nay, that's hard.
    Tim. Rather let *Timon* say, I have a daughter
Beauteous and young, and fair as unsun'd lilies;
Your eye has drank her charms, and strong desire
Knocks at your heart, therefore let *Athens* burn;
Spare not a man that e'er spake *Timon*'s name
But in the way of worship— Oh, 'tis great,
'Tis glorious friendship in his daughter's arms.
    Evan. That daughter is no idle wanton, Sir,
To doat on every form that courts the eye;
Tho' nature fashion'd him with every grace
Which the joint bounty of the Gods cou'd give him,
Yet *Alcibiades* had pass'd unnotic'd,
With *Lucius* and *Lucullus*, and the herd
Of common flatterers, were he that base thing,
Which your description paints him.
    Tim.   Soft you now;
He is a man, and *Flavius* is no more;
Yet he is honest, and you'll say, another
May be so too—Two honest men, ye Gods!—
Can there be two? I know you can do much,
Ye great Divinities! therefore I say,
It may be so; but mark me well, my child,
I vouch it not; that were indeed too much.
    Evan. Does Heav'n cloath falsehood in celestial robes?
See where he comes. Who can survey that form,
And doubt if honour dwells in such a shrine?
Yes, in each glance, each gesture it appears,

429

Lives in his tongue, and lightens in his eye,
Pervades, inspires, and occupies his soul.
Enter Alcibiades
    Alcib. Health to thee, noble *Timon!* health and fame,
Peace and fair fortune! The *Athenian* Senate,
Stung with remorse and shame, present themselves,
Entreating your return with them to *Athens.*
    Tim. Say to the Senate, you have seen me die;
Timon is now no more; here lies their prey.
                [*He sinks down on the steps of the temple, being
                    supported in his fall by* Evanthe *and* Flavius.
The stout old hart they've cours'd so long in view,
Dead, dead you see, and fairly hunted down.
    Alcib. Much injur'd *Timon,* they have seen their faults,
Their former thriftiness they have cast from them;
And now their coffers, like their hearts, stand open
To your free use.
    Tim.   Alas, kind-hearted men!
Oh! they are cunning murderers; fine the wound,
And hard to trace, where sharp unkindness strikes,
Therefore they say I am not struck at all;
But Heav'n rejects their plea, and in my heart
Sees the dire arrow rankle.
    Alcib.   Live, oh live!
Shake off despair and live, most worthy *Timon;*
See on all sides my soldiers fence thee round.
Athens I've humbled to thy meanest use,
And driv'n to shameful flight that loathsome crew,
Whose black ingratitude corrodes thy heart.
    Tim. And what in recompence can *Timon* give to *Alcibiades?*
    Alcib.   More than the Gods did,
When they gave life; thou can'st bestow *Evanthe.*
    Evan. O *Alcibiades,* forbear to urge
At this sad hour thy inauspicious suit:
Hence must we date our nuptials? this a time
To ask a blessing in? this awful moment,
For mourning, for misfortune only fit,
Can this be happy when a father dies?
    Timon. No more: give me your hands; come on each side:
The overshadowing heavens shower down upon you

Infinite blessings; make you one in heart,
In mind, faith, truth, contentment! shun mankind:
Live to yourselves and to the Gods alone.
    Evan. Break, break, my heart!
    Timon. Weep not for me, my child; death is my cure,
Life my disease. Son, daughter, friend, farewell.
Bring not my corps within the walls of *Athens*,
But lay me on the very hem of the sea,
Where the vast *Neptune* may for ever weep
On my low grave—Remember—Oh! 'tis past. [*Dies.*
    Evan. There fled his spirit: waft it, immortal Gods,
Up to your heavenly mansions: yes, my father,
We will entomb thee by the ocean's edge
On the salt beach; and when the thronging waves,
Which every morn shall bow their curled heads
To kiss thy tomb, shall, like the flattering friends
Of this base world, fall off and leave thee bare;
Then will I come down to the vacant strand,
Washing thy grave with never-ceasing tears,
Till the sea flows again.
    Alcib.   Ah turn, *Evanthe*,
Turn from that mournful sight and look upon me;
Damp not the blessing which his dying breath
Pronounc'd upon us, and lament not him,
Who, freed from this bad world, rests from his cares.
Now let us bear him to the neighbouring beach;
And with such rites, as soldiers use, inter him
Under the vaulted cliff, (such was his will)
Strong in extremes, from love to hatred tost,
In the fierce conflict he was whelm'd and lost.

233. John Potter, Shakespeare in the theatre

1771–2

From *The Theatrical Review; or, New Companion to the Play-House* (2 vols, 1772). These reviews first appeared in the *Public Ledger* and other newspapers, under the title 'The Theatrical Review. By a Society of Gentlemen, independent of Managerial Influence'. Potter was identified as the author in lampooning verses in the *St. James's Chronicle* for 19–22 and 24–6 October 1771. On Potter see C. H. Gray, *Theatrical Criticism in London to* 1795 (New York, 1931), pp. 193–7.

John Potter (*c.* 1734–1804), miscellaneous writer, published a volume of poetry in 1754, and in 1756 established a newspaper, the *Devonshire Inspector*, at Exeter. Through Garrick he was introduced to Tyers, proprietor of Vauxhall Gardens, and wrote for the entertainments there several hundred songs, cantatas, etc. In his later years he published a number of novels, travel books, political pamphlets, worked as an intelligence agent abroad, and practised medicine in Ireland. His Shakespeare criticism (totalling over 160 pages, but padded out with many quotations) owes much to Johnson and Kames, debts often unacknowledged.

CYMBELINE: *A Tragedy, by Shakespeare*

This pleasing Dramatic Romance (for it cannot be considered in any other light) is one proof amongst many of the amazing fertility of *Shakespeare*'s unbounded fancy; for though the Plot as far as it relates to *Posthumus* and *Imogen* is taken from *Boccace*'s *Decameron*, and the rest from the ancient traditions of the *British* History, there is little historical besides the names.

[Quotes Johnson's concluding note: above, pp. 150f.] Whoever places himself in the Critic's chair must subscribe to these sentiments. But then it should be considered of whom we are speaking:

Of *Shakespeare*, the first Dramatic Author in the World; who, scorning to be bound by any Laws, gave a loose to the workings of the most extensive imagination that ever possessed the mind of Man. The irregularities in this Piece are numerous, we confess; yet notwithstanding all these it contains an infinity of Beauties, both with respect to Language, Character, Passion, and incident; and the severity of Criticism must abate of its rigour by contemplating on those wonderful strokes of Genius with which it abounds. So that while the Judgment is displeased with the improbability of the Plot, and inconsistency of the Dramatic Action, the Mind must receive the highest satisfaction from the pleasing excursions of Fancy; and though it is impossible we can be inattentive to the obvious defects of the Piece the pleasure we receive from it, on the whole, naturally inclines us to behold them with an eye of favour.

This Piece was revived some years since with great Alterations,[1] consisting chiefly of a removal of the most glaring Absurdities with respect to Time and Place, an omission of some Characters and Scenes not necessary to the general Design, and which only increased the number of its Perplexities and retarded the progress of the main Design. As it now stands its Merit is sufficiently known, and the satisfaction it has constantly given in the Representation has always been exprest with the highest applause. (I, 15–17)

[On *The Merchant of Venice*]

The Plot is well contrived, notwithstanding it is irregular; but the Unities of Time and Place are materially broken. The Characters are well chosen, and in general supported in a masterly Manner. The Incidents are not only numerous but pleasing and affecting, and many of the Sentiments are truly sublime. In short, tho' this Piece hath many defects its beauties are infinitely more numerous.—With what art and perfect knowledge of human Nature in her most degenerated State has the Poet drawn the Character of *Shylock*! How nobly has he availed himself of the general Character of the *Jews*, the very Quintessence of which he has displayed in a delightful manner in order to enrich this Cha-

---

[1] This is presumably Garrick's cut version of 1762. See Hogan, *Shakespeare in the Theatre* (2.167).

racter. And though he has evidently deviated from a Matter of fact (according to Tradition), in representing the Jew the Hero of Villainy and Barbarity instead of the Christian, popular Prejudice will sufficiently vindicate him; not that we think he was absolutely bound to adhere to the matter of fact, if it really was so. After all, the Picture here drawn is so disgraceful to human Nature, that we doubt whether it ever had an Original. (36–7) ...

[Quotes Shylock's divided reactions at the loss of his daughter and his ducats: 3.1.72ff.]

How admirably are the dissimilar Emotions arising from unconnected Causes here brought on in quick succession, and producing opposite effects. The Emotions being unequal in force the stronger, after repeated conflicts, extinguish the weaker. *Jessica*'s elopement and infidelity make no figure in opposition to his intended revenge on *Antonio*; for after a few slight vibrations his mind settles in joy, and his loss is forgot. This Scene is a master-stroke. (39) ...

[On *Romeo and Juliet*, in Garrick's adaptation; see Vol. 3, No. 117]

We think this learned Editor [Johnson] has been rather sparing in his Remarks on this Play; for though it is far from being the Masterpiece of this great Author it has singular Merit with respect to the Plot, Characters, Incidents, Language, and moral Sentiments. The Catastrophe is affecting, and sufficiently Dramatic. The Characters of the unfortunate Lovers are very highly painted; and that of *Mercutio* is so boldly touched and so truly original as to do great honour to the inimitable Author of its Creation.

We shall now proceed to speak of the Alteration.—We have heard of five, if not of six Attempts to render this Piece more regular and better adapted to the Stage, some of which we have seen, but as all of them fall short of Mr. *Garrick*'s Alterations, and as that is the only one in possession of the Stage we shall confine ourselves to it—Mr. *Garrick* found what must be obvious to a Person so well skilled in the properties of effect as he undoubtedly is, that *Shakespeare* had neglected to heighten the Catastrophe to so great a degree of distress as it was capable of being carried. This was an Object worthy attention, in the Management of which it is but just to observe he has succeeded wonderfully. As *Juliet*'s awaking before *Romeo*'s death, and the transports of the latter on seeing her revive, overcoming even the remembrance of the very late Act of desperation he had committed, give scope for that sudden transition from rapture to despair which make the recollection that death is approaching infinitely more affecting and the distress of *Juliet*, as well as his own, much deeper than it stands in the Original Play, where she does not awake till after the Poison has taken its full effect in the death of *Romeo*. Besides this material Alteration Mr. *Garrick* has rendered the whole more uniform and regular, without taking any great liberties more than restoring *Shakespeare* to himself, as it were, so thoroughly has he discovered himself acquainted with the genius of this inimitable Poet.

When the Play was revived with these Alterations the funeral Procession of *Juliet* was first introduced, the Music to which was composed by Dr. *Boyce*. It is a Piece of Stage Pageantry we confess, but it adds very little, in our opinion, to the importance of the Tragedy. (62–3) . . .

[On *King Lear*]

With respect to *Tate*'s alteration, we cannot help being of opinion with Dr. *Johnson* that the happy change in the catastrophe, if not more natural, is abundantly more pleasing. . . . *Tate*'s alteration is adapted at this Theatre, greatly to the praise of the Managers and the wishes of humanity. And though we think the Piece might have been more considerably improved by reducing many of the irregularities still retained, the alterations to be placed to his account are so very respectable as to do him considerable credit. What mind is so pleased with melancholy Ideas, or the struggles of injured virtue in distress, as not to receive much heart-felt satisfaction in the last Scene, where *Edgar* and *Cordelia*, surmounting all difficulties, are made happy in each others love as a reward for their loyalty and virtue?

The Character of the *Fool* is entirely omitted in this alteration, and the under-Plot of the loves of *Edgar* and *Cordelia* is wholly *Tate*'s. For which, and the happy change in the catastrophe, though brought about by probable circumstances, he has been severely censured by those who determine with great boldness upon the various degrees of literary Merit, but too frequently give their opinion without much knowledge of the cause before them.

At *Covent Garden Theatre* Mr. *Colman* has introduced another alteration of this Play, in which he has availed himself of some of *Tate's* errors, or rather over-sights, omitted the episode of the loves of *Edgar* and *Cordelia* and considerably heightened the distress of the catastrophe; but we doubt very much whether humanity will give him her voice in preference to *Tate*. (211–13) . . .

[On *The Tempest*]

With respect to the Language put into the mouth of *Prospero* there are many Passages truly sublime, enriched with the finest images and dressed in the most nervous expression, which time will not permit us to cite. But there is one instance which sets a few objects before the eye without much pomp of Language, yet it is truly beautiful. It operates its effect by representing these objects in a climax, raising the mind higher and higher till it feels the emotion of grandeur in perfection.

> The cloud-capt tow'rs, the gorgeous palaces,
> The solemn temples, the great globe itself,
> Yea all which it inherit, shall dissolve, &c.   [4.1.152ff.]

The cloud-capt tow'rs produce an elevating emotion, heightened by *the gorgeous palaces*, and the mind is carried still higher and higher by the images that follow. Successive images, making thus stronger and stronger impressions, must elevate more than any single image can do.

As on the one hand no means directly applied have more influence to raise the mind than grandeur and sublimity so, on the other, no means indirectly applied have more influence to sink and depress it; for in a state of elevation the artful introduction of an humbling object makes the fall great in proportion to the elevation. The above Passage is a beautiful example of this observation. The elevation of the mind in the former part of it makes the fall great in proportion when the most humbling of all images is introduced, that of an utter dissolution of the earth and its Inhabitants.[1]

The above mentioned celebrated Speech is inscribed on *Shakespeare's* Monument in *Westminster-Abbey*; but the famous soliloquy in the Tragedy of *Hamlet*, viz. *To be or not to be* was intended to be placed on his Monument, only it was objected to by the Clergy as improper. (244–5) . . .

---

[1] This passage is plagiarized from Kames, *Elements of Criticism*, 1785 edition, I, pp. 240f.

[On *Timon of Athens* and Cumberland's adaptation, No. 232 above]

This Tragedy, as we have it from *Shakespeare*, is extremely faulty in point of Regularity, many of the Passages being very perplexed, while others appear to have been corrupted through the ignorance or inattention of Transcribers. It contains many beautiful Passages; but, upon the whole, it is not one of those Plays in which either the extent of *Shakespeare*'s views or elevation of his fancy is fully displayed, for he has not exerted much invention in the Conduct of his Plot. Tho' it must be confessed that he has diversified his Characters so as to make a very pleasing and interesting variety, and preserved most of them with great exactness.—The most remarkable Character in the Piece is that of *Apemantus*, which is probably as highly finished as any thing to be met with in the whole of *Shakespeare*'s Works; and must be allowed to be a Master-Piece of Ill-nature and satirical Snarling. Some of his Strokes discover great knowledge of Men and Things, and afford many useful hints to the vain, the extravagant, and the profligate.

With respect to the Alteration of this Play, it is the Work of Mr. *Cumberland*, the Author of the *Brothers* and the *West-Indian*, of whose abilities as a Dramatic Writer we have made mention in some former Numbers.—As the Piece now stands some of the original Scenes are omitted; others considerably reduced for the sake of brevity, and many of the Speeches stripped of those obsolete and indelicate Passages with which they too frequently abounded. These Omissions having greatly reduced the Piece with respect to length, it became necessary to add somewhat to fill up the *Hiatus* which these Omissions had occasioned. With this view Mr. *Cumberland* has rejected the Characters of *Phrynia* and *Timandra*, the Mistresses of *Alcibiades* (who only appeared in one Scene, in the fourth Act); and by giving *Timon* a Daughter, viz. *Evanthe*, he has interwoven a Love-Plot between her and *Alcibiades* in order to give a further extent to the Piece.

With respect to the Omissions some of them are commendable; but we by no means approve of the Banquetting Scenes being rejected in the first Act, it being absolutely necessary to the Plan in order to heighten the succeeding ingratitude of *Timon*'s false friends; besides that, it is one of the principal Scenes in which *Apemantus* appears. In the room of this we are presented with a Dance, and the Banquet is only spoke of.—The new Character of

437

Evanthe is not badly drawn; she is a good example of filial picty, tho' of but little service to the main Design of the Piece.—And we do not think Mr. *Cumberland* has greatly improved the Character of *Alcibiades*, except that it is more laudable for him to marry a virtuous woman than to keep two mistresses. But tho' this may be more moral, we are afraid it is departing from the truth of History, for we do not recollect that any of the Authors who have spoke of him make the least mention of his being married. He was a man of libertine principles who, indeed, became reclaimed in the latter part of his life through the instruction of *Socrates*.

Mr. *Cumberland* has shewn himself but a very feeble hand in writing Love-Scenes, and the event of *Alcibiades'* union with *Evanthe*, though with the consent of *Timon* in his last moments as a reward for his services, is brought about in a strange bungling manner. He has made a great part of the fourth and fifth Acts his own, but we think he has left them full as languid as they were originally; though perhaps he imagines the humour thrown into the Character of the *Soldier* in the fifth Act will in some measure remove this disagreeable circumstance; but we cannot help thinking he will find himself mistaken, for his attempts to be witty are very despicable. . . .

Upon the whole, as far as we were able to judge of the Piece in its altered state from the first night's Representation, we do not think the Improvements very important. There still seems to be somewhat more wanting than the Mutilations mentioned above, or than these Additions, to render this Play what we could wish it to be. And as we think Mr. *Cumberland*'s Additions very inadequate to the Sterling of *Shakespeare* we cannot help wishing that some Writer of sufficient ability would think it worth his while once more to revise this Tragedy; and, by treating it with a more sparing hand than Mr. *Cumberland* has done, and improving it upon *Shakespeare*'s original plan, render it sufficiently interesting; which would entitle it to an equal immortality with the best of this celebrated Author's Pieces. This would be paying a pleasing and a grateful tribute to the memory of the greatest Dramatic Writer, the world ever produced.

The new Scenes are well executed, and the Dresses are pleasingly imagined; nor is the Illumination in *Timon*'s hall inconsistent with that ostentatious *Athenian*'s extravagance and love of splendour. The truth and perfection of Theatrical Representations in a great measure depends on proper Decorations; otherwise all that the Player can inculcate will prove ineffectual. In this particular, even envy must allow, Mr. *Garrick* has generally discovered great judgment, and we recollect few instances of his erring with respect to this point, which is more than we can say of any other Manager within our knowledge. Scenery and Decorations are very important auxiliaries to the keeping up the illusion and carrying on an appearance of reality in Theatrical Representations. But it requires great knowledge to introduce them properly; because they should never engross that attention in an Audience which is primarily due to the Player. (250–4) . . .

[On *Twelfth Night*: quotes Johnson's end-note, above p. 109]

We acknowledge ourselves of the Doctor's opinion with respect to the last particular, but we think he has been somewhat sparing of praise in his general Character of this pleasing Comedy. It is true, it does not exhibit a just picture of life, and on this account fails to produce instruction, which should be the grand aim of the Drama; but as all amusements do not professedly unite themselves with instruction, tho' it is best when they do, surely a Piece full of exquisite entertainment, founded on innocent circumstances, displaying Characters inoffensive in themselves, and Dialogue untainted either with licentiousness or obscenity is entitled to a considerable degree of approbation.—The Plot of this Piece is well contrived, and the Incidents in general are sufficiently probable to be pleasing. The Characters are numerous, and marked with great variety; and tho' some of them are not exact portraits of nature they are not so much on the extreme as either to disgust or be unpleasing. A more innocent set of beings were probably never grouped together. If any one of them can be said to be reprehensible it is *Olivia*, whose sudden love for *Viola* in man's attire, and precipitate marriage with *Sebastian* thro' the mistake of dress, is not altogether consistent with a woman in her exalted situation; and yet we frequently meet with instances of this sort in real life, which derive their origin from chaste love and have their foundation in the principles of honour and virtue. She could not entertain a passion for the *Duke*, tho' she was assured of his love; but this is no uncommon case; and his repeated solicitations form some excuse for the sudden choice of an object which appeared to her to be lovely, and worthy of her esteem and affection. *Shakespeare* seems to have been aware that *Olivia*'s hasty love for the disguised *Viola* would be considered in an unfavourable light, when he put the following lines into her mouth.

> ————————How now?
> Even so quickly may one catch the plague!
> Methinks, I feel this youth's perfections,
> With an invincible and subtle stealth,
> To creep in at mine eyes.   [1.5.278ff.]

Thus much of *Olivia*.—With respect to the Character of *Sir Toby Belch*, it may be objected that he is a drunkard. This we acknowledge, but in other respects he is inoffensive. What is observed above [by Johnson] of *Sir Andrew Ague-cheek* is undoubtedly just; and *Malvolio* is drawn rather in the extreme. Yet surely, tho' there is something singularly ridiculous in this fantastical Character it is rather deserving of applause than censure, and the trick played him by *Sir Toby*, and *Maria* exhibits such contrivance and contains so much true humour as cannot fail of affording exquisite entertainment to the Spectators.—*Clowns* were Characters in which *Shakespeare* delighted; and tho' there was hardly a Play wrote in that time without one, he has varied the *Clown* in this Play with considerable distinction from those in his other Pieces.—*Viola* is a very pleasing Character, yet her conduct is very singular and unaccountable. She forms a deep design with very little premeditation. She is thrown by shipwreck on an unknown Coast, hears that the Prince is a Batchelor, and resolves to supplant the Lady whom he courts.[1] This is not a little extraordinary, and the only excuse to be made is that her resolution was necessary to *Shakespeare*'s Plan.

If it be agreed (and surely it may) to excuse the few inaccuracies and imperfections mentioned above for the sake of the real and intrinsic beauties with which this Play abounds, we think the Piece now before us does not fall greatly short in point of merit of the best of *Shakespeare*'s Comedies, the *Merry Wives of Windsor* excepted. For a greater variety of original Characters is not exhibited in any of his Pieces, all admirably furnished and proportioned to the employments designed them, and each differing from the other. How are they all dressed from the stores of his luxurious imagination, without being the Apes of mode or borrowing

[1] These two sentences are in fact Johnson's: see p. 108 above.

from any foreign wardrobe; for each of them are the standards of fashion for themselves. (276–9) . . .

[On *Othello*]

The Fable of this Play is founded upon one action only, which is conducted with great skill; and if from the distress of the Catastrophe it is not the most pleasing of *Shakespeare*'s Tragedies, it is undoubtedly the most perfect. All the Characters are admirably drawn; the Sentiments, where it is required, are sufficiently elevated; and the Moral is excellent: viz. enforcing in the most natural yet powerfull manner the fatal effects of endulging the pernicious and ungovernable passion of jealousy.—Some Critics have been disgusted with the distresses and unhappy fate of the virtuous and innocent *Desdemona* because, say they, she had not been guilty of the least fault or failing, and therefore her fate is too horrible to be born. To this we answer that though she is from first to last an object of pity, and her fate greatly to be lamented, yet her misfortunes are owing to a cause extremely natural, and not at all uncommon, viz. the jealousy of her husband.

Others have objected greatly to the Character of *Iago*; particularly the learned Author of the *Elements of Criticism*, who says that not even *Shakespeare*'s masterly hand can make the picture agreeable, and that it is so monstruous and satanical as not to be sufferable in the Representation.[1] This opinion, however, has been sufficiently proved to be too far strained by the applause with which the Play has always been received whenever it is performed. *Iago* never fails to engage the attention of an Audience, though his Character is so conducted as to render him detestable; in which the Poet has shewn great judgement. (310–11) . . .

If there is any fault in the Character of *Iago* it is that of his grounding his resentment against *Othello* on very trifling circumstances, viz. his having set a younger Officer over his head on a particular and singular vacancy, notwithstanding he himself still stands most high in his esteem and confidence, and consequently in the fairest light for being immediately preferred by him to a post of equal if not greater advantage. To this indeed is added a slight suspicion, which he himself declares to be but bare surmise, of

[1] Kames, *Elements of Criticism*, 1785 edition, II, p. 368: 'Iago's character in the tragedy of *Othello* is insufferably monstrous and Satanical: not even Shakespeare's masterly hand can make the picture agreeable'.

Othello's having been too familiar with his wife, a particular which *Othello*'s Character and cast of behaviour seems to give no authority to; and on these slight motives he involves in the ruin he intends for the General three innocent persons besides, viz. *Cassio*, *Roderigo* and *Desdemona*.—We are aware that it may be said in answer to this that the more trifling the motives of his resentment, the greater is the art of the Poet in working them up to such an amazing height. But this, we believe, will not bear a very strict examination; for the greater his resentment is heightened on trifling circumstances the more unnatural it certainly must be.

With respect to *Othello*, his military Character is admirably sustained; but though his jealousy is finely wrought up by the machinations of the designing and plausible villain *Iago*, yet from first to last it is raised by trifles, *viz.* the loss of a paultry hand-kerchief which *Desdemona* knew not was of value, and her pleading for *Cassio*'s forgiveness, who had been cashiered on a most trivial fault. These are all the circumstances which corroborate the vile insinuations of *Iago* against the innocent *Desdemona*, and produce so fatal a Catastrophe. *Othello*, therefore, is drawn rather too credulous, and forfeits by such conduct some of our pity. (312–13) . . .

No Writer ever discovered a more accurate or extensive know-ledge of the emotions and passions of the human mind than *Shakespeare*. We shall quote one instance wherein the passion of anger is admirably exhibited and finely painted, and that in an uncommon appearance. [Quotes 'Villain, be sure thou prove my love a whore', 3.3.363ff.] (317). . . .

[On *The Merry Wives of Windsor*]

[This play] is generally allowed to be the most perfect of all his Dramatic Pieces in the Comic way. Even *Dryden*, who was not fond of praising other Writers, acknowledges it to be exactly formed. [Vol. 1, p. 137] And surely nothing can be a more convinc-ing proof of the force of this great Writer's Genius, or how capable he was of executing any hint given him, than the Piece now before us? Which is as perfect in its kind as any thing to be met with in our own or any other Language. This will appear the more extra-ordinary if we consider that it was written before a taste for Regu-larity was established in this Nation. A more perfect set of high-finished Characters was never exhibited in any Play. The double Plot is admirably contrived, for the under Plot is not only finely connected with the principal one and employs the same persons, but it occupies the intervals of the main action and is brought to a conclusion at the same time; which ought always to be the case, though it has been neglected by many of our best Dramatic Writers.—We have here a proof that Wit and Sprightliness are better suited to a virtuous than a vicious Character, and nothing can be more highly entertaining than the conduct of Mrs. *Ford* and Mrs. *Page*, two Ladies not more remarkable for mirth and spirit, than for the strictest purity of manners. (II, 25–6) . . .

[On *Macbeth*]

This excellent Tragedy has generally been considered as one of the *Chef d' Oeuvres* of our inimitable *Shakespeare*, and it has been the subject of much controversy whether the preference should be given to this Play or the *Othello* of the same Author. As a perfect Piece *Othello* deserves the preference most undoubtedly, but the Genius and invention displayed in *Macbeth* is almost superior either to description or praise; and the numberless Beauties it contains are important and wonderful, notwithstanding the whole Piece is so extremely irregular as to disregard every rule of the *Drama*. (59–60) . . .

[The discussion of Lady Macbeth's evil, pp. 65–6, is plagiarized from Kames's *Elements of Criticism*: See Vol. 4, p. 476.] The Poet has shewn great art in the third Scene of the second Act, where, speaking of the murder, he makes Lady *Macbeth* say,

> ——Had he not resembled
> My father as he slept, I had done't.   [2.2.12f.]

This is very artful: for as the Lady and her Husband are drawn it was natural to suppose the act should have been done by her. That it is otherwise shews great judgment, and is highly just; for though ambition had subdued in her all the sentiments of Nature towards *present* objects, yet the likeness of one *past*, which she had been accustomed to regard with reverence, made her unnatural passions for a moment give way to the sentiments of instinct and humanity. (70)

[Two succeeding discussions are plagiarized from Kames: that of Macbeth's apostrophe to sleep, p. 72, with its disapproval of metaphors and similes, comes from the passage given in Vol. 4, p. 491; that on Macduff's reaction to the murder of his children, pp. 78–82, comes from the passage in Vol. 4, pp. 491–2.]

234. George Steevens, Shakespeare in the theatre

1771–2

From the *St. James's Chronicle*.

This column of 'Dramatic Strictures' by *Hic et Ubique* ran from 21–4 December 1771 to 3–5 March 1772. Gray, *op. cit.* in headnote to No. 233, pp. 197–208, discusses the theatre criticism in this newspaper from 1771 to 1779 and attributes many of the reviews between 1774 and 1777 to George Steevens, using such external evidence as the Garrick *Correspondence*. Steevens is known to have written much for this journal (see *DNB*), and became one of the proprietors in 1775. I attribute these notices from the earlier period to him on the grounds of the many correspondences with his views on *Hamlet* expressed in the next item, in Nos 237, 238, and his edition of 1773 (No. 240).

[a] No. 1690, Dec. 21/24 1771

To the Printer of the S. J. CHRONICLE.

SIR. The ignorant and unjustifiable Abuse that is thrown out continually in the Daily Papers, both in Prose and Verse, upon the Gentlemen who write for the Stage, those who conduct it, and those who perform upon it, have induced me to offer my Services in Behalf of the Public and their Servants. Let me not be misunderstood, I don't mean to flatter those who are grosly injured, or to satirize those who are unreasonably praised. I will endeavour to bear the Ballance with a steady Hand; I mean simply to do my Duty as an impartial, independent Critick of our public Diversons, and of Things and Persons connected with them. I will, as far as in me lies, and by your assistance Mr. Printer (if you are not under any undue influence) rescue Dramatick Criticism from the ignorant and illiberal Hands it is in at present. In short, let my observations speak for themselves. I love the Theatres, and attend them; I see many Things to correct, and many Things to commend. If I am right, the Publick will applaud me; if I am not, I shall sink into the same deserved Neglect and Contempt with my Brother Scribblers. What I intend to do will be seen by my Observations, which shall be communicated to you as often as I make them: Though I will not discover to you what I *shall* do, I have no Objection to give you a Hint of what I will *not* do.

I will not criticize Players or Performances I have not seen.

I will not prejudge new Performances before Exhibition, nor be inhuman to new Performers before they have got rid of their Fears.

I will not abuse a modern Author for the Dullness of his fourth Act, which is chicfly Shakespeare's, nor praise Shakespeare for his Beauties in the fifth Act, which are wholely another's.

I will not offend, if I can help it, against Grammar, Truth, Candour, and Common Sense.

I will not receive this Christmas Time, nor at any other Time, any Presents from Actors or Actresses, nor the Freedom of the Theatres from the Managers: for I will speak my Mind, not in the Manner of certain *Gentlemen* Criticks (as they are pleased to call themselves) but with great Regard to the Publick and myself, and with great Justice and Candour to the Performers of both Houses.

And now, Mr. Baldwin, all I have to request of you for my critical Favours is this; that you will appoint a particular Place in your Paper for my Observations, and let them always be published there—that you will not suffer any of your Friends to curtail, lengthen, alter, or garble them—that you will be a little careful to print them that they may be understood, and that if these Terms are complied with, I am your humble Servant; if not, I shall vanish from the *St. James's Chronicle*, and appear again in some other Evening Paper.

Your's, &c.

Hic et Ubique.

Let my Observations be called Dramatic Strictures.

[b] No. 1704: Jan 23/25, 1772

DRAMATIC STRICTURES Upon the Comedy of *Twelfth Night* ... One of the most entertaining Plays in any Language, or upon any Stage is now to be considered; and let me remark, by the Bye, that it is become almost a Term of Reproach that a Comedy should have any Resemblance of a Novel. ... Without justifying or condemning the Practice at present, I shall only remark that Shakespeare, in the Play under our Consideration, as well as in *As you like it*, *All's well*, &c. *Much ado*, *Measure for Measure*, *Merchant of Venice*, &c. has chosen Novels for the Foundations on which to erect the most extraordinary and exquisite Edifices of Art and Nature! The late Dr. Akenside, whose Genius and Taste are well known by various Performances, pronounced this Comedy of *Twelfth Night* the Perfection of the Comic Drama. The Doctor, perhaps, was too warm in his Admiration; but surely when we consider the Variety and proper Contrast of Characters, the many uncommon Situations to unfold and bring forth the several Humours, Passions, and Peculiarities of the *Dramatis Personæ*, there is no Performance of five short Acts which contains such Matter for Mirth, arising from the happy Disposition of the Scenes and from the natural, though unexpected, Mistakes of the Characters. All the Parts being thus well and easily connected with the whole commands that Attention, mixed with Pleasure, which real Criticks acknowledge to be the best Proof of the Genius of a Comic Writer.

Twelfth Night is an admirable Comedy; and first let us pay our Respects to that most consummate Coxcomb, that ridiculous Composition of stiff Impertinence and uncommon Conceit— *Malvolio*—masterly represented from Top to Toe, with inflexible Muscles, by that Arch Comedian Mr. Thomas King.

Sir *Toby Belch*, never sober but always delightfully mischievous, is the true Picture of an old shameless Debauchee, reduced by his Intemperance to be a Hanger-on, and distressing his Niece by his Love of Drink, Noise, and Quarrelling. ...

446

Sir Andrew Ague-cheek, who admires Sir Toby, and without any one Requisite to keep him Company adds much to the *Vis-comica* of the Piece. He quarrels without Courage, drinks himself sick, and becomes the Maudlin Echo of Sir Toby, without Wit, Humour, Spirit, Fancy, or Force; and yet Shakespeare has shewn all of 'em in the Production of this most inimitable Nothing!

I should have attacked Mr. G——k upon the motley Manner of his dressing this Play when it was first revived, had he not been pleased to produce afterwards his Love-sick Duke, Sea Captain, &c. in their proper Accoutrements. We shall allow a Manager, as well as an Author, to correct their Errors, without finding Fault too hastily either with the one or the other.

Hic et Ubique.

[c] No. 1716: Feb. 18/20, 1772
DRAMATIC STRICTURES *on the Composition and Performance of* HAMLET.
The famous Cheselden (as it is reported) never went upon any important Operation in Surgery, even upon common Subjects, but he felt in Spite of Experience a very singular Anxiety upon the Occasion. What then must be my Sensations, when unguided and unexperienced, I have not only promised to *operate* upon the greatest Genius that ever existed, but likewise to take a Cut or two at his *Representer* into the Bargain?—Let us quit Figure, and to Business.

Hamlet is a curious Instance of the noblest Exertion of Dramatic Powers, and the greatest Abuse of them.—Considered as a Composition it is more, and less than Human. It rises to Inspiration, and sinks into Buffoonery. Greece, Rome, nor all the Kingdoms of the Earth, ancient and modern, can produce such Proofs of Genius as those Scenes where the Ghost appears, and those which are preparatory to them.—Perhaps the immortal Author, in his more finished and consistent Dramas, has not any Parts superior, I may say equal to the Nature, Terror, Pathos, and Character, of those astonishing Exertions of his Powers! With this Consideration it is almost impious to mention his Errors, and yet they lie open to the Observation of every common Eye.

Now to his moral Part. *Hamlet,* a most exquisite Dramatic Character, young, warm, full of Grief for his Father's Death, and fuller of Resentment at his Mother's Marriage—before he sees the Ghost, and before he knows of his Father's Murder, expresses all the combined Passions of Rage, Sorrow, and Indignation, and yet when he is assured by his Father's Spirit that Murder has been added to Adultery and Incest, and he pledges himself— *with Wings as swift as Meditation, or the Thoughts of Love to sweep to his Revenge* [1.5.29ff.]—yet from that Moment—(notwithstanding all the Bitterness of Expression, his filial Tenderness and Horror at his Uncle's Crimes, with his Father's sacred Injunctions to spur him on—*'If thou hast Nature in thee bear it not'* [1.5.81]—Revenge, and all his former Passions are stagnated, and he goes on from Act to Act playing the Fool (inimitably I must confess), always *talking, threatening,* but never *executing.* He himself indeed, in one of the finest Soliloquies that can be imagined, produces a Kind of Excuse for his Cowardice, as he calls it, in *not fattening all the region Kites with the Slave's Offal!* [2.2.573f.] which is, that the Devil might have appeared to him, *assumed his Father's Shape, and abused him to damn him* [2.2.594ff.]; but when, by another Proof, he is convinced of his Uncle's Guilt, his Father again appears to him, *to whet his almost* BLUNTED *Purpose* [3.4.111] (the best Critique upon the Play.)[1] Why does he not *then* bring about the Catastrophe? or why suffer himself to be tamely and unnaturally sent out of the Kingdom, to which he returns as unaccountably and as ineffectually as he left it. He does indeed make one Effort to kill the King before that divine Scene with his Mother in the 3d Act, but it is attended with such an abominable Reason for not doing it that it had better have been omitted, as it is in the Representation. [Quotes 'Up, Sword, and know thou a more horrid Time . . . ' 3.3.88ff.]

All the remaining Part of the Play, from the 3d Act, seems as if his Genius, quite exhausted in the *Conception, Pregnancy,* and *Delivery* of such Wonders had wanted rest, fall'n asleep,[2] and dreamt of going to England, coming back, Churchyards, Graves, Burials, Fencing Trials, Poison, Stabbing, and Death—all which are indeed

> ——*Velut ægri somnia, vanæ*
> *Fingentur species:*[3]

---

[1] Cf. Steevens below, p. 477.
[2] Cf. Steevens, below, pp. 452, 456, 472, 488 and 540.
[3] *Ars Poetica,* 7f.: 'idle fancies, . . . shaped like a sick man's dreams'.

But they are Dreams of Genius! I shall speak of the Characters, in which Shakespeare seldom is wanting, when I speak of the Representation. In short, let it be said, more to the Honour of the Abilities of this astonishing Man, that notwithstanding all the Errors, Absurdities, and Extravagancies of this Play he alone could make it interesting without Progress in the Fable, and engage the Attention of an Audience by the Magic of his Imagery and Sentiments, by the wild irregular Sallies of an inspired Imagination, unassisted by Probability, or even Connection of Events.—This wonderful Secret no other Writer ever possessed, from the Beginning of the World to this Day! We may truely say of him, both as a Poet and a Man, what Antony so well declares of Brutus, with a small Alteration of the Words:

> This was the noblest Poet of 'em all!
> His Life was gentle, and the Elements
> So mix'd in him, that Nature might stand up,
> And say to all the World, THIS WAS A GENIUS!

Hic et Ubique.

[d] No. 1717: Feb. 20/21, 1772
DRAMATIC STRICTURES *on the Performance of* HAMLET.
[by Garrick]
Though it is confessed by the most conversant and oldest Attenders upon this Performer, that he never played better than he has done in this Character, yet let me not be thought ill-natured if I wish that with the same Judgement, Skill, and Experience, he was some Years younger to represent the *young* Hamlet: This Fault, if it is one, he cannot amend, and we can only lament.

His Entrance upon the Stage speaks every Circumstance of his Situation; but let me differ, with great Deference to him, about the Manner of speaking the Speech to his Mother—*Seems, Madam! nay it is*, &c. [1.2.76] Mr. G. in my Opinion, takes away from the Dignity, Solemnity and Manhood of the Character by giving a Kind of feminine Sorrow to it. The Son, though ever so tender, should not sink the Prince in his Grief. Besides, is not his a more confirmed Melancholy from the Conduct of his Mother, than from the immediate Bursting of Sorrow for his Father, who has been dead two Months—'*But I have that* WITHIN *which passeth Show*' [1.2.85]——therefore the *inward* not *external* Exhibition of Sorrow must be the Guide to the Actor through the first Scene.—The

Space allowed me in the Paper will not permit me to express my Approbation, and therefore my Silence denotes my Consent.— As no Writer in any Age *penned* a Ghost like Shakespeare, so in our Time no Actor ever *saw* a Ghost like Garrick. For my Part I must confess he has made me believe my old Friend Bransby (who is tolerably substantial) to be incorporeal—and I think for the Time with my Friend *Partridge* in *Tom Jones*. But, not to be frightened out of my Wits, why will not the Actor speak *Angels and Ministers!* &c. upon the immediate Entrance of the Ghost? and why will he suffer his Friends Hor. and Mar. to destroy a graceful Attitude of Terror, by holding him directly?—The Seperation of the three Persons in different Positions would be more terribly Picturesque, and they should take hold of him only at—

> *Hamlet*—*I'll follow thee!*
> *Horatio*—You shall not go, my Lord—   [1.4.79f.]

Fear then gets the better of Ceremony, and they lay hold upon him, 'till he breaks from them at—'*I say away—go on—I'll follow thee*—' [1.4.86] In the following Scene with the Ghost I approve much of Hamlet's speaking the Line—'*O horrible, horrible, most horrible*'—[1.5.80] which divides the long Speech of the Ghost, and gives a Line of Energy to Hamlet, who is too long silent without it——yet I doubt whether Shakespeare intended it.

In Act the Second, our Actor makes a small Mistake, which I should not have remarked had he not repeated it.—Speaking to Polonius of the *God-kissing Carrion* [2.2.181]—he points to the *Sun*, when it is the *dead Dog* that is the *God kissing Carrion*.—I must repeat it that it is much to the Honour of a Poet, and of the Actor, who can support Scenes of no Action or Interest to the Play (as the second Act is) and render them entertaining even after the most interesting and sublime Scenes of the Ghost in the first.— The Soliloquy which finishes the second Act is a Master-piece of Reasoning and Passion—and is a Model of this Kind of Writing— there is no Scene of Dialogue more interesting or impassioned.— May I venture to ask, if Mr. G. would not please the Judicious more by exerting his Powers less, in this Soliloquy?

Act III. *To be or not to be*—has not the Fault in the Execution which I hinted at above—the same with Ophelia, if not played with Levity, will appear too severe for the Character of Hamlet.— Shakespeare, by asking the Question, *Ha, ha! are ye honest?* with a Laugh, is a Direction for the Player.—It is not natural to think that Hamlet in Love with Ophelia would be too rough with her.—She has done nothing to deserve it, and it is the best Distinction of feigned from true Madness that he would choose from his Feelings to support it with as little Outrage as possible to her he loves; of the two Ways in his Power, he would naturally choose that which would give her and himself the least Pain.—The Advice to the Players (never more wanted, and less attended to than at present) is *well spoken, with good Accent, and good Discretion.*—It is Pity that Hamlet is obliged in his Rant at Ophelia's Grave to contradict himself. If I were Hamlet, I would give up the Rant and the Applause together.—Mr. G. may do as he pleases.

We are now come to the great Scene of this wonderful Play.—It has been Matter of much Dispute in the News-papers and Coffee-houses whether the two Pictures should not be large ones hanging up in the Queen's Closet, rather than Miniatures taken out of his Pocket.—As there was no Cessation from Playing but in the fanatical Times, from Charles the First 'till the Restoration, the Manner of performing the Scenes in the Author's Time is undoubtedly handed down to us—Besides, has not he taken Care to give us a Hint that the Pictures should be in little? *Those that would make Mowes at him while my Father lived, give twenty, forty, fifty, an hundred Ducats apiece for his* PICTURE IN LITTLE. [2.2.360ff.] A Critick who sat near me on the 2d Night of performing this Play, and whom I judged from his Discourse, to be an Antiquarian, very significantly assured us that the two Pictures should be golden Medals in Cases, which, he said, would put an End to the Dispute by convincing every Body of the Propriety of his Thought.— This Gentleman slept more than half the Play.

—Let me just mention, that there was a particular Look of that excellent Actress, the late Mrs. Pritchard, when Hamlet says—*Do you see nothing there?* which was much wanted—She turned her Head slowly round, and with a certain *Glare* in her Eyes, which looked every where, and saw nothing, said, '*Nothing at all; yet all that's here I see!*' [3.4.133] which gave an Expression and Horror to the Whole, not to be described. That Circumstance excepted, I was contented, and expressed my Satisfaction as warmly as any gaping Spectator of 'em all. As I mean nothing but to search after Truth, and to be of as much Service as I can to the rising Generation of Criticks and Actors (who will always take their Favourite for their

Standard to judge and act by) let me propose a Doubt, which Mr. G. himself has begot in me.—As he must have felt the good Effects of a low tremulous Manner in many Parts of this Scene with his Mother, would not the Whole executed in the same Manner affect an Audience more deeply? I am aware that the Actor might urge the great Effect of Contrast, and that acting, like a Picture without Light and Shade, or a certain Variety, would fail in Art; it may be so—But could I be as expressive and audible in that under-speaking as I could in a louder Exertion of my Powers, I would follow Nature wherever she guided me, though the two Galleries should fall asleep at the Performance! *Dixi!*

Nothing can be said in Praise of the remaining Parts of the Play, notwithstanding that many Pearls may be found among the Rubbish. If I had my Will, I would quit the Theatre at the End of the 3d Act, though Roscius himself were to perform the Part of Hamlet. It is some Comfort to us little Beings that the most sublime Genius can sink from Heaven below the Earth, that our greatest Philosopher, *Bacon*, and our greatest General, *Marlborough*, could descend to the Weaknesses of the lowest Minds; and that our greatest Poet, *Shakespeare*, could produce the two last Acts of Hamlet.[1]

Hic et Ubique.

[e] No. 1720, 27/29 Feb. 1772 [Letter to the Editor]

SIR, Your Correspondent *Hic et Ubique* is one of those few Writers who think themselves obliged to treat Authors with Candour and Politeness, and to behave with Decency and good Manners to the Players.

I have read his Letters with Pleasure; they convey Instruction with Politeness; they abound with judicious Remarks; they convince us that the Writer is at once a Master of his Subject, an easy well-bred Man, and an agreeable Companion.

Will you permit me, Mr. Baldwin, to give my Opinion of some passages in his last Letter, in which he censured, or at least pretended to censure, the Performance of Hamlet by our matchless Roscius. In my Opinion he makes but a mock Fight of the Business; for if he has no stronger Objections to Mr. Garrick's Hamlet than

[1] Cf. Steevens, pp. 456, 472 and 540 below.

what are contained in those Strictures, I will venture to pronounce that the Actor is not only inimitable, but infallible.

His first Attack is on the Behaviour of the Actor in his first Speech to his Mother. Here he complains that he is too feminine in his Grief, too defective in solemn Dignity. Mr. Hic et Ubique knows very well that the Passions will not stand upon Ceremony, and that the Prince has very little Advantage over the Peasant in the Expression of strong and settled Grief. . . .

Our Critic seems to rise in his Remarks upon Mr. Garrick's Action at the Appearance of the Ghost. Why will not, says he, the Actor speak 'Angels and Ministers,' upon the Entrance of the Ghost? Why! Because if he understood his Situation he could not possibly utter a Syllable. Nothing is left to him or any Man, who sees or thinks he sees a wonderful and terrible Spectre, but an almost breathless Astonishment! If any Time can justify the *vox faucibus haesit*,[1] this is the Time.

The Soliloquy at the End of the second Act is admirable, and perhaps the most impassioned and animated in all Dramatic Poetry. As Mr. Garrick never amuses us with false Fire, I should be sorry to damp his noble Ardour by a cold Recipe from the Critical Standish.

Hamlet, on seeing Ophelia in the third Act, assumes an extravagant Behaviour which distinguishes feigned from real Madness. How he could possibly convince Ophelia that he was distracted by a more delicate Behaviour, I am as much at a Loss to know, as I am to distinguish in this Place real Criticism from that which is feigned and ironical.

I will tell your comical Friend Mr. *Hic*, that the Dispute about the Pictures of the two Kings was not confined to News-Papers and Coffee-Houses; the learned Dr. Armstrong, in a Pamphlet abounding with excellent Criticism, which was published many Years ago,[2] asserted that Hamlet should not in that Scene produce two Pictures in Miniature; no, he ought to point at two large Family Portraits in the Room; *sed pace tanti viri*, he is all wrong. Our Critick's Authority from Shakespeare is excellent: Doubtless Wilks saw Hamlet acted by Betterton a hundred Times, and copied him in that Scene. Betterton played soon after the Restoration, and knew some of the old Actors, the immediate Successors of

[1] *Aeneid*, 2.774, 3.48, etc.: 'the voice clave to my throat'.
[2] See 4.315.

Hemings and Condell, the Friends of Shakespeare. It cannot be doubted that he was instructed by them in all the mechanical Part of his Business.

What follows is so comical that I hope I shall be pardoned for not treating the Gentleman's *Doubt*, as he calls it, seriously. He would submit it to Mr. G. if he should not act the Scene between him and his Mother in a *low, tremulous Voice*. Your Servant, Mr. *Hic*; a Scene of half an Hour in a Whisper would furnish an excellent Entertainment to the Audience: Mr. Garrick, as Mr. Bayes, knew how to pen a Whisper very well; but I will answer for him, if he will permit me, that it will never be in his Power to act such a Scene as that between Hamlet and his Mother in such a Manner as to make it a Secret to the Audience. This brings to my Mind a ridiculous Message from a ridiculous Messenger in *The Rehearsal*:

> The Army's at *the Door*, and *in Disguise*,
> Desires to speak a Word with both your Majesties.
> QUOLIBET.

[f] No. 1722: 3/5 March, 1772
DRAMATIC STRICTURES *continued upon* HAMLET.
Though I fear my indulgent Readers may be tired with three Lectures upon the same Play, yet as I promised to say something of the other Characters, I shall always think it incumbent upon me to keep my Word with the Public.—The King, guilty of Adultery, Incest, and Murder, has nothing particularly to distinguish him from other Royal Villains, but one of the most pathetic and highly finished repentant Struggles, in the third Act, which ever fell from the Pen of Genius! '*O my Offence is rank!*' &c.—[3.3.36] . . .

Polonius, though a Crust for the Criticks, is a most common natural Court Character.—He is a perfect old Courtier, tripping and dangling after the Heels of Royalty, who, with Buffoonery and Experience of the World, having picked up by Time trite Sentiments and superficial Knowledge, blends them ridiculously with his own peculiar Cast of thinking, and Manner of acting, which (without naming Names) have been realized within these few Years by some Noblemen we all remember. Mr. *Baddely* avoids that common Fault of making the Character nauseously ridiculous; but there is a certain mock Importance, and vacant Stare of ignorant Astonishment, which I contrive to be spread over Polonius's Features, when Hamlet sports with him, that I never yet saw quite executed to my Mind.—In short, it is one of those mixed Characters which appears with almost contradictory Qualities, yet all in Nature, requiring the Genius of Shakespeare to write and a great Actor to perform—His busy Curiosity and Willingness to be employed in that meanest of Characters, a Court Spy, has been judiciously thrown in by Shakespeare, that his Death might not be too much felt by the Audience.

Horatio, the Friend and Companion to Hamlet, is kept down, as the Painters phrase it, in proper Subordination to the Prince.—Whenever an Horatio shall have a Set of Features to express Terror, he will have it in his Power, by seeing the Ghost first, to forestal (if I may be allowed the Expression) in some Degree the very great Effect of Hamlet's Terror and Astonishment when he is put into the same Situation.

Laertes is more a marked Character than Horatio, and though he is blackened by plotting with the King against Hamlet's Life, yet his Rage upon his Father's Death, and pathetic Heart-breaking over the Madness and unfortunate End of his Sister, is truely dramatic.

The two Friends, *Guildenstern* and *Rosencranz*, are, as they ought to be, two very pliant, courtly young Men, full of passive Obedience, who think themselves honoured by a King's Command to do the meanest, and most contemptible Actions.—Good Cloaths, tolerable Persons, and well-powdered Wigs (which is not always the Case) are the requisite Qualities for these two young well-bred Gentlemen.

The *Queen* is an extraordinary Personage, if one could forget that she was not an Adultress (for Incest was not so great a Crime in those Times, and whether she was Accessary to the Murder is doubtful); she appears otherwise amiable throughout the Play.

Ophelia—The first theatrical Impression made upon the Author of these Strictures was by the late Mrs. Cibber in this Character. The Propriety of her Deportment, her Expression of Grief mixed with Terror at the Behaviour of Hamlet, and the Whole completed by a Harmony and Pathos in her Scenes of Madness is only to be conceived by those who have seen her. That I may not be thought to have taken all for granted at that Time, I confess, at the Setting-out of the Character with her Father and Brother she did not

455

charm my Ear, for Want of Simplicity in her Manner; she rather spoke too tragically, and with a Sort of Stage Cant. But as the Part proceeded, the Actress grew warm, and when once she was seized with a Passion, Whining and Monotony sunk before it; and the fourth Act, with all its Imperfections, had its Effect upon the Audience even after the Masterpiece of Genius at the End of the third. ...

Hic et Ubique.

235. George Steevens, advice to Garrick on adapting *Hamlet*

1771

From *The Private Correspondence of David Garrick*, ed. James Boaden (2 vols, 1831), I, pp. 451–4. The letter is dated 'Hampstead, Saturday Evening, 1771'.

... I expect great pleasure from the perusal of your altered *Hamlet*. It is a circumstance in favour of the poet which I have long been wishing for. Dr. Johnson allots to this tragedy the praise of variety; but in my humble opinion, that variety is often impertinent, and always languishing on the stage. In spite of all he has said on the subject, I shall never be thoroughly reconciled to tragi-comedy; for if the farce of theatrical deceptions is but short-lived at best, their slightest success ought not to be interrupted. This play of Shakespeare, in particular, resembles a looking-glass exposed for sale, which reflects alternately the funeral and the puppet-show, the venerable beggar soliciting charity, and the blackguard rascal picking a pocket.

I am sure when you personate the Danish Prince, you wish your task concluded with the third act, after which the genius of Shakespeare retires, or only plays bo-peep through the rest of the piece.[1] I confess I am talking a kind of poetical blasphemy; but

[1] Cf. Steevens's similar comments, pp. 448, 452 above, and 472, 540 below.

I am become less afraid of you, since you have avowed your present design.

I think you need not fear that the better half of your audience, (as Othello says,) *should yawn at alteration*.[1] No performer whatever would be able to recite all that Shakespeare has put into the mouth of his prince with equal energy. You are therefore furnished with a plea for declaring that performers must either check their powers, or shorten the drama where it grows to an unreasonable length. Every man in his senses must think you had done right in making the latter your choice; for you will then be enabled to do justice to all you retain, and to retain no more than deserves that justice. I cannot answer for our good friends in the gallery. You had better throw what remains of the piece into a farce, to appear immediately afterwards. No foreigner who should happen to be present at the exhibition would ever believe it was formed out of the loppings and excrescences of the tragedy itself. You may entitle it, *The Grave-Diggers; with the pleasant Humours of Osrick, the Danish Macaroni*.

As you intend to stab the usurper I beg, for your own sake, you will take care that this circumstance is not on his part awkwardly represented. Those who die on the stage either in single combat or by suicide generally meet with applause; but Henry the Sixth standing still to receive the dagger of Richard too often excites merriment. Poor Gibson was sure to convulse the audience with laughter whenever he fell in that character: and yet it is no more than justice to his memory to observe that all who knew him were sincerely sorry when he died a natural death. A stab given to an unarmed or a defenceless man has seldom a very happy effect. An Englishman loves a spirited, but abhors a phlegmatic exit.

Excuse this liberty I have taken with you in your profession; but the idea struck me immediately on reading your intended change in the catastrophe of *Hamlet*, which I am very impatient to see.

I think myself much obliged to you, both for a letter which is highly flattering to my vanity, and for the entertainment I expect from your promised communication. That I may not appear totally ungrateful I will cease to trespass on your patience any longer, and once more assure you that I am, with great truth, your much obliged.

G. STEEVENS.

[1] Cf. No. 237, p. 477.

['MR. STEEVENS'S REMARKS As to the *text* of Shakespeare's play, and Mr. Garrick's alteration of HAMLET']

As a proof that this play was written before 1597, of which the contrary has been asserted by Mr. Holt in Dr. Johnson's Appendix, the following passage from Mr. Farmer's pamphlet may be brought. 'Shakespeare is said to have been no extraordinary actor, and that the top of his performance was the Ghost in his own *Hamlet*. Yet this *chef-d'oeuvre* did not please. I will give you an original stroke at it. Dr. Lodge published in the year 1596, a pamphlet called *Wits Miserie, or the World's Madness, discovering the incarnate devils of the age*, 4to. One of these devils is *Hate Virtue, or sorrow for another man's success*, who (says the Doctor) *looks as* pale as the vizard of the GHOST, *which cried so miserably at the theatre*, HAMLET, REVENGE!'

It appears from a MS. note of Dr. Gabriel Harvey (a name well known to us who rake over the dunghill of antiquity) that he was well acquainted with the play of *Hamlet*, in the year 1598. His words are these:—'The younger sort take much delight in Shakespeare's *Venus and Adonis*; but his *Lucrece*, and his tragedy of *Hamlet Prince of Denmark*, have it in them to please the wiser sort. 1598.'

This is sufficient to prove that *Hamlet* had been performed seven years at least before it was published, as the first known edition is in 1605; the title-page of which declares it to have been much augmented and corrected by the author. I have not the copy by me, so that Mr. Garrick will do well to consult his own for fear of mistakes.

Shakespeare was always adding, without the least consideration whether his additions were consistently made or not. If it were necessary to bring proofs of this, the task would be easily performed. All his amplifications &c. were, I suppose, communicated to the Hopkins of his theatre, who not having the judgment or the caution of our friend in the easy chair published them indiscriminately; nay, what the poet had rejected as well as what he had added. This may account for the immoderate length of *Hamlet*; but as no copy of it in its first state is preserved, our conjectures are little better than guess-work. . . .

In the *Personæ Dramatis* remember to leave out the names of the characters omitted in this alteration of the play.

[On 1.1.12f.]

> If you do meet Horatio, and Marcellus
> The rivals of my watch.

The true reading is,

> If you do meet Horatio and Marcellus,
> The *rival* of my watch.

There is but one person on each watch. Bernardo relieves Francisco, and Francisco waits to be relieved by Marcellus. Horatio watched only through curiosity.

[On 2.2.140]

> Lord Hamlet is a prince out of thy sphere.

All princes alike were out of her sphere. The passage should be printed thus:—

> Lord Hamlet is a prince—out of thy sphere.[1]

[On 3.2.132] Mr. Garrick speaks—'Miching Malicho,' and yet it is scratched out in the copy.

[On 3.2.287f.]

> For if the King likes not the comedy,
> Why then belike—he likes it not perdy.

Is it necessary to retain these lines?
[On 4.2.30] 'Hide fox and all after.' Should not this be omitted?
[On 4.4.53f.] 'Rightly to be great,' &c. This is not printed as Mr. Garrick spoke it. He delivered it with a variation which obviates the inconsistency of the speech.
Why the alteration and omission[2] of

> This army of such mass and charge,
> Led by a delicate and tender prince.? [4.4.47ff.] . . .

[On 5.1.277f.]

> Nay and *you'll* mouth it, Sir,
> I'll rant as well as *thou.*

Endorsed, 'Mr. Steevens of Hampstead, about "Hamlet," &c.'

---

[1] Steevens included this note in the 1773 edition, X, p. 209; other notes from this letter appear at X, pp. 211 and 222.
[2] This soliloquy is to be found in the 'Good' quarto (1604–5), but not in the Folio text.

236. David Garrick, adaptation of *Hamlet*

1772

First performed at Drury Lane on 18 December 1772. Text from Folger Library manuscript, first printed by George Winchester Stone, Jr, 'Garrick's Long Lost Alteration of *Hamlet*', *PMLA*, 49 (1934), pp. 890–921; this excerpt on pp. 916–21.

To facilitate comparison with Shakespeare I have added in the right-hand margin act, scene, and line-references to the original. Whole or part lines marked with an asterisk are Garrick's own invention.

In the preceding scene (4.4 in the original) Garrick had omitted Fortinbras and his army, substituting Guildenstern for the Captain. At the end of the scene, as a conclusion to Hamlet's 'How all occasions do inform against me', Garrick's alteration reads:

> O from this Time forth,
> My Thoughts be bloody *all! the hour is come—*
> *I'll fly my Keepers—sweep to my revenge.*   [Exit.

(ed. Stone, p. 912; cf. 4.4.65; Garrick's alteration italicized)

Hamlet thus does not leave Denmark, hence the sea voyage, the pirates, and the deaths of Rosencrantz and Guildenstern, can be omitted. In the next scene Garrick altered the report that Laertes 'is in secret come from France' to

> Her Brother *tempest-beaten back to Denmark*

(ed. Stone, p. 914; cf. 4.5.85)

presumably to reduce the violation of the Unities. Ophelia's first mad-scene follows, then Laertes' rebellion (4.5.1–124, omitting 17–20, 89–93, 102, 106–7, 122). The adaptation proceeds as follows.

[Act IV, scene 5]

Laertes. Where is my father?		[4.5.125
King.	Dead.	
Queen.	But not by him.	

King. Let him demand his fill.   126
Laertes. How came he dead? I'll not be juggled with,   127
To Hell Allegiance, Vows to the blackest Devil,[1]   128
                To this Point I stand,   130
That both the Worlds I give to Negligence,   131
Let come what comes; Only I'll be reveng'd,   132
Most throughly for my Father.   133
    King. Who shall stay you?   134
    Laertes.   My Will, not all the World:
And for my Means, I'll husband them so well,   135
They shall go far with little.   136
    King.   Will you in Revenge of your   *
Dear Father's Death, destroy both Friend and Foe?[2]   *
    Laertes. None but his Enemies.   140
    King.   Will you know them then?   141
    Laertes. To his good Friends thus wide I'll ope
                my Arms,   142
And like the kind Life-rend'ring Pelican   143
Repast them with my Blood.   144
    King.   Why now you speak,
Like a good Child, and a true Gentleman.   145
That I am guiltless of your Father's Death,   146
And am most sensible in Grief for it,   147
It shall as level you your Judgment pierce,   148
As Day does to your Eye:[3] Go but a-part,   149; 199
Make Choice of whom your wisest Friends you will,   200
And they shall hear and judge 'twixt you and me;   201
If by direct or by collat'ral Hand   202
They find us touch'd, we will our Kingdom give,[4]   203
To you in Satisfaction: But if not,   205
Be you content to lend your Patience to us,   206

---

[1] Garrick cuts lines 129f.
[2] These lines are substituted for 136–40.
[3] Garrick transfers lines 199–215 to this point.
[4] Garrick cuts line 204.

And we shall jointly labour with your Soul,	207
To give it due Content.	208

    Laertes.   Let this be so.

His Means of Death, his obscure Funeral,	209
No Trophy, Sword, or Hatchment o'er his Bones,	210
No noble Rite, nor formal Ostentation,	211
Cry to be heard, as 'twere from Earth to Heaven,	212
That I must call't in question.	213

    King.   So you shall;

And where th'Offence is, let the great Ax fall.	214
I pray you go with me.	

        [*Noise within as they are going to see Ophelia.*[1]   *

Laertes. [within] O my poor Ophelia!—Let her come in.   *

Enter Ophelia.

By Heav'n, thy Madness shall be paid with Weight,[2]	153
Till our Scale turn the Beam. O Rose of May!	154
Dear Maid, kind Sister, sweet Ophelia!	155
O Heav'ns! is't possible a young Maid's Wits	156
Should be as mortal as a sick Man's Life?[3]	157

    Ophelia.

They bore him bare-fac'd on the Bier,	[*Sings.*	161
And in his Grave rain'd many a Tear;		163
Fare you well, my love.		164

Laertes. Hadst thou thy Wits, and did'st persuade	
Revenge,	165
It could not move thus.	166
Ophelia. You must sing, Down a-down,	167
and you call him a-down-a. O how the	168
wheel becomes it! It is the false Steward	169
that stole his Master's Daughter.	170
Laertes. This nothing is much more than Matter.	171
Ophelia. There's Rosemary, that's for Remem-	172
brance; Pray you, Love, remember: And	173
there's Pansies, that's for Thoughts.	174
Laertes. A document in Madness, Thoughts,	175
and Remembrance fitted.	176

---

[1] Garrick's autograph stage-direction.
[2] Garrick now reverts to the earlier part, omitting 150-2.
[3] The Folio reads 'old man's'; Garrick cuts 158-60.

Ophelia. There's Fennel for you, and Columbines;   177
there's Rue for you, and here's some for me.   178
We may call it Herb of Grace o'Sundays; O you may   179
wear your Rue with a Difference. There's a Daisy: 180
I would give you some Violets, but they all wither'd   181
when my Father died: They say he made a good End.   182

For bonny sweet Robin is all my Joy.   *[Sings.*   183

Laertes. Thought and Affliction, Passion, Hell itself!   184
She turns to Favour, and to Prettiness.   185
   Ophelia.

     And will he not come again?   *[Sings*   186
     And will he not come again?   187
     No, No, he's dead,   188
     Go to thy Death-bed,   189
     He never will come again.   190

     His Beard as white as Snow,   191
     All Flaxen was his Pole;   192
     He is gone, he is gone,   193
     And we cast away Moan;   194
     And peace be with his Soul, and with all Lovers Souls.   *
                   [Exit.[1]

   Laertes. O treble Woe   5.1.240
Fall ten Times double on that cursed Head,   241
Whose wicked Deed depriv'd thee of   242
Thy most ingenious Sense!— let me but see him Heav'n!   243; *
'Twould warm the very Sickness of my heart,   *; 4.7.55
That I should live and tell him to his teeth,   56
Thus didst Thou!   57

Enter Hamlet

   Hamlet. What is he, whose Griefs   5.1.248
Bear such an Emphasis? Whose Phrase of Sorrow   249
Conjures the wand'ring Stars, and makes them stand   250
Like wonder-wounded Hearers? This is I,   251
Hamlet the Dane!

---

[1] Garrick now cuts 4.5.197–9; 4.6 (Horatio with Hamlet's letter); 4.7 (Claudius and
Laertes, with Hamlet's letter; the murder plot; the report of Ophelia's death), all but lines
55–7, inserted above; 5.1.1–239, 243–7 (the gravediggers; the funeral scene).

Laertes. Then my Revenge is come.   *

                     [*Draws his sword*

Hamlet. I prithee take thy Fingers from thy sword,   254; *

For though I am not splenetive and rash,   255

Yet have I in me something dangerous,   256

Which let thy Wisdom fear.   257

     King. Keep them asunder.   258

     Hamlet. Why, I'll fight with him upon this Theme   260

Until my Eye-lids will no longer wag.   261

     Queen. O my Son! What Theme?   262

     Hamlet. I lov'd Ophelia; forty Thousand Brothers   263

Could not with all their Quantity of Love   264

Make up my Sum. What wilt thou do for her?   265

     King. O, he is mad, Laertes.   266

     Hamlet. Shew me what thou wilt do.   268

Wilt weep? Wilt fight? Wilt fast? Wilt tear thyself?   269

Wilt drink up Eisel? Eat a Crocodile?   270

I'll do't! and More—nay and you'll mouth it, Sir,[1]   271*; 277*

I'll rant as well as Thou—   278

     Queen. O Hamlet—Hamlet—   259

For Love of Heav'n forbear him!   [*To Laertes*   267

     King.[2] We will not bear this Insult to our Presence,   *

Hamlet, I did command you hence to England,   *

Affection hitherto has curb'd my Pow'r,   *

But you have trampled on Allegiance,   *

And now shall feel my Wrath—Guards!   *

     Hamlet. First feel mine—   [*Stabs him*   *

Here thou Incestuous, Murd'rous, damned Dane   5.2.317

There's for thy treachery, Lust and Usurpation!   *

     King. O yet defend me, friends, I am but hurt—   5.2.316

                     [*Falls and dies*

     Queen. O Mercy Heav'n!—Save me from my Son—   *

                         [*Runs out.*

Laertes. What Treason ho! Thus then do I revenge   *

---

[1] Here Garrick has added the words 'and More' and 'it, Sir'.

[2] Garrick now cuts 5.1.278–93; 5.2.1–395, all but five lines (Hamlet and Horatio on Claudius' plot to have him killed in England; the deaths of Rosencrantz and Guildenstern; Osric and the wager; the duel; the poisoned rapier; the poisoned drink; the death of Gertrude from Claudius' poison; the death of Laertes; the return of Fortinbras, and his assumption of rule).

My Father, Sister, and my King—   *
    [*Hamlet runs upon Laertes's sword and falls*
  Horatio. And I my Prince, and Friend—   [*Draws*   *
  Hamlet. Hold good Horatio—'tis the Hand of Heav'n,   *
Administers by him this precious balm   *
For all my Wounds. Where is the wretched Queen?   *

Enter Messenger.

  Messenger. Struck with the Horror of the Scene, she fled—   *
But ere she reach'd her Chamber door, she fell   *
Intranc'd and Motionless—unable to sustain the Load   *
Of Agony and Sorrow—   *
  Hamlet. O my Horatio—watch the wretched Queen,   *
When from this Trance she wakes—O may she breathe   *
An hour of Penitence, ere Madness ends her.   *
Exchange forgiveness with me brave Laertes,[1]   5.2.321
Thy Sister's,[2] Father's Death, come not on me,   *
Nor Mine on thee!—   *
  Laertes. Heav'n make us free of 'Em!   *
  Hamlet. O I die Horatio—but one thing more,   344; *
O take this hand from me—unite your Virtues—   *
    [*Joins Horatio's hand to Laertes'*
To calm this troubled Land—I can no more,   *
Nor have I more to ask but Mercy, Heav'n.   [*dies.*   *
  Horatio. Now cracks a Noble heart—Good Night
                         sweet Prince,   351
And Flights of Angels sing thee to thy rest: 352
Take up the Body, such a Sight as this[3]   393
Becomes the Field, but here shews much Amiss.   394

              END

---

[1] In Shakespeare's text this line is spoken by Laertes to Hamlet.
[2] In the extant text Garrick does not seem to have made provision for Ophelia's death.
[3] In Shakespeare these two lines are spoken by Fortinbras.

237. Various writers, Garrick's *Hamlet* reviewed

1772–3

(a) Arthur Murphy, 'Shakespeare's ghost protests'. From *Hamlet, with Alterations*; *A Tragedy, in Three Acts. Dated December* 15, 1772. First published in Jesse Foot's *Life of Murphy* (1811), pp. 256–74; reprinted, with some annotation, by M. Lehnert, *Shakespeare Jahrbuch* (Weimar), 102 (1966), pp. 97–167. On Murphy see the head-note to No. 124 (Vol. 3).

This satire is directed against the contemporary theatre, and against Garrick's alleged motives for making the adaptation.

[Act III, scene 2]

Scene,—another part of the Theatre.
[*Enter* Ghost, *and* Garrick.
    Ghost. .... I am Shakespeare's Ghost,
For my foul sins, done in my days of nature,
Doom'd for a certain term to leave my works
Obscure and uncorrected; to endure
The ignorance of players; the barbarous hand
Of Gothic editors; the ponderous weight
Of leaden commentator; fast confin'd
In critic fires, till errors, not my own,
Are done away, and sorely I the while
Wish'd I had blotted for myself before:
But that I am forbid to tell the pangs,
Which Genius feels from ev'ry blockhead's pen,
I could a tale unfold, whose lightest word
Would make that idiot-laughter keep the cheeks
Of ev'ry scribler; thaw thy frozen blood,
And bid a puny whipster's pen, like thine,
Deal out thy paragraphs and crude conceits

In Morning Chronicles, till ev'ry name
Should be begrim'd, and black as BARRY's face,
When he, my best Othello, walks the stage.
But this effect of malice must not be
To ears of modern scriblers. List, list, O list!
If thou didst ever the fam'd Shakespeare love—
     Garrick. O Heav'n! 'my little loves like bees
Cluster and climb about your knees!'[1]
     Ghost. Revenge his foul and most unnatural murder.
     Garrick. Murder?
     Ghost. Murder most foul, as in the best it is;
But this most foul, strange, and unnatural.
     Garrick. Haste me to know it; that I, with haste as great
As Stratford's town-clerk at the Jubilee,
May sweep to my revenge.
     Ghost.   I find thee apt;
And duller shouldst thou be than the flat lines
That coldly creep in modern playwrights' page,
Wouldst thou not stir in this. Now, Garrick, hear:
'Tis giv'n out, that in a barb'rous age
Shakespeare arose, and made th'unskilful stare
At monstrous farces: so the ear of Europe
Is by the forged process of a Frenchman
Rankly abus'd. But know, ungrateful man!
The serpent that did sting thy poet's fame
Has made his fortune by him.
O think what a sad falling-off was there!
From me, whose name was of that dignity
That it went hand in hand with time himself,
My honour blooming fresh:—and to decline
Upon a wretch, whose natural gifts were poor
To those of mine!
But public taste, the sport of fickle fashion,
May sate itself in a celestial page,
And prey on garbage.
But, soft!—methinks, I scent the morning air;—
Brief let me be:—My works have made your fortune;
And Hamlet brought to you, the mere reciter,
The organ of another's sense, more money,

[1] From Garrick's Jubilee *Ode*: above, p. 350.

Than e'er it did to me, who wrought the tale.
Yet on my scenes, by ages sanctified,
In evil hour thy restless spirit stole,
With juice of cursed nonsense in an inkhorn,
And o'er my fair applauded page did pour
A Manager's distilment, whose effect
Holds such an enmity with wit of man,
That each interpolating word of thine
Annihilates the sense, and courses through
The natural turns of fable and of thought;
And, with a sudden stupor, it doth damp
And chill, like sheets of water on a fire,
The clear and glowing lines: so did it mine;
And a most instant numbness crept about,
Most blockhead-like, with vile and paltry phrase,
All my smooth writings.
Thus was I, ev'n by thy unhallow'd hand,
Of *both my grave-diggers* at once dispatch'd,
Cut off in the luxuriance of my wit,
Unstudied, undigested, and bemawl'd:
No critic ask'd,—but brought upon the stage
With all your imperfections on my head!
 Garrick. O, horrible! O, horrible! most horrible!
 Ghost. If thou hast nature in thee, dare it not;
Let not th'immortal page of Shakespeare be
A place for ev'ry puny whipster's trash.
But, howsoever thou pursuest this act,
Attempt no more, nor let your soul conceive
Aught 'gainst my other plays; I leave thee now
To the just vengeance critics will inflict,
And to the thorns that in your bosom lodge,
To goad and sting thee. Fare thee well at once!
Yon window shews the morning to be near,
And thy once glow-worm eyes, with age grown dim,
Begin to pale their ineffectual fire.
Reflect in time; farewell! remember me [*Exit* Ghost.
 Garrick. Hold, hold my heart;
And you, my sinews, though you are grown old,
Yet bear me stiffly up.—Remember thee?
Ay, thou fierce ghost! while memory holds a seat

In this distracted globe. Remember thee?
Yea, from the stock of plays i' th' Prompter's list,
I'll wipe away all trivial modern bards,
And thy remembrance all alone shall live
Within the book and volume of my brain,
Unmix'd with other matter than my own.
'Tis gone, and now I am myself again.
My tables,—meet it is, I set it down,
That, by the alteration of a play,
I can demand a benefit from Lacy.
I'm sure it's so, while I can act myself.

George
and   } *within.* Illo! ho, ho!
Becket.

Garrick. Illo! ho, ho! come, boy, come.
Enter George *and* Becket.[1]
 George. How is 't? what news?
 Becket. Good Sir, tell it—
 Garrick. No, you'll reveal it.
 George. Not I.
 Becket. Nor I.
 Garrick. How say you then? would heart of man once
           think it?
But you'll be secret?
 Both.   By Heav'n, we will!
 Garrick. There's ne'er an actor strutting on the stage
That can do Shakespeare justice, but myself.
 Becket. There needs no ghost, good Sir, come from the grave
To tell us this.
 Garrick.   Why right; you say right;
And so, without more circumstance at all,
Insert it in the *St. James's Chronicle;*
And circulate it wide in ev'ry paper.
I'll draw the paragraphs; and be it yours,
My trusty Becket, in your own fair hand
To copy all, and give it to the press.
This Ghost is pleas'd with this my alteration,
And now he bids me alter all his Plays.

---

[1] George Garrick, the actor's brother, and Thomas Becket, London bookseller.

His plays are out joint;—O *cursed spite!*
That ever I was born to set them right!

END OF THE TRAGEDY.

(270–4)

(b) From the *General Evening Post*, 15–17 December 1772.[1]

The lovers of the Drama are greatly pleased with the advertisment issued by the Managers of Drury-lane theatre relative to an alteration of *Hamlet*, which is to-morrow evening to be exhibited at that house. Few of our great poet's pieces are more generally admired, upon the whole, than the tragedy in question; yet the glaring inconsistencies in the character of the hero have been long very painful objects of reflection to the warmest advocates of Shakespeare; and therefore an attempt to remove such palpable imperfections must be well entitled to the approbation of the public.

There are many people, it is true, who are such enthusiastic admirers of Shakespeare that they start at the least liberty taken with his works, and hold it a kind of dramatic sacrilege to meddle with his very imperfections. This, however, is too great a degree of theatrical veneration; we reverence Shakespeare for his beauties, not for his blemishes; and the more highly we esteem him as a writer the more careful we should be to retrench every defect which has a tendency to injure him in the opinion of his auditors. Some of his plays have been already altered with success; *Romeo and Juliet*, *Lear*, and *Cymbeline*, are evidently improved by the alterations they have undergone; and we may safely venture to affirm that *Hamlet* cannot sustain any change derogatory to the character of its celebrated author.

In the present state of the play a review of the principal persons in the drama must strike us with horror. Hamlet knows that his father has been barbarously murdered by his uncle, and even his father's ghost appears to urge him on revenge; Hamlet seems perfectly well acquainted with what is proper to be done, yet never attempts to do it till he himself is mortally wounded.[2] On the contrary, though he is incessantly execrating his bloody, his incestuous uncle he is continually executing his commands, and

---

[1] For the ascription to Steevens see the head-note of No. 238.
[2] Cf. Steevens, No. 234 above, p. 448, and below, pp. 488, 540.

470

even in the last act undertakes to win the wager for him, which proves the cause of his death.

The King is an incestuous murderer, yet is struck with remorse at the greatness of his guilt, and in agony of contrition prays most fervently to Heaven for its mercy. From praying he rises to the perpetration of new crimes, and sends the son of that brother whose life he has taken, and whose Queen he has espoused, under the appearance of an honourable embassy to be butchered in England.

Laertes is a man of the highest spirit and the nicest honour, yet while complimented publicly with these two distinguished qualities he basely undertakes to murder Hamlet, though he has the moment before not only accepted the Prince's excuse for the involuntary injuries done to his family, but even embraced him as his most particular friend.

The Queen is painted a woman of virtue, just as Laertes is drawn a man of honour. Her virtue permits her to marry her husband's brother in two months, and though she is a matron yet 'Rebellious Hell', to borrow an expression from her son,—'so mutinies in her bones' that she never once considers the rapidity, or the incest of her marriage as the smallest impropriety. Such are the characters who in the present state of the tragedy under consideration have the principal business of the fable in their hands. Who can be justly interested for their fate, elevated at their success, or depressed by their misfortune? The Prince himself, the least culpable of the four (for he can claim no degree of *positive* praise) is more calculated to excite our contempt, than to wake our sensibility.[1] *Any* alteration therefore *must* be for the better; and when we recollect how judiciously Mr. Garrick has hitherto altered our favourite poet we may be certain where he has so much room to amend, that he will produce nothing either unworthy of himself or disagreeable to the public.

(c) From *ibid.*, 17–19 December 1772 (by Steevens).

Last night the alteration of *Hamlet*, which we announced to our readers, was performed for the first time at Drury-lane theatre, to a most brilliant audience, and received universally with the loudest peals of approbation. Indeed we never saw the public applause

[1] Cf. Steevens below, p. 541.

more generally or more justly bestowed since our acquaintance with the stage; and it is Mr. Garrick's singular felicity that his acting has not only been of infinitely greater service to Shakespeare than all the eulogies of his various commentators, but that his corrections have likewise given some of our celebrated poet's chief pieces a certainty of maintaining their ground in the catalogue of exhibiting plays, which, without an assistance of such a nature has probably slept in oblivion, notwithstanding the exalted reputation of their author.

The first act of *Hamlet* was formerly intolerably long, and lost much of its fine effect from this particular circumstance of tediousness. Mr. Garrick, therefore, has judiciously divided it into two acts, and concludes his present first at that passage where Hamlet declares an intention of watching with Horatio to see his father's spirit. By this means we are filled with expectation for the appearance of the ghost in the second act; and it must be confessed that the apparition now has a double degree of importance and solemnity. The second act terminates with these lines:

> The time is out of joint; O! cursed spight,
> That ever I was born to set it right.   [1.5.189f.]

In the third act we are presented with the usual scenes between Hamlet and Ophelia; the Players are also introduced as formerly, and the circumstance of having a play to catch the conscience of the King determined upon. The play, however, is not brought on till the fourth act. This act is concluded with the fine closet-scene between Hamlet and his mother, which originally finished the third, and materially weakened the play by throwing every succeeding incident into a state of the most palpable inferiority.[1] Hitherto little liberties are taken with Shakespeare, besides a regular division of the acts, and a just omission of several passages which, with all our veneration for the Swan of Avon, were absolutely necessary to be expunged. The fifth act contains the great alterations, and gives us almost a new catastrophe; yet such a catastrophe as perfectly agrees with the main fable of the play, and appears, from a particular speech, to have been at one time the intention of the author. When the King, on the death of Polonius, has resolved to send Hamlet to England, the Prince, as the tragedy was lately represented, went off very quietly, and though urged by every

[1] Cf. Steevens below, p. 540, and No. 234 above, pp. 448, 452.

motive of nature, honour, and justice, to revenge his father's murder, contented himself with unlading his 'heart in curses, like a very drab.' Shakespeare was sensible of this capital defect in the character of his hero, and endeavoured to save him by putting the following soliloquy in his mouth, just as he is going to embark:

> How all occasions do conspire against me,
> And spur my dull revenge!　　　　　　[Quotes 4.4.32–66]

Notwithstanding a speech so full of self-condemnation for his tardiness to punish his uncle, Shakespeare sent Hamlet for England; and though he made the Prince acquainted with the King's design to have him murdered there, and satisfied him that on his return to Denmark his life must be in danger, Hamlet not only returns without apprehension, but without resentment, and readily undertakes to win a wager for the incestuous murderer.[1] Mr. Garrick, however, corrects this egregious absurdity in a masterly manner. He adds three or four lines to the foregoing soliloquy, in which Hamlet, after calling upon vengeance, nature and manhood to wake, declares his resolution to slip his keepers (Rosencranz and Guildenstern) and flies back to the palace to seek his revenge. Just as he reaches the palace Laertes, who is tempest-beaten back, and just pacified by the King for Polonius's death, seeing Ophelia's distraction, breaks again into a violent rage, and execrates Hamlet as the author of the general calamity. At this time Hamlet enters, and addresses Laertes with the speech which formerly was spoken in the grave scene:

> What is he whose griefs
> Bear such an emphasis, &c.　　　　　　[5.1.248f.]

Laertes on this prepares to attack him; but the King interposes, and telling Hamlet in a rage that tho' his affection has hitherto screened him from the severity of the laws he will no longer prevent the operations of justice, but make him feel her heaviest rod for his disobedience in refusing to go to England. Having said this, he calls for his guards to arrest the Prince, on which Hamlet drawing his sword, upbraids him with his crimes, and desires him to stand on his defence. The King instantly draws; the Queen runs screaming off the stage, at seeing her son engaged in so bloody a conflict with her husband, and the latter is killed.

[1] Cf. Steevens, No. 234 above, p. 448.

Hamlet has no sooner dispatched his uncle, than Laertes prepares to assail him; they engage, and the former is mortally wounded. Hamlet now, in the last agonies, exchanges forgiveness with Laertes, recommends a strict friendship between him and Horatio, and dies with a request that both will attend not only to the recovery of the miserable Queen, but labour to heal the divisions of their unfortunate country. Such now is the bold, the warm, the animated catastrophe of *Hamlet*. All the buffoonry of the Grave-diggers, the reader will see, is necessarily omitted, as well as all that cowardly, unnatural plot of the poison to take off Hamlet if he should escape the envenomed sword of Laertes. It is inconceivable how the audience were charmed with the manliness of these alterations. When Hamlet attacked his uncle with so much spirit, the house was a continued roar of the most extravagant applause; and perhaps a finer dramatic situation could not be contrived than the Queen's agony at the combat between her son and husband. Essential as these alterations are, Mr. Garrick has not introduced above twenty lines himself; and it is needless to say what force the play, in its present improved state, acquired from his admirable acting.

(d) From *ibid.*, 19–22 December 1772 (by Steevens).

When we attended the representation of *Hamlet*, so judiciously altered by Mr. Garrick on Friday evening, we were much pleased at the propriety with which that great master changed a particular expression in the character of the Prince, as it has been long censured as a gross violation of decency, and ranked among the number of those illiberal jests which offend the ear without contributing to the amusement of the public.

The expression we allude to is introduced when the Court is present at the exhibition of the play ordered by Hamlet, and the Prince, with an affected air of gallantry, throws himself at the feet of Ophelia. Having condemned the expression on account of its indecency, we can by no means think of disgusting our readers[1] with a mention of it; but those who are acquainted with the play, and hear Mr. Garrick now ask the young lady when she rallies him in that scene whether she means '*foolish matters*,' will immediately recollect the term formerly used in the room of '*foolish*' ['country'], and approve, with us, the justice of the alteration.

[1] Cf. Steevens in his 1773 edition, p. 539 below, Note 65.

It is universally acknowledged by our most celebrated Critics that nothing is so shamefully improper on the stage as an indecent sentiment; the author who hazards it can plead neither peculiarity of taste nor ignorance of the world for his offence against purity; he must be previously sensible that he is committing a palpable error, and must suppose that the minds of his audience are as depraved as his own to suppose that they can be possibly delighted with what should excite their utmost indignation. In the contrivance of a fable, in the painting of a character, or the unravelling of a catastrophe, a poet may be mistaken; he may think that a beauty which is a glaring defect, and consider that as a defect which is a singular felicity. About the decency of a sentiment, however, he can have no hesitation; it must be decent or indecent, proper or reprehensible; and to lay it before us if it is the latter is tacitly to tell us that we encourage a dramatic kind of brothel for the entertainment of our wives and daughters.

It would therefore be highly worthy Mr. Garrick's known good sense and solicitude for the honour of the stage to extend his attention to the circumstance of decency. There is scarcely one of our old plays which is not scandalously culpable in this point, and if our modern Roscius thinks (as he certainly does, with a delicacy greatly creditable to his character) that a single word is not too minute an object of alteration, the public would deem themselves still more essentially obliged to him if he would make a general reform in the article of theatrical licentiousness. The labour would not be altogether so herculean as may be imagined at a first glance; little more than omissions would be necessary to effect this salutary purpose, and then indeed he would be more than ever entitled to the admiration of his country. . . .

(e) From the *St. James's Chronicle*, 19–22 December 1772 (by Steevens).

OBSERVATIONS *upon the* ALTERATIONS *of* HAMLET.

To endeavour to overcome Prejudices which are connected with our Passions and Pleasures is, according to the celebrated Baron Montesquieu, one of the greatest and most difficult Tasks that Philosophy can undertake. Should this Maxim be true, I will venture to affirm that the boldest dramatic Stroke was given last Friday Night at the Theatre Royal in Drury-Lane, and that it should succeed is as unaccountable as it is unexpected. To compare small Things to great, our Reformation in religious Matters was not more surprising, in Proportion to its Importance, than that an Alteration of the most revered Tragedy of *Hamlet* should be received with that *universal Approbation* which the News-Papers proclaim to us. I will not give my Opinion upon the Merit of the Alteration till I have seen its Effects and considered the Whole with its *Restorations, Omissions, Divisions, Transpositions, Connections,* and *Additions* in my Closet, should the Alterations be ever published. My Design is only to give some Account of the Criticisms upon *Hamlet,* to consider how far we should give Ear to too great Refinements, and in what Circumstances we may venture to touch even the hallowed Reliques of our immortal Bard.

The Tragedy of *Hamlet* has been long the Object of severe Criticisms both at home and abroad. Shakespeare's Cotemporaries have attacked him; and as the greatest Genius will always have the most inveterate Enemies, they have endeavoured to ridicule perhaps the first Piece of dramatic Writing extant, viz. the Soliloquy of *To be or not to be.* Beaumont and Fletcher are the sacrilegious Persons who have dared to do it.[1] Jonson too had his Sarcasms upon his Friend, and added great Weight in the critical Scale. It is impossible that such a Giant of Genius should stalk abroad without some Endeavours from lesser Powers to make him stop a little; but should a Host of the mightiest Criticks assail him, he will stride on through all Ages to astonish, and, in Spite of Opposition, *sublimi feriet sydera vertice.*[2] Should it be asked if this Giant may not at Times be too much incumbered, and that he would have more Strength, Vigour, and Spirit to be relieved from some of his Weight, I should answer without Doubt; but let it not be done by common Hands wantonly or rashly. Has not *Macbeth* (perhaps the first Drama in any Language) been almost annihilated by Alteration? Has not the clumsy Pen of *Tate* grievously wounded *King Lear?* and the coarse Daubing of *Shadwell* disfigured *Timon of Athens?* In short, have we hitherto

---

[1] Compare Steevens in his 1773 edition, p. 538 below, Note 63.
[2] Horace, *Odes,* 1.1.36: '[he] shall touch the stars with [his] exalted head'.

got any Advantages from any of the Alterers of our Bard? and may we not say with Othello, that we have

———*Yawn'd at Alteration.*[1]

With regard to *Hamlet*, it is certain that there are some fundamental Blemishes among the greatest and most exquisite Beauties that were ever turned out of the Hands of Genius. *Voltaire* with great Ridicule, some Justice, and unparalleled Falshood and Effrontery, has dissected this Play like a Butcher, and has scarcely left a single Feature unmaimed throughout the Whole. A celebrated Lady indeed [Mrs Montagu], has washed the Wounds her favourite Shakespeare so inhumanly received, and by Applications with her fair Hands she has quite rescued our mangled Dramatist from the Frenchman's Malice, and turned the Tables upon him. She has proved that *Voltaire* is as unable to judge of the Merits of Shakespeare as a blind Man of Colours; the Want of Eyes in one, and of English Language in the other, equally incapacitates both. However, though this French Wit can little taste the Beauties of Diction, which is the Colouring of the Poet, and without which there can be no Poetry, yet he may undoubtedly judge of the Construction of a Fable, and we must own, to shew our Impartiality, that his Objections against the unaccountable Delay of Hamlet's Revenge (to which *he is prompted by Heaven and Hell*) have great Force, and have been felt by every Englishman of Understanding even before *Voltaire* had Existence. If this Objection could be removed, with the Language of Shakespeare, the greatest Admirers of him would be satisfied; but to have the discordant Notes of a Sow-Gelder's Horn mixed with the animated Silver Tone of the Trumpet can never be endured. Hamlet's going to England and attempting nothing against his Uncle, though *his blunted Purpose is whetted by* a second Visitation of his Father's Ghost, is certainly a great Fault.[2] But then the next Question that will arise is this—whether or no the Scenes of Delay, and the Fifth Act of the Original, (though allowed unartful and improbable) will not entertain an Audience more than any modern Refinement or Alteration, though perhaps according to Rules, and in the Spirit of Aristotle, Bossu, Dennis, &c. &c. &c.

I shall say no more for or against this lopping of Shakespeare

---

[1] Cf. Steevens's letter to Garrick, p. 457 above.
[2] Cf. Steevens, No. 234 above, p. 448, and Steevens's edition, p. 540 below, Note 70.

till I can see, hear, and read it. I particularly insist upon *reading* it before I shall give my Judgement. I have been deceived often by the Power of Action; and let a good Actor perform the coldest modern Tragedy, and a bad one the best of Shakespeare's, Dulness may have a short-lived Triumph, and nothing but Time, the best Critic of them all can set every Thing to Rights again. I am a great Admirer of Shakespeare, I had almost said of his Errors.

JOHN BULL.

(f) From the *Macaroni and Theatrical Magazine, or Monthly Register of Fashions and Diversions of the Time*, i (December 1772). 'Macaroni' was a contemporary expression for an actor.

On Friday, December 18, *was performed, for the First Time, at* Drury-Lane Theatre, *the Tragedy of* HAMLET, *with* ALTERATIONS; *the Part of* Hamlet *by Mr.* GARRICK.

This celebrated tragedy of Shakespeare's has ever been considered as one of his most capital productions in respect to *sentimental declamation*. But however willing the critical world were disposed to subscribe to this opinion, a proportionable degree of censure was ever extorted from them in deciding on the *incidents of the fable*. Foreigners who were, consequently, divested of those prejudices we entertain in favour of our immortal countryman saw the absurdities which disgraced this piece with half an eye; and either not being *qualified*, or not *willing* to judge of the poet's merits on the whole, have never hesitated to pronounce it a fabrication of monstrous incongruities.

To clear the piece of these charges (which were in part not ill founded) has been the task of the present *revisor:* how far he has succeeded the applauses of a crowded and judicious audience have already testified.—We shall, therefore, for the entertainment of those who happened to miss so *mental an entertainment*, lay before them a sketch of the alterations.

In the first act the Ghost has hitherto made his appearance to Hamlet: this is judiciously deferred to the second, as there is not only full matter enough in the first without this but it gives that necessary pause to the next meeting, when Hamlet tells his friend Horatio he'll meet him in the platform between eleven and twelve.

478

In the second act the Ghost appears; and the remainder of this act makes out the second.

The former second act makes out the present third act; as does the third, in the same manner the fourth: so that the three original acts now make four, on account of dividing the first.

In the fourth and fifth act, which are now united, instead of Hamlet's return to England being merely *accidental*, and thereby defeating his own *pre-determined* purpose of killing the king, it is now an act of his *own* arising from the recollection of the much superior business he had to do in revenging his father's death than going on a needless expedition.—The grave-digging scene in the fifth act is likewise very properly expunged: it is the distress of Ophelia which contributes to the catastrophe, not the *mode of her interment*. Laertes's fencing-match with Hamlet has suffered the same *deserved* fate; and is now very properly changed into a duel, where, after Hamlet kills the king, Laertes kill him. In short, instead of the critical part of the audience being obliged to deduct the absurdities and improbabilities of this piece from its real merits, the chain of entertainment is now conducted, unbroken and connected.

It is almost needless to speak of so established an actor's merit as Mr. Garrick in the character of Hamlet: yet, great as it hitherto has been in this part, we think he topped it on the present occasion: probably arising from the new disposition of the drama, which might have lent an additional fire to his imagination.

Mrs. Smith made her first appearance in Ophelia the same night; and gave us some hopes that her great talents in music have not precluded her a reputable situation as an actress. Her first song in this part put it beyond a doubt she may be ranked as one of the leading singers in this kingdom; which an enraptured audience gave strong testimonies of: and no wonder—for such harmony (as Milton expresses it) was sufficient 'to have created a soul under the ribs of death.' (119–20)

(g) From the *General Evening Post*, 22–4 December 1772 (by Steevens).

Though the late alteration of *Hamlet* has given universal satisfaction to all Critics of true taste, yet there are some people so blindly attached to every thing which is Shakespeare's that they lament the removal of capital defects, and are particularly sorry that the famous scene of the grave-diggers is now discontinued in the representation of this celebrated tragedy. For our own parts, though we entertain a just admiration for the genius of our immortal author, we are nevertheless such downright advocates for common sense that we do not profess to admire him where he commits any outrage upon nature and probability. The Grave-diggers' scene shall, for the sake of argument, be admitted a masterly piece of writing; but unless we adopt Bayes's opinion, and think that the plot of a play is good for nothing but to introduce fine things, we must certainly acknowledge that the interlude of the gravediggers' has no more business in the performance than a funeral sermon, a tumbler's exhibition on the tight rope, or a hornpipe by Mr. Atkins.[1] In dramatic composition it is not enough that a scene is *exquisitely* written. It must be *properly* written, that is it must have a natural affinity to the fable, or it can by no means be entitled to our approbation. The finest thing which the mind of man can possibly conceive, without it is naturally related to the plot, without it has a tendency to advance the great business of the play, is at best no more than a shining mistake, or a glaring absurdity.

If we try the Grave-diggers' scene in *Hamlet* by this criterion, we shall soon cease to hold it in esteem as a dramatic instance of excellence, however favourably we may be inclined to consider it as a piece of writing. Yet if we weigh the point a little farther, we shall find that the particular act in which this scene is introduced makes it additionally improper for exhibition, and doubly supports the propriety of Mr. Garrick's suppressing it. In proportion as the catastrophe of any play advances, in that proportion the poet should confine himself closely to the essential business of the fable, and avoid every useless excursion into the airy regions of the imagination. The Grave-diggers' scene in *Hamlet* is actually too long, too heavy, too uninteresting for a first act. What a trespass, therefore, must it not be on our feelings to bring it in upon us in the fifth? We are all burning with impatience for the winding up of the plot, and anxious beyond conception to know in what manner the poet means to dispose of his principal characters. Yet, instead of finding our wishes gratified in this respect we are to put up with the buffoonry of two clowns on the important

[1] Cf. Steevens's letter to Garrick, pp. 456f. above.

question of professional superiority between a gallows-builder and a grave-maker. Surely the determination of the two Kings of Brentford is not more ridiculous than this.

> *First King.* And now to serious business let's advance—
> *Second King.* I do agree; but first let's have a dance.

We want of all things to go to the serious business of the plot; the poet says I agree, but first let's have a joke or two about the gallows-maker and a grave-maker. *Risum teneatis amici!*[1]

Having thus delivered an en passant opinion with respect to the *propriety* of the Grave-diggers' scene, we should be very glad if any of its enthusiastic admirers would kindly tell us wherein its excellence, as a piece of writing, consists. For our own parts we think the silly jokes between the Clowns too trifling for the entertainment of a serious audience; and the round of punning between Hamlet and the principal grave-digger too trivial for any audience at all. Hereafter we may possibly produce reasons in support of this opinion; for the present our limits will allow us only to repeat our wishes that the idolators of Shakespeare, by controverting these hasty remarks, may oblige us to enter more minutely on the subject.

(h) From the *General Evening Post*, 16–19 January 1773 (by Steevens).

It is with no little astonishment we hear, notwithstanding the universal applause which distinguished the alteration of *Hamlet* in three several representations, that a number of *judicious* critics are determined on the next exhibition to testify their discontent, and in particular to call for the Grave-diggers' scene, about which so much has been said in the news-papers. If we had not seen some publications in our prints exhorting the town to a measure of this kind, we should have considered the report as one of those idle rumours which are fabricated every hour to supply a want of interesting intelligence; but having observed various attempts of a literary nature to prejudice our audiences against the alterer of *Hamlet*, common candour obliges us to say a few words more in respect to this play, and to point out the general ill consequences that

---

[1] *Ars Poetica*, 5: 'could you, my friends, . . . refrain from laughing?'

must result to our drama if it is once suffered to fall the victim of critical assassination.

Since the original institution of our stage the town has justly exercised a right of praising or condemning every new performance as it appeared; and though many have survived the severity of a first repulse still, to the credit of our good sense very few have been driven from the theatre which have once passed the fiery ordeal of public examination. Indeed public applause would be a very precarious, nay a very ridiculous object of pursuit if what was approved one night was to be condemned the next, and if the audience fixed no certain kind of standard for the merits of our dramatic entertainments. If those very *exquisite* judges who claim the government of our theatrical taste are really offended at what they call the massacre committed upon *Hamlet*, why did not they attend on the first night the alteration was performed, and manifest their enthusiastic attachment to the very errors of Shakespeare? This was the proper time of preventing the violation they complain of; the alterer, whoever he was, stood then upon his trial, and a jury of good and lawful critics might have easily convicted him in a court of common understanding. But the idolators of Shakespeare either neglected to do this, or entirely gave up the point; they suffered the literary culprit to be acquitted with the highest honour, and now, after he has been conducted with triumph from the bar, they gravely talk of calling him to an account for his malefactions.

The Town, which has three times bestowed the loudest approbation on the altered *Hamlet*, is not only on this occasion bound to support its own repeated award, but bound, by its general regard for the interests of literature, to repel any cowardly attempt which may be made by these bush-fighters in criticism to deprive us of so valuable an entertainment. If a piece which has been thus distinguished by a more unanimous applause than any perhaps ever exhibited in our theatres is now to be attacked by the wantonness of malignity, or the inconsideration of caprice, our stage is virtually annihilated. The same spirit of turbulence which opposes the performance of one approved play may oppose the performance of every play in the acting catalogue of both houses; 'tis impossible to draw a line, or to say where the mischief will terminate; a playhouse riot is a delicious feast to the young and the unreflecting. We hope therefore that the public will remember how far their own honour is considered in this remarkable case; and we hope also that every friend to our political rights will also stand forth a champion for our literary privileges. The Town has decided, and its decision should be implicitly obeyed; this is the great principle of our dramatic Magna Charta, and if once given up, we are theatrically enslaved.

(i) Unsigned review, from the *Westminster Magazine*, i (January 1773), the theatrical review for December 1772.

This despicable comedy [*The Duel*, by Mr O'Brien] was succeeded by more pleasing Scenes—the tragedy of *Hamlet*, with alterations by Mr. Garrick. The tedious interruptions of this beautiful tale no longer disgrace it; its absurd digressions are no longer disgusting. The meeting of Hamlet with his Father's Ghost, in the first Act (when the Story leapt forward twenty-four hours in the space of ten minutes) is now protracted to the end of the second Act. The second Act in the original becomes the Third in the Alteration; the Third is converted into the Fourth; and the Fourth, by the judicious addition of certain Passages in the Fifth, constitutes the last Act in the new Edition. Hamlet, instead of embarking for England, is prevented by the arrival of young Fortinbras, whose business suggests to him, that he has forgot his almost-blunted purpose, and that it is time for him to fulfil his promise to his Father's Spirit, and sweep to his revenge. Laertes too, who had embarked for France, is tempest-beaten upon his own coast, and returns to Court in sufficient time to be revenged of Hamlet for the death of his father. These, and many other inaccuracies are obviated by the simple effects of transposing, expunging, and the addition of a few lines.—Necessary innovations! when introduced by the acquisition of such splendid Advantages. We have now to boast, that this brilliant Creation of the Poet's Fancy is purged from the Vapours and Clouds which obscured it; and, like his own Firmament, it appears to be finely fretted with Golden Stars. (34–5)

(j) Horace Walpole, from his manuscript 'Book of Materials'; first printed by W. S. Lewis, *Notes by Horace Walpole on Several Characters of Shakespeare* (Farmington, Conn., 1940); and in

Horace Walpole's Correspondence, ed. W. S. Lewis *et al.*, xxix, pp. 368–70. This notebook contains material written between 1770 and 1779. The present excerpt can be dated 1773: it follows a note made on 11 September 1772; the next note but one is dated 21 November 1774.

Some of these notes were intended for Malone's edition; but Walpole seems finally not to have communicated them to Malone.

On Walpole as a Shakespeare critic see articles in *Studies in Philology* by J. M. Stein, xxxi (1934), pp. 51–68, and C. S. Kilby, xxxviii (1941), pp. 480–93. With the completion of W. S. Lewis's magnificent edition of the *Correspondence* a fresh assessment is due.

In 1773.[1] Mr Garrick produced his *Hamlet* altered, in which he had omitted the scene of the grave diggers, from injudicious complaisance to French critics, and their cold regularity, which cramps genius. Objections made to that admirable scene of nature is, that it is burlesque, unheroic, and destroys and interrupts the interest of the action, and diverts Hamlet from his purpose on which he ought only to think, the vengeance due to the murder of his father. Not one of these objections are true. If Garrick had really been an intelligent manager, he would have corrected the vicious buffoonery which lay in his actors, not in the play. The parts of the grave-diggers have long been played by the most comic and buffoon actors in the company, who always endeavoured to raise a laughter from the galleries by absurd mirth and gesticulations. The parts ought to be given (to them) who could best represent low nature seriously, and at most the jokes between the men themselves previous to Hamlet's entry might have been shortened, tho those very jests are natural and moral, for they show that habit can bring men to be cheerful even in the midst of the most melancholy exercise of their profession. That the scene is not unheroic, tho in prose, is clear from the serious remarks it draws from Hamlet. Is every low character inconsistent with heroic tragedy? What has so pathetic effect as the fool in

[1] The correct date is 1772: Walpole perhaps means the season of 1772–3.

Lear? in how many Greek and modern tragedies are the nurse, a shepherd, a messenger, essential to the plot? Mirth itself, especially in the hands of such a genius as Shakespeare, may excite tears not laughter, and ought to do so. The grave-digger's account of Yorick's ludicrous behaviour is precisely an instance of that exquisite and matchless art, and furnishes an answer too to the last objection, that the humour of the grave-digger interrupts the interest of the action and weakens the purpose of Hamlet. Directly the contrary; the skull of Yorick and the account of his jests could have no effect but to recall fresh to the Prince's mind the happy days of his childhood, and the court of the King his father, and thence make him (see) his uncle's reign in a comparative view that must have rendered the latter odious to him, and consequently the scene serves to whet his *almost blunted purpose.* Not to mention that the grave before him was destined to his love Ophelia—what incident in this scene but tends to work on his passions?—O ignorance of nature, when the union of nature and art can make critics wish for art only!

Is it not amazing that as all rules are drawn from the *conduct* of great genius's, not from their *directions,* nobody should have thought of drawing up rules from Shakespeare's plays, rather than of wishing they had been written from rules collected from such subaltern genius's as Euripides and Sophocles? I maintain that it was likely we should have had finer tragedies, if Shakespeare's daring had been laid down for a rule of venturing, than by pointing out his irregularities as faults. Let me add that the Witches in *Macbeth* are by the folly of the actors, not by the fault of Shakespeare, represented in a buffoon light. They are dressed with black hats and blue aprons, like basket women and soldiers' trulls, which must make the people not consider them as beings endowed with supernatural powers.

Addison is a glaring proof that pedantry and servility to rules could dishabilitate a man of genius. Compare his *Cato* and Shakespeare's *Julius Cæsar.* There is as much difference as between the soul of Julius and the timidity of Addison. A school boy of parts might by 19 have written *Cato.* The other was written by a master of human nature, and by a genius so quick and so intuitive, so penetrating, that Shakespeare from the dregs and obstacles of vile translations has drawn finer portraits of Cæsar, Brutus, Cassius, Antony and Casca than Cicero himself has done, who lived with and knew the men. Why? because Cicero thought of what he should say of them; Shakespeare of what they would have said themselves.

But Shakespeare has not only improved on Cicero, but on the founders of his art, Euripides and Sophocles, for he has done what they did not, he has introduced a chorus properly and speaking and acting in character. The Roman mob before whom Brutus and Antony plead, is just. They did plead before the Roman mob, and the mob is made by Shakespeare to display the effect that eloquence has on vulgar minds. Shakespeare does not make Brutus and Cassius disclose their plot to the Roman people—that would not have been a stroke of nature or of art, but of absurdity. Shakespeare never introduces a chorus but with peculiar propriety. Fluellen &c in *Henry 5th* are in effect a chorus: but they are not a parcel of mutes unconcerned in the action, who by the mouth of one representative draw moral and common place reflections from the incidents of the piece. A chorus was the first idea; to incorporate the chorus in the body of the drama, was an improvement wanting. Instead of observing that Shakespeare's enlightened mind had made that improvement, we have had men so absurd as to revert to the original imperfection—just as some men have wished to revive the feudal system—for some men cannot perceive the discrimination between original principles and original usages. (5–9)

238. George Steevens, Shakespeare in the theatre

1772–3

From the *General Evening Post*.

The earlier theatre criticism in this newspaper had been John Potter's *Theatrical Review* (No. 233 above). It was replaced in December 1771 with a column which bore various pseudonyms ('Longinus', 'Crito', 'Jeremy Collier', 'Animadvertor', 'Lorenzo', and 'Rusticus'), but which is evidently the work of one pen. C. H. Gray (*op. cit.* in head-note to No. 233, pp. 214–20) also noted the resemblances between the various pseudonyms, and judged the reviews of the period 1771–3 to be 'the critical writing of importance' that appeared in this journal, representing a critic of 'vigorous personality'. From numerous resemblances with his 1773 edition, the letters to Garrick, and subsequent work I ascribe these reviews to George Steevens, who is known to have written for the *General Evening Post* (*DNB*).

[a] [1–2 January 1772]
It is generally observed of Shakespeare that however incongruous the plots of his plays may be, he is always peculiarly happy in the preservation of his *Characters*, and never represents the same person in an inconsistent point of view to his readers. Thus, through all the changes and chances of the dramatic world his villains are still villains, his men of honour men of honour, and his women of virtue, examples of remarkable purity.—Few people are greater admirers of the immortal bard than myself, yet I can by no means subscribe to the universal encomium pronounced in this respect upon his accurate preservation of *character*; and if you please to insert the following stricture upon the part of Hamlet, which I saw performed very lately in an astonishing manner by Mr. Garrick, possibly the public may not much condemn the singularity of my sentiments.

487

The character of Hamlet is evidently designed by its illustrious author as a picture of an amiable prince, an affectionate son, a fast friend, and a fine gentleman.—Yet in no one of these respects is it by any means intitled to our approbation. From the beginning of the play till his killing the King at the end of the fifth act we find him irresolute, unnatural, inconstant and brutal.—He assumes the appearance of madness to answer no purpose, and is perpetually talking of what he *ought* to do, without a single attempt of proceeding to action.[1] His father has risen from the grave to call for vengeance upon a *kindless* murderer, and Hamlet promises solemnly to revenge his death, but never makes the smallest effort to effect it. On the contrary, after the veracity of the Ghost has passed the ordeal of the play our hero continues to unload his griefs in curses like a very *drab*, and even sets out quietly for England, instead of *fatting all the region kites* with the offals of his uncle; nay, though the Ghost reappears, 'to whet his almost blunted purpose,' Hamlet still continues to *talk*, and confines himself to the littleness of *safe* reproach, uttered under the pitiable guise of 'A *sore* distraction:' [5.2.222] At the end of the fifth Act, indeed, when he finds himself mortally wounded and hears that he has not half an hour to live, then he proceeds to revenge his own death, and the inconsiderate are highly charmed with his heroism. Whereas in fact common sense stands astonished at his cowardice, and wonders that a father bursting from the tomb cannot rouse him to a deed of manly resolution.

Characters assumed upon the stage should never be taken up but to answer some essential purposes. One half of the play in question is employed by Hamlet's madness; yet what individual consequence does this madness produce? The hero, to be sure, insults Ophelia (whom he tenderly loves) in the grossest manner, under the appearance of insanity; and he abuses her brother in the grossest manner, likewise under the same appearance, merely for the very conduct which should excite his esteem. In short, he does every thing wrong during his pretended madness, but never attempts any thing right; and after an outrageous violence on Laertes, in his sober senses, descends to the baseness of a serious lye to excuse himself by the plea of his '*sore distraction.*'

I do not point out these noon-day imperfections in the character

---

[1] Compare the following sequence with No. 234 above (p. 448), No. 237 (pp. 470f.), and with Steevens's 1773 edition, pp. 540f. below, Note 70.

of Hamlet so much with a view of finding fault as with a hope that some of our many commentators will endeavour to make Hamlet a little more consistent with himself. 'Tis strange that he should have *spirit* enough to kill the innocent, and yet want resolution to punish the guilty; 'tis strange he should lament Ophelia's death, and yet insult her brother for lamenting it; and 'tis above all things strange that his rage is chiefly turned against *meritorious* objects, while the great object of his horror goes unpunished till he himself, by being in the agonies of death, has nothing farther to apprehend. *Hamlet* is generally stiled one of our dramatic *classics*; I could therefore wish to see it *somewhat* correct, and rendered really worthy of those tears which we usually conceive the due of superior virtue plunged into superior calamity.

LONGINUS.

[b] [6–8 February 1772]
However the various commentators on Shakespeare's tragedy of *Hamlet* may differ about particular parts of that celebrated piece, there is one scene which they all allow to be masterly, though certainly the very reason which they assign for calling it eminently excellent is the very reason why they should pronounce it peculiarly reprehensible.

The scene which I here allude to is that in which Hamlet instructs the player in the minutenesses of his profession, and exclaims against the absurdity of those actors who let the necessary business of the play stand still to introduce some impertinent witticism of their own, and forfeit the applause of the judicious to excite the risibility of a few ignorant spectators. This practice, says Shakespeare, 'is infamous, and shews a most pitiful ambition in the fool who uses it.' [3.2.40f.]

That the lesson which Shakespeare thus gives to the players is admirable I shall readily acknowledge; and I shall also as readily acknowledge that the actors who fall into the error which he complains of deserve to be mentioned with the utmost severity of animadversion. Yet, with all possible deference to the genius of this great writer, I cannot help thinking that time and place are palpably wanting to render this scene in question a little more consonant to the laws of propriety. For if the reader considers but a moment he will find Shakespeare himself running into the very fault which incurs his own censure, and making the necessary business of the play stand still to dazzle the auditor's imagination with the lustre of his critical accuracy.

To say in the poet's defence that the scene at present under consideration is replete with knowledge, and eminent for justice, is saying nothing, because in dramatic writing it is neither the *wisdom* nor the *truth* of a passage which makes it agreeable to propriety. A scene to be *proper* must advance the great business of the play; must serve to complicate the intrigue, or to develope the catastrophe. Unless it does this it is *impertinent*, however exquisite in itself, because we can only estimate its theatrical value by the relation which it bears to the piece, and are by no means to consider its merit as a separate composition, but its worth in a state of evident dependency. . . .

It is not, therefore, enough for a scene in a play to be well *written*, it must be well *applied*; whatever impedes the progress of the plot is an error of the first magnitude; and as in life we say the wisest villain is the most dangerous, so on the stage the most glittering defect, by being the last defect observed, becomes the most capital imperfection. To comprehend the force of this reasoning it is not necessary to be a Critic by rule, nor to be deeply read in the institutes of the Stagyrite; every man who sees *Hamlet* is impatient during the performance of this scene, and burns with expectation of the vengeance which he hopes the young Prince will wreak on his father's murderer. What is Hecuba to Hamlet, or what is Hamlet to Hecuba? Yet, notwithstanding Shakespeare's own text manifestly rises against himself, the commentators *will* have the theatrical instruction a diamond of the finest water, though, *from the nature of its situation*, it is obviously a whiting's eye set in mud.

LONGINUS.

[c] [8–11 February 1772]
In pursuance of my promise, I now come to mention *Timon of Athens*, which I pronounced in my last letter so radically wrong as to affirm that it must speedily return to the oblivion from whence it was lately called forth by the industry of the Drury-lane managers.

When I speak of this play it is not my intention to examine whether the alterations made by Mr. Cumberland are, or are not, judicious: I will suppose them, for argument sake, to be as masterly as the hand of human nature could form them; yet still I must contend that a dramatic edifice reared on a tottering foundation can never stand the smallest storm of criticism, but on the contrary at the first shock must instantly crumble into dust.

The two grand passions to be excited in tragedy are pity and terror; pity for the miseries of the worthy, and terror at the punishments inflicted upon guilt: neither of these passions however is excited in *Timon of Athens*. The hero, held out as an object of compassion, is an object only of ridicule; when he talks of his misfortunes we actually smile at his follies, and see him so undistinguishing a prodigal that we no way detest the ingratitude of his parasites; Timon's sole merit consists in giving away his money profusely, and in entertaining every man at his table with magnificence who stoops to be his flatterer. This is not generosity but weakness; it is not benevolence, but dishonesty; for he lets many of his lawful creditors go unpaid while he is squandering mines of wealth upon a gang of contemptible rascals. When, therefore, Timon, in the hour of adversity, lays claim to our sympathy in the character of a liberal man ruined by his virtues, our hearts indignantly refuse to participate in his distress. We consider him as a blockhead very properly undone by his extravagance, and even rejoice in his sufferings as in the natural execution of poetical justice.

The man who is to interest us most strongly in his misfortunes being thus palpably no object of pity, it necessarily follows that every thing said to raise our emotion is a false attack upon the passions, and, like the woman's absurd wish for the ladle, turns what should be great into absolute farce. Decorate the play, therefore, as we may; act it as we will; and subscribe as we chuse to the beauty of the language; still the main principle on which the whole rests, the great axis upon which all is to turn, Timon's distress, not being of a nature either to affect or terrify, the representation at the best must freeze upon the mind, and move us little more than the fate of Macheath in the *Beggar's Opera*.

To encrease the absurdity of this play besides, Timon himself runs into the very crime for which he not only execrates his sycophants but at last forsakes the society of mankind. The people that most oblige him he insults with the grossest brutality, and even arraigns the equity of Providence because he has acted the part of an ungrateful spendthrift in prostituting the bounties which Heaven graciously poured upon his head. Thus in prosperity he is an idiot, in calamity he is a blasphemer; he behaves foolishly when surrounded by flatterers, and wickedly when abandoned. Yet in the midst of all his lunacy on the one hand, and all his impiety on the other, we are to commiserate his sufferings and to think that both men and Gods have treated him very dirtily.

The poet who would interest us for his hero should always take care that his distresses are of a natural kind, and such as may properly operate upon the feelings. A man madly throwing his treasures into the sea, and afterwards desiring the world to pity him because he wants a guinea is too ridiculous a character to wake the sensibility even of the most compassionate heart. But if to folly so egregious he adds ingratitude, nay, irreligion; if he detests all the worthy, merely for having been the voluntary dupe of the profligate, and questions the justice of Omnipotence because he has himself shamefully abused its bounty;—the author who desires us to weep for such a fellow strikes no less at the morality than the reason of the stage, and will in the end commit a dramatic suicide if in the beginning he is not sacrificed to the honest indignation of the public.

Pall-Mall.   JEREMY COLLIER.

[d] [3–5 March 1772]

Whenever our modern critics take up the pen to point out any defect in the prince of our dramatic poets, they deliver themselves with the utmost diffidence, as if actually fearful of speaking the truth, and always qualify the severity of their animadversion with some compliment which gives censure the air of approbation. For my own part, however, I think if we take *Shakespeare* with all his faults, he will still have beauties enough left to deserve our highest applause, and in the midst of his defects unquestionably remain the most exalted genius of our country.

Among the many plays of this great man which have undergone the ordeal of criticism, I know of none which has escaped more unhurt than the tragedy of *Othello*, notwithstanding the attempts of *Rymer* to render it universally ridiculous on account of the handkerchief. Yet, though this play has had the good fortune to be treated very gently by our critics in general, and though the exquisite manner in which its inimitable author has painted the passion of jealousy throws a seeming veil over a variety of imperfections, an accurate observer will nevertheless find many absurdities in the piece, besides the object of *Rymer*'s disapprobation, which strike materially at the probability of the fable, and destroy that agreeable appearance of nature which constitutes the chief source of our theatrical satisfaction.

In the first place, the circumstance of Emilia's waiting upon Desdemona in the capacity of a chambermaid is utterly indefensible. Iago maintains the rank of a gentleman in the Venetian service, is the second-in-command after Othello on the expedition to Cyprus, and could by no means suffer his wife to be placed in so humiliating a situation. If therefore we suppose it unlikely for one officer's lady to be the servant of another, we overset the whole fable at once, and immediately defeat all the purposes of the catastrophe. Yet we must do this if we are governed by the rules of real life, where disparity of rank in certain degrees creates no difference in gentility, but leaves the youngest Ensign of a regiment as respectable individually as the Chief Commander of an army. I must on this account repeat that if Emilia is taken away from the service of Desdemona, in which it is grosly improper to place her, she can have no opportunity of stealing the handkerchief which gives rise to all the bustle of the play, no opportunity of hearing Desdemona's dying confession, nor any opportunity of discovering her husband's villainy to Othello. But the violence offered to common sense by no means terminates here; for unless we subscribe to farther incongruities we must inevitably give up the tragedy before us. We must suppose Roderigo a greater fool than the poet has painted him, as he fancies that a woman who receives his whole fortune in presents will not admit of his addresses, and entertains the most respectful idea of her purity while he believes her to be scandalously mercenary. The sudden drunkenness of Cassio besides, which constitutes a principal incident of the play, is ridiculous to extravagance; and Desdemona's speaking after she is dead, an Hibernianism of the first magnitude. In short, the handkerchief, which is usually deemed the most obnoxious is the least offensive particular of the performance in question. But in some future stricture I shall possibly proceed with my remarks, and endeavour to shew how the errors now pointed out may be removed. For the present, fearful of trespassing on your limits, I conclude here, and am, your's, &c.

LORENZO.

[e] [14–17 March 1772: on *Richard III*]

... There is no fault of which our tragic writers are more generally guilty than thus '*out-heroding Herod*' when they paint a tyrant, and giving him unnecessary wickedness in order to render him detestable. Shakespeare himself is frequently reprehensible on this account; and in Richard the Third particularly makes so needless a devil of the crook'd-back monster (since we must subscribe to the general opinion of Richard's deformity) that he actually raises our ridicule, where he obviously wishes to excite the abhorrence of his auditors. Who, for instance, can resist the impulses of risibility when Richard, as a reason for his crimes, acquaints us that he wants to make his mind a fit companion for his body—

> Why then, since Heav'n has shap'd my body thus,
> Let Hell make crook'd my mind to answer it.   [3 *Henry VI*, 5.6.78f.]

If Richard was a weak as well as a wicked man, perhaps a language of this nature might admit of some extenuation; but though made a villain of the deepest dye the poet by no means intends him for a foolish character. On the contrary, fraud no less than cruelty distinguishes all his operations: he is as able as he is remorseless; and when we see how industriously he labours to save appearances, even in the very midst of his crimes, it cannot be imagined that the mere satisfaction resulting from the consciousness of criminality would plunge him into perfidy and blood. The worst men have some ends to answer when they commit an outrage upon justice or humanity, and are more prudent factors in wickedness than to destroy without a prospect of advantage. Shakespeare therefore, in the character before us has painted a fiend too black, and indulged his pencil with a freedom at the evident expence of propriety. This prevents the great effect he intended to produce. He wants, as I have already observed, to awake our horror, but by a trespass upon credibility he provokes us to laugh; and I appeal to the reader's own recollection if the galleries are not sure to be in a broad grin whenever Richard is so wantonly over-doing Termagant.

The circumstance of giving unnecessary blackness in this manner to the Devil is not however the only fault in Richard's poetical creation. This Prince, who is upon all occasions represented as subtle, cautious, and politic to a proverb, is idle, trifling, and foolish to a fault where there is the greatest necessity for the exertion of his understanding. What man of common sense, for instance, would ask the woman he passionately loved, when upbraiding him with the murder of her father, whether he was not kind in sending him to heaven? What man of common sense would urge as meritorious to a lady of virtue his having killed her husband, and publicly solicit her hand as a reward for so *laudable* an action? Indeed Shakespeare seems perfectly sensible of the objections to which this unnatural scene is exposed, for he makes Richard immediately exclaim, on Lady Anne's retiring,

> Was ever woman in this humour wooed?
> Was ever woman in this humour won? [1.2.227f.]

A question which criticism must undoubtedly answer in the negative, especially if we suppose the woman, like Lady Anne, to have the smallest pretensions to decency or reputation.

I have seen many actors in the character of Richard, but scarcely any one, if I except Mr. Garrick, who seemed to conceive him properly. Odious as he is drawn by the poet, the generality of our performers labour to render him, if possible, a more shocking dog than he really is, and Mr. Smith of Covent-garden, particularly, makes him stab King Henry after he is dead,[1] which is highly offensive to a spectator of the least generosity. The lines

> ——if any spark of life remains,
> Down, down to hell, and say I sent thee thither [3 *Henry VI*, 5.6.66f.]

may surely be spoken without so barbarous a violence upon a breathless body. Richard is a brave man, though a bad one, and he would have deemed a conduct of that kind below the dignity of a soldier. But this is not the only place in which he is injured by his Covent-garden representative. Mr. Smith makes him a comical fellow on many occasions, and delivers those lines of bluntness which are scattered through the part with all the humour he is master of, and upon the whole with a sufficient share to circulate a loud laugh among his admirers in the gallery. When he tells us how the midwife was astonished to find him born with teeth, he is uncommonly arch, and makes us quite forget that we are looking at the hero of a tragedy.

LORENZO.

---

[1] But the Folio text has the stage-direction '*Stabs him againe.*' at this point.

[f] [17–19 March 1772]

It is commonly observed of Shakespeare that as he flourished in the reign of a Lancastrian Princess, and was much encouraged by the Court, it was natural enough for him in those plays which relate to the unhappy feuds between the Houses of York and Lancaster to be extremely partial to the latter, and to exaggerate the failings of the former to the utmost height of poetical description. Upon this principle many of his commentators have undertaken to extenuate, if not to justify, his character of Richard the Third, and because that Prince was really a bad man, to contend for the propriety of exhibiting him as a deformed one out of compliment to the general prejudices of vulgarity.

I am led into these reflections from the freedom I took in my last letter with the character of Richard the Third, which I ventured to pronounce unnatural to the last degree, and affirmed to be coloured up to such a caricature of wickedness as absolutely excited our ridicule, where the poet only meant to rouse our detestation. Yet if we comply with the warmest admirers of Shakespeare, and even overlook in the play alluded to his glaring partiality to the House of Lancaster, still that will by no means rescue him from those charges which I urged against the superlative wickedness of his atrocious characters, nor excuse the absurdity of painting his villains in so shocking a light as to stagger the belief of credulity. We will, if you please, Mr. Editor, give up the play of *Richard the Third*, and in the aims of the politician wholly forget the prostitution of the poet. But what shall we say, Sir, to the unnecessary blackness of his Cloten in *Cymbeline*, of his Bastard in *Lear*, or of his Macbeth, which surely had nothing to do with the York and Lancastrian broils, and which therefore might be represented with some little degree of probability?

Cloten is a very whimsical composition; he is drawn foolish and wise, brave and insignificant, suspicious to an excess, yet weak beyond the toleration of credibility.[1] In his vices he keeps no bounds whatsoever with the instruments he wishes to employ, but on the contrary describes the villainy he wants executed in the most detestable terms. Thus in his attack upon Pisanio, to discover where Imogen is, he tells that faithful servant if he is desirous to be thought *a true man*, that is, if he is ready to commit every crime which Cloten thinks proper to advise, this *gracious*

---

[1] Compare the very similar critique by Steevens, p. 534 below, Note 53.

Prince will at once receive him into his highest favour, and neither spare his purse nor his interest to advance him in Cymbeline's Court. Other villains, when they endeavour to corrupt the weak or the wavering, behave with some share of caution and break their infamous purposes gradually, to lessen the horror of their intentions. Thus Richard himself speaks only by innuendo for a time to Buckingham about the murder of his nephews; thus John deals almost wholly in metaphors with Hubert when he recommends the sacrifice of Arthur; and thus even Macbeth thinks it necessary to make use of qualifying arguments to the assassins of Banquo. But Cloten, though uninvested with a regal power of defending his deeds, is a plain, undisguised, self-condemning monster. Like Lord Ogleby in the *Clandestine Marriage*, he is above all consideration the moment his desires are kindled, and instead of tediously beating the bush comes to his point at once, with an impudence that actually puts guilt out of countenance. The murder of Posthumus and the rape of Imogen he mentions as mere trifles, and tells us after he has slaughtered the first and forced the latter that the King may *possibly* be angry but that the Queen his mother, having power over the destiny of Cymbeline, shall turn every thing into his commendation. This is not all. Cloten's fury is as ridiculous as it is criminal, for after he has *tied up his horse* in a most royal stile to look after Posthumus he enters into a foolish, preposterous quarrel with one of the disguised young Princes under Bellarius's care, and risques the disappointment of his own views because he takes the Prince to be a mountaineer [4.2.72ff.] 'Yield thee, villain, or thou diest,' is his language to a man who has given him no shadow of offence, and whose only culpability consists in being the inhabitant of a mountain.

Aliquando dormitat Homerus[1] is a common adage, and therefore as much excuse is to be made for the naps of the English Homer as for the celebrated Greek of Antiquity. Men of sense however, if they overlook defects, should not convert them into beauties, but be at least spirited enough to decide between the result of the indulgence and the fervor of their approbation.

LORENZO.

---

[1] Horace, *Ars Poetica*, 359: 'quandoque bonus dormitat Homerus': 'whenever good Homer nods.'

[g] [2–4 June 1772]

An opinion is universally prevalent with respect to the writings of Shakespeare, that he was no friend to the fair sex, but that on the contrary he embraced every opportunity of treating the ladies with the utmost severity, and represented them as often as possible in a disagreeable light to the public. How a charge so unjust should be so generally credited would appear to me a matter of much surprize, if I was not perfectly sensible that nine-tenths of our modern Critics take their opinions entirely upon trust, and never once prudently examine whether their theatrical belief is really orthodox.

The gentlemen who are thus pleased to censure our immortal poet for his cruelty to the ladies tell us triumphantly of Goneril and Regan in *Lear*, of Lady Anne in *Richard the Third*, of the Queen in *Cymbeline*, of the Queen in *Hamlet*, and ascend the climax of critical exultation with a mention of the Queen in *Macbeth*. In the several characters here enumerated I readily grant that Shakespeare has by no means drawn a flattering picture of the softer sex, and even acknowledge that a Devil more incarnate than the latter could not possibly be coloured by the pencil of human imagination.[1] Yet while I make this acknowledgement I shall enter also with confidence into Shakespeare's defence, and beg to ask what the reader thinks of Juliet, Imogen, Ophelia, Portia in the *Merchant of Venice*, Portia in *Julius Cæsar*, Veturia and Volumnia in *Coriolanus*, Isabella in *Measure for Measure*, of Rosalind and Cælia in *As You Like It*, of Hero and Beatrice in *Much Ado*, of Helena, Diana, and the Countess of Roussillion in *All's Well that Ends Well*, of Constance in *King John*, Desdemona in *Othello*, of Cordelia in *Lear*, and several other women of less importance in these and the different pieces, which I have not particularly pointed out. I fancy a great majority, even from this trifling retrospect of parts, will be found in favour of the fair; and our bard of course will not only be rescued from the imputation of injustice to the sex but be allowed the title of strenuous advocate for the dignity of female reputation.

The charge, however, of making his women generally depraved is not the only one which the Critics have brought against Shakespeare; they insist that as vehicles for dramatic action his feminine characters are most insignificant, and even Colley Cibber admits

---

[1] Cf. Steevens in the 1773 edition, p. 524 below, Note 23.

the justice of this accusation so far that he enters into a laboured justification of the poet from his total want of actresses. But instead of granting the conclusion drawn I deny the premises absolutely, and declare that Shakespeare has no need of an excuse. His women are always as important as the nature of his fable requires them, and if in some places his men engross the principal business of a play there are other places where his women have equally the advantage. If Falstaff for instance not only banishes all brothers from the throne of humour in the *Merry Wives*, Rosalind is no less distinguished in the comedy of *As You Like It*. If Othello renders Desdemona comparatively insignificant, Imogen throws all the male characters at a considerable distance behind her in *Cymbeline*; in *Much Ado*, there is no knowing where to place the superiority—and in *Romeo*, capital as the lover is made, Juliet is entrusted with the most interesting part of the business. Possibly indeed, upon a minute comparison of character and character the scale will preponderate in favour of the men, and that too essentially; but won't it do the same in real life? Are not men the grand agents in the fall of empires, as well as in the management of domestic duties; and don't they settle the marriage of a child, no less than direct the revolutions of Government? Shakespeare consequently gave them only that natural pre-eminence which they possess in the unavoidable course of things, and the Critics expose themselves constantly to contempt in asserting that his women are palpably contemptible.

From the foregoing observations a reader of common sense will see the indispensible necessity of judging for himself in every thing relative to the stage. No error is more general than what I have here endeavoured to expose, yet none is more obvious to the meanest capacity; and I dare say that many, on the perusal of these indigested hints, who think that Shakespeare's women are not only depraved in the majority but dramatically insignificant also, will be astonished at the grossness of a mistake into which they never could have fallen, if they had merely exercised a moderate portion of reflection.

ANIMADVERTOR.

[h] [23–26 January 1773]
On the Tragedy of KING LEAR, *performed last night at* Covent-Garden Theatre.
It has been a matter of much debate among the critics whether a

play could be successfully constructed without being either immediately founded upon a love story, or having such a collateral relation with the business of love that the chief incidents of the piece shall spring from that passion.

Had the critics, however, turned to *Macbeth* or *Julius Cæsar* they might have seen that a very excellent play could have been written without the assistance even of a love episode. Lady Macbeth has no conjugal struggles of tenderness on her husband's account. She is his accomplice in guilt, and is therefore anxious for her own sake that his villainy is successful. But none of the finer feelings are alarmed for his safety; they are all rooted up in her soul, and no one incident in the piece arises from the source of female affection.[1]

Julius Cæsar, in the circumstance of Portia's anxiety about Brutus, is to be sure an instance of conjugal tenderness which seems at a first view to refute the assertion with which we set out. But when the reader recollects that the scene between Portia and Brutus is rather a *preparation* for a situation than a real situation, and when he moreover recollects that no circumstance of consequence is produced by the heroism of Portia to advance the piece, he will probably think with us that *Julius Cæsar* is no more to be set down as a play of tenderness than the bloody usurper of the Scottish diadem.

Mr. Colman, in the tragedy of *King Lear*, has given us a fresh proof that a play, and even that play a tragedy, can be written successfully without any share of a love plot, as he totally excludes Tate's alteration and does not suffer any idea of a reciprocal affection to exist between Edgar and Cordelia. Yet, though he brings the piece to a catastrophe, and interests us as warmly in the distresses of Lear as Shakespeare himself intended we should be interested, it must nevertheless be acknowledged that Tate's addition of the love scenes renders the dependent parts of the tragedy considerably more pleasing than we find them in their original state; and that wherever the tender passions can be introduced with propriety they should always engage a material share of the poet's consideration. . . .

[1] Cf. Steevens in the 1773 edition, p. 524 below, Note 23.

[i] [16–18 February 1773]

On the performance of KING LEAR *last night at Drury-lane Theatre.*
We some time ago took notice of this celebrated tragedy as a piece
of writing, and declared that Tate's alteration in our opinion had
considerably improved the great original; we shall now speak of
the representation at Drury-lane theatre, where we attended
last night to see Mr. Garrick in the principal character, and absolutely experienced an *agony* of pleasure from the performance of
this inimitable actor.

Were we to enquire in what particular scene Mr. Garrick is pre-
eminently excellent it would be a difficult circumstance to point it
out; he enters so fully, so entirely into the meaning of his author
that though we are unquestionably most affected by the passages
which are most distressful, he satisfies us equally in the delivery
of a common command or in the recital of the plainest observation. In short, every syllable being spoken with the nicest degree
of propriety, we see the master as much in a simple *yes* or *no* as in
the wildest whirlwind of the passions; and while he continues
before us never recollect that we are sitting at no more than an
imaginary tale of affliction.

Mr. Garrick's mode of speaking the curse at the end of the first
act in the play has been always highly applauded, yet we think he
improved, if possible, in the settled solemnity of the execration.
Other actors in this capital passage are loud, turbulent, and
ostentatious; they seem to demand our attention for something
very extraordinary, and tacitly desire us to be ready with our
warmest approbation. Mr. Garrick, however, conducts himself
without the smallest shadow of parade, and is pouring out the
effusions of his afflicted bosom before a less skilful actor would
have been ready in his attitude. His voice, besides, is lowered in a
manner that not only makes the curse more bitterly determined
but makes us inwardly shudder at the air of religion which accompanies the imprecation. Shakespeare, indeed, has written the
curse exquisitely; Garrick, however, gives it additional energy,
and it is impossible to hear him deliver it without an equal mixture
of horror and admiration.

> Hear nature, hear, dear goodess, hear a father,
> Suspend thy purpose, ...   [1.4.275ff.]

We have quoted the curse for the reader's perusal, but it is not in
language to convey the tone, the air, and the fervency with which

it was pronounced last night. In fact, when we aim at describing any part of Mr. Garrick's performance in Lear, we feel a most melancholy want of expression, and unavoidably fall again and again into the beaten road of an interjective applause. We cry 'tis *fine! prodigious! astonishing!* yet we have no sober term by which we can critically impress the reader with our ideas of its excellence in the *extreme*, and therefore the little which our scanty limits allow us to say, must be very inadequate to his merit in the character. . . .

[j] [20–3 February 1773]
Though on Thursday last we spoke solely of the *performance* of *Lear*, that is of the manner in which it is *exhibited* at Drury-lane theatre, yet upon recollection we are of opinion that some little alterations are necessary in this tragedy to give it a more probable appearance on the stage. The profligate characters are made unnecessarily flagitious. They commit the most atrocious crimes out of a downright regard for villainy, and the Bastard, for instance, unlike the generality of monsters, who when alone at least have their bosoms harrowed up by conscience, not only exults in his crimes but speaks of them as so many sources of real satisfaction. It may perhaps be requisite for the catastrophe, as Tate has altered the play in question, to make the Bastard entertain a resolution of violating Cordelia at midnight, on a blasted heath, and in the midst of a storm uncommonly dreadful; we say it may perhaps be requisite to trespass thus far upon probability because otherwise Edgar could have no opportunity of rendering a service to his mistress. It may also be requisite for him to rejoice when his father's eyes are pulled out, because he is elevated to the Earldom of Gloster; and it may be requisite to make the two Queens passionately in love with the Bastard, because they poison each other in consequence of their mutual jealousy. But surely it cannot be in the least requisite to retain the despicable farce of leading the eyeless Gloster up to the imaginary cliff of Dover, nor requisite to abuse his judgment that he may be continued in the undisturbed possession of his senses. The circumstances of solemnity, besides, by which this incident is attended encreases the ridicule beyond conception. Edgar, indeed, says,

> Why do I trifle thus with his despair?
> 'Tis done to cure it.   [4.6.33f.]

The remedy, however, is here likely to be worse than the disease, and when, after the following pathetic address to heaven we see Gloster taking a jump upon the boards, nay, find him fancying that he has fallen from the very top of the cliff, our laughter is infinitely more provoked than than our sensibility.

> *Glost.* O you mighty Gods,
> This world I do renounce,   [4.6.34ff.]

Edgar, who attends his father on this notable exploit, heightens the horror of the scene previously with this celebrated description. [Quotes 4.6.11–24]

The *pious* Edgar, if really concerned at the miseries of his father, could neither have the power nor the inclination to play the fool in this ridiculous manner, especially as the moment the old man takes his absurd leap, he says

> And yet I know not how conceit may rob
> The treasury of life . . .   [4.6.42ff.]

As the defect pointed out is so very gross, and is not all necessary to advance the catastrophe of the play, we hope that Mr. Garrick will judiciously expunge this mummery in future, and prevent us from looking with contempt upon a passage which is meant to excite our warmest admiration.

[k] [6–9 March 1773][1]

To the Editor of the GENERAL EVENING POST.

SIR,

Who it is that, through the channel of your Paper, *favours* the public with the Dramatic Strictures, I neither know nor care. For an *impartial* writer (as, I think, he has more than once stiled himself) he is the most *curious* one I ever remember. There is (if you will believe him) neither Tragedy or Comedy, modern or ancient, performed at Covent-garden, but it is '*void* of sentiment,' '*filled* with incongruities,' or the 'historical truth is not attended to,' or some such fatal error. When it has so happened that the same play has been acted at Covent-garden which he has puffed off from Drury-lane, he then belabours the *poor* actors, and says that however ill it might be performed, it would be be difficult at

---

[1] Shortly after this date the 'Dramatic Strictures' ceased, being replaced by a shorter, less individualized column of 'Theatrical Intelligence', probably shared by more than one newspaper.

Covent-garden to supply their places with more pleasure to the public, and that he is SORRY to say the *merits* of the play are lost in the *performance*. In short, your correspondent appears to be neither more nor less than Trumpeter in Ordinary to Drury-lane, or you may, without much fear of hurting his reputation, invert the order of the words, and make him *Ordinary Trumpeter* to the said Theatre.

I. P.

239. Tate Wilkinson, adaptation of *Hamlet*

1773

From *The Wandering Patentee; or, A History Of The Yorkshire Theatres, From* 1770 *To The Present Time.* .... (4 vols, York, 1795).

Tate Wilkinson (1739–1803), whose career as actor and manager lasted for 40 years, performed in provincial theatres throughout Great Britain, becoming best known while managing a circuit of theatres in the north of England. He was an exemplary manager, who recruited good actors and reformed abuses. Breaking his leg for the second time at the age of 50, he 'was thenceforward prevented from playing juvenile characters'. He was celebrated as one of the most extraordinary mimics ever known, exceeding even Samuel Foote. He published his *Memoirs* in four volumes (York, 1790). His adaptation of *Hamlet* was evidently an attempt to cash in on a London success for the provinces. As with Garrick's version I have marked inserted lines with asterisks.

Mr. Garrick's alteration of *Hamlet* was that season [1772–3] tried at Drury-Lane, and to the astonishment of every one well received, even by the Galleries, though without their favourite acquaintances the Grave Diggers. I made application to

Mr. Garrick for the copy, he did not choose to oblige me; so I set to work, and will here insert my compilation. I do it with less fear, for though the jumble is my putting together yet as it is on the plan of Colley Cibber's alteration of *Richard the Third*, so the reader here will meet several obsolete passages from Shakespeare, that to one not very familiar with all that author's wonderful productions may afford some entertainment.

HAMLET with alterations.

In my alteration, the FIRST ACT ends with the line, 'Earth o'erwhelms 'em to man's eyes.' [1.2.267] The SECOND with 'That ever I was born to set it right. [1.5.190]

The THIRD ACT is the second in the original, and the FOURTH is the third in the original. The fifth act in the alteration begins with the line 'There's matter in these sighs,' [4.1.1] and goes on regularly to Laertes's speech.

Laer. Too much of water hast thou, poor Ophelia,	4.7.186
And therefore I forbid my tears.	187
Tears! Wherefore tears? They rather should convert	*1
To sparks of fire.—Let me but meet him, Heav'n.	*
Enter QUEEN.	
Till that hour comes, time moves on drooping wings:	*
Revenge, revenge!	*
Queen. Calmly, good Laertes.	4.5.113
Laer. That drop of blood that's calm, proclaims me	
bastard,	114
Cries cuckold to my father, brands the harlot	115
Even here, between the chaste and unsmirched brow	116
Of my true mother.—For daring will I tell him,	117
Front to front—thus didst thou.	
Ham. [*without*] What's he whose phrase bears such an	
emphasis?	5.1.248–9
Enter HAMLET *and* HORATIO.	
Ham. Here am I, Hamlet the Dane.	251–2
Laer. Perdition catch thee! [*Lays hold of Hamlet.*	*
Ham. Thou pray'st not well.	253
I pr'ythee, take thy fingers from my throat,	254
For though I am not splenetic and rash,	255

---

1 But cf. *Henry VIII*, 2.4.72f.: 'my drops of tears/I'll turn to sparks of fire'.

Yet I have in me something dangerous,   256
Which let thy wisdom fear.   257a
    Hor. Good, my Lord!   259
    Ham. Hold off your hands!   257b
    King. Pluck them asunder.   [*They are parted.*   258
    Hor. Good Sir, be temperate.   [*To Hamlet.*   *
    Ham. Thou know'st my wrongs;—thou know'st my
                  soul is fixed.   *
I charge thee on thy friendship not to impede me.   *
    King. [*Laying hold of Laertes*] Laertes, hold!—on thy
                 allegiance hold!   *
Claims not our royal person here respect?   *
Traitor! [*To Hamlet*] how cam'st thou hither against our will?   *
Against our sovereign express command?   *
(Now soft-ey'd pity hence, and keen remorse.) [*Aside.*   *
Thou must rely on other shores for safety: *
The cries of blood, blood all innocent,   *
Here loudly claim thee as a victim due.   *
I will not screen a murd'rer. Call officers. [*To Laertes.*   *
Thy father's death shall instant be revenged.   *
    Laer. My rage will urge me on with lightening's speed.   *
And my tumultuous grief pour balsam on my wrongs.
                 [*Exit Laertes.*   *
    Queen. Oh! let me kneel, and plead for gentle Hamlet.   *
    King. Unworthy Queen, to call him gentle Hamlet!   *
Begone, nor let humanity attempt to thwart   *
The will of Heaven.   *
    Ham. The will of Heaven!—Behold   *; 3.4.173–5
In me Heaven's minister—in me my father.   *
    King. Thy father, idle railer! What's thy meaning?   *
             [*Enthusiastically alarmed.*
    Ham. Meaning! Ask thy conscience; let that answer.   *
I have not time to wage a war of words,   *
I must appear a blaze of vengeful terror.   *
By me my father speaks; by me he warns thee: *
In me behold his dread, assur'd avenger.   *
The sword of Heaven is drawn—prepare—prepare—   *
The hour is come that sinks thee to perdition.   *
    King. Curse on thy arrogance.   *

Ham. Would curses kill, as doth the Mandrake's
                               groan,[1]   [3.2.310

I would invent as bitter searching terms,   311
As curst, as harsh, as horrible to hear,   312
Deliver'd strongly through my fixed teeth,   313
With full as many signs of deadly hate,   314
As lean-faced Envy in her loathsome cave: 315
My tongue should stumble in mine earnest words; 316
Mine eyes should sparkle like the flint-struck steel; 317
Mine hair be fixed on end, like one distract;   318
Ay, every joint should seem to curse and ban: 319
And even now my burthen'd heart would break,   320
But that its sacred, just revenge doth claim thee.   *

    King. [*Aside*] His words alarm! My fears must make me
                              daring—   *
If he lives I fall.   *
    Queen Sure guilt doth sink me.   [*Aside.*   *
Son—husband—I've no power of utterance. [*Queen pleading.*   *
    King. Hence, Gertrude.—Traitor, have at thy heart!   *
    Ham. Heaven bids at thine: *
Thou art not worthy of so fair a combat;   *
But in this arm let justice strike thee. [*They fight round.*   *
    Queen. Oh, horror, horror, help!—Son—husband—   *
Oh, mercy—mercy!   *
    [*Queen runs out shrieking, after which the King falls.*
    Hor. My Lord, how fare ye?   *
    King. Curse on thy stripling hand —In this dread hour   *
My crimes o'erwhelm—Reason forsakes—and furies rend me.   *
Death, thou hast snar'd me.   *
If thou be'est Death, I'll give thee Denmark's treasure,   *
So thou wilt let me live and feel no pain.   *
    Ham. Oh! What a sign it is of evil life   *
When Death's approach appears so terrible.   *
    King. [*Madly*] Bring me unto my trial when you will.[2][3.3.8
Can I make men live, whether they will or no?   10
I'll give my treasures but to look upon him: 13
He hath no eyes, the dust hath blinded them.   14

---

[1] Wilkinson inserts here the speech of Suffolk to Queen Margaret from 2 *Henry VI*, 3.2.310–20.
[2] Wilkinson here inserts the death of Cardinal Beaufort from 2 *Henry VI*, 3.3.8–31.

Comb down his hair.—Look! look! it stands upright!   15
Like lime-twigs set to catch my winged soul.   16
    Ham. Oh, thou eternal Mover of the heavens!   19
Look with a gentle eye upon this wretch: 20
O beat away the busy meddling fiend   21
That lays strong siege unto his wretched soul,   22
And from his bosom purge this black despair.   23
    Hor. See how the pangs of death encompass him!   24
    Ham. Peace to his soul if Heaven's good pleasure be.   26
O uncle, if thou think'st of heaven's bliss,   27
Hold up thy hand, make signal of thy hope.   28
               [*King looks without a sign and dies.*
He dies and makes no sign:—O Heaven, forgive him!   29
    Hor. So bad a death argues a monstrous life.   30
    Ham. He's dead—forbear to judge,   31]
For we are sinners all.
LAERTES, *as entering with* Soldiers.
    Laer. [*Without*] This way my friends,—the King, the
                         King's in danger.   *
Guard well each avenue,—let him not pass,   *
But kill him rather—[*Enters*]—How, thou bloody villain!   *
The king too murdered! Heavens my tardy hand   *
Should wither from its trunk for this delay   *
Of vengeance for an honoured father's murder;   *
My dear lov'd sister's hapless fate by thee,   *
Even in her earliest bloom destroy'd;   *
To me they call, loud shrieking from their graves,   *
With piercing cries, and claim thy forfeit blood.   *
    Ham. Yet hear, Laertes! how canst thou use me thus,   5.1.282
I lov'd you ever.   283
    Hor. Good Laertes, hear.   [*Earnest.*   *
    Laer. No more—his breath is poison, and his sight   *
Is loathsome.—This for my king and sister: *
This for my father's death.   [*Fight.*   *
    Hor. My Prince in danger!   *
Let me bare my breast.
    [*Horatio rushes between, Hamlet receives a first, then a second wound, and falls into Horatio's arms.*
    Hor. Oh heavens, my master falls.—Within there!—
      help!—   *

Enter Captain *and* Guards.

    Ham. Rash youth, thou'st slain thy king, nay more, thy
                        friend.   *

The loss of life afflicts me not, Laertes;   *

My blood is due for thy dear father's death,   *

A fated unknown victim—Poor Ophelia.   *

For her my agonizing heart weeps faster   *

Than all the crimson drops thy sword has drawn.   *

    Hor. It may be yet within the power of art—   *

    Ham. Dream not of art, nor stir in my last moments; *

I feel Death's arm, nor shrink within his grasp.   *

    Laer. I'm lost.—Thy ways, oh Heaven! are intricate: *

If I have err'd, impute it not—   *

    Ham. When thou hast learnt the mystery from Horatio, *

Thou'lt pity and forgive.—All I request is,   *

Comfort my hapless mother—ease her sorrows—   *

Relieve my country from distracting broils.   *

I could disclose—but oh,—I die,—Horatio,   *;5.2.330

Thou liv'st—report me and my cause aright   331

To the unsatisfy'd.   332

    Hor. Sweet Prince, whilst life dost course its vital stream, *

My trusty love shall tend thy memory ever.   *

    Ham. Thou noble youth, exchange forgiveness with me, 321

Thy father's death dwell not on me, nor mine on thee.[1] 322

    Laer. Heaven make thee free of it.   324

    Ham. Oh, I cannot live to hear what news from
                   England!   346

But I do prophecy the election lights on Fortinbrass. 347

If so, tell him he has my dying voice,   348

With the occurents, more or less, that have solicited— 349

The rest is silence—oh!   [*Dies.* 350

    Hor. There cracks the cordage of a noble heart. 351

Adieu, sweet Prince!   351

And choirs of angels sing thee to thy rest.   352

    Laer. My rage is gone, and I am struck with
                   sorrow.[2]   [5.6.147–8

Bid the drum beat, the silver clarion sound;   150

---

[1] In Shakespeare these two lines are spoken by Laertes.

[2] Wilkinson inserts here part of the closing speech by Aufidius over the corpse of Coriolanus.

Let them speak mournfully—trail your steel pikes. 150–1
Yea, he shall have a noble memory. 154
Take up the bodies—such a night as this, 393
Becomes the field, but here shews much amiss. 394

DIRECTIONS.—*The soldiers turn their spears to the ground. Laertes not to bow at the conclusion, but continue looking over Hamlet— Horatio kneeling over the Prince. Drums beat muffled. Trumpets and the band play a dead march. The bell tolls and curtain drops very slow.*——

This was acted at all my Theatres, and well received, whether with any degree of desert, I will not presume to say. It was first acted at York, on Saturday April 3, 1773. (I, 166–73)

240. George Steevens and Samuel Johnson, edition of Shakespeare

1773

From *The Plays of William Shakespeare. In ten volumes. With the Corrections and Illustrations of Various Commentators; To which are added notes by Samuel Johnson and George Steevens. With an Appendix* (10 vols, 1773).

At the end of his Preface, reprinted from the 1765 edition, Johnson added this sentence: 'Of what has been performed in this revisal, an account is given in the following pages by Mr. Steevens, who might have spoken both of his own diligence and sagacity in terms of greater self-approbation, without deviating from modesty or truth' (Sig. E$_2$^{r}). Johnson usually gave most credit for the edition to Steevens, but Arthur Sherbo has computed that he wrote 84 new notes for this edition (including end-notes to several plays which he had failed to provide in 1765), and altered some 70 other notes

(*Johnson on Shakespeare*, p. xxxix). For the progress of the edition see the Garrick *Private Correspondence* and *Letters*; Johnson's *Letters* and Boswell's *Life*; and for a study of Johnson's revisions see Sherbo, *Johnson, Editor*, pp. 102–13, and '1773: The Year of Revision', *Eighteenth-Century Studies* 7 (1973), pp. 18–39.

ADVERTISEMENT TO THE READER. [by Steevens]

The want of adherence to the old copies, which has been complained of in the text of every modern republication of Shakespeare, is fairly deducible from Mr. Rowe's inattention to one of the first duties of an editor. Mr. Rowe did not print from the earliest and most correct, but from the most remote and inaccurate of the four folios.[1] Between the years 1623 and 1685 (the dates of the first and last) the errors in every play at least were trebled. Several pages in each of these ancient editions have been examined, that the assertion might come more fully supported. It may be added that as every fresh editor continued to make the text of his predecessor the ground-work of his own (never collating but where difficulties occurred), some deviations from the originals had been handed down, the number of which are lessened in the impression before us as it has been constantly compared with the most authentic copies, whether collation was absolutely necessary for the recovery of sense or not. The person who undertook this task may have failed by inadvertency, as well as those who preceded him; but the reader may be assured that he who thought it his duty to free an author from such modern and unnecessary innovations as had been censured in others, has not ventured to introduce any of his own.

It is not pretended that a complete body of various readings is here collected; or that all the diversities which the copies exhibit are pointed out; as near two thirds of them are typographical mistakes, or such a change of insignificant particles as would

[1] Steevens takes this, and many subsequent points, from Capell's edition: see p. 308 above. His plagiarisms from Capell were exposed by John Collins in *A Letter to George Hardinge on the subject of a passage in Mr. Steevens's preface to his impression of Shakespeare*, the preface to which is dated September 1774, the letter (48pp.) being published in 1777. I quote from the copy in Capell's library; Collins, *op. cit.*, p. 23.

crowd the bottom of the page with an ostentation of materials, from which at last nothing useful could be selected.

The dialogue might indeed sometimes be lengthened by yet other insertions than have been made, but without advantage either to its spirit or beauty; as in the following instance.

Lear. No.

Kent. Yes.

Lear. No, I say.

Kent. I say, yea.

Here the quartos add:

Lear. *No, no, they would not.*

Kent. *Yes, they have.*   [*King Lear*, 2.4.15ff.]

By the admission of this negation and affirmation would any new idea be gained?

The labours of preceding editors have not left room for a boast that many valuable readings have been retrieved; though it may be fairly asserted that the text of Shakespeare is restored to the condition in which the author, or rather his first publishers appear to have left it, such emendations as were absolutely necessary alone admitted.

> *Multa dies, variusq; labor mutabilis ævi*
> *Retulit in melius, multos alterna revisens*
> *Lusit, et in solido rursus fortuna locavit.*[1]

Where a particle indispensably necessary to the sense, was wanting such a supply has been silently adopted from other editions; but where a syllable or more had been added for the sake of the metre only, which at first might have been irregular, such interpolations are here constantly retrenched, sometimes with and sometimes without notice. Those speeches which in the elder editions are printed as prose, and from their own construction are incapable of being compressed into verse without the aid of supplemental syllables, are restored to prose again;[2] and the measure is divided afresh in others, where the mass of words had been inharmoniously separated into lines.

The scenery, throughout all the plays, is regulated in conformity to a rule which the poet, by his general practice, seems to have

---

[1] *Aeneid*, 11.425ff.: 'Many an ill has time repaired, and the shifting toil of changing years; many a man has Fortune, fitful visitant, mocked, then once more set up upon firm ground'.

[2] Collins, *op. cit.*, pp. 24f., notes the similarity to Capell (p. 305 above).

proposed to himself. Several of his pieces are come down to us divided into scenes as well as acts. These divisions were probably his own, as they are made on settled principles, which would hardly have been the case had the task been executed by the players. A change of scene with Shakespeare most commonly implies a change of place, but always an entire evacuation of the stage. The custom of distinguishing every entrance or exit by a fresh scene was adopted, perhaps very idly, from the French theatre.[1]

For the length of many notes and the accumulation of examples in others some apology may be likewise expected. An attempt at brevity is often found to be the source of an imperfect explanation. Where a passage has been constantly misunderstood, where the jest or pleasantry has been suffered to remain long in obscurity, more instances have been brought to clear the one or elucidate the other than appear at first sight to have been necessary. For these it can only be said that when they prove that phraseology or source of merriment to have been once general which at present seems particular, they are not quite impertinently intruded; as they may serve to free the author from a suspicion of having employed an affected singularity of expression, or indulged himself in allusions to transient customs which were not of sufficient notoriety to deserve ridicule or reprehension. When examples in favour of contradictory opinions are assembled, though no attempt is made to decide on either part such neutral collections should always be regarded as materials for future critics, who may hereafter apply them with success. Authorities, whether in respect of words or things, are not always producible from the most celebrated writers; yet such circumstances as fall below the notice of history can only be sought in the jest-book, the satire, or the play; and the novel, whose fashion did not outlive a week, is sometimes necessary to throw light on those annals which take in the compass of an age. Those, therefore, who would wish to have the peculiarities of Nym familiarized to their ideas must excuse the insertion of such an epigram as best suits the purpose, however tedious in itself; and such as would be acquainted with the propriety of Falstaff's allusion to *stewed prunes*[2] should not be disgusted at a multitude of instances which, when the point is once known to

[1] Collins, *op. cit.*, pp. 25f., notes that Capell (above, p. 312) is the source for this whole paragraph.
[2] See Note 37 below.

be established, may be diminished by any future editor. An author who *catches* (as Pope expresses it) at *the Cynthia of a minute*, and does not furnish notes to his own works, is sure to lose half the praise which he might have claimed had he dealt in allusions less temporary, or cleared up for himself those difficulties which lapse of time must inevitably create.

The author of the additional notes has rather been desirous to support old readings than to claim the merit of introducing new ones. He desires to be regarded as one who found the task he undertook more arduous than it seemed, while he was yet feeding his vanity with the hopes of introducing himself to the world as an editor in form. He who has discovered in himself the power to rectify a few mistakes with ease is naturally led to imagine that all difficulties must yield to the efforts of future labour; and perhaps feels a reluctance to be undeceived at last.

Mr. Steevens desires it may be observed that he has strictly complied with the terms exhibited in his proposals,[1] having appropriated all such assistances as he received to the use of the present editor, whose judgment has in every instance determined on their respective merits. While he enumerates his obligations to his correspondents it is necessary that one comprehensive remark should be made on such communications as are omitted in this edition, though they might have proved of great advantage to a more daring commentator. The majority of these were founded on the supposition that Shakespeare was originally an author correct in the utmost degree, but maimed and interpolated by the neglect or presumption of the players.[2] In consequence of this belief alterations have been proposed wherever a verse could be harmonized, an epithet exchanged for one more apposite, or a sentiment rendered less perplexed. Had the general current of advice been followed the notes would have been filled with attempts at emendation apparently unnecessary, though sometimes elegant, and as frequently with explanations of what none would have thought difficult. A constant peruser of Shakespeare will suppose whatever is easy to his own apprehension will prove so to that of others, and consequently may pass over some real perplexities in silence. On the contrary, if in consideration of the different abilities of every class of readers he should offer a comment on all harsh inversions of phrase or peculiarities of expres-

[1] See No. 212 above.   [2] Cf. Capell, pp. 306f. above.

sion he will at once excite the disgust and displeasure of such as think their own knowledge or sagacity undervalued. It is difficult to fix a medium between doing too little and too much in the task of mere explanation. There are yet many passages unexplained and unintelligible which may be reformed, at hazard of whatever licence, for exhibitions on the stage, in which the pleasure of the audience is chiefly to be considered; but must remain untouched by the critical editor, whose conjectures are limited by narrow bounds, and who gives only what he at least supposes his author to have written.

If it is not to be expected that each vitiated passage in Shakespeare can be restored till a greater latitude of experiment shall be allowed; so neither can it be supposed that the force of all his allusions will be pointed out till such books are thoroughly examined as cannot easily at present be collected, if at all. Several of the most correct lists of our dramatic pieces exhibit the titles of plays which are not to be met with in the completest collections. It is almost unnecessary to mention any other than Mr. Garrick's, which, curious and extensive as it is, derives its greatest value from its accessibility.

To the other evils of our civil war must be added the interruption of polite literature, and the suppression of many dramatic and poetical names, which were plunged in obscurity by tumults and revolutions and have never since attracted curiosity.[1] The utter neglect of ancient English literature continued so long that many books may be supposed to be lost; and that curiosity which has been now for some years increasing among us wants materials for its operations. Books and pamphlets printed originally in small numbers, being thus neglected were soon destroyed, and though the capital authors were preserved they were preserved to languish without regard. How little Shakespeare himself was once read may be understood from Tate, who in his dedication to the altered play of *King Lear* speaks of the original as of an obscure piece recommended to his notice by a friend; and the author of the *Tatler*, having occasion to quote a few lines out of *Macbeth*, was content to receive them from Betterton's alteration of that celebrated drama, in which almost every original beauty is either aukwardly disguised or arbitrarily omitted. So little were the defects or peculiarities of the old writers known, even

1 Collins, *op. cit.*, p. 27, notes Steevens's debt to Capell (above, p. 308) for this paragraph.

at the beginning of our century, that though the custom of alliteration had prevailed to that degree in the time of Shakespeare that it became contemptible and ridiculous, yet it is made one of Waller's praises by a writer of his life that he first introduced this practice into English versification.

It will be expected that some notice should be taken of the last editor of Shakespeare, and that his merits should be estimated with those of his predecessors. Little, however, can be said of a work, to the completion of which both the commentary and a large proportion of the various readings are as yet wanting. *The Second Part of King Henry VI.* is the only play from that edition which has been consulted in the course of this work; for as several passages there are arbitrarily omitted, and as no notice is given when other deviations are made from the old copies, it was of little consequence to examine any further.[1] This circumstance is mentioned lest such accidental coincidences of opinion as may be discovered hereafter should be interpreted into plagiarism.

It may occasionally happen that some of the remarks long ago produced by others may have been offered again as recent discoveries. It is likewise absolutely impossible to pronounce with any degree of certainty whence all the hints which furnish matter for a commentary have been collected, as they lie scattered in many books and papers which were probably never read but once, or the particulars which they contain received only in the course of common conversation; nay, what is called plagiarism is often no more than the result of having thought alike with others on the same subject.

The dispute about the learning of Shakespeare being now finally settled, a catalogue is added of those translated authors, whom Mr. Pope has thought proper to call

The classics of an age that heard of none.

The reader may not be displeased to have the Greek and Roman poets, orators, &c. who had been rendered accessible to our author exposed at one view; especially as the list has received the

---

[1] Collins took this passage as the basis for his exposure of Steevens's grossly unfair misrepresentation of Capell, which was used as a cover for many silent plagiarisms from him. Collins refuted Steevens's accusation with a detailed collation of 2 *Henry VI*, showing that Capell was a far more accurate editor than Steevens, and that it was Steevens, not Capell, who (often following Warburton) had 'deviated from the old copies'.

advantage of being corrected and amplified by the Reverend Mr. Farmer, the substance of whose very decisive pamphlet is interspersed through the notes which are added in this revisal of Dr. Johnson's Shakespeare. .... (I, $E_2{}^v$–$E_6{}^r$)

[From the Notes]

[1] [On *The Tempest*, 1.2.28ff.]

> *I have with such provision in mine art*
> *So safely ordered that there is no soul—*
> *No, not so much perdition as an hair*
> *Betid to any creature in the vessel*

Such interrupted sentences are not uncommon to Shakespeare:[1] he sometimes begins a sentence, and before he concludes it entirely changes the construction, because another more forcible occurs. As this change frequently happens in conversation it may be suffered to pass uncensured in the language of the stage. STEEVENS. (I, 9)

[2] [*Ibid.*, 1.2.218: 'their sustaining garments']
—*sustaining*—] i.e. Their garments that bore them up and supported them. So *K. Lear*, 'In our *sustaining* corn.' [4.4.6]
Mr. Edwards was of opinion that we should read *sea-stained* garments; for (says he) it was not the floating of their cloaths but the magic of Prospero which preserved, as it had wrecked them. Nor was the miracle that their garments had not been at first discoloured by the sea-water, which even that *sustaining* would not have prevented, unless it had been on the air not on the water; but, as Gonzalo says, 'that their garments being (as they were) drenched in the sea, held notwithstanding their freshness and gloss, being rather new-dyed than stained with salt-water.'
For this, and all such notes as are taken from the MSS. of the late Mr. Edwards, I am indebted to the friendship of Benjamin Way, Esq; who very obligingly procured them from the executors of that gentleman with leave for their publication. Such of them as are omitted in this edition had been sometimes forestalled by the remarks of others, and sometimes by my own. The reader, however, might have been justly offended had any other reasons

[1] Cf. Heath's *Revisal* (4.551) and Barclay, No. 209 above, p. 233.

prevented me from communicating the unpublished sentiments of that sprightly critic and most amiable man, as entire as I received them. STEEVENS.

This note of Mr. Edwards, with which I suppose no reader is satisfied, shews with how much greater ease critical emendations are destroyed than made, and how willingly every man would be changing the text, if his imagination would furnish alterations. JOHNSON. (I, 17)

[3] [*Ibid.*, 1.2.306ff.]

The strangeness—] Why should a wonderful story produce sleep? I believe experience will prove, that any violent agitation of the mind easily subsides in slumber, especially when, as in Prospero's relation, the last images are pleasing. JOHNSON. [1765]

The poet seems to have been apprehensive that the audience, as well as Miranda, would sleep over this long but necessary tale, and therefore strives to break it. First, by making Prospero divest himself of his magic robe and wand; then by waking her attention no less than six times by verbal interruption; then by varying the action when he rises, and bids her continue sitting: and lastly, by carrying on the business of the fable while Miranda sleeps, by which she is continued on the stage till the poet has occasion for her again. WARNER. (I, 22)

[4] [*Ibid.*, 3.1.73f.]

I am a fool,/—To weep at what I am glad of.] This is one of those touches of nature that distinguish Shakespeare from all other writers. It was necessary, in support of the character of Miranda, to make her appear ignorant, that excess of sorrow and excess of joy find alike their relief from tears; and as this is the first time that consummate pleasure had made any near approaches to her heart, she calls such an expression of it, *folly*. STEEVENS. (I, 58f.)

[5] [*Ibid.*, 3.1.91]

A thousand, thousand!] It is impertinent to be for ever pointing out beauties which the reader of taste will of course distinguish for himself; and yet I cannot quit this scene without observing that it is superior in its kind to any of those that pass between Romeo and Juliet; and holds up the most captivating picture of juvenile affection that has been exhibited, even by Shakespeare himself. The prince behaves through the whole with a delicacy suitable to his birth and education; and his unexperienced mistress pours forth her soul without reserve, without descending from the soft elevation of maiden dignity, and apparently derives her confidence from the purity of her intentions. STEEVENS. (I, 59)

[6] [*Ibid.*, 5.1.90ff.]
Shakespeare, who, in his *Midsummer Night's Dream* has placed the light of a glow-worm in its eyes, might, through the same ignorance of natural history, have supposed the bat to be a bird of passage. Owls cry not only in winter. It is well known that they are not less clamorous in summer. STEEVENS. (I, 90)

[7] [End-note to *The Tempest*]
It is observed of *The Tempest*, that its plan is regular; this the author of *The Revisal* thinks, what I think too, an accidental effect of the story, not intended or regarded by our author.[1]

But whatever might be Shakespeare's intention in forming or adopting the plot, he has made it instrumental to the production of many characters, diversified with boundless invention, and preserved with profound skill in nature, extensive knowledge of opinions, and accurate observation of life. In a single drama are here exhibited princes, courtiers, and sailors, all speaking in their real characters. There is the agency of airy spirits, and of an earthly goblin. The operations of magick, the tumults of a storm, the adventures of a desart island, the native effusion of untaught affection, the punishment of guilt, and the final happiness of the pair for whom our passions and reason are equally interested. JOHNSON. (I, 100-1)

[8] [On *The Two Gentlemen of Verona*, 5.4.7ff.]

> *O thou, that dost inhabit in my breast,*
> *Leave not the mansion so long tenantless;*
> *Lest, growing ruinous, the building fall,*
> *And leave no memory of what it was!*

It is hardly possible to point out four lines in any of the plays of Shakespeare more remarkable for ease and eloquence than these. STEEVENS. (I, 183)

[1] The first sentence originally appeared in Johnson's Appendix to his 1765 edition: see p. 167 above, Note 227.

[9] [End-note to *The Two Gentlemen of Verona*]

That this play is rightly attributed to Shakespeare, I have little doubt. If it be taken from him, to whom shall it be given? This question may be asked of all the disputed plays, except *Titus Andronicus*; and it will be found more credible that Shakespeare might sometimes sink below his highest flights, than that any other should rise up to his lowest. JOHNSON. (I, 189)

[10] [End-note to *The Merry Wives of Windsor*]

Of this play there is a tradition preserved by Mr. Rowe, that it was written at the command of queen Elizabeth, who was so delighted with the character of Falstaff that she wished it to be diffused through more plays; but suspecting that it might pall by continued uniformity, directed the poet to diversify his manner by shewing him in love. No task is harder than that of writing to the ideas of another. Shakespeare knew what the queen, if the story be true, seems not to have known, that by any real passion of tenderness the selfish craft, the careless jollity and the lazy luxury of Falstaff must have suffered so much abatement, that little of his former cast would have remained. Falstaff could not love, but by ceasing to be Falstaff. He could only counterfeit love, and his professions could be prompted not by the hope of pleasure but of money. Thus the poet approached as near as he could to the work enjoined him; yet having perhaps in the former plays completed his own idea, seems not to have been able to give Falstaff all his former power of entertainment.

This comedy is remarkable for the variety and number of the personages, who exhibit more characters appropriated and discriminated than perhaps can be found in any other play.

Whether Shakespeare was the first that produced upon the English stage the effect of language distorted and depraved by provincial or foreign pronunciation, I cannot certainly decide. This mode of forming ridiculous characters can confer praise only on him who originally discovered it, for it requires not much of either wit or judgment: its success must be derived almost wholly from the player, but its power in a skilful mouth even he that despises it is unable to resist.

The conduct of this drama is deficient; the action begins and ends often before the conclusion, and the different parts might change places without inconvenience; but its general power, that power by which all works of genius shall finally be tried, is such that perhaps it never yet had reader or spectator who did not think it too soon at an end. JOHNSON. (I, 311–12)

[11] [Head-note to *Measure for Measure*]
Shakespeare took the fable of this play from the *Promos and Cassandra* of George Whetstone, published in 1598. See Theobald's note at the end [2.495f.].
A hint, like a seed, is more or less prolific according to the qualities of the soil on which it is thrown. This story, which in the hands of Whetstone produced little more than barren insipidity, under the culture of Shakespeare became fertile of entertainment.[1] The curious reader will find that the old play of *Promos and Cassandra* exhibits an almost complete embryo of *Measure for Measure*; yet the hints on which it is formed are so slight that it is nearly as impossible to detect them, as it is to point out in the acorn the future ramifications of the oak. STEEVENS. (II, 3)

[12] [On *Measure for Measure*, 3.1.98]
Princely guards mean no more than the ornaments of royalty, which Angelo is supposed to assume during the absence of the duke. The stupidity of the first editors is sometimes not more injurious to Shakespeare, than the ingenuity of those who succeeded them. STEEVENS. (II, 70)

[13] [*Ibid.*, 3.2.170; Folio reads 'He's now past it, yet']
Sir Thomas Hanmer, *He is not past it yet.* This emendation was received in the former edition, but seems not necessary. It were to be wished that we all explained more and amended less.
JOHNSON. (II, 87)

[14] [End-note to *The Comedy of Errors*]
In this play we find more intricacy of plot than distinction of character; and our attention is less forcibly engaged because we can guess in great measure how it will conclude. Yet the poet seems unwilling to part with his subject, even in this last and unnecessary scene, where the same mistakes are continued till they have lost the power of affording any entertainment at all. STEEVENS. (II, 221)

---

[1] Cf. Capell's note, above p. 325. Collins, *op. cit.*, pp. 28–33, lists other 'borrowings' from Capell's discussion of the sources.

[15] [End-note to *Much Ado About Nothing*]

This play may be fairly said to contain two of the most sprightly characters that Shakespeare ever drew. The wit, the humourist, the gentleman, and the soldier are combined in Benedick. It is to be lamented, indeed, that the first and most splendid of these distinctions is disgraced by unnecessary prophaneness; for the goodness of his heart is hardly sufficient to atone for the licence of his tongue.[1] The innocent levity which flashes out in the conversation of Beatrice receives a sanction from that steadiness and spirit of friendship to her cousin, so apparent in her behaviour when she urges her lover to risque his own life by a challenge to Claudio. In the conduct of the fable, however, there is an imperfection similar to that which Dr. Johnson has pointed out in the *Merry Wives of Windsor*:—the second contrivance is less ingenious than the first:—or, to speak more plainly, the same incident is become stale by repetition. I wish some other method had been found to entrap Beatrice than that very stratagem which before had been successfully practised on Benedick.

This play (as I understand from one of Mr. Vertue's MSS.) formerly passed under the title of *Benedict and Beatrix*. Heminge the player received, on the 20th of May, 1613, the sum of forty pounds, and twenty pounds more as his majesty's gratuity for exhibiting six plays at Hampton-Court, among which this was one. STEEVENS. (II, 337)

[16] [On *The Merchant of Venice*, 5.1.83ff. 'The man that hath no music in himself', a speech praised by Warburton (2.477) and others.]

This passage, which is neither pregnant with physical or moral truth, nor poetically beautiful in an eminent degree, has constantly enjoyed the good fortune to be repeated by those whose inhospitable memories would have refused to admit or retain any other sentiment or description of the same author, however exalted or just. The truth is, that it furnishes the vacant fidler with something to say in defence of his profession, and supplies the coxcomb in music with an invective against such as do not pretend to discover all the various powers of language in inarticulate sounds.

It is no uncommon thing to see those who would think half a

---

[1] Compare Steevens's similar attacks on profanity in his theatre reviews: No. 237d above, pp. 474f.

day well spent in reconciling a couple of jarring strings to unison, and yet would make no scruple to employ the other half in setting two of the most intimate friends at variance. So much for the certitude of being taught morality in the school of music.

———*ite*
Ferte citi flammas, date tela———[1]   STEEVENS. (III, 206)

[17] [On *As You Like It*, 5.4.189f.]

> *Jaques. To see no pastime, I:———what you would have I'll stay to know at your abandon'd cave.*]

Amidst this general festivity the reader may be sorry to take his leave of Jaques, who appears to have no share in it, and remains behind unreconciled to society. He has, however, filled with a gloomy sensibility the space allotted to him in the play, and preserves that respect to the last which is due to him as a consistent character, and an amiable tho' solitary moralist.

It may be observed, with scarce less concern, that Shakespeare has on this occasion forgot old Adam, the servant of Orlando, whose fidelity should have entitled him to notice at the end of the piece, as well as to that happiness which he would naturally have found in the return of fortune to his master. STEEVENS. (III, 339)

[18] [On *All's Well That Ends Well*, 1.1.153ff.: '*Not my virginity yet*'.]
I do not perceive so great a want of connection as my predecessors have apprehended, nor is that connection always to be sought for in so careless a writer as ours. . . . STEEVENS. (IV, 12)

[19] [On *Twelfth Night*, 1.5.240: '*With groans that thunder love, with sighs of fire.*']
This line is worthy of Dryden's *Almanzor*, and is said in mockery of amorous hyperboles. STEEVENS. (IV, 166)

[20] [On *The Winter's Tale*, 4.1. Chorus: Time's apology '*that I slide/O'er sixteen years*',———]
This trespass, in respect of dramatic unity, will appear venial to those who have read the once-famous Lyly's *Endymion*, or (as he himself calls it in the prologue) his *Man in the Moon*. This author

[1] *Aeneid*, 4.593f.: 'Go, fetch fire in haste, serve weapons'.

was applauded and very liberally paid by queen Elizabeth. Two acts of his piece comprize the space of forty years; Endymion lying down to sleep at the end of the second, and waking in the first scene of the fifth, after a nap of that unconscionable length. Lyly has likewise been guilty of much greater absurdities than ever Shakespeare committed; for he supposes that Endymion's hair, features, and person, were changed by age during that sleep, while all the other personages of the drama remained without alteration. STEEVENS. (IV, 320–1)

[21] [Head-note to *Macbeth*]

I have taken a liberty with this tragedy which might be practised with almost equal propriety in respect of a few others, I mean the retrenchment of such stage-directions as are not supplied by the old copy. Mr. Rowe had trick'd out *Macbeth*, like many more of Shakespeare's plays, in all the foppery of the reign of queen Anne. Every change of situation produced notice that the scene lay in an anti-chamber, a royal apartment, or a palace, and even some variations and starts of passion were set down in a manner no less ostentatious and unnecessary. STEEVENS. (IV, 392)

[22] [On *Macbeth*, 1.3.32; quoting a cantankerous note by Warburton attacking Theobald's explanation of 'weird sisters'.]

Must we for ever controvert the truth, only because it has been brought to light by another?—Or can it be worth while to equivocate or misrepresent on an occasion so little interesting as the elucidation of a passage merely poetical? STEEVENS. (IV, 408)

[23] [On *Macbeth*, 1.5.12ff.: '*Great Glamis! worthy Cawdor!*']

Shakespeare has supported the character of lady Macbeth by repeated efforts, and never omits any opportunity of adding a trait of ferocity, or a mark of the want of human feelings, to this monster of his own creation.[1] The softer passions are more obliterated in her than in her husband, in proportion as her ambition is greater. She meets him here on his return from an expedition of danger with such a salutation as would have become one of his friends or vassals; a salutation apparently fitted rather to raise his thoughts to a level with her own purposes than to testify her joy at his return, or manifest an attachment to his person: nor does any

[1] Cf. Steevens above, p. 498.

sentiment expressive of love or softness fall from her throughout the play.[1] While Macbeth himself in the midst of the horrors of his guilt still retains a character less fiend-like than that of his queen, talks to her with a degree of tenderness, and pours his complaints and fears into her bosom, accompanied with terms of endearment. STEEVENS. (IV, 424)

[24] [On *Macbeth*, 2.1.7ff.

————*Merciful powers*
Restrain in me the cursed thoughts that nature
Gives way to in repose.]

It is apparent from what Banquo says afterwards that he had been solicited in a dream to do something in consequence of the prophecy of the witches that his waking senses were shock'd at; and Shakespeare has here finely contrasted his character with that of Macbeth. Banquo is praying against being tempted to encourage thoughts of guilt even in his sleep; while Macbeth is hurrying into temptation and revolving in his mind every scheme, however flagitious, that may assist him to complete his purpose. The one is unwilling to sleep lest the same phantoms should assail his resolution again, while the other is depriving himself of rest through impatience to commit the murder. STEEVENS. (IV, 434)

[25] [On *Macbeth*, 2.1.55: on 'Tarquin's ravishing strides' and Johnson's note, Vol. 3, pp. 174f.]
I cannot agree with Dr. Johnson that a *stride* is always *an action of violence, impetuosity, or tumult.* Whoever has been reduced to the necessity of finding his way about a house in the dark, must know that it is natural to take large *strides*, in order to feel before us whether we have a safe footing or not.[2] The ravisher and the murderer would naturally take such *strides*, not only on the same account but that their steps might be fewer in number, and the sound of their feet be repeated as seldom as possible. STEEVENS. (IV, 439)

[26] [*Ibid.*, 2.2.62f.]
—*incarnardine*,] To *incarnardine*, is to stain any thing of a flesh colour. STEEVENS. (IV, 444)

1 Cf. Steevens in No. 238h above, p. 500.
2 Cf. Heath, *Revisal* (4.561).

Making the green, one red———]

[Steevens cites classical parallels, from Catullus,[1] Sophocles' *Oedipus Tyrannus*[2], and Seneca's *Hippolytus*[3].] The same thought occurs in *The Downfal of Robert E. of Huntingdon*, 1601: 'He made the *green sea red* with Turkish blood.' STEEVENS. (IV, 445)

[27] [*Ibid.*, 2.3.115: Warburton had emended 'Unmannerly breech'd with gore' to 'reech'd' ('soiled with a dark yellow') and Johnson had tentatively agreed: cf. T. Edwards (Vol. 3, pp. 405f.).]

I apprehend it to be the duty of an editor to represent his author such as he is, and explain the meaning of the words he finds to the best advantage, instead of attempting to make them better by any violent alteration.

The expression may mean that the daggers were covered with blood quite to the *breeches*, i.e. their *hilts* or *handles*. The lower end of cannon is called the *breech* of it. STEEVENS. (IV, 453)

[28] [*Ibid.*, 3.1.54ff.

> *Macbeth* [on Banquo] . . . under him
> My genius is rebuk'd; *as, it is said,*
> *Antony's was by Cæsar.*

In his 1745 *Observations* (Vol. 3, p. 177), as in the 1765 edition, Johnson had rejected the italicized lines as being 'an Insertion of some Player'.]

This note was written before I was fully acquainted with Shakespeare's manner, and I do not now think it of much weight; for though the words which I was once willing to eject seem interpolated I believe they may still be genuine, and added by the authour in his revision. The authour of the *Revisal* cannot admit the measure to be faulty. There is only one foot, he says, put for another. This is one of the effects of literature in minds not naturally perspicacious. Every boy or girl finds the metre imperfect, but the

---

[1] Cat., 88. 5–6: 'more [guilt] he incurs than furthest Tethys can wash away, or Ocean, father of the nymphs'.

[2] *O. T.*, 1227f.: 'Neither the Ister nor the Phasis river could purify this house . . .'.

[3] *Hippolytus*, 715ff.: 'What Tanais will cleanse me, what Maeotis, with its barbaric waves rushing into the Pontic sea? Not great Father Neptune's self with his whole ocean, could wash away so much of guilt'.

pedant comes to its defence with a tribrachys or an anapaest, and sets it right at once by applying to one language the rules of another. If we may be allowed to change feet, like the old comic writers, it will not be easy to write a line not metrical. To hint this once is sufficient. JOHNSON. (IV, 460)

[29] [*Ibid.*, 4.3.160]

My countryman; but yet I know him not.] Malcolm discovers Ross to be his countryman while he is yet at some distance from him, by his dress. This circumstance loses its propriety on our stage, as all the characters are uniformly represented in English habits.[1] STEEVENS. (IV, 508)

[30] [*Ibid.*, 5.8.35f.: stage-direction in Folio, *Enter Fighting, and Macbeth slaine*]

This stage-direction is taken from the folio, and proves that the players were not even skilful enough to prevent impropriety in those circumstances which fell immediately under their own care. Macbeth is here killed on the stage, and a moment after Macduff enters as from another place, with his head on a spear. STEEVENS. (IV, 530)

[31] [End-note to *Macbeth*]

It may be worth while to remark that Milton, who left behind him a list of no less than CII. dramatic subjects, had fixed on the story of this play among the rest. His intention was to have begun with the arrival of Malcolm at Macduff's castle. 'The matter of Duncan (says he) may be expressed by the appearing of his ghost.' It should seem from this last memorandum that Milton disliked the licence that his predecessor had taken in comprehending a history of such length in the short compass of a play, and would have new-written the whole on the plan of the ancient drama. He could not surely have indulged so vain a hope as that of excelling Shakespeare in the *Tragedy of Macbeth*. STEEVENS. (IV, 532)

[32] [On *King John*, 3.3.19ff.: John's persuasion of Hubert to kill Arthur.]

This is one of the scenes to which may be promised a lasting

---

[1] Steevens had made similar points in his theatre-reviews: see, for example, the *General Evening Post*, 21–4 March 1772.

commendation. Art could add little to its perfections, and time itself can take nothing from its beauties. STEEVENS. (V, 63)

[33] [End-note to *King John*]
There is extant another play of *King John*, published in 1611. Shakespeare has preserved the greatest part of the conduct of it, as well as a number of the lines. Some of these I have pointed out in the notes, and some I have omitted as undeserving notice. What most inclines me to believe it was the work of some cotemporary writer is the number of quotations from Horace, and other scraps of learning scattered over it. There is likewise a quantity of rhiming Latin and ballad-metre in a scene where the Bastard is represented as plundering a monastery; and some strokes of humour which seem from their particular turn to have been most evidently produced by another hand than that of Shakespeare. .... I admitted this play some years ago as Shakespeare's own among the twenty which I published from the old editions; but a more careful perusal of it, and a further conviction of our poet's custom of borrowing plots, sentiments, &c. disposes me to recede from that opinion. STEEVENS. (V, 111)

[34] [On *Richard II*, 2.2.105]
Come, sister—cousin, I would say.] This is one of Shakespeare's touches of nature. York is talking to the queen his cousin, but the recent death of his sister is uppermost in his mind. STEEVENS. (V, 155)

[35] [*Ibid.*, 3.2.27ff.; Carlisle on the divinity of the king]
Shakespeare has represented this character of the bishop as he found it in Holinshed. The politics of the historian were the politics of the poet. STEEVENS. (V, 191)

[36] [On 1 *Henry IV*, 2.4.494ff.: Hal's lie to the Sheriff, concealing Falstaff]
The man, I do assure you, is not here,] Every reader must regret that Shakespeare would not give himself the trouble to furnish prince Henry with some more pardonable excuse for the absence of Falstaff than by obliging him to have recourse to an absolute falshood, and that too uttered under the sanction of so strong an assurance. STEEVENS. (V, 295)

[37] [*Ibid.*, 3.3.113]

There's no more faith in thee than in a stew'd prune, &c.] The propriety of these similies I am not sure that I fully understand. . . . JOHNSON. [1765: Note 77 above, p. 120.]

Dr. Lodge, in his pamphlet called *Wit's Miserie, or the World's Madnesse*, 1596, describes a bawd thus: 'This is shee that laies wait at all the carriers for wenches new come up to London; and you shall know her dwelling by a *dish of stew'd prunes* in the window, and two or three fleering wenches sit knitting or sowing in her shop.'

In *Measure for Measure*, act ii. the male bawd excuses himself for having admitted Elbow's wife into his house by saying 'that she came in great with child, and longing for *stew'd prunes*, which stood in a dish,' *&c.* [2.1.86f.]

Slender, who apparently wishes to recommend himself to his mistress by a seeming propensity to love as well as war, talks of having measured weapons with a fencing-master for a *dish of stew'd prunes*. [*Merry Wives*, 1.1.258]

In another old dramatic piece entitled *If this be not a good Play the Divel is in it*, 1612, a bravo enters with money, and says, 'This is the pension of the stewes, you need not untie it; 'tis stew-money, Sir, *stew'd-prune* cash, Sir.'

Among the other sins laid to the charge of the once celebrated Gabriel Harvey by his antagonist Nash, 'to be drunk with the sirrop or liquor of *stew'd prunes*,' is not the least insisted on.

In *The Knave of Harts*, a collection of satyrical poems, 1612, a whoring knave is mentioned as taking 'Burnt wine, *stew'd prunes*, a punk to solace him.'

In *The Knave of Spades*, another collection of the same kind, 1611, is the following description of a wanton inveigling a young man into her house:

> ———He to his liquor falls,
> While she unto her maids for cakes,
> *Stew'd prunes*, and pippins, calls.

So in *Every Woman in her Humour*, a comedy, 1619: 'To search my house! I have no varlets, no *stew'd prunes*, no she fiery,' *&c.*

The passages already quoted are sufficient to shew that *a dish of stew'd prunes* was not only the ancient designation of a brothel but the constant appendage to it.

From *A Treatise on the Lues Venerea*, written by W. Clowes, one of her majesty's surgeons, 1596, and other books of the same kind, it appears that *prunes* were directed to be boiled in broth for those persons already infected, and that both *stew'd prunes* and roasted apples were commonly, though unsuccessfully, taken by way of prevention. So much for the infidelity of *stew'd prunes*. STEEVENS. (V, 319–20)

[38] [On 2 *Henry IV*, 2.2.21ff.: Hal's witticisms on the state of Poins's linen.]

—*and God Knows*, &c.] This passage Mr. Pope restored from the first edition. I think it may as well be omitted. It is omitted in the first folio, and in all subsequent editions before Mr. Pope's, and was perhaps expunged by the author. The editors, unwilling to lose any thing of Shakespeare's, not only insert what he has added but recall what he has rejected. JOHNSON. [1765]

I have not met with positive evidence that Shakespeare rejected any passages at all. Such proof may indeed be inferred from those of the quarto's which were published in his life-time, and are declared (in their titles) to have been enlarged and corrected by his own hand. These I would follow in preference to the folio, and should at all times be cautious of opposing its authority to that of the elder copies. Of the play in question there is no quarto extant but that in 1600, and therefore we have no colour for supposing a single passage was omitted by consent of the poet himself. When the folio (as it often does) will support me in the omission of a sacred name, I am happy to avail myself of the choice it offers; but otherwise do not think I have a right to omit what Shakespeare should seem to have written, on the bare authority of the player editors. I have therefore restored the passage in question to the text. STEEVENS. (V, 402–3)

[39] [*Ibid.*, 3.1.30f.]

> *Then, happy low, lie down!*
> *Uneasy lies the head that wears a crown.*

... Had not Shakespeare thought it necessary to subject himself to the tyranny of rhime, he would probably have said—'then happy low, sleep on!' STEEVENS. (V, 432)

[40] [On *Henry V*, 3.6.114ff.: the French herald's speech]

—*so much my office.*] This speech, as well as another preceding it, was first compress'd into verse by Mr. Pope. Where he wanted a syllable he supplied it, and where there were too many for his purpose he made suitable omissions. Shakespeare (if we may believe some of the old copies) meant both speeches for prose, and as such I have printed them. STEEVENS. (VI, 77)

[41] [On 3 *Henry VI*, 3.2.193: *And set the murderous Machiavel to School*]

This is not the first proof I have met with that Shakespeare in his attempts to familiarize his ideas has often diminished their propriety. STEEVENS. (VI, 445)

[42] [On *Julius Cæsar*, 4.3.145ff.]

And, her attendants absent, swallow'd fire.] This circumstance is taken from Plutarch.

It may not, however, be amiss to remark that the death of Portia wants that foundation which has hitherto entitled her to a place in poetry as a pattern of Roman fortitude. She is reported, by Pliny I think, to have died at Rome of a lingering illness while Brutus was abroad; but some writers seem to look on a natural death as a derogation from a distinguished character. STEEVENS. (VIII, 86)

[43] [On *Timon of Athens*, 2.2.174f.]

> *No villainous bounty yet hath past my heart;*
> *Unwisely, not ignobly, have I given.*]

Every reader must rejoice in this circumstance of comfort which presents itself to Timon, who, tho' beggar'd thro' want of prudence, consoles himself with reflection that his ruin was not brought on by the pursuit of guilty pleasures. STEEVENS. (VIII, 314)

[44] [*Ibid.*, 4.3.274ff.: *Apemantus*, 'Art thou proud yet?']

I have heard Mr. Burke commend the subtilty of discrimination with which Shakespeare distinguishes the present character of Timon from that of Apemantus, whom to vulgar eyes he would now resemble. JOHNSON. (VIII, 367–8)

[45] [Head-note to *Titus Andronicus*]

The work of criticism on the plays of this author is, I believe, generally found to extend or contract itself in proportion to the value of the piece under consideration; and we shall always do little where we desire but little should be done. I know not that this piece stands in need of much emendation; though it might be treated as condemned criminals are in some countries,—any experiments might be justifiably made on it.

The author, whoever he was, borrowed the story, the names, the characters, &c. from an old ballad, the age of which cannot be exactly ascertained. The reader who is curious about such a wretched piece, will find the original in Dr. Percy's collection. STEEVENS. (VIII, 404)

[46] [On *Titus Andronicus*, 5.1.21]

To gaze upon a ruinous monastery.] Shakespeare has so perpetually offended against chronology in all his plays that no very conclusive argument can be deduced from the particular absurdity of these anachronisms, relative to the authenticity of *Titus Andronicus*. And yet the *ruined monastery*, the *popish tricks*, &c. that Aaron talks of, and the French salutation from the mouth of Titus are altogether so very much out of place, that I cannot persuade myself even our hasty poet could have been guilty of their insertion, or have permitted them to remain, had he corrected the performance for another. STEEVENS. (VIII, 473–4)

[47] [End-note to *Titus Andronicus*]

The testimony produced at the beginning of this play,[1] by which it is ascribed to Shakespeare, is by no means equal to the argument against its authenticity arising from the total difference of conduct, language, and sentiments by which it stands apart from all the rest. Meres had probably no other evidence than that of a title-page, which, though in our time it be sufficient was then of no great authority; for all the plays which were rejected by the first collectors of Shakespeare's works, and admitted in later editions, and again rejected by the critical editors had Shakespeare's name on the title, as we must suppose by the fraudulence of the

---

[1] Steevens had quoted Tyrwhitt's argument (p. 240 above), that the presence of the title *Titus Andronicus* in the list of Shakespeare's plays given by Francis Meres in his *Palladis Tamia* (1598) guaranteed its authenticity.

printers, who, while there were yet no gazettes, nor advertisements, nor any means of circulating literary intelligence could usurp at pleasure any celebrated name. Nor had Shakespeare any interest in detecting the imposture, as none of his fame or profit was produced by the press. JOHNSON. (VIII, 492)

[48] [End-note to *Titus Andronicus*]
It may not be amiss to remark that this tragedy which (setting aside the feebleness of composition) would be regarded as too bloody on the modern stage, appears to have been highly relished in 1686, when it was revived with alterations by Ravenscroft. Instead of diminishing any of its horrors he seized every opportunity of making large additions of them, insomuch that when Tamora stabs her child the Moor utters the following lines:

> *She has out-done me, ev'n in mine own art,*
> *Out-done me in murder——kill'd her own child.*
> *Give it me—I'll eat it.*[1]   STEEVENS. (VIII, 493)

[49] [On *Troilus and Cressida*, 1.3.296]
I'll hide my silver beard in a gold beaver] Shakespeare, who so wonderfully preserves character, usually confounds the customs of all nations, and probably supposed that the ancients (like the heroes of chivalry) fought with beavers to their helmets. STEEVENS. (IX, 34)

[50] [On *Cymbeline*, 1.5.33ff.: a soliloquy by Cornelius on the Queen's evil; Johnson dismissed it as 'very inartificial': Note 172, p. 149 above.]
This soliloquy, however inartificial in respect of the speaker, is yet necessary to prevent that uneasiness which would naturally arise in the mind of the audience on the recollection that the queen had mischievous ingredients in her possession, unless they had been undeceiv'd as to their quality; and is no less useful to prepare them for the return of Imogen to life. STEEVENS. (IX, 176)

[51] [*Ibid.*, 2.2.38f.: ' ... *like the crimson drops/I'th' bottom of a cowslip*']
This simile contains the smallest out of a thousand proofs that

[1] See 1.247.

Shakespeare was a most accurate observer of nature. STEEVENS. (IX, 192)

[52] [*Ibid.*, 3.4.4. 'Where is Posthumus?']
Shakespeare's apparent ignorance of quantity is not the least, among many proofs of his want of learning. Throughout this play he calls Posthŭmus, Posthūmus; and Arvirăgus, Arvirāgus[1]. STEEVENS. (IX, 223)

[53] [*Ibid.*, 4.2.101]
Yield, rustic mountaineer.] I believe, upon examination, the character of Cloten will not prove a very consistent one. Act i. scene 4.: the lords who are conversing with him on the subject of his rencontre with Posthumus represent the latter as having neither put forth his strength or courage but still advancing forwards to the prince, who retired before him; yet at this his last appearance we see him fighting gallantly, and falling by the hand of Arviragus. The same persons afterwards speak of him as of a mere ass or idiot; and yet, act iii. scene 1, he returns one of the noblest and most reasonable answers to the Roman envoy; and the rest of his conversation on the same subject, though *it may lack form a little* by no means resembles the language of folly. He behaves with proper dignity and civility at parting with Lucius, and yet is ridiculous and brutal in his treatment of Imogen. Belarius describes him as not having sense enough to know what fear is (which he defines as being sometimes the effect of judgment); and yet he forms very artful schemes for gaining the affection of his mistress by means of her attendants, to get her person into his power afterwards; and seems to be no less acquainted with the character of his father, and the ascendancy the queen maintained over his uxorious weakness. We find him, in short, represented at once as brave and dastardly, civil and brutal, sagacious and foolish, without that subtility of distinction which constitutes the excellence of such mixed characters as the Nurse in *Romeo and Juliet* and Polonius in the tragedy of *Hamlet*.[2] STEEVENS. (IX, 250)

---

[1] Christopher Smart had already made this point: see 4.201; also Farmer, Note 85 below.
[2] Compare the very similar critique by 'Lorenzo' of the *General Evening Post*, pp. 496f. above.

[54] [*Ibid.*, 5.5.163ff.: '. . . for feature, laming/The shrine of Venus, or straight-pight Minerva'. Warburton had written an erudite but irrelevant note to prove that 'our author was not ignorant of the fine arts'.]

I cannot help adding that passages of this kind are but weak proofs that the poet was conversant with what we call at present *the fine arts*. The pantheons of his own age (several of which I have seen) give a most minute and particular account of the different degrees of beauty imputed to the different deities; and as Shakespeare had at least an opportunity of reading Chapman's translation of *Homer*, the first part of which was published in 1596, and with additions in 1598, he might have taken these ideas from thence without being at all indebted to his own particular observation or knowledge of the fine arts. It is surely more for the honour of our poet to remark how well he has employed the little knowledge he appears to have had of statuary or mythology, than from his frequent allusions to them to suppose he was intimately acquainted with either. STEEVENS. (IX, 295)

[55] [On *King Lear*, 1.2.1: '*Thou, Nature, art my goddess*']

Dr. Warburton says that Shakespeare has made his *bastard* an *atheist*; when it is very plain that Edmund only speaks of *nature* in opposition to *custom*, and not (as he supposes) to the existence of a *God*.[1] Edmund means only as he came not into the world as *custom* or *law* had prescribed so he had nothing to do but to follow *Nature* and her laws, which make no difference between legitimacy and illegitimacy, between the eldest and the youngest. STEEVENS. (IX, 328)

[56] [*Ibid.*, 1.2.4]

to deprive me,] To *deprive* was, in our author's time, synonymous to *disinherit*. The old dictionary renders *exhæredo* by this word: and Holinshed speaks of *the line of Henry before deprived*. STEEVENS. (IX, 329)

[57] [*Ibid.*, 2.2.163ff.: Kent reading Cordelia's letter aloud; modern editions add inverted commas to this passage.]

---

[1] The first sentence of this note appeared originally in the Appendix to the 1765 edition (VIII, Sig. Kk$_4$^{v}).

————————and shall find time
From this enormous state, seeking to give
Losses their remedies.————)

I confess I do not understand this passage, unless it may be considered as *a part of Cordelia's letter*, which he is reading to himself by
moonlight: it certainly conveys the sense of what she would
have said. In reading a letter it is natural enough to dwell on that
part of it which promises the change in our affairs which we most
wish for; and Kent, having read Cordelia's assurances that she
will find a time to free the injured from the *enormous* misrule of
Regan, is willing to go to sleep with that pleasing reflection
uppermost in his mind. But this is mere conjecture. STEEVENS.
(IX, 376)

[58] [*Ibid.*, 3.6.24: '*Wantest thou eyes at trial, madam?*']
It may be observed that Edgar, being supposed to be found by
chance, and therefore to have no knowledge of the rest, connects
not his ideas with those of Lear but pursues his own train of
delirious or fantastic thought. To these words, *At trial, madam?*
I think therefore that the name of Lear should be put. The process
of the dialogue will support this conjecture. JOHNSON. (IX, 416)

[59] [*Ibid.*, 4.6.184: 'This a good block!': Johnson suggested
'flock', i.e. pieces of 'wooll moulded together ... kneaded to a
mass'.]
Dr. Johnson's explanation of this passage is very ingenious; but,
I believe, there is no occasion to adopt it, as the speech itself,
or at least the action which should accompany it, will furnish all
the connection which he has sought from an extraneous circumstance. Upon the king's saying *I will preach to thee* the poet seems
to have meant him to pull off his *hat*, and keep turning it and feeling
it, in the attitude of one of the preachers of those times (whom
I have seen so represented in old prints) till the idea of *felt*, which
the good *hat* or *block* was made of, raises the stratagem in his brain
of shoeing a troop of horse with a substance soft as that which he
held and moulded between his hands. This makes him start from
his preachment.[1]—*Block* anciently signified the *head part* of the
hat, or *the thing on which a hat is formed*, and sometimes the hat

[1] Steevens has taken this explanation from an article by 'S. W.' in the *London Magazine* for
May 1756 (xxv, p. 234).

itself.—See *Much ado*, &c. 'He weares his faith but as the fashion of his *hat*; it changes with the next *block*.' See Beaumont and Fletcher's *Wit at several Weapons*;

> I am so haunted with this broad-brim'd *hat*
> Of the last progress *block*, with the young hatband.

Greene, in his *Defence of Conny-catching*, 1592, describing a *neat companion*, says, 'he weareth a hat of a high *blocke*, and a broad brimme.'—So in *The Revenger's Tragedy*, 1609. 'His head will be made serve a bigger *block*.' So in Dekker's *Honest Whore*, 1635 'we have *blocks* for all heads.' Again, in Greene's *Tu Quoque*, 1599.

> ————Where did you buy your *felt?*
> Nay, never laugh, for you're in the same *block*.

Again, in *Law Tricks*, &c. 1608, 'I cannot keep a *block* private, but every citizen's son thrusts his head into it.'
Again, in *Histriomastix*, 1610· 'Your hat is of a better *block* than mine.' Again, in *The Martial Maid* of Beaumont and Fletcher, 'Tho' now your block-head be cover'd with a Spanish *block*.' STEEVENS. (IX, 455–6)

[60] [*Ibid.*, 5.3.266, stage-direction: *Cordelia dead in his arms*.]
This princess, according to the old historians, retired with victory from the battle which she conducted in her father's cause, and thereby replaced him on the throne; but in a subsequent one fought against her (after the death of the old king) by the sons of Goneril and Regan she was taken and died miserably in prison. The poet found this in history, and was therefore willing to precipitate her death, which he knew had happened but a few years after. The dramatic writers of this age suffered as small a number of their heroes and heroines to escape as possible; nor could the filial piety of this lady, any more than the innocence of Ophelia, prevail on Shakespeare to permit her to outlive the time allotted her in the construction of his play. STEEVENS. (IX, 484)

[61] [On *Romeo and Juliet*, 2.6.16f.:

> *Here comes the lady, O, so light a foot*
> *Will ne'er wear out the everlasting flint.*]

537

However the poet might think the alteration[1] of this scene on the whole to be necessary, I am afraid, in respect of the passage before us he has not been very successful. The violent hyperbole of *the everlasting flint* appears to me not only more reprehensible but even less beautiful than the lines as they were originally written, where the lightness of Juliet's motion is accounted for from the cheerful effects the passion of love produced in her mind. However, *the everlasting flint* may mean the circular paths paved with flint, which those who were enjoined penance were obliged to tread barefoot; yet on that supposition whatever is gained in propriety is lost in beauty. STEEVENS. (X, 70)

[62] [*Ibid.*, 3.5.213ff.: *Faith, here it is*:—]
The character of the Nurse exhibits a just picture of those whose actions have no principles for their foundation. She has been unfaithful to the trust reposed in her by Capulet, and is ready to embrace any expedient that offers to avert the consequences of her first infidelity. STEEVENS. (X, 102)

[63] [On *Hamlet*, 3.1.60:—*To die,—to sleep,*—]
This passage is ridiculed in the *Scornful Lady* of B. and Fletcher, as follows:—be deceas'd, that is, asleep, for so the word is taken. *To sleep, to die; to die, to sleep*; a very figure, Sir.' &c. &c. STEEVENS. (X, 234)[2]

[64] [*Ibid.*, 3.1.75f.:—'might his *Quietus* make/With a bare *bodkin?*'—]
This first expression probably alluded to the writ of discharge, which was formerly granted to those barons and knights who personally attended the king on any foreign expedition, which was called a *Quietus*.

The word is used for the discharge of an account by Webster, in his *Dutchess of Malfy*, 1623.

---

[1] Steevens's discussion of this play is vitiated by his assumption that the three early texts, Q_1 (1597), Q_2 (1599), and F_1 (1623) represent a sequence of composition and revision by Shakespeare. Modern scholarship has shown that the first Quarto is a pirated version, put together from the memory of theatre performances, eked out with the help of actors' 'parts'; while the other two texts derive from the authentic manuscript by legitimate routes, the second Quarto from the author's 'foul papers', the Folio from the play-book. The three texts, then, represent three versions of a work composed at one time, not revised piecemeal. Steevens had rejected theories of Shakespeare's 'revision' of 2 *Henry IV* in Note 38 above.
[2] Cf. No. 237e above, p. 476.

You had the trick in audit time to be sick
Till I had sign'd your *Quietus.*

A *bodkin* was, I believe, the ancient term for a *small dagger.*
Gascoigne, speaking of *Julius Cæsar,* says,

At last with *bodkins,* dub'd and doust to death
All, all his glory vanish'd with his breath.

In the margin of *Stowe's Chronicle,* edit. 1614, it is said, that
Cæsar was slain with *bodkins;* and in *The Muses Looking-glass,* by
Randolph, 1638.

Apho. A rapier's but a *bodkin.*
Deil. And a *bodkin*
Is a most dang'rous weapon; since I read
Of Julius Cæsar's death, I durst not venture
Into a taylor's shop for fear of *bodkins.*

Again, in *The Custom of the Country,* by B. and Fletcher:

——Out with your *bodkin,*
Your pocket-dagger, your stilletto.— STEEVENS. (X, 236)

[65] [*Ibid.,* 3.2.140:—'*Be not you asham'd to shew,* &c.]
The conversation of Hamlet with Ophelia, which cannot fail
to disgust every modern reader,[1] is probably such as was peculiar
to the young and fashionable of the age of Shakespeare, which
was by no means an age of delicacy. The poet is, however, blameable; for extravagance of thought, not indecency of expression
is the characteristic of madness, at least of such madness as should
be represented on the scene. STEEVENS. (X, 250)

[66] [*Ibid.,* 3.4.209ff.: ' . . . I'll lug the guts into the neighbour
room.']
I heartily wish any of the copies would have authorized me to
leave out the seven following lines. STEEVENS. (X, 277).

[67] [*Ibid.,* 3.4.216f.; Hamlet's exit with the body of Polonius]
Shakespeare has been unfortunate in his management of the
story of this play, the most striking circumstances of which arise
so early in its formation as not to leave him room for a conclusion
suitable to the magnificence of its beginning. After this last

[1] Cf. Steevens's theatre-review, No. 237d above, p. 474.

interview with the *Ghost* the character of Hamlet has lost all its consequence.[1] STEEVENS. (X, 277)

[68] [*Ibid.*, 4.5.178ff.: '*There's rue for you, and here's some for me,*' &c.] I believe there is a quibble meant in the passage; *rue* anciently signifying the same as *Ruth*, i.e. sorrow. Ophelia gives the queen some, and keeps a proportion of it for herself. There is the same kind of play with the same word in *Richard the Second* [3.4.104ff.]. STEEVENS. (X, 298)

[69] You may wear your rue *with a difference*.] This seems to refer to the rules of heraldry, where the younger brothers of a family bear the same arms *with a difference*, or mark of distinction. STEEVENS. (X, 298)

[70] [*Ibid.*, 5.2.351f.:

> *Now cracks a noble heart. Good night, sweet prince;*
> *And flights of angels sing thee to thy rest!*]

Let us review for a moment the behaviour of Hamlet, on the strength of which Horatio sounds this eulogy, and recommends him to the patronage of angels.

Hamlet, at the command of his father's ghost, undertakes with seeming alacrity to revenge the murder; and declares he will banish all other thoughts from his mind.[2] He makes, however, but one effort to keep his word; and on another occasion defers his purpose till he can find an opportunity of taking the murderer when he is least prepared for death, that he may insure damnation to his soul. Though he may be said to have assassinated Polonius by accident, yet he deliberately procures the execution of Rosencrantz and Guildenstern, who appear to have been unacquainted with the treacherous purposes of the mandate which they were employed to carry. Their death (as he declares in a subsequent conversation with Horatio) gives him no concern, for they obtruded themselves into the service, and he thought he had a right to destroy them. He is not less accountable for the

---

[1] Cf. Steevens's theatre-review, No. 234d above, p. 448; also his letter to Garrick, p. 456 above; and 'Longinus' in No. 237c above, p. 472.
[2] Compare the very similar criticism made by Steevens in No. 234c above, pp. 447f., 452, and 'Longinus' in the *General Evening Post*, Nos 237b, 238a above, pp. 470f., 488f.

distraction and death of Ophelia. He comes to interrupt the funeral designed in honour of this lady, at which both the king and queen were present; and by such an outrage to decency renders it still more necessary for the usurper to lay a second stratagem for his life, though the first had proved abortive. He comes to insult the brother of the dead, and to boast of an affection for his sister which before he had denied to her face; and yet at this very time must be considered as desirous of supporting the character of a madman, so that the openness of his confession must not be imputed to him as a virtue. He apologizes to Horatio afterwards for the absurdity of this behaviour, to which, he says, he was provoked by that nobleness of fraternal grief, which indeed he ought rather to have applauded than condemned. Dr. Johnson has observed that to bring about a reconciliation with Laertes he has availed himself of a dishonest fallacy; and to conclude, it is obvious to the most careless spectator or reader that he kills the king at last to revenge himself, and not his father.[1]

Hamlet cannot be said to have pursued his ends by very warrantable means; and if the poet, when he sacrificed him at last, meant to have enforced such a moral it is not the worst that can be deduced from the play.

I have dwelt the longer on this subject because Hamlet seems to have been hitherto regarded as a hero not undeserving the pity of the audience, and because no writer on Shakespeare has taken the pains to point out the immoral tendency of his character. STEEVENS. (X, 343–4)

[71] [On the play-scene (2.2.446ff.) and Warburton's long commendation of it (Vol. 3 above, pp. 252–7).]

The praise which Hamlet bestows on this piece is certainly dissembled, and agrees very well with the character of madness which, before witnesses, he thought it necessary to support. The speeches before us have so little merit that nothing but an affectation of singularity could have influenced Dr. Warburton to undertake their defence. The poet, perhaps, meant to exhibit a just resemblance of some of the plays of his own age, in which the faults were too many in number to permit a few splendid passages to atone for a general defect. The player knew his trade, and spoke the lines in an affecting manner because Hamlet had

[1] Cf. 'Longinus' above, p. 488, and for Johnson's note see above, p. 161.

declared them to be pathetic; or might be in reality a little moved by them. . . . The mind of the prince, it must be confessed, was fitted for the reception of gloomy ideas, and his tears were ready at a slight solicitation. It is by no means proved that Shakespeare has *employed the same thoughts cloathed in the same expressions, in his best plays.* If he bids *the false huswife Fortune break her wheel,* he does not desire her to *break all its spokes*; nay, *even its periphery, and make use of the nave afterwards for such an immeasureable cast.* Though if what Dr. Warburton has said should be found in any instance to be exactly true, what can we infer from thence but that Shakespeare was sometimes wrong in spite of conviction, and in the hurry of writing committed those very faults which his judgment could detect in others? Dr. Warburton is inconsistent in his assertions concerning the literature of Shakespeare. In a note on *Troilus and Cressida* he affirms that his want of learning kept him from being acquainted with the writings of Homer; and in this instance would suppose him capable of producing a complete tragedy *written on the ancient rules*; and that the speech before us had sufficient merit to intitle it to a place *in the second book of Virgil's Æneid, even though the work had been carried to that perfection which the Roman poet had conceived.*

Had Shakespeare made one unsuccessful attempt in the manner of the ancients (that he had any knowledge of their rules remains to be proved) it would certainly have been recorded by contemporary writers, among whom Ben Jonson would have been the first. Had his darling ancients been unskilfully imitated by a rival poet he would at least have preserved the memory of the fact, to shew how unsafe it was for any one who was not as thorough a scholar as himself to have meddled with their sacred remains.

'Within that circle none durst walk but he.' He has represented Inigo Jones as being ignorant of the very names of those ancients whose architecture he undertook to correct: in his *Poetaster* he has in several places hinted at our poet's injudicious use of words, and seems to have pointed his ridicule more than once at some of his descriptions and characters. It is true that he has praised him, but it was not while that praise could have been of any service to him; and posthumous applause is always to be had on easy conditions. Happy it was for Shakespeare that he took nature for his guide, and, engaged in the warm pursuit of her beauties, left to Jonson the repositories of learning: so has he escaped a contest which might have rendered his life uneasy, and bequeathed to our possession the more valuable copies from nature herself. STEEVENS. (X, 352–3)

[72] [On *Othello*, 1.3.140]
Idle is an epithet used to express the infertility of the chaotic state, in the Saxon translation of the Pentateuch. JOHNSON. (X, 382)

[73] [*Ibid.*, 3.3.457 ff.: —'*Like to the Pontick sea*,' &c.]
'This simile is omitted in the first edition: I think it should be so, as an unnatural excursion in this place.' POPE. [Vol. 2, p. 418]

Every reader will, I durst say, abide by Mr. Pope's censure on this passage. As Shakespeare grew more acquainted with such particulars of knowledge he made a display of them as soon as an opportunity offered. I find this very account of the Euxine sea, and almost couched in the same words, in a book intitled, *A Treatise on the Courses of Rivers*, &c. printed by Felix Kingston, in 1595.

Mr. Edwards, in his MSS. notes, conceives this simile to allude to Sir Philip Sidney's device, whose impress, Camden in his *Remains* says, was the Caspian sea, with this motto, SINE REFLUXU. STEEVENS. (X, 453)

[74] [*Ibid.*, 4.2.68 ff.]
Oh thou weed!] Dr. Johnson has been censured for having stifled difficulties where he could not remove them.[1] I would therefore observe that this speech is printed word for word from the folio edition, though the quarto reads,

O thou black *weed!*

Had this epithet, *black*, been admitted, there would still have remained an incomplete verse in the speech: no additional beauty would have been thereby introduced; but instead of it a paltry antithesis between the words *black* and *fair*. I have been a careful reader of many of the plays and other books of the age of Shakespeare, but such a word as *blache* has never yet occurred; and I know not by what rule of criticism a commentator is obliged to adopt difficulties which (on the authority of copies) he may fairly

[1] Cf. Guthrie above, pp. 229f.

avoid. Though the quarto, 1622, affords assistance to an editor, yet the copy in the folio is in many places at once the most ample and correct. STEEVENS. (X, 482–3)

[75] [*Ibid.*, 5.2.1f.]

> It is the cause, it is the cause, my soul;
> Let me not name it— —]

The abruptness of this soliloquy makes it obscure. ... JOHNSON. [1765]

Othello, full of horror at the cruel action which he is about to perpetrate, seems at this instant to be seeking his justification from representing to himself *the cause*, i.e. the greatness of the provocation he had received. STEEVENS. (X, 499)

[76] [*Ibid.*, 5.2.87: the 1st Quarto (1622) gives to Desdemona, before Othello smothers her, the words 'O Lord, Lord, Lord.']
After this speech of Othello the elder quarto adds an invocation from Desdemona, consisting only of a sacred name thrice repeated. As this must be supposed to have been uttered while she is yet struggling with death, I think an editor may fairly be excused from inserting such a circumstance of supererogatory horror, especially as it is found in but one of the old copies.[1] STEEVENS.

This alteration was probably made by the author in consequence of a statute of the 21st of James I. to reform prophane cursing and swearing. HAWKINS. (X, 503)

[77] [*Ibid.*, 5.2.215: '*A thousand times committed.*' and 3.4.104: "*Tis not a year or two shews us a man*'. Steevens quotes Johnson's supposition (1765, Notes 220 and 225 above, pp. 163, 165) that the action of *Othello* is longer than is represented in the play.]
I cannot suppose from these passages that a longer space is comprised in the action of this play than the scenes include.

What Othello mentions in the first instance might have pass'd still more often before they were married, when Cassio went between them; for she who could find means to elude the vigilance of her father in respect of Othello might have done so in respect of Cassio, when there was time enough for the thing supposed to have happened. A jealous person will aggravate all he thinks or

1 It is in the 1622 Quarto, but not in the 1623 Folio.

speaks of, and might use a *thousand* for a much less number only to give weight to his accusation: nor would it have answered any purpose to have made Othello a little nearer or further off from truth in his calculation. We might apply the poet's own words in *Cymbeline*:

> ————spare your arithmetic
> Once, and a million.   [2.4.142f.]

The latter is a proverbial expression, and might have been introduced with propriety, had they been married only a day or two. Æmilia's reply means no more than, 'that is too soon to judge of her husband's disposition, or that she must not be surprized at the discovery of his jealousy, for it is not even a year or two that will display all the failings of a man.' STEEVENS. (X, 509)

APPENDIX.

Some apology perhaps is necessary for the inconvenience of an Appendix, which, however, we can justify by the strongest of all pleas, the plea of necessity. The Notes which it contains, whether communicated by correspondents, or collected from published volumes, were not within our reach when the plays were printed, to which they relate. Of that which chance has supplied, we could have no previous knowledge; and he that waited till the river should run dry, did not act with less reason than the Editor would do, who should suspend his publication for possibilities of intelligence, or promises of improvement. Had we foreseen the *Oxford* edition, the assistance we expected from it might have persuaded us to pause; but our volumes were completely finished before its publication.[1] (X, Sig. L1$_2^r$)

[78] [On *Macbeth*, 2.3.115: see Note 27 above]

UNMANNERLY] Whether the word which follows be *reech'd*, *breech'd*, *hatch'd*, or *drench'd*, I am at least of opinion that *unmannerly* is the genuine reading. Macbeth is describing a scene shocking to humanity: and in the midst of his narrative throws in a parenthetical reflection, consisting of one word not connected with the sentence, '(O most *unseemly* sight!' For this is a meaning of the word *unmannerly*: and the want of considering it in this *detached* sense

[1] The 1771 revision of Hamner was by T. Hawkins (see No. 241 below).

has introduced much confusion into the passage. The Latins often used *nefas* and *infandum* in this manner. Or, in the same sense, the word may be here applied adverbially. The correction of the author of the *Revisal* is equally frigid and unmeaning. 'Their daggers *in a manner lay* drench'd with gore.' The manifest artifice and dissimulation of the speech seems to be heightened by the explanation which I have offered. WARTON. (X, Sig. Mm$_2^v$–Mm$_3$)

[79] [On *Antony and Cleopatra*, 4.12.28]

> Like a right *gypsy* hath at *fast and loose*
> Beguil'd me, &c.

There is a kind of pun in this passage, arising from the corruption of the word *Egyptian* into *Gipsey*. The old lawbooks term such persons as ramble about the country and pretend skill in palmistry and fortune-telling *Egyptians*. *Fast and loose* is a term to signify a cheating game, of which the following is a description. A leathern belt is made up into a number of intricate folds, and placed edgewise upon a table. One of the folds is made to resemble the middle of the girdle, so that whoever should thrust a skewer into it would think he held it fast to the table; whereas, when he has so done, the person with whom he plays may take hold of both ends and draw it away. This trick is now known to the common people by the name of *pricking at the belt* or *girdle*, and perhaps was practised by the Gypsies in the time of Shakespeare. Sir J. HAWKINS. (X, Sig. Nn$_2^v$)

[80] [On *Troilus and Cressida*, 5.2.55ff.]

'How the devil *Luxury*, with his fat rump and *potatoe* finger, tickles these together.'

Luxuria was the appropriate term used by the school divines, to express the crime of incontinence, which accordingly is called *Luxury*, in all our old English writers. In the *Summæ Theologiæ Compendium* of Tho. Aquinas II. 2. Quæst. CLIV. is *de Luxuriæ Partibus*, which the author distributes under the heads of *Simplex Fornicatio, Adulterium, Incestus, Stuprum, Raptus*, &c. and Chaucer, in his *Parson's Tale*, descanting on the seven deadly sins, treats of this under the title, *De Luxuria*. Hence in *K. Lear* our author uses the word in this peculiar sense.

To't *Luxury* pell-mell, for I want soldiers.   [4.6.116f.]

But why is *luxury*, or lasciviousness, said to have a *potatoe finger?*—This root was in our author's time but newly imported from America, was considered as a rare exotic, and esteemed as a very strong provocative. As the plant is so common now, it may entertain the reader to see how it is described by Gerard in his herbal, 1597. p. 780.

'This plant which is called of some Skyrrits of Peru, is generally of us called *Potatus*, or *Potatoes.*—There is not any that hath written of this plant—therefore, I refer the description thereof unto those that shall hereafter have further knowledge of the same. Yet I have had in my garden divers roots (that I bought at the Exchange in London) where they flourished until winter, at which time they perished and rotted. They are used to be eaten rosted in the ashes. Some, when they be so rosted, infuse them and sop them in wine; and others, to give them the greater grace in eating, do boil them with prunes. Howsoever they be dressed, they comfort, nourish, and strengthen the bodie, procure *bodily lust, and that with greediness.*' Shakespeare alludes to this quality of *potatoes*, in the *Merry Wives of Windsor*.

> ——Let the sky rain *potatoes*,
> Hail kissing comfits, and snow eringoes; let
> *A tempest of provocation* come.   [5.4.16ff.]

Ben. Jonson mentions *potatoe pies* in *Every Man out of his Humour*, among other *good unctuous meats*.

In the *Good Huswives Jewell*, a book of cookery published in 1596, I find the following receipt *to make a tarte that is a courage to a man or woman*.

'Take twoo *Quinces* and twoo or three *Burre* rootes and a POTATON and pare your POTATON and scrape your rootes and put them into a quarte of wine, and let them boyle till they bee tender and put in an ounce of *dates*, and when they be boiled tender, drawe them through a strainer, wine and all, and then put in the yolkes of eight egges, and the braynes of three or four *cocke-sparrowes*, and straine them into the other, and a little rose-water, and seeth them all with sugar, cinnamon, and ginger, and cloves and mace, and put in a little sweet butter, and set it upon a chafing-dish of coles between two platters, to let it boyle till it be something bigge.'

Gerard elsewhere observes in his herbal, that '*Potatoes* may serve as a ground or foundation whereon the cunning confectioner or sugar-baker may worke and frame many comfortable conserves and *restorative* sweetmeats.'

The same venerable botanist likewise adds, that *the stalk of Clot-Burre* 'being eaten rawe with salt and pepper, or boiled in the broth of fat meat, is pleasant to be eaten and *stirreth up venereal motions.*' It likewise 'strengtheneth the *back,* &c.' Speaking of *dates,* he says, that 'thereof be made divers excellent cordial comfortable and nourishing medicines, and that procure *lust of the body very mightily.*' He also mentions *Quinces* as having the same virtues.

I suppose every one to be acquainted that *Sparrows* on account of their salaciousness were sacrificed to Venus. The remarks on the other articles that compose this medical piece of pastry, are inserted, to prove that they are all consistent in their operation and tend to promote the same purposes as the POTATON. It must by this time have occurred to the reader that in the kingdom where *potatoes* are eaten in their greatest quantities, the powers of the body are supposed to be found in their highest degree of perfection. Some accounts given by ancient travellers of the *Rhizophagi* might be introduced on this occasion; but perhaps enough has been already said on the subject. ... COLLINS.[1] (X, Sig. Nn$_3^r$–Nn$_4^r$)

[From Appendix II]

[81] [On *A Midsummer Night's Dream,* 2.1.98]
    The *nine mens morris is fill'd up with mud.*

In that part of Warwickshire where Shakespeare was educated, and the neighbouring parts of Northamptonshire, the shepherds and other boys dig up the turf with their knives to represent a sort of imperfect chess-board. It consists of a square, sometimes only a foot diameter, sometimes three or four yards. Within this is another square, every side of which is parallel to the external square; and these squares are joined by lines drawn from each corner of both squares and the middle of each line. One party

---

[1] 'A worthy harmless apothecary, whose name Mr. Steevens took the liberty of subjoining to a very *provocative* note in his Shakespeare, written obviously by himself' (James Boaden, note to his edition of Garrick's *Private Correspondence,* I, 581). Presumably this is the 'Mr. Collins of Hampstead' to whom Steevens credits other serious, and scholarly, notes in the 1773 and 1778 editions.

or player has wooden pegs, the other stones, which they move in such a manner as to take up each other's men as they are called, and the area of the inner square is called The Pound, in which the men taken up are impounded. These figures are by the country people called *Nine Men's Morris*, or *Merrils*, and are so called, because each party has nine men. These figures are always cut upon the green turf or leys, as they are called, or upon the grass at the end of ploughed lands, and in rainy seasons never fail to be *choaked up with mud*. Dr. JAMES. (X, Sig. O₀)

A LETTER FROM THE REV. Mr. FARMER of Emanuel College, Cambridge, AUTHOR OF '*An Essay on the Learning of Shakespeare*', TO MR. STEEVENS.

Dear Sir, I have long promised you a specimen of such observations as I think to be still wanting on the works of our favourite poet. The edition you now offer to the publick approaches much nearer to perfection than any that has yet appeared; and, I doubt not, will be the standard of every future one. The track of reading which I sometime ago endeavoured to prove more immediately necessary to a commentator on *Shakespeare*, you have very successfully followed, and have consequently superseded some remarks which I might otherwise have troubled you with. Those I now send you are such as I marked on the margin of the copy you were so kind to communicate to me, and bear a very small proportion to the miscellaneous collections of this sort which I may probably put together some time or other: if I do this I will take care by proper references to make them peculiarly useful to the readers of your edition.

An appendix has little room for quotation—I will be therefore as concise as possible. (X, Sig. O₀2ᵛ)

[82] When we meet with an harsh expression in Shakespeare, we are usually to look for a *play upon words* (Sig. Oo₃ᵛ)

[83] [On *Love's Labour's Lost*, 3.1.57]
Swift is here used as in other places, synonymously with *witty*. I suppose the meaning of *Atalanta's better part* in *As you like it* is her *wit*—the swiftness of her mind. (Sig. Oo₇ᵛ)

[84] [*Ibid.*, 3.1.67ff.]

I can scarcely think that *Shakespeare* had so far forgotten his little school learning as to suppose that the *Latin* verb *salve* and the *English* substantive *salve*, had the same pronunciation; and yet without this the quibble cannot be preserved. (Sig. Oo$_7^r$)

[85] [*Ibid.*, 4.2.2ff.]

Dr. *Warburton* is certainly right in his supposition that *Florio* is meant by the character of *Holofernes*. *Florio* had given the first affront. 'The plaies, says he, that they plaie in *England*, are neither *right comedies*, nor *right tragedies*; but representations of *histories* without any decorum.'——The scraps of *Latin* and *Italian* are transcribed from his works, particularly the proverb about *Venice*, which has been corrupted so much. The *affectation of the letter*, which *argues facilitie*, is likewise a copy of his manner. We meet with much of it in the sonnets to his patrons.

> In Italie your lordship well hath seene
> Their manners, monuments, magnificence,
> Their language learnt, in sound, in stile, in sense,
> Prooving by profiting, where you have *beene*.
> To adde to fore-learn'd facultie, facilitie.

We see then, the character of the schoolmaster might be written with less learning than Mr. *Colman* conjectured; nor is the use of the word *thrasonical* any argument that the author had read *Terence*. It was introduced to our language long before *Shakespeare*'s time. *Stanyhurst* writes, in a translation of one of Sir *Tho. More*'s epigrams, 'Lynckt was in wedlocke a loftye *thrasonical* hufsnuffe.'

It can scarcely be necessary to animadvert any further upon what Mr. *Colman* has advanced in the Appendix to his *Terence*.[1] If this Gentleman, at his leisure from modern plays, will condescend to open a few old ones, he will soon be satisfied that *Shakespeare* was obliged to learn and repeat in the course of his profession such *Latin fragments* as are met with in his works. The formidable one *ira furor brevis est*, which is quoted from *Timon*, may be found not in plays only but in every *tritical* essay from that of King *James* to that of Dean *Swift* inclusive. I will only add that if Mr. *Colman* had previously looked at the panegyrick on *Cartwright* he could not so strangely have misrepresented my argument from it: but thus

[1] See No. 217 above.

it must ever be with the most ingenious men when they talk *without-book*. Let me however take this opportunity of acknowledging the very genteel language which he has been pleased to use on this occasion.

Mr. *Warton* informs us in his Life of Sir *Tho. Pope*, that there was an old *Play of Holophernes* acted before the Princess *Elizabeth* in the year 1556. (Sig. Oo$_7$$^{r-v}$)

[86] [On *Hamlet*, 2.2.195ff.: Warburton had suggested that Shakespeare alluded to Juvenal, *Satire* 10, ll. 188ff.]

Had *Shakespeare* read *Juvenal* in the original, he had met with '*De temone Britanno, Excidet Arviragus*,' and '*Uxorem, Posthume, ducis?*' We should not then have had continually in *Cymbeline*, *Arvirugus* and *Posthumus*. Should it be said that the *quantity* in the *former* word might be forgotten, it is clear from the mistake in the *latter* that *Shakespeare* could not possibly have read any one of the *Roman* poets.

There was a translation of the 10th Satire of *Juvenal* by Sir *John Beaumont*, the elder brother of the famous *Francis*: but I cannot tell whether it was printed in *Shakespeare*'s time. In that age of quotation every classic might be picked up by *piece-meal*.

I forgot to mention in its proper place that another description of *Old Age* in *As you like it* has been called a parody of a passage in a *French* poem of *Garnier*. It is trifling to say any thing about this, after the observation I made in *Macbeth*: but one may remark once for all that *Shakespeare* wrote for the *people*; and could not have been so absurd to bring forward any allusion which had not been familiarized by some accident or other. (Sig. Qq$_5$^{r})

241. Thomas Hawkins, English drama before Shakespeare

1773

From *The Origin of the English Drama, Illustrated in its Various Species, viz., Mystery, Morality, Tragedy, and Comedy, by specimens from our earliest writers* ... (3 vols, Oxford, 1773).

Thomas Hawkins (1730–72), appointed chaplain of Magdalen College, Oxford, in 1754 (cf. J. Foster, *Alumni Oxonienses* 1715–1886, 2 vols, London, 1891–2), edited the second edition of Hanmer's six-volume Shakespeare in 1771 (cf. B. H. Davis, *A Proof of Eminence. The Life of Sir John Hawkins*, Bloomington, Ind., 1973, pp. 105–8). Hawkins died on 23 October 1772, just as his book was in the press.

The PREFACE.

It is by no means necessary here to enter into a Dispute which has already engaged the pen of many able writers concerning the ORIGIN of the MODERN DRAMA in Europe; for whether it arose in France or in Italy, among the Troubadors of Provence or the Shepherds of Calabria, or started up nearly at the same time in different kingdoms, it will be sufficient for our purpose to contend that it was a Distinct Species of itself and not a Revival of the ANCIENT DRAMA, with which it cannot be compared and must never be confounded. If this point be clearly proved we shall place our admirable SHAKESPEARE beyond the reach of Criticism, by considering him as the poet who brought the drama of the Moderns to its highest perfection, and by dispensing with his obedience to the RULES of the ANCIENTS, which probably he did not know, but certainly did not mean to follow. ... (III, i)

There existed then in Europe at the opening of the sixteenth century two distinct species of Drama; the one formed upon the ancient CLASSIC model, and confined like the sacred dialect

552

of the Ægyptian priests to men of learning; the other merely popular and of a GOTHIC original, but capable of great improvement. In the same manner there prevailed sometime afterwards two kinds of Epic Poetry, the first, like the LUSIAD, on the plan of Virgil and the ancients, the second, like ORLANDO FURIOSO and THE FAIRY QUEEN, of a very different nature, but more diffuse, more various, and perhaps more agreeable. This distinction will place the works of Spenser and Shakespeare in their true class, and prevent a great deal of idle criticism. 'Confound not predicaments,' says lord Bacon, 'for they are the mere-stones of reason.' (III, vi) . . .

The prevailing-turn for drollery and comic humour was at first so strong that in order to gratify it even in more serious and solemn scenes it was necessary still to retain the VICE or artful Buffoon, who (like his contemporary the privileged FOOL in the courts of princes and castles of the great men) was to enter into the most stately assemblies and vent his humour without restraint. We have a specimen of this character in the play of CAMBYSES where Ambidexter, who is expressly called the VICE, enters 'with an old capcase for a helmet and a skimmer for his sword,' in order, as the author expresses it, 'to make pastime.'*

Soon after Comedy the ancient TRAGEDY began likewise to be revived, but it was only among the more refined Scholars that at first it retained much resemblance of the Classical Form. For the more popular audiences it was debased with an intermixture of low gross humour, which has long continued under the name of TRAGI-COMEDY. Even where a series of grave solemn scenes was exhibited without much interruption of buffoonery or farce still our Poets were content to imitate the old MYSTERIES in giving only a tissue of interesting events simply as they happened, without any artful conduct of the fable, and without the least regard to the three great unities. These they called HISTORIES†, and these would probably have long continued the only specimens of our heroic Drama if a few persons of superior education and more

---

* Shakespeare's CLOWNS are genuine successors of the old VICE: And, as the late learned editor of that poet has well observed, PUNCH still exhibits the intire character.

† See a very curious account of these peculiar productions of the English theatre, in the 2d vol. of *Reliques of Anc. Eng. Poetry* (2d edit.) p. 135, 136.[1] Which vindicates our great poet Shakespeare for his neglect of the unities from the impertinence of criticism, and places many of his best productions in a new but just light.

[1] See 4.544–5.

refined taste had not formed their scenes upon the classic models, and introduced legitimate Tragedy in the ancient form. But these at first were only composed for private and learned audiences, at the inns of court, or the universities. (ix–x) . . .

This was the state of the English Theatre when SHAKESPEARE rose, who by the force of his genius, without any assistance from learning, brought the Modern Species of Drama to so high a degree of perfection that it rivals or surpasses the severer and more elegant models of old Greece and Rome. The charms of his versification (from which our dramatic Blank Verse has been gradually degenerating), the beauty of his speeches and descriptions, but above all the great art of expressing the vehement passions, in which no writer of any age ever equalled him, have supported his reputation, notwithstanding some human blemishes, for near two centuries; and whatever praise be due to the Tragedies of the Ancients in the light of pure and finished compositions we cannot consider them as the only models of the drama, but SHAKESPEARE still remains the Dramatic Poet of the English.

It was thought that a work which should tend to illustrate the beauties and extenuate the faults of this great man, the boast and wonder of our nation; which should exhibit in a distinct view the rise and gradual improvements of our Drama before his time; which should contain, as it were, a History of our Language and Versification, and bring to light the productions of several ingenious men, would not be unacceptable to an English reader; and it is in this view principally that the Editor hopes for his indulgence. . . . (xv)

242. Edward Capell, notes on Shakespeare

1774

From *Notes and Various Readings to Shakespeare, Part the first* ... (1774).

These are the notes promised in the 1768 edition (above, No. 220). The nine plays dealt with in this first volume are: *All's Well that Ends Well, Antony and Cleopatra, As You Like It, The Comedy of Errors, Coriolanus, Cymbeline, Hamlet,* 1 *Henry IV,* and 2 *Henry IV.* Capell's book is an odd mixture, consisting of (a) an Advertisement; (b) a Glossary (79 pages); (c) Notes (184 pages); (d) an Errata slip; (e) Various Readings (55 pages).

---

[1] [On *The Comedy of Errors*, 5.1.329]

The note must not be ended without first pointing out to the reader's observance the great and unparalell'd excellence of the fable's catastrophe; which breaks upon the fancy like lightning at the very instant of the Abbess's entry with her son in her hand. For all parties see the cause of their several errors and express it by looks, and the abbess's relation to three of them is discover'd in the face of her husband. (80) ...

[2] [On *Coriolanus*, 1.1.21: 'Let us revenge this with our pikes ere we become rakes']

The humour of [this] line ... lyes in the equivocal meaning of the words '*pike*' and '*rake*,' which the speaker of them had in his head: intending by one of them both the military weapon a pike and the countryman's pitchfork; by the other that same countryman's rake and a person emaciated. (81) ...

[3] [*Ibid.*, 1.1.161f.: 'Thanks.']

The address of the Author is wonderful in the entry of Marcius; giving us in one single word, and that his first and a monosyllable, a thorow insight into his character and a preparation for what is to follow. (82)

[4] [*Ibid.*, 1.9.19ff.]

In the first part of the speech of Cominius ... hyperbole is stretch'd to the utmost; perhaps more than a point or two beyond the bounds of good sense; and the poet himself might be puzzl'd to reduce them to that standard or, in other words, to strip his speech of the metaphor and make of it a sensible reply to that of Marcius; at least the task is too hard for the editor, and shall not be attempted by him. (84) ...

[5] [*Ibid.*, 2.1.115ff.]

Brings' a victory in his pocket?] Here's another of Menenius' speeches, damag'd of the moderns by length'ning it,—*Brings he a victory* &c?∞ The excess of Volumnia's joy breaks out, as nature wills that it should do, in indirect answers and broken expressions: '*On's brows, Menenius;*' speaking exultingly, and instead of *he has it on his brows, Menenius*, meaning the oaken garland that follows. And Menenius is not much behind her in extasy, showing it in short questions and quick passings from person to person. His sudden turn to the Tribunes [ll. 136ff.] (who are retir'd, and not gone as some editors make them) and then again to Volumnia [l. 137] is of this nature; and so is the abruption in his tale of the wounds [ll. 142ff.] (85–6). ...

[6] [*Ibid.*, 2.2.77]

The opposite page affords a signal example of that negligent boldness of phrase which is one of the characteristicks of Shakespeare. For what sense can be extracted grammatically out of '*That's thousand to one good one?*' Yet to those who are conversant with him enough is spoken to make his meaning conceiv'd, and as much too as suited the character to whom the sentence is given. (87) ...

[7] [On crowd-speeches: *ibid.*, 5.6.121ff.]

... in other respects the passage is as it should be, for the word that stands before it, '*confusedly*,' the words themselves of this passage, and the breaks that are in it denote sufficiently that the several members of it belong to as many several persons, all speaking at once or quick upon the heels of each other.

And here the editor will risque the imputation of trifling by making another remark upon speeches that are akin to the present, which may have it's use on the stage if not in reading. What is spoken by several persons, be they many or few, ought to be very short; little more than a word or two, and those such as the occasion requires, and as a number might well be consenting in. A greater length of words is unnatural, for not only no multitude, but no two persons whose thoughts must be deliver'd in many, ever lit upon the same. Yet we have a number of this sort of speeches that exceed the limits prescrib'd to them, to which if we would give some propriety we must imagine a little scenical management: an example shall speak for us. In the opening of this play we have six speeches prefac'd by '*all*;' the three first of them proper and natural, the other three not so without the aid of that scenical management, which has many ways of affording it: by actions, and looks; by a murmur expressing assent; by repetition of some words of their principal speaker (as in the second of those we are talking of by repeating '*a very dog*,' and that from several mouths), or new-modeling some of his words, and giving only their import, and that in their own way and confusedly. One or more of these methods we must conceive us'd in the action, if we would not do injustice to Shakespeare by supposing him to have neglected in such articles that attachment to nature for which he is so remarkable. (101) . . .

[8] [On *Hamlet*, 1.3.58ff.: Polonius' advice to Laertes]

And these few precepts &c.] It has been observ'd (but where is not remember'd at present) that the '*precepts*' are much too good for the speaker, and that we have no other way of making them consistent with character but to imagine them things he has con'd, and comes prepar'd with to make a figure at parting. And the observation is not ill-grounded, for the moment he's at the end of his lesson we are regal'd with a style very different, and flowers of speech is his way; of which '*invests you*' is one, by which he means straitens you, presses urgently on you. (124) . . .

[9] [*Ibid.*, 4.5.172ff.]

There's rosemary, &c.] Many, or most of Ophelia's speeches are pregnant with that kind of sense which is so finely describ'd in

[4.5.7ff.], but in the distribution of her flowers this sense is so strong that her brother observes upon't—'*a document in madness.*' Her first are given to him, '*pansies for thoughts,*' for a reason obvious enough, the word signifying thoughts in the French (*pensées*); and '*rosemary*' is made '*remembrance,*' meaning of death, the dead corpse being anciently stuck with it (*v. R & J.* [4.5.79f.]). Her '*fennel*' is bestow'd on the King and also her '*columbine,*' the reason not apparent in either unless for the columbine, whose flower is a faint kind of purple and therefore given to him. Her '*rue*' she gives the Queen and herself, being an emblem of repentance and sorrows. Of the latter it might remind her at all times, but '*on Sundays,*' or when the thoughts are bent Godward, it is an emblem of penitence; and then, she tells the Queen, it might be call'd '*herb of grace*' (which is a popular name for it), sorrows leading to penitence and being given by Grace for that purpose. All flowers are funereal, and herbs likewise, as being emblems of the shortness of life: (see the fourth act of *Cym.* [4.2.219ff.]) and their scattering, as it were, in this place upon persons who were all to be swallow'd up in short time flows from that prophetical spirit which antiquity thought inherent in madness, and the East is said to think so at present. By '*wear your rue with a difference,*' l. 25, is meant that more repentance was necessary for the Queen than for her, and of a different kind (144). . . .

[10] [*Ibid.*, 4.7.166ff.]

There is a willow &c.] In this natural and affecting description of Ophelia's misfortune the folio's, and the editions succeeding, give us three lines (the third, the fifth, and the ninth) all beginning with '*There,*' a fault of no little size in good writing, which Shakespeare could not fall into. But this is not all. By reading '*come*' in l. [169], instead of '*make*' (as they all do), we lose the cause that brought Ophelia down to this '*willow.*' For she did not come with *ready-made* garlands, only to hang them there, but *to make* garlands of the flowers she had gather'd by stringing them upon boughs of that willow, pluck'd and broken off for that purpose; and when her garlands were finish'd a thought takes her to make the tree fine with them, and this produces the accident. (145) . . .

[11] [On 2 *Henry IV*, 4.2.93ff.]

let your trains] The certainty of this correction is evinc'd both by the following words and the reply to them. The true reason of the Prince's request seems to have been that he might know as soon as possible the actual state of those *'trains'* which, from the shouts he had heard, he imagin'd might be disbanding already; and when certify'd of the truth of his thought by the return of the Archbishop's messenger his concerted project breaks out. Marks of it have appear'd all along: first, in Westmoreland's address to prince John in [4.2.52f.], where he puts him upon an instant agreement to the Archbishop's demands, stopping him in a heat he saw rising that might break off the treaty; but more evident marks of it shew themselves in the three sneering speeches that follow, which come from that Westmoreland. Blameable as this behaviour will seem at this time of day,[1] no disapprobation is shewn of it by the historians that Shakespeare follow'd, which historians (it should be noted) were his cotemporaries, the passive-obedience doctrine running so high with them that all proceedings with rebels were reckon'd justifiable. (179)

A Select Bibliography of Shakespeare Criticism

1765–74

Most of the relevant works have been referred to in the Preface, Introduction, and head-notes above, and in the bibliographies to previous volumes.

For collections of criticism see D. N. Smith (ed.), *Eighteenth Century Essays on Shakespeare* (Glasgow, 1903; repr. with slight corrections, Oxford, 1963) and his volume in the World's Classics series, *Shakespeare Criticism. A Selection* 1623–1840 (1916). Nichol Smith's history, *Shakespeare in the Eighteenth Century* (Oxford, 1928), is the best concise study; R. W. Babcock, *The Genesis*

[1] Cf. Heath (4.556f.), Dr Johnson and Mrs Montagu (pp. 122 and 334 above).

of Shakespeare Idolatry 1766–1799 (Chapel Hill, N. C., 1931) is much fuller, but suffers from an excess of detail and a paucity of analysis, while its bibliography is at times both peripheral and inaccurate. It remains, however, essential reading. Books by the following authors listed in previous bibliographies are recommended: C. C. Green, R. G. Noyes, C. H. Gray, A. C. Sprague, L. Strauss, C. Price, G. C. D. Odell, G. Branam, as are the articles by T. N. Raysor, D. Lovett, R. B. McKerrow, and J. Isaacs.

On Dr Johnson, in addition to the works listed in the notes to the Introduction, the following contain discussions of his Shakespeare criticism, of varying length and quality:

RALEIGH, W., 'Johnson on Shakespeare', *Six Essays on Johnson* (Oxford, 1910), pp. 75–97.

KRUTCH, J. W., *Samuel Johnson* (New York, 1944), pp. 265–336.

HAGSTRUM, J. H., *Samuel Johnson's Literary Criticism* (Minneapolis, 1952).

BATE, W. J., *The Achievement of Samuel Johnson* (New York, 1955).

WIMSATT, W. K., (ed.), *Dr. Johnson on Shakespeare* (New York, 1960), Introduction.

INGHAM, P., 'Johnson's use of "elegance"', *Review of English Studies*, n. s., 19 (1968), pp. 271–8.

TUCKER, S. I., 'Johnson and Lady Macbeth', *Notes and Queries*, n. s., 3 (1956), pp. 210–11.

FLEISCHMANN, W. B., 'Shakespeare, Johnson, and the Unities', in *Essays in English Literature of the Classical Period Presented to D. Macmillan*, ed. D. W. Patterson *et al.* (*Studies in Philology*, extra series, no. 4; Chapel Hill, N. C., 1967), pp. 124–38.

SHERBO, A., 'Johnson's *Shakespeare* and the Dramatic Criticism in the *Lives of the English Poets*' in G. B. Evans (ed.), *Shakespeare:Aspects of Influence* (Cambridge, Mass., 1976), pp. 55–69.

Addenda. W. JACKSON BATE, *Samuel Johnson* (New York, 1977), puts Johnson's Shakespeare criticism authoritatively in its biographical context. D. T. SIEBERT, JR., 'The Scholar as Satirist: Johnson's Edition of Shakespeare', *Studies in English Literature* 1500–1900, 15 (1975), pp. 483–503, is an important study of Johnson's rhetorical strategies for vindicating his own work as an editor at the expense of his rivals.

Index

The Index is arranged in three parts: I. Shakespeare's works; II. Shakespearian characters; III. General index. Adaptations are indexed under the adapter's name, in III below. References to individual characters are not repeated under the relevant plays.

II SHAKESPEARIAN CHARACTERS

III GENERAL INDEX

THE CRITICAL HERITAGE SERIES

GENERAL EDITOR: B. C. SOUTHAM

Volumes published and forthcoming